GENIUS

GENIUS

A MOSAIC OF
ONE HUNDRED
EXEMPLARY
CREATIVE MINDS

HAROLD BLOOM

Ah that our Genius were a little more a genius!
—*Ralph Waldo Emerson*, "Experience"

WARNER BOOKS

An AOL Time Warner Company

Warner Books, Inc., 1271 Avenue of the Americas, New York, NY 10020

Visit our Web site at www.twbookmark.com.

⦿ An AOL Time Warner Company

Printed in the United States of America

First Printing: October 2002

10 9 8 7 6 5 4 3 2 1

Library of Congress Cataloging-in-Publication Data

Bloom, Harold.
    Genius : a mosaic of 100 exemplary creative minds / Harold Bloom.
        p. cm.
    Includes bibliographical references.
    ISBN 0-446-52717-3
        1. Genius. 2. Gifted persons. I. Title.

    BF412 .B58 2002
    153.9'8—dc21   2002016808

Book design by Giorgetta Bell McRee

To the beloved memory of Mirjana Kalezic

Contents

PREFACE

Why these one hundred? At one point I planned many more, but one hundred came to seem sufficient. Aside from those who could not be omitted—Shakespeare, Dante, Cervantes, Homer, Vergil, Plato, and their peers—my choice is wholly arbitrary and idiosyncratic. These are certainly *not* "the top one hundred," in anyone's judgment, my own included. I wanted to write about these.

Since my competence extends only to literary, and to some extent, religious, criticism, there is nothing in this book about Einstein, Delacroix, Mozart, Louis Armstrong, or whom you will. This is a mosaic of geniuses of language, though Socrates is in the oral tradition, and Islam affirms that Allah dictated the Koran to Muhammad.

There are evidences of wavering among those who have dismissed genius merely as an eighteenth-century fetish. Groupthink is the blight of our Age of Information, and is most pernicious in our obsolete academic institutions, whose long suicide since 1967 continues. The study of mediocrity, whatever its origins, breeds mediocrity. Thomas Mann, descendant of furniture manufacturers, prophesied that his Joseph-tetralogy would last because it was well made. We do not accept tables and chairs whose legs fall off, no matter who carpentered them, but we urge the young to study mediocre writings, with no legs to sustain them.

This book, *Genius*, differs from my previous work in that I seek only to define, as best I can, the particular genius of my one hundred personages. I have mixed biographical and literary criticism, but have avoided almost all historicizing.

With contextualizing or backgrounding a work, no one could quarrel. But reducing literature or spirituality or ideas by an historicizing overdetermination tells me nothing. The same social and economic and cultural stresses produce, side by side, immortal works and period pieces. Thomas Middleton and Philip Massinger and George Chapman shared the same cultural energies that supposedly shaped *Hamlet* and *King Lear*. But Shakespeare's best twenty-five (out of thirty-nine) plays are not period pieces. Since we do not know how else to account for Shakespeare (or Dante, Cervantes, Goethe, Walt Whitman), what can we do better than return to the study of the ancient idea of genius? Talent cannot originate, genius must.

*   *   *

I am grateful to my research assistants: Tara Mohr, Kate Cambor, Yoojin Grace Kim, Aislinn Goodman, and Mei Chin. I thank also my editors, Jamie Raab and Larry Kirshbaum, my literary agents, Glen Hartley and Lynn Chu, and my wife, Jeanne.

Harold Bloom
Timothy Dwight College, Yale
December 8, 2001

ON THIS BOOK'S ARRANGEMENT:

Genius and Kabbalah

I have juxtaposed these one hundred geniuses of language in ten sets of ten each, and then divided the sets into subsets of five. All genius, in my judgment, is idiosyncratic and grandly arbitrary, and ultimately stands alone. A contemporary of Dante could have had precisely his relation to tradition, his exact learning, and something like his love for quite another Beatrice, but only Dante wrote the *Commedia*. Each of my hundred is unique, but this book requires some ordering or grouping, as any book does. I have arranged it as a mosaic, believing that significant contrasts and illuminations emerge.

From the time, years back, when I first conceived of this book, the image of the Kabbalistic *Sefirot* has been in my mind. My ten headings are the commonest names for the *Sefirot*. Kabbalah is a body of speculation, relying upon a highly figurative language. Chief among its figurations or metaphors are the *Sefirot*, attributes at once of God and of the Adam Kadmon or Divine Man, God's Image. These attributes or qualities emanate out from a center that is nowhere or nothing, being infinite, to a circumference both everywhere and finite. The idea of emanation is founded upon Plotinus, greatest of Neoplatonists, but in Plotinus the emanations proceed out and away from God, whereas in Kabbalah the *Sefirot* stay within God or the Divine Man. Since the Kabbalists believed that God created the world out of himself, he being *Ayin* (nothing), the *Sefirot* chart the process of creation; they are the names of God as he works at creating. The *Sefirot* are metaphors so large that they become poems in themselves, or even poets. The Hebrew *sappir* ("sapphire") is the probable origin of the word *Sefirot*. One can think of the *Sefirot* as lights, texts, or phases of creativity. Here I have grouped my hundred brief studies of genius under the *Sefirot* that seemed most relevant to me, but no two souls ever agree upon what is most relevant to them.

My placement of the hundred geniuses is hardly one that fixes them in place, since all the *Sefirot* are images constantly in motion, and any creative spirit must move through all of them, in many labyrinths of transformation.

Gershom Scholem, the founder of modern scholarship on the Kabbalah, identified Kabbalah with the genius of the Jewish religion. Moshe Idel, Scholem's successor, finds in Kabbalah, despite its apparently sudden eruption among the Jews of thirteenth-century Provence and Catalonia, the recurrence of ancient Jewish speculations. In a sense, Scholem and Idel agree with Kabbalah's assertion that it takes us back to an unfallen Eve and Adam in Eden, as well as its equally intense claim that Moses received it as the esoteric element in the Oral Law conveyed by Yahweh to Moses on Sinai.

The *Sefirot* are the center of Kabbalah, since they purport to represent God's inwardness, the secrets of divine character and personality. They are the attributes of *God's genius,* in every sense that I use "genius" in this book.

Keter, the first *Sefirah,* could be called the crown, since it is visualized as the crowned head of Adam Kadmon, the God-Man, before his fall. Yet, like all the *Sefirot, Keter* is a paradox, since Kabbalists also called it *Ayin* or nothingness. Borges remarked that Shakespeare was everyone and no one, which I modify to everything and nothing, the crown of literature, and yet the primal nothingness. As a Bardolator-in-Chief, I find it no audacity to consider Shakespeare's genius a kind of secular godhead, which is why I place him foremost among my hundred representatives of the geniuses of language.

I have followed Shakespeare here, under *Keter,* with four almost comparable figures: Cervantes the "first novelist," Montaigne the first personal essayist, Milton the reinventor of epic poetry, and Tolstoy, who fused epic and novel. In a second group I give a sequence of great autobiographers of the self: the poets Lucretius and Vergil, the psychologist-theologian Augustine, and the supreme poets (with Shakespeare and Homer) Dante and Chaucer. These five figures are arranged in a sequence of influence, since each was inspired by the one before, except for Lucretius, who proudly stemmed from the philosopher Epicurus.

Since the ten *Sefirot* form a system in constant motion, all of my hundred persons could be illuminated *almost* equally well by the other nine *Sefirot,* beyond the one where I group them, and I intend this book to be a kind of mosaic-in-perpetual-movement. Still, print demands a sequence, and mine is intended to be suggestive, rather than fixed or arbitrary.

Hokmah, the second *Sefirah,* is frequently translated as "wisdom," for which one should invoke the general aura of "wisdom literature" in the Hebrew Bible and its commentaries. I have given Socrates, Plato, the Yahwist, Saint Paul, and Muhammad as a first group of wisdom figures, and then juxtaposed a second sequence of Dr. Samuel Johnson, his biographer Boswell, the sages Goethe and Freud, and the ironist Thomas Mann as a panoply of secular wisdom.

The third *Sefirah, Binah,* is intellect in a receptive mode, an intelligence not so much passive as dramatically open to the power of wisdom. For me, Nietzsche, Kierkegaard, and Kafka represent mind in this openness, as do Proust, the last of the great novelists, and the Anglo-Irish seer Beckett. In a second sequence, I have grouped five of the major European dramatists—Molière, Ibsen, Chekhov, Wilde, and Pirandello—all of whom have the swiftness of understanding that Kabbalists associate with *Binah.*

With *Hesed,* the bountiful covenant love that issues from God (or from women and men), I have found an initial set of representatives in five great ironic writers, really ironists of love: John Donne, Alexander Pope, Jonathan Swift, and—gentler in their mastery of ironic longing—Jane Austen and Lady Murasaki. A second grouping are also geniuses of eros, but deal more with the anguish of covenant: Hawthorne and Melville, the Brontë sisters, Virginia Woolf.

Din, which comes next, is also called *Gevurah. Din* means something like strict judgment, while *Gevurah* is the power that enables such rigor. Here I have begun with a severe line of great American poet-seers of genius: Emerson, Emily Dickinson, Frost, Wallace Stevens, T. S. Eliot, all exemplars of our native strain, that once was a kind of Puritanism. After them I have placed five High Romantic poets who manifested the power of rigorous imagination: Wordsworth, Shelley, Keats, Tennyson, and the Italian Leopardi.

With *Tiferet,* beauty, also known as *Rahamin* or compassion, I have turned first to five great figures of the Aesthetic movement—Swinburne, the Rossettis, Walter Pater, and the Austrian Hofmannsthal—and then gone on to major poets of French Romanticism and its heirs: Victor Hugo, Nerval, Baudelaire, Rimbaud, and Valéry.

The seventh *Sefirah, Nezah,* can be rendered as God's victory, or as the eternal endurance that cannot be defeated. Here I have begun with three giants of epic: Homer, Camoens of Portugal, and James Joyce, and added to them the superb Cuban epic novelist Alejo Carpentier and the Mexican poet Octavio Paz, most powerful in his "brief epics." A second group shares perhaps less in victory and more in a superb endurance: Stendhal, Mark Twain, Faulkner, Hemingway, Flannery O'Connor, all of them also ironists of eternity.

Hod, the splendor or majesty that has prophetic force, is seen here as governing first a sequence of poet-prophets, commencing with Walt Whitman and three poets he influenced: Pessoa of Portugal, Hart Crane, and Federico García Lorca of Andalusia (southern Spain). A great modern Spanish poet-in-exile, Cernuda, completes this majestic group. Since *Hod* is the emblem of moral splendor, it has sway also over the novelistic sequence of George Eliot, Willa Cather, Edith Wharton, Scott Fitzgerald, and the late philosopher-romancer Iris Murdoch.

With *Yesod*, the ninth *Sefirah*, sometimes translated as "foundation," we have an attribute akin to the initial Roman meaning of "genius," a fathering force. I have placed under *Yesod* first a sequence of masters of erotic narrative: Flaubert, Eça de Queiroz of Portugal, the African-Brazilian Machado de Assis, Borges the Argentine, and Italo Calvino, the modern Italian fabulist. A second sequence is constituted by five heroic vitalists: the prophet-poet William Blake, the prophetic novelist D. H. Lawrence, the major American dramatist, Tennessee Williams, strongly influenced by Lawrence and by Hart Crane, and two foundational modern poets, the Austrian-German Rilke and the Italian Montale.

The tenth and final *Sefirah* is *Malkhut*, the kingdom, also known as *Atarah*, the diadem. Though *Malkhut* is identified with the descended *Shekhinah*, the female radiance of God, I have relied upon its deep inwardness as an attribute, and have grouped under it ten male geniuses who transcend sexuality. *Malkhut* is, to me, the most fascinating of the *Sefirot*, since it displays divine immanence in the kingdom of this world. You reach the other *Sefirot* only through *Malkhut*, so that I employ it here first to group the diverse but curiously interfused sequence of those who created their own human comedies: Balzac, Lewis Carroll, the psychologist-novelist Henry James, Robert Browning, inventor of the dramatic monologue, and W. B. Yeats, Irish dramatic lyricist. A second, allied group is constituted by Dickens and Dostoevsky, visionary novelists of the grotesque, and by Isaac Babel, Russian-Jewish storyteller, and Paul Celan, Romanian-Jewish inventor of a post-Holocaust poetry in German that matches the radiance of Kafka's German narrative prose. The late African-American novelist Ralph Waldo Ellison, whose visionary genius achieved a perfection in his *Invisible Man*, completes this descent of *Malkhut* into our time, and is the last of the hundred geniuses studied in this book.

THE LUSTRES

Each of my ten groups governed by a particular *Sefirah* is subdivided into two sets of five, that I have chosen to call "Lustres." A paragraph or two at the start of each Lustre attempts to indicate something of my process of associating these five figures with one another.

"I read for the lustres," Emerson said, echoing Plutarch and other ancients in the Platonic tradition. "Lustres" in this sense refer to the condition of shining by reflected light, the gloss or sheen that one genius imparts to another, when juxtaposed in my mosaic.

GNOSTICISM:

The Religion of Literature

This book has two paradigms, both rather less esoteric than they may seem: Kabbalah and Gnosticism. I may as well add a third, the Hermetic Corpus or *Hermetica*, a remarkable group of tracts composed in Hellenistic Alexandria in the first century C.E. Scholars call this Greco-Egyptian pagan mystical sect "Hermetism," so as to distinguish it from its Renaissance and modern offshoots, generally called Hermeticism.

Hermetism became immensely influential in the Renaissance because of the mistaken notion that its founding texts were pre-Mosaic, rather than contemporary with the Gospel of John, as they were. The Hermetists were Platonists who had absorbed the allegorical techniques of Alexandrian Jewry, and who developed the Jewish speculation concerning the first Adam, the Anthropos or Primal Man, called the Adam Kadmon in Kabbalah, and "a mortal god" by the Hermetists: "the human on earth is a mortal god [while] god in heaven is an immortal human" (translated by Brian P. Copenhaver). This is a Hermetist gnosis or knowing and results from the Creation-Fall we will see elaborated by the Christian Gnostics a century later, but never quite with the eloquence of the Hermetist first tract, the *Poimandres*, where the mortal god falls into our sorrow of "love and sleep":

When the man saw in the water the form like himself as it was in nature, he loved it and wished to inhabit it; wish and action came in the same moment . . . Even though he is immortal . . . mankind is affected by mortality . . . although . . . above the cosmic framework, he became a slave within it. He is androgyne because he comes from an androgyne father, and he never sleeps because he comes from one who is sleepless. Yet love and sleep are his masters.

(translated by Brian P. Copenhaver)

This is a Narcissistic rather than an Oedipal Creation-Fall, Platonic rather than Judeo-Christian, and is akin to Emerson's "Self-Reliance," where the oldest and best aspects of the self are seen as not being part of nature. Ancient Gnosticism named these elements in the self as the *pneuma*, authentic spirit or breath, the true person.

"Gnosticism" was first employed in the seventeenth century to describe the ancient "heresy" that existed among later first-century pagans, Jews, and Christians. Nearly all our indisputably Gnostic texts are second-century Christian, but earlier Jewish tradition had worshipped the primal Adam as the authentic prophet. The great living Israeli scholar of Kabbalah, Moshe Idel, speculates that Gnosticism, like Jewish medieval Kabbalah, renewed ancient Jewish controversies about Adam, God, Creation, and Fall.

Christian Gnostic literature should be read in Bentley Layton's translation, *The Gnostic Scriptures,* with an emphasis upon Valentinus, the poetic genius among the Alexandrian Gnostics. From Valentinus through the German Romantic poet Novalis, the French Romantic Nerval, and the English William Blake, Gnosticism has been indistinguishable from imaginative genius. I venture, after a lifetime's meditation upon Gnosticism, the judgment that it is pragmatically *the religion of literature.* There are, of course, nonheretical Christian poets of genius, from John Donne through Gerard Manley Hopkins on to the neo-Christian T. S. Eliot. And yet the most ambitious poets in Romantic Western tradition, those who have made a religion of their own poetry, have been Gnostics, from Shelley and Victor Hugo on to William Butler Yeats and Rainer Maria Rilke.

I propose a simplifying definition of Gnosticism in the apprehension of genius: it is a knowledge that frees the creative mind from theology, from historicizing, and from any divinity that is totally distinct from what is most imaginative in the self. A God cut off from the inmost self is the Hangman God, as James Joyce called him, the God who originates death. Gnosticism, as the religion of literary genius, repudiates the Hangman God.

Hans Jonas, for me the most incisive guide to Gnosticism, said of the ancient Gnostics that they experienced "the intoxication of unprecedentness." I recall remarking to Jonas, an intensely brilliant and genial person, that he had described what strong poets always sought for: freedom for the creative self, for the expansion of the mind's consciousness of itself.

INTRODUCTION:

What Is Genius?

In employing a Kabbalistic grid or paradigm in the arrangement of this book, I rely upon Gershom Scholem's conviction that Kabbalah is the genius of religion in the Jewish tradition. My one hundred figures, from Shakespeare through the late Ralph Ellison, represent perhaps a hundred different stances towards spirituality, covering the full range from Saint Paul and Saint Augustine to the secularism of Proust and Calvino. But Kabbalah, in my view, provides an anatomy of genius, both of women and of men; as also of their merging in *Ein Sof,* the endlessness of God. Here I want to use Kabbalah as a starting-point in my own personal vision of the name and nature of genius.

Scholem remarked that the work of Franz Kafka constituted a secular Kabbalah, and so he concluded that Kafka's writings possess "something of the strong light of the canonical, of that perfection which destroys." Against this, Moshe Idel has argued that the canonical, both scriptural and Kabbalistic, is "the perfection which absorbs." To confront the plenitude of Bible, Talmud, and Kabbalah is to work at "absorbing perfections."

What Idel calls "the absorbing quality of the Torah" is akin to the absorbing quality of all authentic genius, which always has the capacity to absorb *us.* In American English, to "absorb" means several related processes: to take something in as through the pores, or to engross one's full interest or attention, or to assimilate fully.

I am aware that I transfer to genius what Scholem and Idel follow Kabbalah in attributing to God, but I merely extend the ancient Roman tradition that first established the ideas of genius and of authority. In Plutarch, Mark Antony's genius is the god Bacchus or Dionysus. Shakespeare, in his *Antony and Cleopatra,* has the god Hercules, as Antony's genius, abandon him. The emperor Augustus, who defeated Antony, proclaimed that the god Apollo was *his* genius, according to Suetonius. The cult of the emperor's genius thus became Roman ritual, displacing the two earlier meanings, of the family's fathering force and of each individual's alter ego.

Authority, another crucial Roman concept, may be more relevant for the study of genius than "genius," with its contradictory meanings, still can hope to be. Authority, which has vanished from Western culture, was convincingly traced by Hannah Arendt to Roman rather than Greek or Hebrew origins. In ancient Rome, the concept of authority was *foundational. Auctoritas* derived from the verb *augere,* "to augment," and authority always depended upon augmenting the foundation, thus carrying the past alive into the present.

Homer fought a concealed contest with the poetry of the past, and I suspect that the Redactor of the Hebrew Bible, putting together his Genesis through Kings structure in Babylon, struggled to truncate the earliest author that he wove into the text, in order to hold off the strangeness and uncanny power of the Yahwist or J writer. The Yahwist could not be excluded, because his (or her) stories possessed authority, but the disconcerting Yahweh, human-all-too-human, could be muted by other voices of the divine.

What is the relationship of fresh genius to a founded authority? At this time, starting the twenty-first century, I would say: "Why, none, none at all." Our confusions about canonical standards for genius are now institutionalized confusions, so that all judgments as to the distinction between talent and genius are at the mercy of the media, and obey cultural politics and its vagaries.

Since my book, by presenting a mosaic of a hundred authentic geniuses, attempts to provide criteria for judgment, I will venture here upon a purely personal definition of genius, one that hopes to be useful for the early years of this new century. Whether charisma necessarily attends genius seems to me problematic. Of my hundred figures in this book, I had met three—Iris Murdoch, Octavio Paz, Ralph Ellison—who died relatively recently. Farther back, I recall brief meetings with Robert Frost and Wallace Stevens. All of them impressive, in different ways, they lacked the flamboyance and authority of Gershom Scholem, whose genius attended him palpably, despite his irony and high good humor.

William Hazlitt wrote an essay on persons one would wish to have known. I stare at my Kabbalistic table of contents, and wonder which I would choose. The critic Sainte-Beuve advised us to ask ourselves: what would this author I read have thought of me? My particular hero among these hundred is Dr. Samuel Johnson, the god of literary criticism, but I do not have the courage to face his judgment.

Genius asserts authority over me, when I recognize powers greater than my own. Emerson, the sage I attempt to follow, would disapprove of my pragmatic surrender, but Emerson's own genius was so large that he plausibly could preach Self-Reliance. I myself have taught continuously for forty-six years, and wish I could urge an Emersonian self-reliance upon my students, but I can't and don't, for the most part. I hope to nurture genius in them, but can impart only a genius for appreciation. That is the prime purpose of this book: to activate the genius of appreciation in my readers, if I can.

These pages are written a week after the September 11, 2001, terrorist triumph in destroying the World Trade Center and the people trapped within it. During the last week I have taught scheduled classes on Wallace Stevens and Elizabeth Bishop, on Shakespeare's early comedies, and on the *Odyssey*. I cannot know whether I helped my students at all, but I momentarily held off my own trauma, by freshly appreciating genius.

What is it that I, and many others, appreciate in genius? An entry in Emerson's *Journals* (October 27, 1831) always hovers in my memory:

> Is it not all in us, how strangely! Look at this congregation of men;— the words might be spoken,—though now there be none here to speak them,—but the words might be said that would make them stagger and reel like a drunken man. Who doubts it? Were you ever instructed by a wise and eloquent man? Remember then, were not the words that made your blood run cold, that brought the blood to your cheeks, that made you tremble or delighted you,—did they not sound to you as old as yourself? Was it not truth that you knew before, or do you ever expect to be moved from the pulpit or from man by anything but plain truth? Never. It is God in you that responds to God without, or affirms his own words trembling on the lips of another.

It still burns into me: "did they not sound to you as old as yourself?" The ancient critic Longinus called literary genius the Sublime, and saw its operation as a transfer of power from author to reader:

> Touched by the true sublime your soul is naturally lifted up, she rises to a proud height, is filled with joy and vaunting, as if she had herself created this thing that she has heard.

Literary genius, difficult to define, depends upon deep reading for its verification. The reader learns to identify with what she or he feels is a greatness that can be joined to the self, without violating the self's integrity. "Greatness" may be out of fashion, as is the transcendental, but it is hard to go on living without some hope of encountering the extraordinary.

Meeting the extraordinary in another person is likely to be deceptive or delusionary. We call it "falling in love," and the verb is a warning. To confront the extraordinary in a book—be it the Bible, Plato, Shakespeare, Dante, Proust—is to benefit almost without cost. Genius, in its writings, is our best path for reaching wisdom, which I believe to be the true use of literature for life.

James Joyce, when asked, "Which one book on a desert island?", replied, "I would like to answer Dante, but I would have to take the Englishman, because he is richer." The Joycean Irish edge against the English is given adequate expression, but the choice of Shakespeare is just, which is why he leads off the hundred figures in this book. Though there are a few literary geniuses who approach Shakespeare—the Yahwist, Homer, Plato, Dante, Chaucer, Cervantes, Molière, Goethe, Tolstoy, Dickens, Proust, Joyce— even those dozen masters of representation do not match Shakespeare's miraculous rendering of reality. Because of Shakespeare we see what otherwise we could not see, since we are made different. Dante, the nearest rival, persuades us of the terrible reality of his Inferno and his Purgatorio, and almost induces us to accept his Paradiso. Yet even the fullest of the *Divine Comedy*'s persons, Dante the Poet-Pilgrim, does not cross over from the *Comedy*'s pages into the world we inhabit, as do Falstaff, Hamlet, Iago, Macbeth, Lear, Cleopatra.

The invasion of our reality by Shakespeare's prime personages is evidence for the vitality of literary characters, when created by genius. We all know the empty sensation we experience when we read popular fiction and find that there are only names upon the page, but no persons. In time, however overpraised, such fictions become period pieces, and finally rub down into rubbish. It is worth knowing that our word "character" still possesses, as a primary meaning, a graphic sign such as a letter of the alphabet, reflecting the word's likely origin in the ancient Greek *character*, a sharp stylus or the mark of the stylus's incisions. Our modern word "character" also means ethos, a habitual stance towards life.

It was fashionable, quite recently, to talk about "the death of the author," but this too has become rubbish. The dead genius is more alive than we are, just as Falstaff and Hamlet are considerably livelier than many people I know. Vitality is the measure of literary genius. We read in search of more life, and only genius can make that available to use.

What makes genius possible? There always is a Spirit of the Age, and we like to delude ourselves that what matters most about any memorable figure is what he or she shared with a particular era. In this delusion, which is both academic and popular, everyone is regarded as being determined by societal factors. Individual imagination yields to social anthropology or to mass psychology, and thus can be explained away.

I base this book, *Genius*, upon my belief that appreciation is a better mode for the understanding of achievement than are all the analytical kinds of accounting for the emergence of exceptional individuals. Appreciation may judge, but always with gratitude, and frequently with awe and wonder.

By "appreciation" I mean something more than "adequate esteem." Need also enters into it, in the particular sense of turning to the genius of others in order to redress a lack in oneself, or finding in genius a stimulus to one's own powers, whatever these may emerge as being.

Appreciation may modulate into love, even as your consciousness of a dead genius augments consciousness itself. Your solitary self's deepest desire is for survival, whether in the here and now, or transcendentally elsewhere. To be augmented by the genius of others is to enhance the possibilities of survival, at least in the present and the near future.

We do not know how and/or why genius is possible, only that—to our massive enrichment—it has existed, and perhaps (waningly) continues to appear. Though our academic institutions abound in impostors who proclaim that genius is a capitalistic myth, I am content to cite Leon Trotsky, who urged Communist writers to read and study Dante. If genius is a mystery of the capacious consciousness, what is least mysterious about it is an intimate connection with personality rather than with character. Dante's personality is forbidding, Shakespeare's elusive, while Jesus' (like the fictive Hamlet's) seems to reveal itself differently to every reader or auditor.

What is personality? Alas, we use it now as a popular synonym for celebrity, but I would argue that we cannot give the word up to the realm of buzz. When we know enough about the biography of a particular genius, then we understand what is meant by the personality of Goethe or Byron or Freud or Oscar Wilde. Conversely, when we lack biographical inwardness, then we all agree that we are uncertain as to Shakespeare's personality, an enormous paradox since his plays may have invented personality as we now most readily comprehend it. If challenged, I could write a book on the personality of Hamlet, Falstaff, or Cleopatra, but I would not attempt a book upon the personality of Shakespeare or of Jesus.

Benjamin Disraeli's father, the man of letters Isaac D'Israeli, wrote an

amiable volume called *The Literary Character of Men of Genius,* one of the precursors to this book, *Genius,* together with Plutarch's *Parallel Lives,* Emerson's *Representative Men,* and Carlyle's *On Heroes and Hero-Worship.* Isaac
D'Israeli remarks that "many men of genius must arise before a particular
man of genius can appear." Every genius has forerunners, though far enough
back in time we may not know who they are. Dr. Johnson considered Homer
to have been the first and most original of poets; we tend to see Homer as
a relative latecomer, enriching himself with the phrases and formulas of his
predecessors. Emerson, in his essay "Quotation and Originality," slyly observed, "Only an inventor knows how to borrow."

The great inventions of genius influence that genius itself in ways we are
slow to appreciate. We speak of the man or woman in the work; we might
better speak of the work in the person. And yet we scarcely know how to
discuss the influence of a work upon its author, or of a mind upon itself. I
take that to be the principal enterprise of this book. With all of the figures
I depict in this mosaic, my emphasis will be on the contest they conducted
with themselves.

That agon with the self can mask itself as something else, including the
inspiration of idealized forerunners: Plato's Socrates, Confucius's the Duke
of Chou, the Buddha's earlier incarnations. Particularly the inventor of the
Hebrew Bible as we know it, the Redactor of the sequence from Genesis
through Kings, relies upon his own genius at reimagining the Covenant
even as he honors the virtues (and failings) of the fathers. And yet, as Donald
Harmon Akenson argues, the inventor-redactor or writer-editor achieved a
"surpassing wonder," utterly his own. This exile in Babylon could not have
thought that he was creating Scripture; as the first historian he perhaps believed only that he was forwarding the lost cause of the Kingdom of Judah.
And yet he seems too cunning not to have seen that his invention of a continuity and so of a tradition was largely his own.

With the Redactor, as with Confucius or with Plato, we can sense an anxiety in the work that must have communicated itself to the man. How can
one be worthy of the fathers with whom Yahweh spoke, face-to-face, or of
the great Duke of Chou, who gave order to the people without imposing it
upon them by violence? Is it possible to be the authentic disciple of
Socrates, who suffered martyrdom without complaint, in order to affirm his
truth? The ultimate anxiety of influence always may be, not that one's
proper space has been usurped already, but that greatness may be unable to
renew itself, that one's inspiration may be larger than one's own powers of
realization.

*   *   *

Genius is no longer a term much favored by scholars, so many of whom have become cultural levelers quite immune from awe. Yet, with the public, the idea of genius maintains its prestige, even though the word itself can seem somewhat tarnished. We *need* genius, however envious or uncomfortable it makes many among us. It is not necessary that we aspire after genius for ourselves, and yet, in our recesses, we remember that we had, or have, a genius. Our desire for the transcendental and extraordinary seems part of our common heritage, and abandons us slowly, and never completely.

To say that the work is *in* the writer, or the religious idea is *in* the charismatic leader, is not a paradox. Shakespeare, we happen to know, was a usurer. So was Shylock, but did that help to keep *The Merchant of Venice* a comedy? We don't know. But to look for the work in the writer is to look for the influence and effect of the play upon Shakespeare's development from comedy to tragicomedy to tragedy. It is to see Shylock darkening Shakespeare. To examine the effects of his own parables upon the figure of Jesus is to conduct a parallel exploration.

There are two ancient (Roman) meanings of the word "genius," which are rather different in emphasis. One is to beget, cause to be born, that is to be a paterfamilias. The other is to be an attendant spirit for each person or place: to be either a good or evil genius, and so to be someone who, for better or for worse, strongly influences someone else. This second meaning has been more important than the first; our genius is thus our inclination or natural gift, our inborn intellectual or imaginative power, not our power to beget power in others.

We all learn to distinguish, firmly and definitively, between genius and talent. A "talent" classically was a weight or sum of money, and as such, however large, was necessarily limited. But "genius," even in its linguistic origins, has no limits.

We tend now to regard genius as the creative capacity, as opposed to talent. The Victorian historian Froude observed that genius "is a spring in which there is always more behind than flows from it." The largest instances of genius that we know, aesthetically, would include Shakespeare and Dante, Bach and Mozart, Michelangelo and Rembrandt, Donatello and Rodin, Alberti and Brunelleschi. A greater complexity ensues when we attempt to confront religious genius, particularly in a religion-obsessed country like the United States. To regard Jesus and Muhammad as religious geniuses (whatever else they were) makes them, in that regard only, akin not only to one another but to Zoroaster and the Buddha, and to such secular figures of ethical genius as Confucius and Socrates.

Defining genius more precisely than has yet been done is one of my objectives in this book. Another is to defend the idea of genius, currently abused by detractors and reductionists, from sociobiologists through the materialists of the genome school, and on to various historicizers. But my primary aim is both to enhance our appreciation of genius, and to show how invariably it is engendered by the stimulus of prior genius, to a much greater degree than it is by cultural and political contexts. The influence of genius upon itself, already mentioned, will be one of the book's major emphases.

My subject is universal, not so much because world-altering geniuses have existed, and will come again, but because genius, however repressed, exists in so many readers. Emerson thought that all Americans were potential poets and mystics. *Genius* does not teach how to read or whom to read, but rather how to think about exemplary human lives at their most creative.

It will be noted in the table of contents that I have excluded any living instances of genius, and have dealt with only three recently dead. In this book I am compelled to be brief and summary in my account of individual genius, because I believe that much is to be learned by juxtaposing many figures from varied cultures and contrasting eras. The differences between a hundred men and women, drawn from a span of twenty-five centuries, overwhelm the analogies or similarities, and to present them within a single volume may seem the enterprise of an overreacher. And yet there are common characteristics to genius, since vivid individuality of speculation, spirituality, and creativity must rely upon originality, audacity, and self-reliance.

Emerson, in his *Representative Men*, begins with a heartening paragraph:

> It is natural to believe in great men. If the companions of our childhood should turn out to be heroes, and their condition regal, it will not surprise us. All mythology opens with demigods, and the circumstance is high and poetic; that is, their genius is paramount. In the legends of Gautama, the first men ate the earth, and found it deliciously sweet.

Gautama, *the* Buddha, quests for and attains freedom, as though he were one of the first men. Emerson's twice-told tale is a touch more American than Buddhist; his first men seem American Adams, and not reincarnations of previous enlightenments. Perhaps I too can only Americanize, but that may be the paramount use of past geniuses; we have to adapt them to our place and our time, if we are to be enlightened or inspired by them.

Emerson had six great or representative men: Plato, Swedenborg, Montaigne, Shakespeare, Napoleon, and Goethe. Four of these are in this book; Swedenborg is replaced by Blake, and Napoleon I have discarded with all other generals and politicians. Plato, Montaigne, Shakespeare, and Goethe remain essential, as do the others I sketch. Essential for what? To know ourselves, in relation to others, for these mighty dead are among the *otherness* that we can know, as Emerson tells us in *Representative Men:*

> We need not fear excessive influence. A more generous trust is permitted. Serve the great.

And yet this is the conclusion of his book:

> The world is young: the former great men call to us affectionately. We too must write Bibles, to unite again the heavens and the earthly world. The secret of genius is to suffer no fiction to exist for us; to realize all that we know.

To realize all that we know, fictions included, is too large an enterprise for us, a wounded century and a half after Emerson. The world no longer seems young, and I do not always hear the accents of affection when the voices of genius call out to me. But then I have the disadvantage, and the advantage, of coming after Emerson. The genius of influence transcends its constituent anxieties, provided we become aware of them and then surmise where we stand in relation to their continuing prevalence.

Thomas Carlyle, a Victorian Scottish genius now out of fashion, wrote an admirable study that almost nobody reads anymore, *On Heroes, Hero-Worship and the Heroic in History.* It contains the best remark on Shakespeare that I know:

> If called to define Shakespeare's faculty, I should say superiority of intellect, and think I had included all under that.

Adumbrating the observation, Carlyle characteristically exploded into a very useful warning against dividing any genius into its illusory components:

> What indeed are faculties? We talk of faculties as if they were distinct, things separable; as if a man had intellect, imagination, fancy, etc. as he had hands, feet and arms.

"Power of Insight," Carlyle continued, was the vital force in any one of us. How do we recognize that insight or force in genius? We have the works of genius, and we have the memory of their personalities. I use that last word with high deliberation, following Walter Pater, another Victorian genius, but one who defies fashion, because he is akin to Emerson and to Nietzsche. These three subtle thinkers prophesied much of the intellectual future of our century that has just passed, and are unlikely to fade as influences during the new century. Pater's preface to his major book, *The Renaissance*, emphasizes that the "aesthetic critic" ("aesthetic" meaning "perceptive") identifies genius in every era:

> In all ages there have been some excellent workmen, and some excellent work done. The question he asks is always:—In whom did it stir, the genius, the sentiment of the period find itself? Where was the receptacle of his refinement, its elevation, its taste? "The ages are all equal," says William Blake, "but genius is always above its age."

Blake, a visionary genius almost without peer, is a superb guide to the relative independence that genius manifests in regard to time: it "is always above its age." We cannot confront the twenty-first century without expecting that it too will give us a Stravinsky or Louis Armstrong, a Picasso or Matisse, a Proust or James Joyce. To hope for a Dante or Shakespeare, a J. S. Bach or Mozart, a Michelangelo or Leonardo, is to ask for too much, since gifts that enormous are very rare. Yet we want and need what will rise above the twenty-first century, whatever that turns out to be.

The use of my mosaic is that it ought to help prepare us for this new century, by summoning up aspects of the personality and achievements of many of the most creative who have come before us. The ancient Roman made an offering to his *genius* on his birthday, dedicating that day to "the god of human nature," as the poet Horace called each person's tutelary spirit. Our custom of a birthday cake is in direct descent from that offering. We light the candles and might do well to remember what it is that we are celebrating.

GENIUS:

A Personal Definition

I have avoided all living geniuses in this book, partly so as to evade the distractions of mere provocation. I can identify for myself certain writers of palpable genius now among us: the Portuguese novelist José Saramago, the Canadian poet Anne Carson, the English poet Geoffrey Hill, and at least a half-dozen North and Latin American novelists and poets (whom I forbear naming).

Pondering my mosaic of one hundred exemplary creative minds, I arrive at a tentative and personal definition of literary genius. The question of genius was a perpetual concern of Ralph Waldo Emerson, who is the mind of America, as Walt Whitman is its poet, and Henry James its novelist (its dramatist is yet to come). For Emerson, genius was the God within, the self of "Self-Reliance." That self, in Emerson, therefore is not constituted by history, by society, by languages. It is aboriginal. I altogether agree.

Shakespeare, the supreme genius, is different in kind from his contemporaries, even from Christopher Marlowe and Ben Jonson. Cervantes stands apart from Lope de Vega, and Calderón. Something in Shakespeare and Cervantes, as in Dante, Montaigne, Milton, and Proust (to give only a few instances), is clearly both of and above the age.

Fierce originality is one crucial component of literary genius, but this originality itself is always canonical, in that it recognizes and comes to terms with precursors. Even Shakespeare makes an implicit covenant with Chaucer, his essential forerunner at inventing the human.

If genius is the God within, I need to seek it there, in the abyss of the aboriginal self, an entity unknown to nearly all our current Explainers, in the intellectually forlorn universities and in the media's dark Satanic mills.

Emerson and ancient Gnosticism agree that what is best and oldest in each of us is no part of the Creation, no part of Nature or the Not-Me. Each of us presumably can locate what is best in herself or himself, but how do we find what is *oldest?*

Where does the self begin? The Freudian answer is that the ego makes an investment in itself, which thus centers a self. Shakespeare calls our sense of identity the "selfsame"; when did Jack Falstaff become Falstaff? When did Shakespeare become Shakespeare? *The Comedy of Errors* is already a work of genius, yet who could have prophesied *Twelfth Night* on the basis of that early farce? Our recognition of genius is always retroactive, but how does genius first recognize itself?

The ancient answer is that there is a god within us, and the god speaks. I think that a materialist definition of genius is impossible, which is why the idea of genius is so discredited in an age like our own, where materialist ideologies dominate. Genius, by necessity, invokes the transcendental and the extraordinary, because it is fully conscious of them. Consciousness is what defines genius: Shakespeare, like his Hamlet, exceeds us in consciousness, goes beyond the highest order of consciousness that we are capable of knowing without him.

Gnosticism, by definition, is a knowing rather than a believing. In Shakespeare, we have neither a knower nor a believer, but a consciousness so capacious that we cannot find its rival elsewhere: in Cervantes or Montaigne, in Freud or in Wittgenstein. Those who choose (or are chosen) by one of the world religions frequently posit a cosmic consciousness to which they assign supernatural origins. But Shakespearean consciousness, which transmutes matter into imagination, does not need to violate nature. Shakespeare's art is itself nature, and his consciousness can seem more the product of his art than its producer.

There, at the end of the mind, we are stationed by Shakespearean genius: a consciousness shaped by all the consciousnesses that he imagined. He remains, presumably forever, our largest instance of the use of literature for life, which is the work of augmenting awareness.

Though Shakespeare's is the largest consciousness studied in this book, all the rest of these exemplary creative minds have contributed to the consciousness of their readers and auditors. The question we need to put to any writer must be: does she or he augment our consciousness, and how is it done? I find this a rough but effectual test: however I have been entertained, has my awareness been intensified, my consciousness widened and clarified? If not, then I have encountered talent, not genius. What is best and oldest in myself has not been activated.

I

KETER

LUSTRE 1

William Shakespeare, Miguel de Cervantes, Michel de Montaigne, John Milton, Leo Tolstoy

Keter or the crown, in Kabbalah at once everything and nothingness, begins with this first Lustre of masters, each of whom dominates his genre forever. Shakespeare usurps all modern drama, Cervantes the novel, Montaigne the personal essay, and Milton the secondary or postclassical epic. Tolstoy, whether as modern novelist or storywriter, comes close to Shakespeare's other usurpation: of nature itself.

Shakespeare, Cervantes, and Montaigne were contemporaries, yet Shakespeare, open to absorbing any influence, uses both Montaigne and Cervantes in his work (though *Cardenio*, a Cervantine adaptation done by Shakespeare and John Fletcher, is a lost play). Milton uneasily is profoundly influenced by Shakespeare: Satan blends aspects of Iago, Macbeth, even Hamlet. Tolstoy, who hated and condemned Shakespeare as immoral, nevertheless had a fondness for Falstaff, while *Hadji Murad*, the superb short novel of Tolstoy's old age, is Shakespearean in all its varied characterizations.

WILLIAM SHAKESPEARE

> Th'expense of spirit in a waste of shame
> Is lust in action; and, till action, lust
> Is perjured, murd'rous, bloody, full of blame,
> Savage, extreme, rude, cruel, not to trust;
> Enjoyed no sooner but despisèd straight;
> Past reason hunted, and no sooner had,
> Past reason hated as a swallowed bait
> On purpose laid to make the taker mad;
> Mad in pursuit, and in possession so;
> Had, having, and in quest to have, extreme;
> A bliss in proof, and proved, a very woe,
> Before, a joy proposed; behind, a dream.
> > All this the world well knows, yet none knows well
> > To shun the heaven that leads men to this hell.
> > > —Sonnet 129

Shakespeare, who at the least changed our ways of presenting human nature, if not human nature itself, does not portray himself anywhere in his plays. Whether he reveals his inwardness in his one hundred and fifty-four sonnets is disputable, and yet his genius is manifested in them almost unfailingly. Published in 1609, the Sonnets may go back as far as 1593, but if they are in any way autobiographical, they seem deliberately distanced from self-revelation. The most powerful, Sonnet 129, sustains itself at an extraordinary pitch of controlled intensity, while carefully evading all of the personae of the Sonnets: the fair young nobleman, the Dark Lady, the rival poet, and most crucially the "I" who speaks almost all of the other sonnets. Will, desire, even revulsion are impersonalized, but the furious energy of these fourteen lines conveys, with terrible eloquence, a negative judgment upon the indiscriminant element in the male sexual drive, whose orgasmic culmination is "a waste of shame." The sexual "spending" is merely a "waste of spirit" in the "hell," one vagina or another, that concludes the poem.

Shakespeare, who created Rosalind, Falstaff, Hamlet, Iago, Lear, Macbeth, Cleopatra—figures we can know better than ourselves—declines to create himself in his sonnets. He provides us with an almost infinite range of surmise, but he withdraws even from his own apparent erotic humiliations and sufferings. It may be that his own self-estrangement is a hint he gives us so that we can sustain the massive sufferings aesthetically granted us by the high tragedies.

WILLIAM SHAKESPEARE
(1564–1616)

To contemplate Shakespeare's genius is at once to encounter the critic's despair and the critic's ecstasy. One doubts that the dying Shakespeare, barely fifty-two, took comfort in having created Hamlet, Falstaff, Lear, Iago, Cleopatra, Rosalind, and Macbeth: the men and women, whose reality, supposedly fictive, transcends our own. If I could question any dead author, it would be Shakespeare, and I would not waste my seconds by asking the identity of the Dark Lady or the precisely nuanced elements of homoeroticism in the relationship with Southampton (or another). Naively, I would blurt out: did it comfort you to have fashioned women and men more real than living men and women?

Shakespeare's language is primary to his art, and is florabundant. He had a deep drive to coin words anew, and I am always astonished that he employed more than twenty-one thousand separate words. Of these, he invented roughly one out of the twelve: about eighteen hundred coinages, many of them now in common use. Racine, superbly practicing an art antithetical to Shakespeare's, used two thousand words, not many more than Shakespeare coined. Though rhetorical criticism confronts a task both fruitful and formidable in analyzing Shakespeare's great feast of language, he differs in degree rather than in kind from a handful of other poets in English whose verbal resources are virtually endless. The true Shakespearean difference, the uniqueness of his genius, is elsewhere, in his universality, in the persuasive illusion (is it illusion?) that he has peopled a world, remarkably like what we take to be our own, with men, women, and children preternaturally natural. Cervantes rivals him with two giant personalities, Don Quixote and Sancho Panza, but Shakespeare has hundreds. Barnardine, in *Measure for Measure*, speaks only five times, and for a total of seven sentences, and yet we know him completely.

Is there another dramatist who excelled equally at comedy and tragedy? We have no comedies by Sophocles, or tragedies by Aristophanes. Ben Jonson ventured both, but we are grateful for his comedies, *Volpone* and *The Alchemist*, and agree with his contemporaries that *Sejanus* is scarcely playable. We do not expect comedy from Racine, or tragedy from Molière. Ibsen writes a mixed form: *Peer Gynt* is not quite comedy, and *Hedda Gabler* is something other than tragedy. Bernard Shaw certainly should have stayed with comedy: *Pygmalion* is still alive, but *Saint Joan* is an embarrassment. Shakespeare alone can compose a *Twelfth Night* and a *King Lear.* Why?

As Plato's *Symposium* comes to its end, everyone has gone home or fallen into a drunken sleep except for the tragic dramatist Agathon, Aristophanes, and Socrates, who could outdrink all Athens. The three survivors pass around an enormous bowl of wine, and keep drinking while Socrates argues that the same man ought to be able to write both comedy and tragedy. Overcome both by the sage's argument and the wine, first Aristophanes and then Agathon fall asleep. Tucking them both in, Socrates walks forth into the dawn.

Jesting aside, Plato seems to be carrying on his contest with the poets. We can surmise how he would have reacted to Shakespeare, whose comprehensive art would have resulted in the dramatist's immediate exile from the Platonic Republic. Since only Shakespeare meets Socrates' challenge, it may be useful to surmise why and how the playwright of *As You Like It* could become the author of *Macbeth.* There is no family resemblance between Sir John Falstaff and Iago, no clear link between Shylock and Hamlet. Even the supreme clown Feste and the Fool in *King Lear* have nothing in common except their profession.

Shakespeare was not a great tragic dramatist until he wrote *Hamlet* at the turn into the seventeenth century. That made possible the sequence of *Othello, King Lear, Macbeth, Antony and Cleopatra,* and *Coriolanus.* Of the early tragedies, *Titus Andronicus* is both a send-up and a bloody farce, really a parody. *Romeo and Juliet* is a superb lyric, but is a tragedy of circumstance; nothing in Juliet's own character leads to the catastrophe. Dr. Johnson found *Julius Caesar* to be cold, and I agree; the well-crafted tragedy of Brutus does not move us, because he is a hollow man, caught up in the solipsism of his own nobility. Shakespeare had to learn tragedy, and achieved it only the fourth time around. He was not a born tragedian, or an inevitable one, and he paid a high inward cost for his descent into the abyss of Iago, Edmund, Macbeth.

Yet, in comedy, he was wonderful from the start. *The Comedy of Errors* is critically underestimated. It is not only beautifully shaped, but its portrait of Antipholus of Syracuse has psychological resonance and very precise delineation. We misplay and misread *The Taming of the Shrew* as a misogynistic romp: it is quite otherwise in its subtle account of how a true marriage is formed as defense against the world's supposed wisdom. *Love's Labour's Lost* is an almost unknown masterpiece, concealing its comic wealth beneath the baroque splendors of its high rhetoric. Without Shylock, *The Merchant of*

Venice would be one of the most inventive of romantic comedies; with him, it is a severe enigma. The comic triumphs, unmatched even by Molière, are *A Midsummer Night's Dream, As You Like It, Twelfth Night,* and what I regard as the Falstaffiad, the two parts of *Henry IV.* Falstaff darkens in the second part, and ends an outcast, in that limbo inhabited by Shylock and which poor Malvolio will join. And yet Falstaff is what William Hazlitt regarded him as being: the height of comic achievement in all literature, as befits a figure who competes with Hamlet and Rosalind in wit, intelligence, and psychological acuity.

Going with his own impulse, Shakespeare wrote comedy, until shadows envelop *Troilus and Cressida, All's Well That Ends Well,* and *Measure for Measure,* the scherzo that destroys the genre. Against the grain, he composed tragedy, until *Timon of Athens* similarly ended the mode for him. The final phase we have again mistaken, by adopting the late-nineteenth-century Irish critic Edward Dowden's naming of its plays as the "late romances." The Shakespearean parts of *Pericles,* and at the very end, of *The Two Noble Kinsmen,* are tragicomedies, as are *Cymbeline, The Winter's Tale,* and *The Tempest.* All these are comedies with a difference, but comedies nevertheless.

Presumably a blend of commercial and personal notions guided Shakespeare's movement between dramas, though we are unlikely ever to know the personal elements. But we are thinking of the largest consciousness and most incisive intellect in all literature, surpassing even Dante's. Though Shakespeare, unlike Ben Jonson, always mixed genres, and broke all the rules, he is unlikely to have been unaware of the infinite reaches of his own powers. Old-style theatricalists and our current rabblement of directorial and academic advocates of French Shakespeare (the plays as Foucault would have written them) have obscured the literary complexities of the major plays.

Aside from the quartos—authorized and pirated—we still would know that Shakespeare expected to be read if we ourselves will read at all closely. We drown in the visual media; Shakespeare's audience, schooled by church, were better able to absorb intricacies through the ear. Yet even the quickest among them would have had great trouble apprehending the Player King's crucial speech in the play-within-the-play (act 3, scene 2, 183–209), twenty-six densely argued lines that conclude:

> Our wills and fates do so contrary run
> That our devices still are overthrown:
> Our thoughts are ours, their ends none of our own.

To meditate upon genius is necessarily to reflect upon true originality and upon creative primacies. In relation to Homer and the Bible, Shakespeare was belated, but neither Chapman's Homer nor the Geneva Bible was more than a sourcebook for him, both less important pragmatically than Ovid. Except during his earlier years as a dramatist, when Christopher Marlowe was something of a trouble to him, Shakespeare happily accepted contamination by forerunners. The creation of Falstaff and of Hamlet freed Shakespeare from any vestiges of Marlowe, except for those he ironically extended as instruments of parody. Falstaff's prose, and Hamlet's poetry and prose alike, are Shakespeare's celebration of his own genius.

There are other characters than Shakespeare's, in the world's literature, who seem always to have been there, long before their authors brought them into being. And yet it is the peculiarity of Shakespeare's triumph that his women and men, scores of them, give us the illusion that Shakespeare is *their* creature, or at least one of them, another of their company. William Hazlitt said of Falstaff, "he is an actor in himself almost as much as upon the stage." I love almost everything Falstaff says, but I love best his declaration to Hal:

> O, thou hast damnable iteration, and art indeed able to corrupt a saint: thou hast done much harm upon me, Hal, God forgive thee for it: before I knew thee, Hal, I knew nothing, and now am I, if a man should speak truly, little better than one of the wicked.

Does anyone else, in all of literature, enjoy what he is saying as much as Falstaff does? That is Hazlitt's point: Falstaff is an actor in himself, as well as an actor's role. Falstaff always plays the part of Sir John Falstaff, even as his true sister-in-Shakespeare, Cleopatra, never stops playing the part of the old serpent of the Nile. I shake my head in wonder when I try to remind myself that Falstaff and Cleopatra are parts for players, and the reminder barely works.

Nor should it work. The reality of literary and dramatic character is a necessary predicate, if the reader is to sustain a sense of her own reality. There is no death of the author, contra the egregious Foucault. At seventy-one, one rightly becomes impatient at all those who would reduce authors to social energies, readers to gleaners of phonemes, and Falstaff, Hamlet, and Cleopatra to roles for actors and actresses. Our deaths are real enough; should our lives be less real? All that Hamlet, Falstaff, and Cleopatra require of you is that you not bore them.

At whose altar should one worship? Who else is there? If one were

Sancho Panza or Don Quixote, one might choose Cervantes, but those two sublimities are alone with one another. How often can we play a role that is not Shakespeare's? Or should I say: that is not already Shakespeare's? Emerson thought that the creator of Falstaff was the master of the revels to mankind. Yet even Emerson nodded; Falstaff competes with Montaigne's Socrates, as the sage of human consciousness. Despite the qualified praise of Dr. Johnson, and the enthusiasm of Hazlitt, Swinburne, A. C. Bradley, and Harold Goddard, Falstaff still seems to me—in proportion to his gifts and merits—the most undervalued personage in all of Western literature. I will expatiate therefore upon the genius of Sir John Falstaff.

His continuous high spirits, though sublimely charming, belong more to Falstaff's charisma than to his genius, in any sense of "genius." Though Falstaff accurately commends himself for "wit"—a much wider term than our "wit"—Sir John is not wittier in himself than are Hamlet, Rosalind, and Cleopatra, or in a terrifying mode, Iago and Edmund. Falstaff, as always, gets it right when he remarks that he is not only witty in himself but the cause of wit in other men. Falstaff is a teacher, and he teaches wit, even at his own high expense. His raggle-taggle company of irregular humorists are poor students, being merely his imitators. But he has one prize pupil: great, cold, unloving, hypocritical, Machiavellian Prince Hal—a student of authentic genius. Before *Henry IV, Part I* begins, Hal's course of study is complete, and the outrageous Professor Falstaff—irrepressible and omnipresent—needs, in the Prince's judgment, to be terminated, perhaps with maximum prejudice upon the gallows. Shakespeare could not endure handing Falstaff over to the hangman. Indeed he could not tolerate Falstaff (or Macbeth!) dying upon stage. But Hal passionately desires and indeed needs to get Falstaff off the stage, for until Falstaff ceases to distract us, Hal cannot be a star turn. All through *Henry IV, Part I*, Hal battles to make the play part of *The Henriad*, by destroying Hotspur and thus usurping his achieved "honour," and by overgoing Falstaff, by whatever means. Hal, formidable infighter, feels: who can overgo Sir John? Hal and Shakespeare know better by Part II, where Hal shares (hardly the right word!) only two scenes with Falstaff. The Prince spies upon Falstaff poignantly but rather tawdrily courting the whore, Doll Tearsheet, and at the end with horrible moralizing brutality rejects and humiliates his old companion. Shakespeare, in an epilogue, promises to bring Falstaff to France in *Henry V*, but wisely thought better of it. Even a rejected Falstaff would steal Hal's own play from him. Sir John would turn the Battle of Agincourt into a rerun of the Battle of Shrewsbury, and there would be no play. Imagine Henry V ranting, "We few, we happy few" to a company including Falstaff. It is inconceivable.

Agincourt is not a fight that you go into with a bottle of sack in your holster. And neither the audience nor the dramatist would tolerate Sir John replacing poor Bardolph at a hanging to encourage the others.

Shakespeare, though he could not allow Falstaff to die on stage, gives the best speech in *Henry V* to Mistress Quickly, who sings a superb cockney prose aria of the passing of Sir John Falstaff:

> Nay, sure he's not in hell. He's in Arthur's bosom, if ever man went to Arthur's bosom. 'A made a finer end, and went away an' it had been any christom child. 'A parted ev'n just between twelve and one, ev'n at the turning o' th' tide—for after I saw him fumble with the sheets, and play with flowers, and smile upon his finger's end, I knew there was but one way. For his nose was a sharp as a pen, and a table of green fields. "How now, Sir John?" quoth I. "What, man! Be o' good cheer?" so he cried "God, God, God," three or four times. Now I, to comfort him, bid him a should not think of God; I hoped there was no need to trouble himself with any such thoughts yet. So a bad me lay more clothes on his feet. I put my hand into the bed and felt them, and they were as cold as any stone. Then I felt to his knees, and so up'ard and up'ard, and all was as cold as any stone.

"Thou hast prepared a table for me in the midst of my enemies," King David sings in Psalm 23, which gives the confused Mistress Quickly her "table of green fields," which the scholar Theobald wrongly revised into "and 'a babbled of green fields." And so Sir John is given a dying music that rivals Hamlet's as Shakespeare wistfully murmurs of his greatest creations, "Let it be."

Yet I am not willing to let be the educational genius of Falstaff, the Socrates of Eastcheap, who also dies of poison. Henry V destroys what is mortal in Sir John as completely as he cuts down the dazzling Hotspur. But Socrates had his daemon or genius, and so does Falstaff, and the genius is a god, beyond Hal's vengeful reach. Wyndham Lewis and William Empson both insinuated a prior homoerotic relationship between Hal and Falstaff, but I cannot uncover any such insinuation in Shakespeare's text. Alcibiades tells us that he had attempted to seduce Socrates but failed. It seems improbable that Hal should have made so grotesque a venture, in the Falstaffiad's long foreground. Hal and Hotspur have a more persuasive overtone of the homoerotic in their antagonistic relationship, but Falstaff teaches in a style very different from that of Socrates. Socrates professes a wise ignorance, but Sir John knows himself in all things, and teaches by excess, by an overflowing rather than by an *ascecis*. Falstaff's forerunners in Shakespeare are Falconbridge the Bastard in *King John* and the grandly underrated Bottom of *A Midsummer Night's Dream*. Beyond these precursors, Falstaff outfaces every reversal, and triumphs until he dies for love: a teacher's love, I would emphasize.

But I have heard skeptics question this love. Well, what is a teacher's love? In the English-speaking academic world, closely ruled by campus Puritans, we now have knitting-circles of Madame Defarges, sadistically awaiting the spectacle of the guillotine, fit punishment for "sexual harassment," that poor parody of the Socratic Eros. Though seventy-one, and so someone for whom virtue and exhaustion have become synonymous, I continue to believe that an eros more dualistic even than that of Socrates is appropriate, indeed essential, for effective teaching. Emerson cheerfully reminded Americans (and all others) that only the transcendental and extraordinary could suffice. Of Golgotha, Emerson observed: "this was a Great Defeat— we demand Victory, a victory to the sense as well as to the soul." The Emersonian outrageousness is altogether Falstaffian—Sir John also demands Victory, everywhere except upon the battlefield, where the disdainer of honor is dragged despite himself. Why? Prince Hal's motive is clear enough: an honorable death would redeem the now inconvenient teacher. Shakespeare replies, with Falstaff, "Sir Walter Blunt! There's honor for you! I like not such grinning honor as Sir Walter hath. Give me life."

You would not then appoint Falstaff to the faculty at West Point or at Sandhurst. Would you appoint him at Yale? Even if by gift and guile, he were to be tenured there, he would have to become a department of one, a teacher without colleagues, though with students enough. Institutions ask their teachers to be "good academic citizens," which means to vote early and often, and to follow the fashion, whatever it happens to be. Falstaff votes with his feet (one of the finest of American tropes), but he will show up in his classroom tavern, and teach anyone who is qualified that meaning begins by self-overhearing, by the mind's vitality, and also that meaning begins in order for comedy to flourish. Falstaff or Hamlet—which is more Shakespeare's center? Orson Welles, in fierce self-mockery, fantasized that Hamlet went to England, grew old and fat, and became Sir John Falstaff. Bernard Shaw, who loathed both Falstaff and Shakespeare's Cleopatra, sent Falstaff off to Egypt, submitted him to a strict diet and a sex-change operation, and made Sir John, sage of Eastcheap, into the serpent of the Nile. Falstaff, Hamlet, Cleopatra: add Rosalind, Iago, Macbeth, and the fourfold of Lear, Edmund, Edgar, and the Fool, and you have those who are, for me, endless to meditation. I don't mean to yield up Falconbridge the Bastard,

Bottom, Juliet, Feste, Viola, Leontes, Imogen, Prospero, and two dozen more, but Shylock is too painful for my meditation, as are Othello, Desdemona, Antony, Coriolanus, Timon, and some others.

Where shall Shakespeare be found in Shakespeare? We all want to find him in the Sonnets, but he is too cunning for us, and you have to be the Devil himself to find Shakespeare there. He played the Ghost in *Hamlet*, and Old Adam the serving-man in *As You Like It*. Perhaps he played both Antonios, in *The Merchant of Venice* and *Twelfth Night*, and probably a slew of kings and aging nobles besides—Julius Caesar, Henry IV, the Earl of Gloucester—but all this, I grant, is surmise. James Joyce found Shakespeare most at home as the Ghost of Hamlet's father, and Joyce may indeed have been right. Poldy Bloom, Joyce's surrogate, is haunted by two ghosts, his father's and his son's. Shakespeare's father and Shakespeare's only son both died before the final version of *Hamlet* was staged. Hamlet is a haunted man, until he casts off the father's ghost at sea, and returns, superbly different, to endure the catastrophe of act 5.

Hamlet's development from a haunted student on to a master of theatricalism is not wholly unlike Shakespeare's own, but that seems to me a minor matter. What was more consequential for Shakespeare's own art was Falstaff's influence upon Shakespeare, which made Hamlet possible. Even more consequential was Hamlet's subsequent influence upon Shakespeare, which made everything possible.

Goethe's Wilhelm Meister attempts to fully develop his own persona by directing himself as the Prince of Denmark in a performance of *Hamlet*, a play that he believes to be partly a novel. With considerable irony, Goethe centers this supposed novelistic aspect of *Hamlet* entirely upon the Ghost. A mysterious hooded stranger, complete with white cloak, puts on armor and plays the Ghost to Wilhelm's Hamlet. Wilhelm, convinced that this is his own dead father, surpasses himself as an actor, since at last he plays the part of his self.

Perhaps Goethe, in relation to Shakespeare, at last plays himself in the odd essay *Schäkespear und kein Ende!* of 1815, where Shakespeare seems to become the Ghost of Goethe's father. The actual father, Johann Caspar Goethe, who died in 1782, had accumulated wealth and purchased a coat of arms, but then was balked of further social advancement. Caspar Goethe concentrated therefore upon his son, whose cultural success became the father's obsession. No cultural success in one's own lifetime could have surpassed that of the poet-sage Goethe, and yet Goethe went on being haunted by Shakespeare and by *Hamlet* in particular. Goethe could not have known that Shakespeare himself had first played the Ghost of Hamlet's father, but he might have appreciated the irony of Shakespeare's self-casting. Goethe also did not know that John Shakespeare, William's father, had fallen from the status of a gentleman, with a coat of arms, which William subsequently restored.

Goethe had the immense advantage of lacking any strong precursors in German. Shakespeare, though much in the Chaucerian, English tradition, nevertheless translates superbly into German, which bothered Goethe more than he could acknowledge. The magnificently outrageous Second Part of *Faust* is frequently a parody of Shakespeare, particularly of *Hamlet.* Unable to reinvent the human, as Shakespeare had done, Goethe was compelled to ironize all representations of the human, including his Faust, who is a zombie when read side by side with Hamlet. This hardly mattered to Goethe, since Goethe's own personality transcended any inventiveness of which Goethe was capable. Shakespeare is hidden in and behind his work; even *Faust, Part Two* labors to catch up to Goethe.

We owe to Goethe the refreshing idea—now so unfashionable in the English-speaking world—that you receive more by reading Shakespeare than by seeing him staged. Goethe was merely correct, and his speculation that the great plays transcend genre is also essentially correct. The two parts of *Henry IV,* read together, are both a major drama and an extraordinary novel, as much the ancestor of *The Brothers Karamazov* as *Hamlet* is the forerunner of *Crime and Punishment.* What can a playgoer do with the pattern of Falstaff's obsessive allusions to Jesus' parable of the leper Lazarus and the wealthy glutton? Shakespeare is still actively extending that pattern in the rejection scene that ends *Henry IV, Part II,* and then brings the matter to an extraordinary apotheosis in Mistress Quickly's account of the death of Sir John Falstaff in *Henry V.* And the novelistic aspects of *Hamlet* go well beyond the troubling demands of the Ghost. Shakespeare's invention of the human was as large an element in the invention of the novel as was Cervantes's transformation of picaresque into the character analysis of the relationship between the Don and Sancho.

Where do our selves begin? Goethe, an authority upon development, took his own self-origin for granted. Shakespeare, incomparable psychologist, invented a new origin for us, in the most illuminating idea any poet ever has discovered *or* invented: the self-recognition of self-overhearing. When do we begin? Did the Ghost in *Hamlet* father not only Shakespeare and Goethe and all strong writers since, or did the crime of Claudius, which is the crime of Cain, give birth to all of us, particularly in these last two centuries? Would we overhear ourselves, and be shocked into change, if we were not confronted by our father's ghost, prefigured in the Ghost of King Hamlet?

I have found it very easy to be misunderstood upon this idea, and so I desire to elaborate it. John Stuart Mill observed that poetry is overheard, rather than heard, and we are not Prince Hamlet, yet at moments we overhear ourselves, and are startled. Do we awaken into a new self-awareness, or are we merely cognizant that we are not what we thought ourselves to be? Is Hamlet truly as surprised by his father's spirit in arms as he is by overhearing his own?

> O God, I could be bounded in a nutshell, and count myself a king of infinite space—were it not that I have bad dreams.

That is the origin of Samuel Beckett's Ham in *Endgame,* and of Beckett himself, who was mediated by Joyce and Proust, but ultimately, like all of us, by Hamlet, the master overhearer. Kierkegaard, who wanted to learn his ironies from the difficulty of becoming a Christian, actually absorbed them from Hamlet's modes of rarely meaning what he said, or saying what he meant. Proust, another superb ironist, wrote an extraordinary essay on reading as self-overhearing in the preface to his translation of John Ruskin's *Sesame and Lilies.* Reading, Proust says, is not conversation with another. Its difference consists

> for each of us in receiving the communication of another thought, but while we remain all alone, while continuing to enjoy the intellectual power we have in solitude, which conversation dissipates immediately.

Hamlet's intellectual power is never dissipated, since the Prince will talk to everyone but listen to no one, except perhaps the Ghost. It is not clear to me that anyone in Shakespeare really listens to anyone else. Othello is destroyed by Iago's genius for suggestion and insinuation, yet if he listened more closely to Iago, he would be less persuaded. Macbeth, after briefly listening to his wife, is so immersed in self-overhearing that he scarcely notices her loss, first to madness and then to death. Rather hilariously, Antony and Cleopatra do not hear anyone but themselves. Poor Antony cries out, "I am dying, Egypt, dying. Give me some wine and let me speak a while," to which Cleopatra responds, "No, let me speak!" Like Proust after him, Shakespeare has few illusions about either friendship or love.

Self-overhearing, in Shakespeare, is the royal road to change. Hamlet

notoriously changes every time he hears himself speak, which is why there
can be no central passage in this four-thousand-line play, fifteen hundred of
which constitute his part. Hamlet's self-re-creations through self-overhearing
are everywhere in the play, but I turn to act 5, scene 1, lines 66–216, the extraordinary vision of Hamlet in the graveyard, culminating in the Prince's
contemplation of Yorick's skull. We can say that the play—*The Tragedy of
Hamlet, Prince of Denmark*—moves between the grisly relics of Hamlet's two
fathers, from the Ghost of King Hamlet to the skull of the King's jester,
Yorick, who served as a pragmatic father to the neglected young Prince:

> He hath bore me on his back a thousand times, and now how abhorr'd
> in my imagination it is! my gorge rises at it. Here hung those lips that
> I have kiss'd I know not how oft.

The Ghost never speaks of having loved his son, and King Hamlet is not
likely to have borne Prince Hamlet on his back even once, let alone a thousand times. One doubts that the Prince has kissed Ophelia and Gertrude "I
know not how oft." If the child Hamlet was loved, and loved in return, only
Yorick was involved. I do not think that the mature Hamlet loves anyone,
whatever his protestations, which adds to the mystery as to why we join the
Danish populace in loving this alienated charismatic.

Goethe parodies the graveyard scene in his account of the death and burial of Faust, but Hamlet himself leaves nothing for anyone else to parody:

> That skull had a tongue in it, and could sing once. How the knave
> jowls it to the ground, as if 'twere Cain's jaw-bone, that did the first
> murder!

So much for Claudius's Cain-like murder of King Hamlet, which vanishes away in this parodistic excess of negative exuberance. What does it
mean to say that Hamlet overhears himself in making this allusion to Cain?
Is there a difference between hearing and overhearing oneself? When we
are surprised at listening to our tape-recorded voices, are we hearing or
overhearing? Dictionaries define "overhear" as hearing a speech or speaker
without the speaker's awareness or intention. To overhear oneself is to be
initially unaware that one is the speaker. That unawareness is so brief that
self-overhearing seems more metaphoric than not, yet the moment of literal nonrecognition is authentic. Shakespeare, taking a hint I think from
Chaucer, seizes upon that moment to fashion another version of the human
will-to-change.

Is that fashioning of sufficient import to speak of the invention (or rein-vention) of the human? In the most famous of his seven soliloquies, Ham-let hears (or overhears) himself contemplate taking arms against a sea of troubles and, by opposing, end them. All of us with literary interests inherit Hamlet's equivocal assertion of the power of the poet's mind over a sea or universe of death. What Shakespeare invents, most supremely through Hamlet, is that inward assertion of opposition to what most menaces the ever-burgeoning spirit of self. Hamlet's study of himself is an absolute, and diminishes what is outside the self as a sea of troubles. Incessantly ponder-ing his own words, as if they both were and were not his own, Hamlet be-comes the theologian of his own consciousness, which is so wide that its circumference never can be discovered.

Can you lavish what must be all your intelligence upon Hamlet, and not somehow be Hamlet? If Shakespeare played both the Ghost and the Player King, a natural doubling for any actor, then he confronted Hamlet twice: once as father, and once as dramatic student. Shakespeare's own father and only son Hamnet were dead when he staged the definitive *Hamlet* of 1600–1601. Hamlet will die without a son and without a father, and he will die in the strength of his own charisma, asking not for resurrection or for po-etic immortality but only that he not bear a wounded name. A great nihilist, an Iago or a Svidrigailov, could not care less that his name perpetually should be a wounded one.

The Hamlet of act 5 controls our perspectives: we do not know more than he does, and he believes we know less. Did Shakespeare know more than Hamlet did? In the Hegelian sense, Hamlet is the freest artist of him-self, and could tell us much more about what he represents, if only there were time enough. I interpret that to mean that Hamlet is the supreme artist of self-overhearing, and so could teach us at least the rudiments of that disconcerting art. To hear yourself, at least for an instant, without self-recognition, is to open your spirit to the tempests of change. Shakespeare found this opening most largely with Hamlet and with Falstaff, but it is a constant of all his later work. I illustrate it now, as fully as I can, with the dying Edmund in *King Lear*, because his final change seems to me the most drastically persuasive in all of Shakespeare.

No one in Shakespeare is so free of emotion as Edmund, bastard son of the Earl of Gloucester, and half-brother to Edgar, Lear's godson. Iago takes a certain antic glee in his own beautiful wickedness, but Edmund is beyond that. The Dostoevskian nihilists, Svidrigailov and Stavrogin, have learned some lessons from Edmund, but cannot equal his sublime coldness. As the lover of both Goneril and Regan, rival monsters of the deep, and as the betrayer of both his father and his brother, Edmund surpasses himself when he orders the secret execution of Lear and Cordelia. Remorse, pity, affection, even honest lust have no place in Edmund's nature. He lies dying upon the ground, having received his death-wound from Edgar, and he is strangely accepting, once he knows that his slayer is at least his equal in lineage: "The wheel is come full circle—I am here." Somewhat moved by Edgar's account of their father's death, Edmund is almost ready for change, which comes decisively by way of an extraordinary self-overhearing. The bodies of Goneril and Regan are carried onto the stage, and Edmund puzzles it out:

> Yet Edmund was belov'd:
> The one the other poison'd for my sake,
> And after slew herself.

So startled is he by his own "Yet Edmund *was* belov'd," that Gloucester's bastard son can believe what he hears only by adding the painfully obvious: "The one the other poison'd for my sake, / And after slew herself." Self-overhearing is anything but a metaphor in this hearing with only half-awareness and little intentionality. There are no moments like this in Homer or the Bible, Vergil or Dante. This is a new inwardness that creates rather than confronts change. Belatedly, "despite of my own nature," Edmund attempts to save Cordelia and Lear from his own murderousness. For Cordelia, it is too late, and Lear, insane again, will enter with her corpse in his arms. Shakespeare has perfected self-overhearing into a mode that will be crucial in Chekhov and Stendhal, Dostoevsky and Proust, and many more. If to invent the ever-augmenting inner spirit, including its faculty for self-overhearing, is not the invention of the human, as we since have known the human, then perhaps we are too overwhelmed by social history and by ideologies to recognize our indebtedness to William Shakespeare.

MIGUEL DE CERVANTES

"But of all the things I saw while I was there, the most painful happened during this conversation with Montesinos, when one of my luckless Dulcinea's two companions came over to me, without my noticing it, and with tears in her eyes, and her voice shaking and soft, said to me:

"'My lady Dulcinea del Toboso kisses your hands, your grace, and begs me to return and tell her how you are, and also, because the need is great, she also wants me to beg your grace, as urgently as I know how, if you can lend her six dollars, or however much your grace happens to have with you, against the security of this brand-new cotton petticoat which I have right here, and she promises to pay you back very soon.'

"These words absolutely struck me dumb, so I turned to Montesinos and asked him:

" 'My lord Montesinos, is it possible for people of high rank, who have been enchanted, to suffer from want?'

"To which query he replied:

" 'Believe me, your grace, my lord Don Quixote de La Mancha, that the condition we term want is to be found everywhere, knowing no boundaries and in no respect limited, nor does it spare those who have been enchanted, so that if the lady Dulcinea del Toboso has sent you this request for six dollars, and the security she offers is sound, it would seem to me that you should lend her the stipulated sum, for without any question she must need it very badly indeed.' "

> —"Montesinos' Cave," volume 2, chapter 23 of *Don Quixote* (translated by Burton Raffel)

Does the admirable knight, Don Quixote, believe his own fabulous story of his descent into the Cave of Montesinos? He declines poor Dulcinea's offer of her cotton petticoat as security, and rather sadly sends her only four dollars, rather than six, as he has no more. In the midst of the cave's surrealistic marvels, the Knight is himself: shrewd, kindly, chivalrous, gallant, and mad only north-northwest. We cannot know whether he literally *believes* his own stories because, like his creator, Cervantes, he is a genius of narrative, as much metaphysical as romantic.

Don Quixote's defense of his career is both ethical and metaphysical, and tellingly is made against a priest's attack upon him. The unfortunate cleric blunders by accusing the Knight as being devoid of reality: "go home! . . . stop this wandering." The Quixotic response is overwhelming: "I have set injuries and insults straight, righted wrongs, punished arrogance, conquered giants, and trampled on monsters."

The novel, from Cervantes to Proust, created a metaphysical and ethical splendor that wanes only now in the Age of the Screen. What Cervantes brought to that creation was Quixotic courage—literal, moral, visionary. He shares with Shakespeare and Dante a particular aspect of the Kabbalistic *Keter* or crown, the audacity of Adam early in the morning (as Walt Whitman called it), a sharing in the divine will or desire that the Kabbalists called *Razon*. All further literary emanation radiates out from Cervantes, as it does from Shakespeare.

MIGUEL DE CERVANTES
(1547–1616)

THE LIFE OF CERVANTES WAS SO CROWDED with incident and misfortune that much of it now reads like an exemplary tale by the surpassing writer in the Spanish language, an eminence as perpetual as those enjoyed by Dante, Shakespeare, Montaigne, Goethe, and Tolstoy in the other major Western vernaculars. I intend to discuss *Don Quixote*'s influence upon Cervantes, picking up again one of the strands that (for me, at least) tie together my book: the work in the life, rather than the life in the work. In this, I follow Cervantes himself, who at the end of his amazing book-without-limits declared, "And Don Quixote was born only for me, as I for him: he knew how to act and I how to write; only we two are a unity." Here, as throughout, I quote the remarkable translation of Burton Raffel, except that he prefers the more accurate Quijote, which I am too old to absorb; besides, "quixotic" is now an English word, and "quijotic" will not work very well.

So original is *Don Quixote* that nearly four centuries later, it remains the most advanced work of prose fiction that we have. That indeed is an understatement; it is at once the most readable and yet ultimately the most difficult of all novels. This paradox is what Cervantes shares with Shakespeare: Hamlet and Don Quixote, Falstaff and Sancho Panza are universally available, yet finally tease the mind out of thought. The combined influence of Cervantes and Shakespeare (who died on the same date) overdetermines the entire course of subsequent Western literature. A fusion of Cervantes and Shakespeare produced Stendhal and Turgenev, *Moby-Dick* and *Huckleberry Finn*, Dostoevsky and Proust. Harry Levin, thirty years ago, remarked on the paradox "that a book about literary influence, and indeed against it, should have enjoyed so wide and decisive a literary influence." *Don Quixote* is a book about a hero crazed by reading, if we take it at all literally. Yet the Knight is the sanest person in the book, saner than Sancho, depending upon your own perspective on wisdom, folly, and madness. Miguel de Unamuno (1864–1936), a great storywriter and critic, wrote the commentary upon Cervantes I like best, *Our Lord Don Quixote*. As the title suggests, Unamuno urges us to take Don Quixote as our savior, and as the founder of the true Spanish religion of Quixotism as opposed to Catholic Christianity. Cervantes matters to Unamuno only in that Don Quixote is

Cervantes's genius or daemon. Unamuno ironically concedes that Don
Quixote was mad, but only according to the Christian point of view of
Alonso Quixano, from whom Don Quixote rose in the flesh and to whom he
returned only to die:

> Great was Don Quixote's madness, and it was great because the root
> from which it grew was great: the inextinguishable longing to survive,
> a source of the most extravagant follies as well as of the most heroic
> acts. The outstanding benefactors of their fatherland and of their fel-
> low men have been those who dreamed of eternal name and fame.

The Dutch humanist Erasmus (whom Cervantes certainly had read) in
his *The Praise of Folly* (1509) distinguished between two kinds of madness,
one pernicious, the other sublime: "namely the kind which takes its origin
from me and is most desirable. It occurs whenever a certain pleasant mental distraction relieves the heart from its anxieties and cares and at the same
time soothes it with the balm of manifold pleasures." That is more Cervantes than Unamuno, whose Quixote was more desperate to survive than
eager to take pleasure in playing. Unamuno, a great reader, chose as the
book's most beautiful passage a moment in volume 2, chapter 58 where
Don Quixote and Sancho Panza find freedom on the open road again, after
their long sojourn in the sadistic court of the Duke and the Duchess, where
the Knight particularly has suffered the "clinging compliments" of Al-
tisidora, who mockingly has pretended a grand passion for him. The Knight
and Squire come upon some peasants who carry with them bas-relief carv-
ings for an altar decoration. Don Quixote contemplates the images of Saint
George, Saint Martin, Saint Diego Matamoros, and Saint Paul, and is moved
to state the difference between the saints and himself: "they . . . fought in
God's wars, while I am a sinner and fight in humanity's. They conquered
heaven by force of arms, for Heaven does not reject force and violence, and
I do not know, so far, what my own struggles may have conquered, but if my
Dulcinea del Toboso could only be released, my fortunes might be improved, and my mind strengthened, and it might well be that I could direct
myself down some better road than the one I now follow."

The enchanted Dulcinea, visible only as the coarse peasant girl Aldonza
Lorenza, if released from wicked enchantment might also release Don
Quixote from his complex realization of the problematical basis of his quest.
But since Dulcinea is Don Quixote's genius, as Beatrice was Dante's, and
Quixote is Cervantes's, the Knight is also aware of how destructive the re-

lease of the ideal might prove to be. Unamuno, supremely aware, carries us into a further irony:

> For me, Dulcinea del Toboso has always symbolized glory, that is, worldly glory, the inextinguishable thirst to leave behind the eternal name and fame in the world. The ingenious Hildalgo declares, in his fit of sanity, that if he were perhaps to be cured of his thirst for glory, for worldly renown and fame, he would direct his steps toward attaining that other glory, in which his faith as an Old Christian made him believe.

Whether Cervantes—as opposed to Quixote and Sancho—was an Old Christian (that is, not descended from Jewish *conversos*), we simply do not know. I am a little startled when Sancho, listing his merits, cries out, "And I am also a mortal enemy of the Jews!" There was always a shadow upon Cervantes; despite his heroic war record, he never achieved any royal preferment, and perhaps was in disfavor with King Philip II. New Christians were second-class citizens, always under suspicion from the state church. Cervantes had fought magnificently in the great naval victory over the Turks at Lepanto, where his left hand was permanently maimed. His heroic commander was Don John of Austria, bastard son of the emperor Charles V, and the resented half-brother of Philip II of Spain. Whatever the reason, the government did less than nothing for Cervantes. Four years after Lepanto, he was captured by the Turks, and enslaved for five years in Algiers, before the Trinitarian monks (not the royal house) ransomed him. Refused all patronage, he failed commercially as a playwright, and resorted to becoming a tax collector, only to be jailed for supposed arrears in his accounts. *Don Quixote* was begun during a second imprisonment. Despite the immediate success of the first volume of the book (1605), the publisher held all the rights, and poor Cervantes earned nothing, except instant fame. Only the belated patronage of the Count of Lemos, from 1613 until Cervantes's death in 1616, allowed a relative comfort at the end.

Even as Don Quixote sought eternal name and fame in the wonderfully absurd quest for the enchanted Dulcinea, Cervantes sought it in Quixote. Both Knight and author found all that they had desired, in reputation, which Unamuno translated as immortality, the blessing of extending one's signature in space and time. Influenced by Kierkegaard and possibly also by Kafka, Unamuno longed for the indestructible, not an easy notion to define. Cervantes, whose life was endlessly sorrowful and painful, knew that he had triumphed in *Don Quixote*, and his awareness is very poignant:

One of the things most pleasant to a virtuous and distinguished man
is to see himself, while he is still alive, go out among the nations and
languages of the world, printed and bound, and bearing a good reputation.

That is Don Quixote speaking about volume 1 of his history, after being
told, in volume 2, of his international fame. Throughout volume 2, the uncanny moments intervene, when we cannot distinguish the Knight from his
chronicler. I turn to Unamuno again, who fought against the Spanish cult of
death even in his closing moments, when he confronted the pistol-waving
Fascist general Quiepo de Llano, who shouted the mottoes, "Death to the
intelligence!" and "Long live death!" The seventy-two-year-old Unamuno,
deposed as rector of the University of Salamanca, maintained the dignity of
his institution even as the Fascist lunatic threatened him. All the more can
one hear the true Quixotic spirit in *Our Lord Don Quixote:*

I believe it to be an error, in speaking of the so-called Spanish cult of
death, to assert that we do not love life because we find it so hard on
us, or to say that the Spaniard has never felt a great attachment to life.
On the contrary, I believe he has felt a great attachment to life, precisely because it is so hard on him, and that from his intense attachment to life springs what we call the cult of death.

The Quixotic will to survive is Unamuno's religion, which he regards as
the Spanish religion. There are many worse ways of reading *Don Quixote,*
since it legitimately could be called the Bible of Reality. Cervantes throughout directly addresses the solitary reader, who increasingly identifies herself
or himself with the Knight, rather than with the two other protagonists,
Sancho Panza and the ironic narrator. So great is the novelty of this first
novel that the book's immense originality cannot be absorbed, even after
many rereadings. There are as many Don Quixotes as there are readers, just
as there are more Hamlets and Falstaffs than there are actors to play them.
Cervantes and Shakespeare each perform the miracle of bringing together
an infinite consciousness—the two Knights and the Prince—with the order
of play. In a delightful story written late in his career, Anthony Burgess
brought Shakespeare and Cervantes together at "A Meeting in Valladolid,"
the occasion supposed to be a peace treaty between Spain and England,
with Shakespeare's company of players performing several of his works to
Cervantes's ironic disdain. Somewhat nettled, Shakespeare's riposte is startling and satisfactory:

Tomorrow or the next day we play *Hamlet*. But we play it somewhat differently from heretofore. For in it we place Sir John Falstaff. Wonder not nor start so. It is all too easy of disposal. For *Hamlet* is what it already is up to the point of the prince's being sent to England, there to be murdered on the king's orders. In England, having read and destroyed the commission, he hears that the Danish force is to invade England for non-payment of tributes. At last he finds the name of action, and this holds off all thought of self-slaughter, as does the companionship of Falstaff and his crew. Falstaff may call Hamlet sweet Ham for Hal, it is but a letter's difference. The war is called off on the news of the death of King Claudius. Hamlet proceeds to Elsinore to succeed him. Falstaff and his crew follow but are, of course, cast off at the end.

When Shakespeare and Cervantes meet after the performance, the Castilian complains, "the fat man and the thin man you stole from me," to which Will responds, "Ah, no. They were already there in the London playhouses before ever I heard that you exist." And yet Burgess's Shakespeare, as he dies in Stratford, still broods on Cervantes's having stolen a march on him in having devised a universal character, Hamlet and Falstaff amalgamated in one soul, with Sancho Panza as outside chorus, the mundane aspect of Sir John Falstaff.

Burgess, with whom I consumed several bottles of Fundador while we explored the intricacies of Hamlet/Falstaff and Don Quixote/Sancho Panza, remarked once that these were the only novel and group of plays worth comparing. He then went off into a musical analogy I had not the competence to comprehend, presenting Verdi and Mozart as the agents who might have reconciled the Shakespeare-Cervantes differences. Falstaff, to me, is part Don Quixote, part Sancho Panza, while many before me have brought together Don Quixote and Hamlet. W. H. Auden, who disliked Hamlet, decided that Don Quixote and Falstaff both were Christian saints, while wicked Hamlet had faith neither in God nor in himself. I prefer Unamuno to Auden on Quixote, and do not recognize Christian grace in Falstaff or Satanic-pride in Hamlet.

Don Quixote, according to Auden, is the antithesis of Hamlet the player, because the Knight is "completely incapable of seeing himself in a role." This Quixote is "completely unreflective." I confess that I cannot locate Auden's Quixote in the mere book itself. Cervantes's Quixote says, "I know who I am, and who I may be, if I choose." It will not do to sanctify Don Quixote, or to underestimate him. He plays a deep game with reality, with the state and state church and Spain's social and religious history, and an unreflective Quixote is an impossibility.

Cervantes, despite Burgess's charming fantasy, had never heard of Shakespeare, but Shakespeare, in his final phase, had to take Cervantes into account. He read *Don Quixote* in 1611, when the Shelton translation appeared in England, and he observed his friends Ben Jonson and Beaumont and Fletcher coming to terms with Cervantes in their plays. Working with Fletcher, Shakespeare wrote a play, *Cardenio*, on Cervantes's character in *Don Quixote*, but so far the play is lost. I follow Burgess in seeing why Cervantes troubled Shakespeare. Here was the only authentic contemporary rival, whose popular art had created two figures who were forever to be universal. To equal *Don Quixote*, you need to gather all of Shakespeare's twenty-five or so finest plays together, an enterprise not fulfilled until the First Folio, after Shakespeare's death. Burgess's Shakespeare and Cervantes quarrel fascinatingly. Cervantes says, "You will never produce a *Don Quixote*," and Will replies, "I have made good comedy and eke tragedy which is the highest reach of the skill of the dramaturge," to which Cervantes massively scolds:

> It is not and it will never be. God is a comedian. God does not suffer the tragic consequences of a flawed essence. Tragedy is all too human. Comedy is divine.

Shakespeare need not reply; *Twelfth Night* is the answer to *Don Quixote*, and one wonders whether *Don Quixote* is a divine comedy, or comedy of any sort, violently funny as it can be. Certainly, the characterization of Don Quixote as hero by José Ortega y Gasset does not fit any comic hero that I have encountered, at least in Western literature:

> I do not think that there is any more profound originality than this "practical," active originality of the hero. His life is a perpetual resistance to what is habitual and customary. Each movement he makes has first had to overcome custom and invent a new kind of gesture. Such a life is a perpetual suffering, a constant tearing oneself away from that part of oneself which is given over to habit and is a prisoner of matter.

Cervantes's comedy is linked to pain and suffering: it is a mode of comedy still so original that we find it very difficult to describe. But then so much of *Don Quixote* is beyond our literary parameters. I am about to discuss the Knight's descent into Montesinos' Cave, as described by Don Quixote in volume 2, chapter 23, an incident resistant to every kind of analysis. Though this may be the most puzzling chapter of the vast novel, it is profoundly representative of how enigmatic the Knight's consciousness and quest are throughout Cervantes's vision of reality. After eight hundred large pages, we know a great deal about Don Quixote, and yet he remains as unknowable as Hamlet continues to be after a tragedy of four thousand lines, so much of which he himself speaks.

Montesinos' Cave attracts Don Quixote as a prospective adventure worthy of him, since it has a legendary reputation. It allows the Knight to parody the epic descents to the underworld of Odysseus and Aeneas. The Quixotic descent is by a rope tied around him, and he is hauled up again apparently fast asleep, after what cannot be much more than an hour. Though the Knight is a fervent truth-teller, it is unclear whether he believes his own account of his sojourn in the world below. After all, he knows that the incomparable Dulcinea is his own invention, his poem as it were, and he presumably realizes that his version of Montesinos' Cave is another creation of his sublime imagination. Cervantes, however, deliberately evades giving us any certainty on this, as on almost every other matter. Don Quixote tells us that first he slept and then woke up in the cave, and saw Montesinos emerge from a crystal castle to receive him. Within the castle, the great knight Durandarte lies on his tomb, quite dead but highly voluble, rather like Kafka's Hunter Gracchus floating undead on his death-ship. Amidst a bevy of knights and heroines, Durandarte's Belerma goes about weeping for him while holding his heart in her hands. Merlin, wicked enchanter, is responsible, but we have no time to reflect upon this since Dulcinea suddenly appears, in peasant guise, dashes off, and sends two friends back to ask if she can borrow six dollars from the Knight against the collateral of her brand-new cotton petticoat! Her heroic lover has but four dollars, and graciously sends them to her.

Outrageous throughout, this tale or dream-vision is deliberately beyond interpretation, and reminds me frequently of Kafka, whom clearly it influenced. Kafka's narrative drive is to make himself uninterpretable, which means that what needs interpretation is *why* Kafka so renders himself opaque. "The Truth about Sancho Panza," a Kafkan parable, tells us that Sancho was the obsessive reader of chivalric romances, which so diverted his personal devil, Don Quixote, that Quixote went forth in knight-errantry. Sancho, freely and philosophically, followed his devil and was entertained all his days. Cervantes, though he also cheerfully makes himself uninterpretable, is so large a writer that he rewards us, like Shakespeare, with a world of entertainment. Don Quixote is his own demon, and rides out not to save the Spain of Philip III, which like that of Philip II cannot be saved, but to save *us,* as Unamuno insists. Are we to be saved (secularly) by ourselves being turned into fictions? The effect of volume 1 of *Don Quixote* upon the life of Cervantes can be read on almost every page of volume 2. Poor Cervantes—unrewarded hero, failed playwright, Turkish slave, prisoner of the Spanish state, endless unfortunate—has been transformed into a world figure, because Don Quixote and Sancho Panza are famous. Volume 2 of *Don Quixote* never ceases invoking volume 1, while always making clear that volume 1 is a book, and volume 2 is not. Cervantes himself is volume 2; this second *Don Quixote* is what William Blake called "the Real Man, the Imagination." Defending himself against a priest who had scolded him, Don Quixote (in volume 2, chapter 32) proclaims his achievement:

> I have set injuries and insults straight, righted wrongs, punished arrogance, conquered giants, and trampled on monsters.

Cervantes knew how to write, Don Quixote how to act: only these two are a unity, born for one another.

MICHEL DE MONTAIGNE

> Any topic is equally fertile for me. A fly will serve my purpose; and
> God grant that this topic I have in hand now was not taken up at the
> command of so flighty a will! Let me begin with whatever subject I
> please, for all subjects are linked with one another.
>
> —"On Some Verses of Vergil"
> (translated by Donald Frame)

Montaigne's secret is his universality, at least for male readers. Emerson, Montaigne's disciple as an essayist, celebrated his forerunner as "the frankest and honestest of all writers." T. S. Eliot, who disliked Montaigne, ascribed the French essayist's power to his articulation of a universal skepticism. And yet both Emerson and Eliot, admirer and enemy alike, may have mistaken the universality of Montaigne's appeal. Skepticism is not the center of Montaigne's genius, nor of Hamlet's, who clearly is of Montaigne's party. Montaigne is a comic charismatic, a genius of personality, and Shakespeare, prompted by reading the *Essays*, created Hamlet's playful side in the image of Montaigne. Where Hamlet could not follow Montaigne was into the wisdom of knowing how to live, what to do, because Montaigne refused tragedy.

From Montaigne's perspective, Hamlet's madness emerged from the Prince's desire to evade the human condition. Montaigne rejects self-disdain as the craziest of our attitudes, but Hamlet cannot cast it off until act 5. What truly makes Montaigne a universal genius is his eloquent wisdom of self-acceptance founded upon profound self-knowledge. What Freud vainly attempted to teach us, Montaigne, the better teacher, tells us upon virtually every page: humanize your idealism, "play the man well and duly."

At seventy-one, I repeat to myself constantly Montaigne at his strongest:

> I hate that accidental repentance that old age brings. I shall never
> be grateful to impotence for any good it may do me . . . Miserable sort
> of remedy, to owe our health to disease!

That seems to me the universality of Falstaff, rather than of Hamlet, and in it I hear Montaigne summoning us to rejoice in the common life.

MICHEL DE MONTAIGNE
1533–1592

THE FIRST OF ALL PERSONAL ESSAYISTS IS still much the best; Montaigne invented the term "essay," a trial or test of his judgment, founded upon self-study. His *Essays* were an immediate success, and remain so for thoughtful readers of nearly every nation today. A wisdom writer, professedly in the tradition of Seneca and Plutarch, Montaigne remains profoundly original, not so much in this form of the personal essay, but in his own extended, intimate self-portrait, which was without precedent. Augustine gives us a spiritual autobiography, culminating in his conversion. Montaigne gives us his total self; his highest tribute comes from Emerson: "Cut these words, and they would bleed; they are vascular and alive."

Addressing his reader, Montaigne accurately proclaims, "I am myself the matter of my book." He retired from public life (he thought) in 1570, in order to write his *Essays*, but was called out of retirement to serve as mayor of Bordeaux, as mediator between Henry III of France and the Protestant Henry of Navarre, who became Henry IV, most gifted of all French kings. Had death not intervened, Montaigne would have become a crucial advisor at the court of King Henry IV. Despite his admiration for Navarre, his fellow Gascon, Montaigne doubtless would have regretted his lost retirement. The influence of his proliferating *Essays* upon his life is comparable to the effect of *Don Quixote* on Cervantes. After the first edition of the *Essays* (1580), Montaigne's final twelve years were a living out and revising of his book.

The conversionary experience of Montaigne's life came in 1576, and involved Socrates, who remained ever after his mentor. Montaigne's Socrates, like Montaigne's Plato, was "a disconnected poet," which would have been highly unacceptable to the author of the *Republic* and the *Laws*. One has to celebrate Montaigne's shrewdness in perceiving the essential difference between Socrates and Plato. For Plato, nature is scarcely benign, and all sexuality is to be discouraged, unless necessary for propagation. Socrates has a more generous view of the natural man, which after 1576 becomes Montaigne's, who calls Socrates "the wisest man that ever was." Though Socrates wrote nothing, his dialectical stance was the basis for Montaigne's tests of self-judgment, so that the idea of the essay is itself Socratic. To be a free man is "to know how to enjoy our being lawfully." Socrates is beyond anxiety, or fear of any kind. The late essay "Of Physiognomy" (1585–88) quotes at length Socrates' speech to his judges, from Plato's *Apology*, and then comments magnificently:

> Is that not a sober, sane plea, but at the same time natural and lowly, inconceivably lofty, truthful, frank, and just beyond all example . . . He owed his life not to himself, but to the world as an example.

Does that last sentence apply equally well to Montaigne? He would not have said so, since he saw himself as an imitator of Socrates, a belated follower. And yet he hoped that his book might serve the world as an example of what his scholar Herbert Luthy called "the art of being truthful." Montaigne writes for his own sake alone, and yet he needs us, his readers, if he is to reveal himself to himself. Socrates, as Montaigne rightly observed, did not speak for his own sake alone, but for all who could benefit. The author of the *Essays* is canny and modest, but also amiably shocking and is not always popular with our current feminists. One of his masterpieces is the late essay "On Some Verses of Vergil," which meditates upon sexuality. Here is a cento of passages that give the flavor of Montaigne at his most candid:

> Marriage has for its share utility, justice, honor, and constancy: a flat pleasure, but more universal. Love is founded on pleasure alone, and in truth its pleasure is more stimulating, lively and keen: a pleasure inflamed by difficulty. There must be a sting and a smart in it. It is no longer love if it is without arrows and without fire. The liberality of the ladies is too profuse in marriage, and blunts the point of affection and desire.

> Women are not wrong at all when they reject the rules of life that have been introduced into the world, inasmuch as it is the men who have made these without them. There is naturally strife and wrangling between them and us: the closest communion we have with them is still tumultuous and tempestuous.

> Oh, what a terrific advantage is opportuneness! If someone asked me the first thing in love, I would answer that it is knowing how to seize the right time; the second likewise and the third too; it is a point that can accomplish everything.

Everyone shuns to see a man burn, everyone runs to see him die. For his destruction we seek a spacious field in broad daylight, for his construction we hide in a dark little corner.

Montaigne married, and had only one child who survived, a daughter. There are two fleeting references to his mother in the *Essays;* she was Antoinette de Lopes, of a prominent Toulouse family of Spanish-Jewish origin. Montaigne's daughter receives a few, rather slighting references. His love was reserved for his father, and for his best friend, La Boétie, dead in 1563, after four years in which the essayist's inward solitude vanished, to return for the nearly thirty remaining years of his life. Perhaps Henry of Navarre might have filled that void, had Montaigne lived past 1592. One feels that Montaigne, very much the Gascon "average, sensual man" on the outside, was a Shakespearean solitude within, rather like the Hamlet whom undoubtedly he influenced (Shakespeare evidently first read John Florio's translation in manuscript, Florio being of the Earl of Southampton's household). Donald Frame, Montaigne's modern translator and best scholar, remarked that we each have our own Montaigne, as we have our own Hamlet and Don Quixote. I like the remark, because the Montaigne self-portrayed in the *Essays* is so vivid that he eclipses Saint Augustine, Goethe, and Dr. Johnson as an actual personage so powerfully portrayed that he seems fictive, as literary a character as my hero, Sir John Falstaff.

Herbert Luthy emphasized that there is considerable art in Montaigne's ways of being truthful: "this is perhaps the scandal of Montaigne: to content himself with the imperfect and the fragmentary, and yet to be so wholly untragic." Just as I believe there can be no method for literary criticism except oneself (one hopes at its most intelligent), so Montaigne has no method for self-knowledge. He tried to see himself as he would a neighbor, and set aside his successful and honorable public career, in order to get at himself. But he is wonderfully not a reductionist, unlike Wallace Stevens's *grande dame,* "Mrs. Alfred Uruguay," who chants, "I have wiped away moonlight like mud." Montaigne, no romantic, gives you no moonlight, since his view of sex is so pragmatic, but he certainly does not believe that to know what he is really like, you must know the worst of him. He bears himself with equanimity, like Chaucer's Knight in the *Canterbury Tales,* because no one knows better than Montaigne that we are always keeping appointments we never made. A moderate Catholic and dedicated royalist, Montaigne was caught between sides in France's bloody civil wars of religion. Sieges and burning estates were frequent in Gascony, where Protestants and freebooters were strong, and Montaigne experienced his share of such hazards. Resolved to be neither hero nor saint, the rational and orderly Montaigne retired to his library tower whenever he could, and survived to complete the great book 3 of his *Essays* with his masterpiece, "Of Experience" (1587–88). Here I will slow down to a fairly full commentary, since this is sacred ground for me. Emerson's best essay, "Experience," is the child of Montaigne's final essay, and I am one of the many belated children of Emerson.

"Of Experience," in its about forty pages, surveys both Montaigne's and the human condition. I cannot think of another essay, in the tradition that reaches from Montaigne to Freud, that so profoundly searches out the metaphysics of the self, and that so persuasively urges us to accept necessity:

> But you do not die of being sick, you die of being alive. Death kills you well enough without the help of illness. And illnesses have put off death for some, who have lived longer for thinking that they were on their way out and dying.

What do I know? Of death, nothing, and towards that nothing Montaigne adopts the Socratic stance. Like Socrates, Montaigne strengthens as he ages, in total self-acceptance: "It is an absolute perfection and virtually divine to know how to enjoy our being lawfully." That, and not the knowledge of a remote and unknowable God, is much the highest good. And no reduction of our mere being ought to be sanctioned:

> I, who boast of embracing the pleasures of life so assiduously and so particularly, find in them, when I look at them thus minutely, virtually nothing but wind. And even the wind, more wisely than we, loves to make a noise and move about, and is content with its own functions, without wishing for stability and solidity, qualities that do not belong to it.

This is the wisdom that goes beyond disenchantment, beyond the desire not to be deceived. Only Shakespeare, of the strongest Western writers, shows something like Montaigne's pragmatic distrust of transcendence:

> They want to get out of themselves and escape from the man. That is madness: instead of changing into angels, they change into beasts; instead of raising themselves, they lower themselves. These tran-

scendental humors frighten me, like lofty and inaccessible places, and nothing is so hard for me to stomach in the life of Socrates as his ecstasies and possessions by his daemon.

Emerson, with his own daemon, and sundry transcendental yearnings, was properly wary of his father, Montaigne:

Shall we say that Montaigne has spoken wisely, and given the right and permanent expression of the human mind, on the conduct of life?

With reverence for his precursor, Emerson moves towards defending his own ecstasies:

I mean to use the occasion and celebrate the calendar-day of our Saint Michel de Montaigne by counting and describing these doubts and negations.

Emerson means his own doubts and negations of what he takes to be Montaigne's skepticism, but the Montaigne we read in "Of Experience" is what Donald Frame calls "the Whole Man." Yet that man, as he avers, is uneasy with daemonic possession, even if the daemon be that of Socrates. In his own essay, "Experience," Emerson ultimately yields to his own sense that the daemon knows how it is done.

All I know is reception; I am and I have, but I do not get. I say to the genius, if he will pardon the proverb, *In for a mill, in for a million.*

Montaigne is too unitary to address his genius or daemon. For him, it had no separate existence, as it did for Socrates, Emerson, Goethe, W. B. Yeats, and so many others. More than Emerson or Goethe, Montaigne now seems our contemporary, partly because of that image of the whole person that he so uniquely embodies.

JOHN MILTON

> yet not alone, while thou
> Visit'st my slumbers nightly, or when morn
> Purples the east: still govern thou my song,
> Urania, and fit audience find, though few.
> But drive far off the barbarous dissonance
> Of Bacchus and his revellers, the race
> Of that wild rout that tore the Thracian bard
> In Rhodope, where woods and rocks had ears
> To rapture, till the savage clamour drowned
> Both harp and voice; nor could the Muse defend
> Her son.
>
> —*Paradise Lost*, book 7, 28–38

The *sparagmos*, the ripping apart of Orpheus by the wild Bacchantes of Thrace, is an obsessive anxiety in Milton's work. And yet the Orphic identification is stronger in legitimate pride than it is in fear, for the Muse of heroic epic, Calliope, was the mother of Orpheus. To see yourself as a fresh incarnation of Orpheus is to identify your genius with poetry itself. Milton's extraordinary and justified poetic pride hovers near the center of his gift.

Milton, who was haunted by Shakespeare, once contemplated a *Macbeth*, but thought better of it. The strength of *Paradise Lost* and of *Samson Agonistes*, a drama only for the theater of mind, is that they are saved by genre from challenging Shakespeare. Milton's Satan has the shadow of Iago upon him, and yet Milton fights free to impart his highly individual genius to Satan.

In the invocation to book 9 of *Paradise Lost*, the book of the Fall, Milton asks his celestial patroness, the Muse, for "answerable style." By "answerable" he primarily meant a style equal or corresponding to his great subject, but he meant also a style answerable both to his own genius and his highly individual conception of God.

JOHN MILTON
(1608–1674)

JOHN MILTON, THE GLORY OF HIS LANGUAGE, with Shakespeare and Chaucer, was born in his father's house on December 9, 1608. Shakespeare lived until 1616, and it is worth recalling that Milton was a boy of eight when his major precursor died. By the time Milton was sixteen, he was a poet; in 1632, his equivocal poem of praise, "On Shakespeare," was published. Milton devoted himself to the reading of the Greek and Latin writers at his father's country estate of Horton. *Comus*, his superb mythological masque, was acted there in 1634.

Milton's mother (of whom he says little) died in 1637; a year later Milton seized on the death of a classmate, Edward King, to write his superb classical elegy "Lycidas," possibly the single best shorter poem in the language. As I read "Lycidas," it is a pre-elegy for Milton himself, but his mother's death pervades it.

In May 1638, Milton left for his grand tour of the Continent: France, and then Italy, but the outbreak of civil war in England impelled him homewards by July 1639. By 1641, he was a formidable pamphleteer on the Puritan side. His unfortunate marriage to Mary Powell, in 1642, led to his Divorce tracts. By September 1643, his sight began to fail, but this did not prevent the appearance of his *Areopagitica*, on freedom of publication, in November 1644.

His plans to marry again were baffled by the return of his first wife in 1645. Later in that year, his *Poems of Mr. John Milton* was registered for publication, and came forth in January 1646. The next year, his father died. By the spring of 1649, Milton became Secretary for the Foreign Tongues for Cromwell's regime, a position that made him the official spokesperson for the Revolution. After three daughters and a son were born, his first wife died, followed soon by the little boy's death. By February 1652, Milton was totally blind. He remarried in 1656, but his wife died two years later.

In 1659, the Commonwealth broke apart; Milton continued to publish Republican pamphlets, even as the Restoration took place. By May 1659, the poet was in hiding; in August, his books were burned by the hangman in London, and in October he was imprisoned, for about two months. He presented the new regime with a considerable problem; he had defended regicide in print, but was blind, famous throughout Europe, and regarded as the leading scholar-poet. The advisors to Charles II uneasily released Milton rather than be stained by his execution.

The blind poet evidently was on poor terms with his daughters, a problem which was exacerbated by his third wife, when he married in 1663. In August 1667, *Paradise Lost* was published, to be augmented in the second edition of 1674. *Paradise Regained* and *Samson Agonistes* were published together in 1671. Sometime between November 8 and 10, John Milton died.

These are the outer events of the poet-prophet's life, but since he was completely blind for his final twenty years, we are confronted in *Paradise Lost* by an oracle of the inward life. No more deliberate masterpiece exists in English, and "masterpiece" understates it. This epic is a baroque splendor: endless to meditation, overwhelming to read aloud, and an all but infinite challenge even to those who love it best. A new reader, secular and lacking classical learning, is best advised to read it as gorgeous science fiction. "Gorgeous" is a fine word that we have marred: the right meaning is defined in the *American Heritage Dictionary:* "Characterized by magnificence or intrinsic brilliance." Milton's rivals in his own language are few: Shakespeare, Pope, James Joyce—our greater virtuosi. Though Milton once had the status of *the* Protestant poet, as Dante is still *the* Catholic poet, I am increasingly uncertain, after sixty years of reading Milton incessantly, whether he is even a Christian poet, except as William Blake and Emily Dickinson could be called Christian poets. Each of the three is a sect of one, each so original a heretic as to call their Christianity into considerable question. A. D. Nuttall (one of the best critics alive) doubts that the aging Milton believed in the basic tenets of normative Calvinism, while the late historian Christopher Hill suggested that Milton had become a Muggletonian, which *sounds* silly, but the personal inspiration of Lodowicke Muggleton, who died in 1698, forty-odd years after founding his sect, is very close to Milton's version of the Inner Light. We do know that Milton had broken with the Congregationalists or Independents, and Nuttall argues that the poet had Gnostic tendencies, like Christopher Marlowe and William Blake, and had formulated "alternative trinities." What is clear to us is that Milton had heresies enough, all founded upon his rejection of Pauline and Augustinian dualism, with its severe separation between body and soul. As an aggressive monist, Milton embraced at least four major heresies: rejection of Creation out of nothing; Mortalism, or the belief that soul and body died together and would be resurrected together; Anti-Trinitarianism, which affirmed that Yahweh was a single Person; Arminianism, or the denial of Calvinist Predestination. But, like Nuttall, I am skeptical as to whether Milton in his final years *believed* anything. He felt he *knew* certain truths, but they were not creedal.

Milton, like Shakespeare and Dante, is so palpable a genius that it can seem redundant to characterize his gift, rather like attempting to describe the beauty of Sophia Loren in my far-off youth. His power and fecundity are overwhelming and primary, but I am particularly interested in our judgment of his critically maligned, daemonic alter ego, Satan. Unless Satan is a genius, however wicked, there really is no poem, and I have not enjoyed a lifetime of Christian critics emulating C. S. Lewis, one of the stuffed turkeys of modern scholarship, and thus aping his judgment that Satan is stupid. Shelley, as accurate as Borges and Oscar Wilde, got it right when he slyly observed, "The Devil owes everything to Milton." The Satan of *Paradise Lost* is the disciple of Shakespeare's Iago, an extraordinary teacher of entrapment. Satan is not quite of Iago's bad eminence, but he is (as it were) a clean and clever devil doing his best to get on, and the reader owes him every encouragement. Contra C. S. Lewis, do *not* start with a Good Morning's Hatred of Satan, before you attempt the poem. As I remember writing some years ago, regard him as your Uncle Satan, hardly the Bad News in a poem where the Good News, Jesus Christ, is transformed into a Rommel or Patton leading an armored attack, while riding the flame-spewing Merkabah or Chariot of Paternal Deity (after which the Israelis name their main battle tank), in order to burn Satan and his troops out of Heaven.

Poor Satan ends badly of course, and we last see him as a Dead Sea serpent hissing away, but Milton (like most great poets, Shakespeare always excepted) does not play fair. Milton was justly rather embittered: Oliver Cromwell, his chief of men, had his corpse exposed, dangling over London's gates, and Harry Vane, Milton's best friend, was executed as a regicide. It also had to be an ordeal, courageous though Milton was, for a blind man to be locked up while his books were burned, and his enemy Belial, or the Earl of Clarendon, probably had to intercede, urging that Milton be spared out of diplomatic expediency. Milton and his side had lost their war, just as Satan and his gallant demons had lost their war. Losing even a cultural war is not good for the disposition: I was a sweeter person before our universities yielded to supposed social benignity and chose texts for teaching largely on the basis of the racial origin, gender, sexual orientation, and ethnic affiliations of the New Authors, past and present, whether or not they could write their way out of a paper bag.

Satan, like his forerunner Iago, suffers from a Sense of Injured Merit, because he has been passed over for Christ, even as Iago was passed over for Cassio. A Sense of Injured Merit is likely to cause Resentment, and both Iago and Satan are true archetypes for all current Resenters. What, it may be asked, are we to make of Milton's own Sense of Injured Merit? My answer is that he has none whatsoever. What Milton had experienced was counterapocalyptic; the death of national and personal hope. His son was dead, his daughters estranged, two marriages ended, his eyesight departed, his public image disgraced, his friends judicially murdered or fled into exile. *Paradise Lost* and *Samson Agonistes* rise up with preternatural strength and energy from total defeat, and they manifest sublime authority, pride, self-confidence, and astonishing pugnacity. The chained Samson, threatened by the giant Harapha, defies him: "My heels are fettered, but my fist is free," which is one of my favorite lines in Milton.

In 1660, with the Stuart Restoration in progress, Milton spoke as Jeremiah to an unheeding people: "now choosing them a captain back for Egypt, to bethink themselves a little, and consider whither they are rushing." After that, he went deep into internal exile by composing *Paradise Lost*. Contemplating, when young, a Puritan triumph in England, Milton said of the hymns and hallelujahs of the saints, "some one may perhaps be heard offering at high strains in new and lofty measures to sing and celebrate." What that Song of Triumph would have been like, we cannot know, but surmise holds that it would have been a Spenserian romance on the Matter of Britain, raised to the ecstasy of a redeemed nation. Instead, Cromwell died, the Revolution of the Saints failed, and blind Milton composed *Paradise Lost*.

When I was young, *Paradise Lost* was out of favor because the Vicar of Christ for the universities, T. S. Eliot, disliked it (much later on, Eliot allowed it back into the canon). Most critics read it as a poem by C. S. Lewis, an elevated epic of "mere Christianity." I long ago lost count of how many times I have reread *Paradise Lost*, and as a Jewish Gnostic I necessarily am suspect, but my latest rereading, just completed, would not induce me to call this baroque splendor a "Christian epic." Milton is more circumspect than Blake and Emily Dickinson, but his is as much a religion of one as theirs are. Jesus Christ is hardly even a minor character in *Paradise Lost*. God proclaims him as his Son, thus causing all the trouble of Satan's rebellion, according to William Empson. The next appearance of Christ, as armored commander, I have mentioned already. But the crucial passage, almost ludicrous in its uneasiness, is John Milton on the Crucifixion:

> But to the Cross he nails thy enemies,
> The law that is against thee, and the sins
> Of all mankind, with him there crucifies,
> Never to hurt them more who rightly trust
> In this his satisfaction; *so he dies,*
> *But soon revives . . .*
>   —book 12, 415–20.

The italics emphatically are my own. A Christian epic in twelve books and many thousands of lines devotes six words, broken by an enjambment, to the death and resurrection of Jesus Christ! Milton has to put it in, but skips away from it with what one might call hilarious haste; almost even an unbeliever is a touch embarrassed here. I am charmed by a comment of A. D. Nuttall: "For once Milton sounds almost as unforgivably sprightly as Pope." The truth is that Milton is at the least insensitive in regard to the Crucifixion, and in fact appears quite embarrassed about it. If this is a Christian poem, it is not at all Christological. In his *De Doctrina Christiana*, carefully reserved for posthumous publication (it finally appeared in 1825), Milton implacably reveals himself to be an Arian heretic, who accepts the Father but rejects the Trinity. Nuttall again pleases me by pointing out that there is no reference to Prometheus anywhere in *Paradise Lost*, and I suspect that something profound in Milton, which embraced Arianism, was allied to the avoidance of Prometheus. Milton exalted human freedom, including the freedom to fall, but he attempted *not* to exalt human rebelliousness against a heavenly tyrant. That there is an underground Prometheus in Milton was the insight of Blake and of Shelley, but Milton would have been very unhappy with that imputation.

Paradise Lost is magnificent, but its sublime ambition, which is to explain evil definitively and forever, made Milton free to fall in his own epic. He could no more explain the evil of the royalist Restoration than we can explain the death camps of Hitler and the horrors of Stalin and Pol Pot. Yet my concern is not the inevitable failure of the high argument of *Paradise Lost*, but rather the genius of John Milton. Whether normative critics like it or not, something extraordinary happens in and to Milton's poetry every time that Satan speaks. I do not believe that Satan is Milton's own daemon or genius, but Milton's genius is intimately activated by Satan, no matter how often the poem's narrative voice editorializes against him.

Milton is an erotic poet, not so much in Shakespeare's Ovidian way, but in the Hebraic mode of the biblical Song of Songs. It would not be an hyperbole to remark that Milton's genius essentially is erotic; Milton cannot describe Eve without desiring her, and no other male poet is so enchanted by the notion of sporting with the tangles of a beautiful woman's hair. Our mother Eve is a stunner, and poor Satan suffers all the lecherous agonies of a Peeping Tom:

> So spake our general mother, and with eyes
> Of conjugal attraction unreproved,
> And meek surrender, half embraced leaned
> On our first father, half her swelling breast
> Naked met his under the flowing gold
> Of her loose tresses hid: he in delight
> Both of her beauty and submissive charms
> Smiled with superior love, as Jupiter
> On Juno smiles, when he impregns the clouds
> That shed May flowers; and pressed her matron lip
> With kisses pure: aside the Devil turned
> For envy, yet with jealous leer malign
> Eyed them askance, and to himself thus plained.
> "Sight hateful, sight tormenting! Thus these two
> Imparadised in one another's arms
> The happier Eden, shall enjoy their fill
> Of bliss on bliss, while I to hell am thrust,
> Where neither joy nor love, but fierce desire,
> Among our other torments not the least,
> Still unfulfilled with pain of longing pines;
> Yet let me not forget what I have gained
> From their own mouths; all is not theirs it seems:
> One fatal tree there stands of Knowledge forbidden?
> Suspicious, reasonless. Why should their Lord
> Envy them that? Can it be sin to know,
> Can it be death? And do they only stand
> By ignorance, is that their happy state,
> The proof of their obedience and their faith?
> O fair foundation laid whereon to build
> Their ruin! Hence I will excite their minds
> With more desire to know, and to reject
> Envious commands, invented with design
> To keep them low whom knowledge might exalt
> Equal with gods; aspiring to be such,

> They taste and die: what likelier can ensue?
> But first with narrow search I must walk round
> This garden, and no corner leave unspied;
> A chance but chance may lead where I may meet
> Some wand'ring Spirit of heav'n, by fountain side,
> Or in thick shade retired, from him to draw
> What further would be learnt. Live while ye may,
> Yet happy pair; enjoy, till I return,
> Short pleasures, for long woes are to succeed."
>   —book 4, 492–535.

You can argue, I suppose, that the lustful Milton is in Satan's position, since Milton, and the reader, are also Peeping Toms. But Milton's response to his own Eve is immensely passionate and complex, almost as though this fiercely heterosexual poet had to find in his fictive creation all the love that, for whatever reason, his wives and daughters had not given him. After Satan, Eve is the aesthetic glory of *Paradise Lost,* the true manifestation of an otherness in Milton's genius. Feminist critics of *Paradise Lost* sometimes tend to literalize the poem, center upon Eve's representation as a magnificent sexual object, and thus evade Milton's subtle creation of her powerful subjectivity, her lively (and dangerous) consciousness. I am pleased to cite the distinguished Milton scholar Barbara Lewalski, whose admonition reinforces the argument of this book on genius:

> great poets have a way of rising like phoenixes from whatever ashes
> are left in the wake of social and intellectual revolutions, so no doubt
> it will not be long before we can all again read Milton for what is of
> enduring importance rather than what is historically conditioned in
> his conception of man and woman.

Like Shakespeare, the Milton I read burns through history and allows us to see what was and is always there, but which we might never see without him. Nuttall splendidly remarks that "Eve's rebellion against her husband becomes a voyage of discovery, she leading, Adam following." In the shock of Eve's declaration we rightly forget the unfortunate Miltonic line: "He for God only, she for God in him." Something at once radically new and as old as ancient history breaks through when Eve utters one of the epic's greatest ironies:

> "Hast thou not wondered, Adam, at my stay?
> Thee I have missed, and thought it long, deprived

Thy presence, agony of love till now
Not felt, nor shall be twice, for never more
Mean I to try, what rash untried I sought,
The pain of absence from thy sight. But strange
Hath been the cause, and wonderful to hear:
This tree is not as we are told, a tree
Of danger tasted, nor to evil unknown
Op'ning the way, but of divine effect
To open eyes, and make them gods who taste;
And hath been tasted such: the serpent wise,
Or restrained as we, or not obeying,
Hath eaten of the fruit, and is become,
Not dead, as we are threatened, but thenceforth
Endued with human voice and human sense,
Reasoning to admiration, and with me
Persuasively hath so prevailed, that I
Have also tasted, and have also found
Th' effects to correspond, opener my eyes,
Dim erst, dilated spirits, ampler heart,
And growing up to godhead; which for thee
Chiefly I sought, without thee can despise.
For bliss, as thou hast part, to me is bliss,
Tedious, unshared with thee, and odious soon.
Thou therefore also taste, that equal lot
May join us, equal joy, as equal love;
Lest thou not tasting, different degree
Disjoin us, and I then too late renounce
Deity for thee, when fate will not permit."
                              —book 9, 856–85

No two readers, students, critics, take this speech in exactly the same way, as I rediscover each time I attempt to spur a discussion of it. Partly, this is because Milton himself has antithetical attitudes towards it. Adam initially takes it very badly, hearing in it his wife's death sentence, and vowing that he will die with her. And yet he terms her "last and best / Of all God's works." I will give up battering C. S. Lewis (hero, by the way, of our current Southern fundamentalists) after this, but he does allow himself to say that Eve is guilty of plotting Adam's murder! It is true that she dreads being replaced by a second Eve, and that Kabbalists speculated that she herself had inherited Adam, after he and Lilith, his first wife, had an irreconcilable dispute as to the proper position for sexual intercourse.

The question as to Eve's speech is whether knowledge enormous has made a god of her, to adopt a Keatsian phrasing. That returns us to the labyrinth of Milton's imagination, and inevitably to the matter of Satan, which I turn at last to consider. In Shakespearean terms, Satan is a hero-villain, resembling aspects of Macbeth as well as of Iago. Because Milton unites spirit and power in a single concept, he is a theomorphic vitalist, on the model of the Yahwist's Jacob or Tamar. We (most of us anyway) do not take with Miltonic seriousness the idea that we are molded as the image of God. Milton believed in the God within, and not in the Blakean Nobodaddy he nevertheless depicts in *Paradise Lost*. The aesthetic puzzle of his poem is its scalding, taunting God, who is simply a great poet's blunder. Milton should have followed the Yahwist's audacity in rendering a wholly human Yahweh, who sits in the shade of a terebinth tree and devours Sarah's lunch of veal, rolls, curds, and milk, and then happily is moved to prophesy that she will bear a child. Instead, the monistic Milton gives us a dualistic God, prone to spiritual posturings. When truer to himself, Milton would not accept that the human senses could be fallen, because for him all of reality was to be apprehended as sensation, a conviction only strengthened by his blindness. Miltonic genius refuses any distinction between the naturalistic and the transcendental, which is why Satan is so superb a representation.

Milton's freedom of imagination was identified by him with the Inner Light tradition of radical Protestantism, and with his own interpretation of Christian Liberty, the Freedom of the Saints. Miltonic regeneration perfects nature without maiming it. Satan, a Catholic dualist, does not understand his own fusion of spirit and energy, which is his tragedy. My favorite critic of Milton, W. B. C. Watkins, asserts that "passion is always stronger in Milton than reason." *Paradise Lost* is a passionate epic, and not a reasonable one. That is why Satan is aesthetically superior to Adam, though not to Eve. Striving to distance himself from Satan, Milton in book 5 represents himself as the seraph Abdiel, whose name (which means "God's servant") is that of a human, not an angel, in the Hebrew Bible. Abdiel is the only recalcitrant in Satan's vast third of the heavenly host, the only angel who opposes Satan "in a flame of zeal severe." The other angels judge Abdiel "as out of season," as Milton was out of season, from 1660 until his death in 1674.

Abdiel's defiance prompts Satan to the single utterance that seems to me most problematical, because it is near the center of Milton's own genius:

>   . . . who saw
> When this creation was? Remember'st thou
> Thy making, while the Maker gave thee being?
> We know no time when we were not as now;
> Know none before us, self-begot, self-raised
> By our own quick'ning power . . .
>
>   —book 5, 856–61

Satan does not speak for Milton the man, but is this not the stance of the poet Milton? Would he also not have said, "Our puissance is our own," rather than Shakespeare's or Spenser's? The freedom of the poet is Milton's dearest aspiration, the heart of his integrity. You can say, if you wish, that this freedom ensues from true obedience to the will of God, but who is to interpret such a will? Milton interpreted it for himself, relying solely upon his own authority, which he identified with his genius.

LEO TOLSTOY

"Ah, that's a fine fellow!" exclaimed the chief. "He has gained much land!"

Pahóm's servant came running up and tried to raise him, but he saw that blood was flowing from his mouth. Pahóm was dead!

The Bashkirs clicked their tongues to show their pity.

His servant picked up the spade and dug a grave long enough for Pahóm to lie in, and buried him in it. Six feet from his head to his heels was all he needed.

—"How Much Land Does a Man Need?"
(translated by Louise and Aylmer Maude)

James Joyce thought that Tolstoy's late sketch "How Much Land Does a Man Need?" was the best story ever written. I myself vote for Tolstoy's late novella *Hadji Murad,* but no one need doubt that Tolstoy was the best of storytellers, because his art, like Shakespeare's, seems as though the art itself were nature. It is unsurprising that Tolstoy resented Shakespeare. Harriet Beecher Stowe, Tolstoy insisted, was far better.

Tolstoy's narratives are astonishingly rich; Shakespeare is richer. *King Lear* infuriated Tolstoy, who thought it immoral. In all of Shakespeare, Tolstoy cared only for Falstaff. These are the reactions of genius to genius, and are beyond our judgment, but we always can learn from Tolstoy, particularly when he is scandalously mistaken.

The genius of Tolstoy was dangerously akin to Shakespeare's, which on some level of apprehension appalled the creator of *War and Peace* and *Anna Karenina,* of *Hadji Murad* and *The Kreutzer Sonata.* It may be the reader's illusion that Shakespeare and Tolstoy seem the most *natural* of writers, and yet the illusion is nearly universal. Tolstoy and Shakespeare are unmatched in portraying *change,* and what is more natural than a process whose final form is death? Pierre, as *War and Peace* ends, is astonishingly different from what he was at the outset, and yet his continuity is utterly persuasive. Falstaff, in his great arc from joy to rejection, always remains Falstaff, and not a double man. Tolstoy could not forgive Shakespeare for getting there first.

LEO TOLSTOY
(1828–1910)

IN 1882, TOLSTOY TOOK LESSONS IN Hebrew from a rabbi, and worked strenu-
ously at reading the Bible, to his wife's increasing despair. Whenever religion
engrossed him, they were further alienated, and usually they became closer
again when he returned to writing fiction. Tolstoy long since had ceased to
take communion with the Russian Orthodox Church, and had become a Tolstoyan, with many followers, in Russia and abroad. The definitive observation
on Tolstoy's religion was Maxim Gorky's: "With God he has very suspicious relations; they sometimes remind me of the relation of 'two bears in one den.'"
God could not have been comfortable with Count Leo Tolstoy.

Defining Tolstoy's genius is an absurd enterprise; he had the exuberance
and fecundity of Balzac and Hugo with almost none of their self-consciousness
or their outrageousness. His judgments upon great literature are more mysti-
fying than outrageous. He denounces Shakespeare, particularly *King Lear*, but
accepts Falstaff, because the great wit "does not speak like an actor." On some
level he understood that Shakespeare was his true rival as a novelist. Increasingly I have come to see that the two parts of *Henry IV*, taken together, constitute a novel-of-novels.

My favorite Tolstoy remains *Hadji Murad*, but as I have written about it
twice before, I shall take as my instance of genius another short novel, *The
Kreutzer Sonata* (1889), composed several years before he began *Hadji
Murad*. Rereading *The Kreutzer Sonata* is very nearly a traumatic experience:
I do not know whether to praise Tolstoy for mesmerizing me, or to shudder
at the story's mad inner narrator, Pozdnyshev. This crazed personage is not
Tolstoy, who after all never murdered Countess Tolstoy, though clearly he
sometimes wished he had done so. But there is an afterword by Tolstoy in
which he endorses Pozdnyshev's contention that all sexual intercourse is
evil and should cease, even between man and wife. I exempted Tolstoy
from the Balzac–Victor Hugo amiable outrageousness earlier, because this is
beyond outrage, and takes us into the Tolstoyan cosmos, which is governed
by its own principles. So absolute is his genius that one needs to begin with
his cosmological authority, which persuades us that his fiction is like no
other, and the difference in turn reinforces what I have to call his aesthetic
authority, a phrase that would have infuriated him.

Everything Tolstoy ever wrote, including his craziest moral and theological tracts, is madly readable. As with Shakespeare, you fall into the illusion that nature does the writing. The paradox, clear to everyone, is that the high art of Tolstoy's narratives and of Shakespeare's dramas seems not to be art, until you recover from their mimetic force and compel yourself to become analytical. The Marxist critic György Lukács had to regard Tolstoy as a "special case," since a formalistic point of view could not deal with his vision, or his created world. Lukács wanted to see Tolstoy as the final expression of European Romanticism, but being a superb reader, he yielded to those great moments in which Tolstoy "shows a clearly differentiated, concrete and existent world." Such a cosmos transcended the novel, and renewed the epic:

> This world is the sphere of pure social reality in which man exists as man, neither as a social being nor as an isolated, unique, pure and therefore abstract interiority. If ever this world should come into being as something natural and simply experienced, as the only true reality, a new complete totality could be built out of all its substances and relationships. It would be a world to which our divided reality would be a mere backdrop, a world which would have outstripped our dual world of social reality by as much as we have outstripped the world of nature. But art can never be the agent of such a transformation: the great epic is a form bound to the historical moment, and any attempt to depict the utopian as existent can only end in destroying the form, not in creating reality. The novel is the form of the epoch of absolute sinfulness, as Fichte said, and it must remain the dominant form so long as the world is ruled by the same stars. In Tolstoy, intimations of a breakthrough into a new epoch are visible; but they remain polemical, nostalgic and abstract.

Lukács, a great critic both empowered and limited by his Marxism, testifies to Tolstoy's scandalous strength of representation, akin to only a handful of other writers: Homer, the Yahwist, Dante, Chaucer, Shakespeare, Cervantes, Proust. The illusion such strength gives is that Tolstoy is the least "literary" of writers, an illusion because his profound tendentiousness, his unceasing design upon his reader, places him halfway between Saint Augustine and Freud, masters of a rhetoric that is already a psychology. Tolstoy wants both to save you and cure you; in *The Kreutzer Sonata* he is himself at least half-mad, and expects both salvation and healing to result from the universal cessation of sexual intercourse, whether in or out of marriage.

That a story grounded upon such a premise should be more than readable, indeed overwhelming, is a disconcerting proof of the near-uniqueness of Tolstoy's genius. Shakespeare, in his final comedy, *Measure for Measure*, created a mythical Vienna where the law, now to be enforced, calls for the beheading of any male who has indulged in sexual congress outside of marriage. Fully enforced, in mere reality, this would depopulate us rapidly, but not so totally as Tolstoy contemplated in a letter to his hanger-on, Chertkov:

> Therefore let everyone try not to marry and, if he be married, to live with his wife as brother and sister . . . You will object that this would mean the end of the human race? . . . What a great misfortune! The antediluvian animals are gone from the earth, human animals will disappear too.

Maxim Gorky, in his *Reminiscences of Tolstoy*, tells of Tolstoy whistling in tune with a chaffinch, and failing to keep up with it:

> "What a furious little creature! It's in a rage. What is it?"
>
> I told him about the chaffinch and its characteristic jealousy.
>
> "All life long one song," he said, "and yet jealous. Man has a thousand songs in his heart and is yet blamed for jealousy; is it fair?" He spoke musingly, as though asking himself questions. "There are moments when a man says to a woman more than she ought to know about him. He speaks and forgets, but she remembers. Perhaps jealousy comes from the fear of degrading one's soul, of being humiliated and ridiculous? Not that a woman is dangerous who holds a man by his lusts but she who holds him by his soul . . ."
>
> When I pointed out the contradiction in this with his *Kreutzer Sonata*, the radiance of a sudden smile beamed through his beard and he said:
>
> "I am not a chaffinch."
>
> In the evening while walking, he suddenly said:
>
> "Man survives earthquakes, epidemics, the horrors of disease, and all the agonies of the soul, but for all time his most tormenting tragedy has been, is and will be—the tragedy of the bedroom."

Poor Pozdnyshev is a chaffinch, and is converted into a murderer by "the tragedy of the bedroom." The critic John Bayley illuminates Tolstoy by comparing him with Goethe, disputing Thomas Mann's contrast of the two great writers:

> Tolstoy was also a gigantic egoist, but an egoist of a very different kind. If Goethe cared for nothing but himself, Tolstoy *was* nothing but himself; and his sense of what life had come to mean for him is correspondingly more intimate and more moving.

Certainly Tolstoy is uncannily close to his reader, disconcertingly so in *The Kreutzer Sonata*. And yet no reader I know is able to sympathize with the wretched Pozdnyshev, though we cannot be unmoved by the horror and vividness of Tolstoy's description of the jealousy-crazed husband murdering his wife:

> " 'Don't lie, you wretch!' I howled, and seized her arm with my left hand, but she wrenched herself away. Then, still without letting go of the dagger, I seized her by the throat with my left hand, threw her backwards, and began throttling her. What a firm neck it was . . . ! She seized my hand with both hers trying to pull it away from her throat, and as if I had only waited for that, I struck her with all my might with the dagger in the side below the ribs.
>
> "When people say they don't remember what they do in a fit of fury, it is rubbish, falsehood. I remembered everything and did not for a moment lose consciousness of what I was doing. The more frenzied I became the more brightly the light of consciousness burnt in me, so that I could not help knowing everything I did. I knew what I was doing every second. I cannot say that I knew beforehand what I was going to do; but I knew what I was doing when I did it, and even I think a little before, as if to make repentance possible and to be able to tell myself that I could stop. I knew I was hitting below the ribs and that the dagger would enter. At the moment I did it I knew I was doing an awful thing such as I had never done before, which would have terrible consequences. But that consciousness passed like a flash of lightning and the deed immediately followed the consciousness. I realized the action with extraordinary clearness. I felt, and remember, the momentary resistance of her corset and of something else, and then the plunging of the dagger into something soft. She seized the dagger with her hands, and cut them, but could not hold it back.
>
> "For a long time afterwards, in prison when the moral change had taken place in me, I thought of that moment, recalled what I could of

it, and considered it. I remembered that for an instant, before the action I had a terrible consciousness that I was killing, had killed, a defenceless woman, my wife! I remember the horror of that consciousness and conclude from that, and even dimly remember, that having plunged the dagger in I pulled it out immediately, trying to remedy what had been done and to stop it. I stood for a second motionless waiting to see what would happen, and whether it could be remedied.

"She jumped to her feet and screamed: 'Nurse! He has killed me.'"

(translated by Louise and Aylmer Maude)

Perhaps only because this is Tolstoy, can one seek genius here without courting morality or sadism. When I think of Tolstoy, memories crowd upon me. Prince Andrey falling in love with Natasha when she sings at the clavichord; Anna Karenina lying in bed looking at a single burnt-down candle, which flickers and goes out; Hadji Murad, wounded to death, "limping heavily . . . dagger in hand straight at the foe." Together with these, I wince recalling Pozdnyshev's wife seizing the dagger with her hands, cutting them, but unable to hold it back.

It is a valid commonplace of criticism to say that Tolstoy sees everything as if no one ever had seen it before, and yet mixes the strangeness of what he shows with a sense of the universal. It makes one very uncomfortable to test that commonplace against Pozdnyshev's slaughter of his wife, but the maxim seems to hold. So pure a storyteller is Tolstoy that this fictive murder is as memorable as Macbeth's butchery of the sleeping Duncan. Shakespeare troubled Tolstoy because his own detachment as a writer approached Shakespeare's, and when that supreme artistry asserted itself, Tolstoy's ferocious moralizing ceased.

It bewilders me that Tolstoy would regard my comments as those of another victim seduced by Tolstoy's art, which he himself rejects even as he triumphs in it. Gary Saul Morson irrefutably phrases our dilemma: "*The Kreutzer Sonata* is a brilliantly contrived aesthetic masterpiece that teaches us to despise such contrivance and mastery—and that is its duplicitous strategy." Yet Plato's strongest dialogues enact the same duplicity: they are aesthetic splendors that teach us to exile aesthetic experience. Tolstoy, like Plato, condemns art because he is certain he knows the truth, except that Tolstoy is also his own Socrates, and is willing to be a martyr for the truth. Both Plato and Tolstoy, being literary artists upon the heights, can get away with the bad business of seduction while decrying seduction.

The Kreutzer Sonata concludes with a pathos that I can neither resist nor forgive:

> He was going on but, unable to repress his sobs, he stopped. When he recovered himself he continued:
>
> "I only began to understand when I saw her in the coffin . . ."
>
> He gave a sob, but immediately continued hurriedly:
>
> "Only when I saw her dead face did I understand all that I had done. I realized that I, I, had killed her; that it was my doing that she, living, moving, warm, had now become motionless, waxen, and cold, and that this could never, anywhere, or by any means, be remedied. He who has not lived through it cannot understand. . . . Ugh! Ugh! Ugh! . . ." he cried several times and then was silent.
>
> We sat in silence a long while. He kept sobbing and trembling as he sat opposite me without speaking. His face had grown narrow and elongated and his mouth seemed to stretch right across it.
>
> "Yes," he suddenly said. "Had I then known what I know now, everything would have been different. Nothing would have induced me to marry her. . . . I should not have married at all."
>
> Again we remained silent for a long time.
>
> "Well, forgive me. . . ." He turned away from me and lay down on the seat, covering himself up with his plaid. At the station where I had to get out (it was at eight o'clock in the morning) I went up to him to say good-bye. Whether he was asleep or only pretended to be, at any rate he did not move. I touched him with my hand. He uncovered his face, and I could see he had not been asleep.
>
> "Good-bye," I said, holding out my hand. He gave me his and smiled slightly, but so piteously that I felt ready to weep.
>
> "Yes, forgive me . . ." he said, repeating the same words with which he had concluded his story.

Tolstoy, determined to punish us for being unable to resist his genius, has no forgiveness for us. He really means that he (who had fathered thirteen children upon his wife) should not have married, and that we too should not have done so. That writer and reader/critic should have no mutual forgiveness makes not the slightest difference when it comes to apprehending Tolstoy's fiction. This seems to me an apt way of locating his genius.

LUSTRE 2

|

Lucretius, Vergil, Saint Augustine, Dante Alighieri, Geoffrey Chaucer

|

I have arranged this second Lustre of *Keter* as an influence group, so that the sheen of juxtapositioning is highlighted here. Lucretius pervades Vergil to a startling extent, thus accounting for Vergil's more plangent version of Epicureanism. Augustine, thinking his way through to a Christian rhetoric and theory of reading, is haunted by Vergil, the principal non-biblical text that had formed his mind. Dante, who by his strength fits as readily in Lustre 1, is placed here because his self-portrait as Pilgrim echoes Augustine's, and in turn is deliciously mocked by Chaucer the Pilgrim, an ironist who gently deprecated most absolutes. Chaucer too could fit as readily in the first Lustre, since his greatest creations, the Pardoner and the Wife of Bath, are the crucial forerunners of the Shakespearean nihilists and vitalists, though hardly of the titanic blend of nihilist and vitalist, Hamlet the Prince of Denmark.

LUCRETIUS

> The chilling care comes next.
> Your love's not around, for a change? But still her image
> Is, and her sweet name echoes in your ears.
> But we ought to flee these shadows and scare off
> The food of love, and turn our thoughts to another—
> Shooting the juice into any available body,
> Not holding it all in for a single lover,
> Saving up for ourselves sure pain and sorrow.
> If you feed the sore it'll put down roots and fester
> And blister over and drive you mad with trouble—
> Better write off the old wounds with new business,
> Stroll after a street-strolling trollop and cure yourself,
> Shift your thoughts to another while you still can!
>
> (translated by Anthony M. Esolen)

It is hardly a wonder that Lucretius vanished for more than a thousand Christian years, until his great poem was revived in the fifteenth century. Dante may never have heard of Lucretius, and would have been disconcerted by *De rerum natura* (*On the Nature of Things*), particularly since he inevitably would have realized that Vergil had enormous debts to Lucretius.

Lucretian poets, from Vergil through Shelley on to Wallace Stevens, are marked by a turning away from superstition, and yet Lucretius's more crucial effect was upon Christian poets ambivalently shocked by his strenuous materialism: Tasso, Spenser, Milton, Tennyson.

Nothing in Lucretius is more pungent than his disdain for erotic idealism, as in the passage quoted above. Byron, with his amiable arguments in favor of sexual "mobility," was perhaps Lucretius's wisest erotic disciple. The sufferings of romantic love and loss have no better physician than Lucretius, whose sense of the cosmos as a "flaming rampart" is a curing perspective for sexual anguish.

A genius who warns you away from organized superstition and erotic frenzy might well be at a disadvantage these days. But Lucretius matters most because no other poet teaches you so well not to fear death, a teaching in which Montaigne was Lucretius's follower. By bluntly dismissing survival and immortality, Lucretius seeks to bring you a freedom from dread and from melancholy, a freedom that most of us decline to accept.

TITUS LUCRETIUS CARUS
(c. 99–c. 55 B.C.E.)

LUCRETIUS, OUR TRADITION'S MOST eloquent proponent of "atheism" and metaphysical materialism, has been strongly misread incessantly, which is probably inevitable, since the Epicurean philosophy of Lucretius is totally unacceptable to Christianity, Islam, and Judaism, to all of Western religious tradition. Saint Jerome disposed of Lucretius, vilifying him so effectively that he vanished for more than a thousand years, to be recovered only in the fifteenth century. One wishes that Dante could have read Lucretius: would the Epicurean poet not have become the diabolic contrast to Vergil, Statius, Ovid, and Lucan, all crucial elements in the *Commedia*? You cannot Christianize Lucretius, even if you are Dante.

Of the life of Lucretius, we know nothing except Saint Jerome's Christian slander. We are asked to believe that the poet's wife, Lucilia, reacting to his sexual neglect, gave him a love potion that drove him mad. Supposedly, Lucretius composed *On the Nature of Things,* his superb didactic poem, in some lucid intervals, and then killed himself at forty-four. Perhaps it is just as well that Dante probably never even encountered the name of Lucretius. One grimaces at the prospect of the Epicurean master poet, upright in his tomb in the *Inferno,* giving a Dantean account of his life, his theological errors, and his self-slaughter. We have something like that anyway in Alfred, Lord Tennyson's superb dramatic monologue "Lucretius" (1868), where the poisoned bard of philosophical materialism cries out the storm-ridden agony of his hallucinations:

> "A void was made in Nature; all her bonds
> Cracked; and I saw the flaring atom-streams
> And torrents of her myriad universe,
> Ruining along the illimitable inane,
> Fly on to clash together again, and make
> Another and another frame of things
> For ever: that was mine, my dream, I knew it—
> Of and belonging to me, as the dog
> With inward yelp and restless forefoot plies
> His function of the woodland: but the next!

I thought that all the blood by Sylla shed
Came driving rainlike down again on earth,
And where it dashed the reddening meadow, sprang
No dragon warriors from Cadmean teeth,
For these I thought my dream would show to me,
But girls, Hetairai, curious in their art,
Hired animalisms, vile as those that made
The mulberry-faced Dictator's orgies worse
Than aught they fable of the quiet Gods.
And hands they mixed, and yelled and round me drove
In narrowing circles till I yelled again
Half-suffocated, and sprang up, and saw—
Was it the first beam of my latest day?

"Then, then, from utter gloom stood out the breasts,
The breasts of Helen, and hoveringly a sword
Now over and now under, now direct,
Pointed itself to pierce, but sank down shamed
At all that beauty; and as I stared, a fire,
The fire that left a roofless Ilion,
Shot out of them, and scorched me that I woke."

Tennyson has fused together a weird amalgam of himself, Lucretius, and
Vergil's Aeneas in this grand sexual nightmare. Sylla is the mulberry-faced
dictator, Sulla, renowned for his orgies, which appear to have been sensa-
tional, even by Roman standards. The Hetairai (whores) close in on the
Vergilian Tennyson, until he has a vision of Helen menaced by the vengeful
Aeneas, but her fabled breasts unman the clearly phallic Trojan sword. What
has all this to do with Lucretius, and his great poem on the way things are?
Why, very little, except that Jerome's Christian gossip has given Tennyson
a gorgeously strong misreading of the merely actual Lucretius. Tennyson
was reacting also to the contemporary Epicureanism of Algernon Charles
Swinburne's poems and the early essays of Walter Pater.

Epicurus (341–270 B.C.E.) had propounded in Athens a hedonistic rationalism based on a materialist (atomic) theory of matter. Epicureanism denies the soul's immortality, dismisses Divine Providence, and has no use for
Platonic idealism, particularly in the erotic sphere, where a commonsense
promiscuity is cheerfully advocated, not for its own sake but so as to avoid
passionate disasters. Epicurus and his poetic disciple, Lucretius, affirm the
joy of natural existence and urge us to accept the reality of death, without

false religious consolations. The gods exist, but they are irrelevant, being remote from us, and indifferent to our suffering or our pleasure.

Epicurus, like Lucretius after him, has had little good said of him by official Western culture, but Lucretius has been a major, sometimes hidden influence from Vergil to Wallace Stevens. My favorite Emersonian aphorism is purely Epicurean, and is central to Lucretian tradition:

> As men's prayers are a disease of the will, so are their creeds a disease of the intellect.

Lucretius is strong stuff, however, and has provoked ambivalences in his admirers from Vergil through the Renaissance epic poets (Tasso, Spenser, Du Bartas) on through Montaigne, Molière, Dryden, Shelley, and Walt Whitman. Rather amazingly, the hedonistic dogmatism of the fiercely sublime Lucretius always suggests to me the tendentiousness of Augustine and Dante, who were just as passionately convinced of Christian truth as Lucretius was of his Epicureanism. *On the Nature of Things* presents a poetry of belief, taking Epicurus as the founder of an antireligious religion, of which Epicurus essentially was very much a cult leader in the Athens of his day. Lucretius attempts to be the most faithful of Epicureans, but his temperament is highly idiosyncratic, best conveyed in English by the translations of John Dryden (1685), who unfortunately rendered only a few passages of the poem. Dryden accurately noted that "the distinguishing character of Lucretius (I mean of his soul and genius) is a certain kind of noble pride, and positive assertion of his opinions." This could also be said of Dante, the anti-Lucretius, and usefully reminds us that the sensibilities of poets are more important than their ideologies.

George Santayana, in his *Three Philosophical Poets* (1910), brings together Lucretius with his antithesis, Dante, and with Goethe, himself more an Epicurean than a Christian. But Santayana wrote his study nearly a century ago, and I think that none of the three poets was primarily philosophical. Lucretius is not versified Epicurus, Dante is not versified Augustine, and Goethe also versifies only Goethe. Even the rhapsodic invocation of Epicurus that begins book 3 of *On the Nature of Things* offers the particular accent, not of the Greek founder, but of the severe Roman sublimity that marks Lucretius as the anti-Dante:

> As soon as your reasoning, sprung from that god-like mind, lifts up its voice to proclaim the nature of the universe, then the terrors of the mind take flight, the ramparts of the world roll apart, and I see the

march of events throughout the whole of space. The majesty of the
gods is revealed and those quiet habitations, never shaken by storms
nor drenched by rain-clouds nor defaced by white drifts of snow which
a harsh frost congeals. A cloudless ether roofs them, and laughs with
radiance lavishly diffused. All their wants are supplied by nature, and
nothing at any time cankers their peace of mind. But nowhere do I see
halls of Hell, though the earth is no barrier to my beholding all that
passes underfoot in the space beneath. At this I am the seized with a
divine delight, and a shuddering awe, that by your power nature
stands thus unveiled and made manifest in every part.

(translated by R. Latham [1951])

This doubtless ensues from the Gospel according to Epicurus, but the
vision and tone are purely Lucretian. His is a "divine delight" but expressed
with a force that, in the original, is sustained at great intensity, a survey of
the universe's nature taken from very high up. The cosmological self-
confidence of Lucretius allows him to counsel us to put aside the fear of
death as being an irrelevancy. He confronts with serenity the violent world
that his poem could not teach Vergil to bear serenely. His art is less varied
than Vergil's, and its aesthetic effect upon me is not as great as Vergil's, but
it does me more good to read Lucretius.

VERGIL

> —as many souls
> As leaves that yield their hold on boughs and fall
> Through forests in the early frost of autumn,
> Or as migrating birds from the open sea
> That darken heaven when the cold season comes
> And drives them overseas to sunlit lands
> There all stood begging to be first across
> And reached out longing hands to the far shore.
> —*Aeneid,* book 6, 307–14
> (translated by Robert Fitzgerald)

Dante's Vergil has little to do with the actual Roman poet, who did not yearn for the Christian dispensation. Vergil, deeply influenced by Lucretius, had an Epicurean vision of the prevalence of pain and suffering in natural existence, and perceived nothing transcendental in any time to come. Rather than guiding Dante, the actual Vergil would reside in the *Inferno* in one tomb with Farinata, or would run across the burning sands with the sodomites. Dante's choice of a guide was aesthetic, and had no relation to theological allegory.

As a poetic genius, Vergil has nothing in common with Dante, but his affinities with Lucretius and with Tennyson are authentic and revelatory, while aspects of Robert Frost are also very close.

Vergil is the laureate of nightmare: his goddess Juno is the strongest literary embodiment I know of the all-but-universal male dread of female power. Love, in the *Aeneid,* is a kind of suicide. Dido, the epic's most sympathetic figure, destroys herself rather than endure the humiliation of being abandoned by the pious prig Aeneas, who has more to do with Vergil's patron, the emperor Augustus, than with an Achilles or an Odysseus.

All of us, in Vergil, reach out longing hands to the far shore, leaving behind both our natural pleasure and our erotic pain, as we are ferried into the shadowy afterlife. There is no victory in victory for Vergil, and his gods are as poor in spirit as they are powerful in dominance over us. And yet Vergil's eloquence is extraordinary: the litany of loss was never again to be so exquisite.

VERGIL
(70–19 B.C.E.)

POET, PSYCHOLOGIST-THEOLOGIAN, AND poet-of-poets (setting Shakespeare aside), these three are linked forever by a nostalgia for Roman authority, a longing for an order at once transcendental and worldly. And yet, they hardly lived parallel lives. Vergil died with his epic poem, the *Aeneid*, unfinished, and evidently he desired that the manuscript be destroyed. Augustine, Bishop of Hippo, in what is now Algeria, ended his life with the Vandals battering at the gates of his city. Dante died of malaria contracted upon a diplomatic mission for one of his hosts, who had helped sustain him in his long exile from Florence. A common sadness attends these three poignant dyings: Vergil, who wished his achievement to be obliterated; Augustine, who feared for his flock, menaced by heretical barbarians; Dante, who was a quarter-century short of the "perfect" age of eighty-one, that might have seen his prophecy fulfilled. And yet each of these seers had accomplished miracles of genius: the *Aeneid*; the *Confessions* and the *City of God*; the *Divine Comedy*.

In our contemporary terms, Vergil was a professional poet, indeed the imperial laureate, while Augustine was a professor of literature converted into a Catholic bishop, and Dante was a failed Florentine politician transmogrified into a prophetic poet, akin to Isaiah and to Ezekiel. We have no equivalents to those titans in the century just past. Joyce, a renegade Catholic, Proust, a half-Jewish skeptic, and Kafka, ultimate Jewish exile, are our imaginative touchstones, and perhaps do not yield hopelessly to Vergil, Augustine, and Dante as vast imaginative originalities. And yet there is nothing like the nostalgia for Roman order in Joyce, Proust, and Kafka. You need to turn to lesser figures, like Ezra Pound and T. S. Eliot, to find such longings for archaic ideas of order. Pound, despite his occasional eloquence, is no Vergil, and Eliot, for all his rigor, did not equal Augustine as intellect or Dante as poet. If (as W. H. Auden thought) our Dante was Kafka, one could also nominate Proust as our Augustine, visionary of memory and of time, and Joyce as our Vergil, both continuators of Homer. But our twentieth-century triad were masters of chaos, and not questers for order.

The Latin language, which connected the Christian Augustine to the pagan Vergil, was the parent of Dante's Tuscan vernacular, converted by its use in the *Divine Comedy* into the literary tongue of all Italy. For a learned African Roman like Augustine, Vergil was as close after four centuries as Shakespeare remains to us. Augustine was a superb reader, comparable to Dr. Samuel Johnson in the English eighteenth century. In a recent study, *The Shadows of Poetry: Vergil in the Mind of Augustine* (1998), Sabine MacCormack remarks that the Christian theologian "was undoubtedly Vergil's most intelligent and searching ancient reader." I would venture that Augustine's principal attraction to Dante was not so much theological as it was their shared love for Vergil. Modern scholarship mostly errs in emphasizing Dante's Catholic orthodoxy since he imposed his own genius upon the traditional faith of Paul and Augustine. But then, Dante baptized Vergil's imagination, thus converting an Epicurean poet into a proto-Christian celebrant. Augustine had quoted Vergil copiously in Christian contexts, in order to highlight Christian morals, but Augustine held back from anything like Dante's strong, deliberate misreading of Vergil.

The Vergil of the *Divine Comedy* necessarily is a literary character, as is Dante the Pilgrim. So persuasive is Dante in his poetic authority that it can take the reader a considerable while to realize that *all* the persons of the *Comedy* are literary characters, whatever historical names they bear. The Latin poet Statius never converted to Christianity, but Dante wanted him for a crucial and poignant recognition scene with Vergil in the *Purgatorio*, and so the merely historical truth was falsified. Vergil, as we will see, was in many respects the disciple of the great Epicurean poet Lucretius, who evidently was unknown to Dante and who would have appalled the Tuscan master.

There are only three principal characters in the *Commedia:* Dante the Pilgrim, his "father" Vergil, and the magnificent, enigmatic figure of Beatrice, whom Dante elevates to an extraordinary eminence in the celestial hierarchy. The enigma of Beatrice is that she is Dante's own invention, an audacity difficult to match anywhere else in literature. Had Dante been less than one of the two supreme poets of the Western world, then Beatrice would have been an outrageous imposition of a personal myth upon the formidable structure of Roman Catholic theology. I suggest, in the spirit of this book, that we learn to think of Beatrice as the genius of Dante Alighieri, his "interior paramour," to borrow a phrase from Wallace Stevens. Vergil's genius was his nightmare, Juno, horrible bad news in every way. For Dante, Beatrice was the good news, the Gospel according to Dante.

The *Divine Comedy* is a "sacred poem" rather than an epic, and Dante himself can be said to have regarded it as the Third Testament, a completion of Scripture. We cannot find in Shakespeare a single person who could be called his genius: Hamlet, Falstaff, Cleopatra, Iago, Macbeth, Lear, Rosalind might all be nominated, but only as a cluster. Milton's genius, according to Blake and Shelley, was Satan; probably the role should be assigned to the Inner Light invoked by the Protestant poet in the invocation to book 3 of *Paradise Lost.*

All great poetry loses in translation, and the *Commedia*, being the stronger poem, has more to lose than the *Aeneid.* Paradoxically, Dante survives translation better than Vergil does. The *Purgatorio* of the American poet W. S. Merwin, which I have just reread, is able to convey more of Dante's most original invention than is brought across by such equally admirable achievements as the versions of the *Aeneid* by Robert Fitzgerald and by Allen Mandelbaum. Dante, even more than Vergil the master of nuance, has such cognitive strength and sheer force of will and desire that his text can be almost drained of nuance and still be preternaturally powerful. The self-trust of Dante is enormous. It is equaled by the finest poets in England—Shakespeare, Chaucer, Milton—but an irony shared by Shakespeare and Chaucer veils their self-reliance from us. Milton's exuberance-of-being is our nearest approach to Dante's, but it is difficult to think of a poet in English who deeply resembles Vergil. Tennyson and T. S. Eliot have their Vergilian aspects, and each approximates, in somewhat different ways, Vergil's nightmarish eloquence.

The *Aeneid* is an endlessly paradoxical poem, since it partly founds its epic hero upon Octavius Caesar, the emperor Augustus, nephew and heir of Julius Caesar, victor over Antony and Cleopatra, and the indisputable founder of the Roman Empire. Augustus was Vergil's patron and the proud recipient of the *Aeneid*, and indeed the poem's preserver, against the dying wish of its poet. The emperor Augustus needed the poem because it gave his era an idea of order and of greatness, an achieved foundation of authority; Aeneas always looks towards the future, to the rise of a new Troy in Rome, which will end exile and inaugurate justice. Dante, exile-of-exiles, found justice in his *Commedia*, but it is questionable as to whether Aeneas and Vergil are not at variance with one another. What Vergil finds is suffering, and no end to suffering. Aeneas is the poem's hero, but not Vergil's, a divergence that makes the epic only more interesting, for to possess the wrong hero in the right poem is to anticipate the art of Shakespeare.

It is a grand perplexity that no reader I've ever met has preferred the hero Aeneas, admirable as he doubtless is, to Dido, whom Aeneas loves and abandons, and Turnus, whom Aeneas slays, but only after the Italian hero has been numbed into absolute helplessness by an obscene fury sent by

Juno. What was Vergil's purpose in giving his hero the equivocal victory of slaughtering what pragmatically already was a corpse?

The gods of Epicurus and of Lucretius are remote from all human concerns, but the Epicurean Vergil, who read Lucretius as veritable Scripture, gives us a Jove little better than his consort, and Juno is a monster. Vergil's genius is activated by profound pity for all human suffering, his own included, and yet the essence of that genius appears to be constant anxiety, even acute terror, when contemplating the endless wrath of Juno. The figure of Juno in Vergil can be regarded as the nightmare projection of something universal in the male fear of female power. Vergil subtly intimates a homoerotic orientation, sympathetic to Dido, Aeneas's cast-off beloved, but more profoundly moved by Turnus, Aeneas's rival and victim. Vergil, who celebrated Augustus Caesar as the world's hope for order, peace, justice, cannot be said to have confronted reality with anything approaching hope.

The genius of Vergil partly invests itself in his extraordinary expressive power and in his preternatural sensitivity to suffering. Such power and sensitivity compensate for Vergil's relative weakness where genius generally manifests strength: originality. Vergil devotes the first half of the *Aeneid* to imitating the *Odyssey*, the second half to the *Iliad*. And his religious philosophy essentially relies upon the Epicurean fierceness of Lucretius, a poet Dante was never to read, but which may have resided upon Vergil's writing table. Vergil may be the first European writer to demonstrate that genius can be relatively weak as invention, provided that it be tough and varied in sensibility. When I think of the *Aeneid*, without reopening its pages, I recall first the erotic humiliation of Dido, cast off by the virtuous cad Aeneas, insufferable in his nobility. And yet that is only one perspective, since Vergil is both estranged from his female characters and yet dreadfully sensitive to their reality. His young male characters are poignant for him as Dido is not. No woman in Vergil (that I recall) is compared to a flower, but his youths indeed are flowerlike. This transcends his muted homoeroticism, and relates to a worldview that both accepts and starts away from the Lucretian harshness in regard to the realm of Venus. Notoriously on both sides of every divide, Vergil may be the most consistently ambivalent of all great poets, surpassing even Baudelaire.

The *Aeneid* is self-consciously an epic, yet so frequently elegiac in tonality as to be unlike anything else in its genre. Its hero is heartsick, forever mourning Troy, even as he struggles on towards the foundation of Rome. Christian poets from Dante to T. S. Eliot have insisted upon finding in Vergil a poet longing for revelation, but that seems to me as odd as Simone Weil's discovery of affinities between the Gospels and the *Iliad*. Eliot, half a century ago, wrote, "We are all, so far as we inherit the civilization of Europe, still citizens of the Roman Empire, and time has not yet proved Vergil wrong." Weird enough in the aftermath of the Nazi horror, Eliot's observation now seems bizarre. The Augustan ideology of Vergil's work was compatible with the Romanization of Christianity, but is archaic in this current era of the empire of information. Our Emperor Augustus is the second George Bush, who requires no Vergil. That Vergil's genius is still valid, at this time, could only be maintained because of his lasting sensibility, which has little to do with Aeneas, or with Augustus.

Vergil's cosmos is ruled by his rather surprising Jupiter, who is neither Homeric nor Lucretian. In Homer, the gods are our audience; in Lucretius, they have no concern with us. Vergil's Jupiter wills our destinies: his will is our warfare, is Roman domination without end, is the abandonment of Dido by Aeneas. Fate, or Jupiter's will, is masculine, and cannot be distinguished from power and force. Juno, Jupiter's sister *and* wife, is even more of a nightmare image, and can be called the pragmatic Muse of the *Aeneid*, since her angers and resentment propel the poem's death-march aspect, its surging forward towards bright destruction. One of the prime aesthetic strengths of the *Aeneid* is that its action perpetually surges on. Events are properly remorseless, unlike Vergil, who is exquisitely susceptible to every anguish he portrays. This variance between narrative inexorability and the poet's implicit distress is a remarkably original feature of the *Aeneid*, one that I find rarely present elsewhere in the highest imaginative literature. Dante, whose affinities to Vergil were largely his own myth, has nothing (to my ear) of this Vergilian undersong. Vergil was an Epicurean, but unlike Lucretius the poet of the *Aeneid* could find no consolation in the admonitions of Epicurus against fear and anxiety. Is there a more sublimely anguished poet than Vergil? Like his protagonist, Aeneas, Vergil is carried along by a will stronger than his own, which makes heroism seem superfluous. Yet Vergil is not pious, as Aeneas is. We do not feel that Vergil worships fate, any more than he would venerate the terrible Juno.

Dido, Queen of Carthage, supplies Vergil with a glory he might not otherwise possess, this late in literary history. Her love-death retains an energy that still astonishes us: can the colorless Aeneas really have kindled her to that terrifying a passion? One feels she met the wrong man; Turnus, the Italian king slain by Aeneas at the epic's close, would have been a more appropriate match, an Antony to her Cleopatra. Dido and Turnus are fiery temperaments; Aeneas sometimes prophesies George Eliot's Daniel Deronda, most responsible of prigs. But Dido, victimized by Venus and by Juno, and pragmatically by Aeneas, is unforgettable in her authentic outrage:

> "For why hide my feelings? For what greater wrongs do I hold myself back? Did he sigh while I wept? Did he turn on me a glance? Did he yield and shed tears or pity her who loved him? What shall I say first? What next? Now, neither mighty Juno nor the Saturnian sire looks on these things with righteous eyes! Nowhere is faith secure. I welcomed him, a castaway on the shore, a beggar, and madly gave him a share in my throne; his lost fleet I rescued, his crews I saved from death. Alas! I am whirled on the fires of frenzy. Now prophetic Apollo, now the Lycian oracles, now the messenger of the gods sent from Jove himself, brings through the air this dread command. Truly, this is work for gods, this is care to vex their peace! I detain you not; I dispute not your words. Go, make for Italy with the winds; seek your kingdom over the waves. Yet I trust, if the righteous gods have any power, that on the rocks midway you will drain the cup of vengeance and after call on Dido's name."
>
> (translated by H. R. Fairclough)

She has already determined upon suicide, and this faithful, nearly literal translation cannot convey either her humiliation or her trauma, affects of which Vergil is the great master. Dido is trying to cry out everything at once, to express her sensation of going up in flame. Her scorn at the formidable array of divinities carried in so as to jilt one woman-in-love is rather grand, and her fury of betrayed trust is Medea-like. One might like to know how Dante read this passage, since he must have provoked its equivalent several times in his own erotic career. There is no misogyny in Vergil, despite some judgments made by scholars. As always, the poet is not disinterested, but curiously sides both with Dido and with Aeneas, which is virtually impossible. No case can be made for Aeneas: he has enjoyed the virtuous widow, without being in love with her, and the best he can muster as defense for his caddishness is the pathetic: the gods made me do it, and why shouldn't I get to found my own city, just as you did? It is difficult not to wish that Dido would heave a lance at him.

When the Augustan deceiver of widows descends to Avernus, he comes off badly in his encounter with Dido's shade, but then Vergil nods in this scene, as was furiously noted by the Grand Cham, Dr. Samuel Johnson, who regarded Vergil as a mere imitator of the mighty original Homer. When Odysseus had gone down into Hades, he had been scorned by Ajax, whom he had defrauded of Achilles' arms and armor. I relish Johnson's superb zest as he demolishes Vergil:

> When Aeneas is sent by Vergil to the shades, he meets Dido the Queen of Cathage, whom his perfidy had hurried to the grave; he accosts her with tenderness and excuses; but the lady turns away like Ajax in mute disdain. She turns away like Ajax, but she resembles him in none of those qualities which give either dignity or propriety to silence. She might, without any departure from the tenor of her conduct, have burst out like other injured women into clamor, reproach, and denunciation; but Vergil had his imagination full of Ajax, and therefore could not prevail on himself to teach Dido any other mode of resentment.
>
> —*The Rambler* No. 121

This is deliciously unfair to Vergil, but a palpable hit nevertheless. Homer-haunted, Vergil's originalities came in the pathos and negativity that Dr. Johnson shunned, but that should appeal to our quandaries even as they moved and persuaded Vergil's first readers. These negative visions, including the story of Dido, emerge from a conflict in Vergil between Lucretius's dismissal of political, military, and erotic glory, and the *Odyssey*'s romantic exaltation of heroism and the quest for reunion with Penelope. It was poetically fortunate that Vergil could not resolve his ambivalences. Had Lucretius fully converted Vergil to a rigorous Epicureanism, then death would have been of no concern to Vergil, and we would have lost a plangent sublimity that remains forever unique:

> From here a road leads to the waters of Tartarean Acheron. Here, thick with mire and of fathomless flood, a whirlpool seethes and belches into Cocytus all its sand. A grim ferryman guards these waters and streams, terrible in his squalor—Charon, on whose chin lies a mass of unkempt, hoary hair, his eyes are staring orbs of flame; his squalid garb hangs by a knot from his shoulders. Unaided, he poles the boat, tends the sails, and in his murky craft conveys the dead— now aged, but a god's old age is hardy and green. Hither rushed all the throng, streaming to the banks; mothers and men and bodies of high-souled heroes, their life now done, boys and unwedded girls, and sons placed on the pyre, before their fathers' eyes, thick as the leaves of the forest that at autumn's first frost drop and fall, and thick as the birds that from the seething deep flock shoreward, when the chill of

the year drives them overseas and sends them into sunny lands. They
stand, pleading to be the first ferried across, and stretched out hands
in yearning for the farther shore. But the surly boatman takes now
these, now those, while others he thrusts away, back from the brink.

—book 6, 295–316

(translated by H. R. Fairclough)

The metaphor of the leaves as generations of the human is Homer's, but
transformed by Vergil with an inventiveness that has inspired poets from
Dante on to Spenser, Milton, and Shelley, and to Whitman and Wallace
Stevens in the United States. We pass from the autumnal leaves and the
migrating birds to the grand pathos of the pauper souls, the unburied, who
are thrust away, to flutter and roam the wrong side of the black waters for a
century. To stretch out hands in yearning for the farther shore is to desire
oblivion, and is purely Vergilian, not Homeric nor Lucretian. Augustus and
Roman fate recede; what remains is this negative yearning.

SAINT AUGUSTINE

They read, they choose, they love: they read forever, and what they read never passes away. In reading, they choose, and, in choosing, they love. Their codex is never shut, their book never closed; for God is their text in himself and eternally so.

—*Confessions*
(translated by Brian Stock)

The angels need not read, but we have to. They are not caught up in the dilemmas of memory and of time. Augustine's genius defined those dilemmas, particularly in regard to reading, with permanent clarity. Brian Stock, in his *Augustine the Reader* (1996), observes that Augustine's was the first Western theory of reading; I think it may still be the best. If the age of the book now wanes (only for a time, I would hope), it is vital to recall that

Augustine had much to do with making the book the basis for thought. And yet, as a Christian of extraordinary devoutness, Augustine was skeptical as to whether reading would enlighten, though he insisted we could not continue our spiritual flowering without prolonged, deep reading.

Autobiographical memory, as a basis for reflection, essentially is an Augustinian invention. If any of us think of our lives as texts, we are indebted to Augustine.

As the narrator of his *Confessions*, Augustine becomes a Christian Aeneas, and both annoys and impresses us pretty much as Vergil's Aeneas does. Augustine's faithful concubine, mother of his son, is firmly thrown away, like another Dido. If Aeneas can seem a self-righteous prig, Augustine can seem something worse, smugly sanctimonious. But then, great geniuses do not always cheer us with their personalities.

Augustine feared the will, which too often, Hamlet-like, sets itself against the word. God's will is unknowable, at least with any real freedom from error, except by a reading of the Bible that is deeply informed by a sincere will to know God. Augustine knew that the only ideal reader is God himself, and yet no more accomplished Christian reader ever existed.

SAINT AUGUSTINE
(354–430)

SAINT AUGUSTINE WAS A SUPERB WRITER and a formidable intellect, and my mosaic that depicts genius cannot exclude him, however disconsolate he makes me. He believed in scattering Jews, rather than slaying them, but he was also the first theorist of the Inquisition, to cite his definitive biographer, Peter Brown. Many readers of his two most famous works, the *Confessions* and the *City of God*, now tend to a mixed reaction, unless they are dogmatic believers. Garry Wills, in a recent brief study, shrewdly suggests that we retitle the *Confessions* the *Testimony*, so as to avoid irrelevant "true confessions" overtones. Alas, this doesn't work; one reads Wills and is jarred by each reference to the *Testimony*, so familiar is the actual title. Augustine's subject is the making of a Christian, though his story transcends what most Americans now regard as a "conversion" to Christ.

Augustine's originality invents autobiography, yet I would not center his genius there. Thinking is not possible without memory, and memory itself, in a wide consciousness, may well depend upon reading. Augustine still offers more insights into memory than anyone else does, and perhaps he also remains our best teacher of reading. I am a little rueful about that, since I love Samuel Johnson and Ralph Waldo Emerson, and I don't like Augustine, but he is the first great reader in their sense, and in some ways still the best, granted his tendentiousness, which equals Freud's, but to opposite ends. In fashions only now ending, we have been afflicted by rather tiresome "theorists" of reading. Augustine is presented, by Brian Stock, as the theoretician who laid the foundation for a reading culture, and that seems to me incontrovertible. Much of what I myself can understand about my own lifelong obsessions with reading and memory has been learned from Augustine, sometimes reluctantly.

I begin here with Vergil, because that is where Augustine began, in his endless engagement with the Roman poet. Dante was a creative misreader of Vergil, but Augustine read Vergil accurately, which produces the charming oddity that Dante's Vergil is an Augustinian, while Augustine's Vergil decidedly is not. For both Augustine and Dante, Vergil is the idealized precursor (strangely mixed, by Augustine, with Saint Ambrose) but Vergil was not the authentic literary forerunner of either the African bishop or the Florentine poet. For Dante, it was a composite of the humanist Brunetto Latini and the fellow Florentine poet Guido Cavalcanti. For Augustine, the actual originals were the Neoplatonists Plotinus and Porphyry, both of whom had rejected Christ. Vergil, as I've remarked, was shadowed by Homer, but more darkly even by Lucretius. Augustine had read Lucretius and necessarily abhorred him, but it fascinates me that Lucretius was utterly unavoidable to Dante, who would have read him with fury.

Though Augustine became, with Ambrose and Jerome, one of the "founders of the Middle Ages," as E. K. Rand called them, it is important to keep in mind that the theologian-bishop began as what we now call a teacher of literature, whose prime text was Vergil, even as our central work is the complete writings of Shakespeare. Augustine always remained word-drunk, fascinated by figurative language, though increasingly he could approve it only in the Bible. More even than Dante (who was constantly a politician, though in exile), Augustine was a person of letters, a literary personality before he became central to the Western Church. With Augustine as theologian, I am little concerned here, though to emphasize his psychological acuity and his literary insights is also to invoke his spiritual originality, even where its harshness is difficult to accept.

As a student of consciousness, Augustine pragmatically began as a disciple of Plotinus, but broke decisively from Neoplatonism by seeing knowledge of the self as a consequence of memory, rather than of intuition. We see ourselves as continuities by recreating ourselves via memory: autobiography is virtually inconceivable without it, and yet this is largely an Augustinian innovation. Vergil, who was a continuous presence for Augustine from childhood through old age, implicitly contributed to this formulation of memory's role in the forging of an individual consciousness. Yet for Vergil, and for his Aeneas, memory was either nostalgia or nightmare. Vergil is a foretaste of Nietzsche's insistence that pain is more memorable than pleasure. For Augustine, even forgetfulness is a vital part of memory, since this becomes a Christian myth of memory, in which three powers of the soul reflect, in us, the Trinity and its mysterious unity. "Understanding" was an inheritance from classical thought, but the Augustinian "will," like his "memory," is essentially his own creation, startling as that assertion must seem. And yet to transvalue memory, you modify as well your vision of the intellect, and what joins intellect and memory for Augustine is God's will, working in the soul as the Pauline principle of *caritas*, the love of the creator God for his creatures, man and woman. Memory, as the *Confessions* repeatedly emphasize, is the agent through which the soul's other powers are kindled in God's image. I give a cento of passages from *Confessions*, book 10:

The power of the memory is prodigious, my God. It is a vast, immeasurable sanctuary. Who can plumb its depths? And yet it is a faculty of my soul. Although it is part of my nature, I cannot understand all that I am . . .

We even call the memory the mind . . .

The power of the memory is great, O Lord. It is awe-inspiring in its profound and incalculable complexity. Yet it is my mind: it is my self. What, then, am I, my God? What is my nature? A life that is ever varying, full of change, and of immense power. The wide plains of my memory and its innumerable caverns and hollows are full beyond compute of countless things of all kinds . . .

But in which part of my memory are you present, O Lord? What cell have you constructed for yourself in my memory?

. . . You were within me, and I was in the world outside myself. I searched for you outside myself. I searched for you outside myself and, disfigured as I was, I fell upon the lovely things of your creation. You were with me, but I was not with you.

(translated by R. S. Pine-Coffin)

Beautifully implicit in this montage is the almost invisible passage from memory to will, the transition named as conversion. We cannot recall everything that our memory contains, and what we are too likely to forget is the happiness of having known God. Memory is a power stronger than the self, until the self understands: "You were with me, but I was not with you." The will to know God overcomes our weakness at remembering him. That weakness involves the related mystery, time:

What, then, is time? I know well enough what it is, provided that nobody asks me; but if I am asked what it is and try to explain, I am baffled.

We cannot understand eternity, our language being caught by time, and so how can we say precisely what is time's nature? Present time is only a fiction of duration, a poem or a story, and yet all that we know of past or future is in that poem or story, *as we recite it.* I don't find the Trinity in this remarkable passage, as Garry Wills does, but I recall it every time I recite a poem out loud to myself, which means that, unbeliever as I am, I think of Augustine many times each day, for who else has had this insight into the inner experience of reciting a poem that you possess by memory?

Suppose that I am going to recite a psalm that I know. But once I
have begun, my faculty of expectation is engaged by the whole of it.
But once I have begun, as much of the psalm as I have removed from
the province of expectation and relegated to the past now engages my
memory, and the scope of the action which I am performing is divided
between the two faculties of memory and expectation, the one looking back to the part which I have already recited, the other looking
forward to the part which I have still to recite. But my faculty of attention is present all the while, and through it passes what was the future in the process of becoming the past. As the process continues,
the province of memory is extended in proportion as that of expectation is reduced, until the whole of my expectation is absorbed. This
happens when I finish my recitation and it has all passed into the
province of memory.

What is true of the whole psalm is also true of all its parts and of
each syllable. It is true of any longer action in which I may be engaged
and of which the recitation of the psalm may only be a small part. It
is true of a man's whole life, of which all his actions are parts. It is true
of the whole history of mankind, of which each man's life is a part.

—*Confessions*, book 11, 28
(translated by R. S. Pine-Coffin)

I chant a lyric by W. B. Yeats or a meditation by Wallace Stevens, and because of Augustine I find I have to confront my own mortality, and even my
sense of history. Perhaps that is a three-in-one (poem, life, history of
mankind), perhaps not, but Augustine has turned my activity into an act of
consciousness that far exceeds my intentions, which extended only to my
own aesthetic pleasure. It is Augustine's peculiar strength that he can dis-
turb one with his untimely power to heighten the awareness of vulnerability, little as one may care for his transcendences of that abyss.

You can see Augustine, if you will, as a bridge from Vergil to Dante, but
I find that misleading. Dante's piety—like John Milton's or William
Blake's—is very much his own, and converts only the theological addicts
among his Anglo-American scholars. Augustine, personally as idiosyncratic,
essentially was mystical, primarily interested in the soul's ascent to God
through contemplation. Dante lauds the contemplatives, but no one who
reads closely even the *Paradiso* will mistake Dante for Saint Bernard.
Though Saint Augustine fought against the influence of Plotinus and
Porphyry, he never escaped it. Peter Brown again is definitive:

Augustine, however, was a man steeped in Neo-Platonic ways of thought. The whole world appeared to him as a world of "becoming," as a hierarchy of imperfectly-realized forms, which depended for their quality, on "participating" in an Intelligible World of Ideal Forms. This universe was in a state of constant, dynamic tension in which the imperfect forms of matter strove to realize their fixed, ideal structure.

The church is a shadowy image of a truer church far in the unapparent, Eternity. But that Eternity, rather unlike Dante's heavenly system, is Plotinean, to be reached only by recourse to one's own inner soul. This residual Neoplatonism never abandoned Augustine, because it had become his inner nature. Plotinus was an immortal wound for Augustine, even as Vergil gradually evolved from a mortal solace to a beloved opponent in the *City of God*. When Augustine thought of "poetry," he thought of Vergil; the Psalms were beyond poetry, being the truth. Dido was poetry for Augustine, as she is for us. Augustine knew that the historical Dido, Queen of Carthage, had killed herself to escape marrying a somewhat unwholesome African king. The story of Dido's tragic love for the pious cad, Aeneas, is Vergil's invention, one in which Dido serves as the Cleopatra against whom Augustus warred, and as the prophetess of Rome's harrowing wars with the Carthaginian general, Hannibal. Vergil gave one pathos but not truth, a judgment Augustine extended also to the myth universally popular from the age of Constantine, the Christian emperor, on to Augustine's time. In his fourth Eclogue (about 40 B.C.E.), Vergil prophesied a divine child:

> Now is come the last age of Cumaean song; the great line of the cen-
> turies begins anew. Now the Virgin returns, the reign of Saturn re-
> turns; now a new generation descends from heaven on high . . .
>   . . . under your sway any lingering traces of our guilt shall become
> void and release the earth from its continual dread. He shall have the
> gift of divine life.
>
>   (translated by H. R. Fairclough)

The golden age of Saturn returns, and the Virgin Astraea returns also, bringing divine justice back to us. Constantine improbably interpreted Vergil's child messiah as Jesus Christ, thus making the pagan Vergil a prophet of Christian Advent. Augustine, too good a scholar for this absurdity, hardly wanted to add it to Scripture, but was glad to quote it as a conversionary inducement to pagans.

What more genuinely moved Augustine in Vergil was the heroic pathos of Dido, and the general theme of the exile of Aeneas from Troy. But after Rome fell to the heretical Visigoths in 420, Augustine manifested a different stance towards Vergil in the *City of God*. Vergil remained the best and most beloved of poets, but is rejected as the Augustan Vergil, who finds in ancient Rome only corrupt gods and corrupt souls who revered them. The aging Augustine manifested what Peter Brown called "a darkened humanism that linked the pre-Christian poet to the Christian present in a common distrust of sexual pleasure."

The genius of Augustine is not of the literary eminence of Dante's or of Chaucer's, but it rivals the somber eloquence of Lucretius and the elegiac lyricism of Vergil. Finally, it requires to be appreciated (for me, anyway) by standards neither spiritual nor aesthetic. Augustine the Reader (as Brian Stock celebrates him) is one of the heroes of the now endangered art of reading. Any lifelong reader of the best books one can read is a disciple of Augustine, little as he would have cared for such discipleship unless it led to the acceptance of the Christian revelation.

DANTE ALIGHIERI

"O brothers," I said, "who through a hundred thousand perils have
reached the west, to this so brief vigil of the senses that remains to us
choose not to deny experience, in the sun's track, of the unpeopled
world. Take thought of the seed from which you spring. You were not
born to live as brutes, but to follow virtue and knowledge."

> —*Inferno*, canto 26, 112–20
> (translated by John D. Sinclair)

Ulysses makes his final speech to his men, as they near disaster at the
limit of the known world. Many contemporary authorities on Dante ask us
to condemn Ulysses, since they argue that the voyager's language is merely
self-serving, and exalts heroic adventure with no regard for moral obligation.
Do we read Dante for his morality, or for his genius? Benedetto Croce, a
great Italian critic, chose the genius: "No one of his age was more deeply
moved than Dante by the passion to know all that is knowable," which is
the passion of Dante's Ulysses, who nevertheless is placed in deep Hell,
surrounded by other false counselors.

Dante himself, the *Commedia*'s Pilgrim, says absolutely nothing in response
to Ulysses' speech, and forces us to surmise his response to the hero's eloquence. Since Dante's voyage, in the poem, is a "mad flight" akin to that of
Ulysses, the poetic identity between the two outweighs the moral divergence.
As a reader aged seventy-one, I cannot hear Ulysses speak of "this so brief vigil
of the senses that remains" without partly joining him in spirit. Something in
Dante, despite his theological cheerleaders, partly joins Ulysses also.

Nothing destroys Dante's genius more readily than commentary that exalts his supposed piety and his humane virtues. No poet, not even John Milton, was as much a monster of pride as Dante. We do not trust Dante's
reaction to Brunetto Latini, his "teacher," who is placed in Hell for a
sodomy that Dante may have invented. Statius, a bad Roman poet who certainly remained pagan, enters the *Comedy* as a great poet and secret Christian. Not exactly a martyr, Dante's Statius may hint at a certain reticence in
Dante himself, whose own genius mattered more to him than all the pieties
of Augustine and Aquinas.

DANTE ALIGHIERI
(1265–1321)

THE LIFE OF DANTE ALIGHIERI ITSELF can seem a turbulent poem, closer to his *Inferno* than to his *Purgatorio*, quite aside from his *Paradiso*. Biographies so far are mostly inadequate to Dante's genius, with the major exception of the very first, Giovanni Boccaccio's, aptly described by Giuseppe Mazzotta as a "self-conscious fictional work akin to Dante's own *Vita Nuova* (*The New Life*) which responds imaginatively to Dante's steady self-dramatization in his works." This need not surprise anyone; Dante, like Shakespeare, is so large a form of thought and imagination that individual biographers, scholars, and critics tend to see only aspects of an extraordinary panoply. I always recommend to my students, in preference to all biographies of Shakespeare, the late Anthony Burgess's *Nothing Like the Sun*, a rather Joycean novel narrated by Shakespeare in the first person.

The exalted Dante regarded himself as a prophet, at least the equal of Isaiah or Jeremiah. Shakespeare, we can assume, had no such self-estimate; the creator of Hamlet, Falstaff, and Lear has much in common with Geoffrey Chaucer, the maker of the Pardoner and the Wife of Bath, and Chaucer subtly mocks Dante. One has to be of Chaucer's eminence, if Dante is to be treated ironically, and even Chaucer clearly admires far more intensely than he dissents.

One cannot discuss genius in all the world's history without centering upon Dante, since only Shakespeare, of all geniuses of language, is richer. Shakespeare to a considerable extent remade English: about eighteen hundred words of the twenty-one thousand he employed were his own coinage, and I cannot pick up a newspaper without finding Shakespearean turns of phrase scattered through it, frequently without intention. Yet Shakespeare's English was inherited by him, from Chaucer and from William Tyndale, the principal translator of the Protestant Bible. Had Shakespeare written nothing, the English language, pretty much as we know it, would have prevailed, but Dante's Tuscan dialect became the Italian language largely because of Dante. He is the national poet, as Shakespeare is wherever English is spoken, and Goethe wherever German dominates. No single French poet, not even Racine or Victor Hugo, is so unchallenged in eminence, and no Spanish-language poet is so central as Cervantes. And yet

Dante, though he essentially founded literary Italian, hardly thought of himself as Tuscan, let alone Italian. He was a Florentine, obsessively so, exiled from his city in the last nineteen of his fifty-six years.

A few dates are crucial for the reader of Dante, starting with the death of Beatrice, his beloved ideal or idealized beloved, on June 8, 1290, when the poet was twenty-five. By his own account, Dante's devotion to Beatrice was what we call platonic, though nothing concerning Dante ever can be termed anything but Dantesque, including his Catholicism. He set Easter 1300 as the fictive date of the journey he undertakes in the *Divine Comedy*, and he completed the *Inferno*, its first and most notorious part, in 1314. In the seven years remaining to him, he had the sublime fortune of composing both the *Purgatorio* and the *Paradiso*, so that his magnificent poem was fully composed by almost a year before his death.

Shakespeare died as he turned fifty-two, but we lost nothing by it, because he had stopped writing some three years before. Dante, one feels, would have gone on to other literary achievements, had he lived the quarter-century more that he expected in order to reach the "perfect" age of eighty-one, nine nines in a numerological vision of his own, which cannot altogether be deciphered.

Here is Dante in the *Convivio* (book 4, 24) telling us that age ends at the seventieth year, but that there can be sublimity, if we live on:

> Whence we have it of Plato—whom (both in the strength of his own nature, and because of the physiognomiscope which Socrates cast for him when first he saw him) we may believe to have had the most excellent nature—that he lives eighty-one years, as testifies Tully in that *Of Old Age*. And I believe that if Christ had not been crucified and had lived out the space which his life had power to cover according to its nature, he would have been changed at the eighty-first year from mortal body to eternal.

What change did Dante expect at the eighty-first year? Would Beatrice, the Lady Nine, have appeared to him again, in this life? George Santayana found in Beatrice a Platonizing of Christianity; E. R. Curtius saw her as the center of Dante's personal and poetic gnosis. She has some crucial relation to the transfiguration that Christ would have undergone at eighty-one, since her own death, according to her lover's *Vita Nuova*, is dated by him through a process in which the perfect number nine is completed nine times. At twenty-five she changed from mortal to eternal body. Dante, implicitly and explicitly, tells us throughout the *Comedy* that he, Dante, is the truth. The Sufi martyr Hallaj died for proclaiming that he was the truth, though in the American Religion (in its various forms) such an affirmation is almost commonplace. I talk to dissident Mormons, Baptist sectaries, and many Pentecostals who candidly assure me that they are the truth. Neither Augustine nor Aquinas would have said that he was the truth. The *Commedia* would not work if Beatrice were not the truth, and yet, without Dante, none of us would have heard of Beatrice. I think that too much cannot be made of this, and I never quite understand why Dante, who now defines Catholicism for so many intellectuals, overcame the possibility that his personal myth of Beatrice was as much a heresy as the Gnostic myths of a Sophia, or female principle, in the Godhead. Simon Magus found his Helena in a whorehouse in Tyre, and proclaimed her to be both Helen of Troy and the fallen Sophia, or Wisdom of God. The Samaritan Simon, always denounced by Christians, was the first Faustus, audacious and imaginative, but now is universally regarded as a charlatan. Dante found his unfallen Wisdom of God in a Florentine young woman, and raised her to the heavenly hierarchy. Simon the magician, like Jesus the magician, belongs to oral tradition, while Dante—except for Shakespeare—is the supreme poet of all Western history and culture. And yet Dante was not less arbitrary than Simon, as we ought not to forget. Though he says otherwise, Dante usurps poetic authority and establishes himself as central to Western culture.

How different Dante's centrality is from Shakespeare's! Dante imposes his personality upon us; Shakespeare, even in the Sonnets, evades us, because of his uncanny detachment. In the *Vita Nuova*, Dante immerses us in the story of his extraordinary love for a young woman whom he scarcely knew. They first meet as nine-year-olds, though that "nine" is a warning against any literalization of this story. Nine years after the poet first saw Beatrice, she spoke to him, a formal greeting in the street. Another greeting or two, a snub after he poetically professed love for another lady as a "screen" defense, and one gathering where Beatrice may have joined in a gentle mockery of her smitten admirer: this seems to have been their entire relationship. The best commentary on this mere actuality is that of the Argentine fabulist Jorge Luis Borges, who speaks of "our certainty of an unhappy and superstitious love," unreciprocated by Beatrice.

We can speak of Shakespeare's "unhappy and superstitious love" for the fair young nobleman of the Sonnets, but some other phrase would have to be found for Shakespeare's descent into the Hell of the Dark Lady of the same sequence. To call Dante's love for Beatrice Neoplatonic would be insufficient, but how can we define that love? A passion for one's own genius, for a muse of one's own creation, could seem a dark idolatry of self in almost anyone else, but not in the central man. The myth or figure of Beatrice is fused with Dante's lifework; in a crucial sense she *is* the *Commedia*, and cannot be understood if you stand outside the poem. And yet Dante presents her as the truth, though not to be mistaken for the Christ, who is the way, the truth, the light.

Dante scholarship, vastly useful for mastering the complexities of the *Commedia*, nevertheless does not much help me in apprehending Beatrice. She is more Christological in the *Vita Nuova* than in the *Commedia*, though sometimes there she reminds me of what the Gnostics called "the Angel Christ," since she breaks down the distinction between the human and the angelic. A fusion between the divine and the mortal may or may not be heretical, depending upon how it is presented. Dante's vision does not impress me as Augustinian or Thomistic, but though hermetic, it is not Hermetist, as it were. Rather than identifying with theology, Dante strives to identify it with himself. The presence of the human in the divine is not the same as God's presence in a person, and in Beatrice in particular.

That sounds perhaps odd, since Dante was not William Blake, who urged us to worship only what he called the Human Form Divine. Yet Dante early on wrote that Beatrice was a miracle. This miracle was for all Florence, and not for Dante alone, though he was its sole celebrant. His best friend and poetic mentor, Guido Cavalcanti, is later condemned by Dante for not joining the celebration, but Dante has the same relation to Cavalcanti that the young Shakespeare had to Christopher Marlowe, a shadow of influence-anxiety. Are we to believe Dante when he implies that Cavalcanti would have been saved if he had acknowledged Beatrice? Is a shared originality still original?

As readers, we can abandon Dante's supposed theology to his exegetes, but you cannot read Dante without coming to terms with his Beatrice. For Dante, she is certainly an Incarnation, which he declines to see as a being in competition with the Incarnation. She is, he insists, whatever happiness he has had, and without her he would not have found his way to salvation. But Dante is not a Faust, to be damned or saved, or a Hamlet, who dies of the truth. Dante is bent upon triumph, total vindication, a prophecy fulfilled. His "fathers," Brunetto Latini and Vergil, are transcended, with love, but still firmly set aside. His poetic "brothers" are acknowledged (rather darkly, in Cavalcanti's case) but are not his companions on the way. Does he persuade us, in the *Commedia*, that Beatrice is something more than his individual genius? He is both inside and outside his poem, as Beatrice was in the *Vita Nuova*. Has she a reality that might enable her to be invoked by others?

Shakespeare's grandest characters can walk out of their plays and live in our consciousness of them. Can Beatrice? Dante's personality is so large that it allows room for no one else; the Pilgrim of Eternity takes up all the space. This is hardly a poetic fault, as it would be in any other poet whatsoever. In Dante it is poetic strength, energized by absolute originality, a newness that cannot be staled by endless rereadings, and that cannot be assimilated to its sources, literary or theological.

Augustine, opposing the great Neoplatonists, Plotinus and Porphyry, insisted that self-confidence and pride were not sufficient for the ascent to God. Guidance and assistance were necessary, and could come only from God. Is there a fiercer pride or a more resolute self-confidence than Dante's? He portrays himself as a pilgrim, reliant upon guidance, comfort, and assistance, but as a poet he is more a prophet being called than he is a Christian undergoing conversion. Does he bother truly to persuade us of his humility? His heroism—spiritual, metaphysical, imaginative—makes Dante the poet pragmatically as much a miracle as was his Beatrice.

Fortunately, he presents himself as a personality, not as a miracle. We know him so well, in essence rather than in outline, that we can accept his hard-won changes as he develops, throughout the *Commedia*. Indeed, only he can change in the *Commedia*, as everyone else has reached finality, though there is a process of refining that dwellers in the Purgatorio must undergo. Outrageously vivid as everyone is in the *Commedia*, they are past altering, in kind. They will not change because of what Dante has them say or do. This makes total revelation possible: Dante gives us the last word upon them, beyond dispute, and always provoking wonder. Whether you can have personality after a last judgment has been passed upon you, is a very pretty question.

Beatrice, as Dante's creation, possesses little enough personality, because she clearly has had an angelic preexistence before her birth into Florence. Dante shows us, in the *Vita Nuova*, only that she is of unearthly beauty, and is capable of severity, a stance towards him that augments in the *Commedia*, though it is merely rhetorical. There is rather a leap from her relative unawareness of her idealizing lover, in life, and her cosmological concern for his salvation, after her death. So clearly is she Dante's good genius or better angel that the transmutation is easily acceptable. Laertes rather wistfully says that the rejected Ophelia will be a ministering angel after her death, presumably one of those flights of angels that Horatio invokes at the close, to one's surprise, when we brood about it. Dante, long preparing his own apotheosis, has had his Beatrice in training for quite some time.

No other writer ever is nearly as formidable as Dante, not even John Milton or Leo Tolstoy. Shakespeare, a miracle of elusiveness, is everyone and no one, as Borges said. Dante is Dante. No one is going to explain Dante away by historicizing him, or by emulating his own audacious self-theologizing. Cavalcanti, had he lived, would doubtless have written even more powerful lyrics than earlier, but he is not likely to have composed a Third Testament, which is precisely what the *Divine Comedy* appears to be. The question of Shakespeare's genius is forever beyond us, yet Dante's genius is an answer, not a question. With the exception of Shakespeare, who came three centuries later, the strongest poet of the Western world completed its single greatest work of literary art by the close of the second decade of the fourteenth century. To equal the *Commedia,* and in some ways surpass it, you would have to regard the two dozen most remarkable of Shakespeare's thirty-nine plays as somehow a single entity. But Dante and Shakespeare are very difficult to take in sequence: try to read *King Lear* after the *Purgatorio,* or *Macbeth* after the *Inferno:* a curious disturbance is felt. These two most central of poets are violently incompatible, at least in my experience. Dante would have wanted his reader to judge that Beatrice was Christ in Dante's soul; many of us may be uncomfortable with that, for various reasons, but how startled we would be if Shakespeare, in the Sonnets, were to intimate that the fair young lord (Southampton or whomever) was a type of Christ for the poet who would go on to compose *Hamlet* and *King Lear.*

To the common reader who can absorb the *Commedia* in the original, Beatrice is scarcely a puzzle, since Italian critics are very unlike Anglo-American scholars in their approach to Dante, and their more worldly sense of him has filtered down. I treasure the observation of Giambattista Vico, that even Homer would have yielded to Dante had the Tuscan been less erudite in theology. Dante, like Freud (and the mystics), thought that erotic sublimation was possible, differing in this from his friend Cavalcanti, who regarded love as an illness that had to be lived through. Dante, who has Francesca and her Paolo down in Hell for adultery, was widely noted for his venery, in regard to women very different (in his view) from the sacred Beatrice. About the only place where Dante and Shakespeare meet is in their mutual supremacy at rendering erotic suffering, of others and their own:

> Yet shall the streams turn back and climb the hills
> Before Love's flame in this damp wood and green
> Burns, as it burns within a youthful lady,
> For my sake, who would sleep away in stone
> My life, or feed like beasts upon the grass,
> Only to see her garments cast a shade.

That is from Dante Gabriel Rossetti's version of the "stony" sestina "To the Dim Light," one of the "stony rhymes" passionately addressed by Dante to one Pietra. Beatrice is not very Shakespearean; Pietra is, and would have done well as the Dark Lady of the Sonnets:

> Th'expense of spirit in a waste of shame
> Is lust in action; and, till action, lust
> Is perjured, murd'rous, bloody, full of blame,
> Savage, extreme, rude, cruel, not to trust;
> Enjoyed no sooner but despisèd straight . . .

Pious reactions to Dante are not so clearly useless as attempts to Christianize the tragedies of Hamlet and of Lear, but they do the *Commedia* more harm than feminist resentment, which tends to mistrust the idealization of Beatrice. Dante's praise of Beatrice is immensely poignant; his exaltation of an unrequited love is more problematic, unless we think back to the profound visions of early childhood, when we fell in love with someone we scarcely knew, and perhaps never saw again. T. S. Eliot shrewdly surmised that Dante's experience of first loving Beatrice must have come before he was nine, and the numerological paradigm indeed could have induced Dante to set the experience two or three years later than it took place. Not being Dante, most of us can do little with so early an epiphany, and part of Dante's achievement is that he could found greatness upon it.

If Beatrice is universal in her origins, she becomes in the *Commedia* an esoteric figure, the center of Dante's own gnosis, since it is by and through her that Dante asserts knowledge rather less traditional than most of his exegetes will grant. The permanent notoriety of the *Inferno* has not obscured the dramatic eloquence of the *Purgatorio*, which retains a reasonably wide readership. It is the *Paradiso* which is immensely difficult, and yet that difficulty represents Dante's genius at its most indisputable, breaking beyond the limits of imaginative literature. There is nothing else that resembles the *Paradiso*, unless it be certain sequences in the *Meccan Revelations* of the Andalusian Sufi Ibn Arabi (1165–1240), who had encountered *his* Beatrice in Mecca. Nizam, the Sophia of Mecca, like Beatrice of Florence, was the center of a theophany, and converted Ibn Arabi to an idealized, sublimated love.

At seventy-one, I am perhaps not yet ready for the *Paradiso* (where, being of the Jewish persuasion, I am not going to end anyway), and I have begun to recoil from the *Inferno,* an authentically terrifying if sublime work. I do keep going back to the *Purgatorio,* for reasons wonderfully phrased by W. S. Merwin in the foreword to his admirable translation of the middle canticle of the *Commedia.*

Of the three sections of the poem, only *Purgatorio* happens *on* the earth, as our lives do, with our feet on the ground, crossing a beach, climbing a mountain . . . To the very top of the mountain hope is mixed with pain, which brings it still closer to the living present. (xiii).

My friends all differ upon which canto of the *Purgatorio* is their personal favorite; I choose the vision of Matilda gathering flowers, in the Earthly Paradise of canto 28. The first fifty-one lines, beautifully rendered by Merwin, I give here in Percy Bysshe Shelley's ecstatic version, his only extended translation from the *Commedia:*

> And earnest to explore within—around—
> The divine wood, whose thick green living woof
> Tempered the young day to the sight—I wound
>
> Up the green slope, beneath the forest's roof,
> With slow, soft steps leaving the mountain's steep,
> And sought those inmost labyrinths, motion-proof
>
> Against the air, that in that stillness deep
> And solemn, struck upon my forehead bare,
> The slow, soft, stroke of a continuous . . .
>
> In which the leaves tremblingly were
> All bent towards that part where earliest
> The sacred hill obscures the morning air.
>
> Yet were they not so shaken from the rest,
> But that the birds, perched on the utmost spray,
> Incessantly renewing their blithe quest,

With perfect joy received the early day,
Singing within the glancing leaves, whose sound
Kept a low burden to their roundelay,

Such as from bough to bough gathers around
The pine forest on bleak Chiassi's shore,
When Aeolus Sirocco has unbound.

My slow steps had already borne me o'er
Such space within the antique wood, that I
Perceived not where I entered any more,—

When, lo! A stream whose little waves went by,
Bending towards the left through grass that grew
Upon its bank, impeded suddenly

My going on. Water of purest hue
On earth, would appear turbid and impure
Compared with this, whose unconcealing dew,

Dark, dark, yet clear, moved under the obscure
Eternal shades, whose interwoven looms
The rays of moon or sunlight ne'er endure.

I moved not with my feet, but mid the glooms
Pierced with my charmed eye, contemplating
The mighty multitude of fresh May blooms

Which starred that night, when, even as a thing
That suddenly, for blank astonishment,
Charms every sense, and makes all thought take wing,—

A solitary woman! and she went
Singing and gathering flower after flower,
With which her way was painted and besprent.

"Bright lady, who, if looks had ever power
To bear true witness of the heart within,
Dost bask under the beams of love, come lower

"Towards this bank. I prithee let me win
This much of thee, to come, that I may hear
Thy song: like Proserpine, in Enna's glen,

"Thou seemest to my fancy, singing here
And gathering flowers, as that fair maiden when
She lost the Spring, and Ceres her, more dear."

Shelley keeps the *terza rima* (which Dante had invented) at some expense to the original's literal meaning, but he catches the surprises and splendor of the advent of Matilda, who has reversed the fall of Proserpine and of Eve, and who presages the imminent return of the vision of Beatrice to Dante. Shakespeare, in act 4, scene 4 of *The Winter's Tale*, may also hover in Shelley's memory, since Perdita is Shakespeare's equivalent of Matilda.

O Proserpina,
For the flowers now that frighted, thou let'st fall
From Dis's waggon! daffodils,
That come before the swallow dares, and take
The winds of March with beauty . . .

Why Dante named this singing girl of a restored Eden Matilda (Matelda) is something of a puzzle, explained away differently by various scholars. Dante's Matilda makes only a brief appearance, but I perversely prefer her to Beatrice, who scolds and preaches, and is endlessly too good for Dante. Like Shakespeare's Perdita, Matilda charms us. Who but the ferocious Dante could fall in love again with the heavenly Beatrice? Who would not fall in love with Matilda, as translated here by William Merwin?

"and it tastes sweeter than any other,
and although your thirst might be completely
satisfied if I revealed no more.

"I will add a corollary, as a favor,
And I do not think my words will be less dear
To you because they go beyond my promise.

"Those who sang in ancient times of the age
Of gold and of its happy state saw this place,
Perhaps, in their dreams on Parnassus.

"Here the root of humankind was innocent.
Here Spring and every fruit lasted forever;
When they told of nectar this is what each meant."

Gracious and beautiful, the mysterious epitome of a young woman in love, Matilda walks with Dante through the meadows as though the Golden Age had returned. Matilda moves like a dancer, and we need not slow her pace by piling allegories upon her, or by relating her to historical noblewomen or blessed contemplatives. Dante, notoriously susceptible to the beauty of women, clearly would fall in love with Matilda, if the transmogrified Beatrice, as much chiding mother as image of desire, were not waiting for him in the next canto.

William Hazlitt, superb literary critic of British Romanticism, had a far more ambivalent reaction to Dante than Shelley and Byron did, yet Hazlitt caught at the truth of Dante's originality, the effect of Dante's genius:

he interests only by his exciting our sympathy with the emotion by which he is himself possessed. He does not place before us the objects by which that emotion has been excited; but he seizes on the attention, by showing us the effect they produce on his feelings; and his poetry accordingly frequently gives us the thrilling and overwhelming sensation which is caught by gazing on the face of a person who has seen some object of horror.

Hazlitt was thinking of the *Inferno,* and not of Matilda in the *Purgatorio,* where the sensation is that of gazing upon a face who has seen an ultimate object of delight.

GEOFFREY CHAUCER

But, Lord Crist! whan that it remembreth me°	*I think*
Upon my yowthe, and on my jolitee,°	*gaiety*
It tikleth° me aboute myn herte rote.°	*tickles/ heart's root*
Unto this day it dooth myn herte bote°	*good*
That I have had my world as in my tyme.	
But age, allas! that al wol envenyme,°	*poison*
Hath me biraft° my beautee and my pith.°	*bereft of / vigor*
Lat go,° farewel! the devel go therwith!	*Let it go*
The flour is goon, there is namore to telle:	
The bren,° as I best can, now moste I selle.	*bran, husks*

"Unto this day it does my heart good / That I have had my world as in my time." It is difficult not to be enchanted by the Wife of Bath, who is as much emblematic of Chaucer's genius as Sir John Falstaff is of Shakespeare's. That Shakespeare had her in mind as he created Falstaff is ascertainable; the two grand vitalists each allude to Saint Paul when they affirm that there is no sin in their vocation. And yet the Wife of Bath hints that she has disposed of at least one husband, and her childlessness is somewhat disconcerting.

Chaucer the Pilgrim greatly appreciates the Wife, but then he enjoys and admires most of his fellow pilgrims, or rather he delights in telling us that he does. His pervasive irony centers upon his self-portrait as Pilgrim, whose judgments of the other pilgrims we have to doubt, but that is because Chaucer the Poet wishes us to question almost all moral judgments.

Chaucer seems to have had a properly ambivalent stance towards Dante, whose moral judgments are ferocious and incessant. The high deliberation of the Wife of Bath's good humor speaks for Chaucer himself: cheerfulness keeps breaking in. Her desires are unappeased, and her defiance of age is wonderful: "Let go, farewell! the devil go therewith!"

GEOFFREY CHAUCER
(1340?–1400)

NO LAUGHTER ATTENDS THE READING of Lucretius and Vergil, Augustine and Dante. The comic genius of Geoffrey Chaucer, who declined to study the nostalgias, whether chivalric or spiritual, is all the more welcome for the company in which I have placed him. That company is not arbitrary: there is again an influence relationship at work between Dante and Chaucer, though the truer precursor for Chaucer was Boccaccio, whom he never mentions. Profoundly impressed and cheerfully irritated by Dante, Chaucer created a parody of Dante the Pilgrim in Chaucer the Pilgrim of the *Canterbury Tales*.

Scholars of Dante are properly awed by their poet. Chaucer, the strongest writer in English next to Shakespeare, was eager to learn from Dante, but was too magnificent an ironist to be awed. Lucretius was certain he knew the truth: it was Epicurean. Vergil, uncertain of everything, is a kind of sliding Epicurean: he cannot stand in the truth of metaphysical materialism, would like some transcendence, and knows he never will find it. Augustine and Dante knew the truth, but it is a revelation for those to whom it is revealed. Chaucer, most refreshingly, doubts that any writer can catch truth in language. With misgivings, and hesitancy, Chaucer is a secular poet, and as such he is Shakespeare's truest precursor.

I still prefer the Catholic storyteller-polemicist G. K. Chesterton to all other critics of Chaucer, since he has the surest sense of Chaucer's greatness. He sees that Chaucer is of the eminence of Dante and Shakespeare, and acknowledges that Shakespeare, whatever his inward religious persuasion, writes a secular, even pagan poetry, when it suits his purposes. Yet Chesterton would not sever Dante and Chaucer, though I think he knew better. We know exactly Dante's judgment as to every person in his poem, though Dante himself sometimes cannot bear his own judgment, as in regard to Francesca. But no one can know just where Chaucer stands in relation to the Pardoner or the Wife of Bath or the Knight, and who can say how Shakespeare himself felt about Falstaff and Hamlet, Iago and Cleopatra? Chaucer and Shakespeare do not pretend to know finalities, and we can surmise that moral judgments provoked their irony. Dante really does seem to know everything available to be known in 1300, but he also insists that he knows and tells the truth, no more available then than now. In mere fact, Dante invents endlessly, to help fill out the design of his astonishing poem. Was Brunetto Latini a sodomite? We may not care one way or the other (unless we are fundamentalists or Republicans), but Dante appears to have invented his old teacher's sexual orientation. Vergil, as I have observed, was essentially an Epicurean, and not a Christian before Christ, and the merely historical Beatrice evidently did not take Dante very seriously. Dante, like the rest of us, suffered a great deal, but many of us would be hesitant before we peopled Hell with our personal enemies. Chaucer, too ironical to say these things, clearly knows and feels them, and is not willing to speculate that even the Pardoner will be damned.

Are there any ironies in the *Commedia* that are not cruel? I ought to make clear that belief is not the issue here. Shelley, as I will show later, demonstrates a deeper love and understanding of Dante's poetry than any other poet in the language, T. S. Eliot not excepted. Shelley detested Christianity, and found Dante's dogmatism no barrier:

> The poetry of Dante may be considered as the bridge thrown over the stream of time, which unites the modern and ancient world. The distorted notions of invisible things which Dante and his rival Milton have idealized, are merely the mask and the mantle in which these great poets walk through eternity enveloped and disguised. It is a difficult question to determine how far they were conscious of the distinction which must have subsisted in their minds between their own creeds and that of the people. Dante at least appears to wish to mark the full extent of it by placing Riphaeus, whom Vergil calls *justissimus unus,* in Paradise, and observing a most heretical caprice, in his distribution of rewards and punishments.
>
> ... The Divinna Commedia and Paradise Lost have conferred upon modern mythology a systematic form; and when change and time shall have added one more superstition to the mass of those which have arisen and decayed upon the earth, commentators will be learnedly employed in elucidating the religion of ancestral Europe, only not utterly forgotten because it will have been stamped with the eternity of genius.

Shelley's amiable prophecy has been somewhat more fulfilled in Europe (except for Ireland) than in the United States, except that I do not recognize much of "the religion of ancestral Europe" in what I go on urging us to call the American Religion, the original mix of Orphism, Gnosticism, and

Enthusiasm that has powered the spirituality of the United States since 1800. Our Pentecostals, Mormons, Adventists, various Baptists, and other original inventions are the spearhead, but most of the eighty-nine percent of Americans who affirm that God loves them on a personal and individual basis are fairly remote from ancestral Europe, even when they call themselves Catholics, Lutherans, Methodists, Anglicans, or Presbyterians.

Shelley is of course accurate, though few Dante scholars, and fewer who study Milton, would agree. What is Riphaeus doing in Paradise? Rachel Jacoff refreshingly shows that Dante raises the question in order not to answer it:

> Among the six rulers in the eye and eyebrow of the eagle is Ripheus, a character briefly named in the *Aeneid*. Dante asks, as indeed any reader would, "How can this be?" Like the improbable presence of Cato on the shores of Purgatory, the startling presence of Ripheus in the Heaven of Justice makes us think about how Dante read his classical sources and how he rewrites them. Ripheus is a sign of God's inscrutability, but also of the poet's freedom. Vergil had called Ripheus "most just," but Dante's tale of Ripheus abhorring the "stench of paganism" is pure invention. Catholic theology did allow for "baptism by desire," but no one other than Dante would have selected Ripheus as an example of it.

If Riphaeus, why not Vergil? But then, why Beatrice? It is Dante's poem, and he does what is best for it, but surely we should start realizing that Dante was a sect of one, and not a Thomist, an Augustinian, or whatever. Milton clearly is a sect of one, and Shelley perhaps differed from Dante and Milton only by refusing to call himself a Christian. Dante's theology would not have bothered Chaucer one way or the other, but the Florentine's harshness and arbitrariness did not please the compassionate English ironist. We are reluctant to talk about the shattering arrogance of Dante, but he mostly did not find his God to be at all inscrutable. Dante does not tell us all of God's secrets, but he seems to know most of them, and perhaps would have divulged much more if he had been granted the quarter-century he needed to become nine nines.

Chaucer is not so much politely skeptical of Dante's God-like moral judgment as he is wearied by portraits of men and women who are frozen by Dante, beyond change. One could venture that Chaucer is the difference between Dante and Shakespeare because the Wife of Bath fosters the miracle of Sir John Falstaff, and the Pardoner's nihilistic abyss foreshadows the great Shakespearean transvaluers of all values, Iago and the Edmund of *King Lear.* Rather than center upon even the Wife and the Pardoner, I choose here the whole panoply of the "General Prologue" to the *Canterbury Tales.* Dante is the precursor, subtly revised and countered, in Chaucer's other masterwork, *Troilus and Criseyde,* but the *Canterbury Tales* mostly abandon Dante for a hidden struggle with Boccaccio, a much more dangerous influence for Chaucer, whose mastery of narration and of character are greatly indebted to the zestful author of the *Decameron.*

At about forty-six, Chaucer began to write the *Canterbury Tales,* and continued until his death in 1400. Of one hundred and twenty projected tales, he finished twenty-two and started two others. As in the rest of his work, Chaucer wrote in order to read aloud at court and in the homes of great nobles. And yet Chaucer also expected to be read.

It helps locate Chaucer to realize that he lived in the service of Richard II, and then in that of Henry IV. The world of the *Henry IV* plays of Shakespeare is a vision of Chaucer's England. Sir John Falstaff is Chaucer's contemporary, as it were; more important, Falstaff and the Wife of Bath are true contemporaries, and would have had much to say and to do with one another. They shared a chaotic age of civil wars, virulent and uncertain, a time to go on pilgrimages, which doubtless had their spiritual side, but were also an equivalent of our cruises. The Wife of Bath, having buried five husbands, is in search of the sixth, or at least of company upon the way. I wouldn't want to find myself with Dante's characters, even in the *Purgatorio* or the *Paradiso,* but if some earlier strength could return to me, I would want to be with Chaucer the Pilgrim, the Host, and the twenty-eight other seekers. Chaucer's originality, the glory of his genius, emerges vividly in the portraits of the "General Prologue." Their particular mark is vitality, whether they are the swan-eating Monk or the woman-hunting Friar, or the five lowlife rapscallions: the Miller, the Manciple, the Reeve, the dreadful Summoner, and the outrageous and unsettling Pardoner. The most vital of all vitalists, fit to challenge Falstaff or the Panurge of Rabelais, is of course the Wife of Bath, who invites the reader's embrace, and yet has her own equivocal aspects.

What enabled Chaucer to exercise such mastery of characterization, two centuries before Shakespeare? Though I do not yield to the fashions that decree the discrediting of any idea of individual genius, I grant here, as throughout this book, that there must be an intersection of a gifted consciousness and the *kairos,* the opportune time, for original works to come into being. But I do not think we have learned yet how such intersection works. Geoffrey Chaucer was the son of a successful vintner, and moved from that middle-class foreground to joining the royal household when he was seventeen. He served three successive kings—Edward III, Richard II, and Henry IV—as a soldier, diplomat, courtier, and administrator. There was an apparently fruitful tension between Chaucer's modest origins and his lifelong career at court, but he was hardly the only such figure in his England, and only he became the supreme poet of his country before the advent of Shakespeare. His era and position proved fecund in granting him *materia poetica* for his art, but again: why him? As with Vergil and Augustine and Dante, Chaucer presents us with unique gifts of intellect, language, and insight that emerge from purely individual energies, rather than from cultural energies. Chaucer was a perceptive social observer, and yet the Wife of Bath and the Pardoner are poetic visions represented with a realistic panache that is both ingratiating and misleading, artfully so. So large is Chaucer's irony that sometimes we cannot see it, as Chesterton remarked. The Wife of Bath is darker than she seems, and the Pardoner more sincere than he could bear to know. What to make of the Prioress's ghastly tale, I hardly know. Does Chaucer truly write it without irony? Can you doubt language and stories as much as Chaucer did, and then sincerely offer the anti-Semitic violence of this slanderous tale, which makes *The Merchant of Venice* almost benign by comparison? The ladylike Prioress is perfectly vicious in her hatred of the Jews (who had been expelled from England in 1290, for the crime of being victims of the York Massacre), which culminates in a stanza that I have to take as ironic:

With torment° and with shameful deth echon°	*torture / each one*
The provost dooth° thise Jewes for to sterve°	*causes/die*
That of this mordre wiste,° and that anon;°	*knew / immediately*
He nolde no swich cursednesse observe.	
"Yvel shal have that yvel wol deserve."	
Therefore with wilde hors° he dide hem drawe,°	*horses / had them drawn*
And after that he heng° hem by the lawe.	*hanged (probably on pikes)*

Chaucer's subtler ironies may not be as large, but they are wonderfully incessant. Talbot Donaldson aptly compared Chaucer the Pilgrim to Jonathan Swift's Lemuel Gulliver, with his passion for reasonable horses. Chesterton's Chaucer slyly and blandly enjoyed every contradiction he encountered, and savored his own impudence. No one knew better than Chaucer that his world was on the wane, and perhaps no one else knew better how to enjoy it as it went down. An irony that depends upon a sense that a more gorgeous reality has fled forever is both Chaucerian and Chester-tonian. To tell ironic stories whose true subject is storytelling was Boccac-cio's mode before it was Chaucer's, which must be why Chaucer never mentions Boccaccio. What is entirely Chaucer's originality is his kind of irony, which defies almost any description. The erudition of the Wife of Bath is astonishing, but she herself is ironical concerning it. The Pardoner is doom-eager with a relish at self-destructing that is another aspect of irony. Chaucer himself, as poet and as pilgrim, moves towards an ironic vision in which irony becomes a new kind of love for the world and the color-ful zanies who vivify it. A loving irony flowers into ironic love, a beautiful and laughing apprehension of pilgrims and pilgrimage. Whatever this may be, it is antithetical to what Dante celebrates as love.

Preaching to the congregations he fleeces, the Pardoner attains an ecstasy:

> Myn hondes and my tonge goon so yerne°   *rapidly*
> That it is joye to see my bisinesse.

One wants only to make him a televangelist, an American splendor now fading away. And where will we find our Wife of Bath, with her marvelous motto: "a likerous mouth moste han a likerous tayl"? There had to be a sec-ular poetic voice resonant enough, and a humane vision comprehensive enough, to defend the common life against Dante's prophetic urgencies. Chaucer's originality is less sublime than Dante's, but how welcome it is! Pilgrims of the Absolute never stop making moral judgments. Chaucer does not trust absolutes, and ironically persuades us that life is likely to discredit those who are too gifted at damning others.

II

НОКМАН

LUSTRE 3

|

The Yahwist, Socrates and Plato, Saint Paul, Muhammad

|

The hidden center of this Lustre is the figure of Jesus. He *was* here, but has been somewhat withdrawn, partly because of my perplexities, partly through sage editorial counsel. *Genius* is a book about authorial conscious-nesses, and even Socrates is authorial in the oral tradition. But it seems to me that there are two separate persons, the historical Jesus, of whom we know very little, and the literary character who burns through the four Gospels, even as Yahweh is the great literary character in the J writer or Yah-wist. Jesus and Hamlet are the only literary characters who seem to possess an authorial consciousness, yet this book is not devoted to literary charac-ters but to exemplary creative minds.

To regard Muhammad, seal of the prophets, as an authorial genius is to contravene Islam, since God himself speaks every word of the Koran. But the Koran cannot be ignored, as it is a work of genius we badly need to study. *Hokmah,* divine wisdom, cannot be considered in its Western formu-lations without the juxtapositioning of the Yahwist and Plato, Saint Paul and the Koran.

THE YAHWIST

Yahweh appeared to him by the terebinths of Mamre; he was sitting at the entrance of the tent as the day grew hot. Looking up, he saw three men standing near him. As soon as he saw them, he ran from the entrance of the tent to greet them and, bowing to the ground, he said, "My lords, if it please you, do not go on past your servant. Let a little water be brought; bathe your feet and recline under the tree. And let me fetch a morsel of bread that you may refresh yourselves; then go on—seeing that you have come your servant's way." They replied, "Do as you have said."

Abraham hastened into the tent to Sarah, and said, "Quick, three *seahs* of choice flour! Knead and make cakes!" Then Abraham ran to the herd, took a calf, tender and choice, and gave it to a servant-boy, who hastened to prepare it. He took curds and milk and the calf that had been prepared and set these before them; and he waited on them under the tree as they ate.

—*Tanakh*, Genesis 18:1–15
(American Jewish version)

This is the Yahwist or J writer at her (or his, if you prefer) uncanniest. As the day grows hot, Yahweh appears to Abraham by the terebinth trees of Mamre. With this surprising God are two other Elohim, divine beings or angels who are on the road with Yahweh intending to destroy Sodom and Gomorrah, sinful Cities of the Plain. Yahweh, like the others, bathes his feet, reclines under the shade of the terebinths, and enjoys a delicious lunch of veal, cakes, cheese, and milk. Pleased with Abraham's hospitality, and with Sarah's culinary art, Yahweh prophesies a son for the aged Abraham and Sarah, who are too old for such a begetting and birth. When Sarah, concealed in the tent, laughs ironically at this promise, Yahweh is offended and tells the frightened woman, who denies it, that indeed she had the effrontery to laugh.

Who would give up this Yahweh, despite all the wailings of theologians and scholars, since they desire a less human God? The Yahwist is a comic genius, working in an area where we least expect comedy. The impish joy and exuberance of this writer were not to be equaled again until Shake-speare, whose audacities had to be subtler, in an England where heretics were burned, and blasphemers could lose an ear or even a tongue. But the Yahwist knows nothing of heresy or blasphemy. The J writer is a storyteller, of amazing sophistication and yet with a childlike directness.

William Blake said that the history of religion consisted in "choosing forms of worship from poetic tales." Judaism, Christianity, and Islam all emerge from that process, and all of them are endlessly far away from the exuberant beauty of the Yahwist.

THE YAHWIST
(980?–900? B.C.E.)

HEBREW ORIGINS REMAIN DIFFICULT TO date with much exactitude. Abram, who became Abraham, father of the Jews, Christians, and Muslims, may have lived in the eighteenth century before the common era. Israel presumably descended into Egypt a century later, and the Exodus could have occurred about 1280 B.C.E. Canaan was conquered perhaps fifty years later. The prophet Samuel and King Saul can be dated roughly 1020–1000 B.C.E., and David ruled over Judah and Israel from 1000 to 960, when Solomon ascended the throne, and reigned until about 922, after which he died and the kingdom was divided.

The greatest writer in the Hebrew language, known to scholars as J or the Yahwist, wrote the crucial portions of what we now call Genesis, Exodus, and Numbers sometime between 950 and 900. Since this extraordinary author is unknown to us by name, we are free to surmise her or his identity.

The Book of J or the Yahwist is now embedded in the huge Genesis to Kings structure invented by a great writer-editor, the Redactor, in the Babylonian Exile, about 550 B.C.E. I wrote a commentary, *The Book of J* (1990), by which I continue to stand, though I am unhappy with the translation employed by that volume, and so will quote from *Tanakh* (1985), the American Jewish version of the Holy Scriptures, where the Torah or Five Books of Moses (which encloses the J text) was rendered by a distinguished group including Harry M. Orlinsky, H. L. Ginsberg, Ephraim A. Speiser, and others.

Samuel Butler, Victorian novelist who wrote the superb *The Way of All Flesh*, also composed a book in which he argued that the author of the *Odyssey* was a woman. Butler is delightful if not altogether persuasive, and retrospectively I see that he influenced my surmise that the Yahwist was a woman, an aristocrat at the splendid court of Solomon the Wise. I rather like the suggestion of Jack Miles that I ought to be audacious enough to identify this great woman as the Hittite Bathsheba, mother of Solomon. David famously arranged for Bathsheba's husband, Uriah, to be slain in battle, so that he could add Bathsheba to his wives. How droll it would be if the genius out of whose stories the Redactor fashioned the Torah had been a Hittite woman, and not an Israelite male! Since J is a great ironist, not particularly fond of the Hebrew patriarchs, but delighted by their wives, Bathsheba would certainly fit admirably. There is also J's admiration for Hagar and Tamar, like Bathsheba women who are not Israelites.

I wish to make clear that I read the J text as high literature, as I read Homer, Dante, and Shakespeare. Whatever their true history may have been, the vital representations of Abram/Abraham, Jacob/Israel, Judah, Tamar, Joseph, and Moses are all by J, and so I regard them here as literary characters. Rather than treat the figure of Jesus as a literary character created by Mark in his Gospel, I choose to exclude Jesus from this book, though he belongs, at least in part, to the history of Jewish genius, an assertion in which I merely repeat the judgment of the Reverend John P. Meier, the most distinguished Roman Catholic biographer of Jesus.

The genius of the Yahwist has one overwhelming manifestation, that transcends even Shakespeare (though to say that wounds me). J's most surprising character is not Abraham or Jacob or Moses, or even Joseph, who I take to be a surrogate portrait of King David. It is, uncannily, Yahweh, God not just as a literary character but, unforgettably, God. Again, I eschew all outrageousness; J's Yahweh has been a scandal for almost three thousand years, because he is human-all-too-human. I remember remarking, in my *Book of J*, that by normative standards—Judaic, Christian, Islamic—J's representation of Yahweh is blasphemous. I would say now that I understated this: the theologians (ancient and modern) and the scholars call J's Yahweh "anthropomorphic," which is an absurd evasion.

A superb exception, the German scholar Gerhard von Rad gets this right, though I would substitute J for Israel and the Hebrew Bible or *Tanakh* for Old Testament in von Rad's observation:

Actually, Israel conceived even Jahweh himself as having human form. But the way of putting it which we use runs in precisely the wrong direction according to Old Testament ideas, for, according to the ideas of Jahwism, it cannot be said that Israel regarded God anthropomorphically, but the reverse, that she considered man as theomorphic.

J, with all her irony, considered her women and men as being theomorphic, while her dynamic Yahweh is extraordinary and unconfined from the beginning:

When no shrub of the field was yet on earth and no grasses of the field had yet sprouted, because Yahweh had not sent rain upon the

earth and there was no man to till the soil, but a flow would well up
from the ground and water the whole surface of the earth—Yahweh
formed man (*adam*) from the dust of the earth (*adamah*). He blew into
his nostrils the breath of life, and man became a living being.

—*Tanakh*, Genesis 2:5–7,

with "Yahweh" restored for their "the Lord God."

We are too accustomed to this to recognize its enduring strangeness. Yahweh forms the figurine of Adam from the moist red clay of the *adamah*, not
as a potter shapes with his wheel, but as a child makes a mud-pie. Yet this
is a childlike God who blows into his creature the breath of life, and thus
exalts Adam into a living being, not a soul imprisoned within a body, but a
fused entity, like Yahweh himself.

Original as this is, J surpasses it in the more elaborate creation of Eve,
the unique account of how women came to be formed in all the literature
of the ancient Near East:

Yahweh said, "It is not good for man to be alone; I will make a fitting helper for him." And Yahweh formed out of the earth all the wild
beasts and all the birds in the sky, and brought them to the man to see
what he would call them; and whatever man called each living creature, that would be its name. And the man gave names to all the cat-
tle and to the birds of the sky and to all the wild beasts; but for Adam
no fitting helper was found. So Yahweh cast a deep sleep upon the
man; and, while he slept, He took one of his ribs and closed up the
flesh at that spot. And Yahweh fashioned the rib that He had taken
from the man into a woman; and He brought her to the man. Then
the man said,

"This one at last
Is bone of my bones
And flesh of my flesh.
This one shall be called Woman,
For from man was she taken."

The Hebrew here translated as "a fitting helper" means someone alongside of Adam, and equal to him, since the same word is used later for Yahweh's stance towards us. When the King James version rendered this as "I
will make him an help meet for him," it started troubles we may never fully
escape. J is at her most enigmatic when Yahweh casts a deep sleep

(*tardemah,* a heavy, anaesthetic slumber, since Adam is being operated upon by Yahweh). It is palpable (and ironic) that Yahweh does a more beautiful job this time around. Man came out of the clay, woman from a living being, and so is immediately animate.

I leap out of the garden and past our father Abraham to J's saga of the wily Jacob, who became Israel by wrestling a mysterious angel (one of the Elohim or divine beings) to a draw in a desperate all-night struggle:

> That same night he arose, and taking his two wives, his two maid-servants, and his eleven children, he crossed the ford of the Jabbok. After taking them across the stream, he sent across all his possessions. Jacob was left alone. And a man wrestled with him until the break of dawn. When he saw that he had not prevailed against him, he wrenched Jacob's hip at its socket, so that the socket of his hip was strained as he wrestled with him. Then he said, "Let me go, for dawn is breaking." But he answered, "I will not let you go, unless you bless me." Said the other, "What is your name?" He replied, "Jacob." Said he, "Your name shall no longer be Jacob, but Israel, for you have striven with beings divine and human, and have prevailed." Jacob asked, "Pray tell me your name." But he said, "You must not ask my name!" And he took his leave of him there. So Jacob named the place Penuel, meaning, "I have seen a divine being face to face, yet my life has been preserved." The sun rose upon him as he passed Penuel, limping on his hip.

This is a triumph of J's genius but very difficult for us to confront directly, since "Wrestling Jacob" became a Protestant myth in which the patriarch sustains a loving contest with God himself. For the American Jewish version's "you have striven with beings divine and human" I would substitute "with Elohim and men," with men earlier, and one of the Elohim here at the ford of the Jabbok (the pun on Jacob's name is characteristic of J). Is it a benign being whom Jacob battles? Jewish tradition is ambiguous upon this, and some sources suggest the antagonist was the demon Sammael, angel of death, which makes most sense to me. It is the night before Jacob must suffer a reunion with his wronged brother Esau, cheated of the birthright and the Blessing of Isaac. Jacob, no warrior, knows that the volatile Esau is approaching with four hundred of his rough Edomites, a posse of badmen. After sending over the water his household and possessions, Jacob waits to ambush the Angel of his own death, who is hastening to be on the spot tomorrow, and so Jacob blocks the ford. There is something nefarious about this nameless one of the Elohim; like a vampire, he fears the daylight: "Let me go, for dawn is breaking." And note that this is no loving encounter: Jacob is permanently crippled by it. How shall we account for Jacob's obdurate stamina with which he holds off the angel/demon? J does not explain, but rather gives the new Israel a blaze of epiphany as he departs: "The sun rose upon him as he passed Penuel, limping on his hip."

"Israel," to J, may have meant "May God hold firm," or might also mean "May the angel win." Either way, the name is ironic, since it is Jacob who holds firm, and who triumphs. All his life he has battled for the Blessing, and J's genius manifests itself in the hint that the human will, Jacob's, can be stalwart enough to hold off the Angel of Death, at least in one or another pivotal encounter.

I turn to a third episode in the Yahwist's narrative, the most enigmatic and shocking moment in the Hebrew Bible. J's Moses is not the heroic Titan of Deuteronomy, but instead is handled by the Yahwist with loving irony, and by Yahweh with considerable roughness. This Moses is brave but anxious, not very patient, and very dubious about his own qualifications for leadership. He is heavy-tongued, and is reluctant to become Yahweh's prophet:

> But Moses said to Yahweh, "Please, O Lord, I have never been a man of words, either in times past or now that You have spoken to Your servant; I am slow of speech and slow of tongue." And Yahweh said to him, "Who gives man speech? Who makes him dumb or deaf, seeing or blind? Is it not I, Yahweh? Now go, and I will be with you as you speak and will instruct you what to say." But he said, "Please, O Lord, make someone else Your agent." Yahweh became angry with Moses, and He said, "There is your brother Aaron the Levite. He, I know, speaks readily. Even now he is setting out to meet you, and he will be happy to see you. You shall speak to him and put the words in his mouth—I will be with you and with him as you speak, and tell both of you what to do—and he shall speak for you to the people. Thus he shall serve as your spokesman, with you playing the role of God to him. And take with you this rod, with which you shall perform signs."

> > —*Tanakh*, Exodus 4:10–17

Yahweh's anger evidently is not placated by his prophet's agreement to be recruited, and J gives us this shocker, as Moses goes down into Egypt:

> At a night encampment on the way, the Lord encountered him and sought to kill him. So Zipporah took a flint and cut off her son's fore-skin, and touched his legs with it, saying, "You are truly a bridegroom of blood to me!"
>
> —*Tanakh*, Exodus 4:24–25

Confronted by Yahweh's gratuitous attempt to murder Moses, normative commentary has fled off in all directions, leaving the valiant Zipporah to save the day, and her husband. The great interpreter Rashi told us that Moses tarried at an inn, rather than hurrying down into Egypt, but the Hebrew clearly means a night encampment, inevitable in the Negev.

What is Yahweh's motive for his mad rage? J gives us none, and evidently believes there cannot be any explanation. Normative tradition, knowing that Rashi had not done his job, absurdly insisted Moses had to be slain because he had failed to circumcise his infant son! But that is a belated interpretation, based upon what I assume to be the Redactor's tinkering with this astonishing passage. Midrashic tradition, unhappy with the Yahwist's shock-irony, simply rewrote the passage. Satan appears as a great desert serpent and nearly swallows Moses up until Zipporah circumcises her infant son.

Gnostic heretics ancient and modern (myself included) have been delighted with this passage, but the sophisticated and ironic Yahwist was neither a believer nor a heretic. I take it that J wanted us to see yet once more that total identification with the will of Yahweh is impossible: he is not predictable. As I write, the ineffable Falwell and Robertson have suggested that God allowed the World Trade Center to be destroyed because we tolerate abortionists, homosexuals, feminists, and similar riff-raff. I would not care to have the Falwell-Robertson interpretation of why Yahweh attempted to murder Moses.

The genius of the Yahwist is utterly uncanny: she never ceases to surprise us. Homer evidently did not care to surprise his readers, but recreated the past's poetry more memorably than ever it had been rendered. J was a great original, a genius who has never been fully assimilated by the tradition she hardly meant to found, but which would be scandalized by her, if ever they woke up to full awareness.

SOCRATES AND PLATO

As he came in, Agathon, who was sitting by himself at the far end of the table, called out, Here you are, Socrates. Come and sit next to me; I want to share this great thought that's just struck you in the porch next door. I'm sure you must have mastered it, or you'd still be standing there.

My dear Agathon, Socrates replied as he took his seat beside him, I only wish that wisdom *were* the kind of thing one could share by sitting next to someone—if it flowed, for instance, from the one that was full to the one that was empty, like the water in two cups finding its level through a piece of worsted. If that were how it worked, I'm sure I'd congratulate myself on sitting next to you, for you'd soon have me brimming over with the most exquisite kind of wisdom. My own understanding is a shadowy thing at best, as equivocal as a dream, but yours, Agathon, glitters and dilates—as which of us can forget that saw you the other day, resplendent in your youth, visibly kindled before the eyes of more than thirty thousand of your fellow Greeks.

—Plato, *Symposium*
(translated by Michael Joyce)

Socratic irony presents itself as ignorance, and then wittily ensnares you in wisdom. Plato's irony seems to me rather like Chaucer's, which G. K. Chesterton said was too large to be observed. Emerson, meditating upon the genius of Plato, remarked upon its astonishing range of speculation:

Out of Plato come all things that are still written and debated among men of thought. Great havoc makes he among our originalities. We have reached the mountain from which all these drift boulders were detached.

One feels that Montaigne, Emerson's master, preferred Socrates to Plato, while Emerson's own love went more to the chronicler of Socrates: "The great-eyed Plato proportioned the lights and shades after the genius of our life."

Emerson's definition of being a Platonist is very wide: it included Michelangelo, Shakespeare, Swedenborg, and Goethe. I like best Emerson's classification of Hamlet as a Platonist, though I disagree with it:

Hamlet is a pure Platonist, and 'tis the magnitude only of Shakespeare's proper genius that hinders him from being classed as the most eminent of this school.

Emerson meant that Hamlet's remorseless drive was towards transcendence, but that is the Hamlet of act 5, and not the murderous undergraduate genius earlier in the play. Platonists are dangerous men and women, to themselves and to others. Plato's *Laws* makes me uneasier than Deuteronomy does, or the Koran at its fiercest. Great moralities too swiftly turn savage, and I like it less and less, after a half-century at Yale University, that like all the other academic institutions of the English-speaking world, its laws turn more and more into a parody of Platonism.

SOCRATES
(469–399 B.C.E.)

PLATO
(c. 429–347 B.C.E.)

> As they say that Helen of Argus, had that universal beauty that every body felt related to her, so Plato seems to a reader in New England, an American genius.
>
> —Emerson

Emerson did not think of Socrates as an American genius; sages of the oral tradition seem to belong to their own peoples: Confucius to the Chinese, Jesus to the Jews, Socrates to the Athenians. Plato however has the universality of the greatest writers: Homer, Shakespeare, Cervantes, Montaigne among them. Only Plato, of these, fears his own artistry; you have to wait for Tolstoy to meet this phenomenon again. The late novelist Iris Murdoch wrote an admirable monograph that centers upon such fear: *The Fire and the Sun: Why Plato Banished the Artists* (1977). Murdoch is very lucid, as she is also in her most characteristic novels:

> The most obvious paradox in the problem under consideration is that Plato is a great artist . . . He fought a long battle against sophistry and magic, yet produced some of the most memorable images in European philosophy: the Cave, the charioteer, the cunning homeless Eros, the Demiurge cutting the *Anima Mundi* into strips and stretching it out crosswise . . . He wanted what he more than once mentions, immortality through art; he felt and indulged the artist's desire to produce unified, separable, formal, durable objects. (87–88)

One supposes that the principal event in Plato's life was the judicial murder of Socrates. It seems also a valid hypothesis that Plato's highly artistic polemic against art is primarily a contest for cultural supremacy waged against Homer, which is a struggle that Plato was bound to lose. The Platonic dialogue is a great invention, but even the *Republic* or the *Symposium* is not of the aesthetic eminence of the *Iliad*. Doubtless, they would listen to the *Iliad* recited in the Platonic Kingdom of Heaven.

I am a literary critic, neither a philosopher nor a historian, so my competence to write about Plato's genius is limited. Few literary works move me more than the *Symposium*, and so I will confine my remarks about Plato to that single dialogue.

The genius or daemon of Socrates is one of Plato's starting-points. One learns from Socrates that he can prove our ignorance, since he begins with his own formidable "ignorance." To take Socrates as forerunner, as Plato did, seems to me a choice against Homer. Socrates regarded the *Iliad* as tragedy, or so Plato invariably implies. Freud is a kind of antithesis to Plato, who honors the image of the father; Freud does not, but there had been no Socrates in his life. Socratic irony is identical with Socrates' genius, and Platonic irony consequently is very subtle, since like that of his master it is not primarily rhetorical; that is, it does not say one thing while meaning another. Socrates is too natural, too consistent for that, as Montaigne insisted:

> It is he who brought human wisdom back down from heaven, where she was wasting her time, and restored her to man, with whom lies her most proper and laborious and useful business.

Montaigne's own irony is evident. Gregory Vlastos, a major scholar of Socrates, judged Socrates to have shown "a failure of love." What could be more ironic, if Vlastos was accurate, since Socrates, in the *Symposium*, asserts he is an authority only upon love? Here is Vlastos on "The Paradox of Socrates":

> I have already argued that he does care for the souls of fellows. But the care is limited and conditional. If men's souls are to be saved, they must be saved his way. And when he sees they cannot be, he watches them go down the road to perdition with regret but without anguish. Jesus wept for Jerusalem. Socrates warns Athens, scolds, exhorts it, condemns it. But he has no tears for it. One wonders if Plato, who raged against Athens, did not love it more in his rage and hate than ever did Socrates in his sad and good-tempered rebukes. One feels there is a last zone of frigidity in the soul of the great erotic; had he loved his fellows more, he could hardly have laid on them the burdens of his "despotic logic," impossible to be borne.
>
> —*Socrates, Plato, and Their Tradition*, 15

"Despotic logic," as Vlastos observes, is Nietzsche on Socrates in *The Birth of Tragedy*, an early engagement in Nietzsche's lifelong agon with

Socrates. It is somehow more bothersome to nearly everyone (I am not being ironic) that Socrates should have written nothing than that Confucius and Jesus should have confined themselves to sayings. Kierkegaard, though less hostile than Nietzsche, also was concerned with the silence of Socrates. No one ever can know where Socrates breaks off and Plato's Socrates begins, or even if a distinction like that makes sense. Vlastos, after deep study, concluded that the Socrates of Plato's early dialogues indeed was the historical Socrates and not a Platonic fiction. There is only Xenophon's Socrates as an alternative, and the Xenophon of the *Memorabilia* is nowhere as interesting a writer as he is in his *Anabasis*, an account of the heroic forced march of an army of Greek freebooters retreating from Persia to the Black Sea. Just as loyal a disciple of Socrates as Plato was, Xenophon was a professional soldier, and not a dramatic philosopher. Vlastos destroys poor Xenophon, whose Socrates has no irony and no moral originality, by saying that the gallant general would have made an eminent Victorian subject for Lytton Strachey. So, all we have is Plato, who was a great artist, but who nevertheless loved and honored Socrates as a father. Plato's Socrates is the work of a dramatist comparable both to Euripides and (with reservations) Aristophanes, but those who read Plato included many who had heard Socrates. We are not at all in the situation of Saint Paul and the authors of the Gospels, none of whom had ever seen or heard Jesus.

And yet Socrates without Plato (or with him) remains a paradox or permanent enigma. Unlike the later Plato, Socrates had no dogma; he would like to believe in the soul's immortality, but he accepts the possibility that death may involve the annihilation of consciousness. As to Socrates' vocation or mission, it appears self-contradictory. He professes ignorance, and instructs in wisdom and the care of the soul, yet nearly all his activity essentially is destructive: you affirm some position, and he refutes it. Vlastos attempts to resolve the paradox by calling Socrates a searcher, always in quest of truth. But (except very rarely) an ironic quester seems less present than does a searching ironist.

Søren Kierkegaard, nineteenth-century Danish religious writer, is considered elsewhere in this volume. Here I bring in his academic dissertation *The Concept of Irony, with Constant Reference to Socrates*, presented in 1841. The book itself is so ironic that you cannot extract from it a clear account of Socratic irony, but I remain stunned by Thesis XIII:

> Irony is not so much apathy, divested of all tender emotions of the
> soul; instead, it is more like vexation over the fact that others also
> enjoy what it desires for itself.

This seems neither Socratic nor Hegelian, but is perfectly Kierkegaardian, and takes us into the vexations and anguishes of strongly creative souls, competing with all others. Does the paradox of Socrates not include his agonistic stance, always central to Athenian culture? The *Symposium*, where I trust to arrive soon, is certainly a contest: in drinking, in oratory, in eros, in the care of the soul or self, which after all is Socrates' exclusive concern. If he can find virtue in another self, then and only then will he be able to recognize it himself. But since he is much the best of the Athenians, in any regard, he can only go on questing. Kierkegaard's Thesis XIII is thus an ironic reversal of Socratic irony, and a highly deliberate one, because his argument is that the outer Socrates is merely a mask, and that inwardly Socrates was the opposite of what he played at being. The ultimate irony then is that Socrates would be the authentic sophist, as opposed to Gorgias and his followers, whom Socrates denigrated.

Alexander Nehamas, steering in Vlastos's wake, cites Nietzsche's ambivalence towards Socrates, who is both denounced as a searcher for a reasonable morality and immensely praised for dialectical "self-authenticity." This is dizzying, and augments the profound understanding Nehamas brings to Socratic irony:

Often, irony consists in letting your audience know that something is taking place inside you that they simply are not allowed to see. But it also, more radically, leaves open the question of whether you are seeing it yourself.

—*Virtues of Authenticity*, 113

Does Socrates see it himself? If we were speaking of the sublime of ironists, Hamlet, who is aware of everything, the question would he answerable. Hamlet sees everything, in himself and in others. With Plato's Socrates, we are in the abyss of Plato's irony, which seems to me neither rhetorical nor dramatic. Does Plato know more about Socrates than Socrates does? For all Plato's genius, he is not Shakespeare, and Socrates never overhears himself, as though he were somebody else.

We might still be startled by the phrase "Socratic love," but many among us think we know (somewhat smirkingly) what "platonic love" means. In popular idiom, it now is defined by our dictionaries as affection that transcends sexual desire and that moves towards an ideal or spiritual realm. That is not exactly what the *Symposium* advocates, though it is not easy to expound the *Symposium*, a triumph of literary art.

The best foregrounding for the *Symposium* is K. J. Dover's *Greek Homo-*

sexuality (1978), which cheerfully cautions us that Plato may be something of a special case:

> In two works above all, *Symposium* and *Phaedrus*, Plato takes homosexual desire and homosexual love as the starting-point from which to develop his metaphysical theory and it is of particular importance that he regards philosophy not as an activity to be pursued in solitary meditation and communicated in *ex cathedra* pronouncements by a master to his disciples, but as a dialectical progress which may well begin in the response of an older male to the stimulus afforded by a younger male . . . An Athenian aristocrat, he moved in a section of society which certainly regarded strong homosexual desire and emotion as normal . . . Plato's philosophical treatment of homosexual love may have been an outcome of this ambience. We must however leave open the possibility that his own homosexual emotion was abnormally intense. (12)

One rather doubts that Plato was at all unique except for his surpassing genius. The *Symposium* sets itself dramatically in 416 B.C.E., when Plato was only thirteen. If the actual drinking party (which is what symposium then meant) took place at that time, Socrates was fifty-three, and Alcibiades exercised considerable political power in Athens, in what would have been the fifteenth year of the Peloponnesian War. It is doubtful whether this particular drinking party actually occurred, though not impossible. The young tragedian Agathon gives the party to celebrate his victory, with his first play, at an Athenian festival. Present, besides Agathon and Socrates (much the oldest man there) is Aristophanes, superb playwright of farces, including *The Clouds,* an outrageous satire upon Socrates that had already been performed. There are four other speakers: Alcibiades, who arrives late, and Phaedrus, Pausanias, and Eryximachus. What matters most are three speeches—Aristophanes, Socrates, Alcibiades—though Agathon's discourse on love comes between those of Aristophanes and Socrates. Plato breaks the sequence, because there is no continuity between the visions of Aristophanes and Socrates, while Alcibiades is the appropriate coda to the entire work, since he centers upon the enigma of Socrates himself.

Famously, Aristophanes argues that love is the desire and pursuit of the whole, that itself being a grotesque creature with two heads, four arms, and four legs. Desperate fragments, we dart about looking for our original other half. Zeus, as punishment, sundered us, and we long to become "circle-people" again. Perhaps Plato, by this brilliant invention, paid Aristophanes back for *The Clouds*, but he clearly also satirizes heterosexual love and its so-cial resolution, marriage. And yet Plato has given Aristophanes the most memorable myth in the *Symposium*.

Socrates uncharacteristically resorts to a mentor: the wise woman Dio-tima, a supposed priestess but almost certainly Plato's fiction. She refutes Aristophanes (he wants to protest, but just then the intoxicated Alcibiades bursts in upon the party) by shrewdly observing that love is neither of a half or of a whole, but only of the Good. The beauty of a particular boy ulti-mately leads the lover to a ladder that must be climbed. Since love turns out to be another name for philosophy, particular objects—one boy or an-other—are left on the lower rungs, and the authentic quester ascends to revelation, to the astounding Beauty that is also the Good. All this, made so familiar to us by Platonism, Neoplatonism, and Christian Platonism, is Plato's own originality, the signature of his genius, and is not at all likely to have been formulated by the historical Socrates. Literary originality is so as-tonishing here that I am inclined to interpret it as Plato's triumphal reply to Homer and the Athenian tragic dramatists, for nothing in their vision of Eros ever anticipated this, which seems to me Plato's largest *literary* tri-umph in his endless contest with Homer. There is an ecstasy of unprece-dentedness in Diotima's doctrine, in which love is transformed into the ambition to bring forth Beauty *as its child*. Philosophy overcomes poetry, fa-thers and mothers it (as it were), and achieves the immortality of the soul by beholding at last, not poetry or Beauty, but the Form of the Beautiful. An educational justification for pederasty has transcended itself into the ago-nistic victory of Philosophy over all competitors, whatever the human cost may be.

Socrates speaks of his daemon, but the Plato who composed the *Sympo-sium* seems to me even more daemonic, not a genius of personality like Socrates, but a new kind of poet, ancestor of Dante and of John Milton, and of all Romanticism after them, including W. B. Yeats, Wallace Stevens, and Hart Crane in the twentieth century. And yet Plato, faithful to the Socrates who had fathered him as philosopher, does not conclude the *Symposium* with his own triumphalism. Alcibiades, in a marvelous comic entrance, returns us unforgettably to the paradox of Socrates.

Socrates, Alcibiades says, is a Silenus, or a statue thereof: grotesque out-side, but replete with beautiful images of the divine within. Silenus, dae-monic associate of the mime-god Dionysus, is beyond the human, and by implication, so is Socrates, the first true philosopher. However, Socrates ironically only pretends to be in love, with Alcibiades or with other beauti-ful young men. Instead, he is the object of *their* desire, since finally they behold in him the form of the Good. This is the perfection of the Socratic paradox. He incarnates the ideal: to love him is to love wisdom, and thus to learn how to philosophize. As a reader, this makes me personally unhappy, because I do not believe Plato, but aesthetically I yield to this completely, because the genius of Plato overwhelmingly has asserted itself in the hopeless confrontation with Homer.

SAINT PAUL

Now if Christ is preached as raised from the dead, how can some of you say that there is no resurrection of the dead? But if there is no resurrection of the dead, then Christ has not been raised; if Christ has not been raised, then our preaching is in vain and your faith is in vain. We are even found to be misrepresenting God, because we testified of God that he raised Christ, whom he did not raise if it is true that the dead are not raised. For if the dead are not raised, then Christ has not been raised. If Christ has not been raised, your faith is futile and you are still in your sins. Then those also who have fallen asleep in Christ have perished. If for this life only we have hoped in Christ, we are of all men most to be pitied.

But in fact Christ has been raised from the dead, the first fruits of those who have fallen asleep. For as by a man came death, by a man has come also the resurrection of the dead. For as in Adam all die, so also in

Christ shall all be made alive. But each in his own order: Christ the first fruits, then at his coming those who belong to Christ. Then comes the end, when he delivers the kingdom to God the Father after destroying every rule and every authority and power. For he must reign until he has put all his enemies under his feet. The last enemy to be destroyed is death. "For God has put all things in subjection under his feet." But when it says, "All things are put in subjection under him," it is plain that he is excepted who put all things under him. When all things are subjected to him, then the Son himself will also be subjected to him who put all things under him, that God may be everything to every one.

—I Corinthians 15: 12–28

Perhaps all literary and rhetorical genius is enigmatic, but of the hundred figures I comment upon, Saint Paul seems to me the greatest enigma. He addresses the Corinthians not as unbelievers, but as "spirituals," men and women who believe they already *are* resurrected, without the necessity of dying. Perhaps they were precursors of the later Gnostic "heretics" who said of Jesus, "*First* he was resurrected, and *then* he died." Wayne Meeks, an authority on Paul, notes how comparatively gentle the Apostle is with the Corinthians (unlike his thunderings against the Galatians). It may be that Saint Paul saw certain of his own tendencies in the Corinthians, and so argues more urgently, since in a way he argues with himself.

Paul's literary genius is beyond doubt: "The last enemy to be destroyed is death." And yet Paul, a Hellenistic Jew, conceived of the Covenant as the Septuagint, the Alexandrian Greek translation of the Hebrew Bible, called it: *diatheke*, God's testament in grace, an expression of his will, and not as the Hebrew *berith*, a reciprocal covenant. Paul's strong misreading of Judaism is very difficult for me to accept because it is Hellenistic Christianity rather than the Jewish Christianity of James the Just, the brother of Jesus.

Still, it is good to have Wayne Meeks absolve the genius of Paul from the American evangelicism that is carried on in the Apostle's name:

Paul was not a Lutheran pietist nor an American revivalist. Paul did not reduce the gospel to the forgiveness of sins, let alone to the assuaging of guilt feelings.

The genius of Paul, as Meeks says, was protean. As soon as you think you have grasped hold of Paul, he changes shape. He was not "the second Founder of Christianity," but the first, and he had learned "to be all things to all men."

SAINT PAUL
(?–67)

VERY FEW READERS WOULD BE UNTROUBLED by the phrase "the genius of Jesus," though I mean something by it akin to Plutarch's "the *daimon* of Socrates." Quests for the historical Jesus tend to become scholarly quest-romances, spiritual journeys in which scholars find what they want to find. There was an historical Jesus, but we know virtually nothing about him. The only source we more or less can trust is the Jewish historian Josephus, from whom we can glean a few facts: Joshua, the son of Joseph and Miriam, became a disciple of John the Baptist, a charismatic reformer of spirituality. This Joshua (Jeshua in Hebrew, Jesus in Latin) in turn developed into a charismatic wisdom teacher, followed by a number of Jews, but he was then crucified by the Romans, after evidently provoking at least some religious authorities among the Jews. The principal legatee of Jesus, again according to Josephus, was his brother James the Just, who headed the Jerusalem Community that still followed Jesus. James was stoned to death, by order of the high priest of Jerusalem, a few years before the Roman destruction of the Jerusalem Temple in 70 C.E. Since the New Testament is a polemic, rather than a history, everything we are told there is persuasive to the persuaded: it is faith, argument, myth, vision—call it what you will.

There are also the sayings of Jesus, not all of them reported in the New Testament. Here we have no factual basis for accepting some sayings as authentic, while rejecting others. The only criteria for judgment seem to me literary taste and spiritual discernment, and both of these are notoriously disputable. Since many hundreds of millions, throughout the world, accept the divinity of Jesus, it seems to me something of a scandal that we have so little indisputable information about him. Did he speak Aramaic or Greek, or perhaps both? Can he be located accurately in the maelstrom of Jewish beliefs in his own day? Hillel, some of whose sayings are akin to some of Jesus', was a Pharisee, and so a likely ancestor of what we now call rabbinical Judaism. Was Jesus a Pharisee, despite the New Testament's slanders against the Pharisees? The question may be meaningless, because we have about as little factual information about Hillel as we do about Jesus. I remember declining to review Norman Mailer's *Gospel According to the Son* because it was a self-portrait of Mailer, but every book about Jesus, whether or not it purports to be fiction, always turns out to be autobiographical, particularly in regard to the question of faith.

Jesus, though evidently highly literate, wrote nothing, just as Socrates and (probably) Confucius wrote nothing. All three spoke primarily to disciples, knowing that their wisdom would be transmitted, both orally and in writing. We have no way of judging the accuracy of either mode of transmission, in any of these three instances. Irony, which says one thing but means another, necessarily is an indirect mode of communication, and both Jesus and Socrates palpably spoke as ironists. So did Confucius, so far as I can tell. But the ironies of Jesus are more troublesome, since of these three wisdom teachers he alone has been divinized.

Socrates does not speak in the name of a forerunner, unlike Confucius, who exalts the Duke of Chou. What precisely was the relationship of Jesus to John the Baptist? Surely it ought to be more of an embarrassment than it is, for those who insist upon the divinity of Jesus? Should God be baptized by a man? The New Testament writers nervously portray the Baptist as proclaiming his own secondariness in relation to Jesus, but that seems unconvincing. Did Jesus' discipleship to John end with immersion in the Jordan? And why was the baptism necessary, for the incarnate God? Presumably, Jesus' start as John's follower was too well known to be omitted from the Christ-story, just as the Redactor in Babylon had to include Yahweh's shocking attempt to murder Moses, because it too was notorious.

What doctrine, if any, did John teach Jesus? In what sense, again if any, was the baptism of Jesus a kind of conversion? And, if so, from what to what? You can peruse theologians and religious historians extensively, and still find almost nothing to help answer these questions. The early Christians are evasive as to the relation between John and Jesus. In the Gospel of John, the baptism of Jesus goes unnoticed, while the synoptic Gospels are equivocal; in Matthew, John says that Jesus should baptize *him*, and in Luke, Jesus is baptized by a person unknown, since John is already in prison.

Scholars, particularly recently, have tried to envision the orientation of Jesus in regard to first-century Judaistic sects, but their speculations again do not persuade. Something is always missing. Perhaps one should begin further back. Was John the Baptist a sect of one? Did it become two, with Jesus? Clearly not, since John was enough of an unrest-inducer to warrant his execution. But also, John evidently had several disciples, including Jesus (if the reader can forgive that) and the enigmatic Simon Magus, regarded (rather improbably) by Christian tradition as the founder of the Gnostic "heresy."

It depends upon which modern, scholarly authority you decide to trust. John P. Meier, an eminently fair-minded, Roman Catholic rethinker of the historical Jesus, entitles his study *A Marginal Jew*, and concludes that the followers of the Baptist and of Jesus were also marginal. Quite another view is presented by Robert Eisenman, whose fiercely polemical *James the Brother of Jesus* places John the Baptist, Jesus, and James the Just (admirable cognomen!) all together at the heroic center of mass Jewish resistance to the Roman oppressors. Confronted by the rival assertions of questing scholars, the inquiring reader should turn back to Josephus as our only valid historical witness (though the texts of Josephus were worked over by pious Christian exegetes) and most crucially to the sayings of Jesus (if indeed they are his).

At this point I think that I should observe, with diffidence, that God and the gods necessarily are literary characters. Religious believers, scholarly and otherwise, generally react pugnaciously to such an observation, so I hope to be very clear as to what I am saying. The Jesus of the New Testament is a literary character, just as are the Yahweh of the Hebrew Bible and the Allah of the Koran. But then, Socrates and Confucius were not gods, and they also—*as we know them*—are literary characters, though no one need doubt their historical existence. The historical Jesus is something of a phantom, since the Jewish historian Josephus, though gifted with a huge memory, was a Quisling who had sold himself to the Romans, and lied and distorted freely, generally in his own interest.

Knowing Jesus through his purported sayings is closely akin to knowing Confucius through the *Analects* or Socrates through Plato and Xenophon. What we hear, or try to hear, has been mediated by disciples. The author of the Gospel of Mark, a powerful writer, pragmatically created Jesus for most people, believers and unbelievers alike. In the same way, the earliest prime biblical writer, the Yahwist, gave us the literary character Yahweh, who is worshipped as God by normative Jews, Christians, and Muslims. Again, I speak only pragmatically, though it is unnerving to be told that one believes in a literary character. I offer the idea of "genius" as a saving way out of this impasse. One can speak of the genius of Hamlet, or of Milton's Satan, quite apart from the genius of Shakespeare or of John Milton. To speak of the genius of Jesus is to speak of the sayings attributed to him, and some of these authentically manifest an authority, memorability, and individuality that are marks of genius. I turn to them now, questing for the voice of genius, and setting aside all debate as to the historically authentic Jesus.

*   *   *

So as to avoid all churches and their polemics, I will quote Jesus' aphorisms from *The Logia of Jeshua*, translated by Guy Davenport and Benjamin Urrutia (Counterpoint, Washington, D.C., 1996), a little volume blessedly free of theological tendentiousness.

> Our father's kingdom is not going to come with people watching for it. No one is going to be able to say, *Look, here!* or, *Over there!* For the kingdom is inside you, waiting for you to find it.

The kingdom of God is then an undiscovered tract of the inward self, and cannot be located in time or space. But what of those for whom the self is only an abyss?

> Whoever has will be given more, whoever has nothing, it will be taken away. This world is a bridge. Do not build your house on it. Be a traveler passing through.

If we are passersby (like Walt Whitman), then we will find the kingdom inside us. Finding him, Jesus avers, is hardly a problem:

> Look, I'm always with you, until the end of time. Lift up a stone, you'll find me there; split wood, I'm there.

John P. Meier, being a learned Catholic priest, would not accept this last aphorism as having any relation to the historical Jesus, because it is from the second-century C.E. quasi-Gnostic Gospel of Thomas. But, as he knows, this saying may be much older than that, and no one has isolated an historical Jesus anyway. What scholars call Christian Gnosticism frequently strikes me as a belated version of the aphoristic Jesus. The Gospel of Thomas presents Jesus as exalting only two figures: John the Baptist and James the Just. We know more about the historical James the Just, "the brother of Jesus," than we do about Jesus; of John the Baptist we know almost as little as we do of Jesus. Yet informed surmise about the Baptist is certainly possible, and it makes me wonder what doctrine (if any) Jesus entertained when he began as his cousin John's disciple. John the Baptist had other disciples, including Simon Magus, the villain of so many Christian texts, and the ultimate source of the Faust legend. Simon and other early Gnostics presumably learned their way of knowing from the Baptist, who baptized Jews and Samaritans alike. There are still a few Samaritans in

Israel/Palestine, and still a few Mandaeans or Gnostics in Iraq, who like the Samaritans accept John the Baptist as one of their prophets.

Prophet of what? Of Jesus, the church replies, but clearly the Baptist's role—shall we not say his genius?—was larger. The Koran fuses John and Jesus, probably because Muhammad found in the Ebionites or later followers of James the Just the forerunners of his own revelation. We could term John the Baptist the first Ebionite, *before Jesus,* but we have no clear information as to the origins of the Ebionites (the name means "poor men"). We do have Josephus' testimony that John the Baptist, in the '20s before the common era, was a charismatic preacher of righteousness, whose large following frightened Herod Antipas into executing John. Josephus manifested a certain anxiety in writing about John; the Baptist's context, in the Transjordan, is omitted. John had stationed himself not in the Holy Land but in the Wilderness, a new Elijah and perhaps a new Moses. I suspect that John prophesied not his follower Jesus, but Yahweh, who would cross the Jordan to expel the Romans, but only if the Jews had again chosen righteousness, and purified themselves of sin. And I wonder if there was not also a more esoteric element in the Baptist's vision.

Heresiologists in the early Christian centuries insisted that Simon Magus had asserted divinity for himself, but that may be as much a falsification as their naming "simony" after the Baptist's most prominent Samaritan disciple. Simony is still defined by our dictionaries as the buying or selling of spiritual powers, so that the debasement of Simon the Gnostic in the New Testament (Acts 8:9–24) is now embedded in our culture, but then so is the anti-Semitic vilification of the quite mythical Judas Iscariot, where Judas (Judah) quite simply means "the Jew," while Iscariot is a cognomen upon which there is no agreement, though I guess that it is related to the *Sicarii* of Josephus, the Zealots or Jews who most fiercely opposed Rome, and who made their last stand at Masada.

Historians of Gnosticism lament the difficulty of questing for the historical Simon Magus, but this does not move me, since all we know of the historical Jesus (as I have said) is that he was associated with John the Baptist and James the Just, and that he was crucified by the Romans. Paul, who was the earliest New Testament author, had virtually no interest in the historical Jesus, probably because those who had known Jesus were almost all opponents of Paul. The historical Simon Magus has much the same relation to the legendary Faust that the historical Jesus has to Paul's (and Christianity's) Jesus Christ. Christian legend tells that Simon came to Rome, where he took the cognomen of Faustus ("the favored one") and perished there in a rather unlikely levitation attempt. Simonianism lasted for about two generations, and then merged into a larger heterodox Gnosticism, which had its apogee in the second century.

However Simon died, his association with John the Baptist suggests that, like other Samaritan disciples, he had absorbed esoteric knowledge from the Baptist. Was Jesus, another disciple of John, likelier in his vision to resemble Paul, who never knew him, or James the Just, who with Jesus' other disciples formed the Jerusalem Church? That congregation fled to Pella, in Transjordan, after the murder of James and before the destruction of the Temple by the Romans in 70 C.E. The Ebionites, a generation or two later, were descended from the original group around Jesus and James, and the Ebionites lasted until destroyed by Pauline orthodoxy.

Since Simon Magus has left us no sayings and no writings, and we know of him only through his Christian enemies, we have only his legend by which to judge him. And yet the Faust story is so extraordinary that its first incarnation hardly seems obscure. Simon Magus shimmers luridly through the centuries, as a figure of bravura and outrageousness, dramatically given to audacious symbolic acts. John the Baptist, according to a tradition still alive today among the Shiites of Iran, taught a doctrine of "the Standing One," a Primal Adam who never fell. John, a new Elijah, proclaimed the return of the true Adam. The relation of Jesus to that proclamation, whatever Jesus felt it to be, was altered forever by Paul. Simon, though, identified himself directly with the great Power of the Primal Adam, and seems to have been followed by many of the Samaritans. If Simon was a magician, then so was Jesus, since as healers both were open to charges of sorcery. Like the Baptist, Jesus evidently was celibate, but the flamboyant Simon certainly was not. He took as mistress a certain Helena, a prostitute from Tyre, and announced that she was at once the reincarnation of the Homeric Helen of Troy, and the fallen First Thought (Ennoià) of God whom he, Simon, was called to raise up. This Faustian invention is the undying aspect of Simon's legend, and as an imaginative act continues to trouble the Western imagination.

Jesus, in his sayings and in his symbolic acts, was the greatest of all ironists. Simon Magus may have intended some irony by taking up with Helena of Tyre, but since we have no record of Simon's mode of speech, we cannot know. And yet Jesus, though celibate, had his Helena in Mary Magdalena, another repentant whore. The legend of Jesus is the most powerful the West has known, transcending the myths of Homer, the Hebrew Bible, and the Koran. And, despite the long history of Christianity, in all its varied components, the legend founds itself upon a voice:

I have lit a fire on the earth and shall watch over it until it blazes.

Jesus could not have anticipated Paul, who began as the Pharisaic Jew Saul of Tarsus, converted after a vision, and subsequently swept aside the gnosis of Jesus' own family and circle, and proceeded to invent both Jesus Christ and Christianity. Though Jesus *had* lit a fire on the earth, it was Paul who caused it to blaze. "The genius of Paul" is a time-worn but accurate phrase; without Paul, what is now called "Christianity" would not have triumphed, first in the Roman Empire, and then in the realms that came after it. In First Corinthians (9:19–23) he famously proclaimed, "I have become all things to all men." To his early Jewish-Christian opponents, followers of James the Just, Paul was the Enemy, an incarnation of Satan. From the perspective of the Jerusalem Jesus-sect, what else could Saul of Tarsus/Paul the Apostle seem? As a Pharisee, he had led violence, in the Temple, against James himself, and after converting to Christ (rather than to the historical Jesus) Paul continued to quarrel with the family and close associates of Jesus.

Very few accounts of Paul discuss the violent elements in his extraordinary personality. Even Wayne Meeks, Paul's fairest-minded scholar, who shrewdly names Paul "the Christian Proteus," avoids going into the ferocity of the Apostle's nature. Friedrich Nietzsche, most acute of moral psychologists, in 1880 expounded Paul's persecuting drive:

The man suffered from a fixed idea, or rather a fixed question, an ever-present and ever-burning question: what was the *meaning* of the Jewish Law? and, more especially, *the fulfillment of this Law?* In his youth he had done his best to satisfy it, thirsting as he did for the highest distinction which the Jew could imagine—this people, which raised the imagination of moral loftiness to a greater elevation than any other people, and which alone succeeded in uniting the conception of a holy God with the idea of sin considered as an offence against this holiness. St. Paul became at once the fanatic defender and guard-of-honor of this God and His Law. Ceaselessly battling against and lying in wait for all transgressors of this Law and those who presumed to doubt it, he was pitiless and cruel towards all evildoers, whom he would have punished in the most rigorous fashion possible.

Now, however, he was aware in his own person of the fact that such a man as himself—violent, sensual, melancholy, and malicious in his hatred—*could* not fulfil the Law; and furthermore, what seemed strangest of all to him, he saw that his boundless craving for power was continually provoked to break it, and that he could not help yielding to this impulse. Was it really "the flesh" which made him a trespasser time and again? Was it rather, as it afterwards occurred to him, the Law itself, which continually showed itself to be impossible to fulfil, and seduced men into transgression with an irresistible charm? But at that time he had not thought of this means of escape. As he suggests here and there, he had many things on his conscience—hatred, murder, sorcery, idolatry, debauchery, drunkenness, and orgiastic revelry—and to however great an extent he tried to soothe his conscience, and, even more, his desire for power, by the extreme fanaticism of his worship for and defence of the Law, there were times when the thought struck him: "It is all in vain! The anguish of the unfulfilled Law cannot be overcome." Luther must have experienced similar feelings, when, in his cloister, he endeavoured to become the ideal man of his imagination; and, as Luther one day began to hate the ecclesiastical ideal, and the Pope, and the saints, and the whole clergy, with a hatred which was all the more deadly as he could not avow it even to himself, an analogous feeling took possession of St. Paul. The Law was the Cross on which he felt himself crucified. How he hated it! What a grudge he owed it! How he began to look round on all sides to find a means for its total annihilation, that he might no longer be obliged to fulfil it himself! And at last a liberating thought, together with a vision—which was only to be expected in the case of an epileptic like himself—flashed into his mind: to him, the stern upholder of the Law—who, in his innermost heart, was tired to death of it—there appeared on the lonely path that Christ, with the divine effulgence on His countenance, and Paul heard the words: "Why persecutest thou Me?"

—"The Dawn of Day"
(translated by J. M. Kennedy)

The association of Paul with Luther is precise, though Luther's vicious anti-Semitism took him further, into the proclamation, "death to the Law!" Still, the affinity of Luther with Paul certainly was temperamental as well as theological, and Nietzsche cannot be bettered in his characterization of Paul: "violent, sensual, melancholy, and malicious in his hatred." Eight years later, in *The Antichrist*, Nietzsche adumbrated his understanding of Paul:

Paul is the incarnation of a type which is the reverse of that of the Saviour; he is the genius in hatred, in the standpoint of hatred, and in the relentless logic of hatred. And alas what did this dysangelist not sacrifice to his hatred? Above all the Saviour himself; he nailed him to *his* cross.

To be "the genius of hatred" was the role also assigned to Paul by George Bernard Shaw, whose attack upon Paul nevertheless again emphasizes the Apostle's genius:

> He is no more a Christian than Jesus was a Baptist; he is a disciple of Jesus only as Jesus was a disciple of John. He does nothing that Jesus would have done, and says nothing that Jesus would have said.

Even those who hold that Nietzsche and Shaw go too far would have to admit that Paul is totally unconcerned with the merely historical Jesus, but only with Jesus as the Christ. Paul seems to assume that he himself is the Jesus to the Gentiles, as it were, and so a figure who possesses absolute authority. Donald Harman Akenson suggests that Paul takes it for granted that the audience for his epistles knows quite enough about the life of Jesus the man, so that the details of the life and death are not necessary. This has to confuse us now, because Paul's authentic epistles are much the earliest texts in the New Testament, and probably were composed between 49 and 64 C.E. The synoptic Gospels generally are believed to have been written from 70 to 85 C.E., while the Gospel of John *may* be as late as 95 C.E. That means that Paul was executed by the Romans before the destruction of the Temple in 70 C.E., hardly a catastrophe he would have ignored.

Luther, who idealized Paul, in his lectures on Paul's Epistle to the Galatians attacks the Jewish Christians as saying:

> "Who is Paul anyway? After all, was he not the very last of those who were converted to Christ? But we are the pupils of the apostles, and we knew them intimately. We saw Christ perform miracles and we have heard Him preach. But Paul is a latecomer and is our inferior."

Galatians seems to me a very angry epistle indeed, and I think Luther's hint as to the source of Paul's fury is accurate: the apostle Paul would not accept the idea that he was a latecomer. And yet, in relation to the Jerusalem Christians, he *was* a latecomer; unlike them, he had arrived long after the events of Jesus' life and death. Søren Kierkegaard, the nineteenth-century Danish religious philosopher whom I will discuss later in this book, wrote a brilliant pair of essays in his *Philosophical Fragments* (1844): "The God as Teacher and Savior" and "The Case of the Contemporary Disciple." Christ, unlike Socrates, understands himself without the need of disciples, who are there only to receive incommensurable love. A contemporary disciple of God "was not contemporary with the splendor, neither hearing nor seeing anything of it." The ironist Kierkegaard is consonant with the polemicist Paul: neither allows the disciple any immediacy with God. The Jewish Christians of Jerusalem, including even James the Just, neither heard nor saw the great light that burst upon Paul on the road to Damascus.

Where precisely should we locate Paul's genius, setting aside whether we choose to honor or deplore him? Wayne Meeks emphasizes that "Hellenistic Christianity" preceded Paul, since Paul was converted to it. Yet Paul, even if he did not invent a non-Jewish Christianity, captured its images and doctrines forever. Pragmatically Paul's argument became what could be called "Not Jesus but Christ." Paul's genius was his powerful originality as a misreader of the Jewish Covenant with Yahweh, which ceased to be a mutual agreement and became an unilateral expression of the will of God.

It is easy for many Americans to mistake Paul as a revivalist, whose total emphasis is upon rebirth through the forgiveness of sin. That is a weak misreading of Paul, who was more than an apostle of grace. The former Pharisee was a great inventor who transformed Hellenistic Christianity into a new kind of world religion. His nearest equivalent is Muhammad, who founded the next universal religion, and evidently had never heard of Paul, nowhere mentioned in the Koran. A genius for universalism may be the rarest of gifts in Western religion: Paul and Muhammad, otherwise so different, are the largest instances of it that we know.

And yet between Jesus and Paul's Christianity there came a generation of silence. Fresh scrolls have not yet been found to fill *that* silence. Perhaps they never will be found. The General Epistle of James, which Luther wished to expunge from the New Testament, not only insists that "faith, if it have not works, is dead, being alone," but also renews the prophecies of Jesus against the rich:

> Behold, the hire of the labourers who have reaped down your fields, which is of you kept back by fraud, crieth.

We do not speak of "Paul the Just," any more than we would associate his disciples, Augustine and Luther, with social justice. You can read and reread all the authentic epistles of Paul, and never know that Jesus, like Amos and the other prophets, and like William Blake in a later time, spoke for the poor, the ill, the outcast.

MUHAMMAD

Read in the name of your Lord who created,
2. Created man from an embryo:
3. Read
for your Lord is most beneficent,
4. Who taught by the pen,
5. Taught man what he did not know.
6. And yet,
but yet man is rebellious,
7. For he thinks he is sufficient in himself.
8. Surely your returning is to your Lord.

—sura 98, The Embryo

O you, enfolded in your mantle (of reform)
2. Arise and warn,
3. Glorifying your Lord,
4. Purify your inner self,
5. And banish all trepidation.

—sura 74, The Enfolded

—Koran
(translated by Ahmed Ali)

The historian F. E. Peters, a superb student of Islam, remarks that the Koran is a text without context. Therefore it inspires very diverse interpretations, even among those faithful to the Prophet. Islam remains uncertain as to which of the passages above was Muhammad's initial revelation. They are both impressive, being—like everything else in the Koran—direct utterances of God.

Muslims would consider it very odd to speak of the *genius* of the Prophet, but a religious or spiritual genius is hardly a category we should discard. Prophets—be they Isaiah, Muhammad, or Joseph Smith—are persons of enormous gifts, masters of language. There is a later Muslim tradition that Muhammad could not read nor write, but instead recited the Koran (it means "Recitation") in direct recollection of the voice of God, perhaps through the mediation of the Angel Gabriel. A successful merchant before his prophetic revelation, Muhammad presumably was not what we call "illiterate," and Muslim tradition seems primarily to be saying that the Prophet had not read the Hebrew Bible and the Greek New Testament.

Though necessarily Muhammad has literary debts to Jewish and Christian texts no longer extant, his shattering spiritual and imaginative originality cannot be doubted. No one else in human religious history has given us a text in which God alone is the speaker. Audacity, a crucial characteristic of Muhammad in every way, marks the Koran's achievement of a literary effect unlike any other. We can never relax as we read it, or when we recite it, alone or with others.

MUHAMMAD
(570?–632)

THE WESTERN WORLD SPIRITUALLY emerges from three sacred texts: the Hebrew Bible (or "Old Testament," from a Christian perspective), the Greek New Testament, and the Arabic al-Qur'an (less correctly, the Koran). Most of us have read, even studied, the first two, usually in English translation, but, rather shockingly, few have attempted to read the Koran. Some scholars, who ought to know better, still refer to the Koran as a barbarized version of the Jewish and Christian Scriptures. In a good translation, like that of Ahmed Ali (*Al-Qur'an*, Princeton University Press, 1988), which is the one I will cite here, the Koran is very much its own book, fit rival to the strong Scriptures that it knowingly comes after and strikingly reinterprets. Muhammad, the Messenger of God, "the Seal of the Prophets," was active in the seventh century of the common era, dying in 632 at the age of sixty-two. From his fortieth year on, he spoke with the voice of God, mediated to him by the Angel Gabriel. These utterances, memorized by his followers and then written down, became the Koran ("Recitation"); Muhammad supposedly could neither read nor write, and has to be regarded as one of the world's major prose poets in a strictly oral tradition. Islam ("submission" to God) is far more reliant upon the Koran than Christianity is upon the New Testament, or than Judaism truly is upon the Hebrew Bible. The Koran, unlike its parent Scriptures, seems to have no context. Scholars of Judaism and Christianity are able to historicize most (though not all) of the sacred texts, but the Koran (except for its "Jewish Christian" foreground) is an absolute origin in itself. Strangely as the other Scriptures are ordered, they seem models of coherence when first contrasted to the Koran. The Koran has one hundred and fourteen chapters or sections (called suras) which have no continuity with one another, and mostly possess no internal continuity either. Their length varies enormously, their order has no chronology, and indeed the only principle of organization appears to be that, except for the first sura, we descend downwards from the longest to the shortest. No other book seems so oddly and arbitrarily arranged as this one, which may be appropriate because the voice that speaks the Koran is God's alone, and who would dare to shape his utterances?

Overtly, the Koran is the record of Muhammad's prophetic utterances between the age of forty, when he received his call, and sixty-two, when he suddenly died. Perhaps twenty years after the Prophet's death, Uthman, third in line of Muhammad's caliphs, commanded that the Koran be assembled from all the available material, written and oral. There is not much reason to doubt the authenticity of the text, or its composition (for the most part) by Muhammad himself. The nearest American equivalent is the *Doctrines and Covenants* of the Mormon prophet, Joseph Smith, whose revelation had something of the same relation to Judaism and Christianity that Muhammad's vision had to its Jewish and Christian sources. Smith, though a religious genius, had nothing like Muhammad's rhetorical power, a strength of expression that more than survives the Koran's peculiar lack of organization. Sometimes I reflect that the baffling arrangement (or lack of it) of the Koran actually enhances Muhammad's eloquence; the eradication of context, narrative, and formal unity forces the reader to concentrate upon the immediate, overwhelming authority of *the voice,* which, however molded by the Messenger's lips, has a massive, persuasive authority to it, recalling but expanding upon the direct speeches of God in the Bible.

John Wansbrough, in his *Qur'anic Studies: Sources and Methods of Scriptural Interpretation* (Oxford, 1977), makes the important observation that Muhammad's original auditors seem to have had no difficulty in understanding his highly allusive references to biblical materials. Evidently, those who listened to the Prophet at Mecca and Medina, even when they were not Jews (or survivors of the anti-Pauline Jewish Christians?), had a considerable grasp of the biblical stories, frequently in later Jewish versions that we likely do not possess. The Arabs to whom Muhammad prophesied lived side by side with several tribes of Jews (or Judaized Arabs) and were also in contact with Christians, including monastics. Certainly the initial impression that reading the Koran now makes upon Jews and Christians alike is uncanniness: the concepts and stories at once are totally familiar and enormously strange. Islam ("submission" to Allah, the Biblical Elohim) may be the religion of Abraham, as it insists, and the faith of Jesus, as again it asserts, but "Abraham" here means the archaic Jewish religion according to Muhammad, and evidently the Jewish Christianity to which Saint Paul opposed himself, and which retreated across the Jordan and also into Arabia after the Roman destruction in 70 C.E., of the Jerusalem Jewish followers of Jesus, led by James the Just, his brother. Muhammad's Jesus is a man, not God, and does not die upon the cross; someone else dies in his place, as in certain Gnostic accounts, that themselves may go back to Jewish Christian origins.

* * *

Many of us are accustomed to reading "the Bible as literature," which is hardly acceptable to trusting Jews and believing Christians. Here I wish to introduce "the Koran as literature," which is even more unacceptable to faithful Muslims. Still, Muslims themselves speak of "the Glorious Koran" rather than "the Holy Koran," if only because the Koran is seen by them as being uncreated, since it is literally the Word of God. Eloquent as most of the Hebrew Bible is (I would not say that for Leviticus, or for parts of Numbers), and poignant as the Gospel of Mark certainly is, neither Scripture is as reliant upon the authority of God's own voice as the Koran must be. Evidently the rhymed prose of the Koran cannot be rendered properly into English, but there is still real literary power in several of the translations. A reader needs to persist, setting aside repetitions and obscurities, in order to begin hearing the voice that has converted and sustained hundreds of millions who have turned to or kept to Islam throughout the last thirteen centuries. The Koran must be a central book for us, because Islam increasingly will become an influence upon our lives, both abroad and here.

For me, the Koran has a particular fascination, because it is the largest instance I know of what, during the last quarter-century, I have been calling "the anxiety of influence." Strong prophet as Muhammad was, the Koran manifests an enormous (and overtly triumphal) struggle with the Torah and with rabbinical additions to the Five Books of Moses. "The People of the Book," throughout the Koran, refers both to Jews and to Christians, but there seems to have been only one Gospel for Muhammad, and it hardly can be identified with any Gospel we now possess. Jesus, for Muhammad, is another true prophet in the sequence that begins with Adam and that ends with Muhammad himself, yet Jesus is also something more than a prophet, if less than the Son of God. The Koran accepts the Virgin Birth, and regards Jesus as the legitimate Jewish Messiah, who is seen however as another reaffirmation of the religion of Abraham. The Koran's boldest stroke, in its contest with the Torah, is to insist that Abraham was neither Jew nor Christian, but the first instance of Islam, of submission to "the God," Allah. With this act of interpretation, Muhammad subsumes the sacred history of the Jewish people, and gives Ishmael, Arab son of Abraham, at least equal authority with Isaac and Jacob, both of whom are called sons of Abraham in the Koran. As reforming prophet, Muhammad's quest is to overcome both the paganism of his native city of Mecca, and what he sees as the backslidings from the pure faith of Abraham and Ishmael in the rabbinic Judaism of Arabia and the Christianity that followed Saint Paul rather than James the Just of Jerusalem.

This struggle to reclaim Abraham is the center and the majestic strength of the glorious Koran, which identifies spiritual authority with Abraham, and both with Muhammad. More even than the Hebrew Bible and the Greek New Testament, the Arabic Koran stresses authority as its governing principle. Some of the Bible and much of the New Testament is polemical, but *all* of the Koran is a fierce polemic: against the pagans of Mecca, the Jews of Medina, and whatever Christians of Arabia (there cannot have been many) who were not Ebionites or Jewish Christians. This polemical tone of the Koran hardly vitiates its power as prose poetry, but doubtless helps account for the initial impression of many non-Muslim readers that the book's spirituality is less profound than that of the Scriptures it seeks to emulate and overgo. Muhammad's recital is almost continually embattled, resembling in this rhetorical respect the tonalities of the Scrolls from the Dead Sea, where the Covenanters seem to be holding forth (and holding out) against the whole world. The Prophet of Islam may never wholly have gotten beyond his shock and fury that the Jews of Arabia should have refused to accept him as the apostle of God promised them by their own writings and oral traditions. Uncomfortable as Jews necessarily feel as they read the New Testament, the Gospel of John in particular, they frequently are made just as anxious by the Koran's accounts of what Muhammad regarded as Jewish hypocrisy and betrayal, in relation to his mission. His chagrin is quite understandable, since the Koran's vision of submission to God is, theologically speaking, far more a heresy from the perspective of Pauline Christianity than it is from that of the archaic Jewish religion. The Koran has little in common with the Talmud, but, as an interpretation of the Hebrew patriarchs and prophets, it seems to me highly persuasive.

Jesus as the incarnate Word replaced the Torah for Pauline Christianity; Muhammad voids that replacement, not by returning to Torah but by subsuming the Book within his own book. The Koran is neither quite a replacement for the Bible nor a commentary upon it, but rather a devotional recital that never ceases to refer or allude to the stories that are told of the prophets—Adam, Noah, Moses, Jesus—and of some of the patriarchs, kings, and high personages of the Jews, who are taken to belong just as much to the Arabs: Abraham, Joseph, David, and Solomon. Though the Jewish background is always there, nothing in the Koran is at all likely to remind non-Muslim readers of the earlier Book. For Muhammad, the Bible returns from the past bearing the colors, sounds, and meanings of his own revelation, his own creative misunderstanding of the revelations made to Adam and to Noah, to Moses and to Jesus. Part of this transmemberment is a broad movement from narrative to lyric. Everything becomes chant, the prose poems of the God, who glances at this earlier message only to embellish and repoint his definitive rhapsody.

"The people of the Koran," a great multitude compared to the survivors of "the people of the Book," have much the same relation to their Scripture that pious Jews have maintained to theirs. A vast ocean of commentary surrounds both sacred texts, which are treated as works of God and so as living beings. Prayer, and the Divine answer to prayer, move back and forth across both. Yet there is a crucial difference between Bible and Koran, which is that Muhammad himself is taken as the prime interpreter of the book that God, through Gabriel, dictated to him. Traditions of the Prophet and of his companions have a unique authority in determining what the Koran means. There are Judaic analogues to this, but even Moses does not occupy as solitary and crucial a position in Judaism as Muhammad does in Islam. It is therefore something of a puzzle for the non-Muslim reader that so little sense of Muhammad's individual personality is conveyed by the Koran, as opposed to the overwhelming sense of the God's nature and disposition. This is clearly appropriate, from the perspective of Islam, but it probably adds to the initial obstacles that an outsider needs to transcend.

John Wansbrough, in his *Qur'anic Studies,* classifies the imagery of the Koran in four principal groups: retribution, sign, exile, and covenant. Retribution, always the God's, concerns the fate of nations, cities, peoples who fail the God's test. The sign either manifests the God or authenticates the Prophet. Exile, the mark of the righteous Abraham, is repeated in Muhammad's Hegira or flight from Mecca to Medina, which marks the traditional onset of the Era of Islam. Covenant explicitly returns to the former prophets—Noah, Abraham, Moses, and Jesus—with a particular emphasis upon Moses, who seems more of an anxiety for Muhammad than are any of the others. All four imagistic groupings remain powerfully Hebraic, in any case, and the Koran, in my judgment, does not really make them altogether Muhammad's own. The Koran's literary originality clearly is not a matter of imagery or of persons, and resides elsewhere, primarily in the Prophet's absolute, uncompromising stance as the vessel for the voice of the God. Muhammad's shattering rhetorical power shows its exuberance by what can be termed the reinvention of the religion of Abraham, whatever that actually may have been. Weighed down by the immense burden of the voice of the God, the reader is more than persuaded that the covenantal signs of retribution and exile threaten him if submission to the God is not accepted:

In the name of Allah, most-benevolent, ever-merciful.
I call to Witness the Day of Resurrection,

And I call the reprehensive soul to witness:
Does man think
We shall not put his bones together?
Surely We are able to re-form even his finger-tips.
Yet man is sceptical
of what is right before him.
He asks: "When will the Day of Resurrection be?"
Yet when the eyes are dazzled,
The moon eclipsed,
And the sun and moon are conjoined,
That day will man say:
"Where can I find escape?"
Never so, for there will be no escape.
With your Lord alone
will be the retreat on that day.
Then man will be told
what he had sent ahead (of good)
and what he had left behind.

—sura 75:1–13
(translated by Ahmed Ali)

The harshness and directness of this may be unsurpassable, yet is not original in itself, since it follows biblical precedents. What is original is a certain truncation and obliqueness, clearly akin to Muhammad's characteristic allusive, elliptical way of handling his biblical antecedents. The polemical edge never abandons Muhammad's tone, which asserts and achieves authority by never allowing the reader to rest. Urgency is of course also a frequent mark of the rhetoric of the Hebrew Bible and of the New Testament, but rarely is the pace so relentless as it is throughout the Koran. Unbending spiritual authority, whatever its political implications, demands and receives in the Koran an answerable style which is very difficult to resist. Variety, a stylistic demand that we exercise almost everywhere else, has little justification when we are asked to withstand the voice of Allah.

Muhammad's struggle rarely involves any direct confrontation with the text of Torah or Gospel; perhaps he shied away from it, or more likely he just did not know it. He knew rabbinical traditions, oral and written, which were all he needed, or wanted, and these came to him, and left him, on the heights. The early Meccan suras, in particular, have a constant sublimity:

In the name of Allah, most benevolent, ever-merciful.

I call to witness the dawn
And the Ten Nights,
The multiple and the one,
The night as it advances,
Is there not an evidence in this
for those who have sense?
Have you not seen what your Lord
did to the 'Ad
Of Eram with lofty pillars
(erected as signposts in the desert),
The like of whom
were never created in the realm;
And with Thamud
who carved rocks in the valley;
And the mighty Pharaoh
Who terrorised the region,
And multiplied corruption.
So your Lord poured a scourge
of punishment over them.
Your Lord is certainly in wait.
As for man,
whenever his Lord tries him
in order to be gracious
and provide good things for him,
he says: "My Lord has been gracious to me."
But when He tries him by restraining his means,
he says: "My Lord despises me."

—sura 89:1–16

The Ten Nights are both the first and the last ten nights of the lunar months, and so are signs here both of the rising and the waning of everything sublunary, including the legendary gardens of the 'Ad of Eram, the earthquake-ruined lost city of Thamud, and the Pharaoh who defied Moses. The parallel waxing and waning of each human fortune is conveyed, grimly and with great rhetorical economy, in "Your Lord is certainly in wait." Like sura 75, which is also an early Meccan revelation, this chant represents what might be called the primal Muhammad, whose emphasis is upon the incommensurateness of Allah and his creatures. In his earliest declarations,

Muhammad returns to the paradoxes of the Yahwist or J writer, author of the first and most impressive strand of text in what we now call Genesis, Exodus, and Numbers. Allah, "the God," had long been the principal god of pagan Mecca before Muhammad, the only one not represented by an idol. F. E. Peters, in his *Muhammad and the Origins of Islam* (Albany, 1994, p. 107), surmises that this imagelessness of Allah testifies to the growing influence of Jews and Christians in Arabia, before Muhammad. But in the Ka'ba, the Meccan sanctuary reputedly built by Abraham and his son Ishmael, ancestor of the Arabs, the idols of other gods shared the domain of Allah. God's house at Mecca, though founded by Abraham on a visit to his son Ishmael, stood on a site first hallowed by Adam himself. The one stone house in ancient Mecca, the Ka'ba evidently contained pictures of Abraham and of Jesus, and so the pre-Islamic paganism of Mecca was already wildly eclectic, and a clear precursor of Islam, with its Jewish and Christian elements. Yet the Allah of Muhammad's earlier Meccan suras is already not the Allah of the Meccan pagans, but is the biblical God of Abraham, Noah, Moses, and Jesus, the Jewish Christian God who paradoxically is both wholly transcendent and wholly immanent.

Muhammad was a prophet and not a theologian, and while the Koran teaches us the personality and character of Allah, it does not deign to provide us with reasoned, descriptive accounts of the inner nature of the God. Though the two main (and warring) branches of Islam, Sunni and Shiah, both assert their Koranic orthodoxy, and regard the other as heresy, no non-Muslim reader could hope to decide which is truer to the Koran, Cairo or Teheran. Muhammad unconditionally declares that he is the seal of prophecy: "There shall be no further prophets," but Muslims, after him, of whatever mode, do not set up as prophets: their heresies (if they are such) are questions of interpretation, as they are in post-biblical Judaism or Christianity. Still, so stark is the Koran that classical Islamic interpretation is likely to strike us as being much further away from Muhammad's recitation than Jewish and Christian interpretation seem to be from the Bible. There is a rhetorical finality and completeness to the Koran, as well as an awesome apparent simplicity that at first makes the reader impatient of commentary. The Hebrew Bible, in whole as in part, is a very difficult text, and much in the New Testament is confused and contradictory, while the Koran somehow *appears* to be stunningly open and clarified, massively self-consistent, and extraordinarily coherent. Though this rhetorical effect doubtless is somewhat illusive, it is as much a characteristic of the Koran as is Muhammad's oblique, quasi-referential employment of biblical stories and episodes. Both the rugged *nakedness* (to call it that) of the Koran's vision, and

its revisionist return to an authentic religion of Abraham, are so absolute
that a non-Muslim reader is unlikely to associate Islamic theology, when encountered, with its Koranic origins.

In my own experience as a reader of literature, the Koran rarely makes a
biblical impression upon me, particularly of an aesthetic sort. Sometimes,
as I immerse myself in reading the Koran, I am reminded of William Blake
or of Walt Whitman; at other moments, I think of Dante, who would have
found the association blasphemous. Partly the analogues are suggested by
the personal authority of the seer's voice: Dante, Blake, and Whitman in his
most self-confident passages approximate a divine voice, which is what we
hear incessantly in the Koran. There is another part, having to do with the
Prophet's calling, which is an undersong throughout the Koran, and which
is more overt in Dante, Blake, and Whitman. The Koran is a vast, prophetic
prose poem, one that emphasizes the centrality and continuity of the
prophetic tradition. Allah's messenger, solitary at the onset of his mission,
speaks to and for a community of the faithful, and the burden of his
prophecy is both a renewal of tradition and a breakthrough into what will
come beyond tradition, which must mean beyond prophecy itself. Here, the
Koran is mysterious, and perhaps legitimates the Islamic mystics, the Sufis,
more than any of the Islamic theocrats, of whatever branch or nation. For
what is the Koran? It is anything but a closed book, even if it is the seal of
prophecy. As much as the Bible, or Dante, or even Shakespeare, the Koran
is the Book of Life, as vital as any person, whoever she or he is. Since the
God addresses all of us who will hear, it is a universal book, again as open
and generous as the greatest works of secular literature, as the masterworks
of Shakespeare and Cervantes. The Sufis found their center in sura 24:35,
a sublime passage on the God as light, and a paean to the persuasive universalism of the poet-prophet Muhammad:

> God is the light of the heavens and the earth.
> The semblance of His light is that of a niche
> in which is a lamp, the flame within a glass,
> the glass a glittering star as it were, lit with the oil
> of a blessed tree, the olive, neither of the East
> nor of the West, whose oil appears to light up
> even though fire touches it not,—light upon light.
> God guides to His light whom He will.
> So does God advance precepts of wisdom for men,
> for God has knowledge of every thing.

It is a perfect poem in itself, a miracle and yet natural, and in no way sectarian: "light upon light." The niche may be the heart of Muhammad, or finally any discerning heart: "God guides to His light whom He will." That blessed olive tree, neither of the East or of the West, is everywhere and nowhere, wherever and whenever a purified vision alights. Purely as a provocation to aesthetic apprehension, this celebrated rhapsody to light is comparable only to crucial theophanies in Dante and Blake, and to biblical and post-biblical apostrophes that invoke a liberating illumination. Not least, this rapture is an epitome of the Koran, another evidence of its authentic status as a central book for everyone.

LUSTRE 4

|

Dr. Samuel Johnson, James Boswell, Johann Wolfgang von Goethe, Sigmund Freud, Thomas Mann

|

With this second Lustre of wisdom writers I have experimented with dissolving boundaries, allowing these figures to flow into one another, so that even the five Frontispieces are gathered together. Though I do not repeat this procedure in the rest of the book (I would risk a kind of chaos), I deliberately retain it here, because Kabbalistically *Hokmah* is indivisible. Though Dr. Johnson and Boswell were Christian moralists (a touch outrageously, in Boswell) and Goethe, Freud, and Mann were secular, they flow into one another with compelling authority.

Freud would have resented my assertion that, like these other moralists, he relied upon demonstrating the use of literature for life. Yet Freud may be said to have misrepresented himself, both as scientist and as healer. An essay like "Mourning and Melancholia" is closer to Dr. Johnson and to Goethe than it is even to Charles Darwin. Thomas Mann, the novelist as wisdom writer, saw Freud accurately when he associated the Jewish sage with Goethe, wisest of all men of letters.

DR. SAMUEL JOHNSON

... since a genius, whatever it be, is like fire in the flint, only to be produced by collision with a proper subject, it is the business of every man to try whether his faculties may not happily cooperate with his desires, and since they whose proficiency he admires, knew their own force only by the event, he needs but engage in the same undertaking, with equal spirit, and may reasonably hope for equal success.

—Johnson, *The Rambler* No. 25

Samuel Johnson, still the greatest of all literary critics, ever, urges us to find our proper subject, which alone will cause our genius to fire forth. Writing to his biographer, Boswell, in 1763, he enlarged this principle of aesthetic and intellectual ambition:

There lurks, perhaps, in every known heart a desire of distinction which inclines every man first to hope, and then to believe, that Nature has given him something peculiar to himself. This vanity makes one mind nurse aversions and another actuate desires, till they rise by art much above their original state of power and as affectation, in time, improves to habit, they at last tyrannize over him who at first encouraged them for show.

The cost of the enlargement is the tyranny of vanity or the pathos of the failed writer. Genius is a perilous balance between strong emulation of grand forerunners, as Johnson followed Alexander Pope, and the self-deceptions of so many contemporaries included in Johnson's *Lives of the Poets*, because the booksellers (not Johnson) wanted them there. Now they constitute a sad litany of period pieces: Roscommon, Pomfret, Stepney, Sprat, Sheffield, Fenton, Yalden, Tickell, and many more—their name is legion. You can amuse yourself by picking up any anthology of our current poets and choosing your own Sprats and Yaldens, candidates for the iniquity of oblivion.

JAMES BOSWELL

During all this conversation I really behaved with a manly composure and polite dignity that could not fail to inspire an awe, and she was pale as ashes and trembled and faltered. Thrice did she insist on my staying a little longer, as it was probably the last time that I should be with her. She could say nothing to the purpose. And I sat silent. As I was going, said she, "I hope, Sir, you will give me leave to inquire after your health." "Madam," said I, archly, "I fancy it will be needless for some weeks." She again renewed her request. But unwilling to be plagued any more with her, I put her off by saying I might perhaps go to the country, and left her. I was really confounded at her behaviour. There is scarcely a possibility that she could be innocent of the crime of horrid imposition. And yet her positive asseverations really stunned me. She is in all probability a most consummate dissembling whore.

Thus ended my intrigue with the fair Louisa, which I flattered myself so much with, and from which I expected at least a winter's safe copulation. It is indeed very hard. I cannot say, like young fellows who get themselves clapped in a bawdy-house, that I will take better care again. For I really did take care. However, since I am fairly trapped, let me make the best of it. I have not got it from imprudence. It is merely the chance of war.

—The London Journal

James Boswell thus takes leave of his fair Louisa, from whom he had "expected at least a winter's safe copulation." He commends himself for his composure and politeness, and enjoys his display of dignity. We do not have Louisa's account of their farewell, but one can doubt she would have manifested "awe" at Boswell's bearing. Boswell's comic genius anticipates our doubt; he speaks to "a most consummate dissembling whore" with the same dramatizing self-consciousness that he displayed with Dr. Johnson, Voltaire, and Rousseau.

Boswell is the master of the irony of retrospect: instead of murmuring, "I wish I had said that," he proceeds to speak his afterthought as though it has been spontaneous, while subtly acknowledging to the reader that all is reconstructed, including the personality and character of James Boswell.

The *Life of Johnson* is a careful miracle, subtly balancing the formidable Johnson with his biographer's shrewd provocations and stage-management. Still, there are limits to Boswell's opportunism; Boswell is not Shakespeare, and Dr. Johnson is not Sir John Falstaff, a triumph of dramatic imagination. Throughout, Boswell respects and loves the reality of his subject, though certainly he endows the great critic with many Shakespearean touches.

JOHANN WOLFGANG VON GOETHE

To see such life, such glad activity!
To stand with free men upon ground that's free!
Then, then, I might say to the passing moment,
"Linger awhile, you are so fair!
The footprints of my earthly passage cannot
Even after eons disappear."
Foreseeing such scenes of unmatched contentment,
I now enjoy the highest, supreme moment.
[*Faust collapses; the Lemurs catch him and lay him on the ground.*]
—*Faust*, Part Two, act 5, 7122–28
(translated by Martin Greenberg)

More than Goethe's Faust dies here: the entire Western literary tradition from Homer through Dante on to Shakespeare and Goethe attains its conclusion. After Faust's demise, we undergo a post-Enlightenment cavalcade that has several names—Romanticism, Modernism, Postmodernism—but is truly a single phenomenon. Perhaps only now, in a new millennium, can we detect signs of that phenomenon waning. An age of religious warfare, already upon us, is likely to foster a new Theocratic Era, as Giambattista Vico prophesied. What will happen to Western secular literature in such a time is very unclear.

Goethe is the final sage of the old Western secular culture, which can be called humanism, Enlightenment, or what you will. One of Goethe's most refreshing qualities is his irreverence: *Faust, Part Two* is a wonderfully outrageous work, whose primary purpose is to manifest Goethe's genius in its full range and complexity.

Goethe believed in his own daemons, who seem to have endowed him with occult energies, including parodistic appropriation of all his forerunners, from Homer on to Shakespeare's *Hamlet*. Wisdom, according to the later Goethe, consists in renunciation, since to act out all our desires is to court chaos.

And yet Goethe is equivocal in his renunciations, and it is difficult to reconcile his achieved wisdom with his sly outrageousness. Faust is buried in a parody of the graveyard scene in *Hamlet,* as if Goethe would steal some of Hamlet's charismas for his undramatic hero. Shakespeare, evidently a deliberately colorless person, would not have dreamed of competing with Hamlet, his most brilliant and enigmatic creation. Goethe far outshines his Faust, who is allowed no participation in the exemplary genius of his creator.

SIGMUND FREUD

One day the brothers who had been driven out came together, killed and devoured their father and so made an end to the patriarchal horde ... The violent primal father had doubtless been the feared and envied model of each one of the company of brothers: and in the act of devouring him they accomplished their identification with him, and each one of them acquired a portion of his strength. The totem meal, which is perhaps mankind's earliest festival, would thus be a repetition and a commemoration of this memorable and criminal deed, which was the beginning of so many things—of social organization, of moral restrictions and of religion.

Freud was a great mythmaker, never more than in *Totem and Taboo* (1913). And yet I think it an error to distinguish between Freud's "cultural" and his "scientistic" writings. He himself would have been pained by his current reputation, because he firmly believed that his psychoanalysis was a science that eventually would be seen as a contribution to biology. Since it is no such thing, Freud's enemies now once again dismiss him as a charlatan, which is absurd. The practice of psychoanalysis always has been a shamanism, dependent upon the more-or-less occult transference between analyst and patient. But that Freud was archaic from the start, though no more a charlatan than the Socrates of Plato's *Symposium*.

The permanent Freud is the great moral essayist, a writer comparable to Montaigne. The literature of the century now departed had, as its greatest figures, Proust, Joyce, Kafka, and Freud, aside from the major poets contemporary with them. Just as Montaigne is the peer of Cervantes and Shakespeare, so Freud is of the visionary company of Joyce and Proust. Montaigne and Freud marvelously adumbrate the autobiographical fictions of the self: each is his own great subject. Freud again would be unhappy with the comparison, because he sought an authority that would be more than personal. And yet his most useful lesson to us, quite unintended, well may be that only a personal authority still retains authenticity.

THOMAS MANN

Goethe knew that, loud or low, people would be saying "Ouf!" when he died. He felt himself a manifestation of that greatness which oppresses as much as it blesses the earth. He embodied this greatness in the mildest, most placable form which greatness can assume: that of a great poet. But even in such guise it is none too comfortable for contemporaries. Bewilderment and revulsion as well as love and amaze are its portion.

(translated by H. T. Lowe-Porter)

Mann, contemplating "Goethe's Career as a Man of Letters" in 1932, the year before Hitler took power, was still free to consider his forerunner as an aesthetic phenomenon. In 1938, Mann in exile lectured on Goethe's *Faust* at Princeton University, and concluded with a very different emphasis:

A "clear word" and a benevolent, pointing out the better course, seems powerless today; world events pass all such over with brutal disregard. But let us hold fast to the anti-diabolic faith, that mankind has after all a "keen learning," and that words born of one's own striving may do it good and not perish from its heart.

(translated by H. T. Lowe-Porter)

Two generations later, how relevant to us is the enlightened humanism of Goethe and of Mann? In the aftermath of September 11, 2001, there were bleatings of "no more irony," but these have vanished quickly. All is irony in the newest age of religious war and domesticated terror. Mann's emphasis, in 1938, was on the use of literature for life, and that use transcends the work of mourning. Goethe's greatness had much to do with the scale of his speculations, and with his emphasis upon the secular salvation that one's own intellectual striving could induce. Mann, following after, progressed from his ambivalence towards his precursor's genius, and a defensive irony in regard to Goethe, to an embattled sense of the work of humanism at ensuring the survival of value, at maintaining an "anti-diabolic" faith. I urge my students, and the readers who come to my public book presentations, to return to *The Magic Mountain* in this time of trouble. Mann's own genius is to teach "keen hearing," without which we will be more easily seduced by brutality.

SAMUEL JOHNSON, JAMES BOSWELL, JOHANN WOLFGANG VON GOETHE, SIGMUND FREUD, THOMAS MANN

I.

I tend to judge other literary critics partly by their relationship to Dr. Samuel Johnson (1709–1784), who seems to me the canonical critic or standard-setter. Since my method in this book is juxtaposition, I delight in bringing Johnson together here with the universal genius Johann Wolfgang von Goethe (1749–1832), Sigmund Freud (1856–1939), and Thomas Mann (1875–1955). When Johnson died Goethe was thirty-five. Johnson did not know of him, and I suspect he would have rejected Goethe, on moral and religious grounds. For Goethe, English literature meant Shakespeare and Lord Byron, not Johnson. In no real sense were these two geniuses contemporary with one another, though they flourished in the later eighteenth century.

Johnson can be read without regard to his superb biographer and close friend, the Scottish journalist James Boswell (1740–1795), but Boswell gives us another daemonic personality and original genius, to juxtapose with his moral guide, and also with Goethe, Mann, and Freud, all of them diverse authorities upon the melancholia that afflicted Johnson and Boswell alike. Boswell is otherwise odd man out in this chapter, though like Johnson he was a psychologist of genius, and his own authority upon melancholy. Yet Boswell, as a writer, can rival the four sages, formidably as they peal forth: Johnson, Goethe, Mann, and Freud. In calling Boswell a journalist, I intended the description in a double sense: one of the first foreign correspondents, and also the creator of an encyclopedic journal of the self and its vicissitudes. If you add to that Boswell's achievement as a still unmatched literary biographer, then he may seem less exposed in the luminous company of these four seers of our psychology.

Though we now have a fairly complete idea of Mann's life, we necessarily know far less about him than we do about Johnson, Boswell, Goethe, and Freud, since all but everything is known about them. Are they not indeed the four most documented lives of genius that we possess? Compared to these, we know nothing inward about the life of Shakespeare, and not much more about Dante or Cervantes. If we wish, we can absorb the inner selves of Johnson, Boswell, Goethe, and Freud as if they were characters in Shakespearean drama, akin to Falstaff, Prince Hal, Hamlet, and Macbeth. Just as Shakespeare's protagonists of genius seem always to have been there, so it can seem also that Johnson, Boswell, Goethe, and Freud have existed as personalities since time began. Even with Mann, we are given ample evidence of his consciousness of his own genius, a particular mark of the other four.

A book about genius, which emphasizes the influence of the work upon the life, or of genius upon itself, has to discover an inevitable center in this chapter, since these lives tend now to be more widely circulated than the work. Freud tends to be described either as villain or as hero, varying with stances towards psychoanalysis, while poor Boswell is best known to the public because his *London Journal* gives so lively an account of his encounters with whores. Johnson is still relished (when he is recognized at all) as Mr. Oddity, while Mann is now regarded as a closet gay, and Goethe still represents culture in Germany, though not elsewhere. National sages (Johnson in England, Emerson in America, Goethe where German is spoken, Montaigne in France) are not as exportable as formerly, partly because of an international decline of the West's trust in its own canon, and partly because of the universal dumbing-down of wisdom into information. The need for the genius of wisdom remains incessant however, and turns us back towards these sages.

II.

Boswell died at fifty-four, worn out by alcohol, endless venereal infections, and a lifetime of battling his own depressiveness. Whatever his unwisdom, he had studied himself and others minutely, and his insights into melancholia perhaps surpassed those of Johnson, his fellow-sufferer. Elsewhere, I have glanced at the traditional association between Saturn and melancholy, and considered the place of that association in the psychology of genius. Samuel Johnson, of all the sages, was most afflicted with a "vile melancholy," and famously feared "the dangerous prevalence of imagination." His finest poem, *The Vanity of Human Wishes*, alludes in its title to Ecclesiastes, where supposedly King Solomon, wisest of men, confessed that "all is vanity." Johnson, who loved comedy, barely avoids being a tragic moralist, by sheer effort of will. His prose romance, *Rasselas*, burns into many readers' memories the extraordinary sentence: "Human life is everywhere a condition in which much is to be endured, and little to be enjoyed." Johnson's famous, rolling prose style, with its preference for universality and generality, is well illustrated by that beautifully balanced sentence. It is curious that Johnson fiercely disliked the prose style of Jonathan Swift, whose prose seems to me, after Shakespeare's, the best in the language, but Swift's love of fact offended Johnson, who preferred prose to have a more elaborate music. Doubtless Johnson would have found the Victorian critic Walter Pater to be morally decadent, but Johnsonian prose is well on the way to Pater's dying falls. Johnson had a classical sensibility, but his intimation of death as the triumph of fact drove him to compose a more baroque style than we might expect.

As always, my subject is genius, and so I ask the question: what was the genius of Samuel Johnson? Hopeless romantic that I remain, I sometimes ask myself why I prefer Johnson on Shakespeare to William Hazlitt or Pater on Shakespeare, and always realize again that Johnson's voice seems that of literary criticism itself. Johnson is the genius of criticism: his work reverberates with an authority that is a wholly adequate response to the greatness even of Shakespeare or of Milton. And yet his critical genius emerges most strongly when he reminds us what literature is for, as in these comments upon the poet John Dryden's version of Vergil's *Aeneid:*

> Works of imagination excell by their allurement and delight; by their power of attracting and detaining the attention. That book is good in vain which the reader throws away. He only is master who keeps the mind in pleasing captivity; whose pages are perused with eagerness, and in hope of new pleasure are perused again; and whose conclusion is perceived with an eye of sorrow, such as the traveler casts upon departing day.

I quoted this once to an audience, and someone popped up to demand why this could not also be a defense of Harry Potter fans, or of the worldwide admirers of Stephen King. Can anyone really peruse again Rowling or King "in hope of new pleasure"? Johnson wanted *Don Quixote* to be even longer, and so do I. Is it the *mind* that Rowling or King keeps "in pleasing captivity"? Not wishing my audience to be held captive by a leveler, I recall responding by quoting a passage always in my heart, from Johnson's "Preface to Shakespeare":

> The irregular combinations of fanciful invention may delight a-while, by that novelty of which the common satiety of life sends us all in quest; but the pleasures of sudden wonder are soon exhausted, and the mind can only repose on the stability of truth.

There is a marvelous, Shakespearean excess in Johnson's stance and language, yet that excess does not exclude critical justice. Johnson's work is always aggressive; polemic is never far from him. He wants to argue with you, whoever you are, and he desires to convince you that what matters is what is near to you, what you can use. The genius of his criticism is that it forswears disinterestedness, and cultivates the interests of the common reader, of whatever era. Genius, as I constantly assert, must manifest itself as originality, which can seem mere oddity, yet finally defends and defines individuality. I carry around, with other passages of Johnson that will not abandon my memory, this grandly strengthening and possessing paragraph from *The Rambler* No. 125:

> Definitions have been no less difficult or uncertain in criticism than in law. Imagination, a licentious and vagrant faculty, unsusceptible of limitations, and impatient of restraint, has always endeavored to baffle the logician, to perplex the confines of distinction, and burst the enclosures of regularity. There is therefore scarcely any species of writing, of which we can tell what is its essence, and what are its constituents; every new genius produces some innovation which, when invented and approved, subverts the rules which the practice of foregoing authors had established.

Johnson, fierce classicist, would reject our current debasement of the idea of "genius." We still value originality in a scientist or a technocrat, but not in masters of language. Were another James Joyce, Gertrude Stein, or Samuel Beckett to arise, we would be slow to recognize such a figure, though I judge us to have one now in the Canadian poet Anne Carson. Johnson resisted the new poetry of his later years, in such bards of Sensibility as Thomas Gray and William Collins, but still deserves credit for recognizing and encouraging Oliver Goldsmith. Even the greatest of critics sometimes nods, and Johnson unfortunately observed that "*Tristram Shandy* did not last," Laurence Sterne's masterwork being now more alive and influential than ever. Johnson deserves all the indulgences that can be granted, because he was greatly good as well as great-hearted. A more humane critic has never existed, nor one who demonstrates quite so well the true value of the highest literature for life.

Boswell, in his *Life of Johnson*, luminously depicted Johnson's eminence as a critic:

His superiority over other learned men consisted chiefly in what may
be called the art of thinking, the art of using his mind; a certain continual power of seizing the useful substance of all that he knew, and
exhibiting it in a clear and forcible manner; so that knowledge, which
we often see to be no better than lumber in men of dull understanding, was, in him, true, evident, and actual wisdom.

Though Boswell took copious notes of his conversations with Johnson,
he lived well before the age of the tape-recorder, so that the biographer's
art undoubtedly entered into the extraordinary wisdom and pungency of
what we may call the Johnson of oral tradition. Frederick A. Pottle, foremost
of Boswell scholars (and my own revered mentor), gives a definitive account
of this blending of Boswell and Johnson:

Does Boswell, then, report Johnson's conversation verbatim? In particular sentences and in some brief passages of an epigrammatic cast,
yes. In general, no. The crucial words, the words that impart the peculiar Johnsonian quality, are indeed *ipsissima verba*. Impregnated with
the Johnsonian ether, Boswell was able confidently to recall a considerable body of characteristic diction. Words entail sense; and when
elements of the remembered diction were in balance or antithesis,
recollection of words and sense would almost automatically give "authentic" sentence structure. But in the main Boswell counted on im-
pregnation with the Johnsonian ether (that is, on a understanding,
grown intuitive, of Johnson's habits of composition) to help him consciously to construct epitomizing sentences in which the *ipsissima
verba* would be at home.

With that background, we can enter the *Life of Johnson* to encounter the
extraordinary conversations between critical genius and biographical genius. With a subject as formidable as Johnson and a prober as incessant as
Boswell, the exchanges could become stormy, despite the mutual love involved. It cannot have been easy for Boswell to hear his hero cry out, "You
have but two topics, yourself and me, and I'm sick of both." Readers don't
agree with Johnson, but Boswell was seeking information about the sage's
earlier years in London, when he lived hand-to-mouth, frequently in the
company of the minor poet Richard Savage, whose story is told by Johnson
in his *Lives of the Poets*, probably his masterwork. Johnson, who, according to
Boswell, went on "tearing at his meat like a tiger," even in the years of

his prosperity and fame, always evaded discussing his early struggles in London.

For Johnson, the mind should be full of reading, but also of "reflection," both upon human experience, and upon the specific experience of literature. "Reflection," in Johnson, is the process by which natural genius augments its endowment, and produces significant work. In the Johnsonian sense, "reflection" takes on all its meanings, as Robert J. Griffin has adumbrated. The mirror is held up to nature, but then the image is turned back to the mind's meditation upon itself in relation to the image. "Genius," to Johnson, is a wider term than the definition he gave to it in his famous *Dictionary*. Poetic originality is at the heart of Johnson's vision of genius, but this is an originality that arises antithetically, in competition with past achievements, with the great undead poets, to whom reparation must be made. Shakespeare is, for Johnson, the great exception, and more even than Dante, Shakespeare indeed had no strong forerunners, once Marlowe ceased to be a trouble: "Shakespeare engaged in dramatick poetry with the world open before him." There Johnson deliberately echoes the situation of Adam and Eve at the close of *Paradise Lost*, so that Shakespeare is for Johnson the New Adam, only poetically speaking, since this was hardly a position that the pious Johnson theologically could support.

Homer, Shakespeare, and Milton were for Johnson the greatest of poets, but personally he loved best the work of Alexander Pope, who was certainly the major English poet between the death of John Milton and the advent of the great Romantics, William Blake and William Wordsworth. With Johnson's veneration for Pope's satires, particularly *The Dunciad,* no one should quarrel, but Johnson's extraordinary passion for Pope's frigid version of Homer is beyond me. Boswell, after quoting Johnson's hyperbolical "If Pope be not a poet, where is poetry to be found," goes on to a more conversational hyperbole: "Sir, a thousand years may elapse before there shall appear another man with a power of versification equal to that of Pope." The overstating Johnson is one of the glories of Boswell's *Life,* and deliberately allies the critic to Shakespeare's Sir John Falstaff. Johnson morally disapproved of Falstaff (from which I strongly dissent) yet forgave the fat knight, shrewdly observing that Shakespeare's finest comic character "makes himself necessary to the prince that despises him, by the most pleasing of qualities, perpetual gaiety, by an unfailing power of exciting laughter." Johnson and Boswell can be said, at times, each to play Falstaff to the other's Prince Hal, as both needed to exorcise the demon of melancholy.

III.

The associated but very different gifts of Johnson and of Boswell have a particular value for my purpose, which is to demonstrate how inextricable personality and intellect are in questions of genius. Goethe will manifest the same intricate knot of self and mind, but I am not yet ready to abandon the English sage and the Scottish journalist for the German demigod.

Johnson begins the final paragraph of his *Life of Milton* with a central observation: "The highest praise of genius is original invention," which I connect with Shelley's dry sentence: "The Devil owes everything to Milton." Johnson's original invention cannot match Milton's, but then in English who can match and overgo Milton except for Shakespeare and Chaucer? But Johnson, though a remarkable poet and storyteller, was primarily a literary critic, even as Boswell was primarily a literary biographer and autobiographer. The Johnsonian inventiveness, for me, defines what literary criticism ought to be and very rarely is: the appreciation of originality and the rejection of the merely fashionable. Johnson, confronting Shakespeare or Milton, frequently returns us to the perpetual human quest to escape fact or the universe of death. As a critic, Johnson almost always balances our tendency to delude ourselves with our need not to confront too starkly our own demise. Visionary poets like Milton and Blake tend to assert the power of the imagination or poetic mind over a universe of death, but Johnson is far from such an assertion. Profoundly orthodox in his Anglican Christianity, Johnson nevertheless daily dreaded both madness and death. He meets this dread with energy and courage, but vastly distrusts the mind's defense of substituting fantasy for realistic expectation.

As a poet, Johnson found his precursors in Dryden and Pope, whose works he could recite by heart. I think that Pope inhibited Johnson from achieving poetic strength, with the single exception of *The Vanity of Human Wishes*. Who was Johnson's precursor as a literary critic? Sir Francis Bacon had an effect upon Johnson as a moral essayist, yet Bacon was not a critic. Ben Jonson's critical observations in his *Timber or Discoveries* (1640) were known to his namesake, and may have had some effect, but the great comic dramatist, Shakespeare's friend and rival, has little of Johnson's direct confrontation of literary greatness. The earlier neoclassic Jonson was primarily a satirist, and Samuel Johnson's humane largeness transcends satire.

Johnson was too natural, almost too primordial to have invented himself, but James Boswell can be called his own literary invention. In that single regard he has been compared to Norman Mailer (by myself among others), but Boswell did not have novelistic ambitions. His deepest desires were not literary, despite his adulation of Johnson. To be wealthy, powerful, famous, politically prominent: these were Boswell's unfulfilled aspirations, since his vision of Scotland was more feudal even than it was Tory. He died as Lord of Auchinleck, so profoundly snobbish that he brushed aside Robert Burns, who has sought his patronage. Boswell could have been Emerson to Burns's Whitman, but he could not even bother to read the work of a peasant, who happened to be Scotland's greatest poet. But that is the worst of Boswell; his best is self-creation, the invention of Johnson's biographer, and of his own autobiography. That was more than enough to establish his own genius.

IV.

To move from Johnson and Boswell to Goethe is an extraordinary shock, at least for me, since the mature Goethe's hard-won serenity is a universe away from the energetic melancholia of the great critic and his follower. Goethe's daemonic energy is the only immediate link, since his exuberance has the magnitude of Johnson's, and Boswell's. Charismatic geniuses rarely become literary persons: instead they manifest themselves as religious founders, conquerors, politicians, world-destroyers. Lord Byron and Oscar Wilde are exceptions, and there also are false charismatics, like Hemingway (marvelous storywriter that he was), but Goethe must be the only potential messiah who chose to become a poet.

Goethe's extraordinary (and extraordinarily well-documented) personality is a kind of miracle, one not at all easy to describe. Emerson, with customary shrewdness, defined Goethe as the idea "that a man exists for culture, not for what he can accomplish, but for what can be accomplished in him." A charismatic is in herself or himself an idea as well as a person, an idea that goes beyond individual magnetism. Shakespeare is the now be-leaguered Western canon; Goethe is Western culture, now engulfed by the oceanic World Wide Web, by media entertainment, by misplaced guilt, by quasi-literacy, by educational networking that negates deep reading. To his contemporaries, the young Goethe (in his early twenties!) was *the* German genius, who would become their Shakespeare, "creative demiurge," as Nicholas Boyle, Goethe's definitive biographer, phrases it. What had they to base messianic expectations upon, or was Goethe, from the start, primarily a triumph of personality? The enormous poetic gift, more truly lyric than dramatic, was always there, and translates poorly into English. Tieck and Schlegel, in astonishing translations, converted Shakespeare into superb German dramatic verse, but no one (except Shelley, in two scenes from

Faust) has been able to render Goethe's best works into adequate English, and since Goethe, unlike Shakespeare, could create no persons except himself, we are puzzled by his novels and plays. Faust is an idea (or matrix of ideas) but not an individual. Shakespeare invented the human; Goethe hardly needed to invent Goethe, who arrived as nature's masterpiece, the genius of potential happiness. Dante died at fifty-six, a quarter-century short of his "ideal age" of eighty-one, when he believed he could fulfill his own prophecies. Goethe, with more than a year and a half still to go, at eighty-one composed the wildest passages of *Faust, Part Two*, piling outrage upon outrage, in what I regard as the most sublime of all monster movies, and yet a great poem.

Goethe was central to British and American culture in the time of Carlyle and Emerson, yet now he is read (when he is read at all) in English only by a tiny minority, even among scholars. I find this particularly dismal as we begin the third millennium, because Goethe would be healthier for us than ever before, at just this moment in our expiring high culture, when the polemic against genius has achieved the prevalence of a pernicious ideology. Shakespeare created a cosmos of selves, but of Shakespeare's inward self we knew almost nothing. Of Goethe's self, we know everything, and of it we can say that it became the archetype for the individual writer of genius, lasting more than a century. The motto for any new strong writer was provided (perhaps forever) by Goethe, who urged him to have "the persistence, will, and self-abnegation to acquaint himself thoroughly with the tradition while retaining enough strength and courage to develop his original nature independently and to treat the divers assimilated elements in his own way." That advice, though not to be bettered, has to be heard against one of Goethe's darker aphorisms: "Genius is always the enemy of genius by over-influence."

I return to a central question: what is the secret of Goethe's genius? He was middle-class in his origins, though raised to the minor nobility by his long-term patron, the Duke of Saxe-Weimar, and his art spans the transition from an aristocratic age to the post-Napoleonic era. But it is very difficult to assign him to any historical or social period, since his intellectual daring matches his imaginative originality. To this day he remains the glory of his language, as unlikely ever to be surpassed as Shakespeare is in English, Cervantes in Spanish, or Dante in Italian. He may never be restored, in English-speaking countries, to the centrality that he had for Emerson or for George Santayana or for T. S. Eliot. Yet *Faust*, even in translation, remains an essential work, if we are to achieve a final self-understanding as a culture, even as we go down. Faustian women and men are all around us, and there is a Faustian element in all our technological new-fangledness. Perhaps our Age of Information is essentially Faustian, and is the consequence of a Faustian bargain that an Americanized world goes on making. The relevance of Goethe may be obscured, yet remains continuous, since *he* made no Faustian bargain, so rightly confident was he always of his own unsupported genius. His biographer Boyle traces a movement in Goethe from a poetry of desire to one of renunciation, in which poetry's limits are acknowledged, but those limits seem to me transgressed in the amiable outrageousness of *Faust, Part Two*.

Goethe, from his start, was a wholly secularized writer, with little use for God or Christ. His lifelong quest was to free poetry from Christianity, precisely the reverse of T. S. Eliot's hegira. Nietzsche, much influenced by Goethe, like every other post-Goethean German writer, made a shriller but less original stand as Antichrist. Goethe shrewdly declined the role of messiah, and yet proclaimed to Germany that while he indeed had been present at the creation, he could not assert any particular understanding of the world. This theological outrageousness was still with Goethe in his final revisions of *Faust, Part Two*. If it was irony, such irony was wholly Goethean, another original mode, nature's own irony speaking through an individual. There isn't any single term except "Goethean" to characterize Goethe's position. You can try "pantheist," "Spinozist," "naturalist," "vitalist," but he will evade you. Endlessly metamorphic, like nature, Goethe is his own Spirit of the Earth, and lingers always a step or two beyond our understanding. In American terms, he would be an unlikely amalgam of Emerson, Walt Whitman, and Emily Dickinson, though decidedly more scabrous (in certain moods) than any of them. His curious excursions into natural science—the metamorphoses of plants and theory of colors—are reflections of his deep identification of himself with a nature always in the process of becoming, of a non-Godhead waiting to be born. Decidedly refusing to be a prophet, Goethe did not preach a religion of the future. Instead, he sought to embody all of cultural history, Eastern and Western, Christian and classical, Hermetic and secular. In his final phases, he assays the miracle of becoming a Persian poet and a Chinese poet in German, as though he were the rightful inheritor of all the ages.

There is really no one else at all like him, though he played at the roles of Pindar and of Shakespeare. His only rival as a German poet was his disturbed younger contemporary, Hölderlin, whose most characteristic poems Goethe never knew. The exhilaration of unprecedentedness always attended him, since happily he had no strong German forerunners, and cheerfully established a senior partnership with Schiller, a decade younger than himself. Even Shakespeare had to absorb Christopher Marlowe, but the young Goethe was alone with the wind and the weather. So fortunate was his poetic situation that his imaginative happiness may account for his extraordinarily delayed entrance into sexual life, first in his Italian journey in his late thirties, and then with Christiana Volpius, on his return to Weimar. Until then what you might call his erotic career had been a navigation through intense relationships that evaded fulfillment, the most prolonged and self-destructive being his idealized brother-and-sister passion with the virtuous Charlotte Von Stein. Perhaps Goethe's originality extended even into the realms of desire, with considerable benefits to his earlier poetry, yet a good deal of unnecessary personal suffering, for others and for him.

Goethe was too canny not to know that he had constructed his own happiness and harmony, though he sometimes wanted to believe it was a natural endowment. His last disciple of genius, the twentieth-century German novelist Thomas Mann, cunningly gets this right in his essay "Goethe as Representative of the Bourgeois Age" (1932):

> There are in Goethe, on closer examination, as soon as the innocence of the youthful period is past, signs of profound maladjustment and ill humor, a hampering depression, which most certainly have a deeplying uncanny connection with his mistrust of ideas, his child-of-nature indifference . . . Nature does not confer peace of mind, simplicity, single-mindedness; she is a questionable element, she is a contradiction, denial, thorough-going doubt.

Mann might almost be speaking of Johnson or Boswell, or of himself. Goethe associated happiness with astonishment, and delighted in refuting any generalization made about him. He decidedly would have rejected any suggestion that key aspects of Western culture had come to an end, alike in his work and in his personality, but I suspect that they had. To read Goethe is, for me, endlessly fascinating, but the *Wilhelm Meister* novels, *Egmont,* and *The Sorrows of Young Werther* are now museums, transports into past realities. *Faust,* particularly its superb Second Part, is a grotesque fantasy, an erotic nightmare, which I have commented on elsewhere (*The Western Canon,* 1994), and which I urge upon any reader who can sustain it. The problem is not that something is wrong with Goethe (*the* writer himself, as Emerson termed him) but that something is very wrong with us. We have lost not just knowledge, but qualities of spirit that are minimal requirements if Goethe is to be read with pleasure.

E. R. Curtius, the principal German literary critic in the century now ended, usefully indicates that *Faust, Part Two* is more baroque than classical, and that its author embodied an aristocratic individualism, one that believed "the truth was already discovered thousands of years ago." Where? Well, in different ways, in the Bible, and in Plato and Aristotle, but what can Goethe mean by that, since the Hebrews and the Greeks were hardly consonant with one another? Goethe warns us not to be misled by one or two decades, but the counterculture has now been triumphant in the West for at least three decades, and is likely to go on winning in the era of the World Wide Web. Brutally elitist, the old Goethe said to his Boswell, Eckermann, that "My things cannot become popular . . . they are not written for the masses, but only for individuals who have similar desires and aims."

Curtius thought that Goethe, as heir of Dante and of Shakespeare, should be regarded "as a self-concentration of the Western mind in one person," and he found no one after Goethe of whom that could be said. If there has been such a figure, it must be Sigmund Freud, rather than Joyce and Proust, the major literary artists of the twentieth century. No single American creator—not Emerson nor Walt Whitman nor Henry James—gathers the best of tradition together as Goethe did. Such a gathering is not an American enterprise anyway, or at least the Emersonian emphasis is elsewhere. Freud also placed the emphasis elsewhere, but I find myself agreeing with Thomas Mann, in a speech delivered by him in Vienna, May 9, 1936, on Freud's eightieth birthday. Mann concluded by comparing Freud to the final speech of Goethe's Faust, where the hundred-year-old quester declares his own triumph over the sea of death. Freud, like Goethe a wisdom writer, may be the last Western writer in the tradition that sought to assert the power of the creative mind over a universe of death.

V.

Freud's genius is obscured just now because his scientific assertions are castigated, or else because he is defended, as a scientist, by his waning true believers. Both his defamers and his loyalists seem to me irrelevant; drubbing Freud for his mere scientism eventually will seem as aimless as deprecating Goethe for his researches on plants or colors. Or, to vary the analogue, Freud's insistence that psychoanalysis would make a contribution to biology is nearly as interesting to me as are Dante's declarations that the *Divine Comedy* is no less than the truth about God, Hell, Purgatory, and Heaven. One reads Dante with wonder and aesthetic gratitude, while wincing at his theology. So one reads Freud, the major essayist of his era, while shaking off his tendency to literalize his own metaphors. He is as metaphorical as

Goethe or Montaigne, and like them is primarily a writer. Francis Crick cheerfully dismissed Freud as a medical doctor with a very good prose style, which is true enough, but neglects the superb literary uses to which that style is put. Freud joins Johnson, Boswell, and Goethe as another original and vital autobiographer and dramatist of the self. More crucially, he makes a third with Johnson and Goethe as an authentic sage, a moralist validated by possession of the highest intellectual powers.

Throwing Freud out will not get rid of him, because he is inside us. His mythology of the mind has survived his supposed science, and his metaphors are impossible to evade. I am aware that I testify as a person of seventy-one, nine years old at the time of Freud's death, and that younger readers may not be as aware that Freud's speculations remain alive in them. Contemplate the gorgeous panoply of Freud's inventions: libido or the drive, the death drive, the psychic agencies (id, ego, superego), the unconscious, the mechanisms of defense (repression, projection, regression, and many more), and the development of the sexual drive through the phases of orality, anality, and genitality. This dynamic or dramatic psychology is Shakespearean and Goethean, that is to say, rhetorical or literary. "I invented psychoanalysis because it had no literature," Freud announced, but its literature was literature itself, Shakespeare and Goethe in particular. There is, in mere fact, no libido and no death drive, no unconscious (though sometimes I identify that with my back), while the defenses also are remarkable metaphors or tropes.

The philosopher Ludwig Wittgenstein attacked Freud, saying of psychoanalysis that it was speculation, not even hypothesis. Dismissing Freud, Wittgenstein said, "A powerful mythology," but that scarcely seems a dismissal, to me. Freud, in 1933, cheerfully admitted, "The theory of the drives is our mythology. Drives are mythical entities, magnificent in their indefiniteness." This is Freud's Sublime, and has its deliberate humor. Forces drive us, as they did in Homer and in late Shakespeare. There is something unknowable in our erotic lives, and Freud wants to call it the drive. There is no specific object or aim of the drive. It is a frontier concept, and wanders about as an exile between psyche and body, those wanderings being the vicissitudes of the drive. Vicissitudes can be perversions or defenses when they are on the frontier: hence the ambiguous status of sadomasochism, the drive in permanent exile.

What shall we say of this mode of speculation? Does it differ, in kind, from Platonic myths? Freud, not a transcendentalist, held on (involuntarily) to a shred of Platonism, by his exaltation of reality-testing. It was morally necessary to live with reality, the final form of which was death. Weary of such moralizing, Freud's contemporary, the Viennese satirist Karl Kraus, fired off the unanswerable salvo: "Psychoanalysis is itself the illness of which it purports to be the cure." This is worth some serene brooding. Is Christianity that fall of which it purports to be the salvation?

Philip Rieff thought that Freud was the first completely irreligious moralist, but that may be to forget Goethe, and we can wonder about Montaigne, where Socrates is a presence and Jesus an absence. Forty years ago, Rieff could write about Freud as a dominant figure in our culture; that dominance has evaporated. Freud, who wanted to be a third with Copernicus and Darwin, became a third with Montaigne and Goethe. His dwindling psychoanalytical societies will vanish in less than another generation. The phrase "the literary Freud" will become a redundancy, and will sound as odd as "the literary Montaigne" or "the literary Goethe." Science (or scientism) was Freud's defense against anti-Semitism: psychoanalysis was not to be categorized as "the Jewish science," as it became for the disturbed Jung, a mock-Gnostic closer to the original Faust than to Valentinus. Freud, a magnificent personality, does not resemble Goethe's colorless Faust, and was considerably less impish than Goethe and Goethe's Mephistopheles, who saves *Faust* from Faust. Though a frustrated crew of current resenters stigmatize Freud as a charlatan, they do him violence, he being so majestical. The sage of Vienna, who intended to become no less than a new Moses, replacing Judaism by psychoanalysis, became instead a new Prospero, but one who would not break his staff or drown his book.

Freud delighted in calling himself a conquistador, or failing that, a Hannibal, Semitic enemy of Rome, or a Cromwell, throwing over an established church. In his exile, he went to London, not Jerusalem, believing that Palestine always would be the cradle of fresh superstitions. I am delighted by Freud's *The Future of an Illusion,* though it may be his weakest book, if only because I relish the image of T. S. Eliot, respectable anti-Semite, reading it in a fury. Freud too would have been delighted. *Moses and Monotheism,* Freud's novel, makes fairly explicit the identity between the history of Jewish religion and that of the life of the New Moses, Solomon Freud (to give him his Hebrew name, which suited him far better than the Wagnerian Sigmund). Freud's pragmatic motto, in regard both to Catholics and to normative Jews, might well have been: "Outrage, outrage, always give them outrage." T. S. Eliot indeed was outraged, but then even a far less gifted Jew than Freud would have been enough for Eliot to deplore. The only Jewish genius who pleased Eliot was Christopher Marlowe's Barabas, *The Jew of Malta,* who dies in boiling oil, though to be just to the abominable Eliot, one should mention his fondness for Groucho Marx.

Freud prided himself upon his originality, and denied that he had read Schopenhauer and Nietzsche, a denial I don't believe. Shakespeare, authentic precursor, Freud nastily reduced to "the man from Stratford," usurper of the glory of the Earl of Oxford, who wrote all the plays (some from beyond the grave). Oxfordian maligners of Shakespeare are a mean lot, adept at poison-pen letters (I have received a passel). The Freudian map of the mind is his own invention, but Freud had a Hamlet Complex, as Goethe did, with Shakespeare again playing the father's Ghost. Hovering uncannily nearby was Charles Darwin, wisely named by Alexander Welsh as scandalous forerunner of Freud. How chagrined Freud might be that now, in the United States, Darwin goes on outraging fundamentalists, while Freud's provocations are forgotten. Darwin continues to inflict severer wounds than Freud; a number of American states and school boards now require courses in "creation science," but I do not know of any compulsory anti-Freudian courses. Evolution is a live issue; the unconscious, the drives, and repression are stuffed birds on the shelf. I say this not to disparage the enormous genius of Freud, but only to indicate again that we have passed into another time, when the genome and the computer constitute reality, and the Freudian speculation does not.

VI.

Freud, despite his plethora of gifts, was a Viennese Jew, and in the 1870s, when he was a university student, only a few careers were available to him. He attended a public reading of Goethe's hymn to Nature, and decided on medical study. Yet, early and late, he did not think of himself as a healer. His speculation, psychoanalysis, presented itself as a mode of interpretation, yet in itself it is a highly personal interpretation, rather than a method. Of what is it an interpretation? Even that is now in dispute, in our era. Rieff charmingly wrote that "Freud democratized genius by giving everyone a creative unconscious." These days, we blink at so amiable an illusion. Does President George W. Bush have a creative unconscious? I may be an antiquarian in urging us back to less generous ideas of genius, or again Freud, with his own aristocratic disdain for those less intellectually ambitious than himself, may have been more ironical than we yet have realized.

A generation ago, we would speak of this or that "after Freud," but now I think we remain post-Shakespearean but pre-Freud: psychoanalysis arrived, had its equivocal triumph, and departed forever. At last we are freed to see Freud plain, as a genius of expression and as a prophet against cultural decline, rather than as the founder of a discipline or even a universal therapy. Freudians in my youth had a dark idolatry of the father of their analysis; their Talmud was the Welsh Freudian Ernest Jones's three-volume hagiography, and their Bible was the Standard Edition, as translated by James Strachey into an eloquent Edwardian prose that caught the founder's dignity and urgency, somewhat at the expense of his ironies. Though a kind of Freudian for a few years, when I was in the middle of the journey, I took him mixed with large draughts of Emerson, and long since had found my Bible in the poets and my Talmud in the literary critics. But I learned awe when confronting Freud; a proposed study of him called *Transference and Authority* was the one book I have never been able to finish. And I had to abandon an annual graduate course on Freud, because as the term neared its end, my verbal slips, the parapraxes of Freud's *Psychopathology of Everyday Life*, augmented, until the final class became involuntarily hilarious, since I suffered a kind of misspeaking in tongues.

Freud's actual authority, like that of Dr. Johnson, Goethe, and Emerson, was and remains literary. You ought to read him without presuming that he is one who knows. There is no Freudian gnosis or secret wisdom, but there is an abundance of open vision and of pragmatic wisdom. He has some opacities, but so had Saint Augustine, Johnson, and Goethe: sages come flawed.

Broadly, the geniuses juxtaposed in this book divide into wisdom writers and creators of aesthetic splendors, but the division is dubious. Goethe is both, as are many others. Freud is a superb discursive writer, surely the major essayist of the twentieth century, comparable to Emerson, Hazlitt, Pater, John Stuart Mill in the nineteenth. I think of such extraordinary performances as "Mourning and Melancholia," or "On Narcissism: An Introduction," or a splendid shocker like *Totem and Taboo*, but here I want a more serene greatness, as befits Goethe's inheritor. I turn to a later work, *Inhibitions, Symptoms, and Anxiety* (1926), which was in an earlier English translation rendered as *The Problem of Anxiety*. This is Freud's revision of his somewhat crazy first theory of anxiety, in which anxious expectations were roused by transformed libido. Undischarged excitation accumulated, and all this frustrated desire emerged as anxiety. That has a certain popular reverberation, but Freud was wary of discovering a common origin for the drive and anxiety, and boldly admitted his error:

> Whereas the old view made it natural to suppose that anxiety arose from the libido belonging to the repressed instinctual impulses, the new one, on the contrary, made the ego the source of anxiety.

In his *Autobiographical Study* (1935), Freud calls this one of his final analytical insights, and in its dry way it does represent an enormous self-revision. Unconscious anxiety is dismissed; anxiety is a fear knowingly experienced by the conscious ego. The indomitable Macbeth, Freud's favorite character in the Earl of Oxford's plays (Shakespeare's), is the implicit model. As his crimes multiply, Macbeth's anxiety augments, and alerts him to possible danger, and so provokes him to more murderousness. Lady Macbeth breaks down, but Macbeth is kept going by his anxious expectations. Unlike Johnson and Boswell, and certain phases of Goethe, Freud like Macbeth is immune from melancholia. Depression and anxiety (in its Macbethian-Freudian sense) are antithetical to one another. In high irony, anxiety becomes vitalizing for the ego: it provides daemonic energy, and fuels the genius of Macbeth—and of Sigmund Freud.

Freud insisted that his life and work were one:

> This *Autobiographical Study* shows how psychoanalysis came to be the whole content of my life and rightly assumes that no personal experiences of mine are of any interest in comparison to my relations with that science.

Since there is no such science, what happens if we substitute the word "poetry" for the words "psychoanalysis" and "science" in that sentence? Could this be Goethe speaking, or Thomas Mann if we changed "poetry" to "storytelling"? Freud, as much as Montaigne, Goethe, or Mann, indeed shows us the work in the life, rather than the life in the work, but Freud would have been furious to be told that his work was essay-writing. Like Dr. Johnson or Emerson, Freud is a prudential sage, another rather surprising moral essayist. And like Goethe, Freud is an authority upon the relationship between culture and character. I have spent my life teaching literature, and increasingly I have become surrounded by academic impostors who call themselves "cultural critics." They are nothing of the sort: they are resentment-pipers. Freud, as the third millennium begins, remains the last authentic critic of our culture, and is sublimely useful as such. It does not matter that he wanted to be a Darwin, and became a Goethe. His genius, nurtured by nineteenth-century scientism, was activated by his grand self-deception. Wittgenstein, who thought Freud to be almost always wrong, and without wisdom, nevertheless admired him for "having something to say." The cultural judgments of Wittgenstein provoke in me a certain wariness, if only because he joined David Hume among the philosophers in resenting Shakespeare.

What Emerson said of Plato seems to me true of Freud also:

There was never such range of speculation. Out of Plato come all things that are still written and debated among men of thought. Great havoc makes he among our originalities.

I break off the quotation there, because the next sentence is apt for Plato but too large for Freud:

We have reached the mountain from which all these drift boulders were detached.

What then precisely is Freud's originality, the authentic signature of his genius? I find it most clearly in his vision of Eros, not Plato's nor Augustine's nor Dante's but akin to Shakespeare's (thought much more reductive). Freud speculated that we fall in love in order not to become ill, so that effectually we avoid one illness by embracing another. Brilliant as Freud is in describing the sorrows of Eros, he is not particularly original on those vexations of the spirit. But on the central motivation for loving, Freud is grimly original: the spirit withers too gloriously in the air of solitude, and the overfilled inner self threatens to choke on the excess of its own delights:

A strong egoism is a protection against disease, but in the last resort we must begin to love in order that we may not fall ill, and must fall ill if, in consequence of frustration, we cannot love.

The first of those illnesses is the more ironic and the more interesting: one might indeed say the more Freudian. You have to possess a really gorgeous psychic narcissism, a Macbeth-like ambitiousness, to fear that you must love or else expire of your own investment in self. Of all Freudian epiphanies, I find most revelatory an observation that he made in an interleaved copy of an early edition of *The Psychopathology of Everyday Life:*

Rage, anger, and consequently a murderous impulse is the source of superstition in obsessional neurotics: a sadistic component, which is attached to love and is therefore directed against the loved person and repressed precisely because of this link and because of its intensity.—My own superstition has its roots in suppressed ambition (immortality) and in my case takes the place of that anxiety about death which springs from the normal uncertainty of life.

The will-to-immortality here is not less poetic than it is in the sonnets of Petrarch or of Shakespeare. Freud's Eros illuminates again a central component of what tradition has designated by the name of "genius," the drive of the will to achieve and to memorialize. Contrast to Freud's characterization of his "superstition" a famous passage in a letter from Johnson to Boswell:

There lurks, perhaps, in every known heart a desire of distinction which inclines every man first to hope, and then to believe, that Nature has given him something peculiar to himself. This vanity makes one mind nurse aversions and another activate desires, till they rise by art much above their original state of power and as affectation, in time, improves to habit, they at last tyrannize over him who at first encouraged them for show.

For Johnson, all of us are what Freud termed "obsessional neurotics," and "every man" seems not to allow for the exceptions of genius. Johnson however distinguishes between "aversions" and "desires," just as Freud separates "a sadistic component" and "suppressed ambition (immortality)." Ultimately, Johnson and Freud alike return us to the melancholy wisdom of Koheleth (Ecclesiastes):

Whatsoever thy hand findeth to do, do it with thy might; for there is no work, nor device, nor knowledge, nor wisdom, in the grave, whither thou goest.

This biblical Preacher has no "anxiety about death," and no illusions about immortality. It seems odd to characterize either Johnson or Freud as being wistful, but then the massive nihilism of Ecclesiastes is hard for even the strongest to bear.

VII.

In one of his *Last Essays* (published posthumously in 1958), Thomas Mann returned to Goethe in what he called a "Fantasy," in order to brood upon the miracle of Goethe's genius of personality. Mann began (himself nearing eighty) by quoting from the eighty-three-year-old poet's final letter to his friend, Wilhelm von Humboldt, a distinguished philologian:

the best genius is the one which absorbs everything, which is capable of appropriating everything without detriment to its underlying disposition, which we call character. Rather, what comes from outside should improve it and as far as possible add to its potentialities.

Commenting upon this, Mann speaks of a "splendid narcissism," and quotes Goethe's praise of personality as "the supreme bliss of mortal man." Goethe's *charisma* certainly was not inherited by his last major disciple, Thomas Mann, which is the undersong of this very entertaining "Fantasy on Goethe." There is also the sorrow that Mann, famous in the United States when I was young, has faded considerably in recent years, despite the magnificence of *The Magic Mountain* and much of his other fiction. These days, he suffers the irony of being revived as a gay writer, just released from the closet. One would have hoped that the palpable aesthetic merits of his novels and stories would have been enough for literary survival well into the third millennium, but Mann, like his heroic Goethe, was a great ironist, and irony is difficult to preserve in our present moment.

Mann, a genius of irony, could not achieve the art that allows the creation of Shakespearean or Cervantine characters, an art attained in the last century perhaps only by Proust and Joyce. Hans Castorp, the protagonist of *The Magic Mountain*, is immensely admirable and likable, and we learn not to literalize Mann's repeated ironies as to the ordinariness of his best-conceived hero. Irony, in literature as in life, is a defensive gesture, and Mann resented critics who saw his work as primarily ironic, rather than comic. *The Magic Mountain* and *Doctor Faustus* are hardly comic novels, but *Confessions of Felix Krull, Confidence Man* certainly is, and shows a late emergence of Goethean personality into a Mannian protagonist. But I want to hover here on *Doctor Faustus*, a labored novel, certainly flawed by endless ironies, and yet a creation of genius, which I fear may fall into the oblivion of permanent neglect, in all countries. Mann worried fiercely about his *Doctor Faustus*, and even wrote an entire book about it, *The Story of a Novel*. The epigraph to this superbly narcissistic self-study is inevitably taken from Goethe's charming and self-charmed autobiography, *Poetry and Truth*:

At the time of its publication every work of fancy should stand upon its own feet and accomplish its own effect. Hence I have never been fond of supplementing any of mine with prefaces or postscripts, nor have I offered any apologies to the critics. Nevertheless, the more such works recede into the past, the more ineffective they become, in measure to their effectiveness at the moment. Indeed, they are the less esteemed, the more they are bestowed upon the country's culture, as mothers are so easily overshadowed by a bevy of beautiful daughters. Therefore it is meet and fitting to win for them their historical value by discussing their origins with men of understanding and good will.

That "bevy of beautiful daughters" presumably are the works of the post-Goethean writers, though Mann's sly appropriation would indicate American writings that have overshadowed *Doctor Faustus*. It is dismal to recall that Mann, in *The Story of a Novel,* confessed the highest ambitions in regard to the composition of *Doctor Faustus:*

> This one time I knew what I was setting out to do and what task I was imposing upon myself: to write nothing less than the novel of my era, disguised as the story of an artist's life, a terribly imperiled and sinful artist.

Goethe, more than his *Faust,* haunts Mann's *Faustus.* The painstaking artist Mann is darkly conscious that he lacks the Goethean spontaneity, the sublime excess of a charismatic personality. One can conceive Goethe as a Shakespearean character, but not Thomas Mann, who would have presented problems in representation that even Shakespeare might have found daunting. Goethe overheard himself constantly, and delighted in his consequent metamorphoses. Mann changed to survive, particularly in the years of his American exile, but he confined his self-surprise to his work, as opposed to his life. The shadow of Goethe rarely left him, though Mann had the strength not to evade the shadow, but rather to render it even more luminous. *Bildung,* the Goethean vision of self-development, remained Mann's ideal, even when it is parodied savagely, as throughout *Doctor Faustus.*

The 1936 lecture "Freud and the Future" implicitly set forth the design for Mann's lifelong imitation of Goethe:

> Alexander walked in the footsteps of Miltiades; the ancient biographers of Caesar were convinced, rightly or wrongly, that he took Alexander as his prototype. But such "imitation" meant far more than we mean by the word today. It was mythical identification, peculiarly familiar to antiquity; but it is operative far into modern times, and at all times psychically possible.

Two paragraphs on, Mann reveals that his true subject is not Freud but Goethe:

To me in all seriousness the happiest, most pleasurable element of what we call education (*Bildung*), the shaping of the human being, is just this powerful influence of admiration and love, this childish identification with a father-image elected out of profound affinity . . . The *imitatio* Goethe, with its Werther and Wilhelm Meister stages, its old-age period of Faust and *Divan*, can still shape and mythically mould the life of an artist.

Neither Goethe's *Faust* nor Mann's *Doctor Faustus* is now much read in the United States, though the Second Part of *Faust* is grotesquely sublime, and Mann's novel was popular until about my fortieth year (1970). The triumph of the counterculture destroyed public taste for irony, throughout the Western world, and Mann seems fated to wane still further (unless indeed he should be adopted by Gay Studies). This seems to be a great pity, since something of great value ended with Thomas Mann. Only scholars now read Johnson and Boswell, while Goethe is emblematic of culture only where German is spoken. Freud's day has gone by, and it may not be possible to revive him as an essayist, when he so strongly insists that he is more. Mann, who associated Goethe with Freud, may dwindle into a relic of both figures.

III

BINAH

LUSTRE 5

|

*Friedrich Nietzsche, Søren Kierkegaard,
Franz Kafka, Marcel Proust, Samuel Beckett*

|

Even as *Keter* is the height of consciousness, and *Hokmah* that height meditating upon or contemplating itself, *Binah* is intelligence-as-realized-
knowledge, or a prism breaking open illumination into what can be
apprehended. Hence I have gathered together in the fifth Lustre some of
the extraordinary knowers of the breaking of light. Nietzsche's perspectivism, Kierkegaard's attempt to be an apostle rather than merely a genius,
Kafka's desperate visions of indestructibility, are joined by Proust's vast
story of memory recaptured, and by Beckett's post-Protestant sense of how
it is we keep going on, after going on seems as unlikely as is immortality.

What unifies this Lustre is the exacerbated spirituality of these visionaries. Even Marcel Proust, secular dandy, teaches us how the creative mind
converts consciousness into spiritual knowledge, transmuting erotic loss
into the self's transcendence of its own approaching dissolution. The greatest artist of the five, Proust cannot equal the other four as ascetics of the
spirit, but who among us can equal Proust?

FRIEDRICH NIETZSCHE

The Christian conception of God—God as god of the sick, God as spider, God as spirit—is one of the most corrupt conceptions of the divine ever attained on earth. It may even represent the low-water mark in the descending development of divine types. God degenerated into the *contradiction* of life, instead of being its transfiguration and eternal Yes! God as the declaration of war against life, against nature, against the will to live! God—the formula for every slander against "this world," for every lie about the "beyond"! God—the deification of nothingness, the will to nothingness pronounced holy!

—*The Antichrist*, 18
(translated by Walter Kaufmann)

Nietzsche proclaimed Christianity to be a religion of nihilism, and therefore decadent. *The Antichrist* is a rather misleading title, since Nietzsche opposed not Jesus, but historical and institutional Christianity: its morality and theology. The New Testament, and Paul in particular, were rejected by Nietzsche, but he eventually identified himself with the crucified Nazarene.

The Antichrist's most potent argument is that Christianity is the religion of resentment and vengeance, and not of love and forgiveness. However Christianity ought to be judged, Nietzsche is not at his strongest in *The Antichrist*. His genius is radiant in *Toward a Genealogy of Morals*, which usurps the stance Freud attempted to assume later in *Totem and Taboo*:

the ancestors of the most powerful tribes have become so fearful to the imagination that they have receded at last into a numinous shadow: the ancestor becomes a god. Perhaps this is the way all gods have arisen, out of *fear* . . . And if anyone should find it necessary to add, "But also out of piety," his claim would scarcely be justified for the longest and earliest period of the human race.

(translated by Francis Golffing)

We mistake Nietzsche if we do not see that he shares both with Socrates and with Hamlet a profound distrust of language:

We no longer esteem ourselves sufficiently when we communicate ourselves. Our true experiences are not at all garrulous. They could not communicate themselves even if they tried. That is because they lack the right word. Whatever we have words for, that we have already got beyond. In all talk there is a grain of contempt.

(translated by Walter Kaufmann)

Nietzsche's genius is at its most intense when he warns us against expressing what is already dead in our hearts. And no genius ever has alerted us so powerfully to the price we pay for the genius of others:

> The danger that lies in great men and ages is extraordinary; exhaustion of every kind, sterility, follow in their wake. The great human being is a finale; the great age—the Renaissance, for example—is a finale. The genius, in work and deed, is necessarily a squanderer: that he squanders himself, that is his greatness. The instinct of self-preservation is suspended, as it were; the overpowering pressure of outflowing forces forbids him any such care or caution. People call this "self-sacrifice" and praise his "heroism," his indifference to his own well-being, his devotion to an idea, a great cause, a fatherland: without exception, misunderstandings. He flows out, he overflows, he uses himself up, he does not spare himself—and this is a calamitous, involuntary fatality, no less than a river's flooding the land. Yet, because much is owed to such explosives, much has also been given them in return: for example, a kind of higher morality. After all, that is the way of human gratitude: it *misunderstands* its benefactors.

(translated by Walter Kaufmann)

Certainly we go on misunderstanding our benefactor, Nietzsche, but no right understanding is possible, as he taught us. In the madness of his final year and a half, he thought himself transfigured, resurrected from crucifixion. Perhaps he was: his identification with Dionysus became complete. Something ended in him and with him, and we live on partly in his aftermath.

FRIEDRICH NIETZSCHE
(1844–1900)

THE DAWN OF DAY HAS BROUGHT US the Information Age. Where shall wisdom be found? My own answer would be: "In Shakespeare, Goethe, Emerson, Nietzsche, and in their few peers." Nietzsche today is primarily a wisdom writer, a great aphorist. He would have winced at such homage, because he regarded an aphoristic style as being decadent. Still, except for *Toward a Genealogy of Morals*, that was the style his temperament demanded.

At seventy-one, a literary critic has learned that he can speak only for himself, and not for what is fashionable, so let me begin by dismissing "French Nietzsche," and send that off to the dustbin with "French Freud." I will consider only what Nietzsche has done, and goes on doing, for me.

Every word, Nietzsche wrote, is a *Vorurteil*, a bias or inclination, which makes me read Shakespeare very differently. For Shakespeare every word indeed was a *Vorurteil*, which is vital for us when we listen to Hamlet and to Falstaff, Shakespeare's two greatest masters of language. Hamlet, Nietzsche told us, thinks not too much but much too well, and thus exemplifies the grand insight of Nietzsche in *Götzen-Dammerung* that we lose self-esteem when we express ourselves, since what we find words for is something already transcended, so that a kind of contempt enters the act of speaking: "This is most brave, / That I . . . / Must like a whore unpack my heart with words, / And fall a-cursing like a very drab." Thus Hamlet, who I think would not dispute Nietzsche's wisdom, but I wonder if Sir John Falstaff would, since he had a faith in language that Nietzsche and Hamlet deny:

> 'Sblood, 'twas time to counterfeit, or that hot termagant Scot had paid me scot and lot too. Counterfeit? I lie, I am no counterfeit. To die is to be a counterfeit, for he is but the counterfeit of a man who hath not the life of a man, but to counterfeit dying, when a man thereby liveth, is to be no counterfeit, but the true and perfect image of life indeed.

Falstaff marks Hamlet's limits, as Shakespeare marks Nietzsche's, for Shakespeare is richer. Nietzsche sharpens one's ability to read, but Nietzsche himself does not read us as Shakespeare reads us. In *The Antichrist*,

Nietzsche tells us that God, strolling in his garden, is bored and so creates man as entertainment. But man also is bored. To which I murmur: but Sir John Falstaff is never bored, because his inventiveness is endless. Shakespeare, more creative than Nietzsche's God, gave us Falstaff, who never ceases to entertain us. Nietzsche gave us Zarathustra, who is a sublime bore. Without Nietzsche, reading now would lack a certain edge, but we need more than Nietzsche.

Nietzsche loved Emerson, and made the best comment, that I know, upon the American sage:

> Emerson has that gracious and clever cheerfulness which discourages all seriousness; he simply does not know how old he is already and how young he is still going to be; he could say of himself, quoting Lope de Vega: "I am my own heir." His spirit always finds reasons for being satisfied and even grateful; and at times he touches on the cheerful transcendence of the worthy gentleman who returned from an amorous rendezvous, "as if he had accomplished his mission." "Though the power is lacking," he said gratefully, "the lust nevertheless is praiseworthy."
>
> —*Götzen-Dammerung*, section 13

This is both delicious and shrewd, but there is a recognition of loss in the best part of it: "he does not know how old he is already and how young he is still going to be." Emerson, like Lope de Vega, that great monster of literature, was indeed his own heir, while Nietzsche was not, with Goethe's shadow (and Schopenhauer's) upon him. That is why Nietzsche, like Freud after him, was a prophet of the anxiety of influence. From his colleague Jakob Burckhardt, Nietzsche had learned that the Hellenic spirit was agonistic: "Every talent must unfold itself in fighting." Nietzsche's marvelous fragment of 1872, "Homer's Contest," was my own starting-point in writing a little book published almost exactly a century later, *The Anxiety of Influence* (January 1973). In addition to teaching us how to read better, Nietzsche also warns us against the dangers of overidealizing the psychology of creativity.

"Genius" is a term now very much out of fashion. Historicism (against which Nietzsche warned us) triumphed in the Age of Foucault, but that era now passes. Still, the World Wide Web will be no friendlier to the idea of genius. In that great ocean of texts, how many will be able to discern a work of transcendent eminence? Will Nietzsche become only another forlorn, rather belated representative of a Western high culture that may seem like a vast period piece? Goethe is barely read in the United States, and Emerson, as central to American culture as Goethe is to German, is the concern only of antiquarian academics.

The prophetic, Zarathustra-aspect of Nietzsche is now as archaic as Freud's credo: "Where it was, there I shall be." Nietzsche hardly seems to be without a superego; indeed he looks more and more like a version of Hamlet, whom he judged to be the Dionysian hero. Will he dwindle into another Chamfort or Lichtenberg, superb aphorists, but recalled for little else? None of this is a critique of Nietzsche, but only a timely meditation upon what it takes to survive a mindless era, where screens replace books, and sensation negates thinking.

The exemplary role of Nietzsche will fade away, at least as a teacher of reading. What may endure is the critic of religiosity, akin to Kierkegaard. I intend this particularly from an American perspective, as we are a religion-mad nation, where nearly ninety percent (according to recurrent Gallup surveys) believe that God loves them, on a personal and individual basis.

Nietzsche said of Goethe, "he *created* himself." But of God, Nietzsche remarked that either he is the will-to-power, or else he turns good. One thinks of the Nietzschean God of José Saramago's superb novel *The Gospel According to Jesus Christ,* who is quite bad, and cares only to extend his power. Saramago's Jesus Christ, Nietzsche's one Christian, dies on the cross, urging us to forgive God: "Mankind, forgive Him, for He knows not what He does." If there continues to be a Nietzschean legacy, it will be in the imagination of writers like Saramago, or the Canadian poet Anne Carson, whose book *Glass, Irony, and God* rivals Saramago's *Gospel* as a critique of ongoing ideas about God. Perhaps Nietzsche would have accepted the irony of such an aesthetic legacy. "Think of the earth!" is his most powerful admonition, and it may continue to reverberate.

SØREN KIERKEGAARD

The difference between a man who faces death for the sake of an idea
and an imitator who goes in search of martyrdom is that whilst the former expresses his idea most fully in death it is the strange feeling of
bitterness which comes from failure that the latter really enjoys; the
former rejoices in his victory, the latter in his suffering.
—Kierkegaard, *Journals*, March 1936
(translated by Alexander Dru)

Kierkegaard fiercely desired always to be an apostle of the Christ, and
not just a solitary genius. He could not have appreciated the terrible irony
that, for most of us, he is a literary genius, despite his intense spiritual aspirations. We (most among us) remember Kierkegaard as the author of *Repetition, Either/Or, The Sickness Unto Death, The Concept of Dread*, extraordinary
works in which his irony, inventiveness, and psychological acuity dominate,
and his religious insights tend to be secondary.

Kierkegaard's Nebuchadnezzar, recollecting when he was a beast and ate
grass, mused upon the God of the Hebrews, and understood that only this
Mighty One was free of the need for instruction. Speaking for Kierkegaard,
Nebuchadnezzar teaches us where the creative mind has touched its limit,
and where the difficulty of becoming a Christian at last is resolved. "And no
one knoweth anything of Him, who was His father, and how He acquired
His power, and who taught Him the secret of His might."

The God of Kierkegaard is the God of Abraham, Isaac, Jacob, Moses, and
Jesus. But the *Edifying Discourses* of this Danish seer have not affected literary tradition to anything like the degree of his fascinating meditations upon
seduction, repetition, and the dark night of the soul.

SØREN KIERKEGAARD
(1813–1855)

THE MOTTO TO "THE ROTATION METHOD" in Kierkegaard's *Either/Or* is from Aristophanes:

> You get too much at last of everything;
> Of sunsets, of cabbages, of love.

I repeat Heinrich Heine's moving affirmation of faith: "There is a God, and his name is Aristophanes." Kierkegaard, Prince Hamlet come again to Denmark, did not agree theologically with Heine, but as a writer he kept his awareness of Aristophanes. Rather than seek Kierkegaard's genius in a particular work, I will wander about in my lifelong memory of his works, gleaning the lustres that have never abandoned me.

Kierkegaard, master of every concept of irony, compared geniuses to a thunderstorm:

> Geniuses are like a thunderstorm: they go against the wind, terrify people, clear the air.
> The established order has invented various lightning rods.
> And it succeeded. Yes, it certainly did succeed; it succeeded in making the *next* thunderstorm all the more serious.
>
> (translated by H. V. Hong and E. H. Hong)

Was Jesus Christ, in Kierkegaard's view, such a thunderstorm? Roger Poole has charted Kierkegaard's mastery of "indirect communication," generally by complex ironies, as here, when Kierkegaard compares a genius to a Christian:

> That not everyone is a genius is no doubt something everyone will admit. But that a Christian is even more rare than a genius—this has knavishly been totally consigned to oblivion.
> The difference between a genius and a Christian is that the genius is nature's extraordinary; no human being can make himself into one. A Christian is freedom's extraordinary or, more precisely, freedom's

ordinary, except that this is found extraordinarily seldom, is what every one of us should be. Therefore God wants Christianity to be proclaimed unconditionally to all, therefore the apostles are very simple, ordinary people, therefore the prototype is in the lowly form of a servant, all this in order to indicate that this extraordinary is the ordinary, is open to all—but a Christian is nevertheless something even more rare than a genius.

Of Jesus, Kierkegaard remarks that in three and a half years he won only eleven followers, a considerable contrast to evangelical triumphs since. Famously defining the difference between a genius and an apostle, Kierkegaard accurately observed that "as a genius, Paul cannot stand comparison with either Plato or Shakespeare." The difference is one of authority; but who except Kierkegaard (and his later follower, the poet Auden) would want to compare genius and apostle, Plato and Saint Paul? Kierkegaard was palpably a genius; was he an apostle? Since Kierkegaard's central insight was *the immense difficulty of becoming a Christian*, we can relieve him of that calling.

The center of Kierkegaard's genius is his awareness that, in a society ostensibly Christian, it is virtually impossible to become a Christian. I sometimes tell myself that the two most un-American of all thinkers were Spinoza and Kierkegaard. Baruch Spinoza tells us that it is necessary for us to love God without expecting that he will love us in return. Kierkegaard tells us that Christians are not Christians, but something else. Nietzsche, a step on from Kierkegaard, asserts that there was only one Christian, and he died on the cross, but the author of *Christian Discourses* and *Practice in Christianity* fought hard against that despair. Kierkegaard prayed to become a Christian, though he would have understood Emerson's denunciation of prayer as a disease of the will.

Negation of seeming realities in an ostensibly Christian society is the essence of Kierkegaard's genius, but this was an anxiety for him, since Kierkegaard had to be post-Hegelian, even as we have to be post-Freudian. Hegel negates the authority of the fact, of what he regards merely as the given, which he destroys so as to get at the metaphysical truth, by a process he termed "mediation." Though he had a curious sense of humor, Hegel did not like irony. For the Hegelian mediation, Kierkegaard ironically substituted what he called "repetition," the subject of a little book with that title (1843) that was published under the pseudonym Constatin Constantins. Three years before, Kierkegaard was betrothed to Regine Olson; after a year's engagement, he ended the relationship. *Repetition* is a monument to his act of bad faith, since by "repetition" he intended to mean the will to undergo possibilities that could become transcendent, including marriage.

The true hero of repetition is the faithful husband:

> He solves the great riddle of living in eternity and yet hearing the hall clock strike, and hearing it in such a way that the stroke of the hour does not shorten but prolongs his eternity.

That is a sentence of genius, and its irony is turned against Kierkegaard himself, who knew he had failed to solve that riddle: "Irony is an abnormal growth . . . it ends by killing the individual," and so Kierkegaard, like the Young Man of his expiatory book, who also breaks an engagement, becomes a mere parody of repetition. Seduction cannot qualify as repetition because it deprives the seducer of any hope for transcendental experience.

Kierkegaard, a poet of ideas, had set his heart upon originality. Like the Keatsian poet "dying into life," Kierkegaard's quest was to become a Christian, instructed only by the Christ himself. In 1844, he published *Philosophical Fragments*, one of his most extraordinary efforts, under the pseudonym Johannes Climacus. On the title page the reader finds:

> Can a historical point of departure be given for
> an eternal consciousness; how can such a point
> of departure be of more than historical interest;
> can an eternal happiness be built on historical
> knowledge?
>
> The question is asked by one who in his ignorance
> does not even know what provided the occasion
> for his questioning in this way.

The triple question divides Kierkegaard's Christianity from Hegel's Idealism, and from Plato's. Socrates and his student cannot teach one another, but each gives the other a means of self-understanding. Christ understands himself perfectly: his disciples' function is to receive his love, both for themselves and for all mankind. The disciples' mode of repetition is the perpetual renewal of their prospect for becoming a Christian. "Can the truth be learned?" Johannes Climacus asks. One turns to the last work of Kierkegaard for an answer.

Kierkegaard died at forty-two, collapsing in the street after drawing the last funds of his inheritance, his final link to his father. A month later he was dead in hospital, having no reason to live longer. His final essay, "The Changelessness of God," begins with a prayer:

> You Changeless One, whom nothing changes! You who are change-less in love, who just for our own good do not let yourself change—would that we also might will our own well-being, let ourselves be brought up, in unconditional obedience, by your changelessness to find rest and to rest in your changelessness! You are not like a human being. If he is to maintain a mere measure of changelessness, he must not have too much that can move him and must not let himself be moved too much. But everything moves you, and in infinite love. Even what we human beings call a trifle and unmoved pass by, the sparrow's need, that moves you; what we so often scarcely pay atten-tion to, a human sigh, that moves you, Infinite Love. But nothing changes you, you Changeless One! O you who in infinite love let your-self be moved, may this our prayer also move you to bless it so that the prayer may change the one who is praying into conformity with your changeless will, you Changeless One!

I find this unbearably poignant. God, whom nothing changes, neverthe-less is moved to infinite love. We, if we wish not to change, cannot allow ourselves to love at all. We break our engagements, and achieve no authen-tic repetition. After the prayer, Kierkegaard preaches a sermon to us, his readers, for we are his only congregation.

The sermon's text is James 1:17–21, the antithesis of Pauline doctrine, but the word of Jesus as reflected by his brother, James the Just, head of the Hebrew Christians of Jerusalem:

James 1:17–21

> Every good gift and every perfect gift is from above and comes down from the Father of lights, with whom there is no change or shadow of variation. According to his own counsel, he brought us forth by the word of truth, that we should be a first fruit of his creation. Therefore, my beloved brethren, let every person be quick to hear, slow to speak, slow to anger, because a person's anger does not work what is right-eous before God. Therefore put away all filthiness and all remnants of wickedness and receive with meekness the word that is implanted in you and that is powerful for making your souls blessed.

It is marvelous that this humane counsel, universally relevant, should
have been Kierkegaard's last word, together with his eloquent response,
which I take, though not from this sermon-like work, but from the earlier
The Point of View for My Work as an Author, written in 1848 but published
posthumously in 1859. In a new kind of spiritual autobiography, owing nothing to Saint Augustine, Kierkegaard forsakes irony, embraces "direct communication," and allows himself the pathos of having been "a genius in a
market town." He welcomes one among us, the ideal reader or "lover" of his
works:

> Just one more thing. When someday my lover comes, he will readily
> see that when I was regarded as being the ironic one the irony by no
> means consisted in what a highly cultured public thought it did—and of
> course my lover cannot possibly be so fatuous that he assumes that a
> public can be the judge of irony, which is just as impossible as being the
> single individual *en masse.* He will see that the irony consisted in just this,
> that in this esthetic author and under this appearance of worldliness the
> religious author concealed himself, a religious author who at that very
> time and for his own upbuilding perhaps consumed as much religious-
> ness as a whole household ordinarily does. Furthermore, my lover will see
> that irony was again present in connection with the next part, and pre-
> cisely in that which the highly cultured public regarded as madness. For
> the essential ironist there is nothing else to do in an ironic age (that
> great epitome of fools) but to turn the whole relation around and him-
> self become the object of the irony of every one. My lover will see how
> it all tallied at every single point, how my existence-relations turned
> around in altogether accurate correspondence to the change in my writ-
> ing. If I had not had an eye or the courage for that and had changed the
> writing but not my existence-relations, then the relation would have be-
> come undialectical and confused.

That stands aside from the difficulty of becoming a Christian, and perhaps evades a pragmatic truth. Most of us who love Kierkegaard come to
him because of his aesthetic achievements, and not for spiritual sustenance,
and yet I think he addresses us also here, even if we are little concerned
with the difficulties of becoming a Christian. I read Kierkegaard as having
more in common with Nietzsche and with Kafka, even with Beckett, than
he does with Cardinal John Henry Newman and other religious writers of
the nineteenth century. Whatever he may have yearned for, he was a genius
and not an apostle, as he surely knew.

FRANZ KAFKA

Nor is it perhaps really love when I say that for me you are the most beloved; love is to me that you are the knife which I turn within myself.

—*Letters to Milena*
(translated by Tania and James Stern)

Franz Kafka disputes with Rainer Maria Rilke the bad eminence of having been the most exasperating male literary genius for gifted women to have loved during the entire twentieth century. Rilke must have been the most egocentric poet in European history, while Kafka, hopelessly alienated from himself as from everyone else, evaded his lovers until his final relationship with Dora Dymant, when he was dying of tuberculosis.

Kafka, as person and as writer, was a sequence of giant paradoxes. His larger fictions—*The Trial* and *The Castle*—do not challenge Proust's *In Search of Lost Time* and Joyce's *Ulysses,* or even Mann's *The Magic Mountain.* And yet one thinks of the twentieth century as the era of Kafka and Freud, rather than of Proust and Joyce. Kafka's fragments, aphorisms, tales, parables dispute with Freud's essays on culture the central place in the authentic spirituality of their time. Everything about my contention is itself paradox, since Freud would have scorned such a role, while Kafka fled it. But what did Kafka not flee?

In a famous letter to Milena Jesenká (whom the Nazis were to murder), Kafka eloquently denounces letter-writing:

> Writing letters, however, means to denude oneself before the ghosts, something for which they greedily wait. Written kisses don't reach their destination, rather they are drunk on the way by the ghosts. It is on this ample nourishment that they multiply so enormously. Humanity senses this and fights against it and in order to eliminate as far as possible the ghostly element between people and to create a natural communication, the peace of souls, it has invented the railway, the motor car, the aeroplane. But it's no longer any good, these are evidently inventions being made at the moment of crashing. The opposing side is so much calmer and stronger; after the postal service it has invented the telegraph, the telephone, the radiograph. The ghosts won't starve, but we will perish.

The ghostly element that divides lovers cannot be abrogated; whatever value we have, as individuals, renders us estranged from one another. Kafka's genius was for isolation. He taught us that we have nothing in common with ourselves, let alone with one another.

FRANZ KAFKA
(1883–1924)

There is only a spiritual world; what we call the physical world is the evil in the spiritual one.

That is not Meister Eckhart nor Jakob Boehme, but the Czech-Jewish writer Franz Kafka, who died of tuberculosis before he turned forty-one. Had he lived a normal span, he likely would have been murdered in a German death camp, as were his three sisters and his lover Milena Jesenká. W. H. Auden called Kafka the Dante of the twentieth century. Now, early in the twenty-first, Kafka does seem to possess a spiritual authority we do not necessarily associate with his few peers in aesthetic eminence of his own time: Joyce, Proust, Beckett.

How curious, yet how indisputable, that spiritual authority is: Kafka certainly did not experience it, and he denied that he possessed wisdom or religious insight. Nietzsche prophesied, and Kierkegaard sought a truth that edified. Kafka's enterprise was different: his particular genius makes the vocation of writing into a kind of religion. One needs to qualify this: Flaubert, Proust, Joyce were the high priests of literary art. Kafka again is different, and that difference is virtually impossible to describe. He was a writer as Goethe and Heine were incessant and dedicated writers. But, in Kafka, the act of writing has an aura I can only call Kabbalistic, though Kafka was not immersed in Kabbalah. Without belief, beyond belief, in no touch with belief, Kafka writes as his undead Hunter Gracchus perpetually voyages. Kafka too is a ship that has no rudder, and is driven by a wind that rises up from the icy regions of death.

In an age of great originals, Proust and Joyce the foremost, Kafka is more original than the originals, who according to Emerson are never original. Kafka might have changed his mind. Nothing explicable happens in a story or novel by Kafka; even when the works are finished, they must as well be fragments. The dictionaries now have the word "Kafkaesque"; the *American Heritage College Dictionary* defines it as "characterized by surreal distortion and usually a sense of impending danger." That is accurate enough except for "surreal"; Kafka is no surrealist. I might also question "distortion," since

Kafka's descriptions are disturbingly "normal" and "natural," but the quality of impending danger is indeed almost always there. Still, you cannot illuminate Kafka's genius by talking about the "Kafkaesque"; a fresh start must be made, but how and where?

Kafka's appeal to an enormous readership, worldwide, plainly transcends his palpable Jewishness, and yet it seems not possible to think of Kafka or his writing without reflecting upon the dilemmas of Jewish identity. This is allied to but again different from writers like Isaac Babel, Paul Celan, and Philip Roth, where Jewish identity is not at all problematical, or from Mandelstam, where whatever had been an enigma was altered by Stalinist brutality. Kafka is a party of one, the permanent archetype of Jewish solitude, though Paul Celan was to provide a second paradigm.

The extraordinary authenticity of Kafka's writing is unique: its canonical critic remains Walter Benjamin, though the effect upon Gershom Scholem, Benjamin's closest friend, was even larger, and to this day determines any view of Kabbalah through Scholem's kind of personalized historical scholarship. When I was young, literary intellectuals were obsessed with Kafka. I do not find that obsessive an interest among my best students, but he remains more of a preoccupation with them than are Proust and Joyce. Their own struggles of belief and unbelief, in whatever religion, continue to bear stigmata evident in Kafka in ways that do not, perhaps cannot, lose relevance.

Though there are permanent stories by Kafka, and *The Castle* hesitates upon the edge of being a spiritual quest-romance, his crucial achievement is in short tales, fragments, aphorisms, diary entrances, passages in letters, and—above all—parables.

The longish parable "The Great Wall of China" remains a superb introduction to Kafka, and to some degree can be regarded as an extended Jewish joke, but this is the comedy of Prague Jewish literary intellectuals three generations ago. We know that when Kafka read aloud the openings of "The Metamorphosis" and *The Trial* to his circle, everyone was swept by laughter, and that the hilarious Kafka scarcely could continue. *We* don't laugh at those scary beginnings, and we cannot recover the precise irony of the group surrounding Kafka. But who, without Kafka, would think of the Great Wall as the Chinese Tower of Babel? Kafka experienced the enormous influence of Goethe, and sensibly sought to evade it, in a way that anticipates Paul Celan's ambivalences towards German language and literature. I am too weary of misunderstandings across nearly thirty years, but I state again that the anxiety of influence has nothing to do with the Oedipus complex. Kafka did not have an Oedipal relation to Goethe, or Celan to Rilke. Their language was a contest with German, and their German, in very different ways, departed from that of the literary tradition.

The gently ironic narrator of "The Great Wall of China," one of the masons, is aware of the Tower of Babel, the rival but inferior construction, and quotes a scholar's book which "maintained that the Great Wall alone would provide for the first time in the history of mankind a secure foundation for a new Tower of Babel. First the wall, therefore, and then the tower." This seems a wild idea to the narrator, but: "Human nature, essentially changeable, unstable as the dust, can endure no restraint; if it binds itself it soon begins to tear madly at its bonds, until it rends everything asunder, the walls, the bonds and its very self."

Why was the Great Wall built? Supposedly, to keep out the peoples of the North, but we are told that the decision to build the wall existed from all eternity. It could not be the command of the present Emperor, because no one in the South knows who he is, and if, when he is dying, he sends a message to you alone, it never will reach you. In reality, there may be no Emperor, or perhaps "there is also involved a certain feebleness of faith and imaginative power on the part of the people." Otherwise they would gather Emperor and empire to them "but once to feel that touch and then to die."

As a joke about the Jewish people's relation to God, this is a little too good, and so the Kafkan narrator ends with the slyest of jokes:

> This attitude then is certainly no virtue. All the more remarkable is it that this very weakness should seem to be one of the greatest unifying influences among our people; indeed, if one may dare to use the expression, the very ground on which we live. To set about establishing a fundamental defect here would mean undermining not only our consciences, but, what is far worse, our feet. And for that reason I shall not proceed any further at this stage with my inquiry into these questions.

Kafka's genius for uncanny comedy is almost without precedent, though he might have endorsed my obsession with Heinrich Heine's affirmation: "There is a God, and his name is Aristophanes." It is the genius of Philip Roth, particularly in his masterwork, *Sabbath's Theater*, to have taken up Kafka's irony and to have elaborated it. Though I have written about Kafka's magnificent fragment "The Hunter Gracchus" in several previous books, I will revisit it here in some depth, because it manifests Kafkan irony at its most intense. Poor Gracchus, an undead drifter like the Flying Dutchman or the Wandering Jew, is astonishingly patient as he endures his absurd dilemma, floating about from port to port on his death-ship, for no fault and no reason. Impatience is frequently named by Kafka as the only authentic sin, though it is endemic in every strong writer, from Petrarch on, since all of them are impatient for literary immortality. Shakespeare may be a partial exception (except in certain sonnets), but Kafka may be the largest instance of evading this impatience. One of his most celebrated aphorisms plays upon this evasion:

> The crows maintain that a single crow could destroy the heavens. There is no doubt of that, but it proves nothing against the heavens, for heaven simply means: the impossibility of crows.

The name "Kafka" has no specific meaning in Czech, but it sounds like *kavka*, which is a jackdaw or grackle, a bird in the crow family. Gracchus in Latin was a name ultimately meaning "crow," and the Hunter Gracchus, who cannot reach the heavens, is impossible, being neither alive nor dead. Kafka, who said of himself, "I am a memory come alive," was studying Hebrew when he wrote "The Hunter Gracchus," in early 1917, and he continued this study, fitfully, for six years, until his final illness. The wanderings of Gracchus have a perplexed relation to Kafka's Jewishness, very difficult to work through because of the fragment's beautiful and pervasive ironies. But the play upon crow or jackdaw is the starting-point, unusually clear for Kafka, being rather more than a Kabbalistic "K" or "Joseph K." The great hunter's situation is Kafka's, "a butterfly" whose part in the *Jenseits* (eternity) is to be forever on the great stair leading up to it. Gracchus's fate is neither purgatorial nor hellish: he is a vagrant; like little Odradek, in "Sorrows of a Paterfamilias," he has "no fixed abode." And yet Gracchus is wonderfully dignified, and does not complain:

> "I am always in motion. But when I make a supreme flight and see the gate actually shining before me, I awaken presently on my old ship, still stranded forlornly in some earthly sea or other. The fundamental error of my onetime death grins at me as I lie in my cabin. Julia, the wife of the pilot, knocks at the door and brings me on my bier the morning drink of the land whose coasts we chance to be passing. I lie on a wooden pallet, I wear—it cannot be a pleasure to look at me—a filthy winding sheet, my hair and beard, black tinged with gray, have grown together inextricably, my limbs are covered with a great flower-patterned woman's shawl with long fringes. A sacramental candle stands at my head and lights me. On the wall opposite me

is a little picture, evidently of a Bushman who is aiming his spear at me and taking cover as best he can behind a beautifully painted shield. On shipboard one is often a prey to stupid imaginations, but that is the stupidest of them all. Otherwise my wooden case is quite empty. Through a hole in the side wall come in the warm airs of the southern night, and I hear the water slapping against the old boat."

The shawl with long fringes and the sacramental candle are not un-Judaic; the Bushman is an ironic hilarity. Has the image of *Galut* or Diaspora been portrayed this memorably elsewhere? There is no cross displayed, as we would expect for the bier of a hunter from the Black Forest. No, the hunter is the writer, voyaging through language, German and Hebrew, absurdly caught between life and death. Gracchus is wholly admirable: patient, indestructible, above all aware of every irony. He had stepped aboard his death-ship confident that it would carry him to the *Jenseits,* and then came the bad luck, "das Unglück," for which he bears no guilt. The boatman, Gracchus says, must be to blame, but we are not told why or how, and the hunter does not expand upon this. Instead, he utters a prophecy that makes me too aware of the death camps awaiting Kafka's lovers and sisters a quarter-century later, when German culture triumphed:

> "Nobody will read what I say here, no one will come to help me; even if all the people were commanded to help me, every door and window would remain shut, everybody would take to bed and draw the bedclothes over his head, the whole earth would become an inn for the night. And there is sense in that, for nobody knows of me, and if anyone knew he would not know where I could be found, and if he knew where I could be found, he would not know how to deal with me, he would not know how to help me. The thought of helping me is an illness that has to be cured by taking to one's bed.
>
> "I know that, and so I do not shout to summon help, even though at moments—when I lose control over myself, as I have done just now, for instance—I think seriously of it. But to drive out such thoughts I need only look round me and verify where I am, and—I can safely assert—have been for hundreds of years."

"Das hat guten Sinn," Gracchus says, "There is sense in that," because in Jewish interpretation—Talmudic, Kabbalistic, Freudian, Kafkan—there is meaning in everything: each letter of Torah, each moment of Jewish history, requires ransacking for its total significance. There is no white noise, as there is in Shakespeare and Goethe. The admirable Gracchus, condemned to the Burgomastor of Riva as his audience, as Kafka is condemned to us, concludes this unconcludable fragment by remarking that he cannot foretell his death-ship's departure: "My ship has no rudder, and it is driven by the wind that blows in the undermost regions of death."

The genius of Franz Kafka seems less either natural endowment or daemonic otherness than an inhabitant of the rarer, third realm of aspiration. That Kafka is one of the indispensable sages of the three thousand years of Jewish tradition I do not doubt, though his wisdom can only be received as it is conveyed, by irony:

The fact that there is nothing but a spiritual world deprives us of hope and gives us certainty.

MARCEL PROUST

And in a sense I was right to trace them back to her, for if I had not walked on the front that day; if I had not got to know her, all these ideas would never have been developed (unless they had been developed by some other woman). But I was wrong too, for this pleasure which generates something within and which, retrospectively, we seek to place in a beautiful feminine face, comes from our senses: but the pages I would write were something that Albertine, particularly Albertine of those days, would quite certainly never have understood. It was, however, for this very reason (and this shows that we ought not to live in too intellectual an atmosphere), for the reason that she was so different from me, that she had fertilized me through unhappiness and even, at the beginning, through the simple effort which I had to make to imagine something different from myself.

(translated by C. K. Scott-Moncrieff and Terence Kilmartin)

The lost, the wasted years that the narrator, Marcel, devoted to his jealous passion for Albertine, who betrayed him so incessantly with other women, are seen near the close of *In Search of Lost Time* as the fountain of his novelistic art. Albertine "fertilized me through unhappiness," ironically fecund gift to the last great Western novelist in the old, high sense.

Proust is a comic genius, subtler even than James Joyce, though deliberately more limited in his ambiance. Joyce's Poldy refuses to be devoured by jealousy, even when in Nightown he beholds Blazes Boylan ploughing Molly, most unfaithful of wives. Sexual jealousy in Joyce is a sadomasochistic joke, a "raising of the incitement premium," as Freud phrased it. In Proust, as in Shakespeare, sexual jealousy is indistinguishable from creative imagination. Long after Albertine is dead, and Marcel has ceased to love her memory, he carries on his search for every detail of her lesbian career.

In Proust, authentic love can only be experienced in regard to one's mother, which may explain why Nerval was valued so highly by the author of *In Search of Lost Time*. Sexual love, for Proust, is another name for sexual jealousy: reality means nothing to us, in contrast. Freud thought that you fell in love in order to avoid becoming ill, but Proust saw such falling as a descent into the hell of jealousy. One's own sexual jealousy, comic to others, is tragic to oneself, but can be transmuted in retrospect, into something rich and strange.

MARCEL PROUST
(1871–1922)

MARCEL PROUST AND JAMES JOYCE, who with Kafka and Freud constitute the inescapable writers of the twentieth century, met once at a Parisian dinner party attended also by Stravinsky and Picasso, in May 1922, half a year before Proust's death, and soon after the publication of *Sodom and Gomorrah, Part Two* and *Ulysses*. Joyce had read a few pages of Proust, and saw no special talent; Proust had never heard of Joyce. The aristocratic Stravinsky snubbed both, and Picasso admired the women present. Accounts of the conversation between Proust and Joyce vary: evidently Proust lamented his digestion, and Joyce his headaches. That is the only link I know between Proust and Joyce except for Samuel Beckett's brief monograph *Proust* (1931), in which Joyce's greatest disciple negotiates a separate peace with *In Search of Lost Time*.

Beckett remains Proust's classical critic, though I recommend also Roger Shattuck's several studies, and the definitive *Marcel Proust: A Life* by William C. Carter (2000). There is no larger instance, in the century just past, of the work in the life, finally constituting the life, than *In Search of Lost Time* and Marcel Proust. It is hardly surprising that the creators of Charles Swann and of Leopold Bloom had just their bodily complaints to tell one another. Perhaps Shakespeare, resurrected by a necromancer, could write a dialogue for Swann and Poldy, who have in common only that they are Jews, Poldy rather tenuously, though Poldy, son of a Jewish father, thinks of himself as Jewish, presumably because Joyce, his model, was also in exile. Proust, who profoundly loved his Jewish mother, was baptized a Roman Catholic, and never considered himself Jewish.

Proust enormously admired both Balzac and Flaubert, but evaded their influence. The tragedies of Racine, the poems of Baudelaire, and the art criticism (inadequate term for it) of John Ruskin contributed more to *In Search of Lost Time* than did the traditions of the French novel. Ruskin in particular, whose *Bible of Amiens* Proust translated, can be regarded as Proust's prime precursor, and the unfinished Ruskin autobiography, *Praeterita*, seems to me the true starting-point for *In Search of Lost Time*. Proust's Ruskin, quite accurately, is primarily a wisdom writer, and though Proust's wisdom eventually rebels against and surpasses Ruskin's, the catalyst of Ruskin was essential to Proust. Beckett's account of Proust's prophetic vision of time is also, involuntarily, a remarkable commentary upon Ruskin's precursor, Wordsworth, of whom Proust knew nothing.

Proust's genius is vast, almost Shakespearean in its capacity to create diverse characters, though Beckett is very shrewd in comparing Proust to Dostoevsky, "who states his characters without explaining them. It may be objected that Proust does little else but explain his characters. But his explanations are experimental and not demonstrative. He explains them in order that they may appear as they are—inexplicable. He explains them away." I interpret Beckett to mean that Proust, like Dostoevsky, returns to Shakespeare, whose Falstaff and Hamlet, Cleopatra and Lear, Macbeth and Iago indeed are inexplicable. Both in the comic and tragic mode, Proust approaches Shakespeare, as Dostoevsky does, I think rather deliberately. Proust evokes *As You Like It* and *Twelfth Night* in his androgynous vision, and *Hamlet* and *King Lear* in his tragic sense of time. Dostoevsky in Old Karamazov returns us to Falstaff, and in Svidrigailov and Stavrogin intimates aspects of Iago and of Edmund in *King Lear.* I will consider Shakespeare's influence again when I discuss Dostoevsky. Here, in following Beckett on Proust as time's tragedian, I summon up Shakespeare as Proust's true master, as he was Dostoevsky's. Proust's mother was immersed in Shakespeare, and imparted her love for Shakespeare to her son, though he came to see his intense love for her as having a model in Racine's *Phèdre.*

Shakespeare, who began essentially as a comic dramatist, would be the unique master of tragicomedy, were it not for Proust, who makes a second. Roger Shattuck emphasizes Proust's comic vision; Samuel Beckett, himself a tragicomic genius, still speaks of "the Albertine tragedy," by which he means that Proust regards all sexual love as tragic: "Surely in the whole of literature there is no study of that desert of loneliness and recrimination that men call love posed and developed with such diabolical unscrupulousness." Beckett strengthens this severe judgment by insisting upon Proust's complete detachment from moral questions. Proustian tragedy, Beckett explains, is an expiation for the original sin of having been born:

> Tragedy is the statement of an expiation, but not the miserable expiation of a codified breach of a local arrangement, organized by the knaves for the fools.

Beckett might be speaking of *Hamlet,* or of *King Lear.* Addicted as I am to the comedy of sexual jealousy in Proust, I nevertheless tend to agree with Beckett rather than Shattuck: Proustian comedy, like that of Shakespeare's "problem plays," is just a step away from the abyss. Yet my concern here must be with Proust alone. His particular genius, Shattuck suggests, is for particulars as "intermittencies," momentary reprieves from solitude. That seems too large a principle, and could apply to other writers as well. How can we isolate the splendor and wisdom that is uniquely Proust's?

The character Marcel is hardly the answer, at least not until he fuses with the narrator in the closing pages. Critics admire the narrator, rightly, as an implicit genius of perspective: he is anxiously open to every fresh revelation of character, and so is learning his craft as a novelist. The unnamed Marcel, the protagonist, suffers the agonies of love and jealousy (pragmatically indistinguishable), but ironically seems unable to learn anything, until he and the narrator become one. Proust handles this with immense skill, but the *pattern* is Dante's, until Dante the Pilgrim and Dante the poet unite at last in the *Paradiso*.

Then there are what Walter Pater called "privileged moments" and Joyce "epiphanies," for which Proust is noted. Beckett counted the crucial ones as eleven, mordantly calling them "fetishes"; Shattuck restores them as *moments bienheureux*. The greatest, Beckett suggests, is "The Intermittencies of the Heart," which comes between chapters 1 and 2 in *Sodom and Gomorrah, Part Two*. Exhausted and ill, the narrator arrives on his second visit to Balbec, and goes to his hotel room:

> Disruption of my entire being. On the first night, as I was suffering from cardiac fatigue, I bent down slowly and cautiously to take off my boots, trying to master my pain. But scarcely had I touched the topmost button than my chest swelled, filled with an unknown, a divine presence, I was shaken with sobs, tears streamed from my eyes. The being who had come to my rescue, saving me from barrenness of spirit, was the same who, years before, in a moment of identical distress and loneliness, in a moment when I had nothing left of myself, had come in and had restored me to myself, for that being was myself and something more than me (the container that is greater than the contained and was bringing it to me). I had just perceived, in my memory, stooping over my fatigue, the tender, preoccupied, disappointed face of my grandmother, as she had been on that first evening of our arrival, the face not of that grandmother whom I had been astonished and remorseful at having so little missed, and who had nothing in common with her save her name, but of my real grandmother, of whom, for the first time since the afternoon of her stroke in the Champs-Elysées, I now recaptured the living reality in a complete

and involuntary recollection. This reality does not exist for us so long as it has not been recreated by our thought (otherwise men who have been engaged in a titanic struggle would all of them be great epic poets); and thus, in my wild desire to fling myself into her arms, it was only at that moment—more than a year after her burial, because of the anachronism which so often prevents the calendar of facts from corresponding to the calendar of feelings—that I became conscious that she was dead. I had often spoken about her since then, and thought of her also, but behind my words and thoughts, those of an ungrateful, selfish, cruel young man, there had never been anything that resembled my grandmother, because, in my frivolity, my love of pleasure, my familiarity with the spectacle of her ill health, I retained within me only in a potential state the memory of what she had been. At any given moment, our total soul has only a more or less fictitious value, in spite of the rich inventory of its assets, for now some, now others are unrealisable, whether they are real riches or those of the imagination—in my own case, for example, not only of the ancient name of Guermantes but those, immeasurably graver, of the true memory of my grandmother. For with the perturbations of memory are linked the intermittencies of the heart. It is, no doubt, the existence of our body, which we may compare to a vase enclosing our spiritual nature, that induces us to suppose that all our inner wealth, our past joys, all our sorrows, are perpetually in our possession. Perhaps it is equally inexact to suppose that they escape or return. In any case if they remain within us, for most of the time it is in an unknown region where they are of no use to us, and where even the most ordinary are crowded out by memories of a different kind, which preclude any simultaneous occurrence of them in our consciousness. But if the context of sensations in which they are preserved is recaptured, they acquire in turn the same power of expelling everything that is incompatible with them, of installing alone in us the self that originally lived them. Now, inasmuch as the self that I had just suddenly become once again had not existed since that evening long ago when my grandmother had undressed me after my arrival at Balbec, it was quite naturally, not at the end of the day that had just passed, of which that self knew nothing, but—as though Time were to consist of a series of different and parallel lines—without any solution of continuity, immediately after the first evening at Balbec long ago, that I clung to the minute in which my grandmother had stooped over me. The self that I then was, that had disappeared for so long, was once again so close to me that I seemed still to hear the words that had just been spoken, although they were now no more than a phantasm, as a man who is half awake thinks he can still make out close by the sound of his receding dream. I was now solely the person who had sought a refuge in his grandmother's arms, had sought to obliterate the traces of his sorrows by smothering her with kisses, that person whom I should have had as much difficulty in imagining when I was one or other of those that for some time past I had successively been as now I should have had in making the sterile effort to experience the desires and joys of one of those that for a time at least I no longer was. I remembered how, an hour before the moment when my grandmother had stooped in her dressing-gown to unfasten my boots, as I wandered along the stiflingly hot street, past the pastry-cook's, I had felt that I could never, in my need to feel her arms round me, live through the hour that I had still to spend without her. And now that this same need had reawakened, I knew that I might wait hour after hour, that she would never again be by my side. I had only just discovered this because I had only just, on feeling her for the first time alive, real, making my heart swell to breaking-point, on finding her at last, learned that I had lost her for ever. Lost for ever; I could not understand, and I struggled to endure the anguish of this contradiction: on the one hand an existence, a tenderness, surviving in me as I had known them, that is to say created for me, a love which found in me so totally its complement, its goal, its constant lodestar, that the genius of great men, all the genius that might have existed from the beginning of the world, would have been less precious to my grandmother than a single one of my defects; and on the other hand, as soon as I had relived that bliss, as though it were present, feeling it shot through by the certainty, throbbing like a recurrent pain, of an annihilation that had effaced my image of that tenderness, had destroyed that existence, retrospectively abolished our mutual predestination, made of my grandmother, at the moment when I had found her again as in a mirror, a mere stranger whom chance had allowed to spend a few years with me, as she might have done with anyone else, but to whom, before and after those years, I was and would be nothing.

Whether I call this a fetish, an epiphany, or what I will, it has just thrown me into an agony of guilt concerning my own beloved dead or dying. Pushing away from the immediate power of this long paragraph is not easy, but only the detachment Proust teaches can convert this from a dark pain to a difficult pleasure. The narrator's grandmother has been dead for a year, but only now does the reality of her permanent absence wound him. Who does not know the equivalent, and who does not regret our unkindnesses to our dead? And yet I do not recognize a passage in all of literature that resembles this, though I am bewildered that so unhappily commonplace a moment should be so original an imagining. Proust's genius is precisely that he goes on to the severity of: "for as the dead exist only in us, it is ourselves that we strike without respite when we persist in recalling the blows that we have dealt them."

How can this Proustian power be categorized? This supposed high priest of the religion of art of course is nothing of the kind: in his universality and deep awareness of human nature, he is as primordial as Tolstoy, as wise as Shakespeare. Memory, involuntary or voluntary, seems beside the point, which is that blindness we desperately require if we are to go on, but once we see, we wonder if we are worth the going on. Proust, again no moralist, is neither the Christ nor the Buddha: he has not come to teach us how to live, or how to be kinder to those we love while they are still here.

As *In Search of Lost Time* proceeds, we stumble upon these illuminations (if that is what they are) more frequently, and they are not always the eleven to eighteen moments of memory or "resurrections" of the spirit. They come at us in a few sentences, sometimes in just one. Proust famously thought that erotic suffering had no limits, that any intrusion upon our solitude damaged our thinking, that we could focus upon pain only if we kept it at a distance, and that friendship was located somewhere between fatigue and ennui. He does not flatter us, but neither the wit nor the disenchantment seems his essence. His genius enables his language to surround us, so that the privileged moments at last simply are those in which we are fortunate enough to read him.

SAMUEL BECKETT

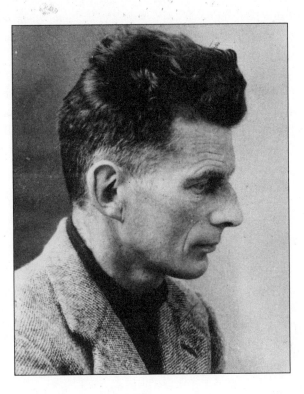

The only fertile research is excavatory, immersive, a contraction of the spirit, a descent. The artist is active, but negatively, shrinking from the nullity of extracircumferential phenomena, drawn into the core of the eddy.

That is from Beckett's monograph on Proust (1931), but describes neither Proust nor the hidden unmentioned presence, Joyce. What we hear is extraordinary self-recognition, and the prophecy of Beckett's later, major work: the trilogy (*Molloy, Malone Dies, The Unnamable*), *How It Is, Endgame, Krapp's Last Tape*. In these excavations, immersions, contractions, descents, Beckett stays within the circumference of the self, and discovers his genius for negation. His authentic affinity is with Kafka, the rival master of the negative.

Can there be a core to an eddy? Nearly every Beckett protagonist resembles Kafka's Hunter Gracchus, whose death-ship is rudderless. Krapp,
playing his last tape, admits he has lost happiness but still exults in the fire
within him. Negative energetics, in Beckett as in Kafka, go back to
Schopenhauer's terrifying Will-to-Live, which blindly seeks to engender
life, to keep going on when you can't go on. One remembers Pozzo in *Waiting for Godot:* "They give birth astride of a grave, the light gleams an instant,
then it's night once more."

Schopenhauer's cosmic pessimism allies him to Buddhism on the one
side, and to Gnosticism on the other. Beckett's Protestantism was, for him,
a dead mythology, but his sensibility remained darkly Protestant. If there
was a core to the eddy, it was a Protestantism emptied out of all faith and
all hope, but not of *caritas.*

SAMUEL BECKETT
(1906–1989)

BECKETT'S GENIUS WAS THAT OF AN exquisitely conscious latecomer. In the European tradition, which he joined by writing so much of his first work in French, he was the heir of James Joyce and Marcel Proust, and to a lesser extent, of Franz Kafka. In Anglo-Irish, Protestant tradition, he came after the Yeats brothers, his friend the painter Jack Butler Yeats and the poet-dramatist William Butler Yeats. Joyce, who was a kind of older brother to Beckett, and Proust, upon whom Beckett wrote a remarkable early monograph, between them would seem to have completed the development of the European novel as an art form. *Ulysses, Finnegans Wake,* and *In Search of Lost Time* had taken tradition to its breaking-point.

Beckett's trilogy—*Molloy, Malone Dies, The Unnamable*—manages an authentic step beyond, and nothing so inaccurately termed Postmodernism has caught up with Beckett. The theater of Ibsen, Pirandello, and Brecht also comes to its finality in Beckett's three great plays: *Waiting for Godot, Endgame,* and *Krapp's Last Tape.* Beyond Beckett, you curve back to the literary past, whatever your intentions. He represents a perfection of what perhaps had begun in Flaubert, and which had no future beyond *How It Is* and *Krapp's Last Tape.*

But the end of Flaubert, or of Proust, or even of Kafka, does not interest me as much as the way Beckett culminates James Joyce. Though *Murphy* (composed 1935–36, published 1938) is the work of a man in his late twenties, and much under Joyce's influence, it remains a novel of permanent genius, and is Beckett's funniest book. Grand comic novels are rare; *Murphy* delighted me when I first read it more than a half-century ago, and makes me happy still, and so I will write about it here. I recall comparing it to Shakespeare's early comedy *Love's Labour's Lost:* both are great feasts of language. Beckett, like Shakespeare, discovers the full range of his verbal resources, and for once allows them unchastened free play.

Beckett writes *Murphy* in London, while undergoing analytic therapy three times a week, and both suffering and enjoying his solitude. Read backwards from *Watt,* the trilogy, and *How It Is, Murphy* is an amazingly traditional novel, written in English and in James Joyce's English at that. It was a book from which Beckett had to progress and develop, but many ordinary readers will feel that something very valuable and beautiful was left behind forever in *Murphy*. Beckett could not have stayed there, but I treasure my worn old cloth copy of *Murphy*, purchased and first read in 1957. The joy and freshness of rereading it has not diminished in all these years.

Only Beckett could base the structure of a novel as wild as *Murphy* upon the procedures of Jean Racine, whose plays the young scholar Beckett zealously had taught. Racine's characters are governed by forces that finally cannot be resisted, as are *Murphy*'s. It is a leap in space and time from Louis XIV's court to the London and Dublin of the mid-1930s, but the agile young Beckett delighted in such incongruities. He delighted also in designing his raffish story along metaphorical lines: Baruch Spinoza joins Joyce as the guiding genius of *Murphy*. For Spinoza's intellectual love of God, Murphy substitutes the love of Murphy, and there is throughout the novel the plangent reverberation of Spinoza's most eloquent principle, which is that we should learn to love God without ever expecting that he will love in return, (which might be called the most un-American of all doctrines).

Deliciously old-fashioned, *Murphy* employs a narrator who never hesitates to interrupt and interpret, while poor Murphy, the protagonist, manifests very little will in comparison. Murphy is a Spinozistic hero (of sorts) at the mercy of a Racinean narrator. And yet the narrator is even more Joycean, and reflects Joyce's efforts in *Ulysses* to distance himself both from Stephen and from Poldy. In *Murphy*, a wonderfully knockabout farce, Beckett has to fight to disengage from his protagonist. His best biographer, James Knowlson, phrases this well:

> But, above all, Murphy expresses in a radical and sharply focused way that impulse toward self-immersion, solitude, and inner peace the consequences of which Beckett was attempting to resolve in his own personal life through psycho-analysis.
>
> —*Damned to Fame* (1996), 203

Just as Joyce can cut clear of Stephen, but not from Poldy (despite art and effort), so Beckett admitted that the death of Murphy involved him too closely: he wished "to keep the death subdued and go on as coolly and finish as briefly as possible. I chose this because it seemed to me to consist better with the treatment of Murphy throughout, with the mixture of compassion, patience, mockery." As Beckett knew, this doesn't quite work, and Beckett remains as Murphy's survivor, indeed a Murphy who survives. But one wants the flavor of the character and his book; here is its superb opening paragraph:

The sun shone, having no alternative, on the nothing new. Murphy sat out of it, as though he were free, in a mew in West Brompton. Here for what might have been six months he had eaten, drunk, slept, and put his clothes on and off, in a medium-sized cage of the north-western aspect commanding an unbroken view of medium-sized cages of south-eastern aspect. Soon he would have to make other arrangements, for the mew had been condemned. Soon he would have to buckle to and start eating, drinking, sleeping, and putting his clothes on and off, in quite alien surroundings.

The first sentence is famous, and Murphy is not free. Seven scarves bind him to his rocking chair. How is he to evade his heart? "Buttoned up and left to perform, it was like Petrouchka in his box." We are told that Murphy had studied recently in Cork with the great Pythagorean, Neary, who is one of the two great delights of the book, the other being his disciple, Wylie. Also pleasing are Celia, the Irish whore who is in love with Murphy, and her paternal grandfather, Willoughby Kelley. As Beckett (in this phase) had to endure his mother's demands that he seek gainful employment, so Murphy is urged by Celia to the same, to no avail, until she threatens to depart. Retrospectively, that Murphy yields to her is the start of his undoing.

Before that decline sets in, Beckett takes us to the heroic location of the General Post Office in Dublin, where MacDonagh and MacBride, and Connolly and Pearse, and their similarly martyred fellows had their last stand against Britain. But now it is the scene of the love-crazed Pythagorean master Neary attempting to bash his brains out against the buttocks of the statue of the dying Celtic hero, Cuchulain. Rescued from the Civic Guard by his pupil Wylie, who pleads Neary's insanity, the sage is led by his disciple to an underground bar and revived by brandy. And here he recounts his erotic despair:

No sooner had Miss Dwyer, despairing of recommending herself to Flight-Lieutenant Elliman, made Neary as happy as a man could desire, than she became one with the ground against which she had figured so prettily. Neary wrote to Herr Kurt Koffka demanding an immediate explanation. He had not yet received an answer.

A comic touchstone, this is the essence of Beckett, however complexly he was to refine his art. Disillusioned by this assimilation of figure to ground, Neary has fallen in love with Miss Cunihan, who proclaims her fealty to Murphy, departed to London. Many misadventures later, when no one any longer loves anyone else, the splendid trio of Neary, Wylie, and Miss Cunihan carry their quest to London, meet Celia, and all together go off to identify the charred remnants of Murphy, victim (to call him that) of a fire at the madhouse where he has been serving as an attendant. But plot is nothing in *Murphy,* where language is everything. Who, to their dying day, will forget "Miss Cunihan's hot buttered buttocks"? And, of all Beckett's allusions to Saint Augustine's double admonition to neither despair nor exult, since one thief was saved, one damned, what surpasses Neary's Pythagorean rag?

"Sit down, the two of you, there before me," said Neary, "and do not despair. Remember there is no triangle, however obtuse, but the circumference of some circle passes through its wretched vertices. Remember also one thief was saved."

James Joyce, who greatly admired *Murphy,* had by heart the grand paragraph of the penultimate section, when Murphy's ashes are scattered upon the floor of a pub:

Some hours later Cooper took the packet of ash from his pocket, where earlier in the evening he had put it for greater security, and threw it angrily at a man who had given him great offence. It bounced, burst, off the wall on to the floor, where at once it became the object of much dribbling, passing, trapping, shooting, punching, heading and even some recognition from the gentleman's code. By closing time, the body, mind and soul of Murphy were freely distributed over the floor of the saloon; and before another dayspring greyened the earth had been swept away with the sand, the beer, the butts, the glass, the matches, the spits, the vomit.

The gusto of this is dreadful, and marvelous. Beckett expiated his belatedness by adding his *Purgatorio* to Kafka's *Inferno.* Together, Kafka and Beckett make up two-thirds of the twentieth-century Dante, which is all we could be given, when the *Paradiso* no longer could be composed.

LUSTRE 6

Molière, Henrik Ibsen, Anton Chekhov, Oscar Wilde, Luigi Pirandello

Five great dramatists who were tragic comedians of the spirit, these apprehend a less elevated knowledge than the saints of literature in the fifth Lustre. The light breaks so sharply through the prism of tragicomedy as to reveal the inaccessibility of the truth. In Molière, hilarity augments as truth wanes, while Ibsen's own bitterness achieves its apotheosis in Hedda Gabler, as much Ibsen as are Solness the master builder and Rubek the sculptor. Chekhov, the most humane of all authors since Shakespeare, shares our love for the three sisters while unrelenting he lets them waste their lives away. No bitterness, and no inward truth, is allowed by Wilde into his social farces, which brilliantly exalt surfaces. With Pirandello, the tradition of Sicilian sophistry extends itself into the Hamlet-like theatricalism of *Henry IV* and *Six Characters in Search of an Author*. All five of these marvelous dramatists themselves are in search of an author who is always absent, the truth that evades representation.

MOLIÈRE

Sir, These are delicate matters; we all desire
To be told that we've the true poetic fire.
But once, to one whose name I shall not mention,
I said, regarding some verse of his invention,
That gentlemen should rigorously control
That itch to write which often afflicts the soul;
That one should curb the heady inclination
To publicize one's little avocation;
And that in showing off one's works of art
One often plays a very clownish part.

(translated by Richard Wilbur)

That is Alceste, protagonist of *The Misanthrope*, winning my heart as he protests my own daily sorrow of being flooded by unsolicited bad verse. Alceste, being a satirist, has not enchanted most critics of Molière, who resent the excesses of this misanthrope's wonderful tirades. Critics tend not to favor ambivalent stage characters anyway, and the passionately sincere Alceste overprotests his own authenticity, and is blind to his own self-love, and to his palpable self-interest.

You could consider Alceste as a comic Hamlet who, unlike Hamlet, has absolutely no sense of humor. And yet Hamlet, even in his madness, does not play the fool's part; Alceste *sometimes* does. Even then, Alceste retains a fierce aesthetic dignity.

Molière's comic genius is both absolute and subtle: Alceste, properly acted, is hilarious and yet, if there were any truth, and if it could be represented on stage, then Alceste might well incarnate one clear aspect of it. Like Shakespeare, Molière began with farce, and developed into a master of intellectual comedy. There the comparison ends: Molière, despite the severe ambiguities of his *Don Juan*, would not go on into tragedy.

Shakespeare's inner life is hidden from us; Molière's was evidently quite miserable. He was a melancholic, a notorious cuckold, and totally reliant upon the protection of the Sun King, Louis XIV, who fortunately had remarkable literary judgment. In a complex sense, Molière is always present in his comedies, and perhaps he was more Alceste than Alceste was.

MOLIÈRE (JEAN-BAPTISTE POQUELIN)
(1622–1673)

AFTER SHAKESPEARE, THE MAJOR Western playwrights are Molière and Ibsen. Racine, Schiller, Strindberg, and Pirandello all have their partisans, and Racine in particular is a superb artist, but Molière seems the only valid alternative to Shakespeare, not that one is needed. Like Shakespeare's, the personality of Molière is unknown to us. We mostly have descriptions of him by his moralizing enemies, who do not interest us. His self-representation in *The Rehearsal at Versailles* is heroically ironic, and contrasts fascinatingly with Hamlet rehearsing the actors, or with Peter Quince directing the undirectable Bottom.

As a general formula, we can venture that Molière's strongest comedies do not cross the border into tragicomedy because he gives us no normative characters whatsoever (except for the implied presence of that mortal god, Louis XIV). Even his most admirable figures are riddled with defects; the most admirable necessarily is Alceste the Misanthrope, who generally takes a drubbing from critics who should know better. I grant that Alceste lacks both humor and love, but he is a great satirist, a superb moral intelligence, caught inside a comedy of genius, the genius being Molière's.

Molière will not let anyone in his plays change, which is the paradox in which he imprisons Alceste. One realizes again why Voltaire crazily considered Shakespeare to be barbarous: Hamlet scarcely can get through a line without changing. Molière was the younger contemporary of Pierre Corneille (1606–1684) and helped the early career of Jean Racine (1639–1699). The court of Louis XIV embraced all three dramatists, the two heroic tragedians and the astonishing comic dramatist, whose plays are totally disconnected from the glory of the Roman Empire. One way of apprehending Molière's singular genius is to read a wise and subtle short book by the admirable novelist Louis Auchincloss. His *La Gloire: The Roman Empire of Corneille and Racine* (1996) never mentions Molière, nor should it, but I brood on the possible relation between Alceste's drive towards authenticity and Auchincloss's splendid definition of *Gloire:*

> *Gloire* might be defined as the lofty ideal that the hero (and more rarely the heroine) has set for himself and which he believes to be his destiny or mission in the world. *Gloire* must be maintained at all costs,

whether of his own life or those of others, and no matter how many of the latter. (4)

I don't think that Alceste's quest is a parody of Corneille and Racine, but a comic redefinition of *Gloire*, while Molière's Don Juan is a precise transformation of *Gloire* into the erotic mode, which wavers uneasily between comedy, satire, and a kind of tragedy. In thirty years of theater, Molière composed only seven plays altogether worthy of his genius: *The School for Wives*, *The Learned Ladies*, *The Miser*, *The Bourgeois Gentleman*, and the great triad of *Tartuffe*, *Don Juan*, and *The Misanthrope*. Despite the benign patronage and protection of the Sun King, *Tartuffe* was banned and *Don Juan* was halted after fifteen performances. Shakespeare's anxieties about authority evidently persuaded him to abandon *Troilus and Cressida* (it was never played), but what if the two parts of *Henry IV*, his great Falstaffiad, had been ruled off stage, with *Antony and Cleopatra* tossed out as well? Would Shakespeare have gone on? Religious hypocrites, scathing at Molière's satire upon them, did serious damage to his career as a playwright. James Joyce was accurate when in *Finnegans Wake* he expressed envy of Shakespeare's audience at the Globe. Molière, whose purposes were so different, might have been grateful for that audience also. Shakespeare wrote thirty-nine plays, of which I would say that two dozen are masterpieces. Molière, frustrated, risked no more *Tartuffe*s and *Don Juan*s, and wasted himself on court entertainments with ballet music by Lully.

I take it that Molière has three characters who fully exemplify his genius: Tartuffe, Don Juan, and Alceste. In *Tartuffe* he played Orgon, in *Don Juan* Sganarelle; only in *The Misanthrope* did he take on the great acting role. Why would he not play Tartuffe, or Don Juan? An anxiety of representation seems to have been involved, lest he expose himself to his many enemies. As Alceste, sometimes termed the Quixote of sincerity, Molière was free to act without inhibitions. The mind lingers over this casting: how preoccupied we would be had Shakespeare himself played Hamlet, and not the Ghost. Did Molière play Alceste as a sublime critique of the playwright himself?

Richard Wilbur, whose versions of Molière are the best and most actable in English, remarks that the protagonist's histrionic intensity is a desperate venture "to believe in his own existence," but that seems to me true of Don Juan yet not of Alceste. The same holds for W. G. Moore's contention that Alceste is unaware of his own drive for "recognition, preference, distinction," perfectly applicable to Don Juan but less so for Alceste/Molière, whose eminence as satirist/playwright requires recognition by the public, preference by the critics, and distinction by the king. The observation by Ramon Fernandez remains acute: "Alceste is a Molière who has lost his awareness of the comic." The satirist's art is not wholly appropriate to comic theater. Society is mad, and if Alceste, like Swift, is contaminated by what he opposes, that may be Molière's pragmatic warning to himself.

I have never seen Molière performed in Paris; in the United States and Britain his three greatest plays tend to be directed at much too slow a pace, but we tend to do that with Shakespeare's comedies also. *Don Juan, Tartuffe,* and *The Misanthrope* are not farce, nor are *As You Like It, Much Ado About Nothing,* and *Twelfth Night,* but all these should move with furious energy, with real touches of zaniness and of repressed forces breaking loose. *The Misanthrope* and *Twelfth Night* in particular should rush by us, forcing us to manifest an answering energy so as to keep up. Nothing is more representative of Molière's genius than Alceste's daemonic energy, mistaken by moralizing critics as hysteria. Richard Wilbur's translation conveys Alceste's agile ecstasy of outrage with superb tact and skill:

> And not this man alone, but all humanity
> Do what they do from interest and vanity;
> They prate of honor, truth, and righteousness,
> But lie, betray, and swindle nonetheless.
> Come then: man's villainy is too much to bear;
> Let's leave this jungle and this jackal's lair.
> Yes! treacherous and savage race of men,
> You shall not look upon my face again.

There is almost as little critical agreement on *The Misanthrope* as there is on *Hamlet.* We are all our own misanthropes. For many, Alceste is merely a monster of vanity, like Don Juan or even the diabolical Tartuffe. And yet, is anyone else in the play to be preferred to Alceste? I am always astonished when academic moralists tell me that Falstaff is wicked. What can they mean? Who, in the *Henry IV* plays, is less wicked than Sir John? Molière, like Shakespeare, is very much a moral realist, and a master of perspectivism. A satirist, confined within a stage drama, is bound to be manic: one thinks of Shakespeare's Timon of Athens, an apocalyptic version of Alceste, or earlier, Mercutio in *Romeo and Juliet* and Jacques in *As You Like It.* The ultimate instance is the apotheosis of rancidity, Thersites in *Troilus and Cressida.* Molière's Don Juan, when swallowed up by hellfire, suffers not so much the libertine's fate, but the doom of the stage satirist. For Molière, the fate of satire became his long martyrdom for having created Tartuffe, prince of pious hypocrites, who should be resurrected to run for high office in the United States.

As an amateur student of American religion, I adore Tartuffe, who would adorn the already refulgent United States Senate, or else achieve fame and wealth as a new kind of televangelist. Here, rendered by Richard Wilbur, is his grand, delayed entrance in act 3, scene 2:

> Hang up my hair-shirt, put my scourge in place,
> And pray, Laurent, for Heaven's perpetual grace.
> I'm going to the prison now, to share
> My last few coins with the poor wretches there.

Soon enough, the healthily lustful Tartuffe is running his hands over Elmire, his foolish patron's wife, while invoking yet more of heaven's grace, after which he embezzles her husband Orgon's fortune—Orgon is a considerable case-study, and I amiably dissent from Richard Wilbur's analysis of him as a middle-aged victim of failing sexuality and authority who resorts to sadism and bigotry as compensation, under the tutelage of Tartuffe. Orgon is a lot sicker than that, and appears to have a transference to Tartuffe that illuminates Freud's clinical essays on the psychoanalytic transference. Tartuffe lusts after Elmire (a sincere lust, his only authentic affect) and repressedly the collapsing Orgon lusts after Tartuffe. When Orgon screams at his daughter, "Marry Tartuffe, and mortify your flesh!" we recognize where we are. If Orgon, under the table, did not hear Tartuffe's outrageously accurate estimate of him, it would have become prophecy:

> Why worry about the man? Each day he grows
> More gullible; one can lead him by the nose.
> To find us here would fill him with delight,
> And if he saw the worst, he'd doubt his sight.

Though the god must descend from his machine through the intervention of the all-knowing, benign Sun King, in order to save everyone and keep *Tartuffe* a comedy, one could wish the hard-pressed Molière had been able to order these matters differently. In literature, as in life, the Tartuffes must triumph, as Molière's genius well knew. The defeat of Tartuffe, like the destruction of Don Juan, requires divine intervention. That is why *The Misanthrope* is the crown of Molière, the purest display of his comic genius. Alceste rejects the only society that can sustain him, and goes off to risk the madness of solitude. We know that he will be back, doubtless to save his sanity by composing comedies, and may take to acting also, being a natural at it. If vice is king (though the king himself is absolute virtue) all that remains is the madness of art.

HENRIK IBSEN

LÖVBORG [*clenching his hands*]. Oh, why didn't you make a job of
it! Why didn't you shoot me down when you threatened to!
HEDDA. Yes . . . I'm as terrified by scandal as all that.
LÖVBORG. Yes, Hedda; you are a coward at bottom.
HEDDA. An awful coward.

(translated by Una Ellis-Fermor)

Hedda's cowardice, like Ibsen's, was social; neither would outrage their
neighbors. Lövborg, being the malign rival, Strindberg is Hedda's perpetual
victim. She will not sleep with him nor shoot him, but she destroys him
nevertheless. We don't much care: he is no Othello or Antony, but Hedda
has both Iago and Cleopatra in her, and her nihilistic self-immolation is permanently fascinating.

What Anna Karenina was to Tolstoy, and Emma Bovary to Flaubert,
Hedda was to Ibsen, but more, much more. If you combined Hedda Gabler
and Peer Gynt in a single consciousness, and threw Brand into the brew,
with a pinch of the Emperor Julian the Apostate, you would get a reasonable likeness of Henrik Ibsen. Solness, Rubek, and the others are mere
snapshots of Ibsen: his soul is with the world-destroyers, and his true love
is the serpentine Hedda.

I am delighted that Hedda has become a feminist heroine: it makes me
want to suggest that Iago is a woman, and so merits joining that pantheon.
Hedda would be trapped in any body—male or female—because nothing
ever could be good enough for General Gabler's daughter, and nothing
comes of nothing.

Ibsen's genius, exemplified by Hedda's, is nihilistic: forget Ibsen-as-
Arthur Miller, the earnest social reformer. Hedda, afraid of society, has no
desire to reform it. She would make a bonfire of it if she could, but her op-
portunities are limited, and so she can burn down only Lövborg, her unborn
child, and herself. We can assume that her last thought, in the instant before shooting herself, was the desire to set fire to Thea's hair. Ibsen, a superb reader of Shakespeare, had noted Iago's pyromania.

HENRIK IBSEN
(1828–1906)

"THERE MUST BE TROLL IN WHAT I write": Ibsen on Ibsen. By thus accurately defining his genius as daemonic, the principal Western playwright since Shakespeare refutes the common notion that he was the Arthur Miller of his day. I pick up a current *Companion to Ibsen* and I find articles on "Ibsen and the realistic problem drama" and "Ibsen and feminism." Why not "Ibsen and orientalism" or "Ibsen and Inuit lesbian studies?" Why not "Ibsen and big media"?

Turn back to where we were when we began: troll. We all have known two or three: nasty destructive women and men who never grew up, and who mask as charismatics or as sexual dynamos. More often we know (or ourselves are) borderline trolls. Ibsen, distinctly not a lovable person, alternated between borderline and pure troll. If you visit the grim, dark Ibsen House in Oslo, you will come away feeling that two or three days of living there would send you into clinical depression. I stood in awe by Ibsen's writing desk, and shuddered to remember that on it he kept a pet scorpion under glass, whom he delighted in feeding fresh fruit.

Not all trolls are geniuses, or geniuses trolls. Ibsen, socially conformist, had the gift of tapping trollish energy from just across the border. His great characters imitate their creator in that daemonic enterprise: Brand, the Emperor Julian, Peer Gynt, Hedda Gabler (marvelous fusion of Shakespeare's Cleopatra and Iago), Solness the master builder. The others I have discussed elsewhere; here I will consider Solness, with a final glance at Rubek the master sculptor, Ibsen's surrogate in his last play, *When We Dead Awaken* (1899). The next year, he suffered his first stroke, and wrote nothing more, though he lived until 1906.

It takes a certain effort to recover Ibsen these days, if only because so many who direct and act him think he is of one substance with *The Crucible* or *All My Sons*. Two early Irish admirers, George Bernard Shaw and James Joyce, had sharply differing visions of him, and the Shavian reduction triumphed and still is with us. Joyce, like Henry James and Oscar Wilde, saw Ibsen as what he was: a Shakespeare of the North, and the only post-Shakespearean dramatist who broke through into a tragic mode of his own. In 1855, when he was twenty-seven, Ibsen gave a lecture in Bergen on

"Shakespeare and his influence upon Scandinavian literature." I would like to read it, but evidently Ibsen destroyed the manuscript. Shaw, who simultaneously feared and loathed Shakespeare (for obvious reasons), absurdly elevated Ibsen over the Englishman, because the Shavian Ibsen was primarily the destroyer of idealistic icons:

> Ibsen supplies the want left by Shakespeare . . . his plays are much more important to us than Shakespeare's . . . they are capable both of hurting us cruelly and of filling us with excited hopes of escape from idealistic tyrannies, and with visions of intenser life in the future.

That isn't Ibsen, but *Man and Superman* or *Saint Joan*. Shaw's Ibsen is a cudgel to use against Shakespeare, which isn't exactly Ibsen's own relation to *Hamlet* and to *Antony and Cleopatra*. James Joyce, reviewing *When We Dead Awaken* in 1900, made clear Ibsen's relation to the Aesthetic Age of Walter Pater:

> At some chance expression the mind is tortured with some question, and in a flash long reaches of life are opened up in vista, yet the vision is momentary.

These are Ibsen's negative epiphanies, dark brothers (or trollish counterparts) of Pater's privileged moments (see my discussion of Pater). Hamlet thinks too well, comes to know the truth of our condition, resurrects, and *then* dies, which is all that truth allows you to do, contra Shaw. "To live is to battle with trolls in heart and mind; to write is to sit in judgment upon yourself." That is Ibsen, but might be Hamlet, had the Prince of Denmark taken up play-botching.

The Master Builder might have as its motto Nietzsche's: "That which does not destroy me strengthens me." That would be an ironic epigraph, since the young troll Hilde Wangel does destroy Ibsen's surrogate, the architect Halvard Solness, who is presumably sixty-four, Ibsen's age in 1892 when the play was composed. Hilde, not quite twenty-three, has arrived after exactly a decade to assert her kingdom, which pragmatically is to be the *sparagmos* of Solness, shattered by his fall from a high tower, after he is rendered dizzy by Hilde's cheerleading from below. This would all be as preposterous as it sounds, except that Ibsen makes it work. His genius makes his great limitation his strength, since fundamentally the troll Hilde and the half-troll Solness are the same person. Again, Bernard Shaw had it all wrong: Ibsen, unlike Shakespeare, can put only himself upon the stage. This was demonstrated, with authority and justice, by Hugo von Hofmannsthal in 1893, in his "The People in Ibsen's Dramas."

Hofmannsthal begins by observing that no one is going to call a lecture "The People in Shakespeare's Plays," because "there is nothing there *except* people." Whereas, "With Ibsen, the entire discussion, the enthusiasms and repudiations, have nearly always been linked with something extraneous to the characters—with ideas, problems, prospects, reflections, moods."

Nevertheless, Hofmannsthal goes on, there is one person in these plays: "a variant of a very rich, very modern, and very precisely observed human type." It is called Julian the Apostate, Peer Gynt, Solness, Brand, Hedda Gabler, Nora, and so on:

> It is by no means a simple being—indeed, it is very complicated; it speaks a nervous, clipped prose, without pathos . . . it takes itself ironically, it reflects about itself.

What this person desires, Hofmannsthal suggests, is to cease writing poetry but to become oneself *materia poetica*, "the stuff of poetry." The different forms of this person name this stuff in various ways: the miraculous, the great Bacchanalia, the sea, or America. And this person—in all her or his permutations—loves an organized death, a particular obsession with Hedda Gabler, but also the mission of Hilde Wangel, who arrives to organize the master builder's death.

Writing a year after the appearance of *The Master Builder*, Hofmannsthal centers upon it:

> Around the creative artist is life, exacting, scornful, confusing. Thus Princess Hilda confronts the vacillating master builder. She is little Hilda, stepdaughter of the Lady from the Sea, now grown up. The master builder once promised her a kingdom, and now she comes to claim it. If he is born a king, this must be quite easy for him. If not, he must simply perish as a result. And that would be tremendously thrilling. Her kingdom lies, like that of Nora and Hedda, in the realm of the miraculous—where one is overcome by dizziness, where one is seized by a strange power, and carried away. He too has this yearning in his soul to stand on the high towers, where in the wind and in the dusky loneliness it is uneasily beautiful, where one talks to God and where one can fall headlong to one's death. But he is not proof against giddiness; he goes in dread of himself, in dread of fortune, in dread of life, mysterious life in its entirety. He is also drawn to Hilda by dread,

a peculiarly alluring fear, the awe felt by the artist for nature, for the merciless, daemonic, sphinxlike qualities inherent in woman, the mystic fear of youth. For youth has something uncanny about it, an intoxicating and dangerous breath of life which is mysterious and disquieting. Everything problematical in him, every repressed mystic quality in him, is roused by her touch. In Hilda he meets himself, he demands a miracle of himself, he wants to force it out of himself, and at the same time watch and feel the awe "when life takes hold of a man and makes him the stuff of poetry." At this point he falls to his death.

The incontrovertible center of this is: "In Hilda he meets himself." Ibsenites (we still have a handful or two) will not agree with Hofmannsthal, but clearly enough Hedda Gabler, Solness, and Ibsen are one, and Hilda, when she matures, will organize her own death as artistically as Hedda does. What keeps it all going, as Hofmannsthal ends by admitting, is that in Ibsen we find ourselves, more beautiful and more strange. In Shakespeare we find others, and otherness, but Ibsen, like Solness, only demanded a miracle of himself. Shakespeare did not need to demand.

Joyce, admiring Irene in *When We Dead Awaken*, all but decided that Ibsen was a woman. Yet this is a perfectly mad play: in summary, or in analysis, it transcends the preposterous, and I do not believe that even Ibsen makes it work. Leaping from a high tower because a troll enchantress is hypnotizing you from below has a kind of persuasiveness to it, though to someone like myself, who cannot walk downstairs without thinking of the fall of Humpty Dumpty, it seems rather baroque. But Rubek, tramping up a mountainside in mist and storm with Irene, his former model who went mad because he never touched her, is beyond stage representation, though an avalanche is a grand challenge for stage designers. As an emblem of resurrection or freedom it hovers near the catastrophe-creation that Ibsen always longed for. As a person, he immolated himself in respectability; as an aesthetic genius, he at last released his trollishness, and ended at the edge of an abyss.

ANTON CHEKHOV

You complain that my characters are gloomy. Alas, it is not my fault! It turns out that way involuntarily, and while I am writing it does not seem to me that I am writing gloomily; in any case, I am always in a good mood when I work. It is noteworthy that gloomy people and melancholiacs always write merry things, while the cheerful depress people with their writings. And I am a cheerful man; at least, as the saying goes, I've enjoyed myself during the first thirty years of my life.

Chekhov's kindliness always mitigated his irony. Like Samuel Beckett, Chekhov is one of the few saints of literature. Both men were irreplaceable writers, and were even more impressive in their lives than in their works. Tolstoy loved Chekhov, both as writer and as man, but considered the man to possess a human greatness surpassing that of the stories and plays. Chekhov's goodness was allied to his respect for simplicity in other persons. Gorky, who like Tolstoy venerated Chekhov, emphasized how merciless Chekhov was towards vulgarity of any kind. Otherwise, Chekhov was a fountain of mercy, towards everyone.

Chekhov's genius is Shakespearean, which is very dangerous praise to extend to any writer, but I intend a precise comparison, without pretending that Chekhov shared in Shakespeare's preternatural powers of characterization. In Shakespeare (as in life) people rarely listen to one another, and even when they do listen, they have enormous trouble in understanding what the other is saying. This frequently eludes us in Shakespeare, because we are so fascinated by the personalities of his characters that we scant the evasions between them. Chekhov cannot create personality as Shakespeare can, but he certainly can and does represent the gaps and evasions between his characters with uncanny power.

Shakespeare's extraordinary detachment towards his personages, even towards Hamlet and Falstaff, is echoed by Chekhov's dramatic principle of restraint, necessarily more evident in the plays than in the stories. It seems odd to designate an author who was as benign as Chekhov *a genius of restraint*, but it also seems accurate.

ANTON CHEKHOV
(1860–1904)

MAXIM GORKY, IN HIS *REMINISCENCES* of his friend Chekhov, said that in the playwright-storyteller's presence "everyone felt an unconscious desire to be simpler, more truthful, more himself." That seems to me the best way to isolate Chekhov's genius, which masks itself by taking banality as prime subject. Dostoevsky, however grim the ambiance he is representing, is always only a step away from the transcendental and extraordinary. Chekhov, Tolstoy's disciple, shared with Dostoevsky only a fierce love for Shakespeare, whom Tolstoy despised. Like Turgenev, Chekhov centered upon *Hamlet*, while Dostoevsky can seem more in the mode of *Macbeth* and *King Lear*. Lev Shestov, a twentieth-century Russian religious sage, compared Chekhov himself to Prince Hamlet, which makes one kind of sense, since Chekhov was obsessed with *Hamlet* as a play, but otherwise Shestov is misleading. Shakespeare's Hamlet is unable to love anyone, though he insists otherwise, and is in fact a killer, with no capacity for remorse. Chekhov, by the testimony of all who knew him well, and by the gratitude of his readers and audiences, was and is someone you have to love. Here is Gorky again, recollecting Tolstoy:

> He loved Chekhov and when he looked at him his eyes were tender and seemed almost to stroke Anton Pavlovich's face. Once, when Anton Pavlovich was walking on the lawn with Alexandra Lvovna, Tolstoy, who at the time was still ill and was sitting in a chair on the terrace, seemed to stretch towards them, saying in a whisper: "Ah, what a beautiful, magnificent man; modest and quiet like a girl. And he walks like a girl. He's simply wonderful."

Tolstoy, a ruthless judge of others, fell and stayed in love with Chekhov, and so do most of us. Robert Brustein eloquently speaks for Chekhov's auditors and readers:

> no one has ever been able to write of him without the most profound affection and love; and he, the author, remains the most positive character in his fiction.

There are great writers one comes to love as personalities, but they seem too uncanny to hold too close: Blake, Shelley, Kafka, Hart Crane. Chekhov is both a good person and warm; Samuel Beckett seems to have been exemplary in every way, yet remote. I am aware that this is not easy to see or to say, but Chekhov can be named as the least daemonic, the most human of all literary geniuses. Like his model, Shakespeare, Chekhov was not a problem-solver, and had no remedies for human predicaments. But we know almost nothing of Shakespeare as a person: he bewilders us because he is everyone at once, including all the characters in all of the thirty-nine plays. Chekhov is always Chekhov, but there is high art in that, and there is also an endowment of a highly individual genius.

You can believe, in *Hamlet*, that Shakespeare is everyone, and yet the Prince stands apart, and in the scene with the actors he perhaps merges with Shakespeare quite directly. As a player himself, Shakespeare stood apart as the royal Ghost, and yet I suspect doubled as the Player King. In *The Seagull* everyone is Chekhov, in a rather different, farcical way. The playwright satirizes himself as the writer Trigorin, but parodies himself also as the young dramatist Treplyov, and I suspect also as the high-minded young actress Nina. All three characters isolate particular elements in Hamlet, though their relation to the Prince is not even parodistic. Treplyov's relationship with his mother, the narcissistic actress Arkadina, is almost too obviously patterned on Hamlet's confrontation with Gertrude, and Nina is a kind of Ophelia. Yet Trigorin is hardly a Claudius, and Treplyov's play-within-the-play is not an attack upon Trigorin, who has more of Polonius in him than of the usurping uncle.

Even in *The Seagull*, Chekhov is sinuously subtle, and always in the interest of more life. Yet, for Chekhov, *The Seagull* is minor. His genius is most luminous in *Three Sisters*, a play Shakespeare might have admired, and in "The Darling," a story that Tolstoy particularly loved. To apprehend what is most Chekhovian in this play and this story may bring us closer to Chekhov's genius, though of all the figures studied in this book, only Shakespeare and Tolstoy, to me, seem more difficult to describe as originals than does Chekhov. All three are miracles of an art that itself is nature, to borrow a Shakespearean phrase. No one truly sustains close comparison in regard to Shakespeare or Tolstoy, and Chekhov would have deprecated any such triangulation. Yet he makes more explicit what unites Tolstoy's Hadji Murad and Shakespeare's Antony as warriors who are magnificent tragic heroes: a passion for life that cannot be diminished by the imminence of death. Chekhov, the poet of the unlived life, is quietly passionate against the wasting of life, while Tolstoy and Shakespeare more massively depict a fullness of life, in protagonists as furiously alive as the Chechen chieftain and the Roman favorite of Cleopatra.

Three Sisters of all Chekhov's works is the most difficult to characterize, partly because it has no genre. We can call it tragedy, tragicomedy, comedy, or what we will. Howard Moss, in the most Chekhovian essay upon the drama, remarked that in it "the inability to act becomes the action of the play." I am always charmed, rereading Moss on *Three Sisters,* by his observation that Chekhov (like Proust) never gives us the portrayal of a happy marriage. But then, I always tell my students that the Macbeths are Shakespeare's happiest couple. Chekhov's deepest lesson from Shakespeare is that none of his characters bother to listen to one another, particularly if they are lovers. Interminable monologues and a really gorgeous solipsism mark Chekhov's characters as they do Shakespeare's. That Chekhov is ironic is plain, but Shakespeare's irony, as Chesterton observed of Chaucer's, is too large to be seen.

Chekhov's three sisters, all of them as familiar to us as are our closest friends, are Olga, Masha, and Irina. The motherly Olga never becomes a mother, and yet compellingly stands for kindness and goodness, though her nerves prevent her from fighting off her sister-in-law, the vitalistic and Napoleonic Natasha. Masha is the Hamlet-like truth-teller, passionate even in her Chekhovian reticences. Chekhov again had learned from Shakespeare the art of leaving things out, and the elliptical Masha, another heroine in mourning for her life, is the most absorbing character in the play. Her lover, Vershinin, is one more Chekhovian self-parody: cultured, benign, weak, finally irrelevant, since he cannot sustain Masha's Ibsenite terror-tactics, in which we are bombarded by truth until it destroys us.

Irina, less complex than Masha, is still both very formidable and lovable, but unable to return love. More even than Olga and Masha, Irina is convinced that a return to Moscow (where the sisters were raised) would heal her stringencies and open Eros for her. Her Moscow, like that of her sisters, is a fiction, and would vanish upon arrival there. Irina and Masha, and even Olga, properly played, induce the audience to fall in love with them, a despairing love, because the three sisters never will reach out for the lives they could have, or find the minimal strength that would set aside their disdain long enough to battle back against their predatory sister-in-law Natasha. All this begins to sound like Chekhovian soap opera, but raised by nuance to an extraordinary level of art. Soap opera in which the three heroines become a chorus lamenting that they do not know enough is something of a new genre, in which Chekhov's imitators have not been able to emulate his dramatic moods and rhythms.

How can one formulate the genius of *Three Sisters*? Moss sums up usefully: "The sisters long to accomplish the opposite of what they achieve, to become the contrary of what they are." The endless enigmas of Hamlet hover here, but the Prince of Denmark can invoke angels and ministers of grace, even though they will not descend. In proportion to his genius, Hamlet accomplishes only the disaster of eight deaths, his own included. Though that is a memorable catastrophe, the waste of the most comprehensive consciousness in all literature would be appalling, were it not for Hamlet's extraordinary music of demise, his overtures to eternity. *Three Sisters* hurts in a very different and indefinable mode. All my esteem for the great Canadian critic Northrop Frye (1912–1991) cannot dispel my unhappiness when his *Anatomy of Criticism* (1957) remarks:

> In those parts of Chekhov, notably the last act of *Three Sisters*, where the characters one by one withdraw from each other into their subjective prison-cells, we are coming about as close to pure irony as the stage can get.

Whether I read *Three Sisters*, or watch it in a theater, I am overwhelmed by pathos as Masha cries out, "We must live . . . We must live . . . ," and Irina proclaims, "I shall work, I shall work . . . ," and Olga embraces both her sisters and ends the play with, "If only we knew; If only we knew!" The sisters are trapped in irony, and yet they certainly do not withdraw from each other. Where there is so much love, including our love for them, how can irony be pure?

"The Darling" (1899), written two years before *Three Sisters*, is the story of a "wonderful and holy" soul, Olenka, who deserves that Tolstoyan description. She is so childlike, and so motherly, at once, that she becomes emptied out, in a state of death-in-life, when she has no one to love. It is as though she has no self, except in loving. Chekhov adores her, as Tolstoy did, and the reader has no other option. Life, in its unkindness, kills both her husbands, but she survives through a foster son, who is left to her care.

Critics have followed Tolstoy in surmising that Chekhov's original emphasis was ironic, possibly even satiric, but that then the story got away from him. Having no personality or ideas of her own, Olenka can be regarded as an outrageous version of a woman, but that seems to me a superficial judgment. I myself have known a few women, and a few men, like

Olenka. Perhaps we all have, even though our society seems not to deal in "holy souls." Olenka is simple-minded, but in no way mentally impaired, and how you choose to read her story is entirely your own judgment upon yourself. In his final phase as a storyteller, Chekhov adopts a Shakespearean perspectivism: what's aught but as it is valued? Olenka's men are absurd, and her foster child is a precarious entity, seething with repressed resentment towards her.

How did Chekhov read his own story? We do not know, and I don't think that it matters. Olenka is difficult to accept, and dangerous to reject, since you do your soul a kind of violence in disdaining her, or even in finding her pitiable. Consumptive and doomed, Chekhov at thirty-nine gave up any attempts to censor his own genius. Poor Olenka is hardly a representation of Chekhov's own genius, and doubtless deserved Gorky's condemnation, from his revolutionary perspective. And yet it is Chekhov, and not Tolstoy, who imagines Olenka. Between the advent of those she can love, Olenka suffers change. You can argue, as some critics have, that Olenka's is a devouring love, which has consumed her husbands, drives away her admirer, and will cause her to lose her foster child, in time. I cannot read the story that way, and Olenka does not seem to me a mere Psyche, waiting for Cupid to arrive again. Confronted by the image of Olenka, something in Chekhov profoundly splits. Perhaps his genius, for all his humane wisdom, was more in the realm of aspiration than his critics have been able to discern. To me, Olenka at last seems an indictment of the ironic hardness of our own souls.

OSCAR WILDE

Mr. Worthing! Rise, sir, from this semi-recumbent posture. It is most indecorous.

—Lady Augusta Bracknell to Jack
The Importance of Being Earnest

The lords of language come in very varied groups, and I like to mingle fictive characters with authors to make up an ensemble. Consider Jane Austen and Shakespeare's Rosalind (*As You Like It*) sharing a tea party, rather more amiably than Cecily Cardew and Gwendolyn Fairfax perform at their tea-confrontation in *The Importance of Being Earnest*. Or envision Mr. Samuel Pickwick encountering Sir John Falstaff at Newgate Prison, and proceeding to discuss debt and imprisonment. Best of all might be an exchange of prose in rolling periods between Dr. Samuel Johnson, and his ornate parodist, Lady Bracknell.

William Butler Yeats thought that Wilde was a frustrated man-of-action, diverted into a literary life. Though Yeats's judgment was an odd one, he reached after something enigmatic in Wilde, who was prodigal of his genius and of his life, and threw them both away. Even in *The Importance of Being Earnest,* something in Wilde himself is always missing.

Though Wilde was the professed disciple of John Ruskin and Walter Pater, he was most at home as a celebrity, a precursor of Truman Capote, Andy Warhol, and a host of other aesthetic superstars. Sadly, his genius was larger than his chosen role could accommodate. Lamenting Wilde's early death at forty-six, I suspect that my sorrow is more personal than literary. *De Profundis* and *The Ballad of Reading Gaol* are overwritten. Had there been more plays, we would have had another *Salomé,* and not another *Earnest.* When Wilde affirmed that he saved his genius for life, and invested only his talent in art, he was accurate, as he always was, but perhaps he came to regret this particular accuracy.

OSCAR WILDE
(1854–1900)

WILDE FOSTERED A CONSIDERABLE ORAL tradition, some of it doubtless apocryphal. His grandson, Merlin Holland, charmingly reminds us that Oscar Wilde "confessed that he lived in permanent fear of not being misunderstood." When the twenty-eight-year-old Oscar the Aesthete arrived at the New York City Customs, he is reported to have said, "I have nothing to declare except my beautiful Genius." If he did not say it, he should have, just as he should have expressed his disappointment with the Atlantic Ocean: "It failed to roar." W. B. Yeats thought that Wilde was always playing the part of Wilde, but that was also true of Lord Byron, Hemingway, and (dare one say it?) the illustrious Goethe. Merlin Holland assigns his grandfather the role of Faust, though whether Marlovian, Goethean, or Mannian is unclear. Since my subject is Wilde's genius, and the divine Oscar is both protean and the object of my lifelong literary worship, I will not confine myself to any single work by him, though that is against my procedure in these pages. Wilde's genius is strongest in *The Importance of Being Earnest* and in two magnificent essays, "The Soul of Man under Socialism" and "The Decay of Lying." I will employ these three at random, while also wandering elsewhere in his work and life.

The cardinal principle in considering Wilde was stated by Jorge Luis Borges: the great Aesthete was almost always right. My self-slain profession, once the scholarly teaching of imaginative literature in the English-speaking world, would still be alive had it learned Wildean wisdom: "All bad poetry is sincere." Alas, it is too late, and the better students rightly flee our undead professors, on every side. We *need* Wilde, even in our ruin; who else can cheer us up in so bad a time? Descending into a mineshaft in Leadville, Colorado, during his American tour, Oscar drilled a new shaft, and then ascended with the miners and their girlfriends to a casino: "and in one corner a pianist—sitting at a piano over which was this notice: 'Please don't shoot the pianist; he is doing his best.' I was struck with this recognition of the fact that bad art merits the penalty of death."

Bad art is now studied in the universities, exalted in the media, and is supposed to be politically good for us. Wilde, accurately prophetic, a century after his death has no rival in describing our literary situation:

In old days books were written by men of letters and read by the public. Nowadays books are written by the public and read by nobody.

Wilde exemplifies the two major senses of genius, an innate fathering-
and-mothering force, and an other self, looking for and finding destruction
for what is innate. A century later, when homosexuality cannot provide social immolation, Wilde would have to find an alternate way down and out,
something beyond imagining. Byron found the Greek rebellion, Hemingway
the various ways to "live your life all the way up" until suicide; I like to
think Wilde might have found an even more individual end. My favorite
among his "maxims for the instruction of the over-educated" is:

One should never listen. To listen is a sign of indifference to one's
hearers.

I haven't won any teaching awards in my half-century career, because I
believe in the passion and intellect embedded in that apothegm. One of
Wilde's truest affinities (shrewdly noted by his editor, Isobel Murray) was
with Emerson, particularly with the central essay "Self-Reliance," which is
echoed both in "The Decay of Lying" and "The Soul of Man under Socialism." Emerson, in "Self-Reliance," says so many things at once as to render
commentary dubious, but Wilde seems to have been most moved by:

I shun father and mother and wife and brother, when my genius calls
me. I would write on the lintels of the door-post, *Whim*. I hope it is
somewhat better than whim at last, but we cannot spend the day in
explanation.

Whim is the royal road to being misunderstood, another aim inherited by
Wilde from Emerson. I suspect that two sentences in "Self-Reliance" had
the same effect upon Wilde that they have had upon many of my students:

In every work of genius we recognize our own rejected thoughts: they
come back to us with a certain alienated majesty.

As men's prayers are a disease of the will, so are their creeds a disease
of the intellect.

On his deathbed, Wilde converted to Roman Catholicism. Perspectives
upon deathbed conversions vary, but Wilde, all his life, held that Jesus

Christ was primarily an artist, and a Gnostic, and Oscar preferred the Gospel of John, on highly heretical grounds, as here in *De Profundis:*

> While in reading the Gospels—particularly that of St. John himself, or whatever early Gnostic took his name and mantle—I see the continual assertion of the imagination as the basis of all spiritual and material life, I see also that to Christ imagination was simply a form of Love, and that to him Love was Lord in the fullest meaning of the phrase.

Wilde recalled remarking to Gide that everything Christ said could be placed immediately in the realm of Art and there be fulfilled completely. "A truth ceases to be true when more than one person believes in it" is a famous Wildean aphorism, which hardly allows room for conversion, except upon the deathbed. The crucial discussion of Christ by Wilde comes in "The Soul of Man under Socialism," and like the rest of the essay is a hymn to personality, to individual self-development. Here is Wilde at his least ironic, and perhaps least understood:

> And so he who would lead a Christ-like life is he who is perfectly and absolutely himself. He may be a great poet, or a great man of science; or a young student at a University, or one who watched sheep upon a moor; or a maker of dramas, like Shakespeare, or a thinker about God, like Spinoza; or a child who plays in a garden, or a fisherman who throws his nets into the sea. It does not matter what he is, as long as he realises the perfection of the soul that is within him. All imitation in morals and in life is wrong. Through the streets of Jerusalem at the present day crawls one who is mad and carries a wooden cross on his shoulders. He is a symbol of the lives that are marred by imitation. Father Damien was Christ-like when he went out to live with the lepers, because in such service he realised fully what was best in him. But he was not more Christ-like than Wagner, when he realised his soul in music; or than Shelley, when he realised his soul in song. There is no one type for man. There are as many perfections as there are imperfect men. And while to the claims of charity a man may yield and yet be free, to the claims of conformity no man may yield and remain free at all.

Though Wilde uses the word "Socialism," he means something much closer to the vision of the Catalan Anarchists who fought against both Franco and

the Communists, and who maintained Catharist (Provençal Gnostic) traditions. Wilde's deepest belief seems to have been that we need to "live each
other's lives and not our own," which is irreconcilable with exalting the individualism of personality, but like Emerson the author of "The Soul of
Man under Socialism" deplored "a foolish consistency."

Wilde's genius was for paradox, and its finest instances in him obliterate
the supposed line between criticism and creation. Here is Wilde at his critical best in the essay-dialogue "The Decay of Lying," speaking through his
surrogate, Vivian:

> No great artist ever sees things as they really are. If he did, he would
> cease to be an artist. Take an example from our own day, I know that
> you are fond of Japanese things. Now, do you really imagine that the
> Japanese people, as they are presented to us in art, have any exis-
> tence? If you do, you have never understood Japanese art at all. The
> Japanese people are the deliberate self-conscious creation of certain
> individual artists. If you set a picture by Hokusai, or Hokkei, or any of
> the great native painters, beside a real Japanese gentleman or lady,
> you will see that there is not the slightest resemblance between
> them. The actual people who live in Japan are not unlike the general
> run of English people; that is to say, they are extremely commonplace,
> and have nothing curious or extraordinary about them. In fact the
> whole of Japan is a pure invention. There is no such country, there are
> no such people. One of our most charming painters went recently to
> the Land of the Chrysanthemum in the foolish hope of seeing the
> Japanese. All he saw, all he had the chance of painting, were a few
> lanterns and some fans.

To be both this wise and this funny is rare enough, but truly outrageous
genius breaks through in a grand assertion: "In fact the whole of Japan is a
pure invention. There is no such country, there are no such people."

This is one of those few passages of memorable literary criticism that
help redeem it as a genre of literature. I am happy to plagiarize myself in
observing that *this* Japan is also that far and wide land where Edward Lear's
Jumblies live, together with his Dong with a luminous nose, Pobble who has
no toes, and the best of all marriages, the Owl and the Pussycat. It is where
Alice goes, whether underground or through the looking-glass, and most
precisely it is the country of cucumber sandwiches, where Lady Bracknell
confronts Miss Prism. The name of the country is the highest criticism:

That is what the highest criticism really is, the record of one's own soul. It is more fascinating than history, as it is concerned simply with oneself. It is more delightful than philosophy, as its subject is concrete and not abstract, real and not vague. It is the only civilized form of autobiography as it deals not with the events, but with the thoughts of one's life; not with life's physical accidents of death and circumstance, but with the spiritual moods and imaginative passions of the mind.

I was told recently that an eminent New Historicist and Cultural Poetician, commencing his large study of Shakespeare, had remarked that *his* book would be about Shakespeare, as opposed to a recent, shaggy monster of a work that only ostensibly concerned Shakespeare, but was just another part of the ongoing autobiography of an aged critic. I cheerfully accept Wilde's wisdom, while hoping to avoid the really gorgeous solipsism of Lady Bracknell, in what remains my favorite passage in *The Importance of Being Earnest,* and so in all of Wilde:

LADY BRACKNELL [*Pulls out her watch*]. Come dear. [*Gwendolyn rises.*] We have already missed five, if not six, trains. To miss any more might expose us to comment on the platform.

LUIGI PIRANDELLO

HENRY IV. Ah, a little light! Sit there around the table, no, not like that; in an elegant, easy, manner! . . . [*To Harold.*] Yes, you, like that! [*Poses him.*] [*Then to Berthold.*] You, so! . . . and I, here! [*Sits opposite them.*] We could do with a little decorative moonlight. It's very useful for us, the moonlight. I feel a real necessity for it, and pass a lot of time looking up at the moon from my window. Who would think, to look at her that she knows that eight hundred years have passed, and that I, seated at the window, cannot really be Henry IV gazing at the moon like any poor devil? But, look, look! See what a magnificent Night scene we have here: the emperor surrounded by his faithful counsellors! . . . How do you like it?

You can salute Pirandello's genius, particularly in his *Henry IV,* by saying that the nameless madman, who only *thinks* that he is Henry IV, is a version of Hamlet, while Belcredi, the practical joker whom "Henry IV" stabs, is both a Claudius figure and a stand-in for Pirandello himself, who was addicted to rewriting *Hamlet*.

The nameless, Hamlet-like character, who would be Henry IV, takes his revenge upon Pirandello for casting him in a farce, rather than a tragedy. Pirandello, a rhetorical genius in the authentic Sicilian literary tradition, grants this moment of high aesthetic dignity to his madman, but subsequently withdraws it, and we return to melodramatic farce.

It is an irony that post-Ibsenite drama achieved its most original moments in this Sicilian sophist, whose essential assumption is that all his characters, ultimately, are quite mad, and not just north-northwest, like Hamlet. Always conscious of Shakespeare and of Ibsen, Pirandello takes their theatricalism and subjects it to near-parody. Even *Six Characters in Search of an Author* borders upon parodistic farce, as though Pirandello could not resolve the struggle between the characters' assertion that the stage belonged to their familial tragedy, and the actors' demand that the stage is theirs, in order to entertain a commercial audience. Ancient sophist that he was, Pirandello always argued on both sides of every dramatic contention.

LUIGI PIRANDELLO
(1867–1936)

ERIC BENTLEY, WHO HAS UNIQUE authority as a critic of modern drama, once told me that my exaltation of Beckett's *Endgame* as the supreme modern drama was mistaken, because it neglected Pirandello, the most important playwright since Ibsen. Interestingly, Bentley quotes Pirandello's judgment: "After Shakespeare I unhesitatingly place Ibsen first." Whether, after Ibsen, one should place Pirandello first is, to me, a puzzling matter; Chekhov and Strindberg, Brecht and Beckett, *read* more powerfully than Pirandello does, but a good, rare staging of Pirandello unsettles me as the other great modern dramatists generally do not. Since tragedy, as a pure form, is no longer possible, while tragic farce demonstrably is feasible, the Sicilian Pirandello can be regarded as the authentic master of tragic farce in the earlier twentieth century, to be followed later by Brecht and Beckett.

Only two plays justify thinking of Pirandello as a dramatic genius: *Six Characters in Search of an Author* (1921) and *Henry IV* (1922). Everything else by him is secondary work, compelling only in flashes. *Six Characters*, summarized, sounds like a theatrical disaster. Eric Bentley's *The Pirandello Commentaries* (1986) gathers up his superb writing on Pirandello, while the most important plays were edited by Bentley as *Naked Masks* (1952). My purpose, as always in this book, is limited to the question of genius. George Bernard Shaw overpraised *Six Characters* as the most original play ever, but Shaw (no genius, in my judgment) merely was fighting his usual rather desperate war against Shakespeare. Pirandello's *Henry IV* is his version of *Hamlet*, and that certainly remains the most original of all plays, and also prompts *Six Characters*.

Shakespeare was his own director and stage-manager, as well as a reliable character actor. Pirandello's characters (two of them anyway) are in search of Shakespeare or his surrogate, the Actor-Manager or director who ultimately declines to write the play that the Father and the Step-Daughter request. We begin with the Actor-Manager trying to start the rehearsal of an incomprehensible comedy by Pirandello, but he is interrupted by the six characters. "We bring you a drama, sir," the Father pleads, and the sexy Step-Daughter vivaciously declares, "We may be your fortune." So far the Mother, third of the characters, is silent, as are the Son, an angry young man, and the unhappy teenage Boy, and the Child, a little girl about four.

The Step-Daughter (rather a grand role, with a touch of musical comedy) is the life of the play, but its center is the desperately guilty Father, whose pathos transcends the rather ghastly melodrama that unfolds among the six characters. To play out that melodrama in one sentence: the Father delivers the Mother to his male secretary, by whom she has three children, having left the Son with Father, who attempts to embrace the Step-Daughter in a bordello, only to be interrupted by the Mother; the secretary having died, the Father takes everyone back, but the little Child drowns, the Boy shoots himself, and the six characters descend upon the Actor-Manager.

Pirandello's genius confutes this farrago and for three acts interweaves the characters and the acting company so inextricably that all is role-playing. His intrinsic model is the extraordinary gap in representation that Shakespeare cuts into *Hamlet,* from the arrival of the players in act 2, scene 2 until Claudius dashes away from the performance of the Prince's *Mousetrap* in act 3, scene 2. For a thousand lines, Shakespeare diverts his audience with plays-within-plays just as all of *Six Characters* consists of roles-within-roles. Shakespeare invents in *Hamlet* the destruction of any boundary between being oneself and playing oneself, and Pirandello converts the invention to Ibsenite uses. Anne Paolucci catches this:

> The actors who play the characters are not supposed to be actors. They are characters that actors are supposed to play but cannot. They emphasize the difference between what they are and what those so-called actors who are trying to play them are ... When the curtain comes down, we applaud the actors who have acted the parts of characters that are too real to be played. We recall, perhaps, Hamlet's speech on the subject, marveling that this mere player could act a part so realistically, so passionately, while I-Hamlet who am *very I,* cannot match the actors' expression of passion. Pirandello's six characters must play a whole play in the mood of that *Hamlet* speech. It is a daring tour de force, but tour de force still, as compared with Pirandello's own version of *Hamlet, Enrico IV.*

Admirable, if we withdraw the "perhaps." Pirandello said he admired "souls that scorn to coagulate or rigidify in this or that predetermined shape," and he found them in *Tristram Shandy* and in *Hamlet.* Discontinuity in the self, endless in Hamlet, is a larger and different matter than role-playing. Only the Father, in *Six Characters,* is a morass of discontinuities, but we touch on Pirandello's prime weakness: Hamlet is a charismatic personality, the Father a sensible emptiness. There is only one personality in *Six*

Characters: not one of the characters or of the acting company. Madame Pace, the bordello operator, whose very name ironically brings peace, is the play's odd card. She arrives on stage as the seventh character, and she certainly is not in search of an author. The six characters no longer seem reality as opposed to the acting's company's illusion, since the vulgar reality of Madame Pace converts the Father and Step-Daughter into illusions. There is only one persuasive character in the play, and she is a bawd.

Bentley's grand assertion for Pirandello insists that the Sicilian playwright gave a new importance to the inescapable nature of role-playing, in life as on stage. Bentley phrases this unequivocally: "Theatre provides an image of life, the image of life, because life is a theatre." I myself don't know that Pirandello or Bentley allow us to argue with them. But I don't think that Sir John Falstaff and Hamlet, Iago and Cleopatra, would agree, which means that Shakespeare also would have dissented from Pirandello and Bentley, despite his astonishing experimentation in Hamlet and elsewhere.

Shakespeare, taking part in the Poets' War against his enemy-friend Ben Jonson, has a lovely time playing theatrical politics in *Hamlet, Twelfth Night,* and *Troilus and Cressida. Twelfth Night,* gloriously but disconcertingly, socially crucifies the wretched Malvolio, but so hilariously that we are slow to see the universal vulnerability that his blow at Jonson exposes in the audience. In *Troilus and Cressida* as in *Hamlet* act 2, scene 2 through act 3, scene 2, Shakespeare does not allow the audience to forget that they are spectators at a play so self-conscious that it no longer asks to be taken as the illusory shadow of truth. Bentley's vision (out of Pirandello) that all is theater is not a Shakespearean formulation. Pirandello went to school with Shakespeare, as Ibsen and Chekhov did, but Pirandello learned too simplistic and reductive a lesson. Life sometimes is a theater, but sometimes it is a war, a school, a purgatory, a descent into hell, a business, or what you will. And doubtless we are all role-players, but only in certain sequences or spasms, and more often than not we are nowhere near a stage. Theater involves stage, actor, and spectator, and for much of our authentic lives we are alone. Try to be actor to your own spectator, and they will carry you off, soon enough.

Henry IV seems to me more interesting than *Six Characters,* because it offers some relief from Pirandello's theatrical metaphysics, though they are present also. Bentley again is our best guide, so dangerously skilled at exposition that he at moments outshines his subject, since *Henry IV* is topheavy with blemishes and confusions, which nevertheless it survives.

The nameless protagonist of *Henry IV* suffers from an unrequited love. A rival admirer of the lady arranges for a riding accident in the midst of a costumed festivity. Our hero, dressed as the German emperor Henry IV, comes back to consciousness with the mad conviction that he indeed is Henry IV. Indulged by a wealthy sister, "Henry IV" lives his delusion in a villa made over into a castle. Twelve years later, sanity returns, but he decides to feign continued madness. As a therapeutic exercise, a psychiatrist introduces into the Emperor's company the daughter of his former beloved, hoping to restore Henry IV to sanity. We are now twenty years since the original lunacy, and Henry IV is supposed to be shocked back to a sense of time. But he has revealed that sanity has returned anyway, and he attempts to embrace the girl. The rival, still the mother's lover after twenty years, intervenes, but is murdered with a sword-thrust by Henry IV.

I suppose that Kleist might have made a tragedy out of that, but of course Pirandello can't and doesn't want to. The historical German Henry IV is remembered for his ordeal of kneeling in the snow at Canossa, slyly submitting to a pope, lest he be dethroned. But that is about all the history that we need. The nameless one is in search of an author, but only as Hamlet is in search of his father's spirit, for Pirandello has rewritten *Hamlet* as a tragic farce by Ibsen. As one of the many revisions of *Hamlet*, this works.

Hamlet in His Modern Guises (2001) by Alexander Welsh does not include Pirandello's *Henry IV* as one of these guises, but does survey a number of novels: Goethe's *Wilhelm Meister's Apprenticeship*, Sir Walter Scott's *Redgauntlet*, Dickens's *Great Expectations*, Melville's *Pierre*, Joyce's *Ulysses*, Iris Murdoch's *The Black Prince*. Welsh's incisive conclusion is that "the Hamletism of modernism attests to the part mourning plays in consciousness," which is a valid clue as to why Pirandello's nameless hero ends his play by murdering his Claudius, Belcredi; Hamlet's mourning for his father, and for what he regards as his mother's lost honor, expands into a sorrow for the human condition, but one doesn't expect Pirandello to be Shakespeare. "Henry IV" mourns his lost youth, and revenges his twenty years of masquerade (twelve mad, eight feigned) upon Belcredi, first author of his misery. And yet the nameless protagonist is left alive, miserable, neither sane nor mad, and totally ruined by having tried to strike through the mask of illusion. Bentley compares him to Beckett's self-immolated characters, and indeed Pirandello has taken us to the border of *Endgame*.

IV

HESED

LUSTRE 7

|

John Donne, Alexander Pope, Jonathan Swift, Jane Austen, Lady Murasaki

|

Hesed, being God's covenant love for men and women, manifests itself either as irony, as in this Lustre, or as the loss of love, in the next. Donne's irony, initially libertine, transmutes into a spiritual irony at his own expense, but the ironies of Pope and Swift are savage and satirical, as is proper for them. In Austen, irony becomes a Shakespearean mode of inventiveness, worthy of *As You Like It*, whose Rosalind is the forerunner of Elizabeth Bennet in *Pride and Prejudice*.

The irony of the subtle and elegant Lady Murasaki is the irony of the oxymoronic "splendor of longing" that is so luminous in *The Tale of Genji*, where longing or incessant desire both vitalizes existence and at last destroys it. John Donne and the Jane Austen of *Persuasion* would have appreciated Lady Murasaki's splendid longing because they also celebrate the complexities of deferred desire.

JOHN DONNE

When by thy scorn, O murderess, I am dead,
And that thou think'st thee free
From all solicitation from me,
Then shall my ghost come to thy bed,
And thee, feigned vestal, in worse arms shall see;
Then thy sick taper will begin to wink,
And he whose thou art then, being tired before,
Will, if thou stir, or pinch to wake him, think
        Thou call'st for more,
And in false sleep will from thee shrink,
And then poor aspen wretch, neglected thou
Bathed in a cold quicksilver sweat wilt lie
        A verier ghost than I;
What I will say, I will not tell thee now,
Lest that preserve thee; and since my love is spent,
I had rather thou shouldst painfully repent,
Than by my threatenings rest still innocent.

"The Apparition" is a superb instance of Donne's art in his *Songs and Sonnets* (1633, published two years after the poet's death). Donne begins by literalizing Petrarch's metaphor of the lover dying of his mistress's scorn, of her replacing him by another admirer. As a ghost bent on vengeance, he will have the sublime bad taste to intrude upon her amorous life. Startled by the apparition, the "murderess" will attempt to wake her current lover, who, worn out in her service, will feign sleep. Alone therefore with the shade of Donne, she will be "a verier ghost," trembling and frightened.

Perhaps the later preacher John Donne, dean of St. Paul's, might have allegorized this delicious lyric by saying that his "murderess" was "the mistress of my youth, Poetry" whom he had abandoned for "the wife of mine age, Divinity," but that would have reversed the plot of the poem. The Dean of St. Paul's found other uses for his libertine wit, displaced into the intellectual agility of his sermons, where doctrine is humanized and rendered accessible.

Donne's genius has a pragmatic element to it, whether his argument was erotic or divine. We praise his "wit," which is palpable, but we should admire him as much for his versatile intellect, a marvelous manager of the transition from one mode of love, secular and salacious, to another, sacred yet still venturesome.

JOHN DONNE
(1572–1631)

BORN EIGHT YEARS AFTER SHAKESPEARE, John Donne in 1595 was living in London, a young gentleman of means, with some reputation as an erotic and satirical poet. A constant theatergoer, he probably attended Shakespeare's *Richard II*, and would have appreciated the progress (or decline) of that martyred monarch from petulant ruler to metaphysical poet, rather in a Donnean mode. *Songs and Sonnets* was not published until two years after Donne's death, but some of the poems circulated widely in manuscript, and perhaps Shakespeare read them, though he is likelier to have read Donne's highly erotic Ovidian elegies. I suspect the influence went the other way; sometimes one feels that *Songs and Sonnets* parodies Shakespeare's Richard II.

Donne's own worldly progress, after his 1602 conversion from Roman Catholicism to the Anglican religion, was at first slow, since he was reluctant to take holy orders until 1615. But after that, he rapidly became a famous preacher, and in 1621 was named dean of St. Paul's. Most of *The Holy Sonnets* were written before Donne's ordination, as was the great meditation "Good Friday, 1613. Riding Westward." The two magnificent hymns "To God My God, in My Sickness" and "To God the Father" probably were written in 1623, during a November-to-December period in which he expected to die. But otherwise, Donne had abandoned poetry for Divinity. His sermons, at their best, are among the strongest in the language.

Dr. Samuel Johnson, my critical paradigm, frequently sought to isolate and define genius (when it could be found), particularly in his *Lives of the Poets* (1779–81). Donne appears in Johnson's *Lives* only as another member of the Metaphysical school, in the *Life of Cowley*. Abraham Cowley is now forgotten, but in the later seventeenth century was the Ezra Pound of his era. Though fading out fast in the Age of Johnson, Cowley still was notorious enough to lead off Johnson's *Lives*, as the supposed founder of the bad old school of poetry that was set aside by John Dryden and Alexander Pope, Johnsonian favorites.

Johnson thought very highly of his *Life of Cowley*, because it broke critical new ground on the Metaphysicals (though Dryden first had named the school). Here is Johnson giving Donne what Dryden gave him, which is rather less than it might seem:

Those however who deny them to be poets, allow them to be wits. Dryden confesses of himself and his contemporaries, that they fall below Donne in wit, but maintains that they surpass him in poetry.

In *The Rambler* No. 125, Johnson observes that "every new genius produces some innovation which, when invented and approved, subverts the rules which the practice of foregoing authors had established." Why could Johnson not see Donne as such a genius? Though the great critic would not say so, he nevertheless was deeply troubled by Donne, whom he called "abstruse and profound," but whose poetry was condemned as "a voluntary deviation from nature in pursuit of something new or strange."

Donne was perpetually revived throughout the nineteenth century, from Coleridge through Arthur Symons, so that his twentieth-century revival by T. S. Eliot needs to be seen as a kind of afterthought. The common reader is Donne's final judge, and Donne is very much alive as we begin the twenty-first century. Here I am concerned to define that vitality, and to demonstrate the genius of Donne, on the wholly Johnsonian ground of invention or perpetual freshness, the originality that cannot be dismissed as a period style. Here, from *Songs and Sonnets,* is Donne at his most popular:

> Go, and catch a falling star,
>   Get with child a mandrake root,
> Tell me, where all past years are,
>   Or who cleft the Devil's foot,
> Teach me to hear mermaids singing,
>   Or to keep off envy's stinging,
>   And find
>   What wind
> Serves to advance an honest mind.
>
> If thou be'est born to strange sights,
>   Things invisible to see,
> Ride ten thousand days and nights
>   Till age snow white hairs on thee;
> Thou, when thou return'st, wilt tell me
> All strange wonders that befell thee,
>   And swear
>   No where
> Lives a woman true, and fair.

If thou find'st one, let me know,
    Such a pilgrimage were sweet,
Yet do not; I would not go
    Though at next door we might meet.
Though she were true, when you met her,
And last, till you write your letter,
        Yet she
        Will be
False, ere I come, to two or three.

This is a libertine's "Song," but very light in tone, and therefore not to be literalized. Its irony implies that the singer himself will be false, ere he comes, to two or three. That "mandrake root" greatly interested Donne, who had devoted four stanzas to the mandrake in his "The Progress of the Soul," where he tells us that the apple plucked by Satan for Eve is abandoned by its soul, and houses itself in the mandrake plant. A long tradition of magic and venery ensues in which the mandrake or May apple or mandragora is employed for inducing lust, sleep, and death. There is thus a shadow or two upon this insouciant song, but the libertine irony dominates.

Donne's genius is manifested more exquisitely in the superb erotic meditation "The Ecstasy," where the title refers to the lovers "standing outside," in a hushed interval before renewed sexual intercourse. What makes this poem so powerful is its doubleness of tone, at once celebrating a metaphysics of love while also constituting a fresh seduction, since the speaker ends by urging the lady to further physical rapture:

As our blood labours to beget
    Spirits, as like souls as it can,
Because such fingers need to knit
    That subtle knot, which makes us man:

So must pure lovers' souls descend
    T'affections, and its faculties,
Which sense may reach and apprehend,
    Else a great prince in prison lies.

To our bodies turn we then, that so
    Weak men on love revealed may look,
Love's mysteries in souls do grow,
    But yet the body is his book.

And if some lover, such as we,
    Have heard this dialogue of one,
Let him still mark us, he shall see
    Small change, when we are to bodies gone.

The Neoplatonic fused soul of the lovers must separate, and then return to a bodily merger, since otherwise their composite soul will be as powerless as a prisoner: "Else a great prince in prison lies." Erotic and divine revelation become one in the Bible of the sexual body: "But yet the body is his book." The two ecstasies are one, whether standing back, or returned to coupling. This doubtless is an invitation to pleasure, but its sophistication touches upon sanctification, Donne's audacity being boundless.

Dr. Johnson's famous (and disapproving) definition of Metaphysical wit states, "The most heterogeneous ideas are yoked by violence together." Donne's genius delights in yoking by subtle insinuation ideas that only *seem* diverse. The mystics, in the long tradition of interpreting the Song of Songs, have found divine union allegorized in erotic play. But Donne is not a mystical poet, even when he composes a devotional masterpiece like "Hymn to God My God, in My Sickness." He lived another eight years, but wrote this extraordinary poem in imminent expectation of dying:

Since I am coming to that Holy room,
    Where, with thy choir of saints for evermore,
I shall be made thy music; as I come
    I tune the instrument here at the door,
    And what I must do then, think here before.

Whilst my physicians by their love are grown
    Cosmographers, and I their map, who lie
Flat on this bed, that by them may be shown
    That this is my south-west discovery
    Per fretum febris, by these straits to die,

I joy, that in these straits, I see my west;
    For, though their currents yield return to none,
What shall my west hurt me? As west and east
    In all flat maps (and I am one) are one,
    So death doth touch the resurrection.

Is the Pacific sea my home? Or are
   The eastern riches? Is Jerusalem?
Anyan, and Magellan, and Gibraltar,
   All straits, and none but straits, are ways to them,
   Whether where Japhet dwelt, or Cham, or Shem.

We think that Paradise and Calvary,
   Christ's cross, and Adam's tree, stood in one place;
Look Lord, and find both Adams met in me;
   As the first Adam's sweat surrounds my face,
   May the last Adam's blood my soul embrace.

So, in his purple wrapped receive me Lord,
   By these his thorns give me his other crown;
And as to others' souls I preached thy word,
   Be this my text, my sermon to mine own,
   Therefore that he may raise the Lord throws down.

The ecstasy of the mystic is lacking; in its place the great wit works it-self out, at its own human expense, and yet with extraordinary vivacity and humor. We should be wary of interpreting "that holy room" as heaven, as the Dean of St. Paul's is too subtle for such presumption. On what he thinks may very well be his deathbed, he writes this hymn to tune his instrument, his poetic gift. Surrounded by attentive cosmographers, he sees himself as a flat map, which becomes the central image of his poem. *Per fretum febris,* through fever's hot strait, he goes southwest to a death, but west and east, flattened out, are one, and so death touches resurrection. That "touch" is very light, and continues so as he plays changes upon the word "straits." Burning with fever, he thinks of Adam's fallen task, to earn bread through the brow's sweat, and he requests the embrace of Christ, as the final Adam.

The controlled pathos of this is extraordinary, and so is its theological reticence. On his supposed deathbed, the Dean must inwardly be aware of his own religious history. Born into a Catholic family, with an uncle and a brother who suffered for the old faith, Donne early on had a Catholic edu-cation, and was slow to abandon the familial tradition, probably not until his thirtieth year. In choosing the Church of England, Donne primarily did not make a theological choice, and his long delay before becoming an Anglican priest demonstrates that expediency was not a prime motive. His poet's temperament complexly determined his career in the church. Critics accu-rately see no great divide between the fervor and wit of the early poetry and the later sermons. Donne wanted continuity with the cultural past and with his own youth, and he found that continuity with the Anglicans, the middle way between Roman Catholicism and Calvinist Protestantism.

His devotional poems, and his sermons, are not theological in their prime emphases, and it can be judged that his genius remained consistent, since "wit" centers all his work. This is "wit" in the older meaning of great intelligence, though Johnson, in following Dryden and Pope, refused to see it as "true wit," an idea of neoclassical order. Ben Jonson, Donne's exact contemporary, both admired and deprecated Donne's poetry, which was too idiosyncratic for him. That extreme personalism, that never left Donne, can be regarded as the particular mark of his genius. His voice still lingers, permanently unmistakable:

> . . . and I am re-begot
> Of absence, darkness, death; things which are not.

ALEXANDER POPE

Others for *language* all their care express,
And value books, as women men, for dress:
Their praise is still—the style is excellent:
The sense, they humbly take upon content.
Words are like leaves; and where they most abound,
Much fruit of sense beneath is rarely found.
False eloquence, like the prismatic glass,
Its gaudy colours spreads on every place;
The face of nature we no more survey,
All glares alike, without distinction gay:
But true expression, like the unchanging sun,
Clears and improves whate'er it shines upon,
It gilds all objects, but it alters none.
Expression is the dress of thought, and still

Appears more decent as more suitable;
A vile conceit in pompous words expressed,
Is like a clown in regal purple dressed;
For different styles with different subjects sort,
As several garbs with country, town, and court.
Some by old words to fame have made pretence;
Ancients in phrase, mere moderns in their sense!
Such laboured nothings, in so strange a style,
Amaze the unlearned, and make the learned smile.

Pope, in his early *Essay on Criticism,* his first important poem, warns critics against the deceptions of false poets. Even the young Alexander Pope assumed a role of literary moralist, one that had not been taken up since Shakespeare's friend and rival, Ben Jonson. A dwarf, twisted in body by childhood tuberculosis, Pope must have seemed an unlikely candidate to become the great English poet of the European Enlightenment. To find equivalents of Pope's precocious technical genius you need to consider John Milton, Alfred Tennyson, and the late James Merrill. Even as children, Pope and these others were verse artists who seemed more like wizards than writers.

Like his friend, Jonathan Swift, Pope was a genius of satire, a dangerous mode for any writer. Readers rarely love satire; bathing in acid is scary, even when salubrious. Pope is not as savage as Swift, but he goes beyond any satirist now alive among us:

Let *Sporus* tremble—"What? That thing of silk,
Sporus, that mere white curd of ass's milk?
Satire or sense, alas! can Sporus feel?
Who breaks a butterfly upon a wheel?"
Yet let me flap this bug with gilded wings,
This painted child of dirt that stinks and stings;
Whose buzz the witty and the fair annoys,
Yet wit ne'er tastes, and beauty ne'er enjoys:
So well-bred spaniels civilly delight
In mumbling of the game they dare not bite.
Eternal smiles his emptiness betray,
As shallow streams run dimpling all the way.
Whether in florid impotence he speaks,
And, as the prompter breathes, the puppet squeaks;

Or at the ear of Eve, familiar toad,
Half froth, half venom, spits himself abroad,
In puns, or politics, or tales, or lies,
Or spite, or smut, or rhymes, or blasphemies.
His wit all seesaw, between *that* and *this,*
Now high, now low, now master up, now miss,
And he himself one vile antithesis.
Amphibious thing! that acting either part,
The trifling head, or the corrupted heart,
Fop at the toilet, flatterer at the board,
Now trips a Lady, and now struts a Lord.
Eve's tempter thus the Rabbins have exprest,
A cherub's face, a reptile all the rest;
Beauty that shocks you, parts that none will trust,
Wit that can creep, and pride that licks the dust.

It doesn't matter just who Sporus was intended to be (Lord Hervey, who had attacked Pope). The reader is invited to substitute her or his favorite contemporary literary malignancy in the reading of this grand passage.

ALEXANDER POPE
(1688–1744)

THERE ARE GREAT POETS WHO RAGE IN the margins, like William Blake, and poets unknown in their own lifetime, like Emily Dickinson and Gerard Manley Hopkins. Alexander Pope's was a public genius, like Ben Jonson's or Lord Byron's or Oscar Wilde's. These figures were *news*, as no living writer of authentic eminence is today, though we have geniuses of publicity, which is not quite what I mean by a "public genius."

Pope began with unusual liabilities. He was a fervent Roman Catholic (though doctrinally dubious) in an England where legally they were excluded from London and from the universities. Like Shakespeare's Richard III he was a hunchback, and a dwarf as well. Yet he was a child prodigy as a poet, with gifts all but universally acknowledged. As a verse-artist in English, he has no superiors, though some peers: Milton, Tennyson, James Merrill among them. There is no inferior verse by Pope: *An Essay on Man* irritates me by its frequent moral platitudes, but it is flawless in expression. Turn Pope's pages at random, and touchstones flash out at you:

> Oh! if to dance all Night, and dress all Day,
> Charm'd the Small-pox, or chas'd old Age away;
> Who would not scorn what Huswife's Cares produce,
> Or who would learn one earthly Thing of Use?

• • •

> Poets themselves must fall, like those they sung
> Deaf the prais'd ear, and mute the tuneful tongue.

• • •

> The Dog-star rages! nay 'tis past a doubt,
> All *Bedlam*, or *Parnassus*, is let out;
> Fire in each eye, and Papers in each hand,
> They rave, recite, and madden round the land.

• • •

Oh! could I mount on the Maenonian wing
Your arms, your Actions, your Repose to sing!
What seas you travers'd! and what fields you fought
Your Country's Peace, how oft, how dearly bought!

• • •

Thus at her felt approach, and secret might,
Art after *Art* goes out, and all is Night.

The marriage of sound and sense in Pope is justly praised, but here I seek his genius, or other self. Though an apostle of Reason, Nature, and Order, and commended as such by Dr. Samuel Johnson, Pope's public persona is in part misleading. A furious energy drives his work, though with nothing like the ironic fury that animates the satires of his close friend Jonathan Swift, who crosses the border into abysses of digressiveness. Pope keeps tight control, as does Racine, but the reader senses throughout a darkness that gathers though it does not fall.

Darkness abounded. Pope was sixteen when a tubercular infection curved his spine in two directions. Four and a half feet tall, racked by headaches and exhaustion, he created art that was a triumph over his deformation. The elegance, power, proportion, and memorability of his poetry strengthened him morally to bear the long disease of his life. Energy, propulsive in his work, actually renders him almost too exuberant a culmination of the neoclassic tradition of Ben Jonson, Denham, Waller, Dryden. Dr. Samuel Johnson, Shakespeare of critics, loved Dryden but regarded Pope as the perfection of poetry, which may be why the formidable Johnson wrote only two major poems, *London* and *The Vanity of Human Wishes*. There is a puzzle here: Dryden, Pope, and Johnson knew that Shakespeare and John Milton were of an imaginative and intellectual eminence well beyond the neoclassic line (Chaucer's language made him less available to them). Pope and Johnson edited editions of Shakespeare, and Dryden preceded them in proclaiming the primacy of Shakespeare. Again, Dryden, Pope, and Johnson esteemed Milton only just below Shakespeare. There is a complex division at work here: Pope's version of Homer, according to Johnson, "tuned the English tongue," and so refined Dryden. Did Shakespeare and Milton then require refinement? Would they yield to it? Is it that they represented something larger than refinement, something that would spur poets of the 1740s, like Collins, Gray, and the Wartons, to a New Poetry, disapproved by Johnson? The question became more urgent with William

Cowper and William Blake, from the 1780s on, and then transformed into a major polemic with Coleridge, Wordsworth, Shelley, and Keats.

Shakespeare, however much Pope venerated him, did not inhibit a writer of moral satire and mock-epic. Pope's masterpieces are *The Rape of the Lock* and *The Dunciad,* both mock-epics, the first brilliantly interwoven with *Paradise Lost,* the second both with Milton and the English Bible. Dr. Johnson esteemed Pope's translation of Homer highest, but this is now a puzzle to almost everyone. Pope's Homer made Pope affluent, the first English poet since Shakespeare to become financially comfortable through his own labors, but I do not know anyone who reads (or can read) it now.

The mock-heroic, central to Pope, was defined by the late Maynard Mack as "the metaphor of tone," ambivalently both comic and destructive. This ambivalence triumphs in *The Dunciad,* Pope's greatest work, which I will center upon here. *The Dunciad* is great comedy, and yet it is as destructive as Swift. I wince as I reread *A Tale of a Tub,* but laugh and grimace at once throughout *The Dunciad.*

William Blake did not like Pope, but as apocalyptic writers they developed curious affinities: it is enlightening to read Blake's "Night the Ninth, Being the Last Judgment" of *The Four Zoas,* side by side with book 4 of *The Dunciad.* Blake is writing prophecy, not mock-heroic, but the mock-heroic is, in Pope, a prophetic mode. Dr. Johnson, fascinatingly, did not much care for *The Dunciad.* He thought that "Pope's irascibility prevailed," because "Pope confessed his own pain by his anger, but he gave no pain to those who had provoked him." Made unhappy by Swift, Johnson accurately saw that *The Dunciad* was Swiftian, containing "petulance and malignity enough" and too many gross images. What *The Dunciad* and *A Tale of a Tub* fear is universal cultural madness. I write in 2001, when the cultural world is now hell, nor are any of us out of it. We don't need a new *Dunciad;* Pope's is precisely relevant, and accurately prophesies the triumph of the Kingdom of the Dull in our countercultural universities and media:

> Beneath her foot-stool, *Science* groans in Chains,
> And *Wit* dreads Exile, Penalties and Pains.
> There foam'd rebellious *Logic,* gagg'd and bound,
> There, strip, fair *Rhet'ric* languish'd on the ground;
> His blunted Arms by *Sophistry* are born,
> And shameless *Billingsgate* her Robes adorn.
> *Morality,* by her false Guardians drawn,
> *Chicane* in Furs, and Casuistry in Lawn,
> Gasps, as they straiten at each end the cord,

And dies, when Dulness gives her Page the word.
Mad *Mathesis* alone was unconfin'd,
Too mad for mere material chains to bind,
Now to pure Space lifts her extatic stare,
Now running round the Circle, finds its square.
But held in ten-fold bonds the *Muses* lie,
Watch'd both by Envy's and by Flatt'ry's eye:
There to her heart sad Tragedy addrest
The dagger wont to pierce the Tyrant's breast:
But sober History restrain'd her rage,
And promis'd Vengeance on a barb'rous age.

That is where I teach, and everyone else now teaches, and that is where
cultural reviewing and speculating go on (consult any issue of the *New York
Times*). The superb concluding passage of *The Dunciad* tells us where all of
us are going and where (evidently) most of us want to go:

In vain, in vain—the all-composing Hour
Resistless falls: The Muse obeys the Pow'r.
She comes! she comes! The sable Throne behold
Of *Night* Primeval, and of *Chaos* old!
Before her, *Fancy's* gilded clouds decay,
And all its varying Rain-bows die away.
Wit shoots in vain its momentary fires,
The meteor drops, and in a flash expires.
As one by one, at dread Medea's strain,
The sick'ning stars fade off th'ethereal plain:
As Argus' eyes by Hermes' wand opprest,
Clos'd one by one to everlasting rest;
Thus at her felt approach, and secret might,
Art after *Art* goes out, and all is Night.
See skulking *Truth* to her old Cavern fled,
Mountains of Casuistry heap'd o'er her head!
Philosophy, that lean'd on Heav'n before,
Shrinks to her second cause, and is no more.
Physic of *Metaphysic* begs defence,
And *Metaphysic* calls for aid on Sense!
See *Mystery* to *Mathematics* fly!
In vain! They gaze, turn giddy, rave and die.
Religion blushing veils her sacred fires,

And unwares *Morality* expires.
Nor *public* Flame, nor *private,* dares to shine;
Nor *human* Spark is left, nor glimpse *divine*!
Lo! thy dread Empire, Chaos! Is restor'd:
Light dies before thy uncreating word;
Thy hand, great Anarch! lets the curtain fall;
And Universal Darkness buries All.

Pope's daemonic laughter at this cultural horror does have a touch in it of a delight in destruction. Book 4 of *The Dunciad* came out in 1742; in 2001, it frightens me.

JONATHAN SWIFT

I began last week to permit my wife to sit at dinner with me, at the farthest end of a long table, and to answer (but with the utmost brevity) the few questions I asked her. Yet the smell of a Yahoo continuing very offensive, I always keep my nose well stopped with rue, lavender, or tobacco leaves. And although it be hard for a man late in life to remove old habits, I am not altogether out of hopes in some time to suffer a neighbour Yahoo in my company without the apprehensions I am yet under of his teeth or his claws.

My reconcilement to the Yahoo-kind in general might not be so difficult if they would be content with those vices and follies only which nature hath entitled them to. I am not in the least provoked at the sight of a lawyer, a pickpocket, a colonel, a fool, a lord, a gamester, a politician, a whoremonger, a physician, an evidence [paid informer], a suborner, an attorney, a traitor, or the like; this is all according to the due course of things: but when I behold a lump of deformity and diseases both in body and mind, smitten with *pride*, it immediately breaks all the measures of my patience; neither shall I be ever able to comprehend how such an animal and such a vice could tally together.

That is Lemuel Gulliver, returned from his Fourth Voyage to the land of the wise and virtuous Houyhnhnms (horses) and the horrible Yahoos (ourselves). Gulliver both speaks and does not speak for Jonathan Swift. Poor Gulliver after all is a Yahoo, as was Swift. Horses, however idealized, remain horses; humans, however debased, retain at least the image of the human. Swift cannot intend us to identify with Gulliver, and yet we cannot quite repudiate him. *Gulliver's Travels* is a satire run wild, and it is a permanent oddity that its First and Second Voyages, to the lands of the Lilliputians and the Brobdingnagians, have achieved permanence as children's literature.

Swift meditated powerfully upon madness, and himself ended insane, victimized by a physiological condition. Though we remember Swift as a satirist, since his grotesque art burns away surfaces to show us the true realities of men and women, the center of his genius is irony, in which one thing is said while quite another is intended.

We are disquieted by Swift because his irony can seem to have no limit. The greatest writers in the language—Shakespeare and Chaucer—are heroic ironists, but their ironies are kept under control, except in extreme instances, such as Shakespeare's *Measure for Measure* and Chaucer's *The Pardoner's Tale*. But in Swift the irony breaks loose, and achieves an unbridled turbulence, particularly in *A Tale of a Tub*. William Blake wrote that "Exuberance is Beauty." By such a measurement, the fierce Swift is the creator of an immense beauty.

JONATHAN SWIFT
(1667–1745)

AT SEVENTY-FIVE, IN 1742, SWIFT WAS declared insane. It is of some importance that we separate this from his eminence as the genius of irony, as
there is nothing of his madness in that. Savage indignation in Swift is a healing affect. The malady that destroyed Swift's mind was a disease of the
middle ear, labyrinthine vertigo, which sometimes gave him the illusion of
hearing great bells ringing in his head and removed his sense of balance.
There is a story that Swift, in his suffering, once picked up a copy of his
masterwork, *A Tale of a Tub*, read a few sentences, put it down, and sighed:
"How great a genius I had when I writ that book!"

I reread *A Tale of a Tub* twice a year, religiously, because it devastates and
so is good for me. Except for Shakespeare's it seems to me the best prose
in the language, and it is also the most salutary corrective for someone of visionary tendencies or Romantic enthusiasms. What *A Tale of a Tub* teaches
are the uses of irony, and these are needed now more than ever, and by us
all, myself not the least.

A Tale of a Tub packs into its hundred pages an intoxicating mix of parody,
satire, endless ironies, and self-aware digressions. I myself have aged into an
infinitely digressive teacher, who all too frequently has to ask his students
where we were before my latest digression. In consequence, I cannot teach
without remembering *A Tale of a Tub*, whose method is to interrupt an allegorical narrative with digressions until all becomes digression. Satires tend
to be digressive; once they get started, something else always turns up for
attack. Swift's digressions exceed those of nearly all other satirists: *A Tale of
a Tub* is nothing but digression. What Freud called the drives (love and
death) are to Swift only digressions. When you digress you turn aside, like
a man walking who never goes straight. In general, though Swift fights many
enemies, his particular devils are Hobbes and Descartes. The "tub" in his
title has several meanings, including an inconsequential object, but it must
also be Swift's private joke. With a large whale bearing down upon them,
sailors would toss forth a tub, hoping to divert the threat, even as Swift
seeks to distract his readers away from the materialist metaphysics of
Thomas Hobbes's *Leviathan*. Descartes, proponent of philosophic dualism,
is slain by Aristotle in Swift's *The Battle of the Books*. The satirist will not even

grant Descartes the honor of a proper death; Aristotle's arrow is aimed at Sir Francis Bacon, but digresses into Descartes.

Everything about *A Tale of a Tub* deliberately disconcerts; its crucial section is not even part of the text, but is attached as an outrider: *A Discourse Concerning the Mechanical Operation of the Spirit.* If spirit and matter are to be radically divided from within another, as by Descartes, then spirit must be transported beyond the realm of matter:

> there are three general ways of ejaculating the soul . . . The first, is the immediate Act of God, and is called, *Prophecy* or *Inspiration.* The second, is the immediate act of the Devil, and is termed *Possession.* The third . . . is the affect of strong Imagination . . . the fourth Method of *Religious Enthusiasm,* or launching out of the Soul, as it is purely an Effect of Artifice and *Mechanick Operation,* has been sparingly handled.

This is now to be remedied, and Swift's speaker has come to tell us that in the Age of Hobbes and Descartes, the Mechanical Operation of the Spirit is indeed digressive: the soul becomes a gaseous vapor, always turning aside as it moves.

Between Swift's savage indignation and ourselves comes his tale-teller, who is a swamp of misinformation, as befits the education of a Grub Street hack, and who embodies many of the views that he attacks. Swift however does not make matters that clear and simple for us; sometimes, in a fury of self, he allows the hack to speak for him, even though the wretch is a former Bedlamite. The hack writes for "the Universal Improvement of Mankind"; Swift's designs are not so exalted, but his mouthpiece has a disturbing tendency to rise into an eloquence that is Swiftian. The high priests of digression, Swift's enemies, acolytes of the wind-god, include "All Pretenders to Inspiration whatsoever," and are dismissed as vulgar apocalyptics:

> It is from this Custom of the Priests, that some Authors maintain these *Æolists* to have been very ancient in the World. Because, the Delivery of their Mysteries, which I have just now mention'd, appears exactly the same with that of other ancient Oracles, whose Inspirations were owing to certain subterraneous *Effluviums of Wind,* delivered with the same Pain to the Priest, and much about the *same* Influence on the People. It is true indeed, that these were frequently managed and directed by *Female* Officers, whose Organs were understood to be better

disposed for the Admission of those Oracular *Gusts,* as entering and passing up thro' a Receptacle of greater Capacity, and causing also a Pruriency by the Way, such as with due Management hath been refined from a Carnal into a Spiritual Extasie. And to strengthen this profound Conjecture, it is farther insisted, that this Custom of *Female* Priests is kept up still in certain refined Colleges of our *Modern Æolists,* who are agreed to receive their Inspiration, derived through the Receptacle aforesaid, like their Ancestors, the *Sibyls.*

Though Swift arms the tale-teller with something of his irony, what follows is astonishing, and is highly offensive to feminists:

The Learned Æolists maintain the Original Cause of all Things to be *Wind,* from which Principle this whole Universe was at first produced, and into which it must at last be resolved; that the same Breath which had kindled, and blew *up* the Flame of Nature, should one Day blow it *out.*

At the close, the Quakers are the target, but the entire passage has mounted to a *King Lear*–like crescendo. Susan Gubar, impatient with scholarly defenders of Swift, sensibly points out the great satirist's horror of a woman's "inescapable physicality." Swift's psychosexual nature was not a happy one, but even had he enjoyed genital transports with "Stella" and "Vanessa," his never-quite mistresses, I don't think that this incarnate genius of irony would have written much differently, and it seems to me absurd to accuse Swift of misogyny, because he is equally outraged by all mankind, male and female. Surely, Swift's central contention is that all of us, of both genders, are subject to the Mechanical Operation of the Spirit. And so of course is Swift, in this magnificent passage, this sublime vapor directed against vapors:

Besides, there is something Individual in human Minds, that easily kindles at the accidental Approach and Collision of certain Circumstances, who tho' of paltry and mean Appearance, do often flame out into the greatest Emergencies of Life. For great Turns are not always given by strong Hands, but by lucky Adaption, and at proper Seasons; and it is of no import, where the Fire was kindled, if the Vapor has once got up into the Brain. For the *upper Region* of Man, is furnished like the *middle Region* of the Air; The Materials are formed from Causes of the widest Difference, yet produce at last the same Substance and Effect. Mists arise from the Earth, Steams from Dunghils, Exhaltations from the Sea, and Smoak from Fire, yet all the Fumes issuing from a Jakes, will furnish as comely and useful a Vapor, as Incense from an Altar. Thus far, I suppose, will easily be granted me; and then it will follow, that as the Face of Nature never produces Rain, but when it is overcast and disturbed, so Human Understanding, seated in the Brain, must be troubled and overspread by Vapours, ascending from the lower Faculties, to water the Invention, and render it fruitful.

If this is still satire, then Swift himself is among the victims, just as he uneasily avoids victimage by dissociating from Gulliver in *Gulliver's Travels*. *A Tale of a Tub* is the greater work, just as *King Lear* surpasses *Othello*, because in the *Tale* and in *Lear* we are carried to a dangerous verge where rhetorical and passional force seem to overflow every consideration of form. Norman O. Brown, in his *Life Against Death* (1959), famously defended what he termed "the Excremental Vision" in Swift, taking the phrase from Middleton Murry and Aldous Huxley. It seems to me, decades later, to require neither pity nor praise, any more than it does in Rabelais and Blake, both of them also satirists imbued with daemonic energies. What frightened Dr. Samuel Johnson in Swift was not so much this force of the ironist's genius, as the "dangerous example" of Swift's satire of so many "religious" tendencies. Swift accurately regarded himself as a devout Anglican priest, serving as dean of the Protestant St. Patrick's Cathedral in Dublin. But he was a parodist, ironist, satirist of unequalled genius. In Dr. Johnson's judgment, those powers swung free from Swift's explicit control: the bells broke down their tower.

I have taken care to distinguish Swift's genius from his eventual madness, but I do not think, as I reread *A Tale of a Tub*, that I can keep apart his genius and his fury. His targets may begin as Hobbes and Descartes, but they expand to include all of us, himself necessarily making one more victim. Goneril and Regan are monsters of the deep, yet Lear's fury transcends even their provocations. It is a struggle not to feel that Swift's rage transcends the Enthusiasm he attacks. Can you manifest prophetic indignation against prophecy? What sanctions Swift's apparent cruelty? "Apparent" is the disputable word in my question:

Last week I saw a Woman flay'd, and you will hardly believe, how much it altered her Person for the worse.

The literary power of this irony is indisputable; it can be read as a parody of sadism, but can we exclude the flavor of sadism itself? *A Tale of a Tub*
is a continuous shock partly because it is one of the handful or so of totally
original books in the language. Its two fundamental, opposing terms are the
"mechanical" and the "spirit," and Swift despises both: the machine is the
corporeal, as designated by Hobbes, and the spirit is consciousness, isolated
and reduced by Descartes. Conceived as a machine, the body seems to
Swift primarily a producer of excrement and sexual fluids, while the Cartesian spirit is wind, a noxious vapor. Swift's Christianity, in contrast, takes
the middle path: reason and truth do not guide us to happiness (an improbable goal, to Swift) but to order and decency. Alas, those terms have
lost much of their luster in the three centuries since *A Tale of a Tub* was published. George W. Bush and the Christian Coalition would not be Swiftian
ideals: he exalted *mind*, the legitimate ground of his ferocious pride.

I go on reading *A Tale of a Tub* because it chastises my own search for the
spirit in Romantic and post-Romantic poetry. Less personally, I recommend
it for its originality, daemonic intensity, and prose splendor. And since my
concern is genius, I scarcely know any other nonfictional prose in the English language that so clearly is a dangerous and astonishing explosion of
genius.

JANE AUSTEN

I must confess that I think her [Elizabeth Bennet] as delightful a creature as ever appeared in print, and how I shall be able to tolerate those who do not like *her* at least I do not know.

— Jane Austen to her sister Cassandra, January 29, 1813

The only person I recall who did not like the heroine of *Pride and Prejudice* was Vladimir Nabokov, who drove me out of his lecture hall at Cornell (in 1947) by his insistence upon Jane Austen's inferiority to Nikolai Gogol. Elizabeth Bennet, Nabokov proclaimed (sounding rather like Humbert Humbert) as insipid. Such a judgment is equivalent to discovering that one is bored by Shakespeare's Rosalind, in *As You Like It*. Nabokov had not yet written *Pale Fire*, the surest demonstration of his own genius, but even that remarkable tour de force is not as hilariously memorable as *Pride and*

Prejudice. What Gogol (who was sublimely mad) would have thought of Jane Austen I cannot imagine, but comparing the two is an absurd enterprise, rather like bringing together Nabokov and George Eliot. The savage ironies of Gogol and Nabokov have nothing in common with Austen's irony, which descended from dramatic inwardness in Chaucer and in Shakespeare.

Elizabeth Bennet, like Rosalind, is witty, amiable, healthy in spirit and in sensibility; she accomplishes the miracle of being at once fascinating and normative, again clearly in descent from Rosalind. Only the highest genius could create delight that menaces only the ill-willed. C. S. Lewis once suggested that Jane Austen was the literary daughter of Dr. Samuel Johnson. Critically, I worship Johnson, the Sublime of my vocation. Austen however is Shakespeare's daughter: her heroines defy historicizing contingencies, and are among our rarest images of inward freedom.

JANE AUSTEN
(1775–1817)

AUSTEN WAS THE SEVENTH OF EIGHT children. Since my concern is her highly individual genius, which distinguished her from her siblings and nearly everyone else in Great Britain, I begin by declaring my pragmatic disinterest in the supposed relationship between her novels and her country's imperial policies and procedures. I have met a remarkable number of persons who teach—I will not say literature, but cultural studies—and who tell me that they never have read *Mansfield Park*, and yet tell me also that what matters most about Austen's novel is its financial "dark side," Sir Thomas Bertram's ownership of a sugar plantation in Antigua.

In our increasingly virtual reality, three authors seem immune to the decline of authentic reading: Shakespeare, Austen, Dickens. This phenomenon is neither cultic nor political: personalities major and minor burst forth from the pages of these writers, in a profusion otherwise unmatched in the language. A very few novelists and fewer dramatists have given us two or three miracles of personality. Shakespeare, by my count, has almost two hundred; Austen, in her five novels that matter, has over thirty. Dead at forty-one, her major phase lasted only six years, 1811–17. Given another decade, she might have achieved an eminence that would startle even her most ardent admirers. *Persuasion*, posthumously published, is to me the most profound of her novels, and demonstrates a fresh mastery of Shakespearean inwardness.

Again like Shakespeare, Austen will reward reading at any level of intensity. Her command of perspectivism is another of her Shakespearean strengths. "What's aught but as it's valued?", Troilus's rhetorical question in *Troilus and Cressida*, is the implicit question also asked by Austen's major protagonists: Elizabeth Bennet, Emma Woodhouse, Fanny Price, Anne Elliot. The matter of estimate and esteem, of self and of others, is central to Austen's vision. Though it is crucial in Shakespeare, his ironies are too large to be seen, like those of Chaucer, and so we can be skeptical as to any one's value or values in the plays. Alistair Fowler protests that Hamlet at best is a hero-villain, but few agree. Austen resolves nearly all doubts before each novel concludes: her art depends upon her reader getting it right. No one, reading *Pride and Prejudice*, will get Mrs. Bennet, Mr. Collins, and Lady

Catherine de Bourgh wrong: they clearly are hilarious bad news. But though
we like Mr. Bennet, we wonder about him. What is the link between his
ghastly choice of Mrs. Bennet and his refusal to entertain any affect that
transcends sardonic amusement? Are the amiable Jane Bennet and Charles
Bingley interesting enough to sustain fully their importance for the story?
So subtle is Austen's irony that we may surmise they are not meant to sustain anything: their blandness highlights the intensities of Elizabeth and of
Darcy. Since I have written elsewhere about *Emma* and *Persuasion,* and am
averse to further polemic against the culturally virtuous who infest the approaches to *Mansfield Park,* I will confine myself to *Pride and Prejudice.*
Austen's genius for inventing personality through the agency of her ironical
powers could not be more happily illustrated than by this flagship of her
achievement. Mr. Collins is one of the comic triumphs of literature: in himself enough to establish Austen's genius forever. Here is Mr. Collins, in
chapter 19, proposing marriage to Elizabeth Bennet:

> "My reasons for marrying are, first, that I think it a right thing for
> every clergyman in easy circumstances (like myself) to set the exam-
> ple of matrimony in his parish; secondly, that I am convinced that it
> will add very greatly to my happiness; and thirdly—which perhaps I
> ought to have mentioned earlier, that it is the particular advice and
> recommendation of the very noble lady whom I have the honour of
> calling patroness. Twice has she condescended to give me her opinion
> (unasked too!) on this subject; and it was but the very Saturday night
> before I left Hunsford—between our pools at quadrille, while Mrs.
> Jenkins was arranging Miss de Bourgh's footstool, that she said, 'Mr.
> Collins, you must marry. A clergyman like you must marry. Choose
> properly, choose a gentlewoman for *my* sake; and for your *own,* let her
> be an active, useful sort of person, not brought up high, but able to
> make a small income go a good way. This is my advice. Find such a
> woman as soon as you can, bring her to Hunsford, and I will visit her.'
> Allow me, by the way, to observe, my fair cousin, that I do not reckon
> the notice and kindness of Lady Catherine de Bourgh as among the
> least of the advantages in my power to offer. You will find her manners
> beyond anything I can describe; and your wit and vivacity, I think,
> must be acceptable to her, especially when tempered with the silence
> and respect which her rank will inevitably excite. Thus much for my
> general intention in favour of matrimony; it remains to be told why
> my views were directed towards Longbourn instead of my own neigh-
> bourhood, where I can assure you there are many amiable young

women. But the fact is, that being, as I am, to inherit this estate after the death of your honoured father (who, however, may live many years longer), I could not satisfy myself without resolving to choose a wife from among his daughters, that the loss to them might be as little as possible, when the melancholy event takes place—which, however, as I have already said, may not be for several years. This has been my motive, my fair cousin, and I flatter myself it will not sink me in your esteem. And now nothing remains but for me but to assure you in the most animated language of the violence of my affection. To fortune I am perfectly indifferent, and shall make no demand of that nature on your father, since I am well aware that it could not be complied with; and that one thousand pounds in the four per cents, which will not be yours till after your mother's decease, is all that you may ever be entitled to. On that head, therefore, I shall be uniformly silent; and you may assure yourself that no ungenerous reproach shall ever pass my lips when we are married."

No comic novelist ever has bettered that! Not even Dickens has quite the match for the egregious Mr. Collins, whose pomposity has found its goddess in the endless vainglory of Lady Catherine de Bourgh. Perhaps the sublime sentence here is: "And now nothing remains for me but to assure you in the most animated language of the violence of my affection." *That* constitutes the assurance, and Mr. Collins passes immediately to the pragmatics of finance, redundantly telling Elizabeth how little she is worth in dowry. Austen almost surpasses this in the stylistic economy of Mr. Collins's rebound to Elizabeth's best friend, Charlotte Lucas:

In as short a time as Mr. Collins's long speeches would allow, everything was settled between them to the satisfaction of both; and as they entered the house he earnestly entreated her to name the day that was to make him the happiest of men; and though such a solicitation must be waived for the present, the lady felt no inclination to trifle with his happiness. The stupidity with which he was favoured by nature must guard his courtship from any charm that could make a woman wish for its continuance; and Miss Lucas, who accepted him solely from the pure and disinterested desire of an establishment, cared not how soon that establishment were gained.

In the background to this comedy, and to the higher humor of the Darcy-Elizabeth dance of courtship, is the poignance of Austen's own personal history. In 1796, when she was twenty, she had fallen in love with Tom Le Froy, the same age, an Irishman of Huguenot lineage. Her lack of sufficient dowry doomed the relationship. There may have been a later such attachment, but the man died. What is certain is that, in the autumn of 1802, Austen accepted the marriage proposal of one Harris Bigg-Wither. After a sleepless night, she informed the young man, twenty-two to her twenty-seven, that she could not marry him. That appears to have been the conclusion of her passional life, but then Bigg-Wither married two years later, and fathered ten children. Austen, had she married, might have left us no finished novels.

Austen's immediate precursors were Samuel Richardson and Fanny Burney, who had shown Austen how to fuse Richardson and Henry Fielding into a new kind of narration. Though Richardson's *Sir Charles Grandison* appears to have been Austen's favorite novel, his masterpiece was *Clarissa*, a fiction as long and as aesthetically magnificent as Proust's *In Search of Lost Time*. *Clarissa* is not read much now, but I do not think even Austen or Dickens or George Eliot or Henry James or Joyce gave us so powerful a book. Austen did not have a religious sensibility, but her temperament was Protestant, and her sense of the Protestant will was influenced by Richardson's novels, William Cowper's poetry, and Dr. Samuel Johnson's moral and literary criticism. The heroines of Austen's novels are exemplars of the Puritan will, which exalts the soul's autonomy. "Pride" in *Pride and Prejudice* is the art of the will. Let us consider what, to me, seems the book's finest passage, Darcy's rebuffed proposal of marriage to Elizabeth, in chapter 34:

> After a silence of several minutes, he came towards her in an agitated manner, and thus began:
>
> "In vain I have struggled. It will not do. My feelings will not be repressed. You must allow me to tell you how ardently I admire and love you."
>
> Elizabeth's astonishment was beyond expression. She stared, coloured, doubted, and was silent. This he considered sufficient encouragement; and the avowal of all that he felt, and had long felt for her, immediately followed. He spoke well; but there were feelings besides those of the heart to be detailed; and he was not more eloquent on the subject of tenderness than of pride. His sense of her inferiority—of its being a degradation—of the family obstacles which judgment had always opposed to inclination, were dwelt on with a warmth which seemed due to the consequence he was wounding, but was very unlikely to recommend his suit.

In spite of her deeply-rooted dislike, she could not be insensible to the compliment of such a man's affection, and though her intentions did not vary for an instant, she was at first sorry for the pain he was to receive; till, roused to resentment by his subsequent language, she lost all compassion in anger. She tried, however, to compose herself to answer him with patience, when he should have done. He concluded with representing to her the strength of that attachment which, in spite of all his endeavours, he had found impossible to conquer; and with expressing his hope that it would now be rewarded by her acceptance of his hand. As he said this, she could easily see that he had no doubt of a favourable answer. He *spoke* of apprehension and anxiety, but his countenance expressed real security. Such a circumstance could only exasperate farther, and, when he ceased, the colour rose into her cheeks, and she said:

"In such cases as this, it is, I believe, the established mode to express a sense of obligation for the sentiments avowed, however unequally they may be returned. It is natural that obligation should be felt, and if I could *feel* gratitude, I would now thank you. But I cannot—I have never desired your good opinion, and you have certainly bestowed it most unwillingly. I am sorry to have occasioned pain to anyone. It has been most unconsciously done, however, and I hope will be of short duration. The feelings which, you tell me, have long prevented the acknowledgment of your regard, can have little difficulty in overcoming it after this explanation."

Mr. Darcy, who was leaning against the mantelpiece with his eyes fixed on her face, seemed to catch her words with no less resentment than surprise. His complexion became pale with anger, and the disturbance of his mind was visible in every feature. He was struggling for the appearance of composure, and would not open his lips till he believed himself to have attained it. The pause was to Elizabeth's feelings dreadful. At length, with a voice of forced calmness, he said:

"And this is the reply which I am to have the honour of expecting: I might, perhaps, wish to be informed why, with so little *endeavour* at civility, I am thus rejected. But it is of small importance."

Some of Austen's best critics exalt the mutual capacity of Darcy and Elizabeth to change, and that thus they earn their later happiness together. Austen's ironic perspectivism opens other possibilities for interpretation. They do not actually change much at all, but they learn to accommodate their complementary prides, which thus are seen to be legitimate. What they see most clearly, after this, is that they are joined in the will, a will to accept esteem where each estimates the value of the other to be uniquely high. Both understand that they must not make an error in the choice of an answering will. This is a displaced Protestantism, but certainly emerges from that tradition, in which one reads the Bible by one's own light, and never loses one's autonomy in a mystic ecstasy. Of the two wills, Elizabeth's is the purer, but Darcy's is the more anxious, and so more insistent upon itself.

How should one define Jane Austen's genius? Henry James, with considerable defensive irony, wrote that "the key to Jane Austen's fortune with posterity has been in part the extraordinary grace of her facility, in fact of her unconsciousness." As with Hawthorne and George Eliot, James tries to deny Austen her conscious artistry, because he needs to defend himself against ancestors. Turn his remark upside down, and speak of the grace of Austen's consciousness, whose circumference, despite her deliberate social limitations, moves out towards Shakespearean dimensions. To regard Austen primarily as an ironist is not enough: she was a genius of the will, and a crucial agent in the secularization of the Protestant will. And yet the direction of that will is its salient aspect: towards personality, towards the acute freedom of individuation.

LADY MURASAKI

And when I play my *koto* rather badly to myself in the cool breeze of the evening, I worry lest someone might hear me and recognize how I am just "adding to the sadness of it all"; how vain and sad of me. So now both my instruments, the one with thirteen strings and the one with six, stand in a miserable, sooty little closet still ready-strung. Through neglect—I forgot, for example, to ask that the bridges be removed on rainy days—they have accumulated dust and lean between the cupboard and a pillar.

There is also a pair of larger cupboards crammed to bursting point. One is full of old poems and tales that have become the home for countless insects which scatter in such an unpleasant manner that no one cares to look at them any more; the other is full of Chinese books that have lain unattended ever since he who carefully collected them passed away. Whenever my loneliness threatens to overwhelm me, I take out one or two of them to look at; but my women gather together behind my back. "It's because she goes on like this that she is so miserable. What kind of lady is it who reads Chinese books?" they whisper. "In the past it was not even the done thing to read sutras!" "Yes," I feel like replying, "but I've never met anyone who lived longer just because they believed in superstitions!" But that would be thoughtless of me. There is some truth in what they say.

(translated by Richard Bowring)

Lady Murasaki, in her *Diary* as in *The Tale of Genji*, conducts an almost Proustian search for lost time, which is appropriate in a writer who truly was the genius of longing. The splendid Genji paradoxically is destroyed by his own incessant longing for the renewed experience of falling in love. When the significantly named Murasaki, the authentic love of his life, wastes away as an involuntary reaction to having been replaced, Genji does not survive her for more than a decent interval.

The Tale of Genji is eons away from Proust, yet I wonder whether Lady Murasaki's incessant longing is not a valid analogue for Proust's search. In Proust, love dies but jealousy is eternal; the narrator still quests for every possible detail of Albertine's lesbian attachments even though his memories of his dead beloved have become very tenuous. Jealousy is subdued in Lady Murasaki, as exclusive female possession of the male is not possible.

I would hesitate to affirm that the perspective of *The Tale of Genji* is entirely female, so firmly does Lady Murasaki identify herself with "the shining Genji." And yet the exaltation of longing over fulfillment throughout the novel may be an indication that the male vision of sexual love is essentially secondary.

Lady Murasaki's own splendor, like Proust's, is her gathering wisdom, in which a mingled spiritual and aesthetic nostalgia takes the place of a waning social order. To be a genius of longing, you must excel in narrative patience, and it is astonishing how well she varies her stories.

LADY MURASAKI (MURASAKI SHIKIBU)
(978?–1026?)

THE AUTHOR OF *THE TALE OF GENJI* IS the only Asian in this book, but her vast romance narrative has been part of literary culture in English since Arthur Waley completed his version in 1933. I read Waley's *Genji* a half-century ago, and retained vivid impressions of it, but have only now read Edward G. Seidensticker's very different translation, though it has been available since 1976. Rereading Waley alongside Seidensticker is instructive: *Genji* is so nuanced and splendid a work that one hopes for many more versions. The German translation by Oscar Benl (1966) provides yet another reflection of Murasaki's immense tale, and enriches a reader who knows neither medieval nor modern Japanese. One gathers that Murasaki's language, in relation to our Japanese contemporaries, is somewhere between Old English and Middle English in regard to us. She is not as distant as *Beowulf*, nor so close as Chaucer; modern Japanese translations therefore are essential for current readers.

Doubtless *The Tale of Genji* is more culturally remote from us than Waley, Seidensticker, and Benl make it seem, but literary genius is uniquely capable of universality, and I have the strong illusion, as I read, that Lady Murasaki is as available to my understanding as Jane Austen is, or Marcel Proust, or Virginia Woolf. Austen is a secular novelist, and so is Murasaki: her romance, as it develops, seems more and more a novel, except that it has a bewildering plethora of protagonists. There are almost fifty principal characters, and keeping clear who has been married and when, or had a sexual relationship, or is secretly someone's father or daughter, can be rather difficult. In reading through Seidensticker's version of nearly eleven hundred pages (it is more faithful and less condensed than Waley's), one never loses interest, but it is difficult not to get lost. Genji, an imperial prince sent into internal exile as a commoner, is an exuberantly passionate personage, whose longings are perpetual, mutable, and impatient when thwarted. It may be more accurate to speak of "longing" than "longings." He *is* a state of longing, and evidently irresistible to the extraordinary (and extraordinarily varied) women of the court and of the provinces.

We are not to consider Genji to be a Don Juan, though he certainly manifests what Lord Byron called "mobility." Lady Murasaki herself, through her narrator, clearly finds Genji more than sympathetic; he is a figure who radiates light, and who ought to be emperor. Eros, in Murasaki and her major contemporary woman writers, is not exactly what we think we mean by "romantic love," but in obsessiveness, self-destructiveness, and over-determination or apparent inevitability there is little pragmatic difference. Though everyone in *The Tale of Genji* is a Buddhist, and so warned by doc-trine against desire, just about all of them are very susceptible indeed, Genji most of all. Renunciation, that "piercing virtue," as Emily Dickinson termed it, is resorted to only after disaster by each lady in turn, and only after many turns by the perpetually passionate Genji.

Genji, who will never be emperor, is particularly liable to sudden (and then lasting) attachments to ladies not of the first rank, thus repeating his imperial father's passion for Genji's mother, forced out of the court by the malice of more aristocratic consorts. Broken by the experience, Genji's mother dies while he is still a baby, and his eagerness for intimacy clearly has a link to this early loss. But Lady Murasaki, who, before her *Tale* is done, will have anticipated Cervantes as the first novelist, is also an accomplished ironist. Her delicious second chapter, "The Broom Tree," gives us a prag-matic symposium on love conducted by Genji and three other courtiers:

> At this point two young courtiers, a guards officer and a functionary in the ministry of rites, appeared on the scene, to attend the emperor in his retreat. Both were devotees of the way of love and both were good talkers. To no Chujo, as if he had been waiting for them, invited their views on the question that had just been asked. The discussion progressed, and included a number of rather unconvincing points.
>
> "Those who have just arrived at high position," said one of the newcomers, "do not attract the same sort of notice as those who were born to it. And those who were born to the highest rank but somehow do not have the right backing—in spirit they may be as proud and noble as ever, but they cannot hide their deficiencies. And so I think that they should both be put in your middle rank.
>
> "There are those whose families are not quite of the highest rank but who go off and work hard in the provinces. They have their place in the world, though there are all sorts of little differences among them. Some of them would belong on anyone's list. So it is these days. Myself, I would take a woman from a middling family over one who has rank and nothing else. Let us say someone whose father is almost but not quite a councillor. Someone who has a decent enough reputa-tion and comes from a decent enough family and can live in some lux-

ury. Such people can be very pleasant. There is nothing wrong with
the household arrangements, and indeed a daughter can sometimes
be set out in a way that dazzles you. I can think of several such women
it would be hard to find fault with. When they go into court service,
they are the ones the unexpected favors have a way of falling on. I
have seen cases enough of it, I can tell you."

Lady Murasaki's irony makes us wonder as to just which are the "rather
unconvincing points." In what may be the *Tale*'s ultimate irony, Genji encounters the major relationship of his life in a ten-year-old girl he calls
Murasaki, whom he adopts and brings up. Her name (and the author's)
refers to the aromatic lavender plant, and Genji's relationship to her is outrageous from the start:

> She thought little of her father. They had lived apart and she
> scarcely knew him. She was by now extremely fond of her new father.
> She would be the first to run out and greet him when he came home,
> and she would climb on his lap, and they would talk happily together,
> without the least constraint or embarrassment. He was delighted with
> her. A clever and watchful woman can create all manner of difficulties.
> A man must always be on his guard, and jealousy can have the most
> unwelcome consequences. Murasaki was the perfect companion, a toy
> for him to play with. He could not have been so free and uninhibited
> with a daughter of his own. There are restraints upon paternal inti-
> macy. Yes, he had come upon a remarkable little treasure.

Again we are given an ironic pathos, which seems to me Lady Murasaki's
most characteristic tonality. She herself came from the second level of court
aristocrats, her family having fallen gradually from much higher rank. When
we first meet the child who will be renamed Murasaki by the infatuated
Genji, her nurse is called Shonagon, which seems to me an irony aimed at
Sei Shonagon, whose *The Pillow Book of Sei Shonagon* is the chief rival to *The
Tale of Genji*, and who is deprecated in Lady Murasaki's *Diary* as being
"dreadfully conceited" in her supposed display of false erudition in the use
of Chinese characters, almost as if she were the Ezra Pound of her day.
   Lady Murasaki, more than nine hundred years before Freud, understood
that all erotic transferences were substitute-formations for earlier attachments. Plato, even earlier, thought the same, though for him the archetypal
relationship was to the Idea, rather than to the parental image. When the
child Murasaki is fourteen, Genji takes her:

It was a tedious time. He no longer had any enthusiasm for the careless night wanderings that had once kept him busy. Murasaki was much on his mind. She seemed peerless, the nearest he could imagine to his ideal. Thinking that she was no longer too young for marriage, he had occasionally made amorous overtures; but she had not seemed to understand. They had passed their time in games of Go and *hentsugi*. She was clever and she had many delicate ways of pleasing him in the most trivial diversions. He had not seriously thought of her as a wife. Now he could not restrain himself. It would be a shock, of course.

What had happened? Her women had no way of knowing when the line had been crossed. One morning Genji was up early and Murasaki stayed on and on in bed. It was not at all like her to sleep so late. Might she be unwell? As he left for his own rooms, Genji pushed an inkstone inside her bed curtains.

At length, when no one else was near, she raised herself from her pillow and saw beside it a tightly folded bit of paper. Listlessly she opened it. There was only this verse, in a casual hand:

"Many have been the nights we have spent together
Purposelessly, these coverlets between us."

As her foster father, Genji has brought a figurative stigma of incest to Murasaki, and she herself will never become a mother. The narrator, as always, makes no judgments, and the violated fourteen-year-old makes the transition into a phase of happiness with Genji, but such a phase is purely ironic. Genji, perpetually questing for what is not to be found, goes on to other consorts, while holding Murasaki in place. But she is a remarkable consciousness, who will not abide with him, and she turns to Buddhist devotion as the path back to herself, and to her own childhood. Since Genji will not permit her to become a Buddhist nun, she arranges a ceremony in honor of the Lotus Sutra, which allows women their part in salvation. And after that, she lapses into a long day's dying to ease her pain, as John Milton might have termed it. With her beauty as a child returned to her, she dies, leaving Genji properly bereft.

Lady Murasaki no more blames Genji than she would chide one season for replacing another. And yet, after this, he is on the path that must lead finally to life's triumph over him. After another year, he begins to make ready to depart, and dies between chapters 41 and 42, as though Lady Murasaki herself were too attached to her creation to represent his dying. Chapter 42 begins, "The shining Genji was dead, and there was no one quite like him." The novel will go on for another three hundred and fifty pages, and the genius of an ironic pathos continues to manifest itself, but it becomes another tale.

The book became, and still is, a kind of secular Bible for Japanese culture. What *Don Quixote* almost uniquely was to Miguel de Unamuno, *The Tale of Genji* has been for a myriad of Japanese men and women of aesthetic sensibility. As a secular scripture, Lady Murasaki's huge romance-novel takes on a very ambiguous status, because it is almost impossible to define the book's relationship to Buddhism. Desire, the longing for another person, is almost the primal fault in most versions of Buddhism. Longing destroys Genji, and the best among his women. But it is the essence of Genji, and as readers we are captured by him, and by the answering passion that he evokes. The best book I have found on Lady Murasaki's masterwork, by Norma Field, accurately and eloquently is titled *The Splendor of Longing in the "Tale of Genji"* (1987). And there, I think, is where Murasaki's genius must be located, in that oxymoronic "splendor of longing." A longing is a yearning that never can be fulfilled, a desire never to be appeased. After reading Lady Murasaki, you never feel the same again about loving, or falling in love. She is the genius of longing, and we are her students even before we come to her.

LUSTRE 8

Nathaniel Hawthorne, Herman Melville, Charlotte Brontë, Emily Jane Brontë, Virginia Woolf

Images of isolation, of madness, and of lost love ally these very different novelists. Hawthorne's Hester, Melville's Ishmael, Charlotte Brontë's madwoman in the attic (Rochester's first wife), Heathcliff, and Virginia Woolf's Septimus Smith (whose suicide prefigures Woolf's own) are all figures of failed covenant. Is Ishmael the exception, since he is saved by Queequeg's coffin? Partly, but Ishmael and Queequeg were involved in the covenant cut with Ahab, to hunt down and slay the great white Leviathan, exalted by God in the Book of Job as the authorized tyranny of nature over man.

Melville professed himself a Gnostic, and *Wuthering Heights* and the final lyrics of Emily Brontë clearly possess Gnostic elements. Hawthorne's Hester is Emersonian but Hawthorne was not, while Charlotte Brontë, profoundly aggressive in her art, also fought through to her own sense of individuality. Virginia Woolf, a Paterian skeptic and aesthete, achieved an art so much her own as to make her a novelistic school of one.

NATHANIEL HAWTHORNE

We will not follow our friend across the threshold. He has left us much food for thought, a portion of which shall lend its wisdom to a moral; and be shaped into a figure. Amid the seeming confusion of our mysterious world, individuals are so nicely adjusted to a system, and systems to one another, and to a whole, that, by stepping aside for a moment a man exposes himself to a fearful risk of losing his place forever. Like Wakefield, he may become, as it were, the Outcast of the Universe.

That is the close of Hawthorne's tale "Wakefield," which Jorge Luis Borges named as his favorite story. A Londoner, Wakefield tells his wife he is going on a journey, rents a lodging in the next street to his house, and stays there twenty years, his whereabouts unknown to Mrs. Wakefield and everyone else. Then he returns home and is "a loving spouse" until death.

Hawthorne ascribes no motive to Wakefield's behavior; halfway through his self-exile, he encounters his wife in the street, and then the throng sweeps them apart. After another decade, Wakefield goes home, and Mrs. Wakefield takes him in. And that is all.

The storytelling genius of Nathaniel Hawthorne has a reputation remote from its actuality. Hawthorne is neither good nor gray; he is as surprising as Kafka, Borges, Calvino. What could his Puritan ancestors have made of him? His grandest achievement, Hester Prynne, subtly conveys a sexuality far more intense, persuasive, and attractive than that of any of her female descendants in American literature. *The Scarlet Letter* is a profoundly vital and disturbing romance precisely because Hester is so vital and disturbing.

Hawthorne's genius confounds expectations, not necessarily by design, but because it obeys the morality of storytelling, and not of history, society, and what one era or another calls nature. Hester Prynne is the outcast of Boston, but hardly of the universe.

NATHANIEL HAWTHORNE
(1804–1864)

WITH THIS SECTION ON *THE SCARLET LETTER* (1850), I begin consideration of the question of genius in a sequence of major American prose fictions, to continue with Herman Melville's *Moby-Dick* (1851), Mark Twain's *Adventures of Huckleberry Finn* (1884), Ernest Hemingway's *The Sun Also Rises* (1926), and concluding with Flannery O'Connor's *The Violent Bear It Away* (1960).

Though Hawthorne subtitles *The Scarlet Letter* "A Romance," and though romance elements abound, Hester Prynne is too complex, too deeply imbued with a divided spirit, to be a heroine of romance. Her affinities are not with Jane Eyre or Catherine Earnshaw but with Clarissa Harlowe, the ancestress of all heroines of the Protestant will. D. H. Lawrence, an authentic critical genius when sufficiently crazed, went after the formidable Hester with a hatchet:

> Hester Prynne was a devil. Even when she was so meekly going round as a sick-nurse. Poor Hester. Part of her wanted to be saved from her own devilishness. And another part wanted to go on and on in devilishness, for revenge.

This is lunatic, but it sees accurately that Hester's will is potentially fearsome. Austin Warren dryly observed that Hester was a pagan, which I would modify to a Protestant pagan, in the tradition of Anne Hutchinson (1591–1643), banished from Boston in 1637 for affirming her personal will as a self-reliant salvation. Religious geniuses who were women fiercely upset colonial Puritans, and Anne Hutchinson went on upsetting Nathaniel Hawthorne, though he did not suffer from a nostalgia for Puritanism. The oddest walking couple in the world's history must be Emerson and Hawthorne, who for years marched around Concord together, mostly in relative silence. Hester is, more or less, Emerson's daughter, but she might have disturbed him even more than she provokes Hawthorne, who is plainly in love with her, as so many male readers are (at least I am, and a number of my friends and students). One gathers, from reading about Anne Hutchinson, that she was sexually compelling, as well as courageous and eloquent. Rather more important: *she repented nothing*. Despite what some scholars affirm, I can locate no repentance in Hester Prynne, not even at the start of the story. That Hawthorne is ambivalent towards her "sin" is universally acknowledged, even if he will not admit it. What matters most about Hester Prynne is that she is the American Eve, which is particularly important because, despite Emerson's prophecies, we have nothing like a rival representation of the American Adam in our literature. Walt Whitman may compare himself to Adam early in the morning, but he is both too large and too diffuse a figure to be properly Adamic. Hester Prynne is an astonishing American answer to Milton's Eve, and I suggest that we think of her as the breakthrough of Hawthorne's own genius. Henry James's Isabel Archer, in *The Portrait of a Lady,* is a superb achievement, but ultimately less poignant than the sublime Hester. Only of a new Eve could Anthony Trollope have written, "I can fancy a reader so loving the image of Hester Prynne as to find himself on the verge of treachery to the real Hester of flesh and blood who may have claim upon him."

Aesthetically, what matters most about *The Scarlet Letter* is Hawthorne's rich and uninterpretable art of conveying Hester's sexual power to us. In *Paradise Lost,* Milton's Eve has an aesthetic rival in Satan, and a not altogether inadequate match in Adam. Hawthorne's Satan, Chillingworth, is far less worthy of Iago's ancestry than Milton's Satan is, and Hawthorne's Adam is the mostly dim and dismal Dimmesdale. The ultimate sorrow of the book is the reader's impulse of wonder: is this the best that the passionate and magnificent Hester could find? In Hawthorne as in Shakespeare, the women must descend in order to find what can be found.

Critics accurately link Hester's rather biblical beauty to that of the Anglo-Jewish Miriam in Hawthorne's *The Marble Faun* (1860), but Miriam is rather mishandled by the novelist, who conveys an irrelevant overtone or two of Beatrice Rappacini. Of Hester's wholesomeness, there can be no doubt whatsoever: she too could be the mother of all living. Like the greatest of Shakespearean protagonists, Hester is too strong for the work to contain her.

These days, Milton catches it from feminist critics who find him patriarchal in regard to his Eve. It is a touch difficult to see how Milton could have portrayed her more lovingly and respectfully, but I have lived to find the temples of learning consigned to amateur social work. Hawthorne learns from Milton how much Eve is to be desired, but he learns little more. The difference between Eve and Hester is not Anne Hutchinson but Emerson, who taught only the one virtue of self-trust. Emersonians, like Nietzscheans, learn to take just one step more in grace. The entire drama of fall and redemption is then acted out in the individual, who has only to forgive herself. Robert Penn Warren, admirable moral critic, read a very different *Scarlet Letter* than I do. Augustinian time is for Warren the lapse that cannot be forgiven. Admirable poet, Warren was a harsh judge. Whether in or out of time, the American Eve forgives herself for nothing, since she comes to believe there is nothing to forgive.

Feminist critics have taken up the defense of Hester as American Eve, partly against D. H. Lawrence and Leslie Fiedler, but both sides are anticipated by Hawthorne's own ambiguous defenses against his passion for Hester. The greatest of the epiphanies in the book is the revelation of Hester's beauty, when she meets Dimmesdale in the forest:

> The stigma gone, Hester heaved a long, deep sigh, in which the burden of shame and anguish departed from her spirit. O exquisite relief! She had not known the weight, until she felt the freedom! By another impulse, she took off the formal cap that confined her hair; and down it fell upon her shoulders, dark and rich, with at once a shadow and a light in its abundance, and imparting the charm and softness to her features. There played around her mouth, and beamed out of her eyes, a radiant and tender smile, that seemed gushing from the very heart of womanhood. A crimson flush was glowing on her cheek, that had been long so pale. Her sex, her youth, and the whole richness of her beauty, came back from what men call the irrevocable past, and clustered themselves, with her maiden hope, and a happiness before unknown, within the magic circle of this hour. And, as if the gloom of the earth and sky had been but the effluence of these two mortal hearts, it vanished with their sorrow. All at once, as with a sudden smile of heaven, forth burst the sunshine, pouring a very flood into the obscure forest, gladdening each green leaf, transmuting the yellow fallen ones to gold, and gleaming adown the gray trunks of the solemn trees. The objects that had made a shadow hitherto, embodied the brightness now. The course of the little brook might be traced by its merry gleam afar into the wood's heart of mystery, which had become a mystery of joy.

One cannot overemphasize that Hawthorne's Hester is a heroically sexual being, that her charisma is implicit sexual power, tragically unfulfilled. Also unfulfilled is her drive towards spiritual autonomy, in the manner of the audacious Anne Hutchinson. Hawthorne has projected her, but then balks her, which spiritually frustrates us, and yet finally gratifies us aesthetically. Perhaps the best clue to Hester is her art of embroidery, a clear analogue to Hawthorne's mixed art of romance and psychological novel. Hester's art is not allowed its full development except in dressing her daughter, Pearl, but Hawthorne persuades us that, in Hester, as in a few of his tales, his own art has fulfilled itself. To have given your nation's literature its most persuasive representation of a woman is to have achieved your genius, once and for all.

HERMAN MELVILLE

"Hark ye yet again,—the little lower layer. All visible objects, man, are but as pasteboard masks. But in each event—in the living act, the undoubted deed—there, some unknown but still reasoning thing puts forth the mouldings of its features from behind the unreasoning mask. If man will strike, strike through the mask! How can the prisoner reach outside except by thrusting through the wall? To me, the white whale is that wall, shoved near me. Sometimes I think there's naught beyond. But 'tis enough. He tasks me; he heaps me; I see in him outrageous strength, with an inscrutable malice sinewing it. That inscrutable thing is chiefly what I hate; and be the white whale agent, or be the white whale principal, I will wreak that hate upon him. Talk not to me of blasphemy, man; I'd strike the sun if it insulted me. For could the sun do that, then could I do the other; since there is ever a sort of fair play herein, jealousy presiding over all creations. But not my master, man, is even that fair play. Who's over me? Truth has no confines."

Captain Ahab addresses his crew in "The Quarter-Deck," chapter 36 of *Moby-Dick*, urging them to join in his Promethean quest to hunt down and destroy the white whale, who has maimed him. Melville's Ahab speaks a Shakespearean prose, metaphysical and dramatic, that has been transformed by the author's genius into a permanent element in the American language.

"Strike through the mask!" is Ahab's directive to us. We are locked within the wall of the visible or natural universe, and Moby-Dick "is that wall, shoved near to me." There may be nothing beyond the wall, but Ahab will not brood upon such a nihilism; Moby-Dick is enough in himself: "He tasks me; he heaps me." We hear the voice of our instinctive American spirituality, affirming itself against a nature it repudiates. What is best and oldest in Ahab cries out its American defiance: "I'd strike the sun if it insulted me."

When Ahab adds, "Who's over me?" then he rejects, not the unknown God, but the tyranny of nature over man.

We do Ahab wrong, he being so majestical, to offer him the show of violence, as many moralizing scholars continue to do. Ahab is no villain, not even a hero-villain like Macbeth. More than our sympathies are with Ahab: *we are Ahab*. He tasks us, he heaps us, for he is the hero as American, our tragic Don Quixote, questing for ultimate justice over the last enemy, death.

HERMAN MELVILLE
(1819–1891)

CAPTAIN AHAB IS THE AMERICAN Prometheus, and not the American Adam. A rugged spirit, both attracted and repelled by Emerson, Melville haunted Emerson's lectures and scribbled fierce marginalia in Emerson's essays. Their affinities outweighed their differences, and the proper answering voice to *Moby-Dick* comes in Emerson's dark *The Conduct of Life*. One might say that Melville reads Emerson rather as Ahab would, seeking out the earliest Emerson, the Orphic adept who is a Gnostic, not an idealist. But *Moby-Dick* is dedicated to the genius of Hawthorne, whom Melville loved, and the dedication implicitly declares: this is my genius, Ahab is my Hester, my vision of the heroic American.

It is certainly the most extraordinary of such visions to date, outsoaring its strongest descendants, Thomas Sutpen in Faulkner's *Absalom, Absalom!* and Judge Holden in McCarthy's *Blood Meridian*. Ahab is a hero-villain, like Macbeth and Hamlet, rather than a genius of villainy, like Iago and Edmund in *King Lear*. And yet Ahab, again like Hamlet, is a genius, he is the genius or daemon of his nation. The United States does not have a single national epic, but an amalgam of three very diverse works: *Moby-Dick, Leaves of Grass*, and *Adventures of Huckleberry Finn*. Ahab is not someone we love; Walt and Huck are. But the awesome Ahab, rightly admired for his greatness by Ishmael and the common reader, joins Milton's Satan and Shakespeare's Falstaff in alienating scholars, old style and new. W. H. Auden, as a Christian critic, disapproved of Ahab: "His whole life, in fact, is one of taking up defiantly a cross he is not required to take up." One gathers that Ahab ought to have played Job, but as Stubbs says, "Ahab's Ahab." Auden is very temperate compared to a papist critic's dismissal of the American Captain: "the world of his acts is strident, assertive, full of repudiation and destruction." Is that not true of Hamlet, Lear, Othello, Macbeth?

Ahab, like Melville, is not a Christian, and like William Blake he believes that the god of this world, called by the names of Jesus and Jehovah, is a botching demiurge, who has set Moby-Dick to reign over us in the same way that Jehovah sends Leviathan and Behemoth against poor Job. Walt Whitman says that the sunrise would kill him if he could not now and always send forth sunrise from himself, but Ahab is even more American and vows that he would strike the sun if it insulted him. Is he not then to strike through the mask that is Moby-Dick? Ahab is the American as ungodly god-like man, indeed he is—with Emerson, Joseph Smith, William James—one of the founders of the American Religion, our unacknowledged blend of Gnosticism, Enthusiasm, and Orphism. What is best and oldest in us is not part of the Creation, but goes back to the Primal Abyss, our foremother and forefather. The chorus that denounces Ahab, when it does not neglect his Gnosticism, deplores it as an ancient heresy, or as a Romantic one. I have argued elsewhere (*The American Religion*, 1992) that from 1800 on, the United States has called itself Protestant while actually following one vari-ant of gnosis or another. In his neglected long poem of 1876, *Clarel*, Melville prophesied a crucial development in the American Religion, currently man-ifested in our Pentecostals, freer Baptists, and black and Hispanic knowers:

> 'Twas averred
> That, in old Gnostic pages blurred,
> Jehovah was construed to be
> Author of evil, yea, its god,
> But Christ revered alone. Herefrom,
> Less frank: none say Jehovah's evil,
> None gainsay that he bears the rod;
> Scarce that; but there's dismission civil
> And Jesus is the indulgent God.

Ahab, a century and a half ago, belongs to a wilder phase of the American Religion, and asks Jesus for no indulgences. For Ahab is an American King Lear, at once democratic and tyrannical, and both pre-Christian and post-Christian. It should be recalled always that the *Pequod*, despite Quaker ownership, has a mostly pagan crew. Starbuck may be the only Christian on board; Fedallah and his group are Parsee Zoroastrians. Ishmael is a Neoplatonist, Stubbs and Flask are atheists, and there are a dozen or more animist faiths scattered among the others. Ahab is an Emersonian who has broken beyond all limits into the Ter-rible Freedom of a hunt for the absolute adversary, the sanctified king over all the children of pride. "Wonder ye then at the fiery hunt?" Ishmael asks us, once he too has been swept up into Ahab's thrust into the watery wastes that the ancient Gnostics called the *kenoma*, a sensible emptiness. A reader must be tone-deaf not to respond to Ahab's appeal:

He tasks me; he heaps me; I see in him outrageous strength, with an inscrutable malice sinewing it. That inscrutable thing is chiefly what

I hate; and be the white whale agent, or be the white whale principal,
I will wreak that hate upon him.

Certainly not a Christian sentiment, it is the credo of a warrior in a metaphysical cause. My subject being genius, and Ahab—despite the critics—
being Melville's own daemon, I seek to define Ahab's genius, which is
spiritual, like Emerson's or Joseph Smith's. Ferociously transcendental,
Ahab blends Emerson and Thomas Carlyle in searching for a true apocalypse, not the path of revolution that always becomes reaction again. Scholars chide Ahab for taking his crew down with him, but who except the
Christian Starbuck ever sees in Ahab a captain back for Egypt? I chafe when
I read our current politicizers and historicizers of literature, and find them
calling Ahab a Napoleon. Melville would rather find Andrew Jackson or Cervantes in Ahab, who commands through charismatic force and preternatural
eloquence. To Melville, Ahab is the genius of democratic America, and the
leader of a band of mariners as high and heroic as tradition affords, and in
Ahab's name Melville invokes the authentic American god, the alien or
stranger God of the Gnostics:

> Thou who didst pick up Andrew Jackson from the pebbles; who didst
> hurl him upon a war-horse; who didst thunder him higher than a
> throne!

You can call an American president what you will—that is our freedom—
but you cannot call him a tyrant, for even an Andrew Jackson or an Abraham
Lincoln is transient, and reliant upon the will of the voters. So, Ahab, American demigod, the Andrew Jackson of whalers: the president of the *Pequod*
rules his wild crew by general consent. Christian moralist critics are as irrelevant as our Frenchified cultural studies rabblement; Ahab is Melville's
longest reach towards Shakespeare, and towards the aesthetic dignity we
must still designate as genius.

Ishmael/Melville enters in the famous meditation that is chapter 72,
"The Whiteness of the Whale," a perspective upon Moby-Dick that is not
so much different from Ahab's but less personally oriented:

> Thus, then, the muffled rollings of a milky sea; the bleak rustlings
> of the festooned frosts of mountains; the desolate shiftings of the
> windrowed snows of prairies; all these, to Ishmael, are as the shaking
> of that buffalo robe to the frightened colt!
>
> Though neither knows where lie the nameless things of which the

mystic sign gives forth such hints; yet with me, as with the colt, some-where those things must exist. Though in many of its aspects, this visible world seems formed in love, the invisible spheres were formed in fright.

But not yet have we solved the incarnation of this whiteness, and learned why it appeals with such power to the soul; and more strange and far more portentous—why, as we have seen, it is at once the most meaning symbol of spiritual things, nay, the very veil of the Christian's Deity, and yet should be as it is, the intensifying agent in things the most appalling to mankind.

Is it that by its indefiniteness it shadows forth the heartless voids and immensities of the universe, and thus stabs us from behind with the thought of annihilation, when beholding the white depths of the milky way? Or is it, that as an essence whiteness is not so much a color as the visible absence of color, and at the same time the concrete of all colors; is it for these reasons that there is such a dumb blankness, full of meaning, in a wide landscape of snows—a colorless, all-color of atheism from which we shrink? And when we consider that other theory of the natural philosophers, that all other earthly hues—every stately or lovely emblazoning—the sweet tinges of sunset skies and woods; yea, and the gilded velvets of butterflies, and the butterfly cheeks of young girls; all these are but subtle deceits, not actually inherent in substances, but only laid on from without; so that all deified Nature absolutely paints like the harlot, whose allurements cover nothing but the charnelhouse within; and when we proceed further, and consider that the mystical cosmetic which produces every one of her hues, the great principle of light, for ever remains white or colorless in itself, and if operating without medium upon matter, would touch all objects, even tulips and roses, with its own blank tinge—pondering all this, the palsied universe lies before us a leper; and like willful travelers in Lapland, who refuse to wear colored and coloring glasses upon their eyes, so the wretched infidel gazes himself blind at the monumental white shroud that wraps all the prospect around him. And of all these things the Albino Whale was the symbol. Wonder ye then at the fiery hunt?

This is one of the permanent centers of American literature, and of the national psyche, and I take it as a critique of Emerson's epiphanies of the Transparent Eyeball and the "ruin or blank" in his *Nature*. The visionary blanks of Emily Dickinson and of Wallace Stevens are also crucial expressions of the American strain. Melville, as almost always, dissents from Emerson, but with a troubled sense of how close he remains to the Concord seer. If there could be a central sentence in the maelstrom of *Moby-Dick*, it would be, "Though in many of its aspects this visible world seems formed in love, the invisible spheres were formed in fright." Ishmael, Spinozistic pantheist or Neoplatonist, has joined Ahab's Gnosticism in his sense of those invisible spheres.

We do not fully know Ahab's spirituality until chapter 119, "The Candles," even as we cannot altogether apprehend his humanity until chapter 132, "The Symphony," which directly precedes the three days of the final chase, and Ishmael's floating return in the "Epilogue." All of *Moby-Dick*, vast as it is, is in the dialectic of the three chapters: 42, 119, 132. The first is the heart of the epic's metaphysics; the second centers Ahab's religion; the third gives us the problem of Ahab's identity, and its relation both to Ishmael's and to Fedallah's. All three chapters are magnificent, but "The Candles" is my favorite because it defines Ahab's genius, and Melville's. In a storm, the men of the *Pequod* behold the corposants, Saint Elmo's fire, an electric discharge flaring from the mast-points. Melville audaciously dares a melodramatic set-piece, akin to Iago's having Othello kneel by his side, as they vow diabolic fealty to one another.

As the corposants flame, Fedallah the Parsee, Zoroastrian fire-worshipper, kneels at Ahab's feet, with his head bowed away from the Captain. Ahab cries out for a mainmast link for his left hand, places his foot upon the Parsee, and with an upward glance and right arm flung high, he chants this magnificent prose poem:

> "Oh! thou clear spirit of clear fire, whom on these seas I as Persian once did worship, till in the sacramental act so burned by thee, that to this hour I bear the scar; I now know thee, thou clear spirit, and I now know that thy right worship is defiance. To neither love nor reverence wilt thou be kind; and e'en for hate thou canst but kill; and all are killed. No fearless fool now fronts thee. I own thy speechless, placeless power; but to the last gasp of my earthquake life will dispute its unconditional, unintegral mastery in me. In the midst of the personified impersonal, a personality stands here. Though but a point at best; whencesoe'er I came; wheresoe'er I go; yet while I earthly live, the queenly personality lives in me, and feels her royal rights. But war is pain, and hate is woe. Come in thy lowest form of love, and I will kneel and kiss thee; but at thy highest, come as mere supernal power; and though thou launchest navies of full-freighted worlds, there's that

in here that still remains indifferent. Oh, thou clear spirit, of thy fire thou madest me, and like a true child of fire, I breathe it back to thee. [*Sudden, repeated flashes of lightning, the nine flames leap length-wise thrice their previous height; Ahab, with the rest, closes his eyes, his right hand pressed hard upon them.*]

"I own thy speechless, placeless power; said I not so? Nor was it wrung from me; nor do I now drop these links. Thou canst blind; but I can then grope. Thou canst consume; but I can then be ashes. Take the homage of these poor eyes, and shutter-hands. I would not take it. The lightning flashes through my skull; mine eye-balls ache and ache; my whole beaten brain seems as beheaded, and rolling on some stunning ground. Oh, oh! Yet blindfold, yet will I walk to thee. Light though thou be, thou leapest out of darkness; but I am darkness leaping out of light, leaping out of thee! The javelins cease; open eyes; see, or not? There burn the flames! Oh, thou magnanimous! now I do glory in my genealogy. But thou art but my fiery father; my sweet mother, I know not. Oh, cruel! What hast thou done with her? There lies my puzzle; but thine is greater. Thou knowest not how came ye, hence callest thyself unbegotten; certainly knowest not thy beginning, hence callest thyself unbegun. I know that of me, which thou knowest not of thyself, oh, thou omnipotent. There is some unsuffusing thing beyond thee, thou clear spirit, to whom all thy eternity is but time, all thy creativeness mechanical. Through thee, thy flaming self, my scorched eyes do dimly see it. Oh, thou foundling fire, thou hermit immemorial, thou too hast thy incommunicable riddle, thy unparticipated grief. Here again with haughty agony, I read my sire. Leap! leap up, and lick the sky! I leap with thee; I burn with thee; would fain be welded with thee; defyingly I worship thee!"

I memorized this involuntarily when I was twelve, and chant it frequently still, though now I love the interpolated stage-direction best. Ahab stands, confronting the fires, as a personality, and if he worships, he does it in defiance. Though Shakespeare hovers in the rhetoric (Hamlet is not far away), Melville's genius triumphs here in Ahab's rhapsodical intensity, which breaks novelistic bounds, but then *Moby-Dick*, as befits its Shakespeareanism, is of no genre. Polonius-like, let us call it a dramatic romance-epic, as appropriate for the Age of Emerson as *Leaves of Grass* was to be five years later. Ahab's invocation of the corposants is marked by his primal ambivalences towards the spiritual realm. Once he had been a convert to Zoroastrianism, but *I now know thee*, and the gnosis makes him free. He confronts one version of genius, the fire's fathering force, with his own personality or daemonic genius, and mocks the fire for not knowing the foremother, the Abyss of the Gnostics, the origin before the Creation-Fall.

Ishmael alone will survive the disaster of the *Pequod,* saved by his lover Queequeg's empty coffin. But where has he been, in between chapter 119, "The Candles," and chapter 132, "The Symphony"? He has disappeared from the book, and vanishes again during the three-chapter, three-day final chase of Moby-Dick. There is no narrator in chapters 120–31, but Melville takes on that role. In the beautiful chapter 132, "The Symphony," Captain Ahab is assimilated to King Lear, and doubts his own identity. Adams Sitney, in a remarkable reading of "The Symphony," notes the transfer of Ishmael's earlier narcissism to the aging Captain, who gazes over the rail to find his reflected eyes merging with Fedallah's in the mirror of the sea. But Fedallah is not Ahab's genius, or even the Mephistopheles of a Faustian bargain. Ahab, in his heroic final moment, yields to the fate of dying in tow to Moby-Dick, because the Captain has replaced the dead Fedallah as his own harpooner:

> let me be then towed to pieces, while still chasing thee, though tied
> to thee, thou damned whale! *Thus,* I give up the spear!

Ahab suffers an Orphic *sparagmos,* towed to pieces by his triumphant enemy. The best tribute is William Faulkner's: "a sort of Golgotha of the heart become immutable in the sonority of its plunging ruin . . . There's a death for a man, now."

CHARLOTTE BRONTË

Folds of scarlet drapery shut in my view to the right hand; to the left were the clear panes of glass, protecting, but not separating me from the drear November day. At intervals, while turning over the leaves of my book, I studied the aspect of that winter afternoon. Afar, it offered a pale blank mist and cloud; near, a scene of wet lawn and storm-beat shrub, with ceaseless rain sweeping away wildly before a long and lamentable blast.

This comes soon after the opening of *Jane Eyre*, and was saluted by Virginia Woolf with exhilaration, in an essay on the Brontës:

It rushes us through the entire volume, without giving us time to think, without letting us lift our eyes from the page. So intense is our absorption that if someone moves in the room the movement seems to take place not there but up in Yorkshire. The writer has us by the hand, forces us along her road, makes us see what she sees, never leaves us for a moment or allows us to forget her. At the end we are steeped through and through with genius, the vehemence, the indignation of Charlotte Brontë.

Woolf speaks of Charlotte Brontë's vehemence and indignation, yet that is too polite. No other narrator is as aggressive towards her reader as is Jane Eyre. Charlotte Brontë is more Byronic than Byron was, and she joyously cudgels her readership. She has a will-to-power of which Jane Eyre is the energetic surrogate. The sexual drive, which we associate with D. H. Lawrence and his protagonists, is closer to the center of Charlotte Brontë's cosmos than it is in the fictive world of Lawrence. Something inchoate in Lawrence, perhaps his problematic psychosexuality, impeded the rhetorical release that subtly but palpably dominates *Jane Eyre*.

EMILY JANE BRONTË

> To-day, I will seek not the shadowy region;
>   Its unsustaining vastness waxes drear;
> And visions rising, legion after legion,
>   Bring the unreal world too strongly near.

Wuthering Heights is a solitary eminence, rising out of a life experience that puzzles me. Emily Brontë seems closer to the contemporary Canadian poet Anne Carson that she does to her sisters Charlotte and Anne. There is a recalcitrant power in *Wuthering Heights* and the best of Emily Brontë's visionary poems, such as "Often rebuked, yet always back returning," whose second stanza heads this frontispiece.

Genius, so frequently adaptable, rarely has been so uncompromising as it was in Emily Brontë. Morality, of any sort, has little to do with *Wuthering*

Heights, a savage romance that retains its capacity to shock the common reader. Presumably, Emily Brontë would not have said, with Catherine Earnshaw, "I *am* Heathcliff!", but she had no need to acknowledge an inner identity that is palpable enough. The meaning of the name "Heathcliff" itself is emblematic of the poet-novelist's being.

In the "Last Lines," she salutes the God within her, who is clearly not the deity of the Judaic-Christian-Islamic normative tradition:

> Vain are the thousand creeds
> That move men's hearts—unutterably vain;
> Worthless as withered weeds,
> Or idlest froth amid the boundless main.

With Emerson, she would have endorsed the defiant manifesto of Self-Reliance, which I knowingly repeat here:

> As men's prayers are a disease of the will, so are their creeds a disease
> of the intellect.

Her private gnosis is more difficult to apprehend than Emerson's, but *Wuthering Heights* allows us to absorb it; indeed we hardly can fail to join ourselves to her private religion as we lose ourselves in *Wuthering Heights*.

CHARLOTTE BRONTË
(1816–1855)

EMILY JANE BRONTË
(1818–1848)

THE PUZZLE OF FAMILIAL GENIUS DEFIES all our modes of reduction just as fiercely as individual genius does. In 1812, the Reverend Patrick Brontë (who was to survive all six of his children) married Maria Bramwell, who died in 1821. The two oldest girls, Maria and Elizabeth, died of tuberculosis in 1825. Bramwell, the only boy, survived until 1848, before yielding to the family malady. Nothing came of his apparent early gifts, but Anne, the youngest child, wrote *Agnes Grey* (1847) and *The Tenant of Wildfell Hall* (1848), both still very readable novels, before her death in 1849. She was a superb talent, but Charlotte and Emily were and always will remain something apart, visionary artists who began a mode that continued in Thomas Hardy and D. H. Lawrence. Charlotte, before she died of toxemia of pregnancy in 1855, wrote four permanent novels: *Jane Eyre* (1847), *Shirley* (1849), *Villette* (1853), and *The Professor* (published in 1857, but actually her first, completed in 1846). Emily, who died of tuberculosis in 1848, at thirty, transcends Charlotte (and very nearly everyone else) in *Wuthering Heights* (1848) and in a handful of extraordinary poems, among all but the strongest in the language.

I have never found *Jane Eyre* a congenial book, since I have the acute sensation throughout that Charlotte Brontë is bashing me over the head, yet I reluctantly agree with everyone else on this, and do not doubt the genius of the novel. But *Wuthering Heights* I have almost by heart, as I do several of the poems. There is sublimity in Emily Brontë as refulgent of genius as are the poems of William Blake or the short stories of D. H. Lawrence. Like so many other readers, I will juxtapose *Jane Eyre* and *Wuthering Heights* by contrasting Charlotte's Rochester with Emily's Heathcliff, and I also will consider, too briefly, her poetry.

All the Brontë sisters, like many other young women of their era, were in love with the image of George Gordon, Lord Byron, who died heroically, leading his Greek brigands, in 1824, at the age of thirty-six. Rochester and

Heathcliff manifestly are Byronic heroes, or hero-villains, and they hardly would be at home in the novel, as such. The fictions of the Brontës, like those of Sir Walter Scott (or of Nathaniel Hawthorne), are romances, but as Byronic romances they necessarily are very different from Scott's work. Northrop Frye is the great authority upon prose romance, as here in his encyclopedic *Anatomy of Criticism* (1957):

> In novels that we think of as typical, like those of Jane Austen, plot and dialogue are closely linked to the conventions of the comedy of manners. The conventions of *Wuthering Heights* are linked rather with the tale and the ballad. They seem to have more affinity with tragedy, and the tragic emotions of passion and fury, which would shatter the balance of tone in Jane Austen, can be safely accommodated here. So can the supernatural, or the suggestion of it, which is difficult to get into a novel. The shape of the plot is different: instead of maneuvering around a central situation, as Jane Austen does, Emily Brontë tells her story with linear accents, and she seems to need the help of a narrator, who would be absurdly out of place in Jane Austen. Conventions so different justify us in regarding *Wuthering Heights* as a different form of prose fiction from the novel, a form which we here shall call the romance. Here again we have to use the same word in several different contexts, but romance seems on the whole better than tale, which appears to fit a somewhat shorter form.
>
> The essential difference between a novel and romance lies in the conception of characterization. The romancer does not attempt to create "real people" so much as stylized figures which expand into psychological archetypes. It is in the romance that we find Jung's libido, anima, and shadow reflected in the hero, heroine, and villain respectively. That is why the romance so often radiates a glow of subjective intensity that the novel lacks, and why a suggestion of allegory is constantly creeping in around its fringes. Certain elements of character are released in the romance which make it naturally a more revolutionary form than the novel. The novelist deals with personality, with characters wearing their personas or social masks. He needs the framework of a stable society, and many of our best novelists have been conventional to the verge of fussiness. The romancer deals with individuality, with characters in *vacuo* idealized by revery, and however conservative he may be, something nihilistic and untamable is likely to keep breaking out of his pages.

If there is a novel in *Wuthering Heights*, it centers upon Catherine Earnshaw, caught between the social reality of Edgar Linton and the daemonic Byronism of Heathcliff. Once Catherine Earnshaw and the Lintons are dead, the book is entirely romance. *Wuthering Heights* is almost uniquely the story of early marriage and early death. Catherine Earnshaw dies at eighteen, Heathcliff's son Linton at seventeen, Hindley at twenty-seven, Edgar at thirty-nine, poor Isabella at thirty-one, and Heathcliff at about thirty-eight (if my arithmetic is right). Edgar Linton is twenty-one and Catherine Earnshaw seventeen when they marry. Hindley marries Frances at twenty, and the marriage made in hell between Heathcliff and Isabella starts when he is nineteen and she is eighteen. The survivors, Hareton Earnshaw and Catherine Linton, make the only happy marriage at twenty-four and eighteen, respectively. Everyone marries very young because they intuit they will not live long. Unless Hareton and the second Catherine can defy their lineage, no protagonist in Emily Brontë's cosmos reaches forty, unhappily prophesying that even the stalwart Charlotte did not attain thirty-nine.

These calculations are a touch numbing, but are meant to count the cost of Emily's remorseless vision. Though the ongoing rabblement of mock-feminists, pretended Marxists, and sub-historicists swarm around *Wuthering Heights*, in order to give us what could be called French Emily Brontë, they scarcely can get near a work that renders void all moral, social, and political contexts. Dante Gabriel Rossetti, with his customary pungent intelligence, got there first with the most:

> It is a fiend of a book, an incredible monster, combining all the stronger female tendencies from Mrs. Browning to Mrs. Brownrigg. The action is laid in Hell, only it seems places and people have English names there.

The ungallant D. G. Rossetti associates the conservative moralism of Elizabeth Barrett Browning with the criminal sadism of the eighteenth-century Mrs. Brownrigg, executed for whipping several young women to death. Rossetti's nasty gusto is accurate enough: *Wuthering Heights*, like *Jane Eyre*, releases an explosive female sadism. Rossetti's friend Algernon Charles Swinburne, himself a sadomasochist, rather surprisingly defended Emily Brontë's romance from such a characterization:

> A graver and perhaps a somewhat more plausible charge is brought against the author of *Wuthering Heights* by those who find here and there in her book the savage note or the sickly symptom of a morbid

ferocity. Twice or thrice especially the details of deliberate or passionate brutality in Heathcliff's treatment of his victims make the reader feel for a moment as though he were reading a police report or even a novel by some French naturalist of the latest and brutalist order. But the pervading atmosphere of the book is so high and healthy that the effect even of those vivid and fearful scenes which impaired the rest of Charlotte Brontë is almost at once neutralized—we may hardly say softened, but sweetened, dispersed and transfigured—by the general impression of noble purity and passionate straightforwardness, which removes it at once and for ever from any such ugly possibility of association or comparison. The whole work is not more incomparable in the effect of its atmosphere or landscape than in the special and distinctive character of its passion. The love which devours life itself, which devastates the present and desolates the future with unquenchable and raging fire, has nothing less pure in it than flame or sunlight. And this passionate and ardent chastity is utterly and unmistakably spontaneous and unconscious.

One could agree with Swinburne if the center of this is taken to be: "The love which devours life itself, which devastates the present and desolates the future." That is the incommensurate love which already has attained the ghastliness of total identification, the love of Catherine Earnshaw and of Heathcliff. "Ghastliness" is my reaction but not at all the view of Swinburne, or of Emily Brontë. When Catherine cries, "I am Heathcliff!", we are taken into Emily Brontë's realm, where none of us could long survive.

Who is Heathcliff? What is he? Despite his Byronic stigmata, Heathcliff is neither a grotesque portrait of Byron nor a repetition of the Byronic heroes: Manfred, Cain, Lara. One can begin by observing that Heathcliff's originality, which makes him so difficult to analyze, itself is the signature or assertion of Emily Brontë's anarchic genius. As a child, she sought literary space for her creative will in her invented Gondal world, which was recovered and reconstructed, but, except for one lyric, no one could have ventured, on its basis, to prophesy her greatness.

Besides Byron—and the inevitable triad of the Bible, Shakespeare, and Milton—who, if anyone, is among Emily's authentic precursors? Some minor gothic romances would seem the only answer: the anonymous *Bridegroom of Barma*, Scott's *The Black Dwarf*, perhaps one or two others. None of these make a difference, and the Bible and Milton are tertiary presences. Byron, greatly transformed, hovers near, but a subtle and rather defensive pattern of Shakespearean allusion emerges in the depiction of Heathcliff: Edmund in *King Lear*, Hamlet, Macbeth, Lear himself are woven together in Emily Brontë's daemonic crossover, or more traditionally Catherine Earnshaw's Demon Lover. Shakespeare is employed to heighten Heathcliff's tragic dignity, but is not allowed to usurp Heathcliff's rather occult origin and ambiance.

It is never clear (by design) in *Wuthering Heights* whether we confront one order of nature, or two. There is Penistone Craggs, which glows in the evening, and has preternatural aspects. More crucially, there is the difficult quest of Heathcliff after Catherine Earnshaw Linton's death: first to find what I suppose might be called (in Gnostic terms) her pneumatic or spiritual form, and then to unite with it. The romance's greatest originality is that there are two modes of reality in it, Heathcliff's and everyone else's, with only Catherine Earnshaw, who is intense but fragile, to mediate between the two. Like Heathcliff, something in her goes back to before the Creation-Fall into nature, but something does not, and is merely natural like the rest of us.

There is little question but that Emily Brontë represents her own lyric persona in Catherine Earnshaw's otherness, in the sense of her "I am Heathcliff!" But it is a mystery, an aesthetically impressive one, that an eighteen-year purgation is imposed upon Heathcliff, in his peculiarly posthumous sojourn as he wants to find and join his Catherine. He is still a child, yearning for a transcendental fulfillment that has no doctrine to explain it. Though she was a clergyman's daughter, there is not an iota of Christianity in Emily Brontë, and the gap between ghostly visions and natural realities in the book is never closed. No critical analysis of Heathcliff will work, because always there is a missing element, which the author declines to name. And yet this is not obscurantism on Emily Brontë's part; she is a knower, though not to be subsumed under the rubric of any historical Gnostic sect.

Heathcliff negates all received tradition, including his Byronic and Shakespearean affiliations. On some level, perhaps never to be apprehended, Heathcliff is Emily Brontë's strong critique of the High Romantic tradition of representing and exalting male desire. But no one has been able to expand that critique; there are almost as many Heathcliffs as there are Hamlets.

Rochester, though disturbing, is a largely conventional figure when juxtaposed to Heathcliff. Jane Eyre is the aesthetic glory of the romance she narrates, while poor Rochester is quite secondary in comparison. Since Jane

Eyre is very close to Charlotte Brontë's self-portrait, one can think of the book as *The Portrait of the Artist as a Young Woman.* Jane is a visionary painter, who portrays in her work her own dreams, and it is illuminating to think of the romance, *Jane Eyre,* as a large, animated visionary painting.

Among novelists, Charlotte most admired William Makepeace Thackeray, but the author of *Vanity Fair* had only a superficial effect upon her writing. The amazingly incompatible precursors are John Bunyan and Lord Byron, and only the combative genius of Charlotte Brontë could have melded *The Pilgrim's Progress* and *Manfred* into the remarkable unity of *Jane Eyre.* Sandra Gilbert and Susan Gubar, doyennes of feminist criticism, invoke the poet Adrienne Rich in order to find traces in Jane of the Great Mother, at once Diana the huntress and Mary the virgin. Though Gilbert and Gubar do not say so, one wonders if it is the Great Mother who blinds and maims Rochester.

Rochester accurately characterizes Jane as indomitable, and certainly she exults in the perpetual freedom of her will. The will's object is Rochester, and Jane will tame him into a virtuously dependent husband, and thus forgive him his past:

> Mr. Rochester has a thoughtful nature and a very feeling heart; he is neither selfish nor self indulgent, he is ill-educated, misguided, errs, when he does err, through rashness and inexperience; he lives for a time as too many other men live, but being radically better than most men, he does not like that degraded life, and is never happy in it. He is taught the severe lessons of experience and has sense to learn wisdom from them. Years improve him; the effervescence of youth foamed away, what is really good in him still remains. His nature is like wine of a good vintage, time cannot sour, but only mellows him. Such at least was the character I meant to portray.

Though that is Charlotte in a letter, it might as well be Jane in the novel. The Byronic energy of Jane Eyre has so worked as to enable Rochester to dwindle into a virtuous husband. Must the male reader not dwindle also, when confronted by the phallic cudgel of Charlotte's style? What are male readers to make of Jane's self-satisfaction in her best of all possible worlds?

> I have now been married ten years. I know what it is to live entirely for and with what I love best on earth. I hold myself supremely blest—blest beyond what language can express; because I am my husband's life as fully as he is mine. No woman was ever nearer to her

mate than I am; ever more absolutely bone of his bone and flesh of his flesh.

I know no weariness of my Edward's society: he knows none of mine, any more than we each do of the pulsation of the heart that beats in our separate bosoms; consequently, we are ever together. To be together is for us to be at once as free as in solitude, as gay as in company. We talk, I believe, all day long: to talk to each other is but a more animated and an audible thinking. All my confidence is bestowed on him, all his confidence is devoted to me; we are precisely suited in character—perfect concord is the result.

Mr. Rochester continued blind the first two years of our union: perhaps it was that circumstance that drew us so very near—that knit us so very close! For I was then his vision, as I am still his right hand. Literally, I was (what he often called me) the apple of his eye. He saw nature—he saw books through me; and never did I weary of gazing for his behalf, and of putting into words the effect of field, tree, town, river, cloud, sunbeam—of the landscape before us, of the weather round us—and impressing by sound on his ear what light could not longer stamp on his eye. Never did I weary of reading to him: never did I weary of conducting him where he wished to go: of doing for him what he wished to be done. And there was a pleasure in my services, most full, most exquisite, even though sad—because he claimed these services without painful shame or damping humiliation. He loved me so truly that he knew no reluctance in profiting by my attendance: he felt I loved him so fondly that to yield to that attendance was to indulge my sweet wishes.

This is the Eve of Genesis 2:24 becoming her Adam's benign master. I am willing to be instructed as to whether that is feminism or not: I am something of a pariah in my profession, and so on such a matter I want advice. But read over those three paragraphs carefully, and see if they don't chill you, whoever you are. I grant them a certain strength and a beautiful modulated aggressivity, but who would be Rochester thrice tamed by the passionate Jane?

I want to conclude this by a contrast of poetry by Charlotte and Emily. Here is the final stanza of Charlotte's "On the Death of Emily Jane Brontë":

> Then since thou art spared such pain
> We will not wish thee here again;
> He that lives must mourn

> God help us through our misery
> And give us rest and joy with thee
> When we reach our bourne!

This is plain dreadful, another demonstration of Oscar Wilde's proclamation that all bad poetry is sincere. In contrast, here is Emily Brontë saluting the "God within my breast" and "affirming the heroism of her own soul":

> There is not room for Death
> Nor atom that his might could render void
> Since thou art Being and Breath
> And what thou art may never be destroyed.

Emily Brontë, remarkably like an ancient Gnostic, addresses "the God within," the pneuma or spark that goes back before the Creation-Fall. Charlotte is a polemical romance writer whose aggressivitiy or drive pragmatically is her genius. Emily is a seer, invoking her own genius as her divinity, very firmly and with a final eloquence.

VIRGINIA WOOLF

If this is so, if to read a book as it should be read calls for the rarest qualities of imagination, insight, and judgment, you may perhaps conclude that literature is a very complex art and that it is unlikely that we shall be able, even after a lifetime of reading, to make any valuable contribution to its criticism. We must remain readers; we shall not put on the further glory that belongs to those rare beings who are also critics. But still we have our responsibilities as readers and even our importance. The standards we raise and the judgments we pass steal into the air and become part of the atmosphere which writers breathe as they work. And influence is created which tells upon them even if it never finds its way into print. And that influence, if it were well instructed, vigorous and individual and sincere, might be of great value now when criticism is necessarily in abeyance; when books pass in review like the procession of animals in a shooting-gallery, and the critic has only one second in which to load and aim and shoot and may well be pardoned if he mistakes rabbits for tigers, eagles for barndoor fowls, or misses altogether and wastes his shot upon some peaceful cow grazing in a further field. If behind the erratic gunfire of the press the author felt that there was another kind of criticism, the opinion of people reading for the love of reading, slowly and unprofessionally, and judging with great sympathy and yet with great severity, might this not improve the quality of his work? And if by our means books were to become stronger, richer, and more varied, that would be an end worth reaching.

"How Should One Read a Book," the final essay in Woolf's *Second Common Reader* (1932), delights me with that penultimate paragraph. Virginia Woolf's genius was double: as a visionary novelist, and as a superb common reader. Her feminist admirers exalt her as the prophet of *A Room of One's Own*, sometimes overlooking that she wanted that room as a place in which to read and write.

Dr. Samuel Johnson gave Woolf, and the rest of us, the idea of the common reader in his *Life* of the poet Thomas Gray:

I rejoice to concur with the common reader; for by the common sense of readers, uncorrupted by literary prejudices, after all the refinements of subtilty and the dogmatism of learning, must be generally decided all claim to poetical honours.

Woolf, in her *literary* judgments, is far closer to Dr. Johnson than she is to the legions who now praise certain books because of the gender, ethnicity, race, sexual orientation, and social ideology of their authors.

To love reading with Woolf's passion is an enabling act of consciousness. Woolf, as a novelist, did not possess the depth and universality of her greatest contemporaries, Joyce and Proust, but her extraordinary insights into consciousness and the darkness just outside its limits constitute her own highly individual mode of genius. Her moments of vision are not so much privileged (as in Walter Pater, and in James Joyce) as they are fatal, poised upon the verge where perception and sensation yield to dissolution.

VIRGINIA WOOLF
(1882–1941)

HERMIONE LEE, WOOLF'S BEST biographer, emphasizes that the novelist-critic "wanted to avoid all categories." Sixty years after her wartime suicide, she is trapped in all manner of categories: Modernist, lesbian, feminist "theorist," but we are in an Age of Categories. As my book is about genius, and the influence of work upon life, I happily can avoid debate. Defining Virginia Woolf's genius, if that I can, will be enough for me.

That genius first fully manifested itself in 1925, and continued in full strength for the sixteen remaining years of Woolf's life. Her absolute works are *Mrs. Dalloway* (1925), *To the Lighthouse* (1927), *The Waves* (1931), *The Years* (1937), and *Between the Acts* (posthumously published, 1941). Five extraordinary novels culminate with her masterpiece; once I preferred *To the Lighthouse*, but at seventy I reread *Between the Acts* more frequently, and with even more pleasure, and so I will center upon it here.

Reuben Brower, in 1951, noted "that in her singleness of vision and in her handling of words, Virginia Woolf has a Shakespearean imagination," and he suggested that the best preparation for understanding *Mrs. Dalloway* was to read *The Winter's Tale*. That would also be the proper prelude for reading *Between the Acts*.

Even had she never written her fantasy *Orlando* (1928), her love letter to the now unreadable Vita Sackville-West, any deep reader of Woolf will discover that her ambitions are Shakespearean, though she carefully approaches him at a very oblique angle. Her Shakespeare is Walter Pater's, and depends upon the theory that the dramatist's incomparable power of reverberation relies upon what Woolf calls "the under-mind" and Pater the "under-texture." Here is Woolf in a memoir brooding on this phenomenon:

Perhaps this is the strongest pleasure known to me. It is the rapture I get when in writing I seem to be discovering what belongs to what; making a scene come right; making a character come together. From this I reach what I might call a philosophy; at any rate it is a constant idea of mine; that behind the cotton wool is hidden a pattern; that we—I mean all human beings—are connected with this; that the whole world is a work of art; that we are parts of the work of art.

Hamlet or a Beethoven quartet is the truth about this vast mass that
we call the world. But there is no Shakespeare, there is no Beethoven;
certainly and emphatically there is no God; *we are the words; we are the
music; we are the thing itself.* And I see this when I have a shock.

We are the words. While she was at work upon *Between the Acts*, Woolf wrote
"The Leaning Tower," her essay upon literary influence:

> Theories then are dangerous things. All the same we must risk making
> one this afternoon since we are going to discuss modern tendencies. Di-
> rectly we speak of tendencies or movements we commit ourselves to the
> belief that there is some force, influence, outer pressure which is strong
> enough to stamp itself upon a whole group of different writers so that all
> their writing has a certain common likeness. We must then have a the-
> ory as to what this influence is. But let us always remember—influences
> are infinitely numerous; writers are infinitely sensitive; each writer has
> a different sensibility. That is why literature is always changing, like the
> weather, like clouds in the sky. Read a page of Scott; then of Henry
> James; try to work out the influences that have transformed the one
> page into the other. It is beyond our skill. We can only hope therefore to
> single out the most obvious influences that have formed writers into
> groups. Yet there are groups. Books descend from books as families de-
> scend from families. Some descend from Jane Austen; others from Dick-
> ens. They resemble their parents, as human children resemble their
> parents; yet they differ as children differ, and revolt as children revolt.
> Perhaps it will be easier to understand living writers as we take a quick
> look at some of their forbears.

Woolf's preface to her *Orlando* lists her own precursors as Defoe, Sir
Thomas Browne, Sterne, Scott, Macaulay, Emily Brontë, De Quincey, and
Pater. The most crucial there is Pater, whose aesthetic stance, precariously
balanced between the major entities of personality and death, became
Woolf's. Shakespeare and Jane Austen are omitted, because they are too
large to acknowledge. Sometimes the whole Leslie Stephen household,
where Virginia Woolf essentially raised and educated herself, seems to have
been written into existence by Jane Austen, particularly in *Emma*. And, in
an implied Woolfian metaphor, Shakespeare can be regarded as the author
of *Between the Acts*, as his cosmos is where it is enacted. And though "Anon,"
the voice of the communal, is replaced by the inauguration of readers and
writers, a deeper residuum of "Anon" survives in Shakespeare.

* * *

Between the Acts is a difficult novel to describe, but beautifully easy to read. The entire continuity of the English cultural tradition is intimated, but mostly by moments of being, epiphanies or privileged moments, until the village audience of the pageant comes to see that they themselves are the conclusion: "Then the curtain rose. They spoke." They are the words, and Woolf, at her most experimental, joins us to them, whether we are English or not. Isa and Giles, wife and husband, rarely are heard speaking to one another, but are indicated indirectly, because they represent the universal condition of marriage itself, where silence and conversation fuse.

Miss La Trobe produces the country pageant outdoors, and begins it with a small girl: "England am I." We pass to Chaucer's Canterbury pilgrims, and on to Queen Elizabeth ("For me Shakespeare sang"), and so to a parody of late Shakespearean romance:

And off he skipped, as if his turn was over.

"Glad that's over," said Mrs. Elmhurst, uncovering her face. "Now what comes next? A tableau . . . ?"

For helpers, issuing swiftly from the bushes, carrying hurdles, had enclosed the Queen's throne with screens papered to represent walls. They had strewn the ground with rushes. And the pilgrims who had continued their march and their chant in the background, now gathered round the figure of Eliza on her soap box as if to form the audience at a play.

Were they about to act a play in the presence of Queen Elizabeth? Was this, perhaps, the Globe theatre?

"What does the programme say?" Mrs. Herbert Winthrop asked, raising her lorgnettes.

She mumbled through a blurred carbon sheet. Yes; it was a scene from a play.

"About a false Duke; and a Princess disguised as a boy; then the long lost heir turns out to be the beggar, because of a mole on his cheek; and Carinthia—that's the Duke's daughter, only she's been lost and in a cave—falls in love with Ferdinando who had been put into a basket as a baby by an aged crone. And they marry. That's I think what happens," she said, looking up from the programme.

"Play out the play," great Eliza commanded. An aged crone tottered forward.

("Mrs. Otter of the End House," someone murmured.)

The parody intensifies with a priest's benediction: .

> *From the distaff of life's tangled skein, unloose her hands.*
> (They unloosed her hands.)
> *Of her frailty, let nothing now remembered be.*
> *Call for the robin redbreast and the wren.*
> *And roses fall your crimson pall.*
> (Petals were strewn from wicker baskets.)
> *Cover the corpse. Sleep well.*
> (They covered the corpse.)
> *On you, fair Sirs,* (he turned to the happy couple).
> *Let Heaven rain benediction!*
> *Haste ere the envying sun*
> *Night's curtain hath undone. Let music sound*
> *And the free air of Heaven waft you to your slumber!*
> *Lead on the dance!*

Other mad parodies follow, mingled with scenes involving audience interplay. The major parody is of Restoration comedy, but no previous comedy
in Woolf matches the moment in which nature comes to the aid of art:

"Louder, louder!" Miss La Trobe vociferated.

Palaces tumble down (they resumed), *Babylon, Ninevah, Troy . . . And Cae-*
sar's great house . . . all fallen they lie . . . Where the plover nests was the
arch . . . through which the Romans trod . . . Digging and delving we break with
the share of the plough the clod . . . Where Clytemnestra watched for her
Lord . . . saw the beacons blaze on the hills . . . we see only the clod . . . Digging
and delving we pass . . . and the Queen and the Watch Tower fall . . . for
Agamemnon has ridden away . . . Clytemnestra is nothing but . . .

The words died away. Only a few great names—Babylon, Nineveh,
Clytemnestra, Agamemnon, Troy—floated across the open space.
Then the wind rose, and in the rustle of the leaves even the great
words became inaudible; and the audience sat staring at the villagers,
whose mouths opened, but no sound came.

And the stage was empty. Miss La Trobe leant against the tree, par-
alyzed. Her power had left her. Beads of perspiration broke on her
forehead. Illusion had failed. "This is death," she murmured, "death."

Then suddenly, as the illusion petered out, the cows took up the burden. One had lost her calf. In the very nick of time she lifted her great moon-eyed head and bellowed. All the great moon-eyed heads laid themselves back. From cow after cow came the same yearning bellow. The whole world was filled with dumb yearning. It was the primeval voice sounding loud in the ear of the present moment. Then the whole herd caught the infection. Lashing their tails, blobbed like pokers, they tossed their heads high, plunged and bellowed, as if Eros had planted his dart in their flanks and goaded them to fury. The cows annihilated the gap; bridged the distance; filled the emptiness and continued the emotion.

Miss La Trobe waved her hand ecstatically at the cows.

"Thank Heaven!" she exclaimed.

It is marvelous, so near to madness and self-immolation, that Woolf summons up this gusto, which returns to her again as the pageant achieves the Victorian period. Yet this is all satire, if it is satire, of a very dark kind. Recognition scenes throng the pageant, in every period, as Woolf happily parodies what Shakespeare himself vehemently parodied at the close of *Cymbeline*. At her best a great critic, Woolf teaches herself, and us, what Shakespearean recognition scenes truly concern: our inability to recognize either ourselves or the other—familial or erotic—in the first place. In a marvelously indirect way, *Between the Acts* is a war novel: England is under Nazi bombardment, but Woolf allows herself no overt references to this. Nor does she permit impressionist suggestions of the wider context that renders her village pageant both somber and hilarious. Forcing herself into an expressionistic mode, she drives us again towards the realization that we are the words.

What results is a novel so violently original that sixty years have not touched its freshness. An elliptical expressionism may sound like a very strange literary mode, but Shakespeare invented it in his final plays, and Woolf extends it in *Between the Acts*. The book is set in 1939, partly to avoid the trauma of bombardment, but partly also to suggest a gathering anxiety, which is now tragically in the immediate past. We have then a war book of a curious sort, which emphasizes not the anxiety of war but "the anxiety of art," as Maria Di Battista indicates:

Between the acts of the village pageant the narrative suggests . . . unfolding sexual tragedy.

This catches the central relationship of the novel, between Isa and Giles, where the poetic Isa is never at all certain whether she loves or hates her husband, though she means something erotic by "hate." Hermione Lee wisely remarks that "all marriages are inexplicable," a Shakespearean and Woolfian recognition. When she was twenty-five, Woolf had anticipated much of her life and art in a rhetorical question plainly marked by the influence of Walter Pater:

> Are we not each in truth the center of innumerable rays which so strike upon one figure only, and is it not our business to flash them straight and completely back again, and never suffer a single shaft to blunt itself on the far side of us?

That isn't exactly a formula for marriage. Let us set aside all questions of bisexuality, and of early sexual abuse: Virginia Woolf, like Pater, had in her enough of a gorgeous solipsism to have made any marriage problematical, just as it ended her sexual relationship with Vita Sackville-West. It seems fair to conclude, following Hermione Lee, that her marriage kept the novelist alive far longer than she might, on her own, have allowed herself to live. In the context of her life, and death, *Between the Acts* is a kind of miracle, as Virginia Woolf herself was.

How can Woolf's genius be defined? Sir Thomas Browne and Thomas De Quincey did not write novels. Walter Pater did, but *Marius the Epicurean* is not a very Woolfian book, nor is the fragmentary *Gaston de Latour*. Yet one of Pater's *Imaginary Portraits*, "Sebastian Van Storck," is a remarkable anticipation of *Mrs. Dalloway*, and Woolf's exquisite art of representing consciousness is profoundly Paterian. Still, it is one thing for poets to be Paterian: Yeats, Wallace Stevens, Hart Crane cultivate lyrics of secular epiphany without compromising their art. Woolf herself was more a lyricist than a storyteller, yet she was able to extend moments of vision into extraordinary narratives. *To the Lighthouse*, *The Waves*, and *Between the Acts* remain among the most original novels of Western tradition. Literary genius, as Dr. Johnson taught us, is manifested by originality, by an inventiveness that also reinvents the author, and to some degree, her readers as well.

V

DIN

LUSTRE 9

Ralph Waldo Emerson, Emily Dickinson, Robert Frost, Wallace Stevens, T. S. Eliot

The *Sefirah* known as *Din* serves as the edge or horizon that marks the limit of *Hesed*'s covenant love. I have grouped an American tradition here and included Eliot, despite his overt rebellion against it. Emerson, too easily categorized as a Transcendentalist, wrote his best book in the severe *Conduct of Life*. Emily Dickinson, rigorously original, is a poet of dark judgments, as Robert Frost is, after her. Wallace Stevens balances such rigor with surges of affirmation.

Those who would follow Eliot at his word, to place him elsewhere with Dante or with Baudelaire, ought to read *The Waste Land* and Whitman's "When Lilacs Last in the Dooryard Bloom'd" side by side, very closely. Poets, that is to say strong poets, cannot choose their tradition; it chooses them, and makes of their work what it will, subject to their agonistic vitality in fighting back.

RALPH WALDO EMERSON

We cannot write the order of the variable winds. How can we penetrate the law of our shifting moods and susceptibility? Yet they differ as all and nothing. Instead of the firmament of yesterday, which our eyes require, it is to-day an eggshell which coops us in; we cannot even see what or where our stars of destiny are. From day to day, the capital facts of human life are hidden from our eyes. Suddenly the mist rolls up, and reveals them, and we think how much good time is gone, that might have been saved, had any hint of these things been shown. A sudden rise in the road shows us the system of mountains, and all the summits, which have been just as near us all the year, but quite out of mind. But these alternations are not without their order and we are parties to our various fortune. If life seems a succession of dreams, yet poetic justice is done in dreams also. The visions of good men are good; it is the undisciplined will that is whipped with bad thoughts and bad fortunes. When we break the laws, we lose our hold on the central reality. Like sick men in hospitals, we change only from bed to bed, from one folly to another; and it cannot signify much what becomes of such castaways—wailing, stupid, comatose creatures,— lifted from bed to bed, from the nothing of life to the nothing of death.

—"Illusions," from *The Conduct of Life*

"Emerson," my late friend Angelo Bartlett Giamatti delighted in saying to me, "is as sweet as barbed wire." The Sage of Concord was not always as harsh as he was in *The Conduct of Life*, but that maturest of his works is the truest Emerson, the finest expression of his considerable genius.

The genius of Emerson remains the genius of America: he established our authentic religion, which is post-Protestant while pretending otherwise. Self-Reliance is not a comforting doctrine, because it admonishes each of us to fall back upon our genius, or else just fall outward and downward.

"Fate," "Power," and "Wealth" join "Illusions" as the great essays in *The Conduct of Life*. "Wealth" tells us, "As long as your genius buys, the investment is safe, though you spend like a monarch." New powers, innate in the self, will emerge.

"All power is of one kind, a sharing of the nature of the world." Such power Emerson calls "original action," another term for Self-Reliance. And yet action, for the mature Emerson, is circumscribed by the sense of fate. He returns to the pre-Socratic conviction that character is fate, ethos is the daemon, and his genius comes to rest in building altars to the Beautiful Necessity:

Why should we fear to be crushed by savage elements, we who are made up of the same elements? Let us build to the Beautiful Necessity, which makes man brave in believing that he cannot shun a danger that is appointed, nor incur one that is not.

RALPH WALDO EMERSON
(1803–1882)

IF EMERSON HAD AN OBSESSION, IT WAS with the question of American genius. "The American Scholar," his oration delivered at Harvard on August 31, 1837, remains the central meditation upon American literary originality: "Our day of dependence, our long apprenticeship to the learning of other lands, draws to a close." A declaration of literary independence becomes a manifesto for genius:

> The one thing in the world, of value, is the active soul . . . In this action, it is genius . . . Genius is always sufficiently the enemy of genius by over influence . . . It is remarkable, the character of the pleasure we derive from the best books. They impress us with the conviction that one nature wrote and the same reads . . . One must be an inventor to read well . . . It is a mischievous notion that we are come late into nature; that the world was finished a long time ago.

All this is aspiration; it kindles, but does not flame out. A year later, in the "Divinity School Address," Emerson caught fire from heaven:

> Jesus Christ belonged to the true race of prophets . . . The understanding caught this high chant from the poet's lips, and said, in the next age, "This was Jehovah come down out of heaven. I will kill you, if you say he was a man." The idioms of his language, and the figures of his rhetoric, have usurped the place of his truth; and churches are not built on his principles, but on his tropes . . . Let me admonish you, first of all, to go alone; to refuse the good models.

This is one of the catalysts of the American Religion, misleadingly called Christianity by churchgoers, ministers, and scholars (who should know better). One of the Scriptures of that religion is Emerson's "Self-Reliance," published in *Essays—First Series* (1841):

> A man should learn to detect and watch that gleam of light which flashes across his mind from within, more than the lustre of the

firmament of bards and sages. Yet he dismisses without notice his thought, because it is his. In every work of genius we recognize our own rejected thoughts: they come back to us with a certain alienated majesty . . . I shun father and mother and wife and brother, when my genius calls me. I would write on the lintels of the door-post, *Whim*.

The first principle for Emersonian genius is implicit here: the lustres we behold in literature already are our own, though we have alienated them from ourselves. Reading should be taking back what is yours, wherever you find it. But this transcends reading, and indeed is transcendence itself:

And now at last the highest truth on this subject remains unsaid; probably cannot be said; for all that we say is the far-off remembering of the intuition. That thought, by what I can now nearest approach to say it, is this. When good is near you, when you have life in yourself, it is not by any known or accustomed way; you shall not discern the foot-prints of any other; you shall not see the face of man; you shall not hear any name;—the way, the thought, the good, shall be wholly strange and new. It shall exclude example and experience. You take the way from man, not to man. All persons that ever existed are its forgotten ministers. Fear and hope are alike beneath it. There is somewhat low even in hope. In the hour of vision, there is nothing that can be called gratitude, nor properly joy. The soul raised over passion beholds identity and eternal causation, perceives the self-existence of Truth and Right, and calms itself with knowing that all things go well. Vast spaces of nature, the Atlantic Ocean, the South Sea,—long intervals of time, years, centuries,—are of no account. This which I think and feel underlay every former state of life and circumstances, as it does underlie my present, and what is called life, and what is called death.

Life only avails, not the having lived. Power ceases in the instant of repose; it resides in the moment of transition from a past to a new state, in the shooting of the gulf, in the darting to an aim. This one fact the world hates, that the soul *becomes;* for that for ever degrades the past, turns all riches to poverty, all reputation to shame, confounds the saint with the rogue, shoves Jesus and Judas equally aside. Why, then, do we prate of self-reliance? Inasmuch as the soul is present, there will be power not confident but agent. To talk of reliance is a poor external way of speaking. Speak rather of that which relies, because it works and is. Who has more obedience than I masters me, though he should not raise his finger. Round him I must revolve by the gravitation of spirits. We fancy it rhetoric, when we speak of eminent virtue. We do not yet see that virtue is Height, and that a man or a company of men, plastic and permeable to principles, by the law of nature must overpower and ride all cities, nations, kings, rich men, poets, who are not.

This is Emersonian genius, or the American Sublime. Emphatically, it is not a social doctrine, and intends no necessary good even to friends and neighbors. Emerson celebrates the Newness, the influx of power, of the daemon who knows how it is done. To take the way from man, not to man, is to discard all societal context. This is the mysticism of genius, as intense in Emerson as in Meister Eckhart or Saint John of the Cross, or of Jakob Boehme and his English disciple, William Law. This life you have in yourself is both your daily breath and that original *pneuma* that was the spark exalted by the ancient Gnostics, because it was what was best and oldest in them, and not part of the Creation-Fall. Unlike an ancient Gnostic speculator, Valentinus or Basilides, Emerson seeks not the fullness, the original *pleroma* from which we fell away in Creation, but the moment of transition, the American Crossing to a perpetual newness. The repose of the *pleroma* excludes power, and power is the Emersonian, American stigma of genius: "it resides in the moment of transition from a past to a new state, in the shooting of a gulf, in the darting to an aim." This produces the most subversive of all Emersonian sentences, when its implications are made apparent: "Speak rather of that which relies, because it works and is." All group morality is voided totally by that principle.

What then is Self-Reliance, or Emersonian genius? It is not so much amoral as nonmoral. The epigraph to the essay, a gnomic quatrain composed by Emerson, makes me think of Judge Holden's outburst in Cormac McCarthy's *Blood Meridian*: "Wolves cull themselves, man!":

> Cast the bantling on the rocks,
> Suckle him with the she-wolf's teat;
> Wintered with the hawk and fox,
> Power and speed be hands and feet.

I used to argue Emerson with my late friends Angelo Bartlett Giamatti, president of Yale and baseball commissioner, and Robert Penn Warren, poet-novelist, and remember well Giamatti's snarl: "Emerson is as sweet as barbed wire!" and Warren's quotation from his friend Allen Tate: "Emerson is the Devil." Giamatti and Warren, both of whom I go on mourning, were classical moralists. Self-Reliance is dangerous though vitalizing doctrine: it gave us Emersonians of the right like Henry Ford, and of the left like John Dewey. And though it is the American Religion, it warns us against set forms of belief: "As men's prayers are a disease of the will, so are their creeds a disease of the intellect," to quote yet again my favorite Emersonian sentence.

Emerson desired all Americans to be poets and mystics, and their curious post-Christian religion he helped to foster *is* their poetry and their mysticism, preached by the *Wall Street Journal* and the *Harvard Business Review*. If the power of American genius resides in transition, in a nervous darting to an aim, then indeed we can avoid ruling the world, because we already have contaminated it. A visit to Portugal or Spain, Italy or Sweden, in essential respects can give you the impression you never left home. Still, if Emerson empowered Henry Ford and activated John Dewey, he also inspired Walt Whitman, and rather more subtly Henry and William James, Emily Dickinson, and Hart Crane.

In "Experience," his most carefully wrought essay, Emerson warily reapproaches the question of genius:

The most attractive class of people are those who are powerful obliquely, and not by the direct stroke: men of genius, but not yet accredited: one gets the cheer of their light, without paying too great a tax. Theirs is the beauty of the bird, or the morning light, and not of art. In the thought of genius there is always a surprise; and the moral sentiment is well called "the newness," for it is never other.

Writing on Montaigne, his master as an essayist, Emerson takes this further:

The genius is a genius by the first look he casts on any object. Is his eye creative? Does he not rest in angles and colors, but beholds the design,—he will presently undervalue the actual object. In powerful moments, his thought has dissolved the works of art and nature into their causes, so that the words appear heavy and faulty.

As Emerson moves in this dangerous direction, he collides with the supreme of art in Shakespeare, and is stopped, but only for some moments. As the visionary of crossings and becomings confronts the limits of thought, language, and imagination, he is overcome by antithetical impulses: "Now, literature, philosophy, and thought, are Shakespearized. His mind is the

horizon beyond which, at present, we do not see." Is that celebration, or
lament? I think it hardly matters, so wise can Emerson be on Shakespeare:

> Shakespeare is the only biographer of Shakespeare; and even he
> can tell nothing, except to the Shakespeare in us; that is, to our most
> apprehensive and sympathetic hour.

This leads on to what, with Dr. Johnson's tributes, remains the best that
has been said about Shakespeare:

> So it fares with the wise Shakespeare and his book of life. He wrote
> the airs for all our modern music: he wrote the text of modern life; the
> text of manners: he drew the man of England and Europe; the father
> of the man in America: he drew the man, and described the day, and
> what is done in it: he read the hearts of men and women, their pro-
> bity, and their second thought, and wiles; the wiles of innocence, and
> the transitions by which virtues and vices slide into their contraries:
> he could divide the mother's part from the father's part in the face of
> the child, or draw the fine demarcations of freedom and of fate: he
> knew the laws of repression which make the police of nature: and all
> the sweets and all the terrors of human lot lay in his mind as truly but
> as softly as the landscape lies on the eye. And the importance of this
> wisdom of life sinks the form, as of Drama or Epic, out of notice. 'Tis
> like making a question concerning the paper on which a king's mes-
> sage is written.
> Shakespeare is as much out of the category of eminent authors, as
> he is out of the crowd. He is inconceivably wise; the others, conceiv-
> ably. A good reader can, in a sort, nestle into Plato's brain, and think
> from thence; but not into Shakespeare's. We are still out of doors. For
> executive faculty, for creation, Shakespeare is unique. No man can
> imagine it better. He was the farthest reach of subtlety compatible
> with an individual self,—the subtlest of authors, and only just within
> the possibility of authorship. With this wisdom of life, is the equal en-
> dowment of imaginative and of lyric power. He clothed the creatures
> of his legend with form and sentiments, as if they were people who
> had lived under his roof; and few real men have left such distinct
> characters as these fictions. And they spoke in language as sweet as it
> was fit. Yet his talents never seduced him into an ostentation, nor did
> he harp on one string. An omnipresent humanity coordinates all his
> faculties. Give a man of talents a story to tell, and his partiality will

presently appear. He has certain observations, opinions, topics, which have some accidental prominence, and which he disposes all to exhibit. He crams this part, and starves that other part, consulting not the fitness of the thing, but his fitness and strength. But Shakespeare has no peculiarity, no importunate topic; but all is duly given; no veins, no curiosities: no cow-painter, no bird-fancier, no mannerist is he: he has no discoverable egotism: the great he tells greatly: the small subordinately. He is wise without emphasis or assertion; he is strong, as nature is strong, who lifts the land into mountain slopes without effort, and by the same rule as she floats a bubble in the air, and likes as well to do the one as the other. This makes that equality of power in farce, tragedy, narrative, and love-songs; a merit so incessant, that each reader is incredulous of the perception of other readers.

This power of expression, or of transferring the inmost truth of things into music and verse, makes him the type of the poet, and has added a new problem to metaphysics. This is that which throws him into natural history, as a main production of the globe, and as announcing new eras and ameliorations. Things were mirrored in his poetry without loss or blur: he could paint the fine with precision, the great with compass; the tragic and comic indifferently, and without any distortion or favor. He carried his powerful execution into minute details, to a hair point; finishes an eyelash or a dimple as firmly as he draws a mountain; and yet these, like nature's will bear the scrutiny of the solar microscope.

In short, he is the chief example to prove that more or less of production, more or fewer pictures, is a thing indifferent. He had the power to make one picture. Daguerre learned how to let one flower etch its image on his plate of iodine; and then proceeds at leisure to etch a million. There are always objects; but there was never representation. Here is perfect representation, at last; and now let the world of figures sit for their portraits. No recipe can be given for the making of a Shakespeare; but the possibility of the translation of things into song is demonstrated.

What is most vital and capacious in Shakespeare is caught here forever. And yet, a page or two later, the undersong becomes the dominant's insistence that must be answered to, as Emerson finds himself dismayed that Shakespeare did not go on to use his wisdom and art to save us; or at least to make us more like himself:

He was master of the revels to mankind. Is it not as if one should have, through majestic powers of science, the comets given into his hand, or the planets and their moons, and should draw them from their orbits to glare with the municipal fireworks on a holiday night, and advertise in all towns, "very superior pyrotechny this evening!" Are the agents of nature, and the power to understand them, worth no more than a street serenade, or the breath of a cigar? One remembers again the trumpet-text in the Koran,—"The heavens and the earth, and all that is between them, think ye we have created them in jest?"

I break in here, not to object to the sacred Emerson, but to hazard Shakespeare's reply, or at least that of the final Shakespeare, in his share of *The Two Noble Kinsmen:* all we can do is to go off and bear us like the time, knowing what Chaucer's Knight teaches us, which is that always we must keep appointments we never made. The choice between the agents of nature and a street serenade is not difficult: the serenade will not destroy us, and understanding destruction may be worth less than the breath of a cigar. As to Allah's eloquent trumpetings, the Shakespearean reply well might be, "Why yes, a jest indeed." And yet Emerson goes on to disarm jesting by his most eloquent tribute:

Had he been less, had he reached only the common measure of great authors, of Bacon, Milton, Tasso, Cervantes, we might leave the fact in the twilight of human fate: but, that this man of men, he who gave to the science of mind a new and larger subject than had ever existed, and planted the standard of humanity some furlongs forward into chaos,—that he should not be wise for himself,—it must even go into the world's history, that the best poet led an obscure and profane life, using his genius for the public amusement.

One honors this, while rejecting it. The question of genius is fierce here: can it transcend, and teach a creedless beyond, give some coherence and significance to its violent order? What Charles Lamb said of Coleridge is for once true of Emerson: he wanted better bread than can be made of wheat.

EMILY DICKINSON

> His mind of man, a secret makes
> I meet him with a start
> He carries a circumference
> In which I have no part—

The genius of isolation is very rare: no other poet, not even Emily Brontë, seems so separate from us as Dickinson. We have no accurate approaches to her. If she was a kind of Emersonian, her difference from him is that she practiced the near-total autonomy that he advocated but could not live, since he was a cultural center in himself.

Emerson evades grief; Dickinson knows it as her atmosphere. Both feared blindness, and had psychosomatic encounters with it. But Emerson's came early and departed; Dickinson's was a deeper trouble.

One learns something of the self's power from Emerson; Dickinson teaches the anguish of a sublime transport through pain. Emerson refused despair; Dickinson is a master of every negative affect: fury, erotic destitution, a very private knowledge of God's exile from himself. Dickinson's is so original a genius that she alters one's sense of what poetic genius can be. She is recognizably a post-Wordsworthian poet, and yet the American difference is as strong in her as it is in Whitman or Melville.

It may be that William Blake, whose own genius was unique, is Dickinson's truest analogue. She is not a post-Protestant American religionist, like Emerson or Whitman, but a sect of one, like Blake. She upsets all our received ideas, as Blake does, without creating a supreme fiction of her own, as he attempted to do. Whether any poet really can start all over again, with each fresh poem, is disputable. Yet if anyone could do it, that poet is Dickinson.

EMILY DICKINSON
(1830–1886)

MY SUBJECT HAPPILY IS DICKINSON'S genius, her originality both in cognitive awareness and in aesthetic stance. I myself do not regard either her personal religion (as much a sect of one as William Blake's) or her sexual orientation as vexed matters, though here, as in all things, I am now part of a minority in what still we pretend are institutions of higher education. One is told, these days, that "the evidence of asterisks" indicates a sexually passionate relationship between Dickinson and her sister-in-law, but I see only that her letters are prose poems, as carefully composed as her poems, and would be evidence for nothing, even if asterisks were something more than asterisks. Much the best biography of Emily Dickinson remains Richard B. Sewall's (1974), which sensibly sums up the relationship between Dickinson and her difficult sister-in-law, Sue. Rather more crucially, Sewall charts Dickinson's frustrated love for Samuel Bowles, and her apparently fulfilled love for Judge Otis Phillips Lord, eighteen years older than herself. Lord died in 1884, at seventy-two; Dickinson was then fifty-four, and lived only another two years, mourning for Lord and the rest of her dead. Since Mrs. Lord died in late 1877, the close relationship between Dickinson and the Judge evidently dates from early 1878 on, when she was forty-seven and he sixty-five. Her letters to him, though composed with her usual preternatural skill at rhetorical elaboration, simply cannot be understood except as sexual passion, though certainly they constitute no evidence for consummation. Wary as one has to be with Dickinson, I follow Sewall in crediting her love for Bowles and what almost became marriage with Lord. We are still in the apprentice state in learning to read Dickinson's poetry, primarily because of her authentic difficulty. She is frequently more allusive than we tend to recognize, as here in a famous quatrain addressed to herself as Lord was dying:

> Circumference thou Bride of Awe
> Possessing thou shalt be
> Possessed by every hallowed Knight
> That dares—to Covet thee
> —Poem 1636, Franklin's edition

This, in aspiration anyway, could be called Dickinson's brief hymn to free love, following Shelley's ecstatic *Epipsychidion,* in which Emilia Viviani, Shelley's momentary beloved, is addressed as "Emily." I expand upon Sewall here, for the Shelleyan allusion is a very deliberate shock conveyed to us by Dickinson. She, in her sublimely enhanced consciousness, is Circumference; Awe is the dying Judge Lord, pragmatically her husband, and she declares herself open to every hallowed Knight that will dare to covet her. The relevant passage in *Epipsychidion* illuminates Dickinson's complex metaphor, "Circumference," by showing its sexual nature:

> Meanwhile
> We two will rise, and sit, and walk together,
> Under the roof of blue Ionian weather,
> And wander in the meadows, or ascend
> The mossy mountains, where the blue heavens bend
> With lightest winds, to touch their paramour;
> Or linger, where the pebble-paven shore,
> Under the quick, faint kisses of the sea
> Trembles and sparkles as with ecstasy,—
> Possessing and possessed by all that is
> Within that calm circumference of bliss,
> And by each other, till to love and live
> Be one:—

Shelley and his Emily, possessing and possessed by each other, also share that mutual possession with everything within the heightened state of their circumference. Turn back to the audacious Dickinson. As Bride of Awe (the Judge) she remains possessing, but after his dying, she anticipates further possession, depending upon the daring of those who will desire or covet her. The poet Dickinson gives us very little room to ironize or allegorize here; she borrows possessing, possessed, and circumference from Shelley's most overt celebration of free love. Whatever enlarged state of being and imagination is involved in Dickinson's self-identification as Circumference, it cannot be taken wholly as metaphor, but implies also the difference in her that has resulted from her love affair with Otis Phillips Lord.

No one can read Dickinson long and deeply without being confronted by her extraordinary self-reliance as a poet, woman, and religious thinker. The expression of that self-trust is a pride in her own poetic authority, and in her highly individual spiritual autonomy. I use the Emersonian self-reliance and self-trust deliberately: what is her relation to her older contemporary Emer-

son? Personally, she evaded him. On December 11, 1857, Emerson lectured
in Amherst, and then dined and stayed overnight next door to the poet, at
her brother's and sister-in-law's house. At twenty-seven, Dickinson was no
recluse; presumably she attended the lecture, and dined with the sage. Sue,
recalling the occasion, said that Emily said of Emerson, "As if he had come
from where dreams were born." And yet she sent her poems not to Emerson but to Thomas Wentworth Higginson, a war hero but a third-rate man
of letters. Writing to Higginson, she asked a question that must have baffled him: "With the Kingdom of Heaven on his knee, could Mr. Emerson
hesitate?" I take this as delicious wickedness, which we are slow to attribute to Dickinson. Confronted by the 1855 *Leaves of Grass*, Emerson's response was precise, critically superb, and a powerful encouragement. Faced
by Dickinson's poems, would we have expected less of Emerson? Her affinities with Emerson were manifold; her difference ultimately larger than
Hawthorne's or Melville's. Like Emerson, she had eye trouble, both literal
and figurative. But she did not share his faithless faith, any more than she
did the faith of her fathers. Self-reliance carried her a long way, but then
failed her, or she it.

It is not possible to define Dickinson's private religion, partly because
she followed Emerson in exalting Whim, which does not belong to the
cosmos of Judaism, Christianity, and Islam. The most subtly intelligent
discussion of Dickinson's spirituality is James McIntosh's *Nimble Believing:
Dickinson and the Unknown* (2000), which takes its title from one of the poet's
letters to Judge Lord:

> On subjects of which we know nothing, or should I say *Beings*—is
> "Phil" [the Judge] a "Being" or a "Theme"—we both believe and dis-
> believe a hundred times an Hour, which keeps Believing nimble—

On that account, it keeps Disbelieving equally nimble, and no one—
including Dickinson herself—could be at all certain just what (if anything)
she believed. I find little in the poems to indicate that she believed in the
Resurrection of Jesus Christ, and she certainly did not accept him as her
redeemer. But the sufferings of Jesus, and his triumph over them, were of
extraordinary interest to her, while they meant nothing to Emerson, who
regarded Golgotha as a Great Defeat, and as an American said, "We demand
Victory, a Victory to the senses as to the soul." Dickinson found a victory at
Golgotha, but only through her outrageous stance as "Empress of Calvary,"
and so as Christ's bride. She intimates that she had married the Holy
Ghost, again a very American realization. McIntosh, perhaps with a touch

more residual Calvinism than Dickinson possessed, thinks that Dickinson's "Awe" is a Calvinist inheritance, and yet it appears to be one of her private names for her near-husband, Judge Lord. And yet, though Dickinson's mature spiritual position is indescribable, McIntosh is surely accurate in saying that it was not self-contradictory. She had worked out a personal religious myth, but she declined to express it fully or consistently, except by dramatizing her place in the myth in her poems. Her Awe, like her Transport, is High Romantic, and we still have not worked out her complex relation to Wordsworth, Shelley, and Keats.

Like Emerson, Dickinson somewhat disconcertingly worships Power, joking that Power stood in Scripture between the Kingdom and the Glory, because it is the wildest of the three. Her "wildness" is Emerson's and, like him, by it she means "freedom." She revered Emerson, but unlike Whitman and Thoreau she cannot be considered Emersonian, because she took such care to keep the sage at a distance. Her supposed struggle with Calvinism—where is it?—has little to do with her wariness. Emerson was too close already, both as a poet and as a reconceptualizer. Some of their poems could be assigned to either poet, hardly a pleasure for Dickinson. To go without models is Emerson's own advice, which Dickinson scarcely needed. Yet both are poets of sudden epiphanies, far more benign in Emerson's case.

How should we confront Dickinson's genius? That shades into: how can we describe a genius so volatile, capricious, conceptually original? Her definitive editor, Ralph Franklin, reminds us that we must go through her idiom to enter her work, as "she conducted no negotiation toward public norms for her poetry." The most useful statement that I have ever read about Dickinson is Franklin's:

> A good citizen of the age of print, she was a committed reader of newspapers, magazines, and books but could not undertake the commercial, impersonal, and fundamentally exposing act of publishing her work. This is the poet who, knowing her boundaries, said, "I do not cross my Father's ground to any House or Town."

I take from this the hint that one had better know one's own boundaries when reading this formidable woman, and when trying to apprehend her genius. How many other American writers are of her eminence? I would say just three: Emerson, Whitman, Henry James. There are others only a touch or two short of that fourfold: Hawthorne, Melville, Mark Twain, Frost, Faulkner, Stevens, Eliot, Hart Crane among them. If asked the desert island question, and could have only one book by an American, I should have to answer Whitman, but Dickinson or Emerson would more than suffice. No one should be foolish enough to condescend to Dickinson, or to enlist her for any ideology or creed whatsoever. Hazlitt rightly said that in Wordsworth you seemed to start anew on a *tabula rasa* of poetry. That is not as strictly true of Dickinson's poetry as of Wordsworth's, but she comes close. And in cognitive originality she surpasses any Western poet except for Shakespeare and Blake. She can think more lucidly and feel more fully than any of her readers, and she is very aware of her superiority. So I am very cautious when, in what follows, I attempt to track her genius.

Though Dickinson is exuberant, and can be comically exhilarating, she is a poet whose central mode is an intense suffering, at times so painful and demanding that she affords only the most difficult kind of pleasure, traditionally associated with the Sublime. When I read her for a prolonged time, and whenever I teach her, the experience exhausts me, the way reading and teaching *King Lear* devastates me. A poet who says that she likes a look of agony, because she knows it is true, risks misprision, as in Camille Paglia's enlisting Dickinson in the ranks of the divine Marquis de Sade. I remember arguing the issue with Paglia (a superb reader) but failing to persuade her. In Dickinson, very difficult pleasures and pains oxymoronically intermingle, and it is also always worth remarking that Dickinson, her reputation aside, can be a very erotic poet, though her genius flourishes wildly in celebrating/lamenting the erotics of loss. Death and passion debate in her, and death necessarily wins.

In 1863, Dickinson reached the Christological age, and experienced the most fecund year her poetry was ever to know. Why it should have been her *annus mirabilis*, I can only surmise. In late April of 1864, she went to Boston for eye treatment, and returned to Amherst on November 28, but the previous year was spent peacefully at home, without major personal losses. In 1862, she chose Higginson as preceptor, long before he went off to be colonel of a black regiment. Her major losses cluster later: her father in 1874, Samuel Bowles in 1878, Charles Wadsworth in 1882, her mother later that year, Judge Lord in 1884, Helen Hunt Jackson in 1885, until on May 15, 1886, Dickinson herself died. With so incredibly inward a genius, as unknown to us as Shakespeare remains, an outward stimulus appears quite unnecessary to prompt the imagination. I take 1863 not quite arbitrarily, since it comprises Poems 499 through 793 in Franklin's edition, nearly three hundred poems and fragments out of 1,789. Its major lyrics include: "A Pit—but Heaven over it" (508), "This is my letter to the World" (519), "It always felt to me—a wrong" (521), "I tie my Hat—I crease my Shawl" (522), "I reckon—when I count at all" (533), "I measure every grief I meet" (550),

"I heard a Fly buzz—when I died" (590), "The Brain—is wider than the sky—" (598), "Much Madness is divinest Sense—" (620), "The Soul's Superior instants" (630), "I saw no Way—The Heavens were stitched" (633), "No Rack can torture me—" (649), "I started Early—Took my Dog—" (656), "A Tongue—to tell Him I am true!" (673), "What Soft-Cherubic Creatures—" (675), "The Tint I cannot take—is best—" (696), "I cannot live with You" (706), "My Life had stood—a loaded Gun—" (764), "Renunciation—is a piercing Virtue—" (782), "Publication—is the Auction" (788). I choose those twenty arbitrarily, following personal taste, and omit many of singular value, but those twenty alone are a body of great poetry. How did they emerge from an outwardly quiet year?

Glancing back a year in Franklin's superb edition, one wonders if 1862 isn't almost as rich, with "Going to Him! Happy letter!" (277), "Of all the Souls that stand create—" (279), "I should have been too glad, I see—" (283), "Of Bronze—and Blaze—" (319), "There's a certain slant of light" (320), "Before I got my eye put out—" (336), "I felt a Funeral, in my Brain" (340), " 'Tis so appalling it exhilarates—" (341), "It was not Death, for I stood up" (355), "After great pain a formal feeling comes" (372), "I cannot dance upon my Toes—" (381), "Dare you see a Soul at the 'White Heat'?" (401), "One need not be a Chamber—to be Haunted" (407), "The Soul selects her own Society—" (409), " 'Twas like a Maelstrom, with a notch" (425), "This was a Poet—" (446), "I died for Beauty—but was scarce" (448), "Our journey had advanced—" (453), "I dwell in Possibility—" (466), "Because I could not stop for Death—" (479), "From Blank to Blank—" (484). That is twenty-one more, each as strong as the twenty after. In 1864, Dickinson suffered extensive eye treatments, and was away from home. The year indubitably shows a falling-off, but one poem at least is equal to any she ever wrote: "This Consciousness that is aware" (817).

The antithetical effect of the Civil War upon Dickinson's flowering in 1862–63 has been argued by Shira Wolosky, who sees the further internalization as a response to national crisis. That seems persuasive, and yet we cannot know. Why did she wane as a poet after 1875? Her last eleven years give us only about three hundred poems, and they read like the work of an imitator, a disciple of the great Dickinson. Only one matters, at least to me: "The Bible is an antique Volume—" (1577). Among the poems Franklin cannot date, there is the wonderful "A word made Flesh is seldom" (1715) and the outrageously erotic "In Winter in my Room" (1742), but little else. One can surmise that her father's death, in 1874, may have destroyed her motive for metaphor. A month after Edward Dickinson's death, she famously wrote to Higginson: "His Heart was pure and terrible and I think no

other like it exists." Their relationship had been overtly remote and profoundly repressed; and perhaps her poetry, at its best, was engendered by
the need to people a void.

Yet I chafe even at so obvious a surmise: Amherst, and New England,
were replete with Calvinist fathers working themselves to death for their
spinster daughters, but yet we do not have a school of Emily Dickinsons,
but only this unique genius. Her sister Lavinia was also a spinster, but was
not a Charlotte or Anne Brontë to her Emily. With so vastly innovative a
consciousness, we need to change completely our usual procedures, and
concentrate on the influence of the work upon the life, rather than the reverse. Everything and everyone, Judge Lord and sister-in-law Sue, failed
Emily Dickinson *except her poetry*. Like William Blake and Gerard Manley
Hopkins, she had only a handful as audience, and she benefited by this isolation, as Blake and Hopkins did also.

Clearly there is an element in lyric poetry that can prosper without an
audience, and that is strongest where society is excluded. I think of African-
American poetry, where much the greatest figure is the reclusive Jay Wright,
who is almost unknown to the reading public, and who is totally free of all
ideological and political cheerleading, unscarred by nationalist rant. Emily
Dickinson was not only a religion of one, but I cannot find in her poetry a
single trace of the Whig politics of her father and of her lover, Judge Lord.
You can observe, if you wish, that only the Dickinson fortune and social position made her possible, but that leaves you exactly nowhere, as Lavinia
Dickinson and so many others show. The academic world, which rewards
cheerleading and loathes genius, is the worst possible audience for, or authority upon, Emily Dickinson, as the vast mass of current contemporaries
pathetically demonstrate. "Hurrah for Emily!" the pom-pom wavers cheer:
"She slept with sister-in-law Sue!"

Very briefly, I will set down what I think I comprehend of Dickinson's genius. Like several other major American poets—Whitman, Frost, Wallace
Stevens—she made a relatively late start. Had she died at thirty, we might
not remember her. There are a few poems that matter before 1861, but her
power is not yet present. There are remarkable scattered phrases, and some
mischievous lyrics of true wit. But, by the conclusion of Poem 243, we recognize her:

> The possibility—to pass
> Without a moment's Bell—
> Into Conjecture's presence
> Is like a Face of Steel—

That suddenly looks into ours
With a metallic grin—
The Cordiality of Death—
Who drills his Welcome in—

"Conjecture" here is what Stevens meant by "an abstraction blooded, as a man by thought." What Dickinson particularly blooded, by her thought, were the hymns of Isaac Watts, though her project was the reversal of the church hymn. She attracted Paul Celan, who translated her beautifully, because in her hymns of negation he recognized something of his own enterprise, though he addresses "No one," and Dickinson makes it difficult to know just whom she invokes. Some of the difficulties of interpreting Dickinson, as I think Celan saw, are surprisingly akin to Kafka's refusal to be interpretable.

There are no daemons or demons in Dickinson (though she has some goblins), and the word "genius" would not be easy to fit into her hymn metric; she uses it only once in a late (1873) comic poem about a spider, no. 1373:

The Spider as an Artist
Has never been employed—
Though his surpassing Merit
Is freely certified

By every Broom and Bridget
Throughout a Christian Land—
Neglected Son of Genius
I take thee by the Hand—

One thinks of Whitman's similarly late "A Noiseless Patient Spider," but this is hardly vintage Dickinson, whereas Poem 381 of 1862 certainly is:

I cannot dance upon my Toes—
No Man instructed me—
But oftentimes, among my mind,
A Glee possesseth me,

That had I Ballet Knowledge—
Would put itself abroad
In Pirouette to blanch a Troupe—
Or lay a Prima, mad,

And though I had no Gown of Gauze—
No Ringlet, to my Hair,
Nor hopped for Audiences—like Birds—
One Claw upon the air—

Nor tossed my shape in Eider Balls,
Nor rolled on wheels of snow
Till I was out of sight, in sound,
The House encore me so—

Nor any know I know the Art
I mention—easy—Here—
Nor any Placard boast me—
It's full as Opera—

She celebrates her own genius, the daemonic exuberance she calls "A
Glee," and she *means* "possesseth." "Glee" and "possession," in the second
word's various forms, are her personal equivalents for genius and the daemonic. "Transport," in its variants, is her favorite term for the Romantic or
daemonic Sublime, though she also plays with the word "Sublime." The
High Romantic "joy" and "delight" are everywhere in her, as legacies from
Wordsworth and Coleridge, Shelley and Keats, but "glee" has a particular
twist for her. One of my secret favorites is Poem 317 of 1862, which I did
not list earlier, because some of my students resist it, yet *here* is her distinct
genius, in a wonderful play-poem:

Delight is as the flight—
Or in the Ratio of it,
As the Schools would say—
The Rainbow's way—
A Skein
Flung colored, after Rain,
Would suit as bright,
Except that flight
Were Aliment—

"If it would last"
I asked the East,
When that Bent Stripe
Struck up my childish

Firmament—
And I, for glee,
Took Rainbows, as the common way,
And empty skies
The Eccentricity—

And so with Lives—
And so with Butterflies—
Seen magic—through the fright
That they will cheat the sight—
And Dower latitudes far on—
Some sudden morn—
Our portion—in the fashion—
Done—

The Glee that possesses her in "I cannot dance upon my toes" becomes
her motive for metaphor here when, "for glee," she manipulates the heavens. A late (1879) fragment, no. 1508, has stayed in my memory since I first
read it in Franklin's edition:

His voice decrepit was with Joy—
Her words did totter so
How old the News of Love must be
To make Lips elderly
That purled a moment since with Glee—
Is it Delight or Woe—
Or Terror—that do decorate
This livid—interview—

This almost certainly depicts the erotic relationship with Judge Lord,
capturing a privileged moment with Dickinsonian detachment. The Glee,
her daemonic intensity, had radiated out to her lover, only to render them
both even older, since the irony of "the News of Love" is its eternal antiquity. "Lived" is appropriate, whether Delight, Woe, or Terror "decorate"
this erotic interview. I know of no one else who writes like this, except for
the final Shakespeare in his part of *The Two Noble Kinsmen*. Shakespeare
and the Bible, both transvalued, are Dickinson's truest precursors, with
whom her mature contest is waged. I return to the Dickinsonian glee for a
final time, in regard to the difficult Poem 365, which I again failed to list,
because of student resistance to what some regarded as opacity:

I know that He exists.
Somewhere—in silence—
He has hid his rare life
From our gross eyes.

'Tis an instant's play—
'Tis a fond Ambush—
Just to make Bliss
Earn her own surprise!

But—should the play
Prove piercing earnest—
Should the glee—glaze—
In Death's—stiff—stare—

Would not the fun
Look too expensive!
Would not the jest—
Have crawled too far!

I don't know whether "He" is Jesus Christ, Charles Wadsworth, or Samuel Bowles, but I don't think that matters. The central word again is "glee," and its origin is in Dickinson, and not in Jesus or in a human love not-to-be. Whether divine or human, He is an alien or alienated god-man, startled by the glee of her "fond Ambush," and yet she fears that the glee, natural to her, but too strong for him, may be a fatal jest. Part of our trouble in reading such a poem is its unprecedentedness. Dickinsonian "glee" is an intoxication of unprecedentedness, her joy and delight in her own autonomy and inventiveness. Did she, after all, turn recluse because she feared her own erotic power? Her idiom was self-consciously gnomic, becoming more difficult as she proceeded. Her poetic power is beyond doubt, as is the Bible's, Shakespeare's, Blake's, Whitman's. She will become only more challenging as the decades and centuries pass. Like Whitman, she stops somewhere waiting for us.

ROBERT FROST

The hurt is not enough:
I long for weight and strength
To feel the earth as rough
To all my length.

This final quatrain of "To Earthward" is central to Frost's sense of himself. Always professedly Emerson's disciple, Frost equals his oracle in spiritual ferocity. "Evil will bless, and ice will burn" is an Emersonian line, but might as well be Frost's. Both these American sages believed in valor, but both also saw plainly that the trial by existence could cost us much of our pride, and so might cause us to conclude in self-mystification and in pain.

Emerson and Frost share an American solitude, a sense that they cannot be free unless they are alone. Frost can be even more severe than Emerson, and particularly upon himself. The poet-critic Yvor Winters, who disdained both Emerson and Frost, said of Frost, "He is an Emersonian who has become skeptical and uncertain without having reformed." Skepticism, as Winters would not see, was central to the vision that Emerson and Frost enjoyed.

Emerson regarded Nature as the Not-Me, and Frost too is no nature poet.

The principal difference between Emerson and Frost is not in poetic argument but in temperament. Frost was prone to terrible depressions, and in many respects was sly, envious, and cruel, hardly capable of comparison to the shrewd but humane and disinterested Emerson. But Frost learned how to convert his melancholy and nihilism into a remarkable poetic originality, a sublime negativity eloquently triumphant in poems like "Directive," "The Most of It," and "The Oven Bird."

ROBERT FROST
(1874–1963)

FROST IS THE PEER OF WALLACE STEVENS, T. S. Eliot, and Hart Crane: these were the principal poets of the United States in the past century. Plainly, Frost, who became a national institution, stands apart from the others. Stevens was a reclusive insurance lawyer and Eliot a voluntary exile in London, where he worked as a publisher. Hart Crane, our Rimbaud and our Christopher Marlowe, was both pariah and prophet. The cracker-barrel Frost, our national sage, was a poor woman's Emerson, which constituted a useful enough public persona, though of no intellectual or aesthetic value in itself. Frost the poet was very different: savage rather than wise; an original revisionist of the later darker Emerson of *The Conduct of Life;* above all, a very difficult, complex artist who in his strongest poems is endlessly surprising.

Emerson always was Frost's touchstone for literature, yet Frost read deeply in the tradition: Emily Dickinson, Keats, Tennyson, Shelley, and Browning were particularly important to him, as was the Roman poet Lucretius, whose Epicurean stance essentially resembled Frost's. The deep friendship with the English poet Edward Thomas had something to do with the authentic affinities between the two poets' works, and reading them together remains illuminating, as I will show.

In a letter to his daughter (1934), Frost remarked that "all poetry has always said something and implied the rest. Well then why have it say anything? Why not have it imply everything? Hart Crane has gone to great lengths here." Presumably Frost referred to Crane's allusiveness and his "logic of metaphor." Frost's way had no affinities with Crane's, or Eliot's or Stevens's, yet he seems to me as difficult a poet, in a mode much his own.

My personal favorites in Frost include "The Wood-Pile," "The Oven Bird," "Design," "The Most of It," "Never Again Would Birds' Song Be the Same," and the shattering "Directive," and so I will confine myself to that arbitrary half-dozen. All of these poems say something, but imply a great deal more, for Frost was one of the geniuses of a particularly dark irony, in which you do not so much say one thing while meaning another, but the meaning itself doubles back and undoes the one thing. How much self-knowledge can we bear? The question was learned by Frost from pondering

Shakespeare, but acquires an iron personalism in Frost that, at its fiercest, is only just to be borne, whether by Frost or by his attentive reader.

In "The Wood-Pile" the poet walks over the hard snow in a frozen swamp on a gray day. This amble is neither pleasant nor safe, but "I was just far from home." There are three enigmatic entities that together comprise the poem: the walker, a frightened small bird, and the wood-pile of the title. The bird is under the misapprehension that Frost is after him for his white tail-feather: "like one who takes / Everything said as personal to himself." That presumably accounts for a husband walking far from home, yet bird and walker fade in comparison to a lonely eminence of wood-pile, an inexplicable presence in the frozen swamp. Someone, a year or two before, has cut, split, piled, measured, and abandoned a cord of maple, held by a stake and prop, now about to fall:

> I thought that only
> Someone who lived in turning to fresh tasks
> Could so forget his handiwork on which
> He spent himself, the labor of his ax,
> And leave it there far from a useful fireplace
> To warm the frozen swamp as best it could
> With the slow smokeless burning of decay.

Sometimes a wood-pile is only a wood-pile; is this one also an abandoned poem, or a dying marriage? We don't know; "The Wood-Pile" is from *North of Boston* (1914), first published in London soon after Frost turned forty, and probably was written in Gloucestershire, when Frost was much in the company of Edward Thomas, the English poet who was killed in France in 1917, when nearing forty. Thomas and Frost exchanged influences, and sometimes I read one of them and am haunted by the other. There is an immensely poignant poem by Thomas called "Liberty" which has a wisdom that Frost, at his rare best, shares and extends:

> There's none less free than who
> Does nothing and has nothing else to do,
> Being free only for what is not to his mind,
> And nothing is to his mind.

That is close to the ethos of Frost's "someone who lived in turning to fresh tasks," which is to live only for the poem that is still to be written. Frost outlived his wife Elinor by a quarter-century; one of their sons died at

three, another killed himself, and a daughter, like Frost's sister, was mentally ill. Frost had a rugged nature, and experienced many sorrows as a husband and a father. Self-awareness, always acute in him, is beautifully
exemplified in the famous "The Oven Bird" of *Mountain Interval* (1916),
where he presumably expects us to know that this warbler builds an oven-
shaped nest, and is also called the "teacher bird," since its call sounds (to
some) like "teacher, teacher":

> The bird would cease and be as other birds
> But that he knows in singing not to sing.
> The question that he frames in all but words
> Is what to make of a diminished thing.

This is one of Frost's signatures: a sustained negativity that reflects his
Emersonian, post-Christian spiritual stance. Pragmatically, Frost is a knowing nihilist, like Emerson. A Gnostic archon or demiurge has brought Frost's
cosmos into being, in a creation that simultaneously was a fall. The argument of the elegantly ghastly "Design" turns upon rhetorical questions that
invert the Christian argument-from-design:

> What brought the kindred spider to that height,
> Then steered the white moth thither in the night?
> What but design of darkness to appall?—

There is a shattering poem, "The Most of It," in *A Witness Tree* (1942)
but written much earlier, which demonstrates Frost's realization both of his
solipsism and his sadism. Emily Dickinson, subtlest of Frost's precursors,
said of her own consciousness that it was aware of neighbors and the sun.
Frost, in one of his many shrewd and oblique self-examinations, portrays a
male figure who "thought he kept the universe alone," and who can hear in
nature only a mocking echo of his own voice:

> Some morning from the boulder-broken beach
> He would cry out on life, that what it wants
> Is not its own love back in copy speech,
> But counter-love, original response.

The "original response" arrives as a violent irony, not so much inhuman
(the general reaction of critics) but even more a male aggressivity, when a
great buck crumples the water:

> And landed pouring like a waterfall,
> And stumbled through the rocks with horny tread,
> And forced the underbrush—and that was all.

"Pouring," "horny," "forced"—all emphasize a male redundancy: the "counter-love" is reduced to "the most of it," and what could the response be but an unoriginal surrender to the masculine? Frost prints directly after this the beautiful and difficult "Never Again Would Birds' Song be the Same," a sonnet whose title is also the poem's penultimate line:

> Never again would birds' song be the same,
> And to do that to birds was why she came.

Eve's fall, in Frost's interpretation, is into language, which in turn becomes the fall of nature, the feminization of birds' song. This is quite Miltonic, and one need not be a feminist to be both poetically impressed and humanly chagrined by it. And yet this complex sonnet was composed soon after Elinor Frost's death, and is a kind of elegy for her. As in "The Most of It," Frost writes as a bereft Adam, and with grim honesty does not assert that much has been learned from the experience of loss.

"Directive," in *Steeple Bush* (1947), seems to me Frost's harshest and most powerful poem, bitter as a judgment upon a personal past, but immensely strong in its capacity to go back to origins on a very painful quest. The quester, upon reaching his waters and watering place, is exhorted to "Drink and be whole again beyond confusion." Frost called Emerson's "Uriel" "the greatest Western poem yet" and his "confusion," here and elsewhere, is ironically appropriated from "Uriel." There the god Uriel (Emerson uttering the "Divinity School Address") affirms that "Evil will bless, and ice will burn," and the outraged heavens split asunder:

> The balance-beam of Fate was bent;
> The bounds of good and evil were rent;
> Strong Hades could not keep his own,
> But all slid to confusion.

"A poem is a momentary stay against confusion," Frost's dictum in his essay "The Figure a Poem Makes," refers back to "Uriel." Emerson and Frost both seem to have known that the Indo-European root of "confusion" initially signified the pouring of a libation to the gods. To drink, and thus to be whole again, beyond confusion, would be to transcend such ancient

worship. "Directive," a poem written by a guide "Who only has at heart your
getting lost," concludes with a startling allusion to a highly problematic passage in the Gospel of Mark:

> I have kept hidden in the instep arch
> Of an old cedar at the waterside
> A broken drinking goblet like the Grail
> Under a spell so the wrong ones can't find it,
> So can't get saved, as Saint Mark says they mustn't.
> (I stole the goblet from the children's playhouse).
> Here are your waters and your watering place.
> Drink and be whole again beyond confusion.

One can feel Frost's unholy delight in Mark 4:11–12: "That seeing they
may see, and not perceive, and hearing they may hear and not understand,
lest at any time they should be converted, and their sins should be forgiven
them." Even so, Frost fiercely splits his readers asunder, challenging them
to read "Directive" aright or be damned. He looks back to a ruined house,
a ruined farm, and an all-but-ruined marriage, and remarks pungently, "This
was no playhouse but a house in earnest." "Directive" exudes "a certain
coolness" and constitutes a "serial ordeal," both directed at his reader.
"When we break laws, we lose our hold on the central reality," Emerson
writes. His disciple Frost, severe and isolate (despite his public status) ultimately addresses an elite, and affords them only difficult pleasures.

WALLACE STEVENS

Tell X that speech is not dirty silence
Clarified. It is silence made still dirtier.
It is more than an imitation for the ear.

He lacks this venerable complication.
His poems are not of the second part of life.
They do not make the visible a little hard.

To see . . .
                    —"The Creations of Sound"

X, we may take it, is T. S. Eliot, not one of Wallace Stevens's favorite
poets. If asked for the particular genius of Stevens's poems, one would say

that they indeed do "make the visible a little hard / To see." Stevens, like Dickinson, is a great unnamer:

> Throw away the lights, the definitions,
> And say of what you see in the dark
>
> That it is this or that it is that,
> But do not use the rotted names.

The visible, like the names, is estranged in Stevens, because his enterprise is to scrub off the varnish, to cleanse the face of his spirit (in Blake's phrase). It remains odd that Stevens, a visionary poet, is rarely read for what he wrote. A High Romantic masking as an insurance lawyer, Stevens confused what public he had. It was only after his death, in 1955, that gradually he came to be seen as the poet of his era, displacing Eliot, Pound, and William Carlos Williams.

Like Shelley and Whitman, Stevens was a Lucretian poet, celebrating a cosmos centered upon inevitable entropy and death. That hardly sounds joyous, but there is an Epicurean joy in Stevens, and an exuberance of language akin to Shakespeare's *Love's Labour's Lost*.

As I grow old, I am most moved by a fine plainness that Stevens also possesses, which gives us the most persuasive defense of poetry in our time:

> From this the poem springs: that we live in a place
> That is not our own and, much more, not ourselves
> And hard it is in spite of blazoned days.

WALLACE STEVENS
(1879–1955)

IT IS DIFFICULT TO ACHIEVE PERSPECTIVE upon someone most of whose poems you have possessed by memory for more than half a century. Wallace Stevens is, after Whitman, Dickinson, and Henry James, the greatest master of nuance in the American language. He is uniquely the poet of "The hum of thoughts evaded in the mind." The subtlest of all major American poets is ill served these days by studies that center upon his social and political contexts, analyses that tell us what a quick perusal of his letters demonstrates, that this insurance lawyer was a Taft Republican who always reflected the values of Bucks County, Pennsylvania, where he grew up in the 1880s. The hard labor of directly confronting the rhetorical wealth of Stevens's poetry has ceased.

I have read Stevens incessantly since I was a boy, taking his genius as a given. This book is not a work of analysis or of close reading, but of surmise and juxtaposition. In this brief revisit to Stevens, about whom I have written very extensively elsewhere, I am not concerned with individual poems, but with his genius, which in his instance means with the power of his aesthetic stance, a power so great that it converted, *in the poems*, an insurance executive into a seer.

Stevens was surly on all questions of influence: Pater and Emerson "were in the attic somewhere," and Walt Whitman had demeaned the status of American poets through his tramp persona. Yet these—with Wordsworth, Coleridge, Shelley, Keats, Tennyson—were the seer of Hartford's prime precursors. Emerson, though deprecated, hovers everywhere in Stevens, whose critical prose can be mistaken for Pater's. Whitman is a deeper and darker presence/absence in Stevens's work. Frequently, if you stare long enough at an ambitious poem by Stevens, a drowned figure will rise up and break the surface, as the swimmer does in Whitman's "The Sleepers." In "The Rock," "The Auroras of Autumn," "The Owl in the Sarcophagus," and a score of other Stevensian visions the shape of the other appears as the shaggy Walt, Stevens's dusky demon and brother.

I am not suggesting that the Good Gray Poet of Brooklyn, Manhattan, and Camden, New Jersey, was the Pennsylvanian aesthete's real Me, but rather that what was strongest in Stevens's poetry found the genius of the shore in the bard of Night, Death, the Mother, and the Sea, the fourfold unison that peals forth in Stevens as urgently and frequently as it does in

Whitman and in Hart Crane. Who after all gave us the most eloquent sum-
ming-up of the national poet in all of our literature?

> In the far South the sun of autumn is passing
> Like Walt Whitman walking along a ruddy shore.
> He is singing and chanting the things that are part of him,
> The worlds that were and will be, death and day.
> Nothing is final, he chants. No man shall see the end.
> His beard is of fire and his staff is a leaping flame.

Whitman is both American Moses and American Aaron, and like them is
an anti-apocalyptic prophet, chanting the harvest of our Evening Land. Inspired by his own vision of Whitman, Stevens momentarily mimics the
voice of Walt himself, singing the song of the self:

> Sigh for me, night-wind, in the noisy leaves of the oak.
> I am tired. Sleep for me, heaven over the hill.
> Shout for me, loudly and loudly, joyful sun, when you rise.

Emerson, greeting the 1855 edition of *Leaves of Grass,* praised Whitman
above all for *power.* Stevens, an all but endless ironist, affirms by tapping
into Whitman's power, frequently without knowing that he does so. In the
great epiphany of *Notes toward a Supreme Fiction,* "It Must Give Pleasure,"
canto 8, that begins, "What am I to believe?", Stevens fuses Whitman with
Wordsworth to extraordinary effect, without I think, being overtly aware of
this allusive interplay: Wordsworth in *The Prelude,* 14, lines 91–120, says of
the great poets that they occupy themselves

> With the whole compass of the universe:
> They from their native selves can send abroad
> Kindred mutations; for themselves create
> A like existence; and, whene'er it dawns
> Created for them, catch it, or are caught
> By its inevitable mastery,
> Like angels stopped upon the wing by sound . . .

"Angel," Stevens writes, "Be silent . . . and hear / The luminous melody
of proper sound." And yet the Wordsworth allusion is a kind of screen memory, veiling Whitman's more kindred mutations in *By Blue Ontario's Shore,*
part 18:

> I will confront these shores of the day and night,
> I will know if I am to be less than they,
> I will see if I am not as majestic as they . . .

"Am I that imagine this angel less satisfied?" is Stevens's rhetorical question, and he goes on to find "a time / In which majesty is a mirror of the self." Without Whitman, Stevens would not have known how to celebrate the self, which (putting his exegetes aside) is a crucial concern of his poetry. His negations (again, like Whitman's) are never final. From Whitman, and from Emerson and Dickinson, Stevens inherited the American program of unnaming. We are to throw away the lights and definitions, and see in the dark this and that: "But do not use the rotted names." The Real me, the Me myself, comprises Night, Death, the Mother, and the Sea; these names do not decay.

It is instructive to note the uneasy parodies and mockeries of Whitman that throng Stevens's poetry. In particular, he could not get "Out of the Cradle Endlessly Rocking" to cease troubling him. We hear in Stevens "An interior ocean's rocking / Of long, capricious fingers and chorals," and of a poet "To whom oracular rockings gave no rest," and we are told, "the night is not the cradle that they cry." And yet the "endlessly rocking" cradle rocks on as Stevens experiences his ordinary evening in New Haven (where there are no other kinds of evening) as an "endlessly elaborating poem."

As much as T. S. Eliot and Henry James, Stevens is haunted by "When Lilacs Last in the Dooryard Bloom'd," though here too he attempts vainly to free himself by mockery. Crispin, the failed poet of *The Comedian as the Letter C,* is "sharply stopped / In the door-yard by his own capacious bloom." By the time that Stevens emerges into his own genius in *Notes toward a Supreme Fiction,* "Lilacs" assumes a positive role, which augments as the poet meditates upon death in "The Owl in the Sarcophagus," "The Auroras of Autumn," and "The Rock." How does an American poet confront "death's own supremest images" without turning to Whitman as vast resource? The mother, "My memory, the mother of us all, / The earthly mother and the mother of / The dead," is joined by "the simplest word," death, and by the lilacs as a saving emblem: "That the lilacs came and bloomed, like a blindness cleaned."

Stevens was a preternaturally strong poet, gifted with a language florabundant enough to recall the Shakespeare of *Love's Labour's Lost.* In the primary, or familial sense, of genius, his poetic vocation is indubitable, and he required as muse only a rather Miltonic "interior paramour." Why then did he require Walt Whitman as a barely repressed daemon, as a genius in the alter ego sense? "I was the world in which I walked" is a Whitmanian formulation, but the line is Stevens's.

When I was young, critics saw Stevens as a kind of poetic dandy, addicted to finicky language. This yielded, during my middle years, to Snow Man Stevens, endlessly negative, and perceiver of "the nothing that is." Now, in old age, I am offered a newly historicized Stevens, socially overdetermined. But none of these is, was, or will be the poetry of Wallace Stevens, who followed, evasively and with massive resistance, the genius of the poems of our climate, which is Emersonian-Whitmanian. Though he scarcely could draw breath without qualifying, Stevens nevertheless edged towards becoming that "more severe, / More harassing master" of "an Ordinary Evening in New Haven." In a lecture at Yale, delivered soon afterwards, he quoted a marvelous little poem, "A Clear Midnight," as an indication of Walt Whitman's power in relation to his subject, his sense of the world:

This is thy hour O Soul, thy free flight into the wordless,
Away from books, away from art, the day erased, the lesson done,
Thee fully forth emerging, silent, gazing, pondering the themes
          thou lovest best,
Night, sleep, death and the stars.

That is neither finicky, nor snowmanish, nor socially energized: it is pure Walt Whitman, and possessed by Stevens's memory. It is merely true to observe that the themes best loved also by Stevens's soul are "Night, sleep, death and the stars." I have loved Stevens's poetry all my life because, in it, "the circles quicken and crystal colors come / And flare." In an underrated poem, "Parochial Theme," Stevens brought together both his turn to Whitmanian affirmation and his (quite Whitmanian) realization of limits:

This health is holy, this descant of a self,
This barbarous chanting of what is strong, this blare.

But salvation here? What about the rattle of sticks
On tins and boxes? What about horses eaten by wind?

The first two lines perhaps defend *Song of Myself* against George Santayana, who had called it "the poetry of barbarism." Salvation, in Whitman as in Stevens, is never the issue: these are not Christian poets, they are Lucretians. Nothing is final, no man shall see the end. Emerson had led Whitman to the shores of America, to found a distinctively American poetry. Wallace Stevens too had realized "The vital, the never-failing genius, / Fulfilling his meditations, great and small."

T. S. ELIOT

> I am moved by fancies that are curled
> Around these images, and cling:
> The notion of some infinitely gentle
> Infinitely suffering thing.

The Eliot of the early "Preludes" is the legitimate inheritor of Tennyson, and of Whitman. After the international success of *The Waste Land* (1922), Eliot slowly began to modify into the Anglo-Catholic royalist and classical conservative of *Ash Wednesday* (1930) and the seer of *The Sacred Wood* and subsequent volumes of critical exclusion. I remember, as a very young man, my fury at Eliot's account of William Blake:

> Blake was endowed with a capacity for considerable understanding of human nature, with a remarkable and original sense of language and the music of language, and a gift of hallucinated vision. Had these been controlled by a respect for impersonal reason, for common sense, for the objectivity of science, it would have been better for him. What his genius required, and what it sadly lacked, was a framework of accepted and traditional ideas which would have prevented him from indulging in a philosophy of his own, and concentrated his attention upon the problems of the poet. Confusion of thought, emotion, and vision is what we find in such a work as *Also Sprach Zarathustra;* it is eminently not a Latin virtue. The concentration resulting from a framework of mythology and theology and philosophy is one of the reasons why Dante is a classic, and Blake only a poet of genius. The fault is perhaps not with Blake himself, but with the environment which failed to provide what such a poet needed; perhaps the circumstances compelled him to fabricate, perhaps the poet required the philosopher and mythologist; although the conscious Blake may have been quite unconscious of the motives.

After a half-century, this seems mere snobbery. Dante is certainly a classic, but not because of "a framework of accepted and traditional ideas"; he was, like Blake, a poet of genius. Eliot's literary and cultural criticism seems to me a blight, but Eliot too was a poet of singular genius, though scarcely comparable in eminence to Dante and to Blake.

A comparison to his American contemporaries, Frost and Stevens just before him, and Hart Crane just after, seems fairer. He cannot wound me, as Frost does, or comfort me, with the Stevens of *The Auroras of Autumn*, nor carry me to the Sublime, as Hart Crane can. And yet Eliot's cadences haunt me:

> You had such a vision of the street
> as the street hardly understands.

Like the Jacobean dramatists he admired so much—Cyril Tourneur and John Webster—Eliot catches the precise nuances of personal betrayal, of bad faith, of our weariness of our own hypocrisies:

> I should find
> Some way incomparably light and deft,
> Some way we both should understand,
> Simple and faithless as a smile and shake of the hand.

THOMAS STEARNS ELIOT
(1888–1965)

ELIOT INDUBITABLY IS ONE OF THE MAJOR American poets, despite some
caveats I will enter here. Emily Dickinson, Walt Whitman, Hart Crane, and
Wallace Stevens mean more to me, but, at their best, Eliot and Robert Frost
achieve that eminence. One ought in any case, as a critic, to be able to say:
I don't love him or her, or this, but genius transcends my literary affections.

I set aside Eliot's verse plays, which are scarcely stageable or readable, and
his criticism, despite its historical importance. As for what now would be called
his cultural criticism, I grimace and pass by. There remains his anti-Semitism,
which is very winning, if you happen to be an anti-Semite; if not, not.

His early poetry is mostly very good, up through 1925 or so. There remained forty years, of which the monument is *Four Quartets*. Remarkable
passages abide in it, and a certain quantity of stuffing. Essentially, Eliot had
a poetic decade, 1915–25, in the tradition of Wordsworth and Whitman,
each of whom had a great decade and then subsided.

There is also the question of Eliot's influence, which was international.
Critically, this has dwindled, but once was enormous. The influence of the
poetry, as late as the mid-century, was equally fierce, but is now spent.

I hope to make a fresh start with Eliot here, in an attempt to isolate his
considerable genius as a poet. Notoriously, he asserted that his precursors
were Dante and Baudelaire, or even minor French poets, rather than anyone
before him who had written in English. But that is the usual poetic spiel:
the central forerunners of *The Waste Land* are Whitman's "When Lilacs Last
in the Dooryard Bloom'd" and Tennyson's *Maud: A Monodrama*. Eliot also
liked to cite lesser Jacobean dramatists, John Webster and Cyril Tourneur,
but his actual poetry is haunted by *Hamlet*, which he hilariously dubbed an
"aesthetic failure." So it goes: trust the poem and not the poet.

One way of reading Eliot, not so prevalent as before but still popular, is to
see all of his work as self-conversionary. Everything up to *Ash Wednesday* then
becomes a seeking for grace, which eventually rains down in *Four Quartets*. As
Eliot said of Tennyson, the quality of his doubt is high, that of his faith less
persuasive. As a master of devotional poetry, Eliot cannot sustain comparison
with George Herbert or even with Christina Rossetti. His strength was elsewhere: in secular irony, self-satire, hallucinatory intensity, the dying fall of later

Romantic lyricism, and in the dramatic monologue, where his considerable debt to Robert Browning has been mostly ignored. His Modernism was still an episode in Romanticism: this was not an Eliotic flaw, but a power he developed against the grain. He learned to acknowledge Shelley as the best adapter of Dante into English poetry. Some of his earlier judgments, never revised, have their own value if you turn them upside down. The essays of Emerson, he said, were already an encumbrance, and William Blake should have been saved (by culture!) "from indulging in a philosophy of his own."

On Walt Whitman, Eliot was, at best, evasive. He exalted the minor French poet Jules Laforgue over Whitman, a judgment that might have surprised Laforgue, who translated and revered Whitman. In 1928, after saying he derived from Laforgue's free verse (without appearing to know that Laforgue's came out of Whitman's), Eliot insisted that "I did not read Whitman until later in life, and had to conquer an aversion to his form, as well as to much of his matter, in order to do so."

This is merely untrue, but wonderfully ambivalent. Two years before, Eliot unfavorably juxtaposed Whitman to Baudelaire, remarking that the American poet blurred the demarcations between self and the world, while the French poet kept the boundaries clear. So, Baudelaire gazed bravely into the abyss, while Whitman saw nothing accurately. Eliot's *Ara Vos Prec* (1920) contained a bad little "Ode," the only poem Eliot ever placed in a volume of his poetry that he finally failed to collect. It appears to be an account of a failed wedding night (presumably his own) and harbors two palpable Whitmanian allusions: "Misunderstood / The accents of the now retired / Profession of the Calamus," and "Io Hymen, Hymenae." Whitman's "Calamus" poems are among his most overtly homoerotic (the calamus is the aromatic perennial herb, sweet flag, and is a Whitmanian phallic emblem), while his brief "O Hymen! O Hymenee!" is a poignant lament to the gods of marriage: "O Hymen! O hymenee! Why do you tantalize me thus?" Eliot thereby associates his sexual failure in his first marriage with a Whitmanian homoeroticism.

I dwell on Whitman and Eliot, who superficially are so different, because in their depths they shared the same genius, the daemon, of the American Sublime. This common genius did not prevent them from going in very different spiritual directions, Whitman into his own version of the American Religion, and Eliot, in 1927, converting to Anglo-Catholicism, and yet Whitman, in Eliot's own true sense of "influence," remained always Eliot's hidden poetic father. He would not, in any sense, overtly admit this until quite late (1953), though as early as 1930 he observed of Whitman, "beneath all the declamations there is another tone, and behind all the illusions there is another vision." Cleo McNelly Kearns, summing up the startling similarities between "When Lilacs Last in the Dooryard Bloom'd" and Eliot's major poem, charts the flow from Whitman's poetry into Eliot's:

> Whitman's poem gives us not only the motifs and images of *The Waste Land*, from the lilacs and flowers through the "unreal city" to the disturbing thought of the body of dead soldiers, the presence of a double self, a dear brother or *semblable*, the "murmur of maternal lamentation," the peering faces, and the song of the hermit thrush over the dry bones.

Eliot's "third who always walks beside you," the risen Christ according to *The Waste Land*'s notes, is either Whitman's "thought of death" or "knowledge of death," or both fused together. *The Waste Land*, like "Lilacs," begins to seem more an elegy for the poet's own genius, rather than a lament for Western civilization. Eliot gives us another American grand song of death, or of the death-in-life that is poetic crisis.

Ash Wednesday and *Four Quartets* doubtless attempt to represent Christian redemption, but not *The Waste Land*, which reflects Eliot's personal breakdown in 1921, a reaction to the strain of his first marriage. The controlled hallucinations of the poem seem to me its authentic magnificence:

> A woman drew her long black hair out tight
> And fiddled whisper music on those strings
> And bats with baby faces in the violet light
> Whistled, and beat their wings
> And crawled head downward down a blackened wall
> And upside down in air were towers
> Telling reminiscent bells, that kept the hours
> And voices singing out of empty cisterns and exhausted wells.

It is as though Eliot had assimilated Bram Stoker's *Dracula* to Tennyson's "Mariana" or *Maud*, with a touch of Oscar Wilde's *Salomé* thrown in. Only a genius of exacerbated sensibility could have given us this unnerving splendor.

Fifty years ago, Eliot was the vicar of neo-Christianity, and *The Waste Land* sang a hymn of salvation to his academic disciples. In those days, Eliot was proclaimed as a moral authority, a veritable sage. I cannot prophesy what Eliot's repute will be a half-century from now, but his daemonic eloquence will not have faded away.

LUSTRE 10

|

William Wordsworth; Percy Bysshe Shelley; John Keats; Giacomo Leopardi; Alfred, Lord Tennyson

|

The High Romantic poets are my second Lustre of *Din*, because their crisis-lyrics of extreme consciousness inhabit the limits of love, the "subtler demarcations, keener sounds" that their descendant Wallace Stevens sought. Wordsworth's rigorous originality cancelled much of prior tradition, and allowed him to begin anew on "a *tabula rasa* of poetry," as the Romantic critic William Hazlitt phrased it.

Shelley, one of my personal favorites since childhood (and the subject of my first book, more than forty years ago), quested in the spirit of *Din* or "severe judgment" to discover the limits of desire. Keats, Shakespearean in his tragic naturalism, has a luxuriant severity that enhances the aesthetic dignity of the Great Odes and the *Hyperion* fragments.

The melancholias of Leopardi and of Tennyson are very different, Leopardi's reflecting his deformity, while Tennyson's ensued from his early loss of Arthur Henry Hallam, his dearest friend and intellectual guide. But there is a Keatsian shadow on Tennyson that augments his sumptuous malaise, and helps produce a ravishing music of poetry.

WILLIAM WORDSWORTH

Paradise, and groves
Elysian, Fortunate Fields—like those of old
Sought in the Atlantic Main—why should they be
A history only of departed things,
Or a mere fiction of what never was?
For the discerning intellect of Man,
When wedded to this goodly universe
In love and holy passion, shall find these
A simple produce of the common day.

That is Wordsworth in 1798, a young man set on revolution, in the marvelous fragment "Home at Grasmere," a manifesto of naturalistic humanism
that deeply affected Keats and Shelley. The earthly paradise can be "a

simple produce of the common day," according to the poet-prophet for whom "simple" and "common" were words of highest praise and honor.

Wordsworth remains, in the twenty-first century, what he has been these last two hundred years: the inventor of a poetry that has been called, at intervals, Romantic, post-Romantic, Modern, and Postmodern, yet essentially is one phenomenon: the replacement of subject-matter by the poet's subjectivity. Goethe was the final poet in a vast sequence that began with Homer; Wordsworth was something different.

After Wordsworth, poets are Wordsworthian whether they know it—as Shelley, Keats, Tennyson, Frost did—or not. Lewis Carroll, parodying Wordsworth's "Resolution and Independence" in his "White Knight's Ballad," and Edward Lear, doing the same in his "Incidents in the Life of My Uncle Arly," make wonderful fun of Wordsworth's egocentricity:

> So, having no reply to give
>   To what the old man said,
> I cried, "Come tell me how you live!"
>   And thumped him on the head.
>   —Lewis Carroll

> O my agèd Uncle Arly!
> Sitting on a heap of Barley
>   Through the silent hours of night,—
> Close beside a leafy thicket:—
> On his nose there was a Cricket,—
> In his hat a Railway-Ticket;—
>   (But his shoes were far too tight.)
>   —Edward Lear

Wordsworth, whether as thumper or as cricket, haunts even his parodists. His genius allowed him

> A mind sustained
> By recognitions of transcendent power.

WILLIAM WORDSWORTH
(1770–1850)

EVERYTHING THAT MATTERS BY Wordsworth was written in one decade, 1797–1807. The last forty-three years of his poetry were lamentable. This is sadly akin to Walt Whitman, all of whose best work was done in the decade 1855–65, to be followed by twenty-seven years of mostly bad verse, until his death in 1892. Wordsworth's genius burned to the socket when he was thirty-seven. Whitman could not get started until he was thirty-six, and his genius had departed at forty-six. I mention these unhappy curtailments because understanding the premature waning of genius may aid in defining the individual nature of genius. Shelley, in *Adonais,* says of Keats:

> From the contagion of the world's slow stain
> He is secure, and now can never mourn
> A heart grown cold, a head grown gray in vain;
> Nor, when the spirit's self has ceased to burn,
> With sparkless ashes load an unlamented urn.

The reference is certainly to Wordsworth, whose agèd narrator of the tale of Margaret, in *The Ruined Cottage* (1797–99), had given the young Shelley an epigraph for his *Alastor* (1815):

> . . . the good die first,
> And those whose hearts are dry as summer dust
> Burn to the socket.

We do not know why Shakespeare abandoned playwriting in the almost three years of life that remained to him after his collaboration with John Fletcher in *The Two Noble Kinsmen* (1613). The foremost of all writers gave up at forty-nine, unlike Dante, Chaucer, Cervantes, Montaigne, Goethe, Tolstoy, Joyce, and Proust, all of whom composed until the end. Whatever Shakespeare's motives may have been, they did not reflect departing powers, judged by his share in *The Two Noble Kinsmen.* How good it would have been had Wordsworth, at thirty-seven, and Whitman, at forty-six, chosen to rest on their oars forever. Elsewhere in this book, I surmise that Whitman's heroic service in the Washington, D.C., war hospitals burned away his genius. But, with Wordsworth, the end was implicit always in the origins of his genius: a visionary radiance fiercely resplendent in his childhood, but then fading into the light of common day. If you invest everything in the "romance of nature," as Geoffrey Hartman called Wordsworth's myth of childhood memory, then you will lose everything when nature eventually betrays the child who loved her.

Wordsworth's genius, A. C. Bradley observed, was in his strangeness, his startling originality. In his great decade, this strangeness is everywhere:

> And I have felt
> A presence that disturbs me with the joy
> Of elevated thoughts; a sense sublime
> Of something far more deeply interfused,
> Whose dwelling is the light of setting suns,
> And the round ocean and the living air,
> And the blue sky, and in the mind of man:
> A motion and a spirit, that impels
> All thinking things, all objects of all thought,
> And rolls through all things.
> —"Tintern Abbey"

> VIII
> Now, whether it were by peculiar grace,
> A leading from above, a something given,
> Yet it befell that, in this lonely place,
> When I with these untoward thoughts had striven,
> Beside a pool bare to the eye of heaven
> I saw a Man before me unawares:
> The oldest man he seemed that ever wore grey hairs.

> IX
> As a huge stone is sometimes seen to lie
> Couched on the bald top of an eminence;
> Wonder to all who do the same espy,
> By what means it could thither come, and whence;
> So that it seems a thing endued with sense:
> Like a sea-beast crawled forth, that on a shelf
> Of rock or sand reposeth, there to sun itself;

X

Such seemed this Man, not all alive nor dead,
Nor all asleep—in his extreme old age:
His body was bent double, feet and head
Coming together in life's pilgrimage;
As if some dire constraint of pain, or rage
Of sickness felt by him in times long past,
A more than human weight upon his frame had cast.

XI

Himself he propped, limbs, body, and pale face,
Upon a long grey staff of shaven wood:
And, still as I drew near with gentle pace,
Upon the margin of that moorish flood
Motionless as a cloud the old Man stood,
That heareth not the loud winds when they call;
And moveth all together, if it move at all.

     —"Resolution and Independence"

IX

  Oh joy! That in our embers
  Is something that doth live,
  That nature yet remembers
  What was so fugitive!
The thought of our past years in me doth breed
Perpetual benediction: not indeed
For that which is most worthy to be blest;
Delight and liberty, the simple creed
Of Childhood, whether busy or at rest,
With new-fledged hope still fluttering in his breast:—
  Not for these I raise
  The song of thanks and praise;
  But for those obstinate questionings
  Of sense and outward things,
  Fallings from us, vanishings;
  Blank misgivings of a Creature
Moving about in worlds not realized,
High instincts before which our mortal Nature
Did tremble like a guilty Thing surprised:
  But for those first affections,

> Those shadowy recollections,
>   Which, be they what they may,
> Are yet the fountain light of all our day,
> Are yet the master light of all our seeing;
>   Uphold us, cherish, and have power to make
> Our noisy years seem moments in the being
> Of the eternal Silence: truths that wake,
>   To perish never;
> Which neither listlessness, nor mad endeavour,
>   Nor Man nor Boy,
> Nor all that is at enmity with joy,
> Can utterly abolish or destroy!
>   Hence in a season of calm weather
>   Though inland far we be,
> Our Souls have sight of that immortal sea
>   Which brought us hither,
>   Can in a moment travel thither,
> And see the Children sport upon the shore,
> And hear the mighty waters rolling evermore.
>   —"Ode: Intimations of Immortality from
>   Recollections of Early Childhood"

You can possess all these by memory, for more than half a century, and have discussed them in print and with students scores of times, but they never lose the shock of newness. Familiarity does not remove their legitimate difficulties: of what precisely does Wordsworth speak, and why? A near-library has been written, and yet the question have not been fully answered. Though his friend Coleridge tried to give Wordsworth a metaphysics, these passages are part of the long war of poetry against philosophy. They speak, Wordsworth insisted, of nothing more than what we are, but then "what we are" had never been seen or felt in such ways before.

I intend to work through these passages from "Tintern Abbey," "Resolution and Independence," and the "Intimations" Ode, not by a "close reading," but by putting to them the question of genius. Wordsworth's greatness is a paradox, one that defies translation into other languages. And yet he is not a baroque Romantic, like Victor Hugo or the Shelley of *Prometheus Unbound*. His most rugged paradox is the mingling of simplicity with the self-consciousness of having a saving prophecy to deliver to everyone. William

Hazlitt, with a certain ambivalence, remarked of Wordsworth, "he may be said to take a personal interest in the universe."

In the passage above from "Tintern Abbey," Wordsworth does not name that "something far more deeply interfused," except to call it "a motion and a spirit." Is it the presence of a wind, albeit metaphoric? Wordsworth is not a biblical prophet, nor is he John Milton, though he is as much Milton's successor as William Blake was. His inspiration is primordial: the breeze rises up from within him. It is the peculiarity of his genius that the presence, motion, and spirit paradoxically are and are not his own. When he encounters the leech-gatherer in "Resolution and Independence" he seems to doubt the initial reality of what he sees, and he does not listen to the old man's reply to the poet's question: "What occupation do you pursue?" Instead, he has a vision:

> XVI
> The old Man still stood talking by my side;
> But now his voice to me was like a stream
> Scarce heard; nor word from word could I divide;
> And the whole body of the Man did seem
> Like one whom I had met with in a dream;
> Or like a man from some far region sent,
> To give me human strength, by apt admonishment.

When the question is resumed—"How is it that you live, and what is it you do?"—the old man smiles patiently, realizing (as we do) that Wordsworth is incapable of listening. This provoked two wonderful parodies of "Resolution and Independence," Lewis Carroll's "White Knight's Ballad" and Edward Lear's "Incidents in the Life of My Uncle Arly." Superb target that Wordsworth's solipsism makes, his inability to focus upon the old man leads to a further sublime vision:

> XIX
> While he was talking thus, the lonely place,
> The old Man's shape, and speech—all troubled me:
> In my mind's eye I seemed to see him pace
> About the weary moors continually,
> Wandering about alone and silently.
> While I these thoughts within myself pursued,
> He, having made a pause, the same discourse renewed.

Wordsworth, like Milton, had every literary gift except humor; comedy in both great poets invariably is involuntary. One does not visualize either poet enjoying the outrageousness of Sir John Falstaff. But allow Wordsworth his own context—a lonely moor, with a pool bare to the eye of heaven—and his genius usurps total control, and invents the modern crisis-poem, the most characteristic new genre in poetry of the last two centuries. Crisis-lyrics have become so profuse that we don't recognize them anymore: they are what we call "poems." In them, the poet speaks to save herself or himself from depression, despair, suicidal negation, in order to get the next poem written. Poetry, as William Empson wrote, has become "a mug's game," played out just before the abyss. "Resolution and Independence," more even than anything else by Wordsworth, created the new genre. Poetry ceased to have any subject except subjectivity itself, carried to extremes of self-consciousness. In this crucial sense, Emily Dickinson, W. B. Yeats, T. S. Eliot, Wallace Stevens, Hart Crane, and so many since have been Wordsworthian poets.

With the "Intimations" Ode, composed between 1802 and 1804, but not published until 1807, we have the paradox of confronting Wordsworth's genius at its strongest, and yet witnessing also the growth of the shadow that will destroy it. I have quoted the ninth of its strophes, composed at least two years after the first four sections. The Ode's burden is the fading away of an earlier, visionary light, which wanes with the maturation into an awareness of one's own mortality. It might indeed be more accurate to call this the "Mortality" Ode, rather than the "Immortality" Ode, as many name it. The flight of the visionary gleam threatens Wordsworth with the sin of those in Dante's *Inferno* who are punished for having been "sullen in the sweet air," and leads to the poem's nadir at the close of the eighth section: "Heavy as frost, and deep almost as life."

The extraordinary breakthrough of the ninth strophe may be the most characteristic expression of Wordsworth's paradoxical genius. By pure intuition, the poet empathizes with, and praises, the infant's resistance to that sense of separateness that eventually must lead to the consciousness of mortality:

> Not for these I raise
>   The song of thanks and praise;
> But for those obstinate questionings
> Of sense and outward things,
> Fallings from us, vanishings;
> Blank misgivings of a Creature

> Moving about in worlds not realized,
> High instincts before which our mortal Nature
> Did tremble like a guilty Thing surprised:

The infant obstinately questions hearing and seeing becoming two senses rather than one, and resists also a world external to himself. Observation could have taught Wordsworth that, but to assert that the infant's "first affections" cannot be disengaged from its "shadowy recollections" of a realm where everything seemed internal is the poet's own insight, or myth. When the "Intimations" Ode is resolved by mingled imaginative gain and experiential loss, we contemplate again Wordsworth's originality. Before Proust, and through John Ruskin an influence on Proust, Wordsworth's genius had created a new myth of involuntary memory.

PERCY BYSSHE SHELLEY

Thy wisdom speaks in me, and bids me dare
Beacon the rocks on which high hearts are wrecked.
I never was attached to that great sect,
Whose doctrine is, that each one should select
Out of the crowd a mistress or a friend,
And all the rest, though fair and wise, commend
To cold oblivion, though it is in the code
Of modern morals, and the beaten road
Which those poor slaves with weary footsteps tread,
Who travel to their home among the dead
By the broad highway of the world, and so
With one chained friend, perhaps a jealous foe,
The dreariest and the longest journey go.

Shelley's lyrical sermon on free love, in his *Epipsychidion,* is also the darkest brief description of marriage that I have read. It gave E. M. Forster the
title for his novel *The Longest Journey,* and it remains the passage I recommend to the hardiest of my students for reading aloud on the evening before their own wedding days.

Shelley's genius was lyrical, to an unsurpassed extent. He converts
nearly every poetic genre—satire, romance narrative, drama, epistle, elegy,
Dantesque inferno—into lyric.

Poetry, Shelley wrote, recorded our happiest and best moments, but he
must have intended that to be figurative, since his lyricism is profoundly
expressive of despair. Shelley's great subjects are the death of love and the
destruction of integrity, both of which he saw as imaginative death, to
which literal death was far preferable.

An epitome of Shelley's lyrical genius is "When the Lamp Is Shattered,"
where the second line—"The light in the dust lies dead"—can be translated as: "Love dies, lust remains." The final stanza eloquently knells the
death of love:

> Its passions will rock thee
> As the storms rock the ravens on high;
> Bright reason will mock thee,
> Like the sun from a wintry sky.
> From thy nest every rafter
> Will rot, and thine eagle home
> Leave thee naked to laughter,
> When leaves fall and cold winds come.

PERCY BYSSHE SHELLEY
(1792–1822)

SHELLEY DROWNED, PERHAPS BY accident, before he turned thirty, which now seems inevitable and appropriate. A skeptical intellect of great power, he was also one of the supreme lyric poets of Western tradition, with both admirers and detractors in every generation. As a revolutionary spirit, he has only a few peers.

I cannot, in 2001, write about Shelley as I did in my springtime of the mid-1950s, but the differences in my perspective will come from my own aging. I have taken Shelley's lyric genius as a given, since I was a boy. It is time to see precisely what it is.

Major lyric poets are rare: English and German literature are most abundant in them. The American tradition really has only a few of true quality; we have also a ghastly procession of bad lyric poets, whose ancestor and dismal exemplar is Edgar Allan Poe, who made an amalgam of Coleridge, Byron, and Shelley, with lamentable consequences. Poe also has his continued admirers, even in countries where critics can read English, but particularly in France, where they can't, as was demonstrated by the distinguished triad of Baudelaire, Mallarmé, and Valéry, all of whom found in Poe the poems that were not there. Never has a poet, and storyteller, benefited so greatly by translation.

Shelley was Wordsworth's younger contemporary, which became both burden and provocation for the Promethean aristocrat and (very wealthy) rebel. Wordsworth had altered permanently the nature of lyric poetry in England: unlike Byron, and even Shelley, Wordsworth has had no influence in non-English-speaking countries, including Germany and Austria, but Wordsworth is not for export. Though he had some effect on William Cullen Bryant, Emerson, and Emily Dickinson, Wordsworth meant little to Whitman or to later American poets like T. S. Eliot and Hart Crane. Wallace Stevens, another solitary brooder, has Wordsworthian affinities, but essentially Wordsworth has become the poet of scholars, as Milton has. For Shelley and Keats, as young poets, that would have seemed impossible, Wordsworth for them being revelation, perhaps a negative one, as Eliot was for Hart Crane.

Elizabeth Bishop (1911–1979), a major American poet, has a remarkable early poem, "The Unbeliever," that contrasts three figures: cloud, seagull, unbeliever, whom I interpret as three kinds of poets. The cloud, a solitary brooder, is Wordsworth or Wallace Stevens, while the seagull, builder of a visionary tower, is Shelley or Hart Crane, and the unbeliever, a nightmare-obsessed sleeper, is Emily Dickinson or Elizabeth Bishop, though disguised as "he." Shelley's lyric genius, like Hart Crane's, finds one of its prime images of freedom, reversible as imaginative ruin, in the tower. The most influential of Shelleyan towers, echoed throughout the poetry of William Butler Yeats, is in the early fragment *Prince Athanase:*

> His soul had wedded Wisdom, and her dower
> Is love, and justice, clothed in which he sate
> Apart from men, as in a lonely tower,
>
> Pitying the tumult of their dark estate.—

Shelley's close friend the novelist Thomas Love Peacock gently satirized him in *Nightmare Abbey,* where the poet Scythrop dwells apart in his not-so-lonely tower, while scattering unheard prophecies among the multitudes. Shelley, himself an urbane ironist, took the satire well, and answered Peacock's mordant tract *The Four Ages of Poetry* with his own vibrant *A Defence of Poetry.*

Peacock's four ages are: iron, gold, silver, and brass. In English poetry, one might speak of *Beowulf,* Shakespeare, Pope, and Wordsworth, following Peacock's lead. Wordsworth, king of brass, is dismissed as a "morbid dreamer," and the essay ends asking us to "smile at the little ambition and the circumscribed perceptions with which the drivellers and mountebanks . . . are contending for the poetical palm and the critical chair."

Shelley's reply is more a prose rhapsody than an essay, and is still the best statement about poetry in the language: "It is at once the centre and circumference of knowledge." I intend to define Shelley's genius upon just that principle of center and circumference, which Emily Dickinson inherited from Shelley, and I take as my proof-text the famous *Adonais: An Elegy on the Death of John Keats.* Since this is a rather elaborate lyric lament in fifty-five nine-line Spenserian stanzas, I am compelled to abstract and condense, which is regrettable since it is part of the achievement of *Adonais* that Shelley beautifully sustains his lyric drive throughout the four hundred and ninety-five lines.

Keats had died of tuberculosis in Rome, on February 23, 1821, aged twenty-five years and four months. Shelley died at sea, off Leghorn, on July

8, 1822, a month short of thirty. *Adonais* was composed in the early days of June 1821, and is as much a prophetic self-elegy as it is a formal hymn celebrating Keats. Though the two poets had met and corresponded, they remained only acquaintances, and so the basis of Shelley's poem is not a personal grief. Nor does the subtly ironic Shelley literally believe that the fiery particle of Keats's mind was snuffed out by a resentful article or two in wintry Scotland. Keats was a pugnacious personality, and while I am nothing of the sort, even I am energized by the endless idiocy of my bad reviewers. "I hate to be praised in a newspaper," remarked the sagacious Emerson, and nothing is more soul-destroying than any praise from the *New York Times Book Review*.

Shelley, thirteen months from his own early death, prophesies his approaching conclusion, and more than comes to terms with it. As precedent, he knowingly has John Milton's "Lycidas," possibly the strongest poem of middle length in the language, which ostensibly elegizes Edward King, a very minor poet, and a friend of Milton's at Christ's College, Cambridge. King drowned in August 1637, and in 1638 his Cambridge contemporaries brought out a volume of elegiac verse, concluding with "Lycidas." Milton, the most ambitious of all poets (together with Dante), was twenty-nine when he composed "Lycidas," which is the age Shelley nears as he writes *Adonais*. What drives "Lycidas" along is not the heroic Milton's fear of death, but his horror of accidental demise that would leave to the world only his minor poems, and not the great works he contemplated creating:

> Alas! What boots it with incessant care
> To tend the homely slighted shepherd's trade
> And strictly meditate the thankless muse
> Were it not better done as others use,
> To sport with Amaryllis in the shade,
> Or with the tangles of Neaera's hair?
> Fame is the spur that the clear spirit doth raise
> (That last infirmity of noble mind)
> To scorn delights, and live laborious days;
> But the fair guerdon when we hope to find,
> And think to burst out into sudden blaze,
> Comes the blind Fury with th'abhorred shears,
> And slits the thin-spun life.

Atropos is the blind sister of the other two Fates; by transforming her into a Fury, Milton heightens the dread of being cut off from canonical achievement. Shelley, in *Adonais*, gives us Milton's triumph:

> —He died,
> Who was the Sire of an immortal strain,
> Blind, old, and lonely, when his country's pride,
> The priest, the slave, and the liberticide,
> Trampled and mocked with many a loathed rite
> Of lust and blood; he went, unterrified,
> Into the gulf of death; but his clear Sprite
> Yet reigns o'er earth; the third among the sons of light.

Homer, Dante, Milton: the epic poets are the sons of light, of Phoebus Apollo, god of poetry and the sun. Keats, who wrote the epic fragment *Hyperion* in this tradition, is therefore elegized as Milton's heir. Shelley, part of whose genius is the mythmaking faculty, brings together the metaphors of Keats's poetry to join in the mourning:

> Thy spirit's sister, the lorn nightingale
> Mourns not her mate with such melodious pain

After Keats's figurations all pass, his fellow poets mourn him, but lament ceases in the final third of *Adonais*, stanzas 38 to 40. Shelley, a lifelong influence upon W. B. Yeats, anticipates the skeptical Hermeticism of Yeats's "Sailing to Byzantium" and "Byzantium," poems in which the aging poet seeks an occult salvation in "the holy fire" of a city of art. Keats's pure spirit flows "Back to the burning fountain whence it came." Having awakened from the dream of life, the spirit "has outsoared the shadow of our night," an image out of Dante: our earth casts its shadow upward into the heavens, but at the sphere of Venus this darkness touches its limit. With a sustained lyricism difficult to equal in Western poetry, Shelley's intense celebration bruises the limits of the Sublime in the four final stanzas:

> The One remains, the many change and pass;
> Heaven's light forever shines, Earth's shadows fly;
> Life, like a dome of many-colored glass,
> Stains the white radiance of Eternity,
> Until Death tramples it to fragments.—Die,
> If thou wouldst be with that which thou dost seek!

Follow where all is fled!—Rome's azure sky,
Flowers, ruins, statues, music, words, are weak
The glory they transfuse with fitting truth to speak.

Why linger, why turn back, why shrink, my Heart?
Thy hopes are gone before: from all things here
They have departed; thou shouldst now depart!
A light is passed from the revolving year,
And man, and woman; and what still is dear
Attracts to crush, repels to make thee wither.
The soft sky smiles,—the low wind whispers near:
'Tis Adonais calls! oh, hasten thither,
No more let Life divide what Death can join together.

That Light whose smile kindles the Universe,
That Beauty in which all things work and move,
That Benediction which the eclipsing Curse
Of birth can quench not, that sustaining Love
Which through the web of being blindly wove
By man and beast and earth and air and sea,
Burns bright or dim, as each are mirrors of
The fire for which all thirst; now beams on me,
Consuming the last clouds of cold mortality.

The breath whose might I have invoked in song
Descends on me; my spirit's bark is driven,
Far from the shore, far from the trembling throng
Whose sails were never to the tempest given;
The massy earth and sphered skies are riven!
I am borne darkly, fearfully, afar;
Whilst, burning through the inmost veil of Heaven,
The soul of Adonais, like a star,
Beacons from the abode where the Eternal are.

The language here suggests the Neoplatonic tradition, but idealism is tempered by what must be called Shelley's own visionary skepticism. Phenomenal existence, the dome of many-colored glass, remains as real as the white radiance of the Eternal One, and "stains" means both "coloring" and "defiling," in balanced measure. Since the fragments of the death-shattered dome of life are identical with the beauties of Rome—azure sky, flowers, ruins, statues, music, the words of poetry—the staining does seem more a valuable coloring than a pollution. And yet all these colors of the spirit are inadequate to express the immutable One that sets itself against the many.

Though Shelley's skepticism lingers with the many, a fierce impulse, animated by personal despair, drives him on to "the fire for which all thirst." Pastoral elegy has transmuted into Gnostic hymn, with the characteristic Gnostic equation of birth with the Fall: "the eclipsing Curse / of birth." In the previous stanza, Eros had become a process that "Attracts to crush," a judgment rendered even more harshly in Shelley's Dantesque death-poem, the fragmentary but persuasive *The Triumph of Life*. Poised upon the verge of a final voyage, Shelley invests all of his lyrical genius in the poem's final stanza.

Shelley's poetic voice is not a solitary outcry, particularly in the baroque richness of *Adonais*, where it is orchestrated into a multiplicity that absorbs and enlists the reader. For whom does Shelley address in the final stanza of *Adonais?* His poetic voice, as Shira Wolosky remarks, is oracular, prophetic, urgent, ferocious in its implications, as in his famous, revolutionary "Ode to the West Wind," which the last stanza of *Adonais* begins by evoking. The image of the inmost self, best and oldest part of one, free of the Creation, is in Gnosticism the *pneuma* or breath, frequently imaged as a spark. That is the breath whose might descends upon Shelley, driving him upon an occult voyage propelled by a tempest—though the cost of Shelley's prophetic confirmation is sounded in "I am borne darkly, fearfully, afar," the gesture here transfers dread to the trembling throng that stays on shore. A brilliant, antithetical allusion to the close of Milton's "Lycidas" helps distinguish Shelley's vision from his Protestant precursor's:

> Now Lycidas the shepherds weep no more
> Henceforth thou art the genius of the shore
> In thy large recompense, and shalt be good
> To all that wander in that perilous flood.

Keats becomes the genius, or protective spirit, of the innermost Heaven, Hermetic realm of poets' souls, and beacons from there, to safeguard final voyages to a transcendent reality. Trelawny, going with Byron to identify their friend's body on the beach, tells us that Keats may have been Shelley's final act of reading:

> The tall slight figure, the jacket, the volume of Sophocles in one pocket, and Keats's poems in the other, doubled back, as if the reader, in the act of reading, had hastily thrust it away.

JOHN KEATS

This living hand, now warm and capable
Of earnest grasping, would, if it were cold
And in the icy silence of the tomb,
So haunt thy days and chill thy dreaming nights
That thou wouldst wish thine own heart dry of blood
So in my veins red life might stream again,
And thou be conscience-calmed—see—here it is—
I hold it towards you.

This dramatic fragment may be the final passage of poetry written by Keats, perhaps in January 1820, a year before his death in Rome, at twenty-five. Expecting his early death by tuberculosis, knowing that his love for Fanny Brawne never would be consummated, Keats lived out a final year, stoically despairing. Like Mozart's death, Keats's end perpetually reminds us of the great works we have lost.

Keats was the genius of tragic acceptance, a stance he shared with Shakespeare, who finally influenced him more profoundly than either Milton or Wordsworth. What Keats called "Negative Capability"—an imaginative stance that could bear strong, competing strains of passion while maintaining disinterestedness—is best exemplified by *King Lear*, and in smaller yet marvelously lucid contexts in odes like "To Autumn" and sonnets like "Bright Star."

The secular, humane consciousness of two subsequent centuries has found no finer representative than John Keats, who teaches us to abide in mysteries while refusing to worship them. He remains the wary celebrant of "The Human Seasons," a sonnet that revives something of Shakespeare's own splendor:

> Four seasons fill the measure of the year;
>   Four seasons are there in the mind of man.
> He hath his lusty spring when fancy clear
>   Takes in all beauty with an easy span:
> He hath his summer, when luxuriously
>   He chews the honied cud of fair spring thoughts,
> Till, in his soul dissolv'd they come to be
>   Part of himself. He hath his autumn ports
> And havens of repose, when his tired wings
>   Are folded up, and he content to look
> On mists in idleness: to let fair things
>   Pass by unheeded as a threshold brook.
>   He hath his winter too of pale misfeature,
>   Or else would forget his mortal nature.

JOHN KEATS
(1795–1821)

KEATS, IN MANY RESPECTS, HAS BECOME the most universally admired English poet since Shakespeare. His memorable passages throng my consciousness with almost Shakespearean plangency and precision:

"On the Grasshopper and Cricket"

The poetry of earth is never dead:
  When all the birds are faint with the hot sun,
  And hide in cooling trees, a voice will run
From hedge to hedge about the new-mown mead;
That is the Grasshopper's—he takes the lead
  In summer luxury,—he has never done
  With his delights; for when tired out with fun
He rests at ease beneath some pleasant weed.
The poetry of earth is ceasing never:
  On a lone winter evening, when the frost
    Has wrought a silence, from the stove there shrills
The Cricket's song, in warmth increasing ever,
  And seems to one in drowsiness half lost,
    The Grasshopper's among some grassy hills.

"On the Sea"

It keeps eternal whispering around
  Desolate shores, and with its mighty swell
  Gluts twice ten thousand Caverns, till the spell
Of Hecate leaves them their old shadowy sound.
Often 'tis in such gentle temper found,
  That scarcely will the very smallest shell
  Be moved for days from where it sometime fell,
When last the winds of Heaven were unbound.
Oh ye! Who have your eyeballs vexed and tired,
  Feast them upon the wideness of the Sea;
  Oh ye! Whose ears are dinned with uproar rude,

Or fed too much with cloying melody—
   Sit ye near some old Cavern's Mouth and brood,
Until ye start, as if the sea-nymphs quired!

"Knowledge enormous makes a God of me.
Names, deeds, grey legends, dire events, rebellions,
Majesties, sovereign voices, agonies,
Creations and destroyings, all at once
Pour into the wide hollows of my brain,
And deify me, as if some blithe wine
Or bright elixir peerless I had drunk,
And so become immortal."—Thus the God,
While his enkindled eyes, with level glance
Beneath his white soft temples, stedfast kept
Trembling with light upon Mnemosyne.
Soon wild commotions shook him, and made flush
All the immortal fairness of his limbs;
Most like a struggle at the gate of death;
Or liker still to one who should take leave
Of pale immortal death, and with a pang
As hot as death's is chill, with fierce convulse
Die into life:

And there she lulled me asleep
   And there I dreamed—Ah! woe betide!
The latest dream I ever dreamed
   On the cold hill side.

I saw pale kings and princes too,
   Pale warriors, death-pale were they all;
They cried—"La Belle Dame sans Merci
   Hath thee in thrall!"

I saw their starved lips in the gloam,
   With horrid warning gaped wide,
And I awoke and found me here,
   On the cold hill's side.

And this is why I sojourn here
   Alone and palely loitering,

> Though the sedge has withered from the lake,
>   And no birds sing.

That is Keats from 1816 into 1819, his year of greatness, when he went on to compose the six Great Odes and *The Fall of Hyperion*. He is only twenty-one when he writes the sonnet "On the Grasshopper and Cricket," and already he manifests an astonishing ear, inner and outer. Like Wordsworth, he had been left alone with the visible and audible world quite early. An accident killed his father when Keats was eight, and his mother died of tuberculosis when he was fourteen. His growth stunted by disease, he was only five feet tall, though in no way disfigured. Like many other short people, he developed a somewhat pugnacious temperament, though not aggressive. Setting aside Shakespeare, concerning whom we know almost nothing that greatly matters, Keats may have been the sanest and most normative of all great poets, ever. Of his major contemporaries, Blake and Shelley were prophets, Wordsworth a sublime egoist, Coleridge a depressive, and Byron a sexual whirligig: incestuous, sadomasochistic, notorious for buggery with both genders, and doom-eager for the heroic death he found in Greece.

In the sonnet "On the Sea" of 1817, Keats reacts to his reading of *King Lear*, act 4, scene 5, where the blinded Gloucester resolves on suicide. Led by the disguised Edgar, his loyal son, Gloucester supposedly is taken to a cliff's edge:

> GLOUCESTER. When shall I come to th' top of that same hill?
> EDGAR. You do climb up it now. Look how we labor.
> GLOUCESTER. Methinks the ground is even.
> EDGAR.   Horrible steep.
>   Hark, do you hear the sea?

Edgar's question, Keats said, was the starting-point for his sonnet. This is an imaginary sea, akin to Hamlet's "sea of troubles" in his most famous soliloquy, "To be or not to be." We can surmise that this is also the sea of poetry, into which Keats had leaped, he noted, in his early long poem *Endymion*. Yet the sea, if the universe of poetry, is also that "universe of death," the chaos through which Milton's Satan made his hero-villain's voyage to discover the New World of Eve's and Adam's Eden. Hence the outcry of Keats's Apollo: "Knowledge enormous makes a God of me," though Apollo dies into life, a painful incarnation, representative of Keats's rebirth into poetry. The dangers involved perhaps are ironized in the four final stanzas of the superb ballad "La Belle Dame sans Merci," where the quester awakens from vision "on the cold hill's side." Poised on the threshold of the "Ode to Psyche," the first of the Great Odes, Keats at twenty-three already had undergone an almost unmatched poetic development.

Keats's genius, as revealed both in his poetry and in his unique letters, probably the most eloquent and wise of any published in the language, is so natural, compassionate, and comprehensive as to call any account of genius into severe question. He asserted that poetry was his daemon, but the poetry did not write itself, and no other poet since Shakespeare is so distant from the state of being possessed, even by the influence of beloved precursors. Keats, with so brief a time remaining to him, turned from Milton and Wordsworth back to Shakespeare, whose presence in the Great Odes and *The Fall of Hyperion* is acknowledged and absorbed with implicit tact. Helen Vendler accurately notes the effect of Hamlet upon the Great Odes, and one senses Hamlet's voice again in the quester's agonies in *The Fall of Hyperion*. But Hamlet is a dangerous figure to invoke, perhaps because he himself is both haunted and haunting. In the "Ode on Melancholy," which was to inaugurate a mode of poetry that goes from Tennyson through the Pre-Raphaelites on to Yeats and Wallace Stevens, Keats evades Hamlet by turning elsewhere in Shakespeare, to *Troilus and Cressida* and the Sonnets. Here is the "Ode on Melancholy":

I

No, no, go not to Lethe, neither twist
    Wolf's-bane, tight-rooted, for its poisonous wine;
Nor suffer thy pale forehead to be kissed
    By nightshade, ruby grape of Proserpine;
Make not your rosary of yew-berries,
    Nor let the beetle, nor the death-moth be
        Your mournful Psyche, nor the downy owl
A partner in your sorrow's mysteries;
    For shade to shade will come too drowsily,
        And drown the wakeful anguish of the soul.

II

But when the melancholy fit shall fall
    Sudden from heaven like a weeping cloud,
That fosters the droop-headed flowers all,
    And hides the green hill in an April shroud;
Then glut thy sorrow on a morning rose,

Or on the rainbow of the salt sand-wave,
  Or on the wealth of globed peonies;
Or if thy mistress some rich anger shows,
  Emprison her soft hand, and let her rave,
    And feed deep, deep upon her peerless eyes.

III

She dwells with Beauty—Beauty that must die;
  And Joy, whose hand is ever at his lips
Bidding adieu: and aching Pleasure nigh,
  Turning to poison while the bee-mouth sips:
Ay, in the very temple of Delight
  Veiled Melancholy has her sovereign shrine,
    Though seen of none save him whose strenuous tongue
Can burst Joy's grape against his palate fine;
  His soul shall taste the sadness of her might,
    And be among her cloudy trophies hung.

The wonderfully abrupt opening results from Keats's decision to cancel an original first stanza, grotesque and excessive, where he warns himself, as quester, that the goddess Melancholy will not be found if she is sought too ardently: "whether she / Dreameth in any isle of Lethe dull." Even if the desired goddess dwells on Lethe, she can be found only by an expanded consciousness, not by poison. Whatever she may be, this Melancholy is not what we now mean by "depression." She may seem closer to the dangerous delights of sadomasochism, and few of my women students have reacted favorably to Keats's sequence of a morning rose, a shore rainbow, peonies, and the peerless eyes of an angry mistress, held on to against her will for the oxymoronic pleasure of hearing her rave. And yet Keats primarily seeks wealth in her anger, a wealth exalted by its evanescence: "She dwells with Beauty—Beauty that must die." In Stevens's "Sunday Morning" this will be transmuted into "Death is the mother of beauty."

Keats moves the emphasis from his equivocal goddess, presumably his Muse, to himself, by invoking not the haunted melancholic, Hamlet, but the anxious Troilus awaiting his sexual fulfillment with Cressida:

  I am giddy; expectation whirls me round;
  Th' imaginary relish is so sweet
  That it enchants my sense; what will it be,
  When that the wat'ry palates taste indeed

> Love's thrice-repured nectar? Death, I fear me,
> Sounding destruction, or some joy too fine,
> Too subtile, potent, tun'd too sharp in sweetness
> For the capacity of my ruder powers.
>   —*Troilus and Cressida*, act 3, scene 2, 18–25

By so clearly echoing this speech, Keats necessarily associates his beloved Melancholy with Cressida, who betrays Troilus with Diomedes. The quester, of "strenuous tongue," will become only one of her relics:

> And he among her cloudy trophies hung.

That resonant final line echoes Shakespeare's Sonnet 31, where the poet addresses the fair young nobleman whom he so self-destructively loves:

> Thou art the grave where buried love doth live,
> Hung with the trophies of my lovers gone . . .

Shakespeare's Troilus overprepares the event; Shakespeare (or the sonnet's speaker) gives the young nobleman an equivocal tribute. Keats, forgetting neither Troilus nor Shakespeare, accepts the danger of a full encounter with his goddess of poetry, who pragmatically may also be a demoness, And yet he shows profound awareness that his acceptance is tragic. This Muse, Melancholy, is herself tragic, because she (and Keats) redefine melancholy as a full consciousness of natural change, whose final form is death. Confronting death at twenty-five, in Rome, Keats was still capable of musing on the fineness of the senses that tuberculosis was obliterating. His genius can be defined by the closing sentences of his last known letter, written from Rome, three months before dying: "I can scarcely bid you good bye even in a letter. I always made an awkward bow." Like his poetry, he is a perpetual greeting of the spirit.

GIACOMO LEOPARDI

No profession is as sterile as that of literature. Yet pretense is so valuable in the world that with its aid even literature becomes edifying. Pretense is the soul, so to speak, of the social life and is an art without which no other art or faculty, considered according to its effects on the human mind, can be perfect. Consider the fortunes of two persons, one of true value in every way, the other of false value. You will find that the latter is more fortunate than the former; indeed the false one is usually fortunate, the true one unfortunate. Pretense makes an effect even if truth be lacking, but truth without pretense can do nothing. Nor does this arise, I think, from our evil inclinations, but because bare truth is always an impoverished thing, and hence if we would delight or move men we must use illusion and heightening, and promise more and better than we can give. Nature herself is an impostor with man, and renders his life likeable and bearable chiefly by means of imagination and illusion.

(translated by Ottavio Mark Casale)

Leopardi is a poetic descendent of Lucretius, sharing this ancestry with Shelley, Walt Whitman, and Wallace Stevens, but he seems closer in spirit to Lucretius than anyone else has been. There is no transcendence for Leopardi, who accepted our condition as nothingness, and who saw all desire as vain. Illusions therefore are our best comfort, aside from the very rare visitations of poetic sublimity.

Leopardi defines genius as that which so vividly renders nothingness as to give us back enthusiasm, even if it is for the void. The exaltation of the soul, in creating or apprehending a work of genius, paradoxically gives fresh life by reaffirming nothingness.

In Lucretius, there is enough positive Epicureanism to allow his great poem to continue its gathering of exuberance. Finding a positive affect in Leopardi is a considerable enterprise, if you confine yourself to his prose. The nuances of the lyric poetry redeem Leopardi: his genius for inevitable phrasing redeems his frightening sense of evil, which for him, as for Keats and for Stevens, is the necessary pain and suffering that we must endure as natural men and women living in a natural entropy that must disintegrate us.

GIACOMO LEOPARDI
(1798–1837)

COUNT GIACOMO LEOPARDI, ITALY'S greatest lyric poet since Petrarch, had a desperate life, and was dead at thirty-nine. Lucretian in his vision, Leopardi wrote with a negative exuberance that is astonishing, proclaiming the bad news of our existence in poems perfect in form, nuance, cognitive music. George Santayana, introducing Iris Origo's classic biography *Leopardi: A Study in Solitude* (1953), memorably caught the paradox of this High Romantic genius:

> The white heat of his anguish burned all anguish away, and cleared the air. Beneath the glorious monotony of the stars he saw the universal mutation of earthly things, and their vanity, yet also, almost everywhere, the beginning if not the fullness of beauty; and this intuition, at once rapturous and sad, liberated him from the illusions of the past and from those of the future.

Leopardi translates very badly, since he is so purely a lyrical poet. The only verse translations in English that convey something of his special quality are by the late English poet John Heath-Stubbs. Sometimes I will cite those here, but more often a plain prose translation by George R. Kay.

In his prose "Dialogue between Torquato Tasso and His Familiar Genius" (*Genio familiare* in the Italian), Leopardi proclaims the center of his dark, creedless creed, as the mad Italian epic poet of the Renaissance confronts his daemon or genius:

> TASSO. . . . the life I lead is nothing but torment, for, apart from grief, *la noia* is also destroying me.
> GENIUS. What is *la noia*?
> TASSO. . . . It seems to me that *la noia* is of the nature of air, which fills up all the spaces between material things and all the voids in each one of them; and whenever a body changes its place and is not at once replaced by another, *la noia* at once comes in. So all the intervals in human life between pleasure and pain, are occupied by *la noia* . . .
> GENIUS. . . . truly I believe that *la noia* means nothing more than a

craving for pure happiness, unsatisfied by pleasure and not percepti-
bly wounded by wretchedness. And this craving . . . can never be gratified . . . Thus the stuff of which human life is made is partly sorrow
and partly *noia;* and we only escape from one of them by falling into
the other . . .

    TASSO. What remedies are there against this *noia?*

    GENIUS. Sleep, opium, suffering . . .

(translated by Iris Origo)

Leopardi sees life as a vertigo in which we alternate between visions of
nulla (nothingness) and the untranslatable *noia* ("spleen" and "ennui" are
inadequate terms). *Noia* is desire when and where there is nothing to desire. Just as "evil" in Wallace Stevens (another Lucretian) means the pain
and suffering that comes to any natural woman or man in a natural world, so
Leopardi's *noia* is natural-all-too-natural.

Leopardi's greatest originality is to engender his own version of the poetic Sublime out of this nightmare of *noia:*

Works of genius have this in common, that even when they vividly
capture the nothingness of things, when they clearly show and make
us feel the inevitable unhappiness of life, and when they express the
most terrible despair, nonetheless to a great soul—though he find
himself in a state of extreme duress, disillusion, nothingness, *noia,* and
despair of life, or in the bitterest and *deadliest* misfortunes (caused by
deep feelings or whatever)—these works always console and rekindle
enthusiasm; and though they treat or represent only death, they give
back to him, at least temporarily, that life which he had lost.

    And so that which in real life grieves and kills the soul, opens and
revives the heart when it appears in imitations or other works of artistic genius (as in lyric poems, which are not properly imitations). Just
as the author, in describing and strongly feeling the emptiness of illusions still retained a great store of illusions—which we proved by so
intensely describing their emptiness—so the reader, no matter how
disenchanted *per se* and through his reading, is pulled by the author
into that very illusion hidden in the deepest recesses of that mind the
reader was experiencing. And the very recognition of the irremediable
vanity and falseness of all things great and beautiful is itself a great
and beautiful thing which fills the soul, when the recognition comes
through works of genius. And the very spectacle of nothingness pre-

sented seems to expand the soul of the reader, to exalt it, and reconcile it to itself and to its own despair. (A tremendous thing and certainly a source of pleasure and enthusiasm—this magisterial effect of poetry when it works to allow the reader a higher concept of self, of his woes, and his own depressed, annihilated spirit.)

Moreover, the feeling of nothingness is that of a dead and death-producing thing. But if this feeling is alive, as in the case I mean, its liveliness dominates in the reader's mind the nothingness of the thing it makes him feel; and the soul receives life (if only briefly) from the very power by which it feels the perpetual death of things and of itself. Not the smallest or least painful effect of the knowledge of great nothingness is the indifference and numbness which it almost always inspires about that very nothingness. This indifference and insensibility is removed by reading or contemplating such a work: it renders us *sensible* to nothingness.

This is Leopardi's *reader's Sublime*, and is the proper work of his poetry, to direct and divert the dangerous prevalence of *noia* in us:

In referring to the absence of pleasure and displeasure, one is referring to *noia* . . . *Noia* always and immediately runs to fill up all the empty spaces left behind in living souls by pleasure and displeasure. The void—that is the passionless state of indifference—cannot exist in such a soul, just as it could not exist in physical nature according to the ancients. *Noia* is like the air on earth, which fills all the spaces among other objects, and races to be where they are not, unless other objects take their place. Or shall we say that the void itself in the human mind, and the indifference, and the absence of every other passion is *noia*, which is itself a passion. Now what do we mean by saying that a living being who is neither enjoying nor suffering is necessarily experiencing *noia*? We mean that he can never stop desiring happiness, that is pleasure or enjoyment. This desire—when it is neither satisfied nor directly thwarted by the opposite of enjoyment—is *noia*. *Noia* is the desire for happiness reduced, as it were, to purity. This desire itself is passion. Thus the mind of a living being can never really be passionless. This passion when found alone, when no other actually occupies the mind, is what we call *noia*. So *noia* is a proof of the perpetual existence of passion in man. If this were not so, *noia* could not really exist, nor could it be present where the others are absent.

How well do Leopardi's poems prepare us for countering this void? Here is John Heath-Stubbs's version of the famous early poem "The Infinite" (1819):

> This lonely hill was always dear to me,
> And this hedgerow, that hides so large a part
> Of the far sky-line from my view. Sitting and gazing,
> I fashion in my mind what lie beyond—
> Unearthly silences, and endless space,
> And very deepest quiet then for a while
> The heart is not afraid. And when I hear
> The wind come blustering among the trees
> I set that voice against this infinite silence:
> And then I call to mind Eternity,
> The ages that are dead, and the living present
> And all the noise of it. And thus it is
> In that immensity my thought is drowned:
> And sweet to me the foundering in that sea.

It may be sweet but it is a foundering: can shipwreck be experienced as a pleasure? We are in an early phase of Leopardi's Sublime, in which, as Shelley says of his, we abandon easier pleasures for more difficult ones. Leopardi, like Lucretius, is a poet of the sky, and again like Shelley, an acolyte of the moon. Here again is Heath-Stubbs translating "To the Moon" (1819):

> O gracious Moon, I call to mind again
> It was a year ago I climbed this hill
> To gaze upon you in my agony;
> And you were hanging then above that wood,
> Filling it all with light, as you do now.
> But dim and tremulous your face appeared,
> Seen through the tears that rose beneath my eyelids,
> My life being full of travail; as it is still—
> It does not change, O my sweet Moon. And yet
> Remembrance helps, and reckoning up
> The cycles of my sorrow. How sweet the thought
> That brings to mind things past, when we are young—
> When long's the road for hope, for memory brief—
> Though they were sad, and though our pain endures.

"It must give pleasure," Wallace Stevens said of poetry as the supreme fiction: how does Leopardi's anguished invocation of the moon give pleasure? Why do an unchanging past and an unchanged present yield pleasure? Can remembrance help, when only anguish is recalled? The clue seems to be the anticipation, either of the same, or of worse to come. At twenty-one, the poet still has hope, though he cites no reason for it. But then, he says only that hope still has a long road ahead, though this evidently is hope without an object. Leopardi was a hunchback who could not attract women, about whom he was passionate. Iris Origo, in her saddest sentence, remarks, "Leopardi had now reached his twenty-first year, and all that was ever going to happen to him, had already happened." Yet nothing had happened. An Epicurean materialist who rejected Christianity yet who was shut out from sensual existence, it was poetic genius alone that kept Leopardi sane. Addicted to language, he quested and achieved purity of diction, which for him had to replace the Christian counsel of purity of heart. What I find to be his secret, his genius, is that uniquely he converted purity of diction into a metaphor, constituted by an entire poem, for a sense of the infinite. Only the vista (to call it that) of the infinite could heal *noia.*

Leopardi's major poem is his sublime ode *La ginestra* (*The Broom*) or *The Flower of the Desert,* set upon Mount Vesuvius, in the final year of his life. It is magnificent, and wholly untranslatable, so my citations of it are from the literal version by George Kay. The *ginestra* dares to bloom upon the arid back of the volcano; does Leopardi, close to the abyss, dare to identify himself with this heroic flower, "the lover of sad places that are abandoned by the world"? The poem's final movement evades the identification, yet does not deny it:

> And you, slow bush of broom, that deck these bare country places with fragrant copses, you too will soon fall to the cruel power of the subterranean fire, which, coming again to its known limit, will stretch its rapacious hem over your soft forests. And you will bend your innocent head beneath the mortal burden without struggling; but a head that has not been bent in cowardly supplication, vainly, before the coming oppressor; nor raised with vainglorious pride towards the stars, nor upon the desert where you sprang and grew not by choosing to, but by chance. But you will have been wiser and so much the less infirm than man, as you did not believe your frail kind made immortal by fate or by yourself.

Nature, in Leopardi's powerful realization, is our ultimate enemy, and our only resource is to be kind to one another. Yet the flower of the volcanic desert is wiser and firmer than we are, with our illusions of immortality. Here purity of diction substitutes, not for the consolation of the infinite, but for our lack of courage in taking up the full burden of our condition.

Leopardi's last poem, "The Setting of the Moon," was completed in Naples on June 14, 1837, just a few hours before his death. Heath-Stubbs, himself a poet of considerable talents, caught fire in translating Leopardi's self-elegy, particularly its final strophe:

> You, banks and little hills,
> Though hidden be the light which from the west
> Had silvered all the mantle of the night,
> Orphaned you shall not long
> Remain, for very soon you may discern
> Once more the eastern skies
> Grow pale with morning, till the dawn arise,
> Whom the sun follows after, and comes forth,
> Blazing and bright again,
> And with his ardent beams,
> His shining streams of light,
> Floods all your summits and the ethereal plain.
> But mortal life, when the fair time of youth
> Has vanished, never then grows bright again
> With any radiance more, or second dawn.
> Widowed until the end; and in the night,
> Where through the dark we come,
> The gods have set a sign for us, the tomb.

Somber and exquisite, this has Lucretian *gravitas*. Leopardi finds no comfort at the end, except for the implicit presence of his own familiar genius. In his vast notebooks, the *Zibaldone* (*Hodgepodge*), he had written:

It seems absurd, yet is precisely true, that since all reality is nought, illusions are, in this world, the only true and substantial things.

As the moon sets and dawn comes again, Leopardi sees that his final illusions are departing, and he departs also.

ALFRED, LORD TENNYSON

Though much is taken, much abides; and though
We are not now that strength which in old days
Moved earth and heaven; that which we are, we are,
One equal temper of heroic hearts,
Made weak by time and fate, but strong in will
To strive, to seek, to find, and not to yield.

Standing in Washington Square Park on September 11, 2001, unbelievingly watching the towers crumble, the final lines of Tennyson's dramatic monologue "Ulysses" came unsummoned. The most Vergilian poet in English, Tennyson saluted Vergil in 1882, at the request of the Mantuans, nineteen centuries after Vergil's death:

> Light among the vanished ages;
> Star that gildest yet this phantom shore;
> Golden branch amid the shadows,
> Kings and realms that pass to rise no more;

Vergil himself has become the golden bough that keeps us safe in the underworld. Tennyson, an elegiac genius saluted by Walt Whitman as "the boss" (though hardly the Springsteen of Queen Victoria), himself is now a golden bough in our possible descent into the darkness that appears to be upon us, at least for a long time to come:

> Dear as remembered kisses after death,
> And sweet as those by hopeless fancy feigned
> On lips that are for others; deep as love,
> Deep as first love, and wild with all regret;
> O Death in Life, the days that are no more.

ALFRED, LORD TENNYSON
(1809–1892)

THE GREAT VICTORIAN "NONSENSE" poets—Edward Lear, Lewis Carroll, William Schwenk Gilbert—all wrote Tennysonian pastiche when they attempted "sincere" verses of affection and regret. Poetically, Tennyson was the style of the age, as John Ashbery long has been in the United States. Now that the twentieth century is over, its deprecation of Tennyson will cease, and his morbid genius again will be recognized by those still capable of reading a poem. The faded "Modernism" of eighty years ago, whose lasting poetic monument is T. S. Eliot's *The Waste Land*, had a grudge against Queen Victoria's laureate. I have demonstrated earlier that *The Waste Land*, which would like to find its forerunners in Dante and Baudelaire, actually was found by its more authentic precursors, Tennyson and Walt Whitman. Tennyson, at his most characteristic, remained in the shadow of John Keats, but he reworked Keats's mode into the idiom of his own genius. With Tennyson, I return to the idea of the daemon, for the best of his poems frequently move against his conscious intentions.

Tennyson at his most inspired is an incantatory poet who should be read aloud. Here is "Mariana," composed when Tennyson was twenty, a complete achievement, a perfection of death-in-life:

> With blackest moss the flower-plots
>   Were thickly crusted, one and all:
> The rusted nails fell from the knots
>   That held the pear to the gable-wall.
> The broken sheds looked sad and strange:
>   Unlifted was the clinking latch;
>   Weeded and worn the ancient thatch
> Upon the lonely moated grange.
>   She only said, "My life is dreary,
>   He cometh not," she said;
>   She said, "I am aweary, aweary,
>   I would that I were dead!"
>
> Her tears fell with the dews at even;
>   Her tears fell ere the dews were dried;

She could not look on the sweet heaven,
    Either at morn or eventide.
After the flitting of the bats,
    When thickest dark did trance the sky,
    She drew her casement-curtain by,
And glanced athwart the glooming flats.
    She only said, "My life is dreary,
        He cometh not," she said;
    She said, "I am aweary, aweary,
        I would that I were dead!"

Upon the middle of the night,
    Waking she heard the night-fowl crow:
The cock sung out an hour ere light:
    From the dark fen the oxen's low
Came to her: without hope of change,
    In sleep she seemed to walk forlorn,
    Till cold winds woke the gray-eyed morn
About the lonely moated grange.
    She only said, "The day is dreary,
        He cometh not," she said;
    She said, "I am aweary, aweary,
        I would that I were dead!"

About a stone-cast from the wall
    A sluice with blackened waters slept,
And o'er it many, round and small,
    The cluster'd marish-mosses crept.
Hard by a poplar shook alway,
    All silver-green with gnarled bark:
    For leagues no other tree did mark
The level waste, the rounding gray.
    She only said, "The day is dreary,
        He cometh not," she said;
    She said, "I am aweary, aweary,
        I would that I were dead!"

And ever when the moon was low,
    And the shrill winds were up and away
In the white curtain, to and fro,

She saw the gusty shadow sway.
But when the moon was very low,
    And wild winds bound within their cell,
    The shadow of the poplar fell
Upon her bed, across her brow.
    She only said, "The day is dreary,
        He cometh not," she said;
    She said, "I am aweary, aweary,
        I would that I were dead!"

All day within the dreamy house,
    The doors upon their hinges creaked;
The blue fly sung in the pane; the mouse
    Behind the mouldering wainscot shrieked,
Or from the crevice peered about.
    Old faces glimmered through the doors,
    Old footsteps trod the upper floors,
Old voices called her from without.
    She only said, "The day is dreary,
        He cometh not," she said;
    She said, "I am aweary, aweary,
        I would that I were dead!"

The sparrow's chirrup on the roof,
    The slow clock ticking, and the sound
Which to the wooing wind aloof
    The poplar made, did all confound
Her sense; but most she loathed the hour
    When the thick-moted sunbeam lay
    Athwart the chambers, and the day
Was sloping toward his western bower.
    Then, said she, "I am very dreary,
        He will not come," she said;
    She wept, "I am aweary, aweary,
        O God, that I were dead!"

It can be self-hypnotic, chanting this to oneself, when it is possessed by memory. Though Tennyson takes this dramatic lyric's speaker, and its epigraph, from Shakespeare's *Measure for Measure* (act 3, scene 1, 212ff.), he has Keats's *Isabella* in mind. That poem's heroine also, like Mariana, waits for the lover who will not arrive: "She weeps alone for pleasures not to be; / Sorely she wept until the night came on . . . / And so she pined, and so she died forlorn." The young Tennyson invents the stanza form, but the feeling-tone of Keats's Great Odes reverberates throughout, a comparison that "Mariana" can almost sustain.

At his poetic start, Tennyson's daemon writes the poem for him. By the time you have read (or intoned) "Mariana" over and over again, you come to understand how deliciously unhealthy this poem is. Though it purports to be a song of despair, a terrible exultation dominates it. Tennyson's Mariana is rather like Blake's Sick Rose, whose bed is "of Crimson Joy" before the invisible worm, flying in the night-storm, has reached it. Acute ambivalence concerning the absent male lover could hardly be more persuasively articulated. Elsewhere in this book, in the section upon Keats, I center upon his "Ode on Melancholy," which I suspect provokes Tennyson's own ambivalences in "Mariana." As much as Goethe, Keats was a firm naturalist, celebrating sensual completion. Tennyson, even as a youth, is impatient with natural process. His surrogate, Mariana, incarnates a daemonic voice, fiercely enamored with itself. The beautiful Laura of Katherine Anne Porter's Mexican story "Flowering Judas" has something of the same erotic self-sufficiency, destructive to the self and others.

The independence of lyric genius from historical determinations is eloquently illustrated by "Mariana." Tennyson's heroine herself is a poet, and she is her own *materia poetica*, and absolutely in no need of the lover she supposedly awaits. His surrogate, the poplar, is disturbing enough, but his presence would destroy the poem. The power of phantasmagoria is threatened by any intrusive element, and the lover would be a most unwelcome intruder.

Tennyson's lyric consciousness tends to center upon the image of a embowered woman, who is his interior paramour or alter ego, which takes us back again to one of the ancient Roman definitions of genius. The exacerbated sensibility of "Mariana" can be found throughout Tennyson's best work. Here I want to center upon the monodrama *Maud*, which appears to have had a permanent effect upon T. S. Eliot. The alienated male speaker of *Maud* cries out, "And my heart is a handful of dust," which becomes *The Waste Land*'s "I will show you fear in a handful of dust." The full title of Tennyson's monodrama is *Maud or the Madness,* and the poem wanders very near to the familial sources of the Laureate's dangerous melancholia. Tennyson's father had been disinherited in favor of a younger brother: the consequences included genteel poverty, a wasted life, acute alcoholism, madness, relatively early death. George Tennyson, rector of a Lincolnshire parish, fathered twelve children, of whom Alfred was the fourth. All his brothers were depressives, one broke down completely, and Alfred, long after he was Queen Victoria's well-financed poet laureate, maintained always a perilous balance.

Maud (1855) was too morbid to be greatly popular, but it deserves Tennyson's descriptive defense:

> This poem of *Maud or the Madness* is a little *Hamlet*, the history of a morbid, poetic soul, under the blighting influence of a recklessly speculative age. He is the heir of madness, an egoist with the makings of a cynic, raised to a pure and holy love which elevates his whole nature, passing from the height of triumph to the lowest depth of misery, driven into madness by the loss of her whom he has loved, and, when he has at length passed through the fiery furnace, and has recovered his reason, giving himself up to work for the good of mankind through the unselfishness of a great passion. The peculiarity of this poem is that different phases of passion in one person take the place of different characters.

That of course is the Laureate and not the daemon speaking, and fortunately the daemon composed most of the poem. *Maud* was published during the Crimean War, and the little Hamlet (who is closer to a little Byron) gives himself up to work for the good of mankind by going off at the close unselfishly to slaughter Russians. I still recall being awed, in London in the mid-1950s, by Beatrice Lillie, who in a music hall kind of show ("An Intimate Evening with Bea Lillie") danced out on stage and shouted at the audience, "Maud, we're rotten to the core." She then spread out her cape to reveal bat-wings and cheerfully darted about while an Irish tenor in evening dress sang the monodrama's most famous number, the song beginning:

> Come into the garden, Maud,
> For the black bat, night, has flown,
> Come into the garden, Maud,
> I am here at the gate alone:
> And the woodbine spices are wafted abroad,
> And the musk of the rose is blown.

The nameless singer is quite paranoid, as we discover, and really is a parody of Tennyson as a young man. His perceptions are lyrically intense, so much so that poor Maud may be judged fortunate to have slipped out of life to evade him:

> There has fallen a splendid tear
> From the passion-flower at the gate.
> She is coming my dove, my dear;
> She is coming, my life, my fate;
> The red rose cries, "She is near, she is near;"
> And the white rose weeps, "She is late;"
> The larkspur listens, "I hear, I hear;"
> And the lily whispers, "I wait."

It is hardly a step from this to the Wonderland or the Looking-Glass world of Lewis Carroll. That seems to me its precarious greatness: where is the edge between sublime passion and sublime nonsense? Tennyson, at his most astonishing, is compelled to let his daemon know how it should be done. In the gorgeously ornate but poetically barren wastes of *Idylls of the King*, the daemonic voice sometimes breaks through, as here in Vivien's song and its afterword, from *Balin and Balan*:

> But now the wholesome music of the wood
> Was dumbed by one from out the hall of Mark,
> A damsel-errant, warbling, as she rode
> The woodland alleys, Vivien, with her Squire.
>
> "The fire of Heaven has killed the barren cold,
> And kindled all the plain and all the wold.
> The new leaf ever pushes off the old.
> The fire of Heaven is not the flame of Hell.
>
> "Old priest, who mumbled worship in your quire—
> Old monk and nun, ye scorn the world's desire,
> Yet in your frosty cells ye feel the fire!
> The fire of Heaven is not the flame of Hell.
>
> "The fire of Heaven is on the dusty ways.
> The wayside blossoms open to the blaze.
> The whole wood-world is one full peal of praise.
> The fire of Heaven is not the flame of Hell.

"The fire of Heaven is lord of all things good,
And starve not thou this fire within thy blood,
But follow Vivien through the fiery flood!
The fire of Heaven is not the flame of Hell!"

Then turning to her Squire "This fire of Heaven,
This old sun-worship, boy, will rise again,
And beat the cross to earth, and break the King
And all his Table . . ."

This hymn to Eros is the true voice of feeling in Tennyson, returning from the repressed. A craggy emanation from the dreary level wastes and mossy marshes of Lincolnshire, the setting of his "Mariana," Tennyson was a walking anomaly, best described (by Thomas Carlyle) as "a man solitary and sad . . . carrying a bit of Chaos about him, in short, which he is manufacturing into Cosmos." But we don't care about that Cosmos; the bit of Chaos can be poetically fascinating. Vivien, who will seduce and destroy Merlin, is part of that bit of Chaos. Tennyson thought that *Maud* was his *Inferno*, and that *In Memoriam* was his *Purgatorio*, and at its very end, his *Paradiso*. What holds on in the memory from *In Memoriam* are precisely those moments that prophesy the urban visions of T. S. Eliot, who particularly admired poem 7, where Tennyson stands in front of what had been the home of Arthur Henry Hallam, the close friend he perpetually mourned:

Dark house, by which once more I stand
Here in the long unlovely street,
Doors, where my heart was used to beat
So quickly, waiting for a hand,

A hand that can be clasped no more—
Behold me, for I cannot sleep,
And like a guilty thing I creep
At earliest morning to the door.

He is not here; but far away
The noise of life begins again,
And ghastly through the drizzling rain
On the bald street breaks the blank day.

Tennyson always remained a daemonic elegist, perpetually mourning, very much in the mode of Vergil, his favorite classical poet, even as Keats was his crucial modern precursor. Christopher Ricks, praising Tennyson's death-poem, the permanently popular "Crossing the Bar," points to the skilled way each of the four stanzas relies upon a "shortened concluding line, reining and subduing the feeling." What stays with me is the second of the four stanzas, which for me epitomizes Tennyson's unique cognitive music:

> But such a tide as moving seems asleep,
>   Too full for sound and foam,
> When that which drew from out the boundless deep
>   Turns again home.

Home is part of the original Chaos, and Tennyson has yielded up all fantasies of societal progress or of manufacturing his daemonic inheritance into a Cosmos.

VI

TIFERET

LUSTRE 11

|

Algernon Charles Swinburne, Dante Gabriel Rossetti, Christina Rossetti, Walter Pater, Hugo von Hofmannsthal

|

The Kabbalah subsumes Aestheticism under the *Sefirah* known as *Tiferet,* the "mercy" of God manifest as God's "beauty," a mediation frequently manifested as the *Shekhinah,* God's presence as a beautiful female form.

English Aestheticism—Swinburne, the Rossettis, Walter Pater—and its Viennese contemporary, best represented by Hofmannsthal, almost inevitably fits this first Lustre of *Tiferet.* Long held in critical disfavor, Swinburne and Dante Gabriel Rossetti are poets of extraordinary accomplishment, as I will demonstrate. Christina Rossetti, a unique and belated triumph of devotional poetry, is also a superb elegist of erotic loss.

The criticism of Walter Pater, much deprecated by T. S. Eliot, profoundly influenced Joyce, Yeats, Virginia Woolf, and many other "Modernists" (how antique that word seems now), while Hugo von Hofmannsthal needs to be rescued from the unfair fate of being remembered only as Richard Strauss's librettist. I attempt that rescue here.

ALGERNON CHARLES SWINBURNE

> None hath beheld him, none
> Seen above other gods and shapes of things,
> Swift without feet and flying without wings,
> Intolerable, not clad with death or life,
>   Insatiable, not known of night or day,
> The lord of love and loathing and of strife
>   Who gives a star and takes a sun away;
> Who shapes the soul, and makes her a barren wife
>   To the earthly body and grievous growth of clay;
> Who turns the large limbs to a little flame
>   And binds the great sea with a little sand;
> Who makes desire, and slays desire with shame;
>   Who shakes the heaven as ashes in his hand;
> Who, seeing the light and shadow for the same,
>   Bids day waste night as fire devours a brand,
> Smites without sword, and scourges without rod;
>   The supreme evil, God.

Swinburne's antireligious audacity, superbly expressed in this chorus of *Atalanta in Calydon,* has a refreshing tonality as we enter more deeply into the twenty-first century, an era in which the wars of religion seem fated to return. But then, Swinburne's was the genius of audacity, whether in his explicit sadomasochism, his polemic against Christianity, or his extraordinary gifts as a parodist. The finest *deliberate* self-parody in the language is Swinburne's "Poeta Loquitor" ("The Poet Speaks"), which, alas, I have not space to quote entire. Here are stanzas 4 through 6 (out of ten) that forestall any Christian critique Swinburne might provoke:

> Mad mixtures of Frenchified offal
>   With insults to Christendom's creed,
> Blind blasphemy, schoolboylike scoff, all
>   These blazon me blockhead indeed.
> I conceive myself obviously someone

Whose audience will never be thinned,
But the pupil must needs be a rum one
   Whose teacher is wind.

In my poems, with ravishing rapture
   Storm strikes me and strokes me and stings:
But I'm scarcely the bird you might capture
   Out of doors in the thick of such things.
I prefer to be well out of harm's way
   When temper makes tremble the tree,
And the wind with omnipotent arm-sway
   Makes soap of the sea.

Hanging hard on the rent rags of others,
   Who before me did better, I try
To believe them my sisters and brothers,
   Though I know what a low lot am I.
The mere sight of a church sets me yelping
   Like a boy that at football is shinned!
But the cause must indeed be past helping
   Whose gospel is wind!

ALGERNON CHARLES SWINBURNE
(1837–1909)

OF ALL THE GENIUSES OF LANGUAGE considered in this book, the poet Swinburne is now the most unfashionable. Doubtless, it is too late to revive him: he was slain by T. S. Eliot and Edmund Wilson, both distinguished hatchetmen. Still, here is his poem "August," which I quote in full because so few now alive have read it. Try chanting it aloud, whether to yourself or to another:

> There were four apples on the bough,
> Half gold half red, that one might know
> The blood was ripe inside the core;
> The colour of the leaves was more
> Like stems of yellow corn that grow
> Through all the gold June meadow's floor.
>
> The warm smell of the fruit was good
> To feed on, and the split green wood,
> With all its bearded lips and stains
> Of mosses in the cloven veins,
> Most pleasant, if one lay or stood
> In sunshine or in happy rains.
>
> There were four apples on the tree,
> Red stained through gold, that all might see
> The sun went warm from core to rind;
> The green leaves made the summer blind
> In that soft place they kept for me
> With golden apples shut behind.
>
> The leaves caught gold across the sun,
> And where the bluest air begun,
> Thirsted for song to help the heat;
> As I to feel my lady's feet
> Draw close before the day were done
> Both lips grew dry with dreams of it.

In the mute August afternoon
They trembled to some undertune
Of music in the silver air;
Great pleasure was it to be there
Till green turned duskier and the moon
Coloured the corn-sheaves like gold hair.

That August time it was delight
To watch the red moons wane to white
'Twixt grey seamed stems of apple-trees;
A sense of heavy harmonies
Grew on the growth of patient night,
More sweet than shapen music is.

But some three hours before the moon
The air, still eager from the noon,
Flagged after heat, not wholly dead;
Against the stem I leant my head;
The colour soothed me like a tune,
Green leaves all round the gold and red.

I lay there till the warm smell grew
More sharp, when flecks of yellow dew
Between the round ripe leaves that blurred
The rind with stain and wet; I heard
A wind that blew and breathed and blew,
Too weak to alter its one word.

The wet leaves next the gentle fruit
Felt smoother, and the brown tree-root
Felt the mould warmer: I too felt
(As water feels the slow gold melt
Right through it when the day burns mute)
The peace of time wherein love dwelt.

There were four apples on the tree,
Gold stained on red that all might see
The sweet blood filled them to the core:
The colour of her hair is more
Like stems of fair faint gold, that be
Mown from the harvest's middle floor.

Swinburne, if noticed at all, still has a certain notoriety because he was a disciple (pragmatically speaking) of the Marquis de Sade, and he certainly wrote a large quantity of masochistic verse, of which the masterpiece is "Anactoria," a dramatic monologue spoken by the Lesbian poet Sappho to the unfortunate Anactoria, her beloved victim (clearly a surrogate for Swinburne himself, as Camille Paglia notes with her customarily pungent accuracy). "August," though, is essentially free of Swinburne's consuming desire to be flogged by a woman, and is perhaps his most Keatsian poem, naturalistic rather than *contra naturam*. At once celebratory and poignant, it goes back to the great unfulfilled love of his life, his quasi-incestuous attachment to his cousin Mary Gordon, with whom he grew up on the Isle of Wight, the apparent setting of "August." Sometimes I am moved to say of "August" what Dr. Johnson said of Alexander Pope: if this be not poetry, then where is poetry to be found?

And yet Swinburne's work, with too few exceptions, demonstrates that verbal genius is not in itself enough, a sadness that alone would justify his inclusion in this book. Here is Swinburne's best critic, the late Ian Fletcher, charting his imperfections, and then bringing on the formidable poet-classicist A. E. Housman to complete the indictment:

> There is, of course, an indictment for his admirers to answer. If Swinburne radiates some of the signs of genius—energy, abundance and a powerful literary identity—his range of subject seems slender. The metrical effects, surprising, stunning even at first, gradually dull the response by reliance on anapests and iambs; the initial effect of wildness is eventually tamed by patterns of expectation; unlike Baudelaire, Swinburne did not dislocate his metres, while his alliterations were continuous, brash, and self-indulgent. The poet has a harem of words to which he remains depressingly faithful: his vocabulary is often heavily Biblical with a manneristic profusion of God, Hell, serpents, stings, rods, flames, and thunders, etc., a surprising characteristic in one who was so determinedly a hammer of the Christians. Swinburne's muse is indeed a kind of inverted Balaam: he curses God in the tones of an Old Testament prophet out of a job, or one perhaps resisting the burdens of office. And the subjects of Swinburne's verse seem to melt into one subject. Whether he is exploring a pungent sado-masochistic psychology or the sea as Mother figure; or the liberation of Italy as emblem of man's liberation from all tyrannies, religious or political; or sounding the bracing moral suasions of the Navy League, it makes little difference. The noxious rhythms, the vocabu-

lary, blurred and generalized, persist, so that we can barely tell if we are meant to admire a battleship or a breast. Housman, one of Swinburne's best and wittiest critics, sums it up: "The sea, like babies and liberty went into the sausage machine into which he crammed anything and everything, round goes the handle and out of the other end comes . . . noise." Housman admired some of the poems, but "there is no reason why they should begin where they do or end where they do; there is no reason why the middle should be in the middle; there is hardly a reason why, having once begun, they should ever end at all; and it would be possible to rearrange the stanzas which compose them in several different orders without lessening their coherency or impairing their effect." But Tennyson's comment has an equal aptness: "He is a reed through which all things blow into music."

Eliot and Wilson on Swinburne do not make me wince as Fletcher and Housman do. A sausage machine that produces noise is a description that, if merited, would sink anyone. In short, Swinburne usually is very annoying, and we don't need a genius to annoy us. Still, there are grand exceptions, besides "August." There is the verse drama *Atalanta in Calydon*, which remains considerably more readable than Eliot's *Murder in the Cathedral* or *The Family Reunion*, and there is Swinburne's best poem, "At a Month's End," thirty-three majestic quatrains in which a man and a woman, who have fallen out of love, walk at night for one last time to gaze together at the sea. The poem evidently commemorates Swinburne's month of an affair with the outrageous Adah Isaacs Menken (1835–1868), actress, adventurer, and poet, out of Memphis, Tennessee, world-famous for her (mostly naked) rides across stage strapped horseback in Lord Byron's *Mazeppa*. Ms. Menken evidently gave Swinburne up because, as she remarked to Dante Gabriel Rossetti, "I can't make him understand that biting's no use." Be that as it may have been, "At a Month's End" has a stately tempo, a death-march of lost Eros:

> Across, aslant, a scudding sea-mew
>   Swam, dipped, and dropped, and grazed the sea:
> And one with me I could not dream you;
>   And one with you I could not be.

The daemonic, as language, goes back to an Indo-European root meaning "to divide." Genius, or the daemon, is the spirit that divides the self, rather than unifies it. Swinburne is one of the signal instances of a nature unable to sustain its own genius. We should value him as one of the few writers adept at depicting the death of love. "At a Month's End" always makes me think of my favorite moments in modern literature that evoke the end of passion. There is Proust's Swann crying out, "And to think I went through all this suffering for a woman who did not even suit me, who was not really my style!" Jack Burden, in Robert Penn Warren's *All the King's Men,* bids farewell in reverie to his former wife: "Goodbye, Lois, and I forgive you for everything I ever did to you." Perhaps best of all, there is Iris Murdoch, somewhere in one of her earlier novels: "Falling out of love is one of the great human experiences; you seem to see the world with newly awakened eyes."

DANTE GABRIEL ROSSETTI

Piled deep below the screening apple branch
They lie with bitten apples in their hands:
And some are only ancient bones that blanch,
And some had ships that last year's wind did launch,
And some were yesterday the lords of lands.

In the soft dell, among the apple trees,
High up above the hidden pit she stands,
And there forever sings, who gave to these,
That lie below, her magic hour of ease,
And those her apples holden in their hands.

This in my dreams is shown me; and her hair
Crosses my lips and draws my burning breath;

Her song spreads golden wings upon the air,
Life's eyes are gleaming from her forehead fair,
    And from her breasts the ravishing eyes of Death.

Much as I love the now neglected poetry of Dante Gabriel Rossetti, his genius transcends melancholia and crosses over into acute morbidity. His fragment "The Orchard-Pit," the opening stanzas of which I quote above, is hardly a tribute to his lifelong adulterous lover, Jane Burden (Mrs. William Morris, the poet-artist Morris also having been Rossetti's lifelong best friend). I have a stuffed wombat on my New Haven living room couch named McGregor, that having been Rossetti's pet wombat, very dear to Morris, who would accompany Rossetti on his frequent visits to the Morrises' house. One account (which I don't doubt) holds that poor McGregor was a decoy. William Morris loved to play with and sketch the little animal for an hour or two at a time, during which the audacious Rossetti and the beautiful wanton Jane Burden Morris would troop upstairs for momentary release of their mutual passion.

Luridity haunts Dante Gabriel Rossetti, and his rather overworked Pre-Raphaelite portrait paintings seem to me greatly inferior to his highly original poetry. His unique blend of naturalism and phantasmagoria works better in the poems, whose tonalities are rarely oppressive, whereas all but the best of the pictures display a heavy sensuality obsessively at play.

Rossetti's poetic masterpiece is *The Stream's Secret*, a long reverie upon his destructive and inescapable desire for Jane Burden. Doubtless Rossetti and Mrs. Morris deserved one another: the thought of a marriage between them can upset Rossetti's reader as much as it undoubtedly disturbed them. Since the Western literary canon has been swept away by the Enlightened Puritanism of the universities of the English-speaking world, Rossetti may be gone forever. But a solitary reader, extremely intelligent, should seek out *The House of Life* sonnets and the translations from Dante and his circle. In our era, being excluded from the universities is quite likely to be a blazon of excellence.

CHRISTINA ROSSETTI

Remember me when I am gone away,
    Gone far away into the silent land
    When you can no more hold me by the hand,
Nor I half turn to go yet turning stay.
Remember me when no more day by day
    You tell me of our future that you planned:
    Only remember me; you understand.
It will be late to counsel then or pray.
Yet if you should forget me for a while
    And afterwards remember, do not grieve:
    For if the darkness and corruption leave
    A vestige of the thoughts that once I had,
Better by far you should forget and smile
    Than that you should remember and be sad.

Her "Remember" sonnet is a superb instance of Christina Rossetti's hushed, understated originality. Few anticipated self-elegies speak so adequately to a survivor in the voice of the beloved dead. Christina's subtle art plays upon the five uses of "remember" in her sonnet, all of them very different from one another. The first is simple or literal remembrance, while the second alludes to the potential guilt of the survivor. "Only remember me," the third, is more plangent with regret, while "afterwards remember" is no reproof, since grieving is inappropriate for the respites granted by erotic loss. The final "remember" is the most gracious, gently testifying to the selfless element in the love that is lost.

Christina Rossetti does not share in the boundless originality of Emily Dickinson, and she is far from the solitary sublimity of the handful of Emily Brontë's apocalyptic lyrics. And yet she is a poet of majestic and permanent genius, with a stance unlike any other elegist of erotic sorrow. Her touch is invariably very light, her voice pitched low, but disturbingly felt. And, though very rarely, she can be ecstatic and celebratory, and we gladly help her celebrate "A Birthday":

> My heart is like a singing bird
>   Whose nest is in a watered shoot:
> My heart is like an apple-tree
>   Whose boughs are bent with thickset fruit;
> My heart is like a rainbow shell
>   That paddles in a halcyon sea;
> My heart is gladder than all these
>   Because my love is come to me.
>
> Raise me a dais of silk and down;
>   Hang it with vair and purple dyes;
> Carve it in doves and pomegranates,
>   And peacocks with a hundred eyes;
> Work it in gold and silver grapes,
>   In leaves and silver fleur-de-lys;
> Because the birthday of my life
>   Is come, my love is come to me.

DANTE GABRIEL ROSSETTI
(1828–1882)

CHRISTINA ROSSETTI
(1830–1894)

CHRISTINA ROSSETTI, A POET OF GENIUS by any standards, remains in many ways an enigma. An Anglo-Catholic devotional writer, original and in some regards esoteric, she does not assimilate easily to the methods and aims of what now regards itself as feminist literary criticism, and which finds in her "the aesthetics of renunciation." The poetry of renunciation in fact need not be either religious or feminine: its major exemplar was the pagan Goethe. A pagan closer up was Christina's remarkable older brother, the poet-painter Dante Gabriel Rossetti, whose intense erotomania provided ample provocation to his sister's ultimate rejection of what our culture still exalts as "romantic love."

Dante Gabriel Rossetti's painting may be regarded as a question of taste; his poetry now enjoys less critical reputation than his sister's, but time will alter that, since the power of his best work transcends fashion, whereas the paintings, for the larger part, may indeed be period pieces. I bring brother and sister together here because they illuminate each other, and the family resemblances (and differences) of genius have their own value and fascination. Elsewhere in this book I juxtapose the James brothers, and two of the Brontë sisters, but neither of these comparisons seem to me so potentially fecund as reading, side by side, the erotic poems of Dante Gabriel Rossetti and the poems of his sister, in their own way sometimes erotic, but always with a difference.

Despite some surface impressions, both Rossettis are difficult poets. Close reading nowadays becomes more problematic: there are few who want to (or can) teach it, and a visually oriented generation is reluctant to learn. Christina (I will use first names so as to stop repeating "Rossetti") is at her strongest when she dissolves all differences between poetry sacred and secular:

Passing away, saith the World, passing away:
Chances, beauty, and youth, sapped day by day:

Thy life never continueth in one stay.
Is the eye waxen dim, is the dark hair changing to grey
That hath won neither laurel nor bay?
I shall clothe myself in Spring and bud in May:
Thou, root-stricken, shalt not rebuild thy decay
On my bosom for aye.
Then I answered: Yea.

Passing away, saith my Soul, passing away:
With its burden of fear and hope, of labour and play,
Hearken what the past doth witness and say:
Rust in thy gold, a moth is in thine array,
A canker is in thy bud, thy leaf must decay.
A midnight, at cockcrow, at morning, one certain day
Lo the Bridegroom shall come and shall not delay;
Watch thou and pray.
Then I answered: Yea.

Passing away, saith my God, passing away:
Winter passeth after the long delay:
New grapes on the vine, new figs on the tender spray,
Turtle calleth turtle in Heaven's May.
Though I tarry, wait for Me, trust Me, watch and pray:
Arise, come away, night is past and lo it is day,
My love, My sister, My spouse, thou shalt hear Me say.
Then I answered: Yea.

This was printed as the third of "Old and New Year Ditties," but it far surpasses the first two. One hesitates to call Christina a mystic, another John of
the Cross or Teresa, because her obsessive emphasis, like Dante Gabriel's,
lingers always on the Inferno of sexual love. Despite her biographers, she has
largely kept her secrets. We know little about her "love life," an oxymoron for
most people, and particularly for her older brother. She declined at least two
marriage proposals, supposedly from religious scruples, but I suspect her pride
and independence determined her single status, her vision of herself as a
writer. Her later religious prose works won her a substantial audience, evidently of women readers. "Passing Away" (to call it that) is a highly personal
poem, written as a superb farewell to the poet's twenties, and on the last day
of the decade of the 1850s. You can chant "Passing Away" aloud many times
(as I recommend) before you notice Christina's artistry in sustaining this

,twenty-eight-line lyric upon one rhyme. There is also the subtle effect of the final stanza's omission of an ending couplet in favor of what then becomes a refrain: "Then I answered: Yea." In the movement from "day by day" through "one certain day" to "and lo it is day," an ecstatic triumphalism emerges, since the day when the poet ceases (in popular view) to be a young woman is also the transfiguring turn away from worldliness. In 1860, Christina had "won neither laurel nor bay," and she cared intensely about her poetical reputation, a care set aside by her beautiful employment of Christ's parable of the wise and foolish virgins: "Watch therefore, for ye know neither the day nor the hour whereon the Son of man cometh." Most of the final stanza plays upon the Song of Solomon:

> For, lo, the winter is past, the rain is over and gone; the flowers appear upon the earth; the time of the singing of birds is come, and the voice of the turtle is heard in our land . . . Arise, my love, my fair one, and come away.

Christina's mode of difficulty, her highly individual fusion of sacred and secular, is very unlike her brother's more "Pre-Raphaelite" kind of difficulty. "Pre-Raphaelite," a confusing term from the start, is best thought of as another wave of Romanticism, the transition from the influence of Keats upon Tennyson, and Shelley upon Browning, to the advent of Aestheticism, of Walter Pater and Oscar Wilde. Dante Gabriel Rossetti, who has to be *the* Pre-Raphaelite poet proper, is endlessly a poetic paradox. Affirmative of his own highly authentic sensualism—Elizabeth Siddal, Fanny Cornforth, Annie Miller, Mrs. William Morris (Jane Burden)—he nevertheless writes a poetry that rejects nature for what has to be called phantasmagoria. Throughout his major sonnet sequence, *The House of Life*, we cannot tell if we are being stationed in remembered natural scenes, or in an unnaturally luxurious Hell, oppressive and fantastic, and illustrative of no morally or religiously sanctioned scheme of judgment:

> Of Adam's first wife, Lilith, it is told
> (The witch he loved before the gift of Eve,)
> That, ere the snake's, her sweet tongue could deceive,
> And her enchanted hair was the first gold.
> And still she sits, young while the earth is old,
> And, subtly of herself contemplative,
> Draws men to watch the bright web she can weave,
> Till heart and body and life are in its hold.

The rose and poppy are her flower; for where
Is he not found, O Lilith, whom shed scent
And soft-shed kisses and soft sleep shall snare?
Lo! as that youth's eyes burned at thine, so went
Thy spell through him, and left his straight neck bent
And round his heart one strangling golden hair.

This is a description of Rossetti's painting of Fanny Cornforth as Lilith, Adam's first wife, who abandoned him (according to the Kabbalah) because she disdained the missionary posture in sexual intercourse. The art historian George Hersey mordantly comments upon Rossetti's later portraits of women, painted after the suicide of his wife, Elizabeth (Lizzie) Siddal:

In features and physique these later women are as different from Lizzie as they are like each other—thick powerful succulent snake-goddesses rather than wasted virgins. Yet the women in these pictures are dead—stiff and staring for all their plump sensuousness. Wreathed in blossoms, bedded in shallow spaces, their loose fingers clasping the tokens such women might well take with them to the tomb, they resemble gorgeous corpses lying in open coffins.

Lilith's bright web is her yellow hair, a strangling snake for the fetish-idolatrous Dante Gabriel. By inverse routes, brother and sister attain to the same vision of sexual fulfillment: death-in-life, or Hell. Both poets share the unhappy conviction that all love between women and men is founded upon mutual betrayal, hardly a Romantic notion. What kind of idea is it, though? It hardly seems to be renunciation, whether in the desperate Dante Gabriel or the contemplative Christina. Neither of them is sado-masochistic, though Christina's *Goblin Market* and "From House to Home" have been so interpreted, and few poems are so extreme as Dante Gabriel's frightening "fragment" called "The Orchard-Pit":

Piled deep below the screening apple branch
They lie with bitter apples in their hands:
And some are only ancient bones that blanch,
And some had ships that last year's wind did launch,
And some were yesterday the lords of lands.

In the soft dell, among the apple-trees,
High up above the hidden pit she stands,

And there for ever sings, who gave to these,
That lie below, her magic hour of ease,
And those her apples holden in their hands.

This in my dreams is shown me; and her hair
Crosses my lips and draws my burning breath;
Her song spreads golden wings upon the air,
Life's eyes are gleaming from her forehead fair,
And from her breasts the ravishing eyes of Death.

Men say to me that sleep hath many dreams,
Yet I knew never but this dream alone:
There, from a dried-up channel, once the stream's,
The glen slopes up; even such in sleep it seems
As to my waking sight the place well known.

My love I call her, and she loves me well:
But I love her as in the maelstrom's cup
The whirled stone loves the leaf inseparable
That clings to it round all the circling swell,
And that the same last eddy swallows up.

Few extended, adulterous love affairs can have been quite as excruciat-
ing, for all concerned, as that between Dante Gabriel and Jane Burden Morris, who appears in this fragment as Proserpina, queen of Hell, a vampire far
outshining Bram Stoker's brides of Dracula. As is almost always true in
Dante Gabriel's poetry, "The Orchard-Pit" is subtly and deliberately *thought
through.* For so sensationally bitter an erotic poem, it is chillingly lucid in its
indictment of Jane Burden, a formidable personality. What Christina
thought of all this, we cannot know, but her own vision of the Hell of Eros
is quite different. Critics rightly point out that there are no human males
in *Goblin Market*—only male goblins.

It is very peculiar that both Rossettis now strike many unthinking readers as rather tame, since both sister and brother frighten me as poets, the
more I ponder them. Christina would not yield to Dante Gabriel's self-
destructiveness: the quality of her Christian faith, severely intellectualized,
saved her. And yet it is not an easy faith to comprehend, whatever your own
beliefs or skepticisms. Here is her extraordinary "Up-Hill," a poem I loved,
but misunderstood, for many years:

Does the road wind up-hill all the way?
Yes, to the very end.
Will the day's journey take the whole long day?
From morn to night, my friend.

But is there for the night a resting-place?
A roof for when the slow dark hours begin.
May not the darkness hide it from my face?
You cannot miss that inn.

Shall I meet other wayfarers at night?
Those who have gone before.
Then must I knock, or call when just in sight?
They will not keep you standing at that door.

Shall I find comfort, travel-sore and weak?
Of labour you shall find the sum.
Will there be beds for me and all who seek?
Yea, beds for all who come.

Jerome McGann first noted the apparent oddness of these two final lines, which can seem a grotesque parody of Christian hope, until you realize—as he shows—that Christina adheres to the strange Adventist doctrine of "Soul Sleep." What happens to the Christian's soul between the moment of her death and the Great Advent of Christ's Second Coming? Does the soul go directly to a Last Judgment, and then wait patiently in Paradise for a Resurrected Body to join it? Or does it sleep a long sleep until at Millennium it wakes up forever? Christina firmly adhered to the latter view, a conviction that governs not only "Up-Hill," but a considerable number of her more interesting poems.

I depart (with gratitude) from McGann's deeply informed historicism to surmise that "Soul Sleep" allowed Christina to hope that her charismatic but self-destructive older brother would yet escape his erotic inferno in the vast slumber before his own resurrection. Her final devotional book, *The Face of the Deep* (1892), is the least judgmental commentary upon the Apocalypse of Saint John the Divine that I have ever read. I give the last word here to her charming memoir "The House of Dante Gabriel Rossetti," also published in 1892, two years before her own death. She recalls the marvelous assemblage of friends and creatures who surrounded her brother in his home on Cheyne Walk in London, ranging from Algernon Swinburne and George Meredith to an owl named Bobby and a wombat called McGregor, and beholds them all as a vision by Lewis Carroll:

> With such inhabitants, Tudor House and its grounds became a sort of wonderland, and once the author of *Wonderland* photographed us in the garden.

It is a comfort to think back to that moment, in the autumn of 1863, when the Reverend Charles Dodgson photographed the Rossettis and the menagerie in Dante Gabriel's garden. After so much erotic travail, one wants to think of Alice, and the Snark.

Frontispiece 54:

WALTER PATER

But the genius of which Botticelli is the type usurps the data before it as the exponent of ideas, moods, visions of its own . . .

But he is far enough from accepting the conventional orthodoxy of Dante which, referring all human action to the simple formula of purgatory, heaven and hell, leaves an insoluble element of prose in the depths of Dante's poetry . . .

One picture of his . . . represented the human race as an incarnation of those angels who, in the revolt of Lucifer, were neither for Jehovah nor for His enemies . . .

. . . the peculiar sentiment with which he infuses his profane and sacred persons, comely, and in a certain sense like angels, but with a sense of displacement or loss about them—the wistfulness of exiles . . .

So just what Dante scorns as unworthy alike of heaven and hell, Botticelli accepts, that middle world in which men take no side in great conflicts, and decide no great causes, and make great refusals.

Walter Pater's essay on Sandro Botticelli in *The Renaissance* doubtless is more of a spiritual and aesthetic self-portrait than it is a portrayal of Botticelli. Pater's vision in *The Renaissance*, like Yeats's after him, is of a supposedly lost Unity of Being, discovered again in the Italian Renaissance, and then adumbrated in British Romanticism, which saw itself as a renaissance of the Elizabethan Renaissance of Shakespeare and his contemporaries. There is a hint of Pater's program of saving aesthetic sensation from British Victorian morality and religion in the epigraph to *The Renaissance:*

Though ye have lain among the pots, yet shall ye be as the wings of a dove covered with silver, and her feathers with yellow gold.

—Psalm 68:13

Henry James knew his Bible, but Pater's subversive use of this eloquent prophecy may have affected James's choice of his title *The Wings of the Dove.* Pater's genius was one of hesitant, evasive insinuation, which nevertheless helped bring about the separation of aesthetic experience and the moral shibboleths of Victorian culture. The greatness of Pater is his secularization of the religious epiphany, a displacement in which so many were to be his heirs: Wilde, Yeats, Joyce, Virginia Woolf, and perhaps all the High Modernists.

WALTER PATER
(1839–1894)

A. C. BENSON, IN A BRIEF LITERARY LIFE, *Walter Pater* (1906), helped carry forward the oral tradition concerning the reclusive Oxford don. I treasure always the vision of the sublime Walter Pater walking the Oxford meadows in the cool of the evening, while murmuring that the exquisite odor of the meadow-sweet gave him pain: "It is the fault of nature, in England, that she runs too much to excess." With this I associate another delicious murmur: "I wish they would not call me a hedonist. It gives such a wrong impression to these who do not know Greek."

Hedonism, which identifies the pleasant with the good, is founded upon the Greek word for "pleasure," and has acquired the aura of sensation-seeking for its own sake. Pater knew that he could not give "hedonism" a good name, and was rather baffled when "aesthete" also achieved a bad eminence, in Gilbert and Sullivan's *Patience* and everywhere after that. Our modern use of "aesthetic" is Paterian in origin, going back to his speaking of the "aesthetic critic" in the preface to his most famous book, *The Renaissance* (1873), and his calling Dante Gabriel Rossetti's and William Morris's work, "aesthetic poetry," in *Appreciations* (1889). We forget what Pater tried to teach us: the Greek *aisthetes* is "one who perceives." The "aesthetic critic" simply is the good or perceptive critic, and the "aesthetic poetry" is the best, most authentic poetry of one's own moment.

Pater is identified forever with what is called the Aesthetic movement in England (roughly 1870 to 1900): the expatriate American painter James Whistler, the poet Swinburne, and Pater's followers, who included Oscar Wilde, Aubrey Beardsley, and William Butler Yeats. But Pater's influence, being sinuous and perpetual, is difficult to chart. Yeats as well as James Joyce acknowledged it, but it pervades Virginia Woolf, Eliot, and Pound, who deprecated Pater, and is strong in Wallace Stevens and Hart Crane. Perry Meisel, in his *The Cowboy and the Dandy: Crossing Over from Romanticism to Rock and Roll* (1999), persuasively ascribes to Pater the crucial formulation of the "psychedelic sublime," familiar to all of us from the later 1960s until now.

In the notorious "Conclusion" to *The Renaissance,* omitted in the book's second edition, and restored in the third (but with a softening of its anti-

Christian implications), Pater's psychedelic sublime is enhanced by the haunting prose cadences that express it, in the elaborate, hesitant, self-conscious baroque style of reverie that Yeats imitated so beautifully in *Per Amica Silentia Lunae*. Here is the genius of Walter Pater at its most insinuating:

> Or if we begin with the inward world of thought and feeling, the whirlpool is still more rapid, the flame more eager and devouring. There it is no longer the gradual darkening of the eye and fading of colour from the wall,—the movement of the shore-side, where the water flows down indeed, though in apparent rest—but the race of the mid-stream, a drift of momentary acts of sight and passion and thought. At first sight experience seems to bury us under a flood of external objects, pressing upon us with a sharp and importunate reality, calling us out of ourselves in a thousand forms of action. But when reflexion begins to play upon these objects they are dissipated under its influence; the cohesive force seems suspended like a trick of magic; each object is loosed into a group of impressions—colour, odour, texture—in the mind of the observer. And if we continue to dwell in thought on this world, not of objects in the solidity with which language invests them, but of impressions unstable, flickering, inconsistent, which burn and are extinguished with our consciousness of them, it contracts still further; the whole scope of observation is dwarfed into the narrow chamber of the individual mind. Experience, already reduced to a swarm of impressions, is ringed round for each one of us by that thick wall of personality through which no real voice has ever pierced on its way to us, or from us to that which we can only conjecture to be without. Every one of those impressions is the impression of the individual in his isolation, each mind keeping as a solitary prisoner its own dream of a world. Analysis goes a step farther still, and assures us that those impressions of the individual mind to which, for each one of us, experience dwindles down, are in perpetual flight; that each of them is limited by time, and that as time is infinitely divisible, each of them is infinitely divisible also; all that is actual in it being a single moment, gone while we try to apprehend it, of which it may ever be more truly said that it has ceased to be than that it is. To such a tremulous wisp constantly re-forming itself on the stream, to a single sharp impression, with a sense in it, a relic more or less fleeting, of such moments gone by, what is real in our life fines itself down. It is with this movement, with the passage and dissolution of impressions, images, sensations, that analysis leaves off—that con-

tinual vanishing away, that strange, perpetual weaving and unweaving of ourselves.

The coherence of our individual consciousness is an assertion against the flux of sensations: otherwise we would dissolve in an indifferent ecstasy. Yet such coherence is a kind of habit we adopt in order to establish a continuous self: our identity is a desperate fiction. Pater, a Lucretian materialist, dangerously urges ecstasy over identity, in a further rhapsody:

> Every moment some form grows perfect in hand or face; some tone on the hills or the sea is choicer than the rest; some mood of passion or insight or intellectual excitement is irresistibly real and attractive for us,—for that moment only . . .
>
> Not the fruit of experience, but experience itself, is the end. A counted number of pulses only is given to us of a variegated, dramatic life. How may we see in them all that is to seen in them by the finest senses? How shall we pass most swiftly from point to point, and be present always at the focus where the greatest number of vital forces unite in their purest energy?
>
> To burn always with this hard, gem-like flame, to maintain this ecstasy, is success in life . . . While all melts under our feet, we may well catch at any exquisite passion, or any contribution to knowledge that seems by a lifted horizon to set the spirit free for a moment, or any stirring of the senses, strange dyes, strange colours, and curious odours, or work of the artist's hands, or the face of one's friend. Not to discriminate every moment some passionate attitude in those about us, and in the brilliancy of their gifts some tragic dividing of forces on their ways is, on this short day of frost and sun, to sleep before evening.

That "hard, gem-like flame" is the principle of fire in the dark Heraclitus: life's essence. We are listening to an aesthetic sermon, but a sermon nevertheless: the religion of art is brought to its birth, a religion that denies immortality, and offers only the ecstasy of what passes:

> we have an interval, and then our place knows us no more . . . our one chance lies in expanding that interval, in getting as many pulsations as possible into the given time.

Like Yeats after him, Pater was fascinated by Blake's "pulsation of an artery . . . in which the poet's work is done." Pater is very close here to what the more occult Yeats will call the Condition of Fire, but to the Epicurean Pater, the occult made no appeal. Both men sought the daemonic moment, when the privilege of genius would burn away apparent surfaces, and reveal the crystal of perfect form, of inevitable expression. Style, for Pater, is the test for perception, and commits him to the aesthetics of the single sentence, however prolonged or elaborated.

And yet a poem or any other literary work is for Pater a *person*, a crystal man or woman forever revealed. His critical genius, out of fashion in our own self-ruined academies of instruction, is most useful now, in my judgment, when he prepares us to meet persons, whether in Shakespeare or in Flaubert. His outrageous reverie or prose poem on Leonardo's Mona Lisa still works magnificently because we certainly meet a person, though she is clearly closer to Dante Gabriel Rossetti's Jane Burden Morris or Yeats's Maud Gonne (as seen by these passionate poets) than to Leonardo's portrait:

The presence that thus rose so strangely beside the waters, is expressive of what in the ways of a thousand years men had come to desire. Hers is the head upon which all "the ends of the world are come," and the eyelids are a little weary. It is a beauty wrought out from within upon the flesh, the deposit, little cell by cell, of strange thoughts and fantastic reveries and exquisite passions. Set it for a moment beside one of those white Greek goddesses or beautiful women of antiquity, and how would they be troubled by this beauty, into which the soul with all its maladies has passed! All the thoughts and experience of the world have etched and molded there, in that which they have of power to refine and make expressive the outward form, the animalism of Greece, the lust of Rome, the reverie of the Middle Ages with its spiritual ambition and imaginative loves, the return of the Pagan world, the sins of the Borgias. She is older than the rocks among which she sits; like the vampire, she has been dead many times, and learned the secrets of the grave; and has been a diver in deep seas, and keeps their fallen day about her; and trafficked for strange webs with Eastern merchants: and, as Leda, was the mother of Helen of Troy, and, as Saint Anne, the mother of Mary; and all this has been to her but as the sound of lyres and flutes, and lives only in the delicacy with which it has molded the changing lineaments, and tinged the eyelids and the hands. The fancy of a perpetual life, sweeping together ten thousand experiences, is an old one; and modern thought has conceived the idea of humanity as wrought upon by, and summing up in itself, all modes of thought and life. Certainly Lady Lisa might stand as the embodiment of the old fancy, the symbol of the modern idea.

In First Corinthians 10:11, Saint Paul warns us against idolatry:

Now all these things happened unto them for ensamples: and they are written for our admonition, upon whom the ends of the world are come.

If Lady Lisa's eyelids are a little weary, the Pauline judgment itself has only an ironic effect upon her, for she subverts Christian categories of moral judgment. Freud saw, in the Mona Lisa, Leonardo's defense against his overwhelming love for his mother, by way of identifying with her totally, and so loving boys in his own image, even as she had loved him. Pater's homoeroticism is never explicit, yet he clearly both desires and dreads his muse (his own mother had died when he was fourteen), in this, the greatest of his epiphanies, a privileged moment of confronting a goddess. Yeats shrewdly said that Pater's Lisa incarnates the doctrine that "the individual is nothing," hardly a comfort to a Romantic poet. But then this goddess is a vampire, hardly a consolation to anyone whatsoever. Something that mocks Pater breaks away from him in this vision: are we to assume that this is the goddess of aesthetic experience?

In his discussion of Plato's genius, Pater isolates again the relationship between knowledge and personality:

For him, truly (as he supposed the highest sort of knowledge must of necessity be) all knowledge was like knowing a *person*. The Dialogue itself, being as it is, the special creation of his literary art, becomes in his hands, and by his masterly conduct of it, like a single living person.

Walter Pater summed up Romantic tradition in what he knew had become Charles Darwin's world. Like his disciple who is writing this book, Pater distrusted all historicisms, which can explain everything except individual genius. It has become the world of the genome, and perhaps we can be engineered away from many of our sorrows; perhaps not. Pater teaches perceptiveness; perhaps genetic engineering will augment other modes of perceptiveness, and perhaps not. His value, at least for the time being, continues to dwell in his vision of literary genius, or the unique perception of unique persons.

HUGO VON HOFMANNSTHAL

DOCTOR. How do you feel, Your Majesty? You give me cause for new hope.

SIGISMUND. Abandon it. I am far too well to hope.

—*The Tower*

(translated by Michael Hamburger)

T. S. Eliot admired *The Tower* more than any of Hofmannsthal's other plays, saying of this prose play that it was essentially poetic drama. From 1918 to 1927, Hofmannsthal reworked this drama, which he had begun in 1902 as an adaptation of the Spanish baroque playwright Calderón's *Life Is a Dream*. There are two final, alternative versions of *The Tower*, the first being the more visionary and truer to Hofmannsthal's divided and complex consciousness.

Hofmannsthal abandoned lyric poetry, for which his genius was absolute, and attempted to become the great dramatist of Vienna in its post–World War I decline. It is an unhappy irony that Hofmannsthal's permanent fame should be as the librettist for Richard Strauss, particularly in *Der Rosen-kavalier.* Freud, the moral essayist of the twentieth century, its Montaigne, transcended his Vienna. Hofmannsthal, whose genius indeed was transcendental, is remembered now as a rococo survivor, which is absurdly unfair.

Hofmannsthal hardly can be dismissed, or relegated to Straussian entertainment, because his quest from aestheticism to a Christianized Neoplatonism is a paradigm for much of twentieth-century Western literature. His affinities with T. S. Eliot were crucial, but I tend to prefer him to Eliot, Hofmannsthal being the more universal imagination. He incarnated the death of an old culture—imperial Vienna—and refused any ideology in its place. I prefer him to Bertolt Brecht's Marxist reductiveness. Besides, though Hofmannsthal adapted freely, he wrote his own adaptations. Increasing evidence indicates that Brecht's authentic plagiarisms were from the devoted women of genius clustered around him, from whom he stole most of the brand name we call "Brecht."

HUGO VON HOFMANNSTHAL
(1874–1929)

HOFMANNSTHAL IS DEEPLY ENJOYED BY tens of thousands of operagoers who know him only as Richard Strauss's librettist, particularly in *Der Rosenkavalier* (1911). It is a curious fate for a genius as bewildering as Hofmannsthal's: poet, dramatist, essayist, storyteller, above all a writer who attempted to live in literature but outside existing conceptions of it. Hofmannsthal is central to the Austro-Hungarian Empire culture that was in crisis long before the end of the Habsburg state in 1918. Since that Viennese lost culture was scandalously fecund in its final phase, it endlessly engages critics and historians. Its writers included Freud, Hofmannsthal, Rilke, Stefan George, Musil, Schnitzler, and Broch, while its composers were Bruckner, Mahler, Schönberg, Alban Berg, Webern. If you add Adolf Loos and Otto Wagner in architecture, and Kokoschka, Schiele, and Klimt as painters, and conclude with the Vienna Circle and Wittgenstein in philosophy, it begins to seem excessive, though I have omitted important writers, quite aside from the Dante of that era, Franz Kafka, in Prague. My distaste for cultural politics is frankly based upon the poverty of Western culture from 1965 to 2000: why bother to explain literature by society when both are so adulterated by aggressive ignorance and its resentful ideologues? Vienna 1880–1918 is a different matter; and yet is now as remote as Alexandria in the second century of the Common Era, another rich culture that it strikingly resembles.

An excellent book, *Fin-de-Siècle Vienna: Politics and Culture*, by Carl E. Schorske (1980), locates Hofmannsthal in his age, and I recommend it strongly to my readers. My own concern, as always, is narrower: how to define the uniqueness of Hofmannsthal's genius? If to some considerable extent it were not, like that of Freud or Kafka, above and beyond the age, it would matter no longer, except to scholars. There is a substance in Hofmannsthal that prevails, and he ought to matter to literate readers, as well as to the lovers of Richard Strauss's operas. In English, Hofmannsthal is best available in the three-volume *Selected Writings: Selected Prose* (1952), *Poems and Verse Plays* (1961), and *Selected Plays and Libretti* (1963). There are also Hermann Broch's ambivalent but strong study *Hugo von Hofmannsthal and His Time*, translated by Michael Steinberg, and Michael Hamburger's fine introductions in the *Selected Writings* volumes.

A reader ought to begin with Hofmannsthal's prose, particularly the famous "Letter of Lord Chandos" (1902), written when the poet was about twenty-six or -seven, about two years after he abandoned the composition of lyric poetry, almost all of it of the highest quality. Lord Chandos is an imaginary young Elizabethan poet-nobleman, who is also two years in retreat from literature, and he writes his older friend, the philosopher-statesman Francis Bacon, to explain his silence:

> I felt, with a certainty not entirely bereft of a feeling of sorrow, that neither in the coming year nor in the following nor in all the years of this my life shall I write a book, whether in English or in Latin: and this for an odd and embarrassing reason which I must leave to the boundless superiority of your mind to place in the realm of physical and spiritual values spread out harmoniously before your unprejudiced eye: to wit, because the language in which I might be able not only to write but to think is neither Latin nor English, neither Italian nor Spanish, but a language none of whose words is known to me, a language in which inanimate things speak to me.
>
> (translated by Tania and James Stern)

John Ruskin had defined a poet as "a man to whom things speak," and Chandos/Hofmannsthal aspires to that impossible condition. Chandos, half-mad, gives up literature; Hofmannsthal, cool and rational, yields up lyric poetry, but only for narrative, drama, prose meditation. Still, there was a loss; when I think of Hofmannsthal I remember first his haunting "Ballad of the Outer Life," as rendered here beautifully by Michael Hamburger:

> And children grow with deeply wondering eyes
> That know of nothing, grow a while and die,
> And every one of us goes his own way.
>
> And bitter fruit will sweeten by and by
> And like dead birds come hurtling down at night
> And for a few days fester where they lie.
>
> And always the wind blows, and we recite
> And hear again the phrases thin with wear
> And in our limbs feel languor or delight.

And roads run through the grass, and here and there
Are places full of lights and pools and trees,
And some are threatening, some are cold and bare . . .

To what end were they built? With differences
No less innumerable than their names?
Why laughter now, now weeping or disease?

What does it profit us, and all these games,
Who, great and lonely, ever shall be so
And though we always wander seek no aims?

To see such things do travelers leave their homes?
Yet he says much who utters "evening,"
A word from which grave thought and sadness flow

Like rich dark honey from the hollow combs.

Hamburger precisely notes that these exquisite lines are written "from the point of view of a man roused from his dream," which echoes Henry V's rejection of Falstaff: "But, being awak'd, I do despise my dream." One thinks (as presumably the erudite Hofmannsthal did) of the mystic Meister Eckhart's lament: "We are all asleep in the outer life." The inanimate things do not speak to us, but how Ruskin and Walter Pater would have loved this poem! At sixteen or seventeen, the baby-poet Hofmannsthal had already transcended the Aesthetic mode, but with a power and plangency still in that mode that surpassed any of his older contemporaries, whether German or French or English.

In his retreat from lyric, Hofmannsthal turned to Browning's dramatic monologues, thus foreshadowing a similar development in Ezra Pound and T. S. Eliot, though for Hofmannsthal the monologue was a way-station on his journey to his major achievement, drama. Whether in verse or prose, Hofmannsthal's dramas remain poems, deliberately in the tradition of the Spanish Golden Age playwright Calderón.

Rather like Goethe before him, Hofmannsthal was too wise to emulate Shakespeare: both the German and the Austrian poet had every literary gift except the prime Shakespearean mystery of creating persons rather than masks. When you read or attend Hofmannsthal, you confront an art of gesture rather than of personalities. Hofmannsthal assimilated actors to dancers: how they spoke was secondary to how they moved. Personality, for

Hofmannsthal, had to be universal and not idiosyncratic. Shakespeare had the wisdom to see otherwise: Hamlet, Falstaff, Cleopatra, Iago are of universal and permanent interest because they are absolute individuals. In fleeing the lyric assertion of a self, Hofmannsthal lost too much, as *The Tower* and *The Difficult Man*—his major plays—reveal. If we and the world are not different things, and the self is only a metaphor, then the dramatic autonomy of Hamlet and of Falstaff would be impossible. Shakespeare's genius participated in the irrationality of the cosmos, and yet peopled the stage with men and with women, which Hofmannsthal never quite does. To believe, as Hofmannsthal (and his Lord Chandos) did, that no aesthetic mode could sustain individual representations, is to forget Shakespeare (of whom Hofmannsthal in fact was highly aware).

The novelist Hofmannsthal admired most was Balzac, whom the poet called "a vast, indescribably substantial imagination, the greatest, most substantially creative imagination since Shakespeare." Balzac, Hofmannsthal asserts, is more immediate, more available than Shakespeare and Goethe: it is "the most complete and multi-articulated hallucination that ever existed." That is a proper introduction to Hofmannsthal's dialogue "On Characters in Novels and Plays," which he subtitles, "An imaginary conversation between Balzac and Hammer-Purgstall, the Orientalist, in a garden near Vienna, 1842," written just after the "Chandos" letter. When Hammer urges Balzac to write for the stage, the novelist replies that "I don't believe that characters exist. Shakespeare believed it. He was a dramatist."

In contrast, this Balzac links himself to Goethe, as wizards who create demons and call them characters. Hofmannsthal, in most of his plays, is a third such wizard. He creates obsessives, ideas, and madnesses, since language and individuality could not be reconciled. It is an unhappy irony that a genius so comprehensive, who should have become another Goethe, is doomed to survive primarily as Richard Strauss's librettist, as though he were Mozart's Lorenzo da Ponte, an estimable figure but no Goethe: Hofmannsthal abandoned his lyric genius, and left his promising novel, *Andreas*, as a fragment. He wrote a few short stories, one of which, "A Tale of the Cavalry," is worthy of Kleist or Kafka. The essays are frequently brilliant, as parts of a world. I come to believe that Hofmannsthal, in giving up lyric and narrative for the theater, wounded his own genius. Ibsen and Pirandello, Brecht and Beckett, hold the theater: you encounter Hofmannsthal there only in Straussian opera. As a dramatist, Hofmannsthal is on the periphery, with Yeats, Claudel, and Eliot.

And yet Hofmannsthal, on a drastically different scale, does not differ from Goethe in kind. Hamburger justly links the two writers in their project:

> to extend an essentially personal and esoteric vision to the most diverse spheres, to cut across established divisions and specializations, to make connections everywhere, and produce not only works, but a literature.

There is an implicit sadness in that comparison, as we begin the twenty-first century with realistic doubts that any one writer ever again will be able to produce a literature.

LUSTRE 12

|

Victor Hugo, Gérard de Nerval, Charles Baudelaire, Arthur Rimbaud, Paul Valéry

|

The major French Romantic poets form a very different Lustre of *Tiferet*. Victor Hugo is now best known as a novelist, but he is *the* poet proper of French literature, the most ambitious. Like Balzac, indeed rather more so, Victor Hugo can seem more a demiurge or minor god than a human, so prodigal were his creative energies.

The Romantic Gnostic Nerval can seem, like Hugo, more at home in the visionary company of Blake and Shelley than in French poetic tradition, which attained a dark epiphany in Baudelaire, frequently judged as the first "modern" poet, a role more precisely filled by the adolescent Arthur Rimbaud, who abandoned literature (in considerable disgust) for a career of adventuring in Africa.

Paul Valéry, the disciple of the poet Stephane Mallarmé, was the most intelligent and accomplished person of letters in twentieth-century France. That may understate Valéry's centrality in modern poetry, where his presence helps place for us such eminent admirers of his work as Rilke, Eliot, and Stevens.

VICTOR HUGO

Well, may at least this book, this somber message, reach
The silence as a murmur
The shore as a wave! May it fall there—sigh or love-tear!
May it enter the grave where youth, dawn, kisses,
Dew, the laughter of the bride,
Radiance and joy have already gone—and my heart along with them:
Indeed, that has never come back! And may it be
A song of mourning, the cry of a hope that can never tell lies,
The sound of a pale farewell in tears, a dream whose wing
We feel brushing against us lightly! May she say:
"Someone is out there—I can hear a noise!"
May it sound in her darkness like the footstep of my soul!

                    —"To the One Who Stayed in France"
                    (translated by E. H and A. M. Blackmore)

In 1843, Hugo's nineteen-year-old daughter Léopoldine drowned, with her husband, in a boating accident. In 1851, Hugo fled into exile, defying Napoleon III, and taking up residence in the Channel Islands (part of England), where he remained until the revolution against Napoleon III in 1870. *Châtiments* (*Chastisements*), a volume of ferocious invectives against the emperor, appeared in 1853, to be followed by the belated laments for Léopoldine, the *Contemplations* of 1856, which concludes with "To the One Who Stayed in France," a major elegy and one of Hugo's grandest poems, representative of his genius.

It is difficult for the titanic Victor Hugo to subdue himself, and it is very poignant that he accomplishes so extraordinary a renunciation here. Unable to continue his annual visits to his daughter's grave, the exile offers his book as surrogate, and asks only a minimal favor of the visionary world; some hope that in her eternal rest his daughter somehow will receive "this strange gift of the Exile to the Dead!"

VICTOR HUGO
(1802–1885)

CONFRONTED BY THE GENIUS OF VICTOR Hugo, a man who accurately believed himself to be Victor Hugo, a critic trying to apprehend genius hardly knows how or where to begin. Balzac's energetic assault upon literary immortality seems a rugged but auxiliary onrush when juxtaposed to Victor Hugo's, though Hugo, three years younger than Balzac, survived him by thirty-five years, so the comparison may be unjust. Given another third of a century, Balzac's *Human Comedy* would have at least doubled in size, so that we would have about one hundred and eighty linked novels, novellas, and stories. And yet Victor Hugo is virtually infinite: has anyone read all of him? There are more than 155,000 lines of poetry, not counting verse dramas, and there are seven novels, twenty-one plays, and an astonishing amount of more-or-less fugitive prose, only now available.

Hugo may have been the last of the universal authors, like Cervantes, Shakespeare, and Dickens. I can think of no twentieth-century equivalent and doubt that one will appear in the twenty-first century. *Les Misérables,* which is to us a musical, was read by everyone in France who could read when it first appeared (1862). At seventy-one, I wonder what will *not* be made into a musical. Will we yet have *Hamlet: A Musical* or, still better, *King Lear: A Musical Extravaganza*? Not that Victor Hugo would be other than delighted by *his* musical, since he wanted to touch as many fellow human beings (women in particular) as he could reach.

I am going to seek Hugo's genius only in his poetry, unfashionable as it now is, particularly in France, where intelligent reading seems to have died with Paul Valéry. But I begin with Hugo's perfectly mad *William Shakespeare* (1864), which is even less about Shakespeare than D. H. Lawrence's *Study of Thomas Hardy* was about Hardy. It is a study of literary genius: Homer, the Bible, Dante, Shakespeare, but primarily Victor Hugo, heir of Shakespeare. Goethe (whom Hugo had never read) is dismissed, and Hugo declares himself to be the true abyss of genius in his era. Hugo's metaphor for genius is that it is an abyss, in the primordial sense of that Tohu and Bohu that preceded Creation in the Priestly account that opens Genesis. The Gnostics, as the esoteric Hugo evidently knew, had exalted that abyss as our Foremother and Forefather, from whom the wicked Demiurge had stolen the stuff of creation. In Kabbalah, as Hugo also knew, God forms the abyss out of himself, by withdrawing (in part) from himself. In Hugo's later poetry we are never far from the *abîme* or *gouffre*, which is both fearful and yet the hiding place of genius.

The critic Georges Poulet, in his book *The Interior Distance* (1959), vividly describes Hugo's abyss-consciousness, in commenting upon a passage in the late poem simply called *God*, published posthumously in 1891: "It is a chaos that returns to chaos and nothingness, not by deficiency but by plethora." In Poulet's judgment, Hugo's later poetry was out of control, but that underestimates Hugo's genius. *God* cannot be called a work of absolute clarity, but Hugo is very aware that he is working at a limit of expression:

I could see, far above my head, a black speck.

It came and went, like a fly on the ceiling.
The darkness was sublime.

      Man, when he thinks,
Is winged; and the abyss was drawing me
Into its night steadily more and more,
Like seaweed dragged by a mysterious tide,
Toward this black speck drifting in the depths;
I felt I was already flying off,
When I was stopped by someone telling me:

"Stay."

      At the same instant, a hand spread out.

I was already high up in the dim cloud.

And I could see a strange figure appearing:
A creature strewn with mouths and wings and eyes,
Alive, vast, almost gloomy, almost radiant.
He was in flight; some of his wings were bald.
The lashes of his fulvous eyes were flickering,
Sending out more noise than a flock of birds;
And his wings made a sound of mighty waters.
Now he resembled animal, now spirit—
Now fleshly nightmare, now apostle's vision,

Depending on which side he showed. He seemed,
In the air where my flight had overtaken him,
To be producing, now light, and now darkness.

He watched me calmly in the dismal mists.

And I sensed something in him that was human.

"Who are you then, to bar my way," I said,
"You half-seen creature shaken by these fogs?"

He answered: "I am one of the feathers of night,
The somber bird composed of clouds and light-rays,
The spread black peacock of the constellations."
                         (translated by E. H. and A. M. Blackmore)

This opens *The Threshold of the Abyss,* the introduction to *God.* Called upon
by the intrepid Hugo to identify himself, this creature asserts a variety of
names: the Human Spirit, Legion, Breath, Wind, Demos, Midst, Limit,
Center, and Reason, and adds a surprising list of human incarnations: Lu-
cian, Aristophanes, Diogenes, Swift, Rousseau, Cervantes, Voltaire—among
others. This Human Spirit is not the spirit that Denies, but the One that
Questions, and Hugo declines to answer, or to see any wonder except *Him,*
which drives the Spirit away. *God* might well have the fuller title of *God; or
the Abyss,* and is a scandalous expression of Hugo's egoistic genius. The
Blackmores, Hugo's exemplary translators, point to the visionary zest the
poet brings to the triumph of the Evil Principle, Ahriman, in part 3,
900–910:

"But Ahriman, dark-eyed, is ever waiting
Till Ohrmazd falls asleep;
And on that day, Chaos and Ill will see him
Seize in his black arms the immense-browed heavens,
Ransack all orbits, penetrate all veils,
And steal the stars from the eternal forehead;
Even in sleep, Ohrmazd will shudder horrified;
The Vast—an ox left lowing by its master
In some dark field—will wake the next day blind;
And, buried in dread space beneath the fog,
Extinguished stars will search for vanished worlds."

Ohrmazd, Zoroastrian god of Good, shudders in his sleep, and two magnificent metaphors memorably convey vastation: the Abyss (or Vast)—like
an ox left lowing by its master in a dark field that wakes up blind—is reduced to a negation. Even more vivid are those extinguished stars searching for worlds that are no longer there. John Porter Houston in his *The
Demonic Imagination* (1968) says of *God* that it demonstrates a greater audacity of metaphor than any other work of Hugo's. What John Hollander has
called Hugo's "grand tone" achieves its sublime not only in *God*, but in *The
End of Satan*, also published posthumously (1886), and in the vast cyclic
poem or sequence *The Legend of the Ages* (1859–83).

In his *William Shakespeare*, Hugo attempted to proclaim his own radical
originality as the prophet of French Romanticism:

> The nineteenth century springs only from itself; it does not receive
> an impulse from any ancestor; it is the child of an idea . . . but the
> nineteenth century has an august mother, the French Revolution.

Even as Shakespeare had no poetic father (though one might argue for
Chaucer, noting the link between the Wife of Bath and Falstaff), so Hugo,
the nineteenth century incarnate, denied any precursor except the Revolution. It is true that the Bible and Shakespeare counted for more in Hugo's
poetry than any French forerunners, at least once the early effect of
Chateaubriand rapidly wore away. Blake, Wordsworth, Coleridge, Shelley,
and Keats, turning themselves away from Pope, had the native tradition of
Spenser, Shakespeare, and Milton to sustain them, but Hugo and his contemporaries could not see themselves similarly as a renaissance of the Renaissance. Boileau could be defied by Keats, charmingly and convincingly,
but French literary culture can no more eliminate the influence of Boileau
than French thought can cease to be Cartesian, despite the tyranny of German philosophy in France since the student upheavals of the late 1960s.

I myself always recall, with amiable zest, a train ride back from Princeton to Yale that I enjoyed decades ago with the leading theoretician of Gal-
lic deconstruction. We were recent friends, had encountered one another
while lecturing separately at Princeton, and fell into cultural debate on the
train. Deploring a belated French modernism that wholly absorbed my
friend, I urged the poetic strength of Victor Hugo as against that of the
more fashionable Mallarmé. In honest amazement, my philosophic companion burst forth, "But, Harold, in France Victor Hugo is a poet read only
by schoolchildren!"

It seems safe enough to prophesy that Hugo, like Shelley, always will bury his undertakers. Hugo is a poet who in some ways fits better into Anglo-American than into French literary tradition. He is, at his strongest, a mythopoetic or visionary poet, akin to Blake and Shelley, as Swinburne first saw. Unfortunately, Hugo has nothing like Blake's conceptual power, and also he does not approximate the subtle, skeptical intellect of Shelley. Since he also lacked epic precursors in his own language, Hugo had the advantage neither of Blake's and Shelley's gifts nor of their agonistic relationship to that mortal god John Milton. Hugo had to become his own Milton, with rather mixed results, one must sadly admit, thinking of *The End of Satan* and *God*. Astonishing as those curious epics are, they lack the authority of Hugo at his strongest, in "To Albrecht Dürer" and "The Melancholy of Olympio," "Sonnez, sonnez toujours," "Boaz Asleep," "For Théophile Gautier," "Orphée," and so many others. This is the authority of a sublime directness: "Qu'il m'exauce. Je suis l'âme humaine chantant, / Et j'aime."

Whether or not table-rappings with assorted spooks sometimes helped to sabotage Hugo's eloquent directness, after 1853, is not clear to me. Séances seem to have been more benign for W. B. Yeats and James Merrill than they were for the already dangerously theomorphic Hugo. The spirits were tricky with Yeats and sometimes wicked with the urbane and kindly Merrill, but they seem to have been as thoroughly cowed by the overbearing Hugo as nearly everyone else was. Apocalyptic poetry is a dangerous genre, particularly if attempted at some length. Yeats shrewdly developed the dialectics of his eschatology in the two versions (1925, 1937) of his prose tract *A Vision* and then based apocalyptic lyrics like "The Second Coming" and "Leda and the Swan" upon the more sequestered exegetical work. Merrill, with insouciant audacity, followed Dante and Blake by incorporating his doctrinal speculations directly into *The Changing Light at Sandover.* Hugo is more puzzling, in that he never worked his preternatural revelations into a system, whether in prose or verse. Instead, he wrote titanic, fragmentary poems, that both expound and refuse to expound his cosmological imaginings. *The End of Satan, God,* and much of *The Legend of the Ages* form together the closest French equivalent to that great mode of English poetry of which *Paradise Lost* is the masterpiece, and Blake's *Four Zoas, Milton,* and *Jerusalem,* Shelley's *Prometheus Unbound,* and Keats's two *Hyperion* fragments are the grand second wave.

The End of Satan began under the title of *Satan pardonné,* which is an oxymoron, since a pardoned Satan could hardly be Satan. But there is much that is oxymoronic in the design and the rhetoric of Hugo's epic fragments. This is accomplished by a consistent parataxis, doubtless biblical in its stylistic origins, but beautifully subversive in Hugo's later rhetoric, since his syntax refuses traditional distinctions between higher and lower orders, up and down, heaven and the abyss. Here is a vision of the Archangel Winter, from *The End of Satan:*

> In the dread circle hemmed by glaciers,
> Pallid wastes where no radiant fathomers,
> Columbuses or Gamas, ever pass,
> In realms of dingy gloom and deep crevasse
> Seized from creation by nonentity,
> Beyond ice floe and berg and ice-bound sea,
> Deep in the fog that quenches every ray,
> In stone waves and rock waters, far from day,
> Amid the gloom, there, on the pole, stands black
> Archangel Winter, darkness on his back
> And trumpet at his lips; nor does he cast
> One flash of eye, or blow one clarion-blast;
> He never even dreams, being sheer snow;
> The winged winds, captives of that age-old foe
> Silence, are in his hand—birds in a snare;
> His sightless eyes horribly watch the air;
> Hoarfrost is in his bones and on his head,
> And he is swathed in ever-petrified dread;
> He terrifies the Vast, he seems so wild;
> He is harsh, dismal, ice—this is, exiled;
> The earth beneath his feet, in its dark cape,
> Is dumb; he is the mute white stony shape
> Set on that tomb in the eternal night;
> Never does any motion, sound, or light
> Brush the lone giant in that somber pall.
> But when, on the timepieces that we call
> Stars, the last day, endless and centerless,
> Will sound, then the Lord's face will luminesce
> And melt the spirit; his mouth will distend
> Suddenly, in a savage, dreadful bend,
> And the worlds—skiffs rudderless, rolling on—
> Will hear the storm-blast of his clarion.

Texture rather than architectonics is the strength of the later Hugo in verse. I remember his apocalyptic poems as individual passages or moments, not as fully achieved designs. If he was not Blake or Shelley or Keats, he remains their peer in great, isolated fragments, visions of an abyss that he had found for himself. He wrote his own elegy partly in his lament for Gautier, where he hymns the departure (though in 1872) of his own century, the Romantic nineteenth:

> We must pass; that is the law; who can escape?
> All things are declining; this glorious age with its light-rays
>   Is entering an immense shadow through which
> We pallid souls are fleeing. What a wild noise those oaks cut down
>   For Herakles' pyre are making in the dusk!
> Death's horses are starting to neigh, are joyful because
>   A brilliant era is ending; this proud age,
> Which was able to quell the opposing winds, is about to expire . . .
>   Yes, Gautier, you are leaving after your peers
> And brothers, after Dumas and Musset and Lamartine.
>   The old rejuvenating spring has dried;
> As there is no longer a Styx, neither is there a Fountain of Youth.
>   The cruel reaper advances, step by step,
> Pensively, with his broad blade, toward the last of the crop;
>   It is my turn; and gloom is filling my
> Troubled sight, as I guess what future the doves must face;
>   I weep at cradles, and I smile at graves.

The Hercules for whose pyre the great oaks are being felled so noisily is hardly Gautier, but is rather Booz (Boaz), whose eyes held light and grandeur, and who turned to God as naturally as he turned to himself, because the timelessness was already his own:

> Old men depart from time and alteration,
> To the eternal fountain they retire;
> In the eyes of the young men there is fire,
> But in the eyes of the old, illumination.

This is "Boaz Asleep" in *The Legend of the Ages,* where Boaz Hugo slumbers while Ruth, bare-breasted, wants to be joined with him, as the poem concludes, with grand erotic suggestiveness:

> While he was sleeping, Ruth, a Moabite,
> Came to his feet and, with her breast bared, lay
> Hoping for some unknown uncertain ray
> When, suddenly, they would waken into light.

Though she was near, Boaz was unaware;
And what God planned for her, Ruth couldn't tell.
Cool fragrance rose from the tufts of asphodel,
And over Galgala, night stirred the air.

The shade was a deep, nuptial, solemn thing;
Angels were flying dimly there, no doubt;
Here and there, in the night, could be made out
Some blueness that appeared to be a wing.

Boaz's breathing mingled in his rest
With muffled streams running through mossy ways.
These things occurred in Nature's gentlest days,
And every hill had lilies on its crest.

The grass was dark; he slept, and she could think;
Some flock-bells tinkled now and then by chance;
Abundant blessings fell from the expanse.
It was the peaceful hour when lions drink.

All slumbered in Jerimadeth and Ur;
The stars enameled the deep, somber sky;
Westward a slender crescent shone close by
Those flowers of night, and Ruth, without a stir,

Wondered—with parting eyelids half revealed
Beneath her veils—what stray god, as he cropped
The timeless summer, had so idly dropped
That golden sickle in the starry field.

No one has ever located Jerimadeth, a Hugolian invention, but that is all the better. The Blackmores catch remarkably the curious exquisiteness of "Boaz Asleep," a poem at once gentle and titanic. Hugo's genius, as *Les Misérables* at its best also demonstrates, is oddly both infinitely gentle and cosmologically stormy. That *sounds* improbable, but Victor Hugo was always improbable.

GÉRARD DE NERVAL

Dream is a second life. I have never been able to cross through those gates of ivory or horn which separate us from the invisible world without a sense of dread. The first few instants of sleep are the image of death; a drowsy numbness steals over our thoughts, and it becomes impossible to determine the precise point at which the *self,* in some other form, continues to carry on the work of existence. Little by little, the dim cavern is suffused with light and, emerging from its shadowy depths, the pale figures who dwell in limbo come into view, solemn and still. Then the tableau takes on shape, a new clarity illuminates these bizarre apparitions and sets them in motion—the spirit world opens for us.

(translated by Richard Sieburth)

That is the opening of *Aurélia or Dream and Life,* Nerval's version of an hallucinating *Vita Nuova,* or Dante reconceived as a French Romantic visionary always in a borderline condition between inspiration and madness. Haunted by the spectral form of his mother, dead since he was two, Nerval attempted in *Aurélia* what Richard Sieburth calls the autobiography of a madness.

Salvation for Nerval was not religious but therapeutic: he vainly attempted the impossible project of writing himself out of a condition of mental illness. He hanged himself before the publication of *Aurélia* was completed. His descent to Avernus was accomplished; he could not manage the arduous task of clambering up out of the underworld.

Nerval had never seen his mother, who died accompanying her husband, a doctor in Napoleon's army that invaded Russia. Doubtless, Nerval's spirit would have been haunted in any case, though to be motherless is an astonishing condition for anyone, let alone a visionary poet. In Wallace Stevens's great poem "The Auroras of Autumn," the toughly rational American, an insurance lawyer and rigorously controlled consciousness, sets down what Nerval would have taken to be his own truth:

Farewell to an idea . . . The mother's face,
The purpose of the poem, fills the room.

Dead at forty-six, Nerval nevertheless proved his genius by transmuting his illness into a permanent literary myth, sustained by the authentic originality and brilliance of his prose reveries "Sylvie" and *Aurélia*, and by the unique sonnets, "The Chimeras."

GÉRARD DE NERVAL
(GÉRARD LABRUNIE)

(1808–1855)

GÉRARD LABRUNIE, AS A YOUNG MAN IN the Romantic Paris of 1830, was a poetic disciple of Victor Hugo, and a ghostwriter, a few years later, for Alexandre Dumas. From 1841 on, Nerval (as he called himself) suffered severe mental illness. In January 1855, he hanged himself. Only two years old when his mother died, Nerval was haunted by her absence, which became central to his malaise. There can be no doubt of Nerval's genius as a visionary poet and prose poet: he went deep into realms where Baudelaire was too circumspect to more than peer, and where Symbolists and Surrealists later were to follow. Nerval, like the German Romantic poet who called himself Novalis, is an anomaly, at once a literary man very much of his moment, and a wild original, ultimately timeless. At nineteen, he had translated Goethe's *Faust, Part One,* and he is a pure instance of Faustian man, obsessed with a daemonic other, his genius and destroyer. This other wrote the stories of *The Daughters of Fire,* and the extraordinary sonnets, "The Chimeras," that concluded that volume.

Richard Sieburth, Nerval's admirable translator and critic, carefully disengages the visionary poet from the Surrealist-influenced scholarly tradition that discovers only one more occult dabbler in the author of "Sylvie" and "The Chimeras":

> Nerval's idiosyncratic system of belief in spiritism, Neoplatonism and the ancient mystery religions is continuously offset (and here he most resembles a Shelley or a Heine) by an intellectual agnosticism inherited from the Enlightenment, leavened by the lucid awareness that the death of God has, as he put it, left but "a number of dark doors opening onto the mind." It is this particular state of *in-betweeness* (or what he calls, like Hölderlin, the plight of the "interregnum") that Nerval most frequently underscores when he addresses the spiritual crisis of his generation of belated romantics.
> —*Selected Writings of Nerval* (1988), xxvi

Like Shelley and Novalis, Nerval is best described as both an intellectual skeptic and a spiritual Gnostic, who lives and writes in the *kenoma,* the catastrophic cosmos that has been abandoned by the Alien God. Nerval saved himself from literary inconsequence by *The Daughters of Fire* (1854), which included the stories (to call them that) "Angélique" and "Sylvie" and the dozen sonnets of "The Chimeras." These, together with *Aurélia*, a visionary reverie left incomplete by his suicide, are the only persuasive testimonies to Nerval's otherness, his genius. All of them call for an uncommon reader, since the prose reveries (they cannot be considered narratives) demand patience and the sonnets dazzle by their extraordinary difference from almost any other poems. They seem at first to have no precursors and yet go back to the French Renaissance, to Ronsard, and to Henry of Navarre's warrior-poet, the Protestant Du Bartas. The most notorious of the sonnets is the untranslatable "El Desdichado" ("The Disinherited One"), which I give in Sieburth's prose version:

> I am the man of gloom—the widower—the unconsoled, the prince of Aquitaine, his tower in ruins: My sole *star* is dead—and my constellated lute bears the *Black Sun* of *Melancholia.*
>
> In the night of the tomb, you who consoled me, give me back Posilpo and the Italian sea, the *flower* that so pleased my desolate heart, and the arbour where the vine and the rose are entwined.
>
> Am I Amor or Phoebus? . . . Lusignan or Biron? My brain still burns from the kiss of the queen; I have dreamed in the grotto where the siren swims . . .
>
> And I have twice victorious crossed the Acheron: modulating on Orpheus' lyre now the sighs of the saints, now the fairy's cry.

The title almost certainly alludes to Scott's Ivanhoe, who took "El Desdichado" as his blazon, in his new identity as the Black Knight. Nerval, romantically identifying himself with the Northern hero, pitches his poem both as triumphant defiance and as regret in nostalgia for lost eros. But there is nothing like a dominant tonality in this astonishing poem, which I read as a summoning of forces in a last stand against madness. The prince of Aquitaine in his ruined tower is at once Nerval, for whom the bells of his gift have broken down the tower of his self, and the troubador-king Richard Lionheart, who claimed Aquitaine, and whom Ivanhoe loyally serves.

There evidently are references to the tarot deck throughout, but a poem is not a pack of cards. The black sun of Dürer's *Melencolia* is the emblem of the "constellated lute," of a troubador lost on the day of the black sun, and in the starless night, cast out into the shadow of the tomb and imploring the return of the Vergilian landscapes of the volcano Posillipo (near Naples) and of arbors where the columbine, flower of consolation, bloomed.

The peculiar magic of Nerval's sudden exuberance burns in his most startling lines, where he ascends to a poetic authority a touch beyond anything else in him:

> Suis-je Amour ou Phébus? . . . Lusignan ou Biron?
> Mon front est rouge encor du baiser de la reine;
> J'ai rêvé dans la grotte où nage la syrène . . .

It is the archetypal passage of all Romantic poetry, akin to Keats's "La Belle Dame sans Merci" (which evidently Nerval did not know). Nerval's questions are purely rhetorical: he is the god of Love and the god of Poetry, he is Lusignan, Crusader King of Jerusalem and the Casanova-like Biron. And yet there is a poignant undersong: the actual loves of Nerval's life, like his devotion to the blowzy actress-singer Jenny Colon, had no such glory. Only in the visionary imagination has he been kissed by the legendary Candace, queen of ancient Ethiopia, or slept in the Siren's grotto. And yet he rouses himself to the status of a new Orpheus in the final triad, where he celebrates two triumphant Orphic descents, one somehow saintlike, the other in search of Daphne or Manto, daughter of the blind prophet Tiresias. Later, become the fairy Melusina, the former oracle of Apollo figured as the ancestress of Lusignan, and so symbolically of Nerval himself.

With the other "Chimeras," this incantatory masterpiece, more than "Sylvie" and the diffuse *Aurélia*, is Nerval's legacy. "Only write a dozen lines and then rest on your oars forever"—the Emersonian adage applies to Nerval as it does to few others. Perhaps the perfect note of Nerval's belated genius is sounded in another of the "Chimeras," "Antéras," who is the brother of Eros, but who opposes love, because it is so often unrequited. Nerval transforms Antéras into a champion of the Amalekite gods who were extinguished by Jehovah:

> Jehovah! the last of the gods to be vanquished by your genius, and who cried out "O Tyranny!" from the pit of hell, is my ancestor Belus or my father Dagon . . .
>
> They plunged me three times into the waters of Cocytus, and sole guardian of my mother the Amalekite, I resow at her feet the old dragon's teeth.

> (translated by Richard Sieburth)

Belus is Baal, god of the Babylonians, and Dagon was lord of the Philistines. Immersion in Cocytus, a river in Hell, alludes either to Nerval's illness, or to medical "treatments" he suffered for it. In an astonishing mythmaking, Nerval emerges from this triple antibaptism as a new Cadmus, to sow dragon's teeth not to birth a new Thebes but to revive Elohistic warriors against the tyrannical Demiurge, Jehovah. One wonders if Nerval, had he permitted himself to live, would have gone on to compose a new Gnostic scripture. In his review of the Parisian spectacle "Diorama" (1844), Nerval hints at the lost traditions of the Gnostics, in a manner reminiscent of Lord Byron's *Cain*.

The impulse, and the genius, to create a countertheology always were implicit in Nerval, but the sorrow of his unmothered and unloved existence destroyed him before his daemon fused all the visionary's contraries together.

CHARLES BAUDELAIRE

> Stupidity, delusion, selfishness and lust
> torment our bodies and possess our minds,
> and we sustain our affable remorse
> the way a beggar nourishes his lice.
>
> Our sins are stubborn, our contrition lame;
> we want our scruples to be worth our while—
> how cheerfully we crawl back to the mire:
> a few cheap tears will wash our stains away!
>
> Satan Trismegistus subtly rocks
> our ravished spirits on his wicked bed
> until the precious metal of our will
> is leached out by this cunning alchemist:
>
> the Devil's hand directs our every move—
> the things we loathed become the things we love;
> day by day we drop through stinking shades
> quite undeterred on our descent to Hell.
>
> (translated by Richard Howard)

These quatrains of "To the Reader" open Baudelaire's *Les Fleurs du mal*, and doubtless helped prompt T. S. Eliot to his conviction that Baudelaire was an authentic precursor of *The Waste Land*. A conviction of damnation seemed to Eliot an admirable enough instance of Christian sentiment, far preferable to skepticism or to a secular humanism.

Tennyson, rather than Baudelaire, is what I frequently encounter in Eliot, just as Walt Whitman pervades *The Waste Land*, to a degree that Eliot would rather have ascribed to Dante. Sartre, hardly devout, joined Eliot in commending Baudelaire's descent to Hell. The best commentary on this odd conjunction of Eliot and Sartre belonged to Nigel Dennis, author of a now-forgotten masterpiece, the satirical novel *Cards of Identity*. "Their top," Dennis remarked of Eliot and Sartre, "is only a German theologian's bottom."

Baudelaire's spirituality is not his prime strength. He possesses cata-strophic wit, the genius of hallucinated vision, and a rhetorical power sec-ond only to that of his demiurgical precursor Victor Hugo, who exasperated Baudelaire to a kind of resentful madness. I know little that is more inven-tive than Baudelaire's transmutation of Hermes Trismegistus into thrice-greatest Satan. The Egyptian Hermes was the putative author of Alexandrian Gnostic tracts of the second century C.E. (though ascribed to far greater antiquity) and became the patron divinity of mystical alchemy. Baudelaire's fusion of Satanism and Hermetism is an act of original genius, though something other than the devious path to God that T. S. Eliot judged it to be.

CHARLES BAUDELAIRE
(1821–1867)

SARTRE ENDED HIS BOOK ON BAUDELAIRE by insisting that this poet, like Emerson's ideal being, made his own circumstances:

> But we should look in vain for a single circumstance for which he was not fully and consciously responsible. Every event was a reflection of that indecomposable totality which he was from the first to the last day of his life. He refused experience. Nothing came from outside to change him and he learned nothing.

Could there have been such a person? Can any poet refuse the experience of reading his precursors? Was Victor Hugo a circumstance for which Baudelaire was fully and consciously responsible? Valéry, who was (unlike Sartre) a theorist of poetic influence, thought otherwise:

> Thus Baudelaire regarded Victor Hugo, and it is not impossible to conjecture what he thought of him. Hugo reigned; he had acquired over Lamartine the advantage of infinitely more powerful and more precise *working materials*. The vast range of his diction, the diversity of his rhythms, the superabundance of his images, crushed all rival poetry. But his work sometimes made concessions to the vulgar, lost itself in prophetic eloquence and infinite apostrophes. He flirted with the crowd, he indulged in dialogues with God. The simplicity of his philosophy, the disproportion of and incoherence of the developments, the frequent contrasts between the marvels of detail and the fragility of the subject, the inconsistency of the whole—everything, in a word, which could shock and thus instruct and orientate a pitiless young observer toward his future personal art—all these things Baudelaire was to note in himself and separate from the admiration forced upon him by the magic gifts of Hugo, the impurities, the imprudences, the vulnerable points in his work—that is to say, the possibilities of life and the opportunities for fame so great an artist left to be gleaned.
>
> With some malice and a little more ingenuity than is called for, it

would be only too tempting to compare Victor Hugo's poetry with Baudelaire's, with the object of showing how exactly *complementary* the latter is to the former. I shall say no more. It is evident that Baudelaire sought to do what Victor Hugo had not done; that he refrained from all the effects in which Victor Hugo was invincible; that he returned to a prosody less free and scrupulously removed from prose; that he pursued and almost always captured the production of *unbroken charm*, the inappreciable and quasi-transcendent quality of certain poems—but a quality seldom encountered, and rarely in its pure state, in the immense work of Victor Hugo . . .

Hugo never ceased to learn by practice; Baudelaire, the span of whose life scarcely exceeded the *half* of Hugo's, developed in quite another manner. One would say he had to compensate for the probable brevity and foreshadowed insufficiency of the short space of time he had to live, by the employment of that critical intelligence of which I spoke above. A score of years were vouchsafed him to attain the peak of his own perfection, to discover his personal field and to define a specific form and attitude which would carry and preserve his name. Time was lacking to realize his literary ambitions by numerous experiments and an extensive output of works. He had to choose the shortest road, to limit himself in his gropings, to be sparing of repetitions and divergences. He had therefore to seek by means of analysis what he was, what he could do, and what he wished to do; and to unite, in himself, with the spontaneous virtues of a poet, the sagacity, the skepticism, the attention and reasoning faculty of a critic.

One can transpose this simply enough into very nearly any of the major instances of poetic influence in English. Let us attempt Wallace Stevens, a true peer of Valéry, but with a more repressed or disguised relation to Whitman than Baudelaire manifested towards Hugo:

It is evident that Wallace Stevens sought to do what Walt Whitman had not done; that he refrained from all the effects in which Walt Whitman was invincible; that he returned to prosody less free and spontaneously removed from prose; that he pursued and almost always captured the productions of *unbroken charm*, the inappreciable and quasi-transcendent quality of certain poems—but a quality seldom encountered, and rarely in its pure state, in the immense work of Walt Whitman.

Valéry, unlike both formalist and Poststructuralist critics, understood that Hugo was to French poetry what Whitman was to American poetry, and Wordsworth was to all British poetry after him: the inescapable precursor. Baudelaire's Hugo problem was enhanced because the already legendary poetic father was scarcely twenty years older than the gatherer of *Les Fleurs du mal.* All French literary movements are curiously belated in relation to Anglo-American literature. French sensibility of the school of Derrida was merely a revival of the Anglo-American literary Modernism of which Hugh Kenner remains the antiquarian celebrant. "Poststructuralist Joyce" is simply Joyce as we read and discussed him when I was a graduate student, thirty-five years ago. In the same manner, the French Romanticism of Hugo in 1830 repeated (somewhat unknowingly) the movement of British sensibility that produced Wordsworth and Coleridge, Byron and Shelley and Keats, of whom the first two were poetically dead, and the younger three long deceased, well before Hugo made his revolution.

Baudelaire started with the declaration that the Romanticism of 1830 could not be the Romanticism (or anything else) of 1845. T. S. Eliot, as was inevitable, cleansed Baudelaire of Romanticism, baptized the poet into an Original Sinner and a neoclassicist, and even went so far as to declare the bard of Lesbos a second Goethe. A rugged and powerful literary thinker, Baudelaire doubtless would have accepted these amiable distortions as compliments, but they do not help much in reading him now.

His attitude towards Hugo, always tinged with ambivalence, became at times savage, but a student of poetic influence learns to regard such a pattern as one of the major modes of misprision, of that strong misreading of strong poets that permits other strong poets to be born. *The Salon of 1845* blames the painter Boulanger on poor Hugo:

Here we have the last ruins of the old romanticism—this is what it means to come at a time when it is the accepted belief that inspiration is enough and takes the place of everything else; this is the abyss to which the unbridled course of Mazeppa has led. It is M. Victor Hugo that has destroyed M. Boulanger—after having destroyed so many others; it is the poet that has tumbled the painter into the ditch. And yet M. Boulanger can paint decently enough—look at his portraits. But where on earth did he win his diploma as history-painter and inspired artist? Can it have been in the prefaces and odes of his illustrious friend?

That Baudelaire was determined not to be destroyed by Hugo was clear enough, a determination confirmed by the rather invidious comparison of Delacroix to Hugo in *The Salon of 1846*:

Up to the present, Eugène Delacroix has met with injustice. Criticism, for him, has been bitter and ignorant; with one or two noble exceptions, even the praises of his admirers must often have seemed offensive to him. Generally speaking, and for most people, to mention Eugène Delacroix is to throw into their minds goodness knows what vague ideas of ill-directed fire, of turbulence, of hazardous inspiration, of confusion, even; and for those gentlemen who form the majority of the public, pure chance, that loyal and obliging servant genius, plays an important part in his happiest compositions. In that unhappy period of revolution of which I was speaking a moment ago and whose numerous errors I have recorded, people used often to compare Eugène Delacroix to Victor Hugo. They had their romantic poet; they needed their painter. Their necessity of going to any length to find counterparts and analogues in the different arts often results in strange blunders; and this one proves once again how little people knew what they were about. Without any doubt the comparison must have seemed a painful one to Eugène Delacroix, if not to both of them; for if my definition of romanticism (intimacy, spirituality and the rest) places Delacroix at its head, it naturally excludes M. Victor Hugo. The parallel has endured in the banal realm of accepted ideas, and these two preconceptions still encumber many feeble brains. Let us be done with these rhetorical ineptitudes once and for all. I beg all those who have felt the need to create some kind of aesthetic for their own use and to deduce causes from their results to make a careful comparison between the productions of these two artists.

M. Victor Hugo, whose nobility and majesty I certainly have no wish to belittle, is a workman far more adroit than inventive, a labourer much more correct than *creative*. Delacroix is sometimes clumsy, but he is essentially creative. In all his pictures, both lyric and dramatic, M. Victor Hugo lets one see a system of uniform alignment and contrasts. With him even eccentricity takes symmetrical forms. He is in complete possession of, and coldly employs, all the modulations of rhyme, all the resources of antithesis and all the tricks of apposition. He is a composer of the decadence or transition, who handles his tools with a truly admirable and curious dexterity. M. Hugo was by nature an academician even before he was born, and if

we were still living in the time of fabulous marvels, I would be prepared to believe that often, as he passed before their wrathful sanctuary, the green lions of the *Institut* would murmur to him in prophetic
tones, "Thou shalt enter these portals."

For Delacroix justice is more sluggish. His works, on the contrary,
are poems—and great poems, *naïvely* conceived and executed with the
usual insolence of genius. In the works of the former there is nothing
left to guess at, for he takes so much pleasure in exhibiting his skill
that he omits not one blade of grass nor even the reflection of a street-
lamp. The latter in his works throws open immense vistas to the most
adventurous imaginations. The first enjoys a certain calmness, let us
rather say a certain detached egoism, which causes an unusual coldness and moderation to hover above his poetry—qualities which the
dogged and melancholy passion of the second, at grips with the obsti-
nacies of his craft, does not always permit him to retain. One starts
with detail, the other with an intimate understanding of his subject;
from which it follows that one only captures the skin, while the other
tears out the entrails. Too earthbound, too attentive to the superficies
of nature, M. Victor Hugo has become a painter in poetry; Delacroix,
always respectful of his ideal, is often, without knowing it, a poet in
painting.

This is grand polemical criticism, deliciously unfair to the greatest
French poet ever. Hugo is now adroit, but not inventive; a correct laborer,
but not creative. Few critical remarks are as effectively destructive as "with
him even eccentricity takes symmetrical forms." Hugo is somehow a mere
earthbound painter of nature, and an academic impostor, doomed from
birth to be an institutional pillar. Baudelaire's stance towards Hugo over the
next decade became yet more negative, so that it is at first something of a
surprise to read his letters to the exiled Hugo in 1859. Yet the complex
rhetoric of the letters is again wholly human, all too human, in the agon of
poetic influence:

So now I owe you some explanations. I know your works by heart and
your prefaces show me that I've overstepped the theory you generally
put forward on the alliance of morality and poetry. But at a time when
society turns away from art with such disgust, when men allow themselves to be debased by purely utilitarian concerns, I think there's no
great harm in exaggerating a little in the other direction. It's possible
that I've protested too much. But that was in order to obtain what was

needed. Finally, even if there were a little Asiatic fatalism mixed up in my reflections I think that would be pardonable. The terrible world in which we live gives one a taste for isolation and fatality. What I wanted to do above all was to bring the reader's thoughts back to that wonderful little age whose true king you were, and which lives on in my mind like a delicious memory of childhood . . .

The lines I enclose with this letter have been knocking around in my brain for a long time. The second piece was written with the *aim of imitating you* (laugh at my absurdity, it makes me laugh myself) after I'd reread some poems in your collections, in which such magnificent charity blends with touching familiarity. In art galleries I've sometimes seen wretched art students copying the works of the masters. Well done or botched, these imitations sometimes contained, unbeknownst to the students, something of their own characters, be it great or common. Perhaps (perhaps!) that will excuse my boldness. When *The Flowers of Evil* reappears, swollen with three times as much material as the Court suppressed, I'll have the pleasure of inscribing at the head of these poems the name of the poet whose works have taught me so much and brought such pleasure to my youth.

"That wonderful little age" doubtless referred to the Romanticism of the revolution of 1830, that enchanted moment when Victor Hugo was king. But the true reference is to nine-year-old Baudelaire, who found in his precursor "a delicious memory of childhood," and no mere likeness. When Baudelaire goes on to speak of imitation he cannot forbear the qualification, "something of their own character, great or common." A few months later, sending his poem "The Swan" to Hugo, he asked that the poem be judged "with your paternal eyes." But, a year later, Baudelaire again condemned Hugo for "his concern with contemporary events . . . the belief in progress, the salvation of mankind by the use of balloons, etc."

The whip of ambivalence lashed back and forth in Baudelaire. Though a believer in salvation through balloons, the bardic Hugo was also, in his bad son's estimate, a force of nature: "No other artist is so universal in scope, more adept at coming into contact with the forces of the universe, more disposed to immerse himself in nature." That might seem definitive, but later Baudelaire allowed himself this diatribe, which hardly dents the divine precursor:

Hugo thinks a great deal about Prometheus. He has placed an imaginary vulture on a breast that is never lacerated by anything more than the flea-bites of his own vanity . . .

Hugo-the-Almighty always has his head bowed in thought; no wonder he never sees anything except his own navel.

It is painful to read this; more painful still to read the references to Hugo in Baudelaire's letters of 1865–66. One moment, in its flash of a healthier humor, renders a grand, partly involuntary tribute to the normative visionary who both inspired and distressed Baudelaire:

It appears that he and the Ocean have quarreled! Either he has not the strength to bear the Ocean longer, or the Ocean has grown weary of his presence.

To confront, thus again, the rocklike ego of that force of nature, your poetic father, is to admit implicitly that he returns in his own colors, and not in your own.

Proust, in a letter to Jacques Rivière, compared Baudelaire to Hugo and clearly gave the preference to Baudelaire. What Wallace Stevens, following Baudelaire, called the profound poetry of the poor and of the dead, seemed to Proust wholly Baudelaire's, and not Hugo's. But as love poets, Hugo and Baudelaire seemed more equal, even perhaps with Hugo the superior. Proust said he preferred Hugo to Baudelaire in a great common trope:

Elle me regarda de ce regard suprême
Qui reste à la beauté quand nous en triomphons.
(She gazed at me with that supreme look
Which endures in beauty even while it is vanquished.)
                                                —Hugo

Et cette gratitude infinie et sublime
Qui sort de la paupière ainsi qu'un long soupir.
(And that sublime and infinite gratitude
which glistens under the eyelids like a sigh.)
                                                —Baudelaire

Both tropes are superb; I too prefer Hugo's, but why did Proust have the preference, or pretend to have it? Both beauties have been vanquished, but Hugo's by the potent Victor himself, while Baudelaire's Hippolyta reflects the triumph of Delphine, who stares at her victim with the shining eyes of a lioness. Proust, perhaps rather slyly, says he prefers the heterosexual trope to the lesbian one, but does not say why. Yet, superb critic that he was, he helps us to expand Valéry's insight. Resolving to do precisely what Hugo had not done, Baudelaire became the modern poet of Lesbos, achieving so complex a vision of that alternative convention of Eros as to usurp forever anyone else's representation of it:

> Pensive as cattle resting on the beach,
> they are staring out to sea; their hands and feet
> creep toward each other imperceptibly
> and touch at last, hesitant then fierce.
>
> How eagerly some, beguiled by secrets shared,
> follow a talkative stream among the trees,
> spelling out their timid childhood's love
> and carving initials in the tender wood;
>
> others pace as slow and grave as nuns
> among the rocks where Anthony beheld
> the purple breasts of his temptations rise
> like lava from the visionary earth;
>
> some by torchlight in the silent caves
> consecrated once to pagan rites
> invoke—to quench their fever's holocaust—
> Bacchus, healer of the old regrets;
>
> others still, beneath their scapulars,
> conceal a whip that in the solitude
> and darkness of the forest reconciles
> tears of pleasure with tears of pain.
>
> Virgins, demons, monster, martyrs, all
> great spirits scornful of reality,
> saints and satyrs in search of the infinite,
> racked with sobs or loud in ecstasy,
>
> you whom my soul has followed to your hell,
> Sisters! I love you as I pity you
> for your bleak sorrows, for your unslaked thirsts,
> and for the love that gorges your great hearts!

Richard Howard's superb translation greatly assists in my inner ear, inadequate for the nuances of Baudelaire's French, in the labor of apprehending what Eric Auerbach memorably spoke of as Baudelaire's aesthetic dignity, that all-but-unique fusion of Romantic pathos and classical irony, so clearly dominant in these immense quatrains. Yet I would place the emphasis elsewhere, upon that psychological acuity in which Baudelaire surpasses nearly all poets, Shakespeare excepted. Freud, speculating upon female homosexuality, uttered the grand and plaintive cry, "we find masculinity vanishing into activity and femininity into passivity, and that does not tell us enough." Baudelaire does tell us enough, almost more than enough, even as Melanie Klein came, after Freud and Karl Abraham, to tell us much more than enough. The "damned women," really little children, play at being masculine and feminine, for Baudelaire's great insight is that lesbianism transforms the erotic into the aesthetic, transforms compulsion into a vain play that remains compulsive. "Scornful of reality," and so of the reality principle that is our consciousness of mortality, Baudelaire's great spirits search out the infinite, and discover that the only infinity is the hell of repetition. One thinks back to Delphine and Hippolyta; Baudelaire sees and shows that Delphine is the daughter revenging herself upon the mother in quite another way. When Hippolyta cries out, "Let me annihilate myself upon / your breast and find the solace of a grave!" then we feel that Baudelaire has made Melanie Klein redundant, perhaps superfluous. The revenge upon the mother is doubtless Baudelaire's revenge upon his mother, but more profoundly it is the aesthetic revenge upon nature. In Baudelaire's own case, was it not also the revenge upon that force of nature, too conversant with ocean, that victorious poetic father, the so often reviled but never forgotten Victor Hugo?

ARTHUR RIMBAUD

So the festering soul, the soul disconsolate,
Will feel Your curses stream upon her head.
She will have made her bed in Your unsoiled Hate,
And left true passion for an image of death,

Christ! O Christ, eternal thief of energy!
God crucified, whose pallor feeds on women
Nailed to the ground with shame and with migraine,
Or else thrown down upon their backs, in pain.

     (translated by Paul Schmidt)

These are the concluding quatrains of "First Communions," one of the
many poems in which Rimbaud, the genius of adolescence, achieved an

astonishing originality, at least in the realm of French poetry. Baudelaire, to Rimbaud, was "the first visionary, the king of poets, *a real God*. And still he lived in too artistic a milieu; and his highly praised form is silly. The inventions of the unknown demand new forms."

What Rimbaud would have made of William Blake, I do not know. Of Victor Hugo, the nearest French equivalent, Rimbaud observed ambivalently, "too many Jehovahs and columns, old worn-out enormities." *A Season in Hell* is a new form, in French, but is it one of "the inventions of the unknown"?

In the long history of poetic gnosis, Rimbaud's *Season* has a considerable lineage, one that he benefited by not knowing. His Gnosticism was not traditional and so cannot be subsumed by the cavalcade that extends from Simon Magus through Victor Hugo. What marks Rimbaud's heresies are their rawness, and their humor:

> From my ancestors the Gauls I have pale blue eyes, a narrow brain, and awkwardness in competition . . . But I don't butter my hair.

Rimbaud lived another eighteen years after abandoning poetry at nineteen. It was not that he wore out his daemon, but that his genius or other self had infuriated him, and drove him into exile.

ARTHUR RIMBAUD
(1854–1891)

RIMBAUD, HEIR OF BOTH HUGO AND Baudelaire, was potentially a stronger poet than either, just as Hart Crane, influenced by Eliot and Stevens, possessed poetic gifts that could have transcended the work of both precursors. Crane's identification with Rimbaud takes on a particular poignancy in this context, reminding us of imaginitive losses as great as those involved in the early deaths of Shelley and of Keats. The scandal of Rimbaud, which would have been considerable in any nation's poetic tradition, was magnified because of the relative decorum in terms of form and rhetoric of French Romantic poetry, let alone of the entire course of French poetic tradition. A crisis in French poetry would seem a ripple in the Anglo-American tradition, which is endlessly varied and heterodox.

Except for Rimbaud, and a few more recent figures, French poetry does not have titanic eccentricities who establish entirely new norms. Rimbaud was a great innovator within French poetry, but he would have seemed less so had he written in the language of William Blake and William Wordsworth, Robert Browning and Walt Whitman. *A Season in Hell* comes more than eighty years after *The Marriage of Heaven and Hell*, and the *Illuminations* do not deconstruct the poetic self any more radically than do the Browning monologues and *Song of Myself*. One must be absolutely modern, yes, and a century after Rimbaud it is clear that no one ever is going to be more absolutely modern than Wordsworth, the poet of *The Prelude* and the crisis-lyrics of 1802. I once believed that the true difference between English and French poetry was the absence of French equivalents of Chaucer and Spenser, Shakespeare and Milton. A larger difference, I now believe, is Wordsworth, whose astonishing originality ended a continuous tradition that had gone unbroken between Homer and Goethe.

Rimbaud had strong precursors in the later Hugo and in Baudelaire, but so great was Rimbaud's potential that he would have benefited by an even fiercer agon, like the one Wordsworth conducted with Milton, and to a lesser extent with Shakespeare. The strongest French poets, down to Valéry, finally seem to confront a composite precursor, Boileau-Descartes, part classical critic, part philosopher. That develops very different urgencies from those ensuing when you must wrest your literary space from Milton or

Wordsworth. The difference, even in the outcast Rimbaud, sets certain limits both to rhetoric and to vision.

Those limits, critics agree, come closest to being transcended, in very different ways, in *Une Saison en enfer* and *Les Illuminations*. Leo Bersani, impressively arguing for the "simplicity" of the *Illuminations*, affirms that Rimbaud's greatness is in his negations. Making poetry mean as little as possible is thus seen as Rimbaud's true ambition. If Rimbaud's "The I is another" is the central formula, then the *Illuminations* becomes the crucial work. But since poetry, like belief, takes place between truth and meaning, the Rimbaldian-Bersanian dream of literary negation may be only a dream. What would a poem be if it were, as Bersani hopes, "nonreferential, nonrelational, and devoid of attitudes, feelings, feelings and tones"? Bersani is the first to admit that the *Saison* is anything but that; it overwhelmingly reveals a coherent self, though hardly one of durable subjectivity. The trope and topos we call "voice" is so strong in *Saison* that we must judge it to be a High Romantic prose poem, whatever we take the *Illuminations* to be.

Saison, far more than Blake's *Marriage,* is always in danger of falling back into the normative Christianity that Rimbaud wants to deny, and that he evidently ceased to deny only upon his deathbed. Kristin Ross, in a brilliant exegesis, reads *Saison* as opening out onto a sociohistorical field of which presumably Marcuse, in the name of Freud, was a prophet. I hear *Eros and Civilization* in Ross's eloquent summation of Rimbaud's stance as "I *will be* a worker—but only at the moment when work, as we know it, has come to an end." If Bersani beautifully idealizes Rimbaud's aesthetic ambition, then Ross nobly idealizes his supposed socialization, though in a post-apocalyptic beyond. I am condemned to read Rimbaud from the perspective of Romanticism, as does John Porter Houston, and the poet I read has all the disorders of Romantic vision, but much of the meanings as well, and they hardly seem to me social meanings.

So much the worse for the wood that finds it is a violin, or the brass that finds it is a bugle, or the French boy of yeoman stock who at sixteen could write "Le Bateau ivre," transuming Baudelaire's "Le Voyage." Rimbaud's violent originality, from "Le Bateau ivre" on, drives not against meaning but against anyone whatsoever, even Baudelaire, bequeathing Rimbaud any meaning that is not already his own. More even than the later Victor Hugo, to whom he grudgingly granted the poetic faculty of Vision, Rimbaud could tolerate no literary authority. Perhaps, if you could combine the visionary Hugo and Baudelaire into a single poet, Rimbaud would have had a precursor who might have induced in him some useful anxiety, but the Anglo-

American poetic habit of creating for oneself an imaginary, composite poetic forerunner was not available to Rimbaud.

Barely two years after "Le Bateau ivre," Rimbaud had finished *Une Saison en enfer.* Blake is supposed to have written "How Sweet I Roam'd from Field to Field" before he was fourteen, but except for Blake there is no great poet as precocious as Rimbaud in all of Western literary history. Like Blake, a poet of extraordinary power at fourteen, Rimbaud, quite unlike Blake, abandoned poetry at nineteen. A trader and gunrunner in Africa, dead at thirty-seven, having written no poetry in the second half of his life, Rimbaud necessarily became and remains the mythical instance of the modern poet as the image of alienation. The myth obscures the deeper traditionalism of *Saison* in particular. Despite the difference implicit in the belated Romanticism of France, Rimbaud is as High Romantic as Blake or Shelley, or as Victor Hugo.

Une Saison en enfer has been called either a prose poem or a *récit;* it could also be named a miniature "anatomy" in Northrop Frye's sense of that genre. Perhaps it ought to be regarded as a belated Gnostic Gospel, like its hidden model, the canonical Gospel of John, a work which I suspect was revised away from its original form, one where the Word became, not flesh, but *pneuma,* and dwelt among us. Of all Rimbaud's writings, the *Saison* is most like a Hermetic scripture. Rimbaud had never heard of Blake, who had promised the world his Bible of Hell, but *Saison* in its form always reminds me of *The Marriage of Heaven and Hell,* though it is very different in spirit from that curiously genial instance of apocalyptic satire.

In no way is it condescending to call *Saison* also the Gospel of Adolescence, particularly when we remember that Rousseau had invented that interesting transition, since literature affords no trace of it before him. To think of Rousseau reading *Saison* is grotesque, but in a clear sense Rimbaud indeed is one of Rousseau's direct descendants. Rimbaud doubtless attempted to negate every inheritance, but how could Rimbaud negate Romanticism? His negation of Catholicism is nothing but Romantic, particularly in its ambivalences.

The pattern unfolded in the nine sections of *Saison* would have been familiar to any Alexandrian Gnostic of the second century C.E. Rimbaud begins with a Fall that is also a catastrophic Creation, abandoning behind him the feast of life, and yet remembering "la clef du festin ancien," the key of charity. The feast must therefore be a communion table, the *pleroma* or fullness from which Rimbaud has fallen away into the Gnostic *kenoma,* or emptiness of Hell that is simple, everyday bodily existence. Satan, in *Saison,* is a Demiurge also, a peasant or serf Demiurge, as it were. Perhaps Rimbaud's largest irony is his "Je ne puis comprendre la révolte," since the serfs rose up only to plunder. The medieval yearnings of the "Mauvais sang" section all resemble the rapaciousness of wolves against an animal they have not killed, and so the wolf Rimbaud, his pagan blood returning, is now passed by:

> Pagan blood returns! The Spirit is at hand . . . why does Christ not help me, and grant my soul nobility and freedom? Ah, but the Gospel belongs to the past! The Gospel, The Gospel . . .
>
> I wait gluttonously for God. I have been of inferior race for ever and ever.
>
> (translated by Paul Schmidt)

The Holy Ghost is near, but the gluttonous waiting for God only guarantees Christ's withholding of charity. Nobility and freedom do not come to the serf lusting for a preternatural salvation. A noble barbarism is therefore preferable to a supposed civilization in a world bereft of revelation. This is the dialectic of libertine Gnosticism, and reminds me that the American work closest to Rimbaud in spirit is Nathanael West's *Miss Lonelyhearts*, with its superbly squalid version of the ancient Gnostic doctrine that Gershom Scholem grimly called "Redemption through Sin." Rimbaud peals throughout the rest of his "Bad Blood" section the iron music of atavism, in a full-scale justification of his own systematic derangement of the senses, only to collapse afterwards into the night of a real hell. Rimbaud's Hell is shot through with glimpses of divinity, and seems to be married to Heaven in a literal way, very different from Blake's ironic dialectic. God and Satan appear to be different names for one and the same spirit of lassitude, and Rimbaud thus prepares himself for his deepest descent, into delirium and its memories of his life of intimacy with Verlaine.

When I think of *Saison* I remember first the sick brilliance of Verlaine, the Foolish Virgin, addressing Rimbaud, the Infernal Bridegroom. If *Saison* has any common readers, in the Johnsonian sense, what else would they remember? Rimbaud, had he wished to, could have been the most consistently savage humorist in the French language. Poor Verlaine is permanently impaled as that masochistic trimmer, the Foolish Virgin, unworthy either of salvation or damnation. The authority of this impaling is augmented by the portrait of the Infernal Bridegroom's forays into poetic alchemy, which are surely to be read as being just as ridiculous as the Foolish Virgin's posturings. So strong is the Rimbaud myth that his own repudiations of divinity and magic do not altogether persuade us. Thinking back to *Saison*, we all grimace wryly at Verlaine as Foolish Virgin, while remembering with aesthetic respect those verbal experiments that Rimbaud renounces so robustly.

To climb out of Hell, Rimbaud discovers that he must cast off his own Gnostic dualism, which means his not wholly un-Johannine Gnostic Christianity. Much of the sections "L'Impossible" and "L'Éclair" are given to the quest away from Christianity, or rather the only Christianity that seems available. But since the quest involves those two great beasts of nineteenth-century Europe, Transcendental Idealism and the Religion of Science, Rimbaud discovers that neither God nor Rimbaud is safely mocked. "Matin," following these dismissed absurdities, first restores Rimbaud's Gnosticism, his sense that what is best and oldest in him goes back to before the Creation-Fall. Hailing the birth of the new labor, the new wisdom, Rimbaud moves into his remarkable "Adieu," with its notorious motto, "Il faut être absolument moderne," the epigraph to the life's work of Rimbaud's Gnostic heir, Hart Crane. No longer a magus or an angel, Rimbaud is given back to the earth, a peasant again, like his ancestors. To think of the earth hardly seems a Gnostic formulation, and the famous closing passage of *Saison* abandons Gnosticism once and for all in an extraordinary breakthrough into visionary monism:

> —I went through women's Hell over there—and I will be able now *to possess the truth within one body and one soul.*
>
> (translated by Paul Schmidt)

I take it that Rimbaud saw *down there*—in his relation with Verlaine—"the hell of women," precisely in the Oedipal romance that he sought to flee. Possessing the truth in a single mind and a single body—one's own—is a narcissistic revelation akin to that of Walt Whitman's at the close of *Song of Myself*. Christianity *and* Gnosticism alike are rejected, and so are both heterosexuality and homosexuality. *Saison* ends with an inward turning closer to Whitman than to Hugo or to Baudelaire:

> Yet this is the watch by night. Let us all accept new strength, and real tenderness. And at dawn, armed with glowing patience, we will enter the cities of glory.
>
> (translated by Paul Schmidt)

It is a passage worthy of the poet whom the late James Wright called "our father, Walt Whitman." We can hardly murmur, "Our father, Arthur Rimbaud," but we can remember Hart Crane's equal devotion to Whitman and to Rimbaud, and we can be grateful again to Crane for teaching us something about our ancestry.

PAUL VALÉRY

For my own part, between the all and the nothing of it, I have oscillated. I knew Mallarmé, *after* having undergone his influence to the limit, and at the very moment when in my own mind I wanted to guillotine all literature.

I worshiped that extraordinary man at the very time when I saw in him the one—invaluable—head to cut off in order to decapitate all Rome. You can easily guess the passion a young man of twenty-two can feel, crazed with contradictory desires, incapable of distracting them, intellectually jealous of every idea that seems to him to combine power with precision: a lover not of *souls*, but of minds the most various, as others are of bodies.

—Letter to Albert Thibaudet, 1917

(translated by Malcolm Cowley and James R. Lawler)

Paul Valéry—the major French poet since Baudelaire, Rimbaud, and Mallarmé—was also the final luminary of the French critical tradition, before its collapse into Roland Barthes and subsequent technicians.

Valéry's conscious ambivalence towards his precursor Mallarmé helped generate his brilliant speculations upon poetic influence. For Valéry, these aesthetic meditations were part of a broader inquiry into the crisis of European culture, into a generic malaise that has spread to the United Sates. The sense of coming very late in an already fulfilled tradition is explored with equal urgency in Valéry's major poems.

To "combine power with precision" is an apt definition of Valéry's genius, which strongly affected the best modern American poets, from Wallace Stevens and T. S. Eliot to James Merrill, whose wonderful version of Valéry's "Palme" ends perfectly with the French master's implicit self-portrait:

> Let populations be
> Crumbled underfoot—
> Palm irresistibly—
> Among celestial fruit!
> Those hours were not in vain
> So long as you retain
> A lightness once they're lost;
> Like one who, thinking, spends
> His inmost dividends
> To grow at any cost.

PAUL VALÉRY
(1871–1945)

IN THE PREFACE TO HIS *LEONARDO POE Mallarmé*, Valéry calls these precursors "three masters of the art of abstraction." "Man fabricates by abstraction" is a famous Valéryan formula, reminding us that this sense of abstraction is Latin: "withdrawn, taken out from, removed." "It Must Be Abstract," the first part of Stevens's *Notes toward a Supreme Fiction*, moves in the atmosphere of an American version of Valéry's insight, but the American is Walt Whitman and not Edgar Poe:

> The weather and the giant of the weather,
> Say the weather, the mere weather, the mere air:
> An abstraction blooded, as a man by thought.

Valéry fabricates by withdrawing from a stale reality, which he refuses to associate with the imaginings of his masters. These "enchanted, dominated me, and—as was only fitting—tormented me as well; the beautiful is that which fills us with despair." Had Valéry spoken of pain, rather than despair, he would have been more Nietzschean. The genealogy of imagination is not truly Valéry's subject. Despair is not a staleness in reality, or an absence of it; it is the overwhelming presence of reality, of the reality principle, or the necessity of death-in-life, or simply of dying. Valéry's beautiful "Palme" concludes with a metaphor that seems central to all of his poetry:

> Pareille à celui qui pense
> Et dont l'âme se dépense
> A s'accroître de ses dons!

The palm is the image of a mind so rich in thinking that the gifts of its own soul augment it constantly. That may be one of the origins of Stevens's death-poem "Of Mere Being," but Valéry's palm is less pure and less flickering than Stevens's final emblem. The two poets and poetic thinkers do not much resemble one another, despite Stevens's yearning regard for Valéry. Perhaps the largest difference is in the attitudes towards precursors. Valéry is lucid and candid, and he confronts Mallarmé. Stevens insists that he does not read Whitman, condemns Whitman for his tramp persona, and yet he cannot cease revising Whitman's poems in his own poems. But then that is how Whitman came to discuss his relation to Ralph Waldo Emerson—clearly they order these matters differently in America.

In a meditation of 1919 on "The Intellectual Crisis," Valéry memorably depicted the European Hamlet staring at millions of ghosts:

> But he is an intellectual Hamlet. He meditates on the life and death of truths. For phantoms he has all the subjects of our controversies; for regrets he has all our titles to glory; he bows under the weight of discoveries and learning, unable to renounce and unable to resume this limitless activity. He reflects on the boredom of recommencing the past, on the folly of always striving to be original. He wavers between one abyss and the other, for two dangers still threaten the world: order and disorder.

This retains its force nearly seventy years later, just as it would baffle us if its subject were the American Hamlet. Valéry's fear was that Europe might "become *what she is in reality:* that is, a little cape of the Asiatic continent." The fear was prophetic, though the prophecy fortunately is not yet wholly fulfilled. When Valéry writes in this mode, he is principally of interest to editorial writers and newspaper columnists of the weightier variety. Yet his concern for European culture, perhaps a touch too custodial, is a crucial element in all his prose writing. Meditating upon Descartes, the archetypal French intellect, Valéry states the law of his own nature: "Descartes is above all, a man of intentional action." Consciousness was for Valéry an intentional adventure, and this sense of deliberate quest in the cultivation of consciousness is partly what makes Valéry a central figure of the Western literary intellect.

Valéry deprecated originality, but his critical insights are among the most original of our century. His *Analects* are crowded with the darker truths concerning literary originality:

> The value of men's work is not in the works themselves but in their later development by others, in other circumstances.

> Nothing is more "original," nothing more "oneself" than to feed on others. But one has to digest them. A lion is made of assimilated sheep.

> The hallmark of the greatest art is that imitations of it are legitimate, worthwhile, tolerable; that it is not demolished or devoured by them, or they by it.

Any production of the mind is important when its existence resolves, summons up, or cancels other works, whether previous to it or not.

An artist wants to inspire jealousy till the end of time.

Valéry's central text on originality is his "Letter about Mallarmé" of 1927, where his relation to his authentic precursor inspired dialectical ironies of great beauty;

> We say that an author is *original* when we cannot trace the hidden trans-formations that others underwent in his mind; we mean to say that the dependence of *what he does* on *what others have done* is excessively complex and irregular. There are works in the likeness of others, and works that are the reverse of others, but there are also works of which the relation with earlier productions is so intricate that we become confused and at-tribute them to the direct intervention of the gods.
>
> (To go deeper into the subject, we should also have to discuss the influence of a mind on itself and of a work on its author. But this is not the place.)

Everywhere else in Valéry, in prose and verse, is the place, because that was Valéry's true topos, the influence of Paul Valéry's mind upon itself. Is that not the true subject of Descartes and of Montaigne, and of all French men and women of sensibility and intellect? What never ceases to engage Valéry is the effect of his thought and writings upon himself. Creative mis-understandings induced in others were not without interest, but Valéry's creative misunderstandings of Valéry ravished his heart away. Texts of this ravishment abound, but I choose one of the subtlest and most evasive, the dialogue *Dance and the Soul*. Socrates is made by Valéry to speak of "that poi-son of poisons, that venom which is opposed to all nature," the reduction of life to things as they are that Stevens called the First Idea:

PHAEDRUS

What venom?

SOCRATES

Which is called: the tedium of living? I mean, understand me, not the passing ennui, the tedium that comes of fatigue, or the tedium of which we can see the germ or of which we know the limits; but that perfect tedium, that pure tedium that is not caused by misfortune or infirmity, that is compatible with apparently the happiest of all conditions—that tedium, in short, the stuff of which is nothing else than life itself, and which has no other second cause than the clear-sightedness of the living man. This absolute tedium is essentially nothing but life in its nakedness when it sees itself with unclouded eyes.

ERYXIMACHUS

It is very true that if our soul purges itself of all falseness, strips itself of every fraudulent addition to *what is,* our existence is endangered on the spot by the cold, exact, reasonable and moderate view of human life *as it is.*

PHAEDRUS

Life blackens at the contact of truth, as a suspicious mushroom blackens, when it is crushed, at the contact of the air.

SOCRATES

Eryximachus, I asked you if there were any cure?

ERYXIMACHUS

Why cure so reasonable a complaint? There is nothing, no doubt, nothing more essentially morbid, nothing more inimical to nature than to *see things as they are.* A cold and perfect light is a poison it is impossible to combat. Reality, unadulterated, instantly puts a stop to the heart. One drop of that icy lymph suffices to slacken all the springs of the soul, all the throbbing of desire, to exterminate all hopes and bring to ruin all the gods that inhabited our blood. The Virtues and the noblest colors are turned pale by it in a gradual and devouring consumption. The past is reduced to a handful of ashes, the future to a tiny icicle. The soul appears to itself as an empty and measurable form. Here then are things as they are—a rigorous and deadly chain, where each link joins and limits the next . . . O Socrates, the universe cannot endure for a single instant to be only what it is. It is strange to think that that which is the Whole cannot suffice itself! . . . Its terror of being what it is has induced it to create and paint for itself thousands of masks; there is no other reason for the existence of mortals. What are mortals for?—Their business is *to know.* Know? And what is *to know?*—*It is assuredly not to be what one is.*—So here are human beings raving and thinking, introducing into nature the principle of unlimited errors and all these myriads of marvels!

The mistakes, the appearances, the play of the mind's dioptric give depth and animation to the world's miserable mass. The idea introduces into what is, the leaven of what is not . . . But truth sometimes shows itself, and sounds a discord in the harmonious system of phantasmagorias and errors . . . Everything straightway is threatened with perdition, and Socrates in person comes to beg of me a cure for this desperate case of clear-sightedness and ennui!

We are close again to Stevens's appropriations from Valéry in *Notes toward a Supreme Fiction.* The "clear-sightedness of the living man" does not belong to Stevens or to us; it is the particular gift of the reductively lucid Valéry, who is capable of seeing "life in its nakedness." If Socrates here is Valéry the writer, then Eryximachus is Valéry the reader of—Valéry! "A cold and perfect light" is what Valéry has taught himself to see—in Valéry. Reality here is not so much the reality principle of Freud, as it is the next step after the nothingness of the abyss or final void in French Poe and in Mallarmé. A pragmatic Gnosticism, implicit in Poe and developed by Mallarmé, triumphs in Valéry's ironic sermon about "what is *to know.*" The universe's terror of its own nothingness causes it to proliferate mortals, as if each one of us were only another desperate figuration. Our errors, our marvels, introduce "into what is, the leaven of what is not."

We encounter here again the vision of "Palme," since we hear the influence upon Valéry himself of

> Parfois si l'on désespère,
> Si l'adorable rigueur
> Malgré tes larmes n'opère
> Que sous ombre de langueur.

"There is a strict law in literature that we must never go to the bottom of anything." Valéry almost did not take his own counsel in his endless quest to explain the preternatural prevalence of his intentional self-awareness. He seems now the last person of letters in the French tradition to have been capable of reconciling acute consciousness of one's own consciousness with the grand fabrications made possible only by abstraction, by a withdrawal from heightened rhetoricity. Compared to him, Sartre and Blanchot, let alone Derrida, come to creation only in the accents of a severe belatedness.

VII

NEZAH

LUSTRE 13

Homer, Luis Vaz de Camões, James Joyce, Alejo Carpentier, Octavio Paz

Nezah is God's victory, and this first of its Lustres groups some instances of epic genius and its twentieth-century variants. Homer is uniquely the poet of victory, and Camões, national poet of Portugal in its Golden Age, devotes himself even more passionately to victory as he celebrates his country's amazing triumphs.

There is a Kabbalistic irony in *Nezah*, since its victory is God's, and not necessarily ours. Joyce, refiguring the *Odyssey* in his *Ulysses*, invokes both Dante and Shakespeare, so enormous are his own aesthetic ambitions, but his irony also invokes Flaubert, the novel's supreme genius in the ironic mode.

The Cuban novelist Alejo Carpentier and the Mexican poet Octavio Paz are surrealistic yet also epic ironists. Overtly Kabbalistic in his symbolism, Carpentier is a historical novelist of authentic genius, still too little known in the United States. Octavio Paz, Mexico's major poet, becomes the plangent elegist of his nation's long martyrdom of its women in *Sor Juana* and in *The Labyrinth of Solitude*.

HOMER

Aye, you shall make those men atone in blood!
But after you have dealt out death—in open
combat or by stealth—to all the suitors,
go overland on foot, and take an oar,
until one day you come where men have lived
with meat unsalted, never known the sea,
nor seen seagoing ships, with crimson bows
and oars that fledge light hulls for dipping flight.
The spot will soon be plain to you, and I
can tell you how: some passerby will say,
"What winnowing fan is that upon your shoulder?"
Halt, and implant your smooth oar in the turf
and make fair sacrifice to Lord Poseidon:
a ram, a bull, a great buck boar; turn back,
and carry out pure hekatombs at home
to all wide heaven's lords, the undying gods,
to each in order. Then a seaborne death
soft as this hand of mist will come upon you
when you are wearied out with rich old age,
your country folk in blessed peace around you.
And all this shall be just as I foretell.

(translated by Robert Fitzgerald)

Beating off all other shades from drinking the blood-sacrifice of the lamb and ewe, Odysseus in Hades allows the prophet Tiresias to drink and speak first. Tiresias concludes his prophecy with this surprising account of a rich old age and gentle seaborne death for Odysseus, after the wanderer has placated Poseidon.

The *completeness* of Homer's genius, as shrewdly noted by James Joyce, is exemplified by Tiresias's beautiful prophecy. We see an aged Odysseus marching inland, where the oar over his shoulder is taken to be a winnowing fan by men who have never seen the sea.

It is fascinating that "a seaborne death" is still Homer's notion of the final adventure of Odysseus. This became the tradition that culminated in the magnificent last voyage of Ulysses in Dante's *Inferno*, when "this so brief vigil of our senses" is extended to the transgression of an attempt to break out of the limits of the known world. The silence of Dante the Pilgrim, after listening to Ulysses, may well be Dante's subtler version of the Homeric completeness.

HOMER

THERE IS A NECESSARY ODDITY IN speaking of the genius of Homer, because much scholarship teaches us that he was a tradition, rather than a particular person. And yet the two epics, the *Iliad* and the *Odyssey*, are highly organized works, put together about 700 B.C.E. by a poet-editor whose genius is beyond question. About a hundred and fifty years later, in the mid-sixth century B.C.E., an editor-author of equal eminence invented the crucial sequence of the Hebrew Bible that goes from Genesis through Kings. This great Redactor, nameless except as R, invented what became the culture of the Jews, utilizing the greatest of older Hebrew writers, J or the Yahwist, but subsuming her (or him) while creating a vast historical chronicle. Compared to that immense labor, the poet-editor of the *Iliad* and the *Odyssey* had a more limited yet equally intricate task. Whereas the Hebrew Redactor was a great reader, working with prior writings, Homer was first an auditor, and then a storyteller burnishing inherited tales that he himself had heard recited, and subsequently improved upon in his own recitations. Someone finally wrote them down, possibly the singer we call Homer. His audience listened to him just as he had listened to the poetry of the past.

The *Odyssey* is a poem of more than twelve thousand lines, written in hexameter verse, and in a highly elaborate language that no one ever could have spoken. A recital of it must have taken several days, and the labor of writing it down must have taken many years, since the alphabet available to Homer was a cumbersome one. But I do not think that committees create great poems, and I think one can surmise that Homer, whoever he was, first perfected his poem's oral version and then wrote it out, presumably revising it in the process. Homer's anxieties, as a poet, concerned the poetry of the past, which has not come down to us. Writing, which he subtly deprecated, was not an anxiety to him, but only a permanent record of his art.

I am willing to believe, with the Hellenistic critic Longinus, that the same Homer composed the *Iliad* and the *Odyssey*, perhaps thirty years or more apart, with the *Odyssey* being the later work. Though very different, the poems could as well be by one master, as *War and Peace* and *Anna Karenina* are Tolstoy in different phases, or as *Romeo and Juliet* and *The Winter's Tale* are Shakespeare with fifteen years of composition in between.

*   *   *

A poet-editor is someone very different from an historian-editor. The Hebrew Redactor, an aristocratic exile in Babylon, in some sense rejoiced in his own belatedness, his gleanings. Judah had been scattered into shards, with the common people allowed to remain in the land, and the learned compelled to remember their stories from afar. In 587 B.C.E., Solomon's Temple had been destroyed by the Babylonians. Scrolls also went into exile, to be arranged comprehensively by the Redactor. Though exile is one of Homer's grand themes, Homer himself refuses to be belated. Like all great poets after him in Western tradition, Homer wishes to be the best and earliest of all singers. Andrew Ford, in his *Homer: The Poetry of the Past* (1992), studies the Homeric conception of poetry as a "song without limits." Such a song voices heroes and gods as a unison, made possible by Homer alone. And yet Homer was perhaps more an end than a beginning: he perfected an ancient performative art, while implicitly denying his indebtedness, whether to prior generations or to contemporary rivals. He had to be just one of many editor-singers of verse tales, chanters who went about selling their performances. But it is central to his art that he evade his guild, and that he tell us his contest is only with the gods and heroes he celebrates.

However many formulae and stock phrases Homer employed, it seems absurd to me—as to many others—that we assume no originalities on his own part, in metaphors and in organization, and in his prideful sense of self as an artist of composition, as well as of performance. His ironies surely are his own inventions, and sometimes superbly reflect his awareness of his own mastery, and so of his superiority to the singers who had come before him. Yet all irony has, in part, a defensive purpose and function, since to say one thing and mean another almost universally is a warding off of technique. Here is a grim, brief tragedy of the bardic Thamyris (*Iliad*, book 2, lines 594–600) in the effectively literal version of Andrew Ford:

> there the Muses
> encountered Thamyris the Thracian and stopped his singing
> as he was coming from Oichalia and the house of Oichalian Eurytus;
> for he made a boastful vow that he would emerge victorious
> even if the Muses, daughters of Zeus, should come to sing in person,
> and they became angry and maimed him, and at once
> took away his divine gift of singing
> and made him forget how to play the lyre.

Thamyris, a mythical early Thracian poet (like Orpheus), has thus a very different relation to the Muses than the one enjoyed by Homer. They would not tolerate rivalry from Thamyris, perhaps because he himself was the son of a Muse. Homer takes care to enter no contest against the Muses; his invocations shrewdly do not quite call upon them for aid, and sidestep any idea of competing with them. "Anger be now your song, immortal one," the *Iliad* begins by addressing the Muse, while the *Odyssey* starts, "Sing in me, Muses, and through me tell the story" (both translated by Robert Fitzgerald). It is as though Homer, culminating a long tradition, persuades us that he is pragmatically first because those who came earlier could not survive the great unwisdom of contesting the Muses. How should one read the unvoicing of Thamyris?

To answer that question, one starts by being skeptical of Homer's voice, which is suspiciously diffident in regard to its own status and limits. Plainly inspired by the Muses, Homer is wary of asserting his own wisdom, even when it is augmented by a Muse's power. And yet he portrays seers and bards whose visions and insights transcend the human depictions that associate the narrative voice of the epics with forerunners who are authentic sages. Plato, doubtless with much irony, refers to "the divine Homer," but the irony of the adjective vanished in Plato's ultimate descendants, the Neoplatonic allegorizers of Homer.

I rely here upon a superb study, Robert Lamberton's *Homer the Theologian* (1986), which traces "the history of perhaps the most powerful and enduring of the strong misreadings . . . that make up our cultural heritage," the Neoplatonist interpretations of Homer from the second to the fifth century of the common era. Fantastic as they were, they were immensely influential, and found their ultimate legatee in Dante.

For nine hundred years before Dante (1265–1321), Homer's work had been available merely as fragments quoted in the writings of others. Only a generation after Dante's death, Homer's poems returned in their full text. When Dante's guide, Vergil, leads him beyond the gates of the Inferno, they enter Limbo, where the virtuous heathens suffer grief without pain, since they were born too early to be saved by Christ. In a blaze of light, Dante and Vergil behold the epic poets, gathered around the armed figure of Homer, chief of poets and precursor of Dante's own precursor, Vergil. Yet this Homer is a poet unread by Dante; he is only a name. When Dante later, deep in Hell, encounters Ulysses, it is indeed Vergil's Ulysses, and not Homer's Odysseus, to whom we listen.

The Neoplatonic or Plotinean Homer allows Dante to learn Ulysses as an allegory of the soul's wandering, but Dante swerves away from the Neoplatonists' version of salvation, since for him Odysseus/Ulysses is thoroughly damned. And yet the Ulysses who speaks out of the fire to Dante can be judged to be Dante's own genius, in one of the senses that I explore throughout this book.

Scholarship probably will never reach full agreement upon Homer, but as an incessant reader of the *Iliad* and the *Odyssey*, they seem to me works by the same poet, though at very different stages of his life and work, with the *Odyssey* evidently the later composition. The story of Odysseus, as told by Homer, is the celebration of a great survivor. The name "Odysseus" (latinized as "Ulysses") means either an avenger who inflicts his curse upon others, or someone who himself is victimized by a curse, here the curse of the earth-shaker, the angry sea god, Poseidon. Poseidon's curse is for Odysseus almost an insurmountable obstacle: how does a hero, however resourceful or enduring, get home to his island kingdom of Ithaca when the world of the waters is ruled by a vengeful god who refuses to be placated?

Of all survivor's stories, this is the most successful, though Homer's Odysseus has so sure a sense of his own identity that it is difficult for many among us not to be somewhat alienated from him. He is formidable and more than a little cold: how else could he prevail? There are many aspects to the genius of Homer (not a Greek phrase or concept), including very complex storytelling skills, but the universality of his Achilles, in the *Iliad*, may be the crown of his excellence. Until the last two centuries, the half-god Achilles (who is also half a child) may have seemed the more conspicuous of the two great Homeric heroes, but Odysseus/Ulysses has meant more to Romantic and modern writers. Perhaps the hero-villain aspect of Odysseus generated his greater appeal, but I suspect it has been more a matter of resourcefulness and guile. Sometimes the wily Odysseus, like Huckleberry Finn, lies merely to keep in practice. Shakespeare's Ulysses, a parody of all politicians, speaks neither truths nor lies, but worldliness, one of the pragmatic qualities that make *Troilus and Cressida* perhaps the most sophisticated of all Shakespeare's plays.

The Homeric gods, though we think of them as definitive for the ancient Greeks, were very troublesome for many who came after Homer, and for Plato in particular, who could not tolerate the idea that the gods of the *Iliad*, in particular, killed for their sport. Apollo, leading the Trojans on in book 15, scatters the Greek rampart in one sweep as a boy, playing on the seashore, knocks down the sand-wall he has built. The Homeric gods in one sense are children, but so is Achilles, hero of the *Iliad*, who nevertheless has the dignity of a tragic figure. The *Iliad* has a unique aesthetic power, difficult to describe, because the tragedy of Achilles is so different from the tragedies of Shakespeare's great warriors: Othello, Macbeth, Antony, Coriolanus. The anger of Achilles has an edge of transcendental bitterness to it, because he is half a god yet mortal. His frenzy to kill is a dialectical protest against mortality itself. Achilles slaughters Trojans almost in the spirit of an outraged child who tortures a wounded kitten. There are translations of Homer into English by the poets George Chapman, Alexander Pope, and William Morris, and more recently by Richmond Lattimore, Robert Fitzgerald, and Robert Fagles, but Tennyson, who translated only one fragment from the *Iliad*, catches elements that no one else does. Here is his "Achilles over the Trench," *Iliad*, book 17, where he calls the hero Aekides:

> Then rose Aekides dear to Zeus; and round
> The warrior's puissant shoulders Pallas flung
> Her fringed aegis, and around his head
> The glorious goddess wreathed a golden chord,
> And from it lighted an all-shining flame.
> As when a smoke from a city goes to heaven
> Far off from out an island girt by foes,
> All day the men contend in grievous war
> From their own city, but with set of sun
> Their fires flame thickly, and aloft the glare
> Flies streaming, if perchance the neighbours round
> May see, and sail to help them in the war;
> So from his head the splendour went to heaven,
> From wall to dyke he stept, he stood, not joined
> The Achaens—honoring his wise mother's work—
> There standing, shouted, and Pallas far away
> Called; and a boundless panic shook the foe.
> For like the clear voice when a trumpet shrills,
> Blown by the fierce beleaguerers of a town,
> So rang the clear voice of Aekides;
> And when the brazen cry of Aekides
> Was heard among the Trojans, all their hearts
> Were troubled, and the full-maned horses whirled
> The chariots backward, knowing griefs at hand;
> And sheer-astounded were the charioteers
> To see the dread, onweariable fire
> That always o'er the great Peleion's head

Burned, for the bright-eyed goddess made it burn.
Thrice from the dyke he sent his mighty shout,
Thrice backward reeled the Trojans and allies
And there and then twelve of their noblest died
Among their spears and chariots.

Achilles, long absent from battle, reenters the war, his purpose directly
being to get back his arms and armor, and the corpse of his beloved Patroklos. Note that Achilles is unarmed, yet he burns with Pallas Athena's fire.
He and Athena shout their battle cries antiphonally, and the effect upon the
Trojans is so terrifying that a dozen of their best warriors die by reeling
backward upon the spears and chariots of their fellows. The savage greatness of the *Iliad* hardly could better be epitomized. Homer's gods are neither Plato's nor our own. Athena's exaltation in battle is akin to the laughter
of Zeus, who rejoices that we slay one another. The otherness of all this is
splendid and also estranging. Yahweh may be a man of war, but he fights the
wars of Yahweh, in which he expects Israel to join.

And yet Achilles stands apart from Athena and the gods, and also from
all the other humans in the poem. Homeric irony is difficult to describe,
particularly in the *Iliad*, but it is generally at work whenever Achilles
speaks. Adam Parry first pointed out that "Achilles is . . . the one Homeric
hero who does not accept the common language and feels that it does not
correspond to reality." And yet Homer shrewdly gives the alienated
Achilles no language of his own, in which his otherness could be explicitly
disclosed. A perpetually implicit irony separates Achilles from the other
Greeks, the Trojans, and the gods. Achilles bruises the limits of language,
with rhetorical questions, redundancies, and demands that never can be
fulfilled. Hamlet, as Parry observes, is the master of overt irony, and can
express the tragedy of his own estrangement, but the heroic Achilles,
barely articulate in comparison, simply cannot, an inability that Homer
brilliantly exploits. How otherwise could we feel the pathos of Achilles'
predicament, since he is the best of the Greeks, and yet doomed by his
own anxious triumphalism? The genius of the poet of the *Iliad* is brilliantly manifested in Achilles.

The *Odyssey*, whether or not it is primarily the work of the same poet, has
a hero extraordinarily different from the tragic Achilles. Resourceful, cunning beyond measure, the great survivor Odysseus is himself a genius, and
a mature one. He is a superb storyteller and charms very nearly all his auditors. It is difficult to speak of Achilles' purposes, if any, until Patroklos is

killed. Odysseus, who never wanted to go off to Troy, wishes only to get home to his wife, father, son, and island kingdom. No one else in all of literature manifests so sustained a drive.

Even the genres of the *Iliad* and the *Odyssey* seem opposed. The *Iliad* is the classical epic, while the *Odyssey*, despite its formal arrangement, is more romance than epic. We have debased the term "romance," but traditionally it meant the literary mode of the marvelous story, idealized or fantastic rather than realistic. Folklore and comedy are central to the *Odyssey*, and hardly exist in the *Iliad*. You can juxtapose the two poems, by saying that, in the *Odyssey*, we are given realistic descriptions of the marvelous, while the *Iliad* describes realities as marvels. Though the *Odyssey* seems anxiously determined not to repeat anything crucial in the *Iliad*, the later poem shyly alludes to and even parodies the epic of Achilles. And yet Odysseus is the same personality in both poems, though he moves to the center, and our consciousness of him expands. We are indeed up so close to Odysseus that we find it odd that the poem actually begins near the end of things, after the hero is set free from his seven-year sojourn with Calypso, enchanting goddess but not his faithful Penelope. The present-time action of the poem occupies only thirty-seven days, but Odysseus frequently revisits his past in his storytelling. One scholar, H. D. F. Kitto, usefully observes that the *Odyssey* never relies upon surprising its reader; even in the hero's homecoming battle with the suitors, Homer does not seek to rouse anxious expectations in us.

There is an element in the *Odyssey* that already is almost Vergilian, a sense of things-in-their-farewell. Though he goes home, Odysseus evidently is aware that he communes with his equals (setting Penelope aside) only when he speaks to ghosts: Agamemnon, Achilles, and the sullen Ajax who turns away, refusing to answer. Since Penelope is not mentioned in the *Iliad*, you could judge that Odysseus is more than fulfilled in getting away from the tragic location of Troy, but Homer perhaps retains nostalgia for the earlier poem. The ironies of the *Odyssey* are more explicit, and Odysseus himself is an overt ironist, absorbing even his own inability at first to recognize Ithaca when he wakes up there after an absence of twenty years.

The genius of Homer (or of this second Homer) pervades the *Odyssey*, though the poem's epiphanies, even its descent into Hades, never have the kinetic force of Achilles and Athena shouting to one another as he returns to the battle. If I think of the *Odyssey*, I always remember first the reunion of Odysseus and Achilles in the world below. I quote here from Chapman's Homer, where Odysseus addresses the greater hero.

"Thou therefore, Thetis' sonne,
Hast equald all that ever yet have wonne
The blisse the earth yields, or hereafter shall.
In life thy eminence was ador'd of all,
Even with the Gods. And now, even dead, I see
Thy vertues propagate thy Empire
To a renewd life of command beneath.
So great Achilles triumphs over death."
This comfort of him this encounter found:
"Urge not my death to me, nor rub that wound.
I rather wish to live in earth a Swaine
Or serve a Swaine for hire, that scarce can gaine
Breath to sustain him, than (that life once gone)
Of all the dead sway the Imperiall throne."
—book 11, 633–46

The equivalent biblical sentiment—better a living dog than a dead lion—lacks the dramatic poignance lent by Achilles as speaker. To have won every contest, the essence of Homeric glory, is still no consolation for the best of the Greeks, who was so outraged by mortality during his lifetime, and remains unappeased in the world of the dead.

LUIS VAZ DE CAMÕES (CAMOENS)

It is here, on the gentle bosom of this same kindly river, that the soaking Cantos of this poem will make harbour after the misery and wretchedness of shipwreck, having survived storms and shallows, privations and perils in compliance with the unjust decree pronounced on one whose harmonious lyre is destined to bring him rather fame than fortune.

(translated by William C. Atkinson)

The Lusiads, the epic of Camoens, the Portuguese Homer or Vergil, must be the most politically incorrect poem ever written, and its poet is clearly guilty of all the sins first named as such in the universities and now deplored by the media: orientalism, racism, sexism, mercantilism, imperialism, and all their variations. And yet Camoens is a great epic poet, whose imaginative force animates the Portuguese literary tradition that emanates from him, which I have chosen to represent throughout this book, including the superb modernist poet Fernando Pessoa, and the nineteenth-century novelist Eça de Queiroz. The Brazilian novelist Machado de Assis has his own relation to that tradition, and also figures in this book. My rule against living geniuses causes me to exclude the marvelous novelist José Saramago, one of the last titans of an expiring literary genre.

The battered Camoens had lost his father to a shipwreck off Portuguese India, at Goa, and himself lost his right eye battling at Crete. Few major poets have been warriors, whatever their cause: Camoens had little literary acclaim in his own lifetime, but ever since has been the national poet, a curious fate for so singular and fierce a Renaissance adventurer.

In our new, ongoing Age of Terror, Camoens is likely to seem too provocative a partisan, since his vision of a world won for Portuguese Catholicism necessarily posits the Muslims as prime rivals. And yet Camoens, though his theme is Portuguese heroism, counts the human cost of everything, and his deep ambivalences reflect a genius as compassionate as it was courageous. His heroic epic is not an antique work, but alas is relevant, all too relevant, as we voyage further into our new age of religious warfare (however we dissimulate by naming it otherwise).

LUIS VAZ DE CAMÕES (CAMOENS)
(1524?–1580)

PROPHESYING THE FUTURE OF LITERARY genius is necessarily to gaze first at the past of genius. One wonders in what form the twenty-first century will behold the return of the gods. Look back at the founders of national literatures. To get *The Lusiads* going, Camoens invokes the Muses, dedicates to the heroic boy-king Sebastian, and then convokes the gods on Olympus. Venus and Mars favor the Portuguese, but Bacchus opposes. Jupiter being in favor, Vasco da Gama's fleet sails up the east coast of Africa and lands at Mozambique, where Bacchus rouses the Muslims against them. Bacchus will try again at Mombasa, but Venus thwarts him. Yet when I reflect on the poem, I remember first canto 5 with the giant Adamastor, who is an invention of genius. Da Gama describes this titanic manifestation:

> "The fearsome monster was proceeding with its prophecies of the fates in store for us when I boldly interrupted. 'Who are you,' I asked, 'for proportions so outrageous take one's breath away?' It rolled its black eyes, contorted its mouth and, uttering a giant roar that filled me with terror, replied in a voice heavy with bitterness, as though the question were one it would gladly have avoided:
>
> "'I am that mighty hidden cape, called by you Portuguese the Cape of Storms, that neither Ptolemy, Pomponius, Strabo, Pliny nor any other of past times ever had knowledge of. This promontory of mine, jutting out towards the South Pole, marks the southern extremity of Africa. Until now it has remained unknown: your daring offends it deeply. Adamastor is my name. I was one of the giant sons of earth, brother to Enceladus, Briareus, and the others. With them I took part in the war against Jupiter, not indeed piling mountain upon mountain but as a sea-captain, disputing with Neptune's squadrons the command of the deep.'"

Adamastor, though so fearsome, is a figure of considerable erotic pathos: he desperately loves Thetis, is tricked by her, and suffers an Ovidian metamorphosis into the Cape of Storms (now called the Cape of Good Hope). Camoens, a very tough, military ironist, has da Gama relate the story, and he is the hero who in canto 9 will enjoy Thetis in that superb erotic paradise, the Island of Love. In a national epic more Portuguese than Roman Catholic (despite its professed piety), the audacious Camoens takes back from the Koran its vision of the sexual bliss awaiting the warriors of Islam in Paradise. Camoens, again ironically, does better than Muhammad; Vasco da Gama and his heroic mariners experience their immortal orgasms with the nymphs without the inconvenience of dying first.

The Lusiads fights a tremendous battle, not only against the Muslims and all the peoples who dispute Portugal's empire, but just as crucially against the poets Vergil and Ariosto. Few poems begin so aggressively as The Lusiads; hardly are we under way when Camoens proclaims, "Let us hear no more then of Ulysses and Aeneas and their long journeying." We are to hear of the even more heroic Vasco da Gama, who has the immense advantage of being a historical figure (related to Camoens by marriage) whom the poet mythicizes.

Like Cervantes, Camoens suffered maiming in battle and the long neglect of patrons, and again like Cervantes, Camoens went to jail, though for public violence rather than the arrears of tax collecting. But Cervantes earned fame, though little money, and eventually, late in life, found benign patronage. The heroic Sebastian granted a poor pension, and seems to have regarded The Lusiads as only an adequate account of Portugal in India. One thinks of the national epic poet of the United States, Walt Whitman, or of Edmund Spenser waiting idly in court hoping for Queen Elizabeth's bounty. The genius who defines a nation will receive posthumous rewards, with a few exceptions like Goethe. Dante was acclaimed throughout Italy, but never was welcomed back to Florence on terms he could accept. William Blake lived and died in obscurity and poverty. The exceptions are the dramatists who understood what their public wanted and needed: Shakespeare, Lope de Vega, Calderón, Molière, Ibsen. John Milton, the epic genius of England, went blind, was imprisoned for a time, and had his books burned by the public hangman. Peron tried to humiliate Borges, and Lorca was murdered by the Falange. Camoens, transcendent genius of his nation, true ancestor of Eça, Pessoa, Saramago, is by no means an anomaly in his worldly fate.

Yet Camoens, like the very different Cervantes, was a tough soldier, and born to endurance, sustained by national pride at the astonishing courage of a tiny nation that had pushed out the Moors, held the Spaniards off, and dominated the oceans of the world, establishing empires in Africa, Brazil, India, and China. In these days of academic "postcolonialism" and of "orientalism," sixteenth-century Portugal is regarded as a villain. I of course would *not* have wished to find myself there and then: they would have made a bonfire of me. But a touch of perspective is needed: the Northmen or Normans do not evoke such censure, presumably because they were more remote in time, and did not sail under the cross of the Catholic Church. One needs to read *The Lusiads* as one reads the Norse sagas or *Beowulf*, or as one reads book 5 of *The Faerie Queen*, where the wild Irish are the enemy. *The Lusiads* was published in 1572, the year of the Saint Bartholomew's Day massacres of Huguenots in Paris and throughout France. Out of that maelstrom came the eventual triumph of Henry of Navarre, and of the Protestant epics of his poets, Agrippa d'Aubigne and Du Bartas. The wars of religion, which we rightly deplore, never cease: Jews and Muslims battle, as they did in the Koran; Roman Catholics, Serb Orthodox, and Muslims fight on in the Balkans; Hindu and Muslim armies contend for Kashmir. Let us dismiss our weak idealisms: the world Camoens describes is still our world, even if Portugal has come home to Portugal, and Brazil is its own realm. Countercultural morality, even if it had an authority beyond that dubiously conferred by Anglo-American universities and media, is simply no guide at all to reading great literature.

Camoens died in terrible depression in 1580, not because *The Lusiads* was still a neglected masterpiece, but because of Sebastian's heroic but crazy African disaster of 1578, in which the body of the boy-king could not be recovered from the battlefield. The national epic poet thus did not have to suffer the myth of Sebastianism, which can be regarded either as a national psychosis or a triumph of the popular imagination, again dependent upon your own perspective. Fernando Pessoa, the Portuguese poet who comes closest to challenging Camoens, embraced Sebastianism, though with a difference, and defensively stays as far away from Camoens as he possibly can. To indicate why, I turn to a brief overview of some of the aesthetic achievements of *The Lusiads*, a poem allusively armored against Vergil and the literary past.

The Lusiads abounds in a mysterious local life, which is too readily tied into the poem's imperial theme by its commentators. I am not much moved when I am told that the delicious orgies of sailors and nymphs on the Island of Love are emblematic of Portugal's dominance of the ocean. But I will commence with some smaller local instances.

At the close of canto 4, King Manuel I sends da Gama off to India, in search of spices, dominion, and glory. As the heroes sail out of Lisbon, a prophetic old man stands on the shore and denounces the expedition:

"Prometheus brought down fire from heaven and, breathing it into the heart of man, set the world ablaze with the clash of arms, dishonour, and destruction. How much better would it not have been for us, Prometheus, and how much less harmful to the world, had you never breathed life into that image of man and fired it with overreaching desires! The luckless Phaethon would then have left Apollo's chariot alone, and Icarus and his father would never have sought to soar through space. A sea commemorates the latter's foolishness, a river the former's. But now there is no undertaking so daring, or so accursed, be it through fire, water, heat, cold or the sword, that man will leave it untried. Wretched in truth is his lot, and strange his nature!"

Portugal is at once Prometheus, Phaethon, and Icarus, and Camoens personally risks the fate of the poet Phaethon, who learned he could not control Pegasus. Perhaps there is a touch of the Homeric Tiresias here, yet Camoens's old prophet is essentially a fresh invention. He presages mad Elijah, in Melville's *Moby-Dick,* warning Ishmael and Queequeg not to sail with Ahab in the *Pequod,* and also the crazy old Mennonite who, in Cormac McCarthy's *Blood Meridian,* admonishes the Kid against the first of his scalp-hunting expeditions. Most importantly, he reveals in Camoens not so much an ambivalence towards Portugal's heroism but a national prophet's sense of the dangers that were to lead to Sebastian's sublime debacle.

Camoens delays his invocation of the epic Muse, Calliope, until the start of canto 3, so as to get the other gods out of the way and be alone with the Muse. John Milton, invoking Urania, is hardly more high-handed than Camoens, who promises the goddess that in return Apollo will be sexually more faithful to her than he has been in the past. Indeed, Camoens's audacity is boundless; the Tagus is the new fountain of the Muses, and the poet somewhat chides the Muse: "You would not have me be afraid for your beloved Orpheus, lest in the result he be overshadowed." Yet this is a two-way thrust, and warns the poet also: Bacchus/Dionysus is the enemy of Portugal, and his Maenads tore Orpheus apart. Is the bard of Portugal to experience an Orphic *sparagmos*?

In life, to some degree; in the poem, his surrogate is the beautiful Inês de Castro, whose tragedy, in canto 3, is the lyrical triumph of *The Lusiads.* Crown Prince Pedro of Portugal takes the charming Inês as his mistress, and begets children upon her, but his father, the aging King Afonso, fears for the legitimacy of his line, and yields to an angry mob, whose security is invested in a state marriage for Pedro:

these cruel assassins now plunged their swords into Inês's neck, that alabaster pedestal for the beauty that first smote her prince with love; and the white flowers at her feet, lately watered with her tears, turned red.

This *frisson farouche* has an unmistakable sadistic component, and the one-eyed Camoens trades in such effects, and without the saving comedy of Ariosto. But there is no way to acquit *The Lusiads* as delighting both in sensuality and in carnage, commonplaces of his time. Canto 4 becomes a litany of slaughters that is resolved only by the appearance of the hero Vasco da Gama, whose overseas ventures turn the Portuguese away from Iberian bloodthirstiness to the export of the Lusitanian drive for dominance.

My favorite episode in *The Lusiads* comes in the erotic canto 9, where Cupid, instructed by his mother, Venus, prepares the nymphs for their ecstasies by the agonies of battle-wounds, in an extraordinary literalization of the Alexandrian metaphor of the arrows of Eros. *The Lusiads* is the most politically incorrect of all epics, and what follows must infuriate feminist critics:

> Such rare praises, the tidings of such outstanding qualities, had their effect on the hearts even of the gods whom Bacchus had inflamed against the heroes, and inclined them somewhat in their favour. The feminine heart, that more lightly abandons its earlier decisions, was already prepared to count it misplaced zeal and cruelty that had led them to wish such bravery ill.
>
> With this, Cupid let fly his arrows one by one, until the sea groaned under the impact. Some went straight through the restless waves, others described a more circuitous course. All found their mark, and the nymphs began to utter most ardent sighs, that welled from the secret depths of their being. Each one was smitten, though none had yet seen the face of him she loved; for the ear in these matters is as vulnerable as the eye.
>
> The indomitable youth then drew bow once again, more vigorously this time than ever, for on Tethys, who was ever the most hostile to the Portuguese, he wanted to inflict the deepest wound of all.
>
> And now his quiver was empty, nor was there left in all the ocean a nymph alive. Wounded, indeed, they still drew breath, but only to the extent of realizing that the wound was fatal.
>
> But let the surging billows make way, for look, Venus has seen to the remedy: riding the blue sea, the bellying white sails come into

view. Now ardent love can make reciprocal answer to the passion that fires the maiden hearts, provided, that is, the native modesty show a due deference to Venus's every behest.

Led by Venus herself, the whole beauteous company of the Nereids had already set out for the island, engaging as they went in the choral dances that were their custom. Once there, the lovely goddess told them of her own behaviour on the innumerable occasions when she fell in love; and they, now completely in thrall to the gentle emotion, hung on her every word.

Manifestly, this is a triumph of male sadism: nothing is intimated of the pain of those fatal wounds, but we feel the poet's satisfaction in "nor was there left in all the ocean a nymph alive." Can this gusto be distinguished from the poet's zest in piling up Castilians, Muslims, Africans, and, by implication, Indians and native Brazilians? Aesthetically, all this works because Camoens understands that a latecomer in literature must rely upon a return of the gods. Though, once the mutual ravishing wears down a bit, nymphs and sailors exchange vows of marriage, there are no Roman Catholic priests on hand to solemnize these raptures.

We proceed to canto 10, with its prophecy of the future, a heroic cavalcade of worldwide Portuguese depredations, replete with possibilities of even more extensive appropriations. This may dazzle us, but we are not moved until the dark close, when Camoens so desperately recommends himself to the boy-king Sebastian:

Should Heaven grant me so much, and should you too one day be moved to embark on an enterprise meet for celebration in song, as something within me, noting the Heaven-sent trend of your designs, whispers prophetically you will, then, whether it be Mount Atlas that comes to dread the mere sight of you more than did Atlas himself the Gorgon's head, or whether, attacking by way of Cape Espartel, you level the fortifications of Morocco and Tarudant, I warrant you that this my Muse, become joyous again with recognition, shall so sing your praises to all mankind that you will be in their eyes a second Alexander, without cause this time to envy Achilles his good fortune in being immortalized by Homer.

Poor Sebastian, in the event, was no second Alexander or Achilles, and vanished in an oceanic onslaught of Moors. Camoens, dying at the beginning of summer 1580, wrote his own epitaph:

All may see that my country was so beloved by me that I am content to die not only in it but with it.

The death of the madly heroic Sebastian became also the death of the great warrior-poet. Camoens left a legacy still vibrant, though disguised, in Fernando Pessoa, and undone, if at all, only by the ironic and compassionate genius of José Saramago. But Camoens gives a vital clue also to the future of the literary imagination, as we move into the twenty-first century. Without Venus and Mars, and the opposing Bacchus, he could not have met the challenge of Vergil and of Ariosto. In what form the gods will return, I cannot prophesy, but in all their cruelty and erotic intensity they certainly must return, if canonical literature is to continue to be composed.

If there was a particular "genius of influence" in the twentieth century, I would award the palm to Fernando Pessoa (1888–1935), whom I consider elsewhere in this book. Here I want only to gaze freshly at his ironic, life-long confrontation with the daemon of influence. Had Pessoa lived forever, he would have peopled the world with thousands of heteronyms. His outrageous denunciations of Shakespeare are prompted by his resentment of the only writer who might be judged to have done just that—though it would be a misjudgment. Pessoa was a great poet, of the eminence of Lorca or of Hart Crane, but he had not an iota of the Shakespearean *otherness* in him. He asserted that he had brought forth a whole company of Hamlets, but no play for them to perform. In his twenty-fifth year, he projected his heteronyms, and stayed with them for more than two decades until he died.

No one better exemplifies Oscar Wilde's warning that all bad poetry is sincere: Pessoa is never sincere. A larger constrast to Camoens could not exist, and I suspect that the combined eminence of Camoens and Walt Whitman prompted Pessoa's genius of insincerity, though Whitman long preceded Pessoa as a master of evasions.

Pessoa, whom scholars call a Modernist, is like all other Modernists a belated Romantic, and his relation to Camoens and Whitman is not much different from Robert Browning's relation to Shelley, or Ezra Pound's to Browning. Belatedness is a literary condition in which, like Wallace Stevens, you believe in a fiction while knowing that what you believe in is not true. Pessoa's fictions of belief included historical Gnosticism, Sebastianism with its vision of a messianic Portuguese Fifth Empire, and Fernando Pessoa as the super-Camoens, eclipsing the major poet in the language.

Richard Zenith wonderfully says that Pessoa was possessed by a genius or daemon—the daemon of detachment. And yet so was Goethe, greatest of European poets since Shakespeare. I am suggesting, not at all in contradiction to Zenith, that Pessoa is rather less a special case than he seems. He is not a postmodernist either, and will survive our still-current French intellectual disease. His authentic originality came in his playing out of the drama of influence. I myself prefer Álvaro de Campos to the other heteronyms, including Fernando Pessoa himself, but I know and love Walt Whitman too well to believe that Campos is of Whitman's eminence, and so I suppose I also suggest, though I know Camoens so less well, that Pessoa and Company is hardly a super-Camoens, just as Campos is not a super-Whitman. Still, to be the major poet in Portuguese since Camoens is an extraordinary distinction, akin to my observing that Wallace Stevens and Hart Crane seem to me the major North American poets since Walt Whitman and Emily Dickinson.

Pessoa's *Mensagem* (*Message* or *Summons*) is a remarkable sequence, aptly compared by Maria Ramaldo Santos to Hart Crane's *The Bridge,* but *The Sea Monster* does not compare adequately with Vasco da Gama's confrontation with the great Adamastor. Camoens has a primal power not in Pessoa's reach. One does not underestimate Pessoa as a poet's poet, but Camoens, like Cervantes, is a larger figure, who endured banishment, war (with the loss of his right eye), street brawls, imprisonment, and further warfare in Malabar, and in the Red Sea, followed by shipwreck in the China Sea. I do not fall, I trust, into the biographical fallacy when I observe that the tough and resilient temperament of Camoens is reflected throughout *The Lusiads.* Confronted by such a figure, Pessoa's detachment became more than an evasion: it became a blessing.

Pessoa's genius is capacious enough to appeal in different modes to different readers. The Horatian struggles of Ricardo Reis do not often enchant me, but they move me differently after I reread *The Year of the Death of Ricardo Reis,* by Saramago. I am a literary critic attempting to reeducate myself, as I go on seventy-one, with the help of the master Saramago. Were I a novelist, I would write *The Year of the Death of Álvaro de Campos* because his gusto fascinates me. That returns me to the genius of influence in Pessoa, and to his affinities to Robert Browning, and, on the other side of time, to Jorge Luis Borges.

Richard Zenith pleases me by his judgment that the flamboyant, rather Falstaffian Álvaro de Campos was the heteronym closest to Pessoa's descent from Marranos on his father's side, but Campos qualifies as a Jewish poet. A naval engineer by profession, Campos was Pessoa without inhibitions, writing letters to Pessoa's friends that Pessoa was too reserved to write. Zenith deliciously informs us that Campos wrote rather negatively to

Ophelia Queiroz, Pessoa's one lady love, who informed Pessoa how much she loathed Campos. Pessoa evidently answered, "I don't know why, since he is rather fond of you!" Overtly bisexual, Campos represented Pessoa's Return of the Repressed, and is closer even to our father Walt Whitman than Pessoa intended him to be: it is Campos who invokes Whitman's extraordinary four-in-one of Night, Death, the Mother, and the Sea.

> So be motherly to me, O tranquil night . . .
> You who remove the world from the world, you who are peace,
> You who don't exist, who are only the absence of light,
> You who aren't a thing, a place, an essence or a life,
> Penelope who weaves darkness that tomorrow will be unraveled,
> Unreal Circe of the fevered, of the anguished without cause,
> Come to me, O night, reach out your hands,
> And be coolness and relief, O night, on my forehead . . .
> You, whose coming is so gentle you seem to be drawing away,
> Whose ebb and flow of darkness, as the moon softly breathes,
> Has waves of dead tenderness, the cold of vast oceans of dream,
> Breezes of imagined landscapes for our inordinate anguish . . .
> You, pallidly, you, faintly, you, liquidly,
> Scent of death among flowers, breath of fever along riverbanks,
> You, queen, you, chatelaine, you, pale lady, come . . .
>
> (translated by Richard Zenith)

JAMES JOYCE

BLOOM

My beloved subjects, a new era is about to dawn. I, Bloom, tell you verily it is even now at hand. Yes, on the word of a Bloom, ye shall ere long enter into the golden city which is to be, the new Bloomusalem in the Nova Hibernia of the future.

• • •

THE MAN IN THE MACINTOSH

Don't you believe a word he says. That man is Leopold McIntosh, the notorious fireraiser. His real name is Higgins.

BLOOM

Shoot him! Dog of a Christian! So much for McIntosh!

We are in the Nightown phantasmagoria of Joyce's *Ulysses,* where Poldy, my amiable namesake, emerges fully as Joyce's genius, rather than the faded aesthete, Stephen Dedalus. There is an antic triple identity forged by the artificer of *Ulysses:* Shakespeare, Bloom, Joyce with Poldy as the mediator, the image of the human linking Shakespeare and Joyce.

Poldy, despite his Homeric model, is the most Shakespearean character in twentieth-century Western literature. He reaches back to the gentlest and most curious Shakespearean clowns: Bottom in *A Midsummer Night's Dream* and Feste in *Twelfth Night.* More crucially, to Joyce himself his Mr. Bloom is an image of citizen Shakespeare, as well as a representative of Dublin's Joyce.

It once was fashionable to describe Leopold Bloom as T. S. Eliot's Jew rather than James Joyce's: decadent, cursed, rapaciously male, depraved relic of a fossil-people. Joyce, unlike Eliot, was not an anti-Semite, and the actual Poldy is vital, gentle, affectionate, endlessly kind, and even heroic when he stands up for his Jewishness in a pub confrontation. Since he has an Irish Catholic mother and grandmother, he is not Talmudically Jewish, but he firmly and openly identifies with his dead father, the Hungarian Jew Virag. All Dublin considers him Jewish, as he does, and Joyce does. For Joyce, he is the Jew-as-Shakespeare, an exiled Shakespeare, and so a maker with whom the exile Joyce can identify.

JAMES JOYCE
(1882–1941)

DEFINING THE GENIUS OF JAMES JOYCE would be an impossible venture: who can define the genius of Shakespeare or Dante or Chaucer or Cervantes? One might speak of the "geniuses" of Joyce, but that doesn't help much. Derek Attridge sensibly points out that people read Joyce without knowing it, since all modern genres and media are almost as Joycean as they are Shakespearean. These early years of the twenty-first century, I would have difficulty in taking apart the tangle of Shakespeare, Joyce, and Freud that manifests endlessly in our media culture.

The great work by Joyce, beyond even the magnificence of *Ulysses*, is *Finnegans Wake*, but a half-century of reading the *Wake* (or more accurately, in the *Wake*) has convinced me that it never will be fully available to even the uncommon reader, whereas *Ulysses* is a pleasure, difficult but available, for the common reader of intelligence and goodwill. Bearing as I do the name of Joyce's Poldy, I assert no affinity to him, but I am happy enough to employ him here as the representative of an essential part of Joyce's genius. My subject therefore will be the personality of Leopold Bloom, which certainly has a considerable relation to the personality of James Joyce. Not that either Poldy's or Joyce's personality is simple to apprehend and to categorize. Sources for Joyce include Richard Ellmann's superb and personal *James Joyce* (revised, 1982), which needs to be supplemented by Brenda Maddox's *Nora* (1988), the biography of Nora Barnacle Joyce, and by Joyce's brother Stanislaus's *My Brother's Keeper* (1958).

Joyce, like everyone in *Ulysses*, Poldy included, regards his protagonist as a Jew, which, from a normative Jewish perspective, would be false. The Talmud defines a Jew as the child of a Jewish mother; Poldy's mother and her mother were Irish Catholics. But Poldy identifies with his dead father, Virag, a Jew who became a Protestant. Though Poldy has been both a Protestant and a Catholic, he has evolved into a non-observant Jew, yet his wife and his daughter are Catholic. His dead son, like the dead father, exists in Poldy's memory as a Jew, an assertion difficult to demonstrate but imaginatively essential, since he is to Poldy what Hamnet Shakespeare was to Shakespeare. If, as Baudelaire remarked, even the janitors in Balzac are geniuses, then the amiable Poldy is closer to being a genius than anyone else in *Ulysses* is, because Poldy has large elements in him both of James Joyce and of Joyce's Shakespeare. I will venture further: of all characters in twentieth-century literature, Leopold Bloom is the most Shakespearean, fit to mingle with Bottom, Falstaff, Hamlet, and Othello, though he does not much resemble any of them. He resembles Shakespeare himself, and is charmingly integrated into Shakespeare in Anthony Burgess's *Nothing Like the Sun,* a boisterously Joycean novel sometimes spoken about Shakespeare in the third person, and sometimes by him in the first.

The representation of genius in *Ulysses* is supposed to be Stephen Dedalus, but he is something of a dry stick, and Poldy steals every scene they share. Joyce, finding the paradigm of *completeness* in Homer's Odysseus (Latin Ulysses), made Poldy the most complete representation of a person in prose fiction. Since Joyce is an astonishing master of what most would consider trivia, we certainly know more details concerning Poldy than we know of Hamlet or Falstaff. And yet it remains a question, which might have annoyed Joyce: is Poldy a more complete representation of inwardness than Hamlet and Falstaff? We listen to them as they change; does Poldy change?

We are given a sequence of eighteen episodes acting themselves out on a single day. Poldy, who earns his living as an advertisement canvasser, has a mind far superior to his occupation. In its variety, quickness, self-revisionary intensity, and amazing capacity for simultaneous detachment and total sympathy, it might well be Joyce's speculative projection of the mind of William Shakespeare. At the least, Poldy's situation in life and his family relationships are strikingly parallel to Stephen's William Shakespeare in the Library scene.

The best book on Joyce I've ever read remains Frank Budgen's *James Joyce and the Making of "Ulysses"* (1934). Budgen, an English painter resident in Zurich, met Joyce there in 1918, and became the closest friend of Joyce's life except for John Francis Byrne, the "Cranly" of *A Portrait of the Artist as a Young Man.* After two-thirds of a century, Budgen's book remains fresh and vivid, and says better and more accurate things about Leopold Bloom than I can find anywhere else. Budgen sketches an exile, cut off from Christians and from Jews, a man neither liked nor disliked, who feels and thinks differently from anyone else in *Ulysses.* Free of religion and of politics, void of ambition, Poldy is prudent, self-contained, gently pessimistic but not unhappy. He is immune to rage, hatred, envy, and malice, and he is above all universally kind and generous. At thirty-eight, he seems three thousand years older than his fellow Dubliners, and though he is a dreamer, he lives in reality. As Budgen notes, he is the most reasonable and humane person in *Ulysses:* could we not add, in all of literature, since Falstaff and Sancho Panza, Hamlet and Don Quixote, are not always reasonable (Hamlet is scarcely humane)? Budgen's conclusion, eloquently phrased, is that Poldy Bloom's true brother is the admirable Uncle Toby in Laurence Sterne's *Tristram Shandy:*

> Bloom is almost as lonely in literature as he is in Dublin, but if there is a kinship it is not with the tragic and uncontained Bouvard et Pécuchet. He is distant from them by the whole space of his scepticism and pessimism. He is cocu, but neither imaginaire like the Moor of Venice, nor like the comic lunatic of the *Cocu Magnifique.* He has neither the authority and passion of the one, nor the insane doubts of the other. Seeing that in the actions he performs and in the thoughts he thinks there is no malice, no envy, no revenge, no hatred, I place him, notwithstanding his prudence, his flirtations, frillies for Raoul and all the rest, in the company of the pure of heart, as near as a father and a husband and a lover may be to Uncle Toby.

Is Poldy then a self-portrait of the inward Joyce? No, for though Joyce was a very good human being, he was not one of the very rare saints of literature, like Samuel Beckett and—for all we know—perhaps William Shakespeare. Poldy of course is no secular saint, but a gentle sinner, and an extraordinary blend of qualities conventionally considered to be both male and female.

In the phantasmagoria of the superb Nighttown sequence, Poldy observes through a keyhole the spectacle of his being cuckolded by Blazes Boylan, exults in his dishonor, and then suffers a vision of William Shakespeare:

LYNCH

(*points*) The mirror up to nature. (*he laughs*) Hu hu hu hu hu!
   (*Stephen and Bloom gaze in the mirror. The face of William Shakespeare, beardless, appears there, rigid in facial paralysis, crowned by the reflection of the reindeer antlered hatrack in the hall.*)

SHAKESPEARE

(*in dignified ventriloquy*) 'Tis the loud laugh bespeaks the vacant mind. (*to Bloom*) Thou thoughtest as how thou wastest invisible. Gaze. (*he crows with a black capon's laugh*) Iagogo! How my Oldfellow chokit his Thursdaymornun. Iagogogo!

This always seems to me the most ambiguous passage in *Ulysses,* and I never find students and friends agreeing on its interpretation. Lynch, very much in Shakespeare's spirit, takes Hamlet's advice to the players—hold the mirror up to nature—and insinuates that nature is cuckoldry, no more, no less. But why do Bloom and Stephen behold there the cuckolded Shakespeare, horned and clean-shaven and frozen-faced? And what is the oddly triumphant Shakespearean outburst on the horror of Othello smothering Desdemona? Shakespeare (deliberately?) misquotes Oliver Goldsmith's poem, "The Deserted Village" (1770), which reads, "And the loud laugh that spoke the vacant mind," Goldsmith intending "vacant mind" as one at rest, enjoying the leisured garland of repose. But Shakespeare mocks the empty minds of Lynch, Blazes Boylan, Molly Bloom, and the whores. Most curiously, Shakespeare addresses the gentle Poldy and unnecessarily warns him not to emulate Othello, murdering Molly as a new Desdemona. Mysteriously, Shakespeare speaks of his father ("my Oldfellow") murdering his Thursday mother ("his Thursdaymornun"), and all this to the rallying-cries of "Iagogo!" and "Iagogogo!"

I would begin by noting that Bloom and Stephen together make up Joyce, and that the augmented Joyce is Shakespeare, or as close to Shakespeare as can be reborn after three centuries. Stephen was a Thursday child, and he feels guilt concerning his dead mother, a guilt augmented by the obscene taunting of Malachi "Buck" Mulligan (Joyce's enemy-friend, the poet and physician Oliver St. John Gogarty). Playing (as he did at the Globe) the Ghost of Hamlet's father, Shakespeare warns the Joycean trio not to compound Hamlet with Othello, which would make the sensual Molly Bloom into a curious brew of Stephen's deceased mother, Queen Gertrude, and Desdemona. And the mockery goes further: staring into the mirror, Bloom/Stephen/Joyce behold not Shakespeare but their composite self: unbearded, impotent, cuckolded, and out of countenance. Like the God of the Calvinists, Shakespeare says to the triple Joyce, "Be like me, but don't attempt to be too like me."

Bloom, declining to understand, asks the whores, "When will I hear the joke?" and receives Zoe's grim rejoinder, "Before you're twice married and once a widower," implying Molly's murder. Poldy, grandly recovering, assures her that, "Lapses are condoned," and implicitly compares his impotence to Napoleon's, but then we are swept away into even wilder phantasmagoria. Frank Budgen recounts that Joyce placed Shakespeare far below Ibsen *as a dramatist*, a weird judgment, but then answered the question, "If on a desert island, what one book?" with the reluctant, "I should hesitate between Dante and Shakespeare but not for long. The Englishman is richer and would get my vote."

If asked who is the most complete character in literature since Shakespeare and Cervantes, I would not hesitate: "Poldy is richest and would get my vote."

ALEJO CARPENTIER

Within two days the century would have rounded out another year, and this would be of no importance to those around me. There the year in which we live can be forgotten, and they lie who say man cannot escape his epoch. The Stone Age, like the Middle Ages, is still within our reach. The gloomy mansions of romanticism, with its doomed loves, are still open. But none of this was for me, because the only human race to which it is forbidden to sever the bands of time is the race of those who create art, and who not only must move ahead of the immediate yesterday, represented by tangible witness, but must anticipate the song and the form of others who will follow them, creating new tangible witness with full awareness of what has been done up to the present.

(translated by Harriet De Onís)

We are on the last page of *The Lost Steps*, first published in Spanish by Carpentier in 1953. I will discuss two other novels by Carpentier in this book, because *The Lost Steps*, while his most ambitious fiction, seems to me a fascinating enigma. And yet it explains Carpentier's relation to history more clearly than his historical novels are able to convey.

"Magical realism," made famous by García Márquez's *One Hundred Years of Solitude*, was primarily Carpentier's invention. The idea that Latin Americans, whether in Cuba or Colombia or wherever, necessarily inhabit a reality more magical than, say, Manhattan's, is dubious. The genius of Borges, of Carpentier, of García Márquez may persuade us otherwise, while we are within their narratives, but we emerge to fresh doubts, both metaphysical and psychological.

Carpentier's authentic genius was for the historical novel, which he approached with the paradigm of the Kabbalah as explicitly as possible. Other modern novelists have used Kabbalistic models, including Thomas Pynchon, Malcolm Lowry, and Lawrence Durrell, but Carpentier uniquely discovered how to fuse Kabbalah and history.

ALEJO CARPENTIER
(1904–1980)

CARPENTIER, A CUBAN NOVELIST WITH A French father and a Russian mother, was one of the founding luminaries of Hispanic-American literature, akin to the Argentine Borges. A scholar of Afro-Cuban culture, particularly of its music, Carpentier's variety of "magic realism" is triumphant in three novels: *The Kingdom of This World* (1949), *The Lost Steps* (1953), and *Explosion in a Cathedral* (1962). The first and third of these are historical romances, *The Kingdom of This World* portraying at its close the downfall of Henri Christophe, king of Haiti, in 1820, while *Explosion* is set in the French Caribbean a generation before, as the guillotine is imported from Paris, to bring over all the benefits of revolutionary terror. *The Lost Steps* is very different, staged in a visionary present that, on a journey to the South American interior, takes one into apparent timelessness. Superb as *The Lost Steps* is, I prefer the two historical extravagances, and so will seek Carpentier's genius in them.

Carpentier is less well known than are Borges, Gabriel García Márquez, Julio Cortázar, and several other Hispanic-American authors of fiction. I am puzzled that this should be, since the three major narratives have literary strengths at least equal to those of Borges's *Ficciones* and García Márquez's *One Hundred Years of Solitude*. Perhaps a political element is at work: Carpentier, who scarcely had lived in Cuba before Castro's revolution, supported Castro's regime up until his death on April 24, 1980, and so was compromised by the new tyranny. His body was flown home from Paris for a state funeral, a dreadful final irony for the visionary who had so brilliantly shown the degeneration of revolution into terrors in both *The Kingdom of This World* and *Explosion in a Cathedral*. Carpentier in that sense was a victim of a still ongoing history.

There are victims abounding throughout *The Kingdom of This World*, a series of tableaux that move between the slave rebellions in what the French called Saint Domingue, and the final moments of Henri Christophe in 1820. There are five major historical events: Macandal leads the first slave revolt, Bouckman the second; then French colonists land in Santiago de Cuba, and General Leclerc conducts his battles, until the empire of Henri Christophe crashes down. Yet these, and many other occurrences, are presented disjunctively, and what the reader experiences is a phantasmagoria, a flow of fabulous incidents. Beneath that flow there is an extraordinarily precise numerology, set forth with gusto and erudition by Carpentier's canonical scholar, Roberto González Echevarría, in his *The Pilgrim at Home: Alejo Carpentier* (1977, 1990). The critic establishes that the narrative moves between 1753 and 1828, seventy-five years, and he shows how deliberate and complex is the cyclic pattern created by Carpentier. None of this need be the concern of the common reader, who will be regaled by a banquet of sense and violence. Perhaps all we need keep in mind as we begin is that *The Kingdom of This World* is ruled by Satan, the god of this world, who always triumphs in history, since he *is* history.

Ti Noel, a young slave, is fascinated by the stories of African kings told by the Mandingo slave Macandal, who also has extensive knowledge of poisonous plants. Santo Domingo is afflicted by an epidemic of poison, destroying first livestock and then many of the whites. A great shaman, Macandal takes the shape of birds, fish, insects, thus evading capture, until at last he is apprehended and burned alive, though in a vision the other blacks see him ascend.

Years later, Bouckman the Jamaican leads an insurrection of the slaves, which is put down with overwhelming force. Ti Noel survives, and is taken off to Santiago de Cuba, to be sold. Once in Cuba, we are in a very different story.

Pauline Bonaparte arrives with her husband, General Leclerc, who subsequently dies of yellow fever. Ti Noel, after years in Cuba, returns as a freed man to Santo Domingo, where slavery has been abolished, but Henri Christophe reigns as king. And Ti Noel, an old man, is impressed into virtual slavery by guards, who whip him into brick-carrying, to build a fortress for the monarch. There is an uprising, Henri Christophe shoots himself, and Ti Noel helps sack the royal palace.

Nothing endures. Republican mulattoes arrive, to whip the blacks into fresh servitude. To escape, Ti Noel becomes a shaman, transforming himself into animals, birds, ants. However, when he joins the geese, he is cast out:

> Ti Noel vaguely understood that his rejection by the geese was a punishment for his cowardice. Macandal had disguised himself as an animal for years to serve men, not to abjure the world of men. It was then that the old man, resuming his human form, had a supremely lucid moment. He lived, for the space of a heartbeat, the finest moments of his life; he glimpsed once more the heroes who had revealed .

to him the power and the fullness of his remote African forebears, making him believe in the possible germinations the future held. He felt countless centuries old. A cosmic weariness, as of a plant weighted with stones, fell upon his shoulders shrunk by so many blows, sweats, revolts. Ti Noel had squandered his birthright, and, despite the abject poverty to which he had sunk, he was leaving the same inheritance he had received: a body of flesh to which things happened. Now he understood that a man never knows for whom he suffers and hopes. He suffers and hopes and toils for people he will never know, and who, in turn, will suffer and hope and toil for others who will not be happy either, for man always seeks a happiness far beyond that which is meted out to him. But man's greatness consists in the very fact of wanting to be better than he is. In laying duties upon himself. In the Kingdom of Heaven there is no grandeur to be won, inasmuch as there is an established hierarchy, the unknown is revealed, existence is infinite, there is no possibility of sacrifice, all is rest and joy. For this reason, bowed down by suffering and duties, beautiful in the midst of his misery, capable of loving in the face of afflictions and trials, man finds his greatness, his fullest measure, only in the Kingdom of This World.

(translated by Harriet De Onís)

This may be too explicit, but in context, a page away from the close of this remarkable romance narrative, it possesses aesthetic dignity, and a kind of wisdom, because it has to be Ti Noel's book, and more now than Macandal or Bouckman he is wholly admirable. His final gesture is poignant:

The old man hurled his declaration of war against the new masters, ordering his subjects to march in battle array against the insolent words of the mulattoes in power.

His "subjects" are the winds and the sea, and after the great green wind blows in from the water, Ti Noel dies what we call a natural death. Only that could end his book, which has condensed seventy-five years of his life into the vision of fewer than two hundred pages. The overwhelming effect of *The Kingdom of This World* is that of a baroque splendor, a spectacular piling on of incredible riches. Carpentier had a genius for visionary condensation, and while his narrative moves rapidly onward, the frequent effect is of a violent spilling over of incongruities, as here at the start of Bouckman's rebellion:

All the doors of the quarters burst open at the same time, broken down from within. Armed with sticks, the slaves surrounded the houses of the overseers, seizing the tools. The bookkeeper, who had appeared, pistol in hand, was the first to fall, his throat slit from top to bottom by a mason's trowel. After bathing their arms in the blood of the white man, the Negroes ran toward the big house, shouting death to the master, to the Governor, to God, and to all the Frenchmen in the world. But, driven by a longstanding thirst, most of them rushed to the cellar looking for liquor. Pick-blows demolished kegs of salt fish. Their staves sprung, casks began to gush wine, reddening the women's skirts. Snatched up with shouts and shoves, the demijohns of brandy, the carboys of rum, were splintered against the walls. Laughing and scuffling, the Negroes went sliding through pickled tomatoes, capers, herring roe, and marjoram on the brick floor, a slime thinned by a stream of rancid oil flowing from a skin bag. A naked Negro, as a joke, jumped into a tub full of lard. Two old women were quarreling in Congolese over a clay pot. Hams and dried codfish tails were jerked from the ceiling. Side-stepping the mob, Ti Noel put his mouth to the bung of a barrel of Spanish wine and his Adam's apple rose and fell for a long time. Then followed by his older sons, he went up to the first floor of the house. For a long time now he had dreamed of raping Mlle Floridor. On those nights of tragic declamations she had displayed beneath the tunic with its Greek-key border breasts undamaged by the irreversible outrage of the years.

Ti Noel is hardly idealized by Carpentier; on the next page we find: "Mlle Floridor lay on the rug, legs sprawled wide, a sickle buried in her entrails." Yet how remarkable the paragraph of the rebellion is. The God of the French does not differ in kind from the master or the governor, and the only "irreversible outrage" is time, which is one with Satan's kingdom of this world. The reader may ask: in what way is Ti Noel ultimately more sympathetic than all of the forces of servitude, since rape and butchery are so natural to him? Carpentier, a Franco-Russian and not a black Cuban, nevertheless inclines towards a black Caribbean perspective. I emphasize "black"; the mulattoes and other mixed-bloods are all portrayed as a new class of masters. But Carpentier never moralizes; the greatness, the fullest measure, found by Macandal, Bouckman, and most of all by Ti Noel, is not at all a moral greatness. The heroism of rebellion, exalted for its own sake, probably reflects the influence of Camus upon the early Carpentier, but I find no humanism and no atheism in *The Kingdom of This World* and Carpentier's later works.

A baroque mysticism, Kabbalistic and Gnostic, will be the burden of Carpentier's most ambitious novel, *The Century of Lights*, known in English as *Explosion in a Cathedral*. The novel's epigraph is from the *Zohar* or *Book of Light* of Moses de Leon, the masterpiece of the Spanish Kabbalah: "Words do not fall into the void." For reasons not always clear to me, Carpentier constructs his novel on a rather tight Kabbalistic grid. Borges plays with Kabbalah, but does not structure his stories on that esoteric model, with the exception of "Death and the Compass."

Carpentier, like the Kabbalists, was an apocalyptic, which must have influenced his adherence to Castro's revolution. To writers currently enduring Castro's Havana, Carpentier's occasional writings on literature and politics must be hard to take; I myself cannot bear them, but politicized literary criticism is my particular hatred, since it has destroyed my profession. *Explosion in a Cathedral* was written in Caracas, Venezuela, from 1956 to 1958, and is a purely Kabbalistic or visionary apocalypse, with very little relation to the Cuba to which Carpentier returned in 1959.

The British occupied Havana in 1762–63, bringing about changes that the Spanish officials could not wholly repair when Havana was theirs again. Carpentier's novel covers two decades, 1789–1809, and is set partly in Havana, partly elsewhere in the Caribbean, also in France, and finally in Spain battling the Napoleonic occupation. On the surface, it is surprisingly (and refreshingly) old-fashioned, almost Conradian in its blend of history and personality. Yet this is deceptive; as González Echevarría argues, in his *Celestina's Brood* (1993), the book is in continuity with the long tradition of Spanish and Latin American baroque writing, which is a history of excess, of wandering beyond limits.

It would have been better to call the translated novel *The Century of Lights*, since the eighteenth-century Enlightenment comes to its conclusion in these pages. There needs to be a new English translation of the book anyway, since *Explosion in a Cathedral* is translated from the French edition, not from the Spanish. Four times in the novel, its central protagonist Esteban refers to the painting he calls "Explosion in a Cathedral" (pages 18, 253, 296, 340 of the translation), this being an actual painting by Monan Desiderio, called however *King Asa of Judah Destroying the Temple*, in the Fitzwilliam Museum of Cambridge University. The painting, or rather Esteban/Carpentier's interpretation of it, is a paradigm for the novel, and sets the apocalyptic pattern by which the slave revolts, the French Revolution, the Terror, Napoleon, and the reenslavement of the blacks (by Napoleonic decree) succeed one another, in what the Kabbalah calls the Breaking of the Vessels, smashed apart by lights too strong for them to contain. When, late in the novel, Esteban is arrested in Havana for sedition by Spanish colonial police, before being deported to prison in Spain he attempts to smash the painting, but it survives.

Carpentier's novel turns upon a triad of major characters: Esteban, his first cousin Sofia, and a brilliantly realized historical personage, Victor Hugues, who is the book's hero-villain, and its only successfully portrayed personality. Esteban, raised as a brother with Sofia and her actual brother Carlos, seems to me a fascinating failure in representation, akin to Martin Decoud, the spoiled idealist of Conrad's great novel *Nostromo*. Though both Esteban and Decoud are aesthetes and *flâneurs*, Esteban does not suffer from Decoud's suicidal detachment, and after a revolutionary career in France and Guadeloupe following the leadership of the Jacobean commissar Victor Hugues, Esteban's idealism survives both disillusionment with Victor and years of imprisonment in Spain. Side by side with Sofia, he goes out to join the common people of Madrid in the lunatic heroism of their uprising against Napoleon, a sublime venture in which both cousins are slain.

Victor Hugues, in the familiar pattern of his hero Robespierre, and of subsequent revolutionary tyrants—Stalin, Mao, Carpentier's Castro—develops from idealism to a passion for the guillotine to the liberator and exploiter of Guadeloupe, until at last he is Napoleon's brutal instrument for reimposing black slavery in French Guiana. There his career in Carpentier's novel concludes; in history he may have died in France circa 1820–22, or he may have gone back to Guiana to die there. Either way, he long outlived Esteban and Sofia, proper fate for a bourgeois "revolutionary" whose obsession always was power and fortune.

The relationship of Sofia to Victor and then to Esteban changes crucially in the final part of the novel. She gives herself to Victor but leaves him as he becomes the Napoleonic butcher of Guiana's blacks, and then goes to Madrid to petition for Esteban's release, to unite with him, and then to lead him out into the proletarian uprising against the army of Joseph Bonaparte in the streets of Madrid, where they die together. As baroque romance, this works well enough, but the occult elements in *The Century of Lights* make for a richer significance. There *may* be another novel besides *Explosion in a Cathedral* that models its three principal characters so closely upon the first three *Sefirot*, but I haven't yet encountered it. Briefly, Esteban is *Keter* or the crown, Victor Hugues is *Hokmah*, not wisdom (despite the word) but will or drive, the "father of fathers," the engendering force that is the initial Roman meaning of "genius," whereas *Keter* (again despite the word) could be interpreted as the other meaning of "genius," the daemon or other self, since in Kabbalistic usage *Keter* has a synonym in *Ayin* or "nothingness." Esteban, as a name, comes from the Greek *stephanus*, which also means "crown," but the Kabbalistic *Keter* or crown is a paradox (precisely like young Esteban), at once the full potential of God, yet also mere passivity, unable to enter the world of action, into which the fathering force of Victor alone is able to propel him.

Sofia, akin to the Gnostic Sophia or fallen figure of wisdom, is for Carpentier the Kabbalistic *Binah*, a word meaning "intelligence" but in Kabbalah only a passive understanding. As a Kabbalistic triad, Esteban is a divine self-consciousness (shared with his creator Carpentier), Victor an active principle of knowing, and Sofia the known, a reflection upon knowledge, a veil through which the light shines. Victor, at the novel's start, arrives in Sofia's and Esteban's house, and takes over as a second father, the actual father being dead.

The reader well may feel a touch bewildered; why does Carpentier need this esoteric armature to write his historical novel of revolution and its sufferings? When Esteban comes home to Havana after undergoing the dictatorial leadership of Victor in France and in Guadeloupe, he is saddened by a new "fall" of his Gnostic Sophia. "His" Sofia has married:

> But the young man was looking at her with an expression of great sadness. He would never have expected to hear such a succession of bourgeois commonplaces from Sofia's lips: "to make a man happy," "the security a woman feels who knows she has a companion." It was terrifying to realize that a second mind, situated in the womb, was now emitting its ideas through Sofia's mouth—Sofia, a name which defined the woman who bore it as possessing a "smiling wisdom." The name Sofia had always appeared in Esteban's imagination as shaded by the great Byzantine dome, wrapped in palms from the Tree of Life and surrounded by Archons in all the mystery of Intact Womanhood. And now the achievement of physical satisfaction, added perhaps to the still concealed joys of incipient pregnancy—whose warning came when the blood which had welled from its deep source since the days of puberty ceased to flow—had sufficed for the Elder Sister, the Young Mother, the pure feminine entelechy of other times, to have become a good, sensible, prudent wife, whose mind was centered on her protected womb and on the future well-being of its fruits, proud that her husband should be related to an oligarchy which

owed its wealth to the age-old exploitation of vast numbers of Negroes. Strange as he had felt—a foreigner—entering *his* house once again, Esteban felt stranger still—even more of a foreigner—confronted by this woman who was too visibly the queen and mistress of that same house, where everything was too neat, too clean for his taste, and too well protected against knocks or damage.

Sofia is *Binah*, the mirror or prism that breaks open the Byzantine dome of divine light into many colors, a Neoplatonic element in Kabbalah. The Tree of Life is formed by the ten *Sefirot*, and the archons surround the fallen Sophia as her ruler-protectors in Gnosticism. Carpentier, here as elsewhere, writes an esoteric counterpoint, in which his three protagonists fuse heretical traditions together. Masonry, the Rosicrucians, and the Templars are all woven into Carpentier's revolutionary web, as they were in the Caribbean and French revolutions. Suggestively, and more than half-seriously, Carpentier portrays the century of Light as the age in which an ancient wisdom returned, generally as an impulse against the state church, allied to the oppressive regimes. The black geniuses of rebellion, Macandal and Bouckman, are Muslims as well as followers of the gods of voodoo.

Carpentier, except for Borges, is clearly the genius of Latin American fiction in its great period, during the second half of the twentieth century. I remember being surprised when Gonzalez Echevarria first told me that Carpentier was French and Russian, with no black ancestors. The genius of Carpentier, in *The Kingdom of This World* and *Explosion in a Cathedral*, had seemed to me precisely attuned to the literary manifestation of a black revolutionary perspective. The lesson, at least for me, is once again the autonomy of literary genius, its freedom from the cultural politics so many seek to impose upon it.

OCTAVIO PAZ

Every moribund or sterile society attempts to save itself by creating a redemption myth which is also a fertility myth, a creation myth . . . The sterility of the bourgeois world will end in suicide or a new form of creative participation.

That is the conclusion of *The Labyrinth of Solitude,* Octavio Paz's shrewd investigation-creation of the myth of Mexico. His implication was that the United States, like Mexico, was another "moribund or sterile society," doomed to "end in suicide or a new form of creative participation."

As a poet and person of letters, Paz emerged from French Surrealism, which he attempted to assimilate to his myth of Mexico. The *Chingada* or violated Aztec woman, raped first by Spanish conquistadors and then by modern Mexican male chauvinists, gave Paz a powerful myth, surrealist in its savage coloring, but hardly an image of redemption, fertility, creation.

Paz is the Mexican national poet because his wisdom reflects the historical cruelty of Mexican experience. All of Mexico's heroes have been murdered, which fosters a vision beyond disillusion. "We are nihilists," Paz said of the Mexicans, "except that our nihilism is not intellectual but instinctive and therefore irrefutable." Perhaps Paz's darkest observation was on Mexican celebration: "The fiesta is at once sumptuous and intense, lively and funereal. It is a vital multicolored frenzy that evaporates in smoke, ashes, nothingness. In the aesthetics of perdition, the fiesta is the lodging place of death."

The poetry of Octavio Paz, remarkable by any standards, both expresses Mexican nihilism and transcends it by resort to Hindu and Buddhist Tantric mysticism, which is a discipline of sexual excess, in which ritual acts are powerful integrations of sexuality, language, and thought. That importation from India was Paz's hope for a "a new form of creative participation," even a myth of redemption. It does not lessen Paz's achievement to see this myth as a belated Surrealism rather than a redemptive program for society, whether Mexican or American.

OCTAVIO PAZ
(1914–1998)

THE MEXICAN POET OCTAVIO PAZ WAS his nation's prime person of letters, perhaps unsurpassable, and he was one of the few recent winners of the Nobel Prize in Literature (1990) who conferred honor upon that award (José Saramago was another). Though I have worked through most of his admirable poetry (with the help of distinguished translators, and several dictionaries), I cannot assert that I have read all of his prose works, which are remarkably varied, so universal were his interests. In pursuit of his genius, I will confine myself mostly to his poetry, and to *The Labyrinth of Solitude,* his attempt at defining Mexican identity, and *Sor Juana: Or, the Traps of Faith,* his critical biography of the first major Mexican and Latin American poet, Sor Juana Inés de la Cruz (1651?–1695). Of his copious writings upon poetry, I find *The Bow and the Lyre* most useful as a supplement to his own work.

Born in Mexico City to a mestizo father and a Spanish mother, Paz inherited revolutionary tradition from his father, who had represented Zapata in the United States. Paz wrote poetry as a child, and began to publish it at seventeen. In 1937, he went to Spain to support the Republic against the Fascists. Persuaded not to join the Loyalist army, but to work for its interests in Mexico, he returned home to devote himself to political journalism. After a year in New York City and San Francisco (1944), he sojourned another year in Paris, frequently in the company of André Breton and the Surrealist group. From 1946 until 1968, when he resigned after the violent repression of the student movement in Mexico City, Paz was in the Mexican Foreign Service, representing his country in Paris, New York City, and Geneva. From 1962 until he ended his diplomatic career in 1968, he served as ambassador to India, where he married.

The remaining thirty years of Paz's life were given wholly to literary composition, in an extraordinary profusion of more than forty books. If you stand back from his work, both poetry and prose, your chief impression will be of a highly individual erotic mysticism, a fusion of Western Hermeticism and Surrealism with Easter traditions, particularly Hindu and Buddhist Tantrism. The short prose volume *Conjunctions and Disjunctions* (1969) seems to me the clearest statement of Paz's visionary eroticism. The book is writ-

ten in the afterglow of the student rebellions of 1968, and its tentative conclusion seems very much a period piece, a third of a century later:

> Or is the rebellion of youth yet another sign that we are living *an*
> *end of time?* I have already expressed my belief: modern time—linear
> time, the homologue of the ideas of progress and history, ever pro-
> pelled into the future, the time of the sign *non-body,* of the fierce will
> to dominate nature and tame instincts, the time of sublimation, ag-
> gression, and self-mutilation—is coming to an end. I believe that we
> are entering another time, a time that has not yet revealed its form
> and about which we can say nothing except that it will be neither lin-
> ear time nor cyclical time. Neither history nor myth. The time that is
> coming, if we really are living a change at times, a general revolt and
> not linear revolution, will be neither a future nor a past, but a present.
> At least this is what contemporary rebellions are confusedly demand-
> ing. Nor do art and poetry seek anything different, although artists
> and poets sometimes do not know this. The return of the present: the
> time that is coming is defined by a *here* and a *now.* It is a negation of
> the sign *non-body* in all its Western versions: religious or atheist, philo-
> sophical or political, materialist or idealist. The present does not pro-
> ject us into any place beyond, any motley, other-worldly eternities or
> abstract paradises at the end of history. It projects us into the
> medulla, the invisible center of time: the here and now. A carnal time,
> a mortal time: the present is not unreachable, the present is not for-
> bidden territory. How can we touch it, how can we penetrate inside
> its transparent heart? I do not know, and I do not believe anybody
> knows . . . Perhaps the alliance of poetry and rebellion will give us a
> vision of it. I see in their conjunction the possibility of the return of
> the sign *body:* the incarnation of images, the return of the human fig-
> ure, radiant and radiating symbols. If contemporary rebellion (and I
> am not thinking only of that of young people) is not dissipated in a
> succession of raucous cries and does not degenerate into closed, au-
> thoritarian systems, if it articulates its passion through poetic imagi-
> nation, in the widest and freest sense of the word poetry, our
> incredulous eyes may behold the awakening and the return to our ab-
> ject world of that corporeal and spiritual reality that we call *the presence*
> *of the beloved.* Then love will cease to be the isolated experience of an
> individual or a couple, an exception or a scandal. The word *presence*
> and the word *love* have appeared in these reflections for the first and

the last time. They were the seed of the West, the origin of our art and of our poetry. In them is the secret of our resurrection.

I shake my head sadly at this, and remember my one meeting with the poet, in New York City in 1971 or 1972, when we clashed on the question of the spiritual authenticity of the events of 1967 to 1970. He invoked Blake, Novalis, and Breton, and I countered that Blake had diagnosed such false dawns as the cyclic rebellion of the titan he named Orc, who always ages into Urizen, a mature captain of business, government, and the media, which indeed has been the destiny of my own rebel students of thirty years ago. Yet Paz was a poet-prophet, a genius who desperately desired to fuse poetry and life. I venerated him then, at the brief, dissenting encounter, and want to expiate now, not so much for my own prophecy, which was that the ultimate consequences of the upheaval would destroy aesthetic standards, but for not having the good sense to keep silent, so as to have heard him say more.

Tantrism is an intensely strenuous erotic mysticism, the mere description of which daunts most of us, yet I perhaps underestimate both the extremity and the prevalence of underground religiosity virtually everywhere. *Conjunctions and Disjunctions* brings together Calvin and Sade, esoteric Buddhisms and Aztec goddesses. Paz always recalls the Asiastic origin of the native Mexicans, and tries to think beyond it, with Lévi-Strauss, to the supposed Golden Age of the Neolithic period: no state, no division of labor, no weapons, no writing, and no priests. It seems a pretty myth, and as such poignant: "Our sex organs tell us that there was a golden age." Blake felt otherwise, and follows Milton's account of angelic love (*Paradise Lost*, book 8, 620–29) in his own *Jerusalem*, which envisions an Eternity where

> Embraces are Cominglings from the Head even to the Feet
> and not a pompous High Priest entering by a Secret Place.

Paz, as *Conjunctions and Disjunctions* makes clear, is a vitalist, in a strange blend of Eastern and Western modes of eroticism. He is the legitimate heir of Góngora and Quevedo, the most disturbing poets of the Spanish baroque seventeenth century. His great poem *Piedra de sol* (*Sunstone*), composed in Mexico City in 1957, founds itself upon the circular Aztec calendar, which measured the cycle of the planet Venus as five hundred and eighty-four days, and so *Sunstone* has five hundred and eighty-four lines, the first six and the final six being identical; the poem therefore is circular and endless (and wonderfully maddening). I quote from Muriel Rukeyser's fiery version:

to love is to struggle, and if two people kiss
the world is transformed, and all desires made flesh
and intellect is made flesh; great wings put forth
and their shoots from the shoulders of the slave, the world
is real and to be touched and the wine is wine,
the bread can taste again, the water is water,
to love is to struggle, is to open the doors,
to stop being a fantasy with a number
condemned to the sentence of the endless chain
by a faceless master;
                    and the world is changed
when two people look at each other, recognizing
to love is to take off our clothes and our names:
"Allow me to be your whore," these are the words
of Heloise, but he gave in to the law,
he took her to be his wife, and as reward,
later, they castrated him;
                    better to have the crime,
the suicidal lovers, or the incest
between two brothers, as between two mirrors
falling in love and loving their reflections,
better to venture and eat the poisoned bread,
better adultery on beds of ashes,
the ferocious passions, and delirium,
its venomous ivy, and the sodomite
who carries for his buttonhole carnation
a gobbet of spit, better be killed by stoning
in the public square than tread the mill that grinds
out into nothing the substance of our life,
changes eternity into hollow hours,
minutes into penitentiaries, and time
into some copper pennies and abstract shit

This baroque excess recalls not only Góngora and Quevedo, but the four-teenth-century Juan Ruiz, whose *Libro de buen amor* is praised in *Conjunctions and Disjunctions. Sunstone* continues and culminates the secularization of the dogma of the Incarnation, now converted into the transfiguration of the flesh by and through the flesh. *The Bow and the Lyre*, completed two years before *Sunstone*, argues for poetry as total revelation, still in the mode of Surrealism. It is a book of wistful affirmations that do not persuade their author. The age-old vexation of poetry and belief is recalcitrant to Paz's asserted solution:

> The poetic word and the religious word are confused throughout history. But the religious revelation does not constitute—at least insofar as it is word—the original act but rather its interpretation. On the other hand, poetry is the revelation of our condition and, for that very reason, the creation of man by means of the image. The revelation is creation. Poetic language reveals man's paradoxical condition, his "otherness," and thus leads him to realize that which he is. It is not the sacred writings of religions that establish man, because they lean on the poetic word. The act by which man grounds and reveals himself is poetry. In sum, the religious experience and the poetic one have a common origin; their historical expressions—poems, myths, prayers, exorcism, hymns, theatrical performances, rites, and so on— are sometimes indistinguishable; in short, both are experiences of our constitutive "otherness." But religion interprets, channels, and systematizes inspiration within a theology, at the same time that churches confiscate its products. Poetry opens up to us the possibility of being that is intrinsic in every birth; it re-creates man and makes him assume his true condition, which is not the dilemma: life or death, but a totality: life and death in a single instant of incandescence.

Blake phrased this more briefly: "choosing forms of worship from poetic tales." As Blake knew (and Paz must have known also), this is eminently reversible. T. S. Eliot, always surprisingly commended by Paz, insisted that European culture had no bulwark except Christianity. Paz is a devotional poet whose religion is not poetry, as he sometimes thought, but a curious blend of Tantric Buddhism, the frightening Aztec sun-worship (which relied upon enormous numbers of human sacrifices), and European Romanticism with its Modernist continuators. The darkest passage I know in Paz's prose comes close to the end of *Conjunctions and Disjunctions*:

> And a nostalgia for Festival. But Festival is a manifestation of the cyclical time of myth; it is a present that returns, whereas we live in the linear and profane time of progress and history. Perhaps the revolt of youth is an empty festival, the summons, the invocation of an event that will always be a future event and never a present one, that never will simply *be*. Or perhaps it is a commemoration: the revolution no

longer appears to be the elusive imminence of the future but rather
something like a past to which we cannot return—yet which we cannot abandon either. In either case, it is not here, but there, always beyond our reach. Possessed by the memory of its future or of its past,
by what it was or what it could have been—no, not possessed but
rather deserted, empty, the orphan of its origin and its future—society mimics them. And by mimicking them it exorcises them: for a few
weeks it denies itself through the blasphemies and the sacrilege of its
young people and then affirms itself more completely and more perfectly in the ensuing repression. A mimetic magic. A victim anointed
by the ambiguous fascination of profanation, youth is the sacrificial
lamb of the ceremony: after having profaned itself through it, society
punished itself. It is a symbolic profanation and castigation and at the
same time a representation. The events of October 2, 1968, in the
Plaza de Tlatelolco in Mexico City evoked (repeated) the Aztec rites:
several hundred boys and girls sacrificed, on the ruins of a pyramid, by
the army and the police. The literalness of the rite—the reality of the
sacrifice—emphasized in a hideous way the unreal and expiatory nature of the repression: the Mexican powers-that-be punished their
own revolutionary past by punishing these young people.

This is Paz at his strongest; his universalism and poetic idealism never
has the force of his returns to Mexico. His two best prose books are his first,
The Labyrinth of Solitude (1950), a search for Mexican identity, and *Sor Juana:
Or, the Traps of Faith* (1988), a superb resurrection of the poet Juana Ramírez,
who became Sor Juana Inés de la Cruz, the great poet of the City of Mex-
ico in seventeenth-century New Spain. The two books, *Labyrinth* and *Sor
Juana*, constitute Paz's authentic otherness, his genius, in conjunction with
his most ambitious poems: *Sunstone, Salamander,* "Maithuna," *Blanco,*
"Vuelta," and scores of somber commemorations, like his poem "Luis
Cernuda."

"Vuelta" ("Return") finds Paz back in Mixcoac, where he lived as a boy,
when it was a village; now it is a part of Mexico City's enormity, the world's
most populous city. My Mexican students tell me of four hours trapped in
a car in a traffic jam, and of subway rides that take two and a half hours,
though scheduled for twenty minutes. Uncannily, Paz echoes T. S. Eliot in
his London "Preludes," as though the Tantric surrealist needs the visionary
of London's decay to help him express the phantasmagoria of Mexico City's
sprawl:

Paralytic architecture
                         stranded districts
rotting municipal gardens
                              mounds of salpeter
deserted lots
          camps of urban nomads
ants' nests worm-farms
                         cities of the city
thoroughfares of scars
                         alleys of living flesh
Funeral Parlor
          by a window display of coffins
whores
          pillars of vain night
                         At dawn
in the drifting bar
          the enormous mirror thaws
the solitary drinkers
contemplate the dissolution of their faces
The sun rises from its bed of bones
The air is not air
          it strangles without arms or hands
Dawn rips the curtains
                         City
heap of broken words
                    Wind
on the dusty corners
                    turns the papers
Yesterday's news
          more remote
than a cuneiform tablet smashed to bits
Cracked scriptures
          language in pieces
the signs were broken
                    atl tlachinolli
                         was split
                    burnt water
There is no center
                    plaza of congregation and consecration
There is no axis
          the years dispersed

horizons disbanded
                    They have branded the city
on every door
                    on every forehead
                              the $ sign
                    (translated by Eliot Weinberger)

Mexico is Paz's Muse, but Mexico is the *Chingada*, as eloquently described in *The Labyrinth of Solitude:*

In contrast to Guadalupe, who is the Virgin Mother, the *Chingada* is the violated Mother. Neither in her nor in the Virgin do we find traces of the darker attributes of the great goddesses: the lasciviousness of Amaterasu and Aphrodite, the cruelty of Artemis and Astarte, the sinister magic of Circe or the bloodlust of Kali. Both of them are passive figures. Guadalupe is pure receptivity, and the benefits she bestows are of the same order: she consoles, quiets, dries tears, calms passions. The *Chingada* is even more passive. Her passivity is abject: she does not resist violence, but is an inert heap of bones, blood and dust. Her taint is constitutional and resides, as we said earlier, in her sex. This passivity, open to the outside world, causes her to lose her identity: she is the *Chingada*. She loses her name; she is no one; she disappears into nothingness; she *is* Nothingness. And yet she is the cruel incarnation of the feminine condition.

If the *Chingada* is a representation of the violated Mother, it is appropriate to associate her with the Conquest, which was also a violation, not only in the historical sense but also in the very flesh of Indian women. The symbol of this violation is Doña Malinche, the mistress of Cortés. It is true that she gave herself voluntarily to the conquistador, but he forgot her as soon as her usefulness was over. Doña Marina [the name given to La Malinche by the Spaniards] becomes a figure representing the Indian women who were fascinated, violated or seduced by the Spaniards. And as a small boy will not forgive his mother if she abandons him to search for his father, the Mexican people have not forgiven La Malinche for her betrayal. She embodies the open, the *chingada*, to our closed, stoic, impassive Indians. Cuauhtémoc and Doña Marina are thus two antagonistic and complementary figures. There is nothing surprising about our cult of the young emperor—"the only hero at the summit of art," an image of the sacrificed son—and there is also nothing surprising about the curse that weighs against La Malinche. This explains the success of the contemptuous adjective *malinchista* recently put into circulation by the newspapers to denounce all those who have been corrupted by foreign influences. The *malinchistas* are those who want Mexico to open itself to the outside world: the true sons of La Malinche, who is the *Chingada* in person. Once again we see the opposition of the closed and the open.

(translated by Lysander Kemp and others)

Mother Mexico is the *Chingada* personified, since her sons revile La Malinche, though acknowledging her as ancestress, indeed as the Mexican Lilith *and* Eve. A great mythmaker, Paz almost persuades us that the "solitude" of the mestizo results from the originary trauma of the Spanish conquest. Monstrous as the Spanish were, they overthrew the equally monstrous Aztec empire, a nightmare of slavery and ongoing, mass sacrifices by torture and slaughter, with ritual cannibalism added as relish. The Spanish slaughters, dedicated to the glory of Jesus Christ, were ritualistic enough, but fell a touch short perhaps of the ritual horrors of the Aztec Empire of the Sun. An historicized trauma could as easily be traced to the Aztecs as to the Spanish.

Still, I do not dispute the mythmaking power of *The Labyrinth of Solitude*, which leads to what is certainly Paz's prose masterpiece, *Sor Juana*, a baroque meditation upon a great poet, her Mexico (or New Spain), and on the further sorrows (for a woman of genius) of Mexican identity. Juana Ramírez was born in what is now Mexico, either in 1648 or 1651. Before she had reached the age of twenty-one, she entered a convent, for reasons still unclear, as she had shown only the signs of a literary calling, and not of a spiritual vocation. Her poetry is not devotional but philosophical, in the Neoplatonist mode of the Hermetic tradition, upon which the late Frances Yates remains the definitive scholar. The Goddess Isis, not the Virgin Mary, was Sor Juana's Muse, and Paz traces the Gnostic heresy throughout her poetry. He leaves unsettled, as it must be, the biographical basis of her love poetry, which certainly *appears* to be lesbian, but in a Neoplatonic mode that may indicate only idealized relationships.

Sor Juana's major poem is *First Dream*, a highly original long quest-romance in which the poet sleeps while her soul voyages through the heavens. Góngora's *Solitudes*, superb poetry of disillusion, is the nearest precursor work, but Paz finds in *First Dream* the anticipation of Valéry, Mallarmé, and of his own *Blanco*. Sor Juana's vision, baroque and Hermetic, owes much to the great heretic Giordano Bruno, burned alive in Rome for his writings.

Whether because of her esotericism, or more likely because of her literary fame, Sor Juana was hounded by the church into an abjuration, in which
she gave up her books and manuscripts, ceased to write poetry, and became
a penitent. A brilliant passage in Paz's epilogue sums up Sor Juana's
tragedy:

> It is scarcely necessary to point out the similarities between Sor
> Juana's personal situation and the obstacles we Mexicans have expe-
> rienced during the process of modernization. There was an insoluble
> contradiction between Sor Juana and her world. This contradiction
> was not merely intellectual; it was fundamental, and can be located in
> three main areas. The first was the opposition between her literary
> vocation and the fact that she was a nun. At other moments, although
> not in New Spain, the Church had been tolerant and had harbored
> writers and poets who, often in blatant disregard of their religious re-
> sponsibilities, had devoted themselves exclusively to letters. Their
> cases, however—the most notable being those of Góngora, Lope de
> Vega, Tirso de Molina, and Mira de Amescua—differ from that of Sor
> Juana in an essential point: they were poets and dramatists but not in-
> tellectuals. Both vocations, poet and intellectual, converged in Sor
> Juana. In late seventeenth-century Spain and its domains, a priest or
> nun with an intellectual vocation was restricted to theology and sa-
> cred studies. This incompatibility was aggravated by the fact that Sor
> Juana's extraordinary intellectual restlessness and her encyclopedic
> curiosity—Sigüenza's also—coincided with a moment of paralysis in
> the Church and exhaustion in Hispanic culture.
>
> The second area of discord was Sor Juana's gender. The fact that a
> woman—what is more, a nun—should devote herself so single-mind-
> edly to letters must have both astounded and scandalized her con-
> temporaries. She was called the "Tenth Muse" and the "Phoenix of
> America": sincere expressions of admiration that must have set her
> head spinning at times. She tells us in the *Response* that no lack of crit-
> icism and censure accompanied this praise. The censure came from
> influential prelates and was founded on a point of doctrine. It was not
> by chance that in his appeal to Sor Juana asking her to forsake secular
> letters the Bishop of Puebla quoted St. Paul. It was one thing to be
> tolerant with Lope de Vega and Góngora, both bad priests, and an-
> other to be lenient with Sor Juana Inés de la Cruz. Although her con-
> duct was beyond reproach, her attitudes were not. She was guilty of
> the sin of pride, a sin to which the vain feminine sex is particularly

susceptible. Pride was the ruin of Lucifer, because hubris leads to rebelliousness. Sor Juana's critics saw a causal relationship between letters, which lead a woman from her natural state of obedience, and rebelliousness. Sor Juana had disproved the inferiority of women in intellectual and literary matters and made her attainments a source of admiration and public applause; to the prelates this was sin, and her obstinacy was rebellion. That is why they demanded a total abdication.

(translated by Margaret Sayers Peden)

Just before this epilogue, poignantly titled "Toward a Restitution," Paz eloquently compresses the church's guilt into a sentence: "She relinquished her books to her persecutor, scourged her body, humbled her intelligence, and renounced the gift that was most her own: the word." A year after her surrender to church discipline, she died at forty-six, broken and humiliated. In telling her story, and reviving the splendor of her poetry, Paz gave his own genius to fullest expression in prose.

Paz's genius nevertheless deserves to be defined in his poetry, and I turn to *Blanco* (1966) as my personal favorite among his major poems. Taking Mallarmé's *Un Coup de dés* as a model, *Blanco* is a meditation upon the paradox of poetic silence, under the direct influence of Tantric Buddhism. The poem, written in New Delhi simultaneously with Paz's wise little book *Claude Lévi-Strauss: An Introduction*, is perhaps best elucidated by that work's concluding paragraph:

The essence of the word is relation, and that is why it is the key, the momentary incarnation of everything which is relative. Every word engenders a word which contradicts it, every word is a relation between negation and affirmation. Relation is to tie together othernesses, it is not the resolution of contradictions. Therefore, language is the realm of dialectic which ceaselessly destroys itself and is reborn only to die. If Buddha's silence were the expression of this relativism, it would not be silence, but word. That is not the way it is: with his silence, movement, operation, dialectic, word, cease. At the same time, it is not the negation of dialectic nor of movement: Buddha's silence is the *resolution* of language. We come from silence and to silence we return: to the word which has ceased to be word. What Buddha's silence says is neither negation nor affirmation. It says *sunyata*: everything is empty because everything is full, the word is not a statement because the only statement is silence. Not nihilism but relativism,

which destroys itself and goes beyond itself. Movement does not resolve itself in immobility: it *is* immobility, and immobility is movement. The negation of the world implies a return to the world,
asceticism is a return to the senses, samsara is nirvana, reality is the
beloved and terrible key to irreality, the instant is not the refutation,
but the incarnation, of eternity, the body is not a window on the infinite: it is the infinite itself. Have we noticed that the senses are at
the same time senders and receivers of all sense? To reduce the world
to meaning is as absurd as reducing it to the senses. The fullness of
the senses: there sense fades away so that a moment later it can contemplate the way in which sensation is dispelled. Vibration, waves,
signals, and responses: silence. Not the knowledge of the void: an
empty knowledge. Buddha's silence is not a knowledge but rather something after knowledge: wisdom. An un-knowing. A being loose and
thus resolved. Quietude is the dance, and the ascetic's solitude is
identical, in the center of the immobile spiral, to the embrace of the
loving couples in the sanctuary at Karli. A knowledge that knows
nothing and that culminates in a poetics and in an erotics. An instan-
taneous act, a form that disintegrates, a word that vanishes: the art of
dancing above the abyss.

(translated by J. S. Bernstein and Maxine Bernstein)

The true motto of Paz's *Blanco* might be: "Not the knowledge of the
void: an *empty knowledge.*" I have my difficulties with apprehending Buddhism, and prefer the analogue in the Gnostic vision of our world as the
kenoma: a sensible emptiness. *Blanco* fascinates me because it contrasts interestingly with the Anglo-American poetic tradition of the "blank," which
goes from Shakespeare and Milton through Wordsworth and Coleridge on to
Emerson, Whitman, Melville, and Emily Dickinson, to culminate in Wallace
Stevens. This tradition also develops the triple meaning of "blank" as the
color white, as an emptiness, and as the center of a target. Following Mallarmé, Paz adds a fourth, a blank left in a text, and a fifth, in the Buddhist
sense, the object or aim of desire.

Blanco can infuriate or intrigue a reader, depending upon temperament.
It can be read as a single work, or just as a poem about "silence," in its central column. But the left-hand column is a love poem, in the Tantric mode,
and the right-hand column is yet another poem, devoted to issues of imaginative understanding. Indeed, you can isolate other, briefer poems within
the columns, an all but endless process. If all this were rendered without
irony, it might be intolerable, and if it were ironic only, that too would be

difficult to accept. *Blanco* fuses throughout Tantric erotic passion, and a distancing irony, very difficult to convey by quotation. It is Paz's hymn to the erotic completion he found, with his wife, and can be compared to D. H. Lawrence's sequence *Look! We Have Come Through!* though Lawrence writes in the mode of Walt Whitman, and Octavio Paz in what I suppose has to be called his unique kind of Mexican Surrealism.

It is not kind to any poet to compare him in any way to Dante, and Paz, though a marvelous artist, could not sustain such a juxtaposition. But I invoke Dante only to indicate that Octavio Paz, despite his universal scope—Paris, India, the United States, Japan—was as attached to Mexico City as the exiled Dante was to Florence. Dante, in his pride, refused to go home on any terms except his own, and so never saw Florence again. Paz, alienated from the Mexican government by the events of 1968, found his own way home, and deserves to be remembered as the genius of his city, and his nation.

LUSTRE 14

|

Stendhal, Mark Twain, William Faulkner, Ernest Hemingway, Flannery O'Connor

|

I have grouped this second Lustre of *Nezah* in order to juxtapose the ironic comedy of Stendhal and of Mark Twain, two superb epic improvisers rarely brought together, but who illuminate one another's capabilities. Twain is not much interested in eros, Stendhal's obsessive concern, but Huck Finn's quest for freedom, from a murderous father and a murderous society, has in it a saving contrast to the Napoleonic self-destructiveness of Julien Sorel in *The Red and the Black*.

Faulkner and Hemingway both asserted Twain's ancestry, different as they were, and the ironic humor of both storytellers has a clear relation to *Huckleberry Finn*. Flannery O'Connor owed much to Faulkner in her novels and stories, but as a theological ironist she is the most remarkable instance I know of what the Kabbalists meant by *Nezah*. In O'Connor, God's victory is all-in-all, and is manifest alike in our damnation (so far as O'Connor was concerned) or in the infrequent salvation that she could ascribe either to her protagonists or to her readers.

STENDHAL

So much pleasure and happiness poured into Lombardy with these Frenchmen, however ill-dressed, that only the priests and certain noblemen remarked this burden of six million, soon followed by many others. These French soldiers laughed and sang all day long, most were not yet twenty-five, and at twenty-eight their commanding general was accounted the oldest man in his army. Such youth, such gaiety, such free and easy ways offered a fine answer to the furious imprecations of the monks who for six months had preached that the French were monsters under orders, on pain of death, to burn down everything and cut off everyone's head; to which end, each regiment marched with a guillotine in its front ranks.

(translated by Richard Howard)

This is Bonaparte's army occupying Milan in 1796, to begin Stendhal's marvelous improvisation of a novel, *The Charterhouse of Parma*. High Romanticism is nowhere higher than in *The Charterhouse*, where Mosca loves Gina, who loves Fabrizio who loves Clélia who loves Fabrizio. Clélia's child by Fabrizio dies, and in turn Clélia, Fabrizio, and the admirable Gina all waste away, each unable to survive without the beloved.

Since everyone involved is both madly honorable and honorably lustful, all this passion is admirably enthralling. Stendhal is a genius of desire, who invests all his powers in Gina, the Duchess Sanseverina, whose extraordinary attachment to Fabrizio, her quasi-nephew, is never fulfilled.

Stendhal, psychologist of passion, charmingly emphasizes that everything in love that is not sickness is vanity. It is, as we all come to know, an immensely difficult truth for us to accept.

There is no gloom in Stendhal's analytics of desire. Whatever despair or paranoia we experience in our amorous life, Stendhal is determined to remain happy, and he maintains his (and thanks to him) *our* high good humor. Very few other novelists are so good for us.

STENDHAL (HENRI BEYLE)
(1783–1842)

NIETZSCHE SALUTED STENDHAL AS "this strange Epicurean and man of interrogation, the last great psychologist of France." Yet Stendhal is both less and more than a psychologist, even in the sense of moral psychologist intended by Nietzsche. If we are unhappy because we are vain, which seems true enough, then the insight seems related to the conviction that our sorrows come to us because we are restless, and cannot sit at our desks. To assimilate Stendhal to Pascal would be tasteless, yet to determine the pragmatic difference between them is a complex labor. Pascal, to me, is the authentic nihilist; Stendhal is something else. Call that Julien Sorel, hero of *The Red and the Black,* who attracts us without compelling our liking. Or do we like him? Robert M. Adams coolly concludes that

> Whether you like Julien Sorel, and for what parts of his behavior, depends, then, in some measure, on who you think you are and what conspiracies or complicities your imagination allows you to join, in the course of reading the book.

That may be giving Stendhal the best of it, since the reader's fundamental mental right, as critic, is to ask the writer, "Who do you think you are, anyway?" The reversal is shrewd, whether Stendhal's or Adams's, since we do not expect the author to be quite as aggressive as ourselves. Stendhal brazenly excels us, and Julien is more his surrogate than many have allowed. We admire Julien for the range of his imagination, and are a little estranged by his extraordinary (if intermittent) ability to switch his affections by acts of will. He is, of course, designedly a little Napoleon, and if one is not Hazlitt or Stendhal that may not move one to affection. But the Napoleonic is only one wave or movement in him, and Stendhal is one of that myriad of nineteenth-century writers of genius who fracture the self. A more crucial movement is the Byronic, and here Adams is very perceptive indeed, marvelously so:

> Most of what we think about Julien depends, of course, on our judgment of his behavior with the two ladies; and here we come up against

the central paradox of the novel, that (like the ladies) we don't really think more highly of our hero the better he behaves. Quite the contrary. The worse he behaves, the more painful the sacrifices he requires of them, the more we are impressed by their determination to love him. Impervious to jealousy, untouched by his effort to murder her, Mme. de Rênal defies public scandal, leaves her husband and children, and comes to be with Julien in the hour of his anguish. Mathilde is in despair that he no longer loves her though she has sacrificed even more prodigally to her love of him. The revelation of Julien is not to be made directly, in the glare of the open daylight, but only through the glow reflected on the faces of these devoted acolytes. As with Christ and Dionysus, the mystery of Julien is performed in the darkness of a prison-tomb, and his resurrection is celebrated in the presence of women. The cenacle of Julien allures its converts by withdrawing its mystery, etherealizing its cult: that is the work of the book's last important section.

One could argue that Julien, like Lord Byron, has that cool passivity which provokes his women into a return to themselves, so that his function is to spur these remarkable (and very dissimilar) ladies on to the epiphanies of their own modes of heroism. This could account for what I myself find most unsatisfactory about *The Red and the Black*, which is the obscurity (perhaps even obscurantism?) of Julien's final state of the soul:

The bad air of the prison cell was becoming insupportable to Julien. Fortunately on the day set for his execution a bright sun was shining upon the earth, and Julien was in the vein of courage. To walk in the open air was for him a delicious experience, as treading the solid ground is for a sailor who has been long at sea. There now, things are going very well, he told himself, I shall have no lack of courage.

Never had that head been so poetic as at the moment when it was about to fall. The sweetest moments he had ever known in the woods at Vergy came crowding back into his mind, and with immense vividness.

Everything proceeded simply, decently, and without the slightest affectation on his part.

Two days before he had told Fouqué:

—As for emotion, I can't quite answer; this dungeon is so ugly and damp it gives me feverish moments in which I don't recognize myself; but fear is another matter, I shall never be seen to grow pale.

He had made arrangements in advance that on the last day Fouqué should take away Mathilde and Mme. de Rênal.

—Put them in the same coach, he told him. Keep the post horses at a steady gallop. Either they will fall in one another's arms or they will fall into mortal hatred. In either case, the poor women will be somewhat distracted from their terrible grief.

Julien had forced from Mme. de Rênal an oath that she would live to look after Mathilde's son.

—Who knows? Perhaps we retain some consciousness after death, he said one day to Fouqué. I should like to rest, since rest is the word, in that little cave atop the big mountain that overlooks Verrières. I've told how several times when I spent the night in that cave and looked out over the richest provinces of France, my heart was afire with ambition: that was my passion in those days . . . Well, that cave is precious to me, and nobody can deny that it's located in a spot that a philosopher's heart might envy . . . You know these good congregationists in Besançon can coin money out of anything; go about it the right way, and they'll sell you my mortal remains.

Julien's superb sense of humor, at the end, enchants us, but what precisely is Stendhal's final attitude towards his hero? I take this sentence as not being ironic: "Never had that head been so poetic as at the moment when it was about to fall." Julien is madly in love with Mme. de Rênal; the sincerity of this madness cannot be doubted, but then the suicidal intensity or sustained drive beyond the pleasure principle of Julien's last days cannot be doubted either. Several critics have remarked upon the supposed similarity between Julien and Don Quixote, but I cannot see it. The Don lives in the order of play until he is battered out of it; then he dies. What others call madness is simply the Don's greatness. But Julien falls into pathology; it is an attractive craziness, because it makes him more likable than before, yet it remains a kind of madness. Stendhal is poor at endings; the conclusion of *The Charterhouse of Parma* is also weak and abrupt. But I feel a certain hesitancy in myself at these judgments. Perhaps I simply like both novels so much that I resent Stendhal's own apparent loss in interest when he nears an end. The best defense of Julien's demise was made by Stendhal's subtle disciple, the Prince of Lampedusa, author of *The Leopard:* "The author hastens to kill the character in order to be free of him. It is a dramatic and evocative conclusion unlike any other." One wants to protest to the Prince that it isn't dramatic enough, but he forestalls the complaint: "The impulsive, energetic handsome Julien spends his last words to tell his friend how he must go about buying back his body." Evidently, this is dramatic in the mode of *The Leopard,* where death takes place in the soul, and the body alone remains living. A Stendhalian pathos, the Prince implies, belongs only to the happy few; it is a pathos more of sensibility than of emotion.

Mathilde and Julien, on the occasion of their first night together, are comic triumphs of sensibility over emotion. "Their transports," Stendhal observes, "were a bit *conscious,*" which is a delicious understatement:

> Mlle. de La Mole supposed she was fulfilling a duty to herself and to her lover. The poor boy, she thought to herself, he's shown perfect bravery, he ought to be happy or else the fault lies in my want of character. But she would have been glad to ransom herself, at the cost of eternal misery, from the cruel necessity imposed upon her.
>
> In spite of the frightful violence with which she repressed her feelings, she was in perfect command of her speech.
>
> No regrets, no reproach came from her lips to spoil this night, which seemed strange to Julien, rather than happy. What a difference, good God! from his last stay of twenty-four hours at Verrières! These fancy Paris fashions have found a way to spoil everything, even love, he said to himself, in an excess of injustice.
>
> He was indulging in these reflections as he stood in one of the great mahogany wardrobes into which he had slipped at the first sounds coming from the next room, which was that of Mme. de La Mole. Mathilde went off with her mother to mass; the maids quickly left the room, and Julien easily escaped before they came back to finish their tasks.
>
> He took a horse and sought out the loneliest parts of the forest of Meudon near Paris. He was far more surprised than happy. The happiness that came from time to time like a gleam of light in his soul was like that of a young second lieutenant who after some astounding action has just been promoted full colonel by the commanding general; he felt himself raised to an immense height. Everything that had been far above him yesterday was now at his level or even beneath him. Gradually Julien's happiness increased as it became more remote.
>
> If there was nothing tender in his soul, the reason, however strange it may seem, was that Mathilde in all her dealings with him had been doing nothing but her duty. There was nothing unexpected for her in all the events of the night, except the misery and shame she had discovered instead of those divine raptures that novels talk about.
>
> Was I mistaken, don't I love him at all? she asked herself.

This hilarity of mutual coldness is the prelude to the novel's most delightful pages, as Stendhal surpasses himself in depicting the agon that springs up between these two titanic vanities. What Hobbes was to the principles of civil society, Stendhal was to the principles of eros. Neither man should be called a cynic. Each is more than a psychologist, because both saw the truth of the state of nature. Hobbes is to Stendhal what Schopenhauer was to the Tolstoy of *Anna Karenina*, the philosopher who confirms the insights so central to the novelist that they scarcely require confirmation. I would prefer to put it more starkly; if you repeatedly read *The Red and the Black*, then *Leviathan* becomes a fascinating redundancy, just as a deep knowledge of *Anna Karenina* renders Schopenhauer's *The World as Will and Representation* almost superfluous. Stendhal, and Tolstoy, are in their antithetical ways the true philosophers of love between the sexes, the dark metaphysicians of the unconscious verities of desire.

MARK TWAIN

That book was made by Mr. Mark Twain, and he told the truth, mainly. There was things which he stretched, but mainly he told the truth. That is nothing. I never seen anybody but lied, one-time or another, without it was Aunt Polly, or the widow, or maybe Mary.

—*Adventures of Huckleberry Finn*, chapter 1

The genius of Huck Finn, American Odysseus, is that he lies "merely to keep in practice." Huck is Twain's own genius, and his book is his author's best, but I have a particular passion for "Journalism in Tennessee," Twain's essence in a sketch of six pages.

Twain goes south for his health, and becomes associate editor of the *Morning Glory and Johnson County War-Whoop*. His employment is brief, caught as he is in the literal crossfire between the chief editor and his opposite number on a rival Tennessee newspaper, Colonel Blatherskite Tecumseh. Various other editors arrive, with pistols and grenades, and Twain resigns his post, with a heartfelt tribute to the spirit of the Tennessee press:

> Take it altogether, I never had such a spirited time in all my life as I have had to-day. No; I like you, and I like your calm unruffled way of explaining things to the customers, but you see I am not used to it. The Southern heart is too impulsive; Southern hospitality is too lavish with the stranger. The paragraphs which I have written to-day, and into whose cold sentences your masterly hand has infused the fervent spirit of Tennesseean journalism, will wake up another nest of hornets. All that mob of editors will come—and they will come hungry, too, and want somebody for breakfast. I shall have to bid you adieu. I decline to be present at these festivities. I came South for my health, I will go back on the same errand, and suddenly. Tennesseean journalism is too stirring for me.

García Márquez insisted that his *One Hundred Years of Solitude* was realism devoid of magic, precisely representing his native clime. Huck Finn's Mississippi River, like Twain's Tennessee journalism, also participates in the extravagance of the real: at his most outrageous, as in the gustatory railroad sketch "Cannibalism in the Cars," Twain maintains the consistency of true lying, which sets itself against time and the state, as Falstaff did, when he turned aside from the world, and bid it pass.

MARK TWAIN
(SAMUEL LANGHORNE CLEMENS)
(1835–1910)

HUCK FINN TELLS LIES "MERELY TO KEEP in practice." He will be forever young, and so never will learn the truth of Nietzsche's warning: to lie incessantly is to expire of exhaustion. James Cox, my favorite critic of Mark Twain, remarked that Huck's mode was "escape and evasion," particularly in regard to conscience or the superego. In Huck's case, there can be little Oedipal in the matter of conscience, because Pap would seem to have been almost free of the superego. Pap or Old Man Finn is terrible bad news: alcoholic, paranoid, racist, ill-tempered, and insanely convinced that his only child, Huck, is the Angel of Death. Harold Beaver, in his lovely book *Huckleberry Finn* (1987), makes the accurate and very useful observation that "the whole of *Huckleberry Finn* is a parody of Christian death and resurrection." Mark Twain, the comic genius of his nation, was seriously hostile towards Christianity, and also had not a trace in him of the Emersonian "God within" of the American Religion. Little Satan, at the verge of fading away in *The Mysterious Strangers*, finally allows himself to blurt out Mark Twain's honest loathing for God:

> who gave his angels painless lives, yet cursed his other children with biting miseries and maladies of mind and body; who mouths justice and invented hell—mouths mercy and invented hell—mouths Golden Rules and forgiveness multiplied by seventy times seven, and invented hell; who mouths morals to other people and has none himself; who frowns upon crimes, yet commits them all; who created man without invitation, then tries to shuffle the responsibility for man's acts upon man, instead of honorably placing it where it belongs, upon himself; and finally, with altogether divine obtuseness invites this poor, abused slave to worship him!

That is a path away from *Adventures of Huckleberry Finn*, a book loved alike by religious and irreligious. The two beacons for the book's glory are Scott Fitzgerald and Ernest Hemingway, both writing in 1935:

Fitzgerald:

Huckleberry Finn took the first journey back. He was the first to look back at the republic from the perspective of the West. His eyes were the first eyes that ever looked at us objectively that were not eyes from overseas. There were mountains at the frontier but he wanted more than mountains to look at with his restless eyes—he wanted to find out about men and how they lived together. And because he turned back, we have him forever.

Hemingway: "All modern American literature comes from one book by Mark Twain called *Huckleberry Finn* . . . it's the best book we've had."

Fitzgerald recalls the stance of *The Great Gatsby*, while Hemingway returns to his early achievement in the Nick Adams stories.

Huckleberry Finn spoke to Fitzgerald and Hemingway in ways he himself did not understand. It is a more profound matter that he was able to speak to Ralph Ellison, who dissented fiercely from all those schools that work to exclude Huck's love for Jim by branding Huck a "racist," a literal-minded mindlessness that is now prevalent in the English-speaking world. But my subject is Mark Twain's comic genius: *Huckleberry Finn* is his masterpiece, though not necessarily in hilarity, since Twain is most outrageous in short sketches, like "Cannibalism in the Cars" and my favorite, "Journalism in Tennessee."

Harold Beaver cites Andrew Lang's 1891 observation:

In one point Mark Twain is Homeric, probably without knowing it. In the *Odyssey*, Odysseus frequently tells a false tale about himself, to account for his appearance and position when disguised on his own island. He shows extraordinary fertility and appropriateness of invention, wherein he is equaled by the feigned tales of Huckleberry Finn.

Huck is not his book's only Odysseus; everyone of any deep interest is a shrewd liar, a concealer of the truth, as when Jim will not tell Huck that Pap is dead, lest Huck go off by himself. And yet it is the truth-tellers, like the amiable Aunt Sally, who are funniest, as in a passage particularly admired by Cox, where the reader notes Huck's deadpan lack of response to the outrageous play upon "save":

"It warn't the grounding—that didn't keep us back but a little. We blowed out a cylinder-head."

"Good gracious! Anybody hurt?"

"No'm. Killed a nigger."

"Well, it's lucky; because sometimes people do get hurt. Two years ago last Christmas, your uncle Silas was coming up from Newrleans on

the old *Lalh Rook*, and she blowed out a cylinder-head and crippled a
man. And I think he died afterwards. He was a Babtist. Your uncle
Silas knowed a family in Baton Rouge that knowed his people very
well. Yes, I remember, now he *did* die. Mortification set in, and they
had to amputate him. But it didn't save him. Yes, it was mortification—that was it. He turned blue all over, and died in the hope of a
glorious resurrection. They say he was a sight to look at."

"No'm. Killed a nigger" is the notorious part of this, coming only a few
pages after Huck's declaration, "All right, then, I'll go to hell," after he tears up
the note that would send Jim back into slavery again. Huck, I suppose, could
be considered a parody of Odysseus, but he is too strong to be reduced to anyone's parody. He has not so much an Homeric as a Whitmanian persuasiveness
to him: Huck and Walt are geniuses of the American language, and use it to
establish their freedom, or at least what freedom they can maintain. Huck's
freedom, in regard to his dreadful Pap, is in flight, which allies him to Jim. Yet
freedom, for Huck, is not an absolute; he is fearful of solitude, and cares intensely for the reality of other selves. Let us distinguish him from Thoreau, of
whom Robert Louis Stevenson observed that he was not surprised that
Thoreau got along best with fish. The great pride of the seer of *Walden* was not
to pay a cent more for anything than it was worth. Huck is willing to overpay.

Huck's essential stance is one of comic decency. Sharing a raft with
Odysseus would be fatal—for you, but Huck does not survive at the expense of others. There are darker, less generous patches in Mark Twain's genius for humor, but they do not get into Huck, just as Kipling, in homage to
Twain, keeps Kim mostly free of what bothers many of us in Kipling. Hatred is alien to Huck, who rivals Joyce's Poldy as the best-hearted fictive
protagonist since Mr. Pickwick.

You don't do Twain a kindness by comparing him to Cervantes (whom he
greatly admired), since no comic novelist can sustain such a juxtaposition,
any more than you help Ibsen or Chekhov by invoking Shakespeare. *Huckleberry Finn* does not batter at the limits of art. All Huck has in common with
Sancho is a certain pragmatism. With the Knight, Huck has few affinities:
he is an American boy, and not a metaphysical quester. But he has something of the Knight's healthy self-consciousness, and of his pride at having
a prominent place in a great story. A twelve-year-old Don Quixote would
not work, and so Twain wisely avoids bringing the paradigm at all close. And
since Huck never will be any older than twelve, he will never turn into the
Knight. More's the pity, for *that* could have been Twain's genius, to send a
mature Huck out into a greater, more fantastic reality.

Frontispiece 68:

WILLIAM FAULKNER

He went to work in the spring. One evening in September he returned home and entered the cabin and stopped in midstride, in complete astonishment. She was sitting on the cot, looking at him. Her head was bare. He had never seen it bare before, though he had felt in the dark the loose abandon of her hair, not yet wild, on a dark pillow. But he had never seen her hair before and he stood staring at it alone while she watched him; he said suddenly to himself in the instant of moving again: "She's trying to. *I had expected it to have gray in it.* She's trying to be a woman and she don't know how." Thinking, knowing. *She has come to talk to me.* Two hours later she was still talking, they sitting side by side on the cot in the now dark cabin. She told him that she was fortyone years old and that she had been born in the house yonder and had lived there ever since. That she had never been away from Jefferson for a longer period than six months at any time and these only at wide intervals filled with homesickness for the sheer boards and nails, the earth and trees and shrubs, which composed the place which was a foreign land to her and her people; when she spoke even now, after forty years, among the slurred consonants and the flat vowels of the land where her life had been cast, New England talked as plainly as it did in the speech of her kin who had never left New Hampshire and whom she had seen perhaps three times in her life, her forty years. Sitting beside her on the dark cot while the light failed and at last her voice was without source, steady, interminable, pitched almost like the voice of a man, Christmas thought, "She is like all the rest of them. Whether they are seventeen or fortyseven, when they finally come to surrender completely, it's going to be in words."

This is the high point of the relationship between Joe Christmas and Joanna Burden in *Light in August* (chapter 11), one of Faulkner's major novels, together with *As I Lay Dying, The Sound and the Fury,* and *Absalom, Absalom!* Difficult as all erotic exchanges between men and women are in Faulkner, the Christmas-Burden affair is the most harrowing, and yet testifies to what most typifies Faulkner's uncompromising genius for character-ization: his disturbing awareness of male misogyny.

Joe Christmas, who passes uneasily for "white," is of mixed race, and is in flight from himself. Acutely ambivalent towards everyone, Joe is fright-eningly negative towards all women, whom he associates with physical corruption and death. And yet Joe Christmas is a doom-eager child—in effect—and hardly establishes Faulkner himself as a misogynist.

Joanna Burden, descended from abolitionists, is already dangerously un-stable before she and Christmas become lovers, an affair that drives her to madness, and to a desire that she and Joe die together. Christmas murders her, flees, and then dies, shot and emasculated, by a posse headed by Percy Grimm, a peculiarly vicious racist.

While that is the violent and terrible story that centers *Light in August*, this gothic turbulence is only part of the novel. Lena Grove, who will be "light in August" when her baby is born, is what I first recall whenever I think of the book. Lena, who evokes imagery of the harvest-girl in Keats's "To Autumn," is Faulkner's Eve, mother of all living. Serene, gracious, gen-tle, simple, constituted of hope, she makes a marvelous contrast to the tor-ments of Joanna Burden and Joe Christmas.

Faulkner's genius is exemplified by his fecundity in creating persuasive if frequently dreadful men and women. We have had no American Dickens: an amalgam of Mark Twain, Henry James, and William Faulkner—sublimely absurd conglomerate—would come closest.

WILLIAM FAULKNER
(1897–1962)

THOUGH SUBJECT TO SUCH DECISIVE influences as Joseph Conrad and James Joyce, Faulkner himself had a considerable genius for narrative innovation. He could blunder badly, but his nineteen novels across thirty-seven years included *The Sound and the Fury* (1929), *As I Lay Dying* (1930), *Sanctuary* (1931), *Light in August* (1932), and *Absalom, Absalom!* (1936). He never equaled those five, but he acquired a second mode of fictive power in the "Old Man" sequence in *The Wild Palms* (1939), and adumbrated this in the fierce humor of his Snopes saga in his later stories and novels. *A Fable* (1954) is the worst of his books; *As I Lay Dying* the best. Since I have written about that marvelous work in *How to Read and Why,* I will use *Light in August* as my proof-text here, it being my second-favorite.

Faulkner was a humanist and not a believer, though this has been obscured by neo-Christian critics. His inversions of Christian typology are frequent, and from *Go Down, Moses* (1942) on, it seems best to characterize Faulkner the novelist as a natural Gnostic, though he was not immersed in the ancient heresy. He was always a *knower,* and not a literary intellectual. Gnostics necessarily are not "secular humanists"; like Herman Melville, who was aware of his own Gnosticism, they have a quarrel with the God of the Hebrew Bible and the Gospel of Mark. Faulkner's quarrel in *Go Down, Moses* and afterwards was also with the God of Southern history, a god who had sanctioned slavery and its familial consequences. White patriarchs fathering children upon their black concubines was the authentic essence of Southern culture, and Faulkner's imaginative apprehension of the world that this produced is without rival.

Faulkner is incontestably the major North American novelist since Henry James, his antithesis, though also a kind of semi-ancestor through the Jamesian effect upon Conrad. No other twentieth-century novelist so definitively joins the great sequence of Hawthorne, Melville, Mark Twain, and Henry James, and yet Faulkner, despite both his national and international influence, stands apart from even his American tradition. To define this solitude is difficult, but that makes *Light in August* an even more useful book for my prime purpose here, which is to isolate Faulkner's daemon, the other self that constituted his genius. Though fascinated by the Bible,

Faulkner subverts it constantly, almost as if something in his genius hopes that truth can be separated out and away from the powerful stories that are the Bible's literary glory. But I will postpone this matter until I have discussed *Light in August.*

Though it will be anything but a pastoral novel, the book begins and ends with Lena Grove, who for Faulkner invoked the imagery of Keats's "Ode on a Grecian Urn," though I suspect he had the harvest-girl of Keats's "To Autumn" more in mind. In search of her faithless lover, the wandering Lena will be "light in August" after her baby is born. But she experiences no anxiety, in this narrative that otherwise is a cauldron of anxieties. Almost as much a process as she is a person, Lena is patient, calm, hopeful, serene, and replete with delight and wonder at whatever she sees on her trek. It has been suggested that Lena is a fallen Eve, mother of all living, but that is too large an identification. Lena Grove is interesting because she may be the only woman in Faulkner who does not frighten or appall her creator. I take it that she is Faulkner's palinode, his self-critique of all those visions of women that rightfully render feminist critics uneasy. She, and Byron Bunch, who falls in love with her, and doubtless eventually will marry her, are the only characters of *Light in August* who need not wait for their dooms to lift. They emerge from the most wholesome element in Faulkner's comedy, an awareness that kindness can prevail, but only for certain favored persons. Never confused or frightened, free of societal stigmas, Lena wanders through *Light in August* like a charmed force, curiously inviolable. Though she will have little to do with the central plot of the book, the agony of Joe Christmas, Faulkner had the aesthetic intuition that she could make the rest of the novel bearable to us.

Faulkner originally intended to call this narrative *Dark House,* and to center it on the Reverend Gail Hightower, one of those hopeless High Romantics who long for the heroic past of their Confederate ancestors. He loses everything—church, wife, sense of purpose—and yet speaks for an aspect of Faulkner's authentic nihilism. By a lovely irony, Hightower delivers Lena's baby and thus returns to life, and achieves a moral heroism by attempting, in vain, to save Joe Christmas from mob violence.

I first read *Light in August* half a century ago (my copy is inscribed March 15, 1951, Ithaca, New York) and have just reread it, for the first time in about a decade. I confess to curiosity as to whether the tragedy of Joe Christmas would hold up in the United States of 2001, rather than of 1932, the year of its publication. Joe Christmas suspects that he is part black, a suspicion he cannot reveal or sustain, and one that will cause him to kill and to be killed. Nearly seventy years after Faulkner wrote it, can the book continue as tragedy, or do our relative social advances reduce it to a period piece? Yet I need not have feared; Faulkner's artistry is permanent and assured, and the social changes, though real enough, are in another sense illusionary. I am impressed to learn that eighty percent of African Americans do not accept the legitimacy of President George W. Bush (and I also do not), and their honorable resistance is a mark that much is unchanged.

Of all Faulkner's protagonists, Joe Christmas is the most doom-eager and the most unknowable: by the other characters, by Faulkner, by the reader, by himself. He constitutes therefore an extraordinary problem in representation, which Faulkner's genius transforms into the book's greatest strength. We cannot like or dislike Christmas, and the other characters cannot interact with him, not even Joanna Burden, civil rights activist who is Joe's lover, and will become his victim. Joe Christmas may be an abstraction, but then so is our universal doom, *until it happens*. And Joe is trapped in all the ambivalences and hatreds that will destroy him: a horror of the African and of the female, which he compounds. For Faulkner, he provides a great challenge, which the novelist meets fully. Shot and castrated by the vigilante stormtrooper Percy Grimm, Joe Christmas dies most memorably:

> Then his face, body, all, seemed to collapse, to fall in upon itself, and from out the slashed garments about his hips and loins the pent black blood seemed to rush like the rush of sparks from a rising rocket; upon that black blast the man seemed to rise soaring into their memories forever and ever. They are not to lose it, in whatever peaceful valleys, beside whatever placid and reassuring streams of old age, in the mirroring faces of whatever children they will contemplate old disasters and newer hopes. It will be there, musing, quiet, steadfast, not fading and not particularly threatful, but of itself alone serene, of itself alone triumphant. Again from the town, deadened a little by the walls, the scream of the siren mounted toward its unbelievable crescendo, passing out of the realm of hearing.

A startling passage, to be echoed by Nathanael West at the end of *The Day of the Locust*, this frightening epiphany asks us to find serenity and triumph in Joe Christmas's martyrdom. As he never, in life, had a serene or undefeated moment, this is plainly too extravagant to be merely paradoxical. What, aside from the horror, renders it memorable for the town's imagination? Dismiss the notion that Joe Christmas, his name notwithstanding, is a figure of Jesus Christ, or even a parody thereof. Does Faulkner control the intense rhetoric here, or are we in the same dilemma we experience at the end of Conrad's *Heart of Darkness*? Much as I admire Conrad elsewhere—in *Nostromo, Victory, Under Western Eyes, The Secret Agent*—I fear that there is nothing to understand in the life *or* death of Kurtz, since Conrad himself does not seem to understand. But the murder and castration of Joe Christmas has too many significances, rather than too few. Christmas has scapegoated himself before anyone else victimizes him, and he has no idea whatever of what he means or possibly believes. He is a pure representation of what Freud called the death drive, but so is Joanna Burden, and Percy Grimm is death itself.

It does not matter, of course, whether Joe Christmas was partly black or not—the book's madness, accurately reflecting the madness of our society, is that suspicion of blackness is more than enough. Faulkner is justified in emphasizing the serenity and triumphalism of Joe's final ordeal, because its memorability is totally fused with the book's, and the nation's, madness. The genius of William Faulkner was fused also, both with that malaise, and with the art that proved almost adequate to it, "almost" only because it is the antithesis of art.

ERNEST HEMINGWAY

They were seated in the boat, Nick in the stern, his father rowing. The sun was coming up over the hills. A bass jumped, making a circle in the water. Nick trailed his hand in the water. It felt warm in the sharp chill of the morning.

In the early morning on the lake sitting in the stern of the boat with his father rowing, he felt quite sure that he would never die.

That is the conclusion of "Indian Camp," one of the Nick Adams stories, in which Nick is a version of the young Hemingway. William Hazlitt, superb English critic, observed that no young man believes he will ever die. Hemingway possessed a particular poignance in the study of death; like his own father, he forestalled death by suicide.

Notoriously, we celebrate Hemingway for his stance and style, as manifested in his prose and his life. Like Byron, Whitman, and Wilde, Hemingway has become a mythical personage. His highly deliberate mythmaking is an aesthetic distraction when one reads his later novels. The short stories, with their remarkable economy, are armored against Hemingway's involuntary self-parodies, which mar *Across the River and into the Trees* and the very popular but inadequate *The Old Man and the Sea.*

Hemingway claimed Mark Twain as American ancestor, and Joseph Conrad as a more distant precursor. Nearly all post-Hemingway American writers have been contaminated by Hemingway, sometimes to their anguish. His stance was precarious, being just this side of sentimental. And yet he remains the unique American master of the short story, and enters that pantheon that includes Chekhov, Turgenev, and James Joyce.

ERNEST HEMINGWAY
(1899–1961)

LIKE LORD BYRON AND OSCAR WILDE, Hemingway is more renowned for his life and personality than for his literary work. Though this palpably undervalues *Don Juan, The Importance of Being Earnest,* and a dozen superb short stories, no one need deplore the charisma of these authors. Goethe, after all, is an even grander example of the genius of personality obscuring (in his case) an enormous achievement. Since my text here is *The Sun Also Rises* (1926), which is not the equal of the best Hemingway stories, there is also the dilemma that what increasingly seems a period piece necessarily suffers by being considered in sequence with *The Scarlet Letter, Moby-Dick,* and *Adventures of Huckleberry Finn.* Still, better this than any other novel by Hemingway, since only here does he maintain, in certain episodes, a significant revelation of his genius, his capacity for inventing a new prose style and stance.

Hemingway asserted that *Adventures of Huckleberry Finn* was his model, and he mentioned also, as American precursors, Stephen Crane and Henry James. He acknowledged Joseph Conrad, who was the crucial forerunner, as he was for Scott Fitzgerald and for Faulkner. Hemingway's relation to Conrad is very subtle: his mode of heroism revises Conrad's without refuting it. It makes me uneasy when I juxtapose Hemingway's novels with Conrad's: *The Secret Agent, Under Western Eyes, Nostromo,* and *Victory* are aesthetic achievements beyond Hemingway's span. The author of *For Whom the Bell Tolls* boasted of taking on Tolstoy, which was unfortunate: Conrad at least was within range.

The Sun Also Rises was published in October 1926, and provides a perfect instance of the work influencing the life, more than the life the work. Like Lord Byron after *Childe Harold,* Hemingway woke up to find himself famous, the charismatic representative of the Lost Generation, forever to be identified with expatriate Paris and Madrid in the 1920s. Brett Ashley became an archetype for restless, destructive young women, and Hemingway became Hemingway, with his credo that only bullfighters, boxers, and big-game hunters lived their lives all the way up.

Of the importance of *The Sun Also Rises* for literary and cultural history, no one retains doubt. Whether the novel still sustains careful rereading is another matter, as is the question of Hemingway's genius, so strongly manifested in just the stories he liked the best: "The Short Happy Life of Francis Macomber," "In Another Country," "Hills Like White Elephants," "A Way You'll Never Be," "The Snows of Kilimanjaro," "A Clean Well-Lighted Place," and "The Light of the World." I would add to these seven "The End of Something," "God Rest You Merry, Gentlemen," and "The Sea Change," and other readers would have different choices. If you go back to any of these after some years away, they leap out at you: they are exemplary stories, in style and in imaginative vision.

Rereading *The Sun Also Rises* is a more complex experience: much of it begins to balance precariously at the verge of the period piece. Perhaps it has toppled over, and *is* now a period piece. One definition of literary genius has to be that its central works do not become period pieces, as Hemingway's best stories, despite parodies and self-parodies, do not. I find I am about to move into a digression on period pieces, and Swift warns against the dangers of digressions, but a book on geniuses of language cannot avoid a meditation upon period pieces, though it is a painful and vexed subject, particularly these crowded days, when so many—in my judgment—period pieces have been canonized by the media and the universities, or to be more accurate, the media-universities.

A period, in the sense relevant here, is an interval of time characterized by the prevalence of a specified culture, ideology, or technology: I quote definition 2 from the *American Heritage Dictionary of the English Language,* fourth edition, 2000. In a literary context, a period piece is not timeless in its aesthetic and intellectual value, but merely reflects a particular moment (or span) when an ideology of culture was dominant. Works of genius of course are both timeless and reflective of an era: you can, if you wish, regard *Hamlet* as a reflection of London in 1601, but you don't need *Hamlet* for such a reflection, as there are plenty of alternatives. I have excluded living writers of genius (and we do have some) from this book, because the media-universities cannot tell them apart from the authors of our ocean of period pieces, and while I *think* I can, I am haunted always by my hero, Dr. Samuel Johnson, who once unfortunately remarked, *"Tristram Shandy* did not last." If Johnson nods, shall not his belated disciple fall asleep?

What incontrovertibly has faded in *The Sun Also Rises* is Lady Brett Ashley, a New Woman perhaps in 1925, but only another destroyer of the self and of others in 2001 (when I write). What has not faded, paradoxically enough, is the period of this period piece (to call it that). The aesthetic Paris of the early and middle 1920s is one of the major centers in the Western movement once uselessly called "Modernism," since every generation necessarily has its own modernism. Picasso, Stravinsky, Proust, Joyce are a matchless fourfold in twentieth-century culture, even if Gertrude Stein (like Ezra Pound a touch earlier) was more important for Hemingway as a catalyst. Though *The Sun Also Rises* has an autobiographical matrix, Hemingway worked hard to free his first major fiction from his life. Jake Barnes, Hemingway's surrogate, is unmarried; Hadley, the novelist's first wife, is removed from the story.

If Brett is now something of a period piece, what is the status of Jake Barnes? He saves the novel, insofar as it can be validated. The reader needs proportion: try rereading *The Sun Also Rises* after rereading Joyce's *Ulysses.* Hemingway cannot change the way you read: he raises your consciousness of style and of sensibility, but does not alter your entire relationship to language.

He is the first instance of a recurrent American phenomenon: a minor novelist with a major style. A genius of sensibility who cannot create deep inwardness in his characters is better suited to the short story, where lyric intensity can replace drama. *The Sun Also Rises* works best as an extended elegy for the self. This is not to make Jake Barnes/Hemingway into Walt Whitman, and yet there is something Whitmanian in Hemingway's stance and mode, the desire to say what cannot be said, the overtones of biblical style even where there are no relevant allusions. I mean a style in which Hemingway, like Whitman, evokes by parataxis, which is a structuring of sentences so that they convey no distinctions of a higher or a lower order. That gives the tone of a withdrawal from all affect, while actually investing affect in the consistency of the withdrawal:

> I thought I had paid for everything. Not like the woman pays and pays and pays. No idea of retribution or punishment. Just exchange of values. You gave up something and got something else. Or you worked for something. You paid some way for everything that was any good. I paid my way into enough things that I liked, so that I had a good time. Either you paid by learning about them, or by experience, or by taking chances, or by money. Enjoying living was learning to get your money's worth and knowing when you had it. You could get your money's worth. The world was a good place to buy in. It seemed like a fine philosophy. In five years, I thought, it will seem just as silly as all the other fine philosophies I've had.

That is characteristic Jake Barnes, and is classic Hemingway. The style has been so influential, from John Steinbeck and John O'Hara through

Nelson Algren and Norman Mailer, that we are in danger of taking it as a commonplace kind of understatement, but Hemingway perfected it. A great style became a period style, and lost some of its flavor.

Jake Barnes calls himself a bad Catholic, since his pragmatic religion is the bullfight, and he searches for Christ in the great bullfighters whose art of courage is one of Hemingway's favored images of "grace under pressure." Reread in 2001, *The Sun Also Rises* can read like a companion to Eliot's *The Waste Land*, though Hemingway was not waiting for grace and did not undergo a conversion, as Eliot did. Clearly there is a nostalgia for a Catholic ordering of spirituality in Jake Barnes, but Hemingway never yielded to it, and, like his father, he ended by shooting himself.

The genius abides steadily in the short stories, some of which, like "God Rest You Merry, Gentlemen," and "The Light of the World," seem to touch the limits of the art. There was a daemon in Hemingway, but he was a lyrical spirit, and was likely to wander away if a narrative became too extended.

FLANNERY O'CONNOR

> I am always having it pointed out to me that life in Georgia is not at all the way I picture it, that escaped criminals do not roam the roads exterminating families, nor Bible salesmen prowl about looking for girls with wooden legs.

That is Flannery O'Connor in a talk she gave called "The Grotesque in Southern Fiction." In our new Age of Terror, with trade towers crumbling and anthrax spilling out of letters, the grotesque in O'Connor's stories and novels almost can seem a comfort.

A genius of the grotesque is relatively rare, and O'Connor and Carson McCullers join Faulkner and Nathanael West in that difficult mastery. "Grotesque" usually is defined as a mode of distortion: bizarre, ludicrous, fantastic. It can seem singular that "grotesque" derives from "grotto," until we think of what permanent residents of a cave or cavern might look like.

In Flannery O'Connor's vision, we are all cavern dwellers, though for her we inhabit not Plato's cave but an American inferno. She wishes to have us terrorized into a state of grace, and she might have rejoiced grimly at our discomfort with the authentic New Age of Islamic fundamentalist terror. As our lives perforce turn more grotesque, her fiction is likely to seem even more relevant.

FLANNERY O'CONNOR
(1925–1964)

LIKE HEMINGWAY, FLANNERY O'CONNOR did her best work in the short story. Even a brief list of her masterpieces would include "A Good Man Is Hard to Find," "Good Country People," "A View of the Woods," "Revelation," "Parker's Back," and "Judgment Day," but there are another five or six nearly as extraordinary.

I have a passion for her second (and last) novel, *The Violent Bear It Away* (1960). Dead at thirty-nine, O'Connor nevertheless achieved something like a total vision in her stories and in her second novel, which I choose to write about here partly because I have discussed some of the stories in *How to Read and Why*, and partly because her genius, always remorseless and turbulent, breaks all bounds in *The Violent Bear It Away*. The novel's epigraph, which would sink most books, is amply proved appropriate by her performance: "From the days of John the Baptist until now, the kingdom of heaven suffereth violence, and the violent bear it away" (Matthew 11:12).

The "now" is Jesus prophesying that the kingdom of heaven is at hand, even as he proclaims that John, still alive but in prison, has inaugurated what appears to be the end time. O'Connor, an apocalyptic Roman Catholic, believed that the violent independent post-Protestant prophets of her native South could take the kingdom of heaven by force. The best comment by O'Connor on her novel requires to be read warily, as we need to read all of her letters and essays when they comment upon her fictions:

> The lack of realism would be crucial if this were a realistic novel or if the novel demanded the kind of realism you demand. I don't believe it does. The old man is very obviously not a Southern Baptist, but an independent, a prophet in the true sense. The true prophet is inspired by the Holy Ghost, not necessarily by the dominant religion of his region. Further, the traditional Protestant bodies of the South are evaporating into secularism and respectability and are being replaced on the grass roots level by all sorts of strange sects that bear not much resemblance to traditional Protestantism—Jehovah's Witnesses, snake-handlers, Free Thinking Christians, Independent Prophets, the swindlers, the mad, and sometimes the genuinely inspired. A charac-

ter has to be true to his own nature and I think the old man is that. He was a prophet, not a church-member. As a prophet, he has to be a natural Catholic. Hawthorne said he didn't write novels, he wrote romances; I am one of his descendants.

Old Tarwater, professional moonshiner and self-called prophet, is hardly a "natural Catholic" unless, by definition, every American religionist is. With her usual cunning, O'Connor renders Old Tarwater a monster, but he passes her test for religious authenticity. The glory of *The Violent Bear It Away* is the fourteen-year-old Francis Marion Tarwater, who inherits from Huck Finn only a recalcitrance that strives for individual freedom, but who is driven both by his great-uncle Tarwater's prophetic training, and by what O'Connor intends to be the voice of the Devil, speaking to the boy Tarwater as an inner voice, "the friend." Eventually, O'Connor externalizes the Devil, who drives a lavender and cream-colored car, and is clearly an unpleasant fellow:

> The person who had picked him up was a pale, lean, old-looking young man with deep hollows under his cheekbones. He had on a lavender shirt and a thin black suit and a panama hat. His lips were as white as the cigarette that hung limply from one side of his mouth. His eyes were the same color as his shirt and were ringed with heavy black lashes. A lock of yellow hair fell across his forehead from under his pushed-back hat.

All that lavender is a little distressing in our age of gay rights, but O'Connor's Catholicism was fierce, normative, and fully formed by the 1940s. After stupefying the boy Tarwater with strong liquor, the Devil rapes him and departs. Awaking in horror, Tarwater sets fire to the woods. When the voice of "the friend" inwardly returns, the young prophet's response is to start another blaze. Subsequently, he beholds a vision of Christ's miracle of the loaves and fishes, and then a burning red-gold tree, and so his prophetic call comes to him: GO WARN THE CHILDREN OF GOD OF THE TERRIBLE SPEED OF MERCY. Having been called, he goes:

> By midnight he had left the road and the burning woods behind him and had come out on the highway once more. The moon, riding low above the field beside him, appeared and disappeared, diamond-bright, between patches of darkness. Intermittently the boy's jagged shadow slanted across the road ahead of him as if it cleared a rough

path toward his goal. His singed eyes, black in their deep sockets, seemed already to envision the fate that awaited him but he moved steadily on, his face set toward the dark city, where the children of God lay sleeping.

That is the impressive end of O'Connor's romance: she intimates that, with his prophecy rejected, young Tarwater will die in a conflagration, doubtless set by himself. The only alternative would be the state asylum, since by the standards O'Connor rejects, the new prophet is schizophrenic. These standards are incarnated in Rayber, the schoolteacher, Tarwater's other uncle, whom O'Connor plainly despises and who is the book's aesthetic disaster, though *The Violent Bear It Away* remains unsinkable. You cannot listen to Rayber's incoherent mix of psychology and sociology without cringing, not because O'Connor's satire is on target, but because she has been too impatient to find out where and what the target is. Her close friend and coreligionist Sally Fitzgerald indicates this difficulty:

> Her weaknesses—a lack of perfect familiarity with the terminology of the secular sociologists, psychologists, and rationalists she often casts as adversary figures, and an evident weighting of the scales against them all—are present in the character of Rayber (who combines all three categories).

The formidable Mrs. Fitzgerald was doing her best, but I think she mistook the point. Even if O'Connor had immersed herself in David Riesman, Philip Rieff, Erik Erikson, and Karl Popper, she could not have managed to make Rayber a more persuasive version of everything she loathed. Her genius was akin to Nathanael West's, whose fictions she greatly admired; like him, she was more a parodist than a satirist. Writing to her friend the novelist John Hawkes, she plainly sees her limitation, which would ruin a novel but not her parodistic romance:

> Rayber, of course, was always the stumbling block. I had a version of this book about a year ago in which Rayber was really no more than a caricature. He may have been better that way but the book as a whole was not. It may just be a matter of giving the devil his due . . . anyway I am usually out of my depth, and I don't really know Rayber or have the ear for him.

Parody, to work, must understand and know its victims, and O'Connor, hardly a saintly temperament, had neither the compassion nor the patience to understand and know Rayber.

She had mistaken her ultimate precursor, who was Jonathan Swift and not Nathaniel Hawthorne. And—as with West and perhaps Swift—there is sadism in O'Connor's temperament. The young prophet Tarwater baptizes Rayber's little idiot son by drowning him, a murder that produces no remorse either in Tarwater or in O'Connor. This Catholic novelist's indubitable genius, her other self, does not seem to me Catholic or even normative Christian. If the Tarwaters are, to O'Connor, "natural Catholics," then O'Connor, in her parodistic propheticism, is yet another oxymoron, a "natural Gnostic." Grace does not arrive in O'Connor's fictions to correct nature but rather to abolish it. We would be good people, O'Connor insinuates, if somebody were there to shoot us every moment of our lives, or to drown us in baptizing us. Regeneration through violence is the doctrine of Shrike in *Miss Lonelyhearts* and of Judge Holden in Cormac McCarthy's *Blood Meridian*. It is, in my judgment, the true vision of what I have learned to call the American Religion, our pragmatic national faith. Her admirers praise Flannery O'Connor as a Roman Catholic moralist, an estimate I find odd. I celebrate her genius as another authentic prophet of the American Religion, at once the source of our individuality in literature and in life, and the origin also of our endemic violence, which West parodied, as O'Connor did also, but with a certain ambivalence.

VIII

HOD

LUSTRE 15

|

Walt Whitman, Fernando Pessoa, Hart Crane, Federico García Lorca, Luis Cernuda

|

When I lectured on this sequence of five great poets in Coimbra, Portugal, an old friend suggested to me that they were, after all, held together by their mutual homoeroticism. That seems to me as little useful as telling me that a particular grouping share their heterosexuality. Eros is infinitely varied, whatever its orientation. This first Lustre of *Hod* or God's "female majesty" is female only in relation to the more severe male attributes of the Divinity.

What holds this Lustre together, for me, is the majesty of Walt Whitman, whose influence engendered Fernando Pessoa's heteronyms, evasions of the presence of Whitman. Hart Crane and García Lorca asserted a more positive relation to Whitman, and yet are more distant from him than Pessoa was. Luis Cernuda, the great modern poet of Spanish exile, owed more to Robert Browning and to T. S. Eliot than to Whitman, but I place him here because *Hod* is the sphere of the Sublime, and Cernuda is one of the last masters of that lonely mode.

WALT WHITMAN

As Adam early in the morning,
Walking forth from the bower refresh'd with sleep,
Behold me where I pass, hear my voice, approach,
- Touch me, touch the palm of your hand to my body as I pass,
Be not afraid of my body.

Whitman is both Adam and Christ, the Old Adam and the New, and like the doubting disciple we are urged to touch the resurrected body as it goes by us.

It is difficult to keep up with Whitman; perpetually he passes and surpasses us.

Walt Whitman is the poem of our climate, the genius of the shores of North America. No other American is so much a world poet, surviving translation and radical revision. He wrote in the American language, and yet seems at home in Portuguese and Spanish, German and Russian.

I doubt that the Whitmanian amplitude has much to do with being the poet of democracy, though Whitman insisted that such was his identity. He actually is a hermetic poet, hesitant and private, and rather more difficult than he proclaims himself as being.

D. H. Lawrence, whose quarrel with Whitman was intimate and familial, praised the American bard as being the only poet who broke a new road. Whitman captured forever the image of the open road; no one else has been able to usurp it.

And yet whenever I think of Whitman and chant him aloud, I encounter the elegist of the self, the poet of the Evening Land. In Whitman, four great images fuse into one: Night, Death, the Mother, and the Sea.

Perhaps the genius of Walt Whitman was more an end than a beginning. The dispossessed found a voice in him, but the actual burden of his song is not so much democracy as it is the high cost of the self's confirmation, which is a total expense.

WALT WHITMAN
(1819–1892)

NORTH AMERICA'S TWO GREATEST POETS, Walt Whitman and Emily Dickinson, achieve universality by centering upon their own selves. Whitman seems not to have been aware that William Wordsworth had inaugurated such an enterprise, since Ralph Waldo Emerson essentially mediated literary culture for Whitman. Dickinson, superbly cognizant of Wordsworth, whom she referred to as the Stranger, resisted Emerson's mediation with more irony than Whitman ever learned towards his master. Dickinson had heard of Whitman as a scandal, and declined to read him, ostensibly for motives of decorum; one doubts that Dickinson's name ever reached Whitman. Yet these two, with their precursor Emerson, and Henry James, remain the strongest writers the United States of America has brought forth, to date. At their best, they are very difficult artists, a view many critics hold of Dickinson and James, but too few of Emerson and of Whitman. Like Emerson, Whitman can be elusive and evasive, and even hermetic. There is also a difficulty peculiar to Whitman: he frequently promises to reveal everything (by which I do not mean his homoeroticism) but actually seems determined to tell you as little about himself as possible. You have to read the poetry very searchingly to grasp Whitman's attitudes towards his father, Walter Whitman Sr., a Quaker carpenter, and you need to read the ellipses in the poetry to intimate why the poet's mother, Louisa Van Velsor Whitman, should so darkly have come to be identified with night, death, and the sea.

Whitman, in his poetry, identifies his genius for us as the "Me myself" of *Song of Myself*, section 4, and "the real Me" of "As I Ebb'd with the Ocean of Life," section 2. I suspect that the mockingbird, "my dusky demon and brother," of "Out of the Cradle Endlessly Rocking," and the hermit thrush of "When Lilacs Last in the Dooryard Bloom'd," are alternate versions of Whitman's genius or daemon. As my subject is the genius of Whitman, and the effect of the work of his poetry upon the life of the man Whitman, I follow the poet himself in thus finding him to have been his own muse. Deeply homoerotic in sexual orientation, and almost certainly devoid of heterosexual experience (though he insisted otherwise), Whitman was truest to his habitual experience by evoking an autoerotic Muse. I quote

here from "Spontaneous Me," an extraordinary pansexual poem (first published in the 1856 second edition of *Leaves of Grass* as "Bunch Poem"):

> The young man that wakes deep at night, the hot hand seeking to
> repress what would master him,
> The mystic amorous night, the strange half-welcome pangs, visions,
> sweats,
> The pulse pounding through palms and trembling, encircling
> fingers, the young man all color'd, red, ashamed, angry;

• • •

> The wholesome relief, repose, content,
> And this bunch pluck'd at random from myself,
> It has done its work—I toss it carelessly to fall where it may.

Most of *Song of Myself* does not concern the genius (real Me or Me myself) or that unknown entity, "my soul," but is rather the poem of "Walt
Whitman, an American, one of the roughs, a kosmos" (the original 1855
reading of what became the first line of section 24). That is the mask or
persona of Whitman, rather than the darker poet of Night, Death, the
Mother, and the Sea. Yet my favorite passage in *Song of Myself* is section 4's
gracious, affectionate description of the Me myself:

> Apart from the pulling and hauling stands what I am,
> Stands amused, complacent, compassionating, idle, unitary,
> Looks down, is erect or bends an arm on an impalpable certain rest,
> Looking with side-curved head curious what will come next,
> But in and out of the game and watching and wondering at it.

When I teach *Song of Myself*, my students divide as to whether this charmingly cool citizen is female or male. No daemon ever can have been gentler
than this Me myself, but in "As I Ebb'd with the Ocean of Life" she/he
turns upon the rough Walt, stingingly mocking his poetic pretensions:

> O baffled, balk'd, bent to the very earth,
> Opress'd with myself that I have dared to open my mouth,
> Aware now that amid all that blab whose echoes recoil upon me I
> have not once had the least idea who or what I am
> But that before all my arrogant poems the real Me, stands yet
> untouch'd, untold, altogether unreached,

Withdrawn far, mocking me with mock-congratulatory signs and
    bows,
With peals of distant ironical laughter at every word I have written,
Pointing in silence to these songs, and then to the sand beneath.

Whitman in 1860 is only forty-one, six years or so along in the great fer-
ment that began in the summer of 1854, when "I was simmering, simmering, simmering—Emerson brought me to a boil." Whitman was to deny
influence later, but in the summer in 1854 he read the essays of Emerson
with considerable care, and to marvelous effect, for that is when he begins
to write what eventually will come to be called *Song of Myself*. The early
Notebook versions record an extraordinary sense of release:

I am your voice—It was tied in you—In me it begins to talk.
I celebrate myself to celebrate every man and every woman alive . . .

We cannot know whether a particular essay of Emerson's, more than the
others, kindled Whitman in the middle of the journey, but I suspect it was
"The Over-Soul," not one of my own favorites. This is an essay about the
question of genius, and it argues for a freshness of revelation beyond any yet
known:

The soul is superior to its knowledge; wiser than any of its works. The
great poet makes us feel our own wealth, and then we think less of his
compositions.

This energy does not descend into individual life on any other condition than entire possession. It comes to the lowly and simple.

"Self-Reliance" and "The Poet," among other essays, are echoed more
overtly in the 1855 *Leaves of Grass*, yet Whitman's sudden sense of his own
Newness is closest to "The Over-Soul." What I cannot trace from Emerson
seems to me Whitman's largest originality, his division of his poethood into
projected self, real Me or Me myself, and soul. Here the 1854 Notebook does
not hold up: something was happening in the winter-to-spring transition of
1854–55 that was a personal catalyst for Whitman, and it seems to have been
the illness and approaching death of his father. A strong nature, the carpenter
Walter Whitman Sr. died hard, slowly, and mostly silently, manifesting his lifelong alternation between fury and stoicism, baffled and embittered. The poet
had returned home to take the failing father's place, and about a week after

Leaves of Grass was offered for sale, the senior Whitman died. A repressed guilt waited a decade before returning in the elegy supposedly for the martyred President Lincoln, "When Lilacs Last in the Dooryard Bloom'd."

Whitman's parents were followers of the charismatic Quaker preacher Elias Hicks, a rebel against normative Quakerism itself, and one of the implicit founders of what I think should be called the American Religion, a post-Christian fusion of Gnostic, Orphic, and Enthusiastic strains. There are few differences between Hicks and Emerson as orators of the Inner Light; Hicks, like Emerson, stressed the divinity of the self, and denied the uniqueness of Christ. Whitman never forgot the experience of hearing Hicks speak, and regarded the Quaker heretic as a hero of American democracy (Hicks was both African-American and Native American). He prepared Whitman for Emerson's vision of genius: "the power to affect the Imagination, as possessed by the orator, the poet, the novelist, or the artist . . . itself representative and accepted by all men as their delegate."

The poet as delegate and as hero was not quite Whitman's central legacy from Emerson. Notebook entries of 1854–55 go beyond their modification in *Leaves of Grass* 1855, in giving us Walt Whitman as the American Christ:

> In vain were nails driven through my hands.
> I remember my crucifixion and bloody coronation
> I remember the mockers and the buffeting insults
> The sepulchre and the white linen have yielded me—
> I am alive in New York and San Francisco,
> Again I tread the streets after two thousand years.
> Not all the traditions can put vitality in churches . . .

When we behold Walt's resurrection in section 38, *Song of Myself*, this has been a touch toned down. Nor does section 41 confess that

> I am myself waiting my time to be a God;
> I think I shall do as much good and be as pure and prodigious as any . . .

Joseph Smith—prophet, seer, and revelator—would not have disapproved, though he might have had a reservation regarding a Notebook draft that failed to enter section 49:

> Mostly this we have of Gods we have man.
> Lo, the Sun;

Its glory floods the moon,
Which of a night shines in some turbid pool,
Shaken by soughing winds;
And there are sparkles mad and tossed and broken,
And their archetype is the sun.

Of God I know not;
But this I know;
I can comprehend no being more wonderful than man . . .

How does Whitman bring together this self-deification and the vexed relationship between his genius, the real Me/Me myself, and his soul? As a God, Whitman carries a complex psychic cartography within him:

I believe in you my soul, the other I am must not abase itself to you,
And you must not be abased to the other.

These opening lines of section 5, *Song of Myself*, seem to me the most difficult in all of Whitman, and potentially among the most revelatory. The poem is called *Song of Myself*, rather than *Song of the Soul* or *Song of the Other I Am* (that is, of the real Me, or Me myself). Whitman has no anxieties about the relationship between Walt Whitman, one of the roughs, an American, and his soul, but evidently he fears that genius and the soul do not marry as readily. To abase oneself to another is to surrender rank, to be degraded in dignity. What then does Whitman conceive of the soul? How would he define it? If the self is personality, inner (real Me) and outer (one of the roughs), then the soul would be character, but I am not certain that Whitman would accept such a distinction. Yet do we ever hear the voice of the soul in his poetry, in the sense that we hear Walt Whitman almost throughout, and his daemon or genius at certain moments or in the voices of mockingbird and hermit thrush?

I think not, and this negation defines the Whitmanian soul. His is a poetry of sublime pathos, and not ethos: even his "real Me" is mutable, but the soul is unchanging, and also largely unknown to him. Whitman was enough of an Epicurean materialist to believe that the *what* is unknowable:

A child said *What is the grass?* fetching it to me with full hands.
How could I answer the child? I do not know what it is any more than he.

Whitman, though spurred on by Emerson, was no Transcendentalist: he has more in common with Lucretius than with Plato or Plotinus. Love, even in the mode of homoerotic "adhesiveness," does not lead Whitman beyond the desired erotic comrade. Like Blake (whom he read only in old age), Whitman believes that the body is all of the soul that the five senses can perceive. One of Whitman's largest paradoxes is that he experiences Emersonian surges of the Newness, while pragmatically evading the Over-Soul. Emerson, in his generous letter saluting *Leaves of Grass*, on July 21, 1855, shrewdly emphasized *power* as Whitman's grand contribution:

> I am very happy in reading it, as great power makes us happy. It meets the demand I am always making of what seemed the sterile and stingy Nature, as if too much handiwork or too much lymph in the temperament were making our western wits fat and mean.

Ten years later, in the aftermath of Lincoln's assassination, Whitman wrote his greatest poem, the last expression of his full genius and of Emersonian power, "When Lilacs Last in the Dooryard Bloom'd." Whitman was only forty-six, but his remaining twenty-seven years represented a long waning of his poetry, parallel to Wordsworth's forty-three years of decline after 1807. Whitman's true life as a poet comprised only the decade 1855–65, even as Wordsworth enjoyed only the Great Decade, 1797–1807. Wordsworth iced over; Whitman, I suggest, was devastated by the Civil War, as Emerson was. Obsessed by hatred for the South, Emerson slipped into senility. Whitman, heroic wound-dresser and unpaid male nurse in the hospitals of Washington, D.C., burned out in devoted service to sick and maimed soldiers, Union and Confederate, black and white, living and dying. There is no comparable figure of such authentic compassionate heroism in our literary culture, and our image of Whitman forever is fixed as "the brother angel" of the study by Roy Morris Jr., who says that this apotheosis "saved" Whitman as a person. It may be, but it destroyed him as a poet, after the final magnificence of the "Lilacs" elegy, which turned out to be a lament not only for President Lincoln, but also for the genius of Walt Whitman. His agony exalted him, and it broke him. If there is an American Christ, then here he is in "The Wound-Dresser":

An old man bending I come among new faces,
Years looking backward resuming in answer to children,
Come tell us old man, as from young men and maidens that love me,
(Arous'd and angry, I'd thought to beat the alarum, and urge endless war

But soon my fingers failed me, my face droop'd and I resigned myself,
To sit by the wounded and soothe them, or silently watch the dead.)

This is the forging of the national poet, undismissable even by the moral authority of Senator Trent Lott, who speaks for what is now the Republican Party when he pronounces that homoeroticism is near allied to kleptomania. They are not about to place Walt Whitman on Mount Rushmore, which will yet be adorned by Ronald Reagan and (dare we hope it?) George W. Bush. Senator Lott can be assured there was no kleptomania brought to the hospital by the Good Gray Poet; he carried instead brandy and ice cream, books and tobacco, pens and paper, with which he wrote letters for the incapable. And he healed: by his presence, his love, his compassion. It is very difficult not to be overwhelmed by this truthful image of Whitman, the prelude at once to his elegiac masterpiece and to his long decline afterwards. How many comparable imitations of Christ have we as a nation?

"When Lilacs Last in the Dooryard Bloom'd" implicitly culminates Whitman's poetry by building upon his five major earlier poems: *Song of Myself*, "The Sleepers," "Crossing Brooklyn Ferry," and the two *Sea-Drift* elegies, "Out of the Cradle Endlessly Rocking" and "As I Ebb'd with the Ocean of Life." It takes from *Song of Myself* the psychic cartography, from "The Sleepers" the gift of controlled phantasmagoria, from "Crossing Brooklyn Ferry" the motif of "face-to-face" communion, and from the *Sea-Drift* elegies the breaking apart of the self, since both the mockingbird and the hermit thrush sing the songs of death. Something in Whitman (call it his genius) knows that this is the grand achievement, and that it comes at a great price to both his selves.

In this book's section on T. S. Eliot, I discuss the complex, suppressed relationship between "When Lilacs Last in the Dooryard Bloom'd" and *The Waste Land*. Here I ruefully admit that Eliot, though no Whitman, is a strong enough poet so that at moments in rereading "Lilacs" I have the hallucinatory sensation that Whitman has been reading *The Waste Land*, fifty-seven years in advance. His quest, in "Lilacs," is both personal and religious, like that of Eliot in *The Waste Land*, but Whitman seeks again his own resurrection, while Eliot seeks Christ's (though Whitman hovers in Eliot's Christ).

I have published sustained readings of "Lilacs" elsewhere, and don't wish to recuperate them now, since my concern is Whitman's genius alone, its crisis and its fate. The death of Father Abraham inevitably recalls the death of Walter Whitman Sr., a decade before, and Whitman's genius seeks to expiate not only its own survival but its genesis, which was so deeply intertwined with the death of the father. In response, the poet directly juxtaposes the song of his "brother," the hermit thrush, with the passage of Lincoln's coffin through the land, and then gives us the "tally," the sprig of lilac that is his own image of voice, as an offering to the dead fathers:

> Here, coffin that slowly passes,
> I give you my sprig of lilac.

The elegy's superb crisis comes as Whitman stands at night near the swamp bordered by "ghostly pines," where "in secluded recesses" the hermit thrush sings to the poet the song of sane and sacred death:

Come lovely and soothing death,
Undulate round the world, serenely arriving, arriving,
In the day, in the night, to all, to each,
Sooner or later delicate death.

Prais'd be the fathomless universe,
For life and joy, and for objects and knowledge curious,
And for love, sweet love—but praise! praise! praise!
For the sure-enwinding arms of cool-enfolding death.

Dark mother always gliding near with soft feet,
Have none chanted for thee a chant of fullest welcome?
Then I chant it for thee, I glorify thee above all,
I bring thee a song that when thou must indeed come, come
    unfalteringly.

Approach strong deliveress,
When it is so, when thou hast taken them I joyously sing the dead,
Lost in the loving floating ocean of thee,
Laved in the flood of thy bliss O death.

From me to thee glad serenades,
Dances for thee I propose saluting thee, adornments and feastings
    for thee,
And the sights of the open landscape and the high-spread sky are
    fitting,
And life and the fields, and the huge and thoughtful night.

The night in silence under many a star,
The ocean shore and the husky whispering wave whose voice I
    know,
And the soul turning to thee O vast and well-veil'd death,
And the body gratefully nestling close to thee.

Over the tree-tops I float thee a song,
Over the rising and sinking waves, over the myriad fields and the
    prairies wide,
Over the dense-pack'd cities all and the teeming wharves and ways,
I float this carol with joy, with joy to thee O death.

The father is doubly gone; the mother—at once midwife, lover, and
shrouder—is open to a joyous Oedipal trespass, an authentic shock, since it
violates the ultimate taboo. Night, Death, the Mother, and the Sea align to
provide the sublime context for the resurrection of Whitman's genius, but
is this a rebirth or a self-immolation?

FERNANDO PESSOA

An imperialism of grammarians? The imperialism of grammarians runs deeper and endures longer than that of generals. An imperialism of poets? Yes, of poets. The phrase sounds ridiculous only to those who defend the old and ridiculous kind of imperialism. The imperialism of poets endures and wins out; that of politicians passes on and is forgotten, unless the poet remembers it in his songs.

(translated by Richard Zenith)

The boy-king Sebastian led the Portuguese army into a slaughter in Morocco, in 1578. Since the royal body was not found on the battlefield, a national myth came into being, Sebastianism, which held that the hero lived on, in a mystic island, and someday would return as the Hidden One, and establish Portugal as the Fifth Empire. After a brief flirtation with the Portuguese Fascist dictator Salazar, Pessoa aestheticized the Fifth Empire, as he does above. The new Portuguese imperialism was to confine itself to the language of literature, and Pessoa, by implication, was to replace Camoens as the national poet.

Pessoa, who was several different geniuses at once, cannot—in my judgment—be said to have overgone Camoens, whether as a lyric or an epic poet. Perhaps Pessoa's relationship to Camoens is parallel to that of William Blake to John Milton, a loving contest against the insuperable.

Pessoa's fascination for his readers has more to do with the example of Walt Whitman than with Camoens. One of Pessoa's "heteronyms"—Álvaro de Campos—vies with Hart Crane, the García Lorca of *Poet in New York*, and with Pablo Neruda as the true heir of "our father Walt Whitman," as the American poet James Wright called him.

FERNANDO PESSOA
(1888–1935)

THE GREATEST PORTUGUESE POET, Luis Vaz de Camões, known in English as Camoens, was born in 1524 or so, and died in 1580. His lyric achievement was remarkable, but he was known as the epic poet of Portugal, the national poet, for *The Lusiads*, a gorgeous Vergilian exaltation of the improbable Portuguese achievement in establishing the first modern international empire, from Africa to Brazil to the shores of China and India, an ascendancy maintained by sea power.

Unlike Spain, which expelled the Moors (and Jews) in 1492, after retaking Granada, the numerically small but fierce Portuguese had cleared their land of Muslims by 1257. They then held off Spain for three centuries until 1580, and regained their independence in 1640. That sixty-year dominance by Spain would not have taken place but for the quixotic, indeed mad invasion of North Africa in 1578 by the boy-king Sebastian. Outnumbered and trapped, the Portuguese army was slaughtered by the Muslims, with Sebastian dying on the battlefield. In the confusion, his body was never recovered, which gave birth to the national myth of Sebastianism, the occult speculation that the heroic boy still lived, beyond time, and someday would return to lead his people again to greatness.

Fernando Pessoa, an enthusiast for Hermetic and Gnostic myths of occultation, necessarily embraced Sebastianism, though with the complex irony he brought to every enterprise. José Saramago, who seems to me the most gifted novelist alive in the world today, entombs Sebastianism in his superb fantasia upon Pessoan themes, *The Year of the Death of Ricardo Reis*, which shows the ultimate withering of Iberian crusading fervor into the movement from the Portuguese Fascism of Salazar to the Spanish Fascism of Franco.

That is almost background enough for venturing into the Atlantic Sublime of Fernando Pessoa, exact contemporary of T. S. Eliot, but a poet rather more to my taste than the abominable Eliot, whose indubitable poetic genius was ultimately allied to his own Fascism. Pessoa, unlike Eliot, did not quest for conversion to Christianity, though he also did not emulate his heroic precursor, Walt Whitman, by presenting himself as the Portuguese Christ. Pessoa, as pure a poet as Paul Valéry, Hart Crane, Federico García

Lorca, and Wallace Stevens, refreshes me, as they do, by his freedom from ideologies. One can add Luis Cernuda and Elizabeth Bishop to this visionary company of the Atlantic Sublime, and more recently the late James Merrill. Of living poets, I would begin with John Ashbery and the Canadian Anne Carson as authentic continuators of Whitman and Emily Dickinson, of Stevens and Elizabeth Bishop, of Pessoa and Hart Crane.

Fernando Pessoa, who was at least three great poets, delights me when he says that he has no proof that Lisbon ever existed. Walt Whitman, Hart Crane, and Federico García Lorca all doubt that New York City ever existed, except in their visions, and Luis Cernuda allowed himself to doubt the very existence of Spain. I live in Connecticut, but I see the visionary landscape of Wallace Stevens's Connecticut only when I recite Stevens. My ordinary evenings in New Haven are far more ordinary than his, since I have yet to confront on the metaphysical streets of the physical town the Lion of Judah, though I thrill to the Stevensian admonition, "The great cat must stand potent in the sun." With Pessoa as with Whitman, Stevens, Crane, we are in the Shelleyan universe of the High Romantic imagination, dismally out of fashion in these days when university critics are consumed by Resentment and by their zeal to save the universe as rapidly as possible.

Pessoa begins with the wonder of his own name, which means "persona" or "mask," and may account for his belief that he was descended from Portuguese *conversos*, which is why, I would think, he makes my favorite heteronym, the flamboyant Álvaro de Campos, a Portuguese Jew. I prefer Campos to the other heteronyms, including Fernando Pessoa, because he extends the projected self of *Song of Myself:* "Walt Whitman, one of the roughs, an American," who is also kosmos. The real Me or Me myself becomes the pastoral Alberto Caeiro, while the unknown Whitmanian soul seems lodged in the Epicurean Ricardo Reis. That allows "Fernando Pessoa" to stand outside the three Whitmanian psychic agencies, but hardly releases his poems from the grand anguish of contamination that Whitman's genius perpetually imparts to those who come after.

Pessoa, though born in Portugal, was raised in English-speaking South Africa, and his literary culture, like that of Jorge Luis Borges, was as much Anglo-American as it was Portuguese or—in Borges's case—Spanish. Though the indisputable poetic influence upon Pessoa was Walt Whitman's, I agree with the suggestions of some scholars that, in a complex way, Pessoa evolved the scheme of his heteronyms from Robert Browning's dramatic monologues. You might say that Pessoa's Álvaro de Campos was his Fra Lippo Lippi, that Ricardo Reis was his Andrea del Sarto, Alberto Caeiro his

Abt Vogler, while "Fernando Pessoa" was his own Childe Roland. You can count as many Browning heteronyms as there are Browning dramatic mono- logues, and it is worth recalling that the poet turned to that form so as to evade his Shelleyan anxiety of influence.

Pessoa's Atlanticism, as deftly recounted by Irene Ramalho Santos, takes on what I regard as too political a coloring, almost as though Pessoa, and his father Walt Whitman, were prophets of the North Atlantic Treaty Organi- zation. Are not Pessoa's politics as visionary as his Rosicrucianism? I am aware that *Mensagem* (*Message* or *Summons*), the one volume of poetry that Pessoa ever published, received a minor award from the Fascist government, but *Mensagem*, as Octavio Paz observed, is an esoteric work, much more Kab- balistic than imperialist. Pessoa can be read as a political poet only if you start with the good morning's conviction that everything is political, in- cluding a good morning.

Whitman and Pessoa matter because, like Hart Crane, García Lorca, and Cernuda, they were great visionary poets, poets of the Sublime. Their At- lantic sublimity is one with Herman Melville's, when Ahab speaks of "the torpedoed Atlantic of my being," which makes me think of Pessoa conceiv- ing of an "Atlantic expansion . . . already present by nocturnal intuition in Walt Whitman's high Atlantic spirit." Ramalho Santos herself cites Hart Crane in a letter where he says of the "Atlantis" canto of *The Bridge*, "it IS the real Atlantis." Pessoa and Crane long for Plato's spiritual Atlantis, and not for the kingdoms of this world. When Pessoa urges us to cross "an At- lantic of soul and spirit," he is not hoping for fresh imperialism.

I grant that the United States of America is now a universal world em- pire in its economic and cultural sway, but Whitman and Hart Crane are seers of the spirit. Alas, I grant also to Ramalho Santos that the United States of George W. Bush begins to have an uncanny resemblance to the Gilded Age of the closing decades of the nineteenth century, but I rather doubt that this George Bush II has read Whitman, or even heard of Hart Crane. The Atlantic Sublime, as I understand it, has no social or political function whatsoever. Shelley, who meant by the "imperial imagination" only the Sublime mode, defined that as poetry which persuaded the reader to surrender easier pleasures in favor of more difficult pleasures. Pessoa's re- sort to the myth of King Sebastian's Fifth Empire is his attempt to replace Camoens as the Portuguese national poet, an ambition more extravagant than Hart Crane's, who never disputed the continued supremacy of Whit- man and of Emily Dickinson. Camoens is never mentioned in Pessoa's *Message*.

Pessoa had the poetic advantage of regarding Shakespeare and Keats,

Shelley and Browning, and Walt Whitman as being his authentic precursors, rather than Camoens, whose *Lusiads* really is an extraordinarily strong poem, a worthy heir to the *Odyssey* and the *Aeneid*. Indeed, Pessoa felt so close to Shakespeare that he astonishingly maligned him, as though one could mock *King Lear* with impunity. But this poetic arrogance joins Pessoa to Emerson's rather wonderful impatience with all poetry *already written,* Shakespeare's included.

Pessoa, marching as a phalanx of poets, remains impatient with what all of them have written. Rather desperately, he proclaims a *poetics of interruption,* but this, though zestful, is only a stalling device. In the spirit of my book, I now must ask: where is the genius of Fernando Pessoa? No quantity of disquietude, no spasms of interruption, can turn that question aside. Let us ask, with Lorca, where finally are we to hear Pessoa's *duende,* the "black notes" of his Atlantic sublimity? Heteronyms away! Where is the daemon?

When I turn to Lorca, I will set aside the great lyrics, and will read the lecture on the *duende* as the great prose poem it is. I once thought that Pessoa had invested all his *duende* in Álvaro de Campos, clearly the most daemonic of the heteronyms, but Campos suddenly can go quite flat. What always revives Campos is the nearest trace of Walt Whitman. The influx of Whitman galvanizes Campos with the acutest ambivalence, and daemonic energy returns, to outrage and be outraged by the sublime Walt. But what of the heteronym, Fernando Pessoa; where are *his* black notes?

As an amateur of Pessoa, I hear the *duende,* sometimes, when Whitman's great fourfold is confronted: Night, Death, the Mother, and the Sea. And sometimes the esoteric summons up the daemon, as it did for Yeats, Rimbaud, Victor Hugo, Blake, even for Hart Crane, the sanest of the five. Pessoa played at Gnosticism and the Kabbalah, but he needed it more consistently. He could have been to the gnosis what John of the Cross was to Catholicism, or Ibn Arabi to Sufism. But why complain? You cannot legislate for great poets; if Pessoa is not Lorca or Hart Crane, he is something else, a master of evasions like Wallace Stevens, whose art allows us "To hear the hum of thoughts evaded in the mind." Like Stevens, Pessoa learned nuances from Whitman: the three are never where you expect them to be. Where, after all, is Atlantis? In the *Critias* of Plato, which is only a fragment, we are told an ancient story that probably was a Platonic invention:

> In the very first place, let us remind ourselves that it is in all nine thousand years since a general war, of which we are now to relate the course, was declared between those who dwelt without and those who dwelt within the Pillars of Heracles. The command of the latter was

taken, and the war conducted throughout, as the story ran, by our own city; the leaders of the other party were the kings of the island of Atlantis. Atlantis, as you will recollect, was once, we said, an island larger than Libya and Asia together; it has now been engulfed by earthquakes and is the source of the impassable mud which prevents navigators from this quarter from advancing through the straits into the open ocean.

(translated by A. E. Taylor)

That seems more Borgesian (or Pessoan) than Platonic, and has an ironic edge. So does much of *Message,* as when Prince John tells us:

> Because it's like the Portuguese, lords of oceans,
> To want, and capable only of this:
> Either all oceans or washed up drift of shores
> Everything, or the nothingess of it all.
> (translated by Edwin Honig and Susan Brown)

Only Portugal, the relic of empire, could have brought forth Pessoa. His gifts were enormous, and his strategies were brilliant, but I wonder if he truly was either the Whitman or the Hart Crane of his nation. Could he have fused his alternate poetic selves, had he tried? The heteronyms are a marvelous invention, but they rise out of the burden of belatedness, the shadow of Walt Whitman. But Pessoa himself deserves the last word on this:

> With such a deficiency of literature as there is today, what can a man of genius do but convert himself, on his own, into a literature? With such a deficiency of coexistable people as there is today, what can a man of sensibility do but invent his own friends, or at least his intellectual companions?

HART CRANE

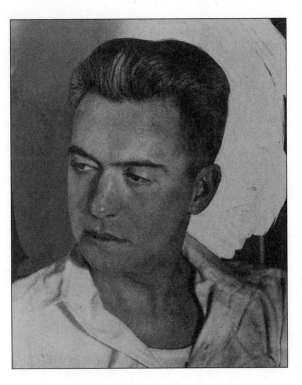

And buzzard-circleted, screamed from the stake;
I could not pick the arrows from my side.
Wrapped in that fire, I saw more escorts wake—
Flickering, sprint up the hill groins like a tide.

That is Crane, in "The Dance" canto of *The Bridge*, identifying himself with a Native American sacrifice, rather than with the death of Saint Sebastian, as in an early, suppressed poem by T. S. Eliot. Various lines reverberate in my memory when I think of Crane: always one of them is, "I could not pick the arrows from my side."

Crane was an Orphic genius, and his life and poetry fused dangerously in the image of Orpheus, the poet torn apart by the ecstatic Dionysiac devotees. That rending or *sparagmos* haunts all of Hart Crane's poetry, from the lyrics of *White Buildings* through *The Bridge* and on to the great death-ode, "The Broken Tower."

Milton, both in the elegy "Lycidas" and in *Paradise Lost,* feared that he himself might suffer an Orphic *sparagmos* before his poetic ambitions could be fulfilled. Crane, drowning himself at thirty-two, mutilated what should have been his achievement, as no American poet (in my judgment) had Crane's extraordinary imaginative endowment.

Crane's intense genius cannot be separated from the authentic difficulties his readers initially encounter. What he called his "logic of metaphor" governs his allusive, word-conscious tonalities, and sometimes demands considerable unpacking. And yet I remember the effect of Hart Crane's poems upon me when I first read them, at the age of ten. My understanding of them had to be imperfect, but the power of his metric and his language, and the sustained sweep of his vision, gathered me in, and made me a wonder-wounded hearer. More than sixty years later, I remain enchanted by Hart Crane's splendor.

HART CRANE
(1899–1932)

WITH CERTAIN FIGURES IN THIS BOOK—Shakespeare, William Blake, Shelley, Hart Crane, Wallace Stevens, W. B. Yeats among them—I return to the poets I first loved when I was a child. Hart Crane, whom I loved first and best, is the only one to whom I have not devoted an entire book, though I contributed a rather comprehensive introduction to the Centennial Edition of his *Complete Poems*. He is stationed here at the midpoint of a sequence of Atlantic poets, with Whitman and Pessoa coming before him, and García Lorca and Cernuda placed after him. That is necessarily an arbitrary stationing for Crane; he groups as readily with Emerson, Emily Dickinson, Stevens, and with T. S. Eliot, with whose poetry Crane's own work engages in a perpetual contest.

With the question of Hart Crane's genius, I feel radically at home, as I have been intoxicated by it for more than sixty years. At last it is time for me to attempt a definition of it, and I find that an odd challenge. Many of my students and friends consider Crane's poetry to be difficult, but six decades of immersion remove most of the varnish that bad and irrelevant criticism placed upon the surfaces of *White Buildings, The Bridge*, and the later poems. "Darkness . . . falls away, / and gradually white buildings answer day."

Crane left a fragment, composed during the last year of his life, called "To Conquer Variety":

> I have seen my ghost broken
> My body blessed
> And Eden
> Scraped from my mother's breast
> When the charge was spoken
> Love dispossessed
> And the seal broken . . .

I hear a touch of Emily Dickinson's cognitive music, and she was a poet who influenced Crane more than we have realized. His sonnet to her, written perhaps five years earlier, memorably praises what she called her "final harvest":

The harvest you described and understand
Needs more than wit to gather, love to bind.
Some reconcilement of remotest mind—

Crane, a superb critic in his poetry and prose alike, knows that—like the rest of us—he cannot fully comprehend Dickinson's cognitive power. The image of the mother, Grace Hart, haunts Crane's poetry, and merges with Whitman's "fierce old mother" in *Voyages.* We are now blessedly released from the burden of reducing homosexuality to its supposed origins, and doubtless all varieties of sexual orientation are influenced by the vagaries of relations between our mothers and our fathers. Crane was the only child of a dreadful marriage, and he lamented "the curse of sundered parentage." I once believed that his most characteristic line was, "I could not pick the arrows from my side," and certainly Tennessee Williams, obsessed with Crane, agreed. Crane identified less with Saint Sebastian than T. S. Eliot did, in his suppressed "The Death of Saint Narcissus":

So he became a dancer to God,
Because his flesh was in love with the burning arrows.
He danced on the hot sand
Until the arrows came.
As he embraced them his white skin surrendered itself to the
    redness of blood, and satisfied him.

Hart Crane's genius, were I now to epitomize it by a single stanza, emerges most clearly in his great chant "Atlantis," the final section of his brief epic *The Bridge,* but the first canto of the poem that he composed. Crane's ecstatic vision, the power of his rhetoric, his superb control of metric, all fuse together;

O thou steeled Cognizance whose leap commits
The agile precincts of the lark's return;
Within whose lariat sweep encinctured sing
In single chrysalis the many twain,—
Of stars Thou art the stitch and stallion glow
And like an organ, thou, with sound of doom—
Sight, sound and flesh Thou leadest from time's realm
As love strikes clear direction for the helm.

I remember being overwhelmed by this when I was a ten-year-old, though I could barely comprehend it. Crane invokes Brooklyn Bridge as Shelley, in *Adonais*, invokes the Neoplatonic One that reconciles "the many twain." But what does "Cognizance" mean? Its primary sense of conscious awareness or knowledge or the secondary import of observance, or taking notice, seem somewhat inadequate for this Atlantic sublimity. Crane appears to desire the tertiary or heraldic meaning: the badge or crest that distinguishes the quester or agonist, the mark of recognition by which *we* are made cognizant of a great presence. Brooklyn Bridge is saluted as chivalric emblem, a gnosis that gathers in the stars, poets, and lovers, and this by the agency of its steeled leap, the vaulting movement that is also the sweep of its lariat, the lasso of Eternity, beyond time's realm.

Crane's poetic gift was astonishing; no other major American poet, dead at thirty-two, could be compared to him. At that age, Whitman and Wallace Stevens would have left nothing, while Emily Dickinson and Robert Frost would have shown mostly promise. Eliot would not have written *The Waste Land*. Crane, at eighteen, already wrote in the lyrical mode that never left him:

> Mine is a world foregone though not yet ended,—
> An imagined garden grey with sundered boughs
> And broken branches, wistful and unmended,
> And mist that is more constant than all vows.

Only a step away are other early lyrics in *White Buildings*, like the extraordinary "Praise for an Urn," written at twenty-two or -three, with its magnificent conclusion, a refusal to mourn that is profoundly mournful:

> Still, having in mind gold hair,
> I cannot see that broken brow
> And miss the dry sound of bees
> Stretching across a lucid space.
>
> Scatter these well-meant idioms
> Into the smoky spring that fills
> The suburbs, where they will be lost.
> They are no trophies of the sun.

Crane's genius was already at home with a compression much like Emily Dickinson's, and also like William Blake's in his lyrics. Dickinson and Blake were associated by Crane, and they combined to provide a model for his

own use of quatrains, one of his favorite forms. It is one of Crane's paradoxes that his prophetic surge of ecstatic vision—Blakean, Shelleyan, Whitmanian—is always melded with a strict poetic formalism. His metric is
Marlovian rather than Shakespearean; one hears Marlowe's mighty line almost throughout, as here in "For the Marriage of Faustus and Helen":

> The earth may glide diaphanous to death;
> But if I lift my arms it is to bend
> To you who turned away once, Helen, knowing
> The press of troubled hands, too alternate
> With steel and soul to hold you endlessly.

I have said that Crane was a superb critic, and I suspect that he surmised
T. S. Eliot's covert relation to Walt Whitman, common ancestor to Hart
Crane and his older contemporary rival. Until almost the end, Eliot denied
Whitman, while Crane affirmed him. And yet *The Bridge* is distant from any
Whitman, even "Crossing Brooklyn Ferry," while *The Waste Land* is very
nearly a rewriting of "When Lilacs Last in the Dooryard Bloom'd." This ren-
ders more complex Crane's open struggle against Eliot's influence, never
ideological but dangerously close in idiom. David Bromwich, in his *Skeptical
Music*, demonstrates the abiding effect of Eliot's early "Preludes" upon
Crane's poetry. Sometimes, in rereading the "Preludes," I could believe
that Hart Crane himself had composed it:

> You had such a vision of the street
> As the street hardly understands.

Crane's idiom is not Whitmanian, but his vision finally is not of the
street, but of Whitman's Atlantic Sublime:

> Atlantis,—hold thy floating singer late!

As a prayer, that is pretty desperate, and Crane is the drowned Orpheus,
not the sea's prophet but its victim. And yet any consideration of the fourfold handful of great poems written by a North American should include at
least four by Hart Crane: "Voyages II," "Repose of Rivers," "Proem: To
Brooklyn Bridge," and "The Broken Tower."

Crane returns us to the question of genius, as does García Lorca. How do
gifts so absolute come into being? Reductive analysis—whether psychoan-

alytic, Marxist, sociobiological, or historicist—will not tell us why the son of a candy manufacturer in Garrettsville, Ohio, became one of the most inspired lyric poets in all of Western tradition. What I can try to do is to isolate and describe the nature of Hart Crane's unique genius.

Crane strongly resembles Arthur Rimbaud, as Crane repeatedly asserted. Yet Rimbaud was actually much the more extreme figure: he represented a rupture with most of French poetic tradition. The prime imaginative lineage of Crane is precisely what he surmised it to be: the American sequence of Emerson, Whitman, Melville, Dickinson, and Stevens, with Eliot as counterstatement. What he added to that sequence was neither dissent nor affirmation, but a personalizing power that surpassed even Whitman and Dickinson in dramatic immediacy. The anguish and pathos of what could be called poetic disincarnation has never been so vividly portrayed, not even in the darkest intensities of Whitman and Dickinson:

> The bells, I say the bells break down their tower;
> And swing I know not where.

The bells are Crane's poetic voice, his unique gift, but the tower they break down is his whole being: consciousness and everything it has intended. What is broken goes back to a primordial catastrophe, the world made and shattered in a single act. King Lear, crying out to Gloucester, shatters us with a lament at the limits of art:

> When we are born, we cry that we are come
> To this great stage of fools—

To rival that, in English, is not possible, but the sublime pathos of Hart Crane comes close:

> And so it was I entered the broken world
> To trace the visionary company of love, its voice
> An instant in the wind (I know not whither hurled)
> But not for long to hold each desperate choice.

The verbal inevitability of that quatrain is Shakespearean. Crane's force is daemonic, in that a greater voice than his own bursts in upon him, and yet his modulation of that sustained rhetorical energy is supreme art, earned through his fifteen years of self-revision, tragically ended at thirty-two.

If genius is a pure endowment, as I believe it to be, the discipline required to give it a permanent shaping is nevertheless an exercise of the aesthetic will. Crane, who refused all ideologies and all received forms of faith, remains an ultimate image of the Sublime, of the high dedication that teaches us to abandon easier pleasures in order to experience the most difficult pleasures, those that activate the mind in all its powers.

FEDERICO GARCÍA LORCA

> Autumn will return bringing snails,
> misted-over grapes, and clustered mountains,
> but none will wish to gaze in your eyes
> because your death is forever.
>
> Because your death is forever,
> like everyone's who ever died on Earth,
> like all dead bodies discarded
> on rubbish heaps with mongrels' corpses.
>
> But no one knows you. No one. But I sing you—
> sing your profile and your grace, for later on.
> The signal ripeness of your mastery.
> The way you sought death out, savored its taste.
> The sadness just beneath your gay valor.
>
> Not soon, if ever, will Andalusia see
> so towering a man, so venturesome.
> I sing his elegance with words that moan
> and remember a sad breeze in the olive groves.
>   (translated by Alan S. Trueblood)

Lorca, like Shelley, is a poet of desire and its limits. Yet Shelley was a formidable intellectual skeptic, and perhaps at last more an Italian than an Englishman. Despite his sojourns in the United States and Cuba, Lorca remained always the archetypal poet of Andalusia, with its complex mixed culture: Christian, Moorish, Jewish, gypsy. The close of his "Lament" for the bullfighter Ignacio Sánchez Mejías, quoted above, conveys Lorca's unique stance as a lyrical genius, where the Andalusian quest for death adds a particular grace to desire and its limits.

Lorca is many poets at once: the singer of the *Gypsy Ballads*, the tragic dramatist of *Yerma* and *Blood Wedding*, the hyperbolical surrealist of *Poet in New York*, the quasi-Moorish elegist of *The Tamarit Divan*. Murdered by the Fascists when he was thirty-eight, Lorca obsesses his admirers, as does Hart Crane, with thoughts of the poems they have lost.

FEDERICO GARCÍA LORCA
(1898–1936)

LORCA IS POPULARLY REMEMBERED AS one of the martyrs of the Spanish Civil War, a victim of Fascist brutality. At least five of his plays remain in the international repertory: *Yerma, Blood Wedding, The House of Bernarda Alba, The Shoemaker's Prodigious Wife, The Love of Don Perlimplín*. Above all, Lorca is properly celebrated as one of the major lyric and meditative poets of the twentieth century, the peer of Montale, Yeats, Valéry, Rilke, Stevens, Pessoa, Hart Crane, Eliot, Trakl, Mandelstam, Celan, Alberti, Cernuda, Frost, Akhmatova, Tsvetayena, Ekelöf, Cavafy—among others. I have listed eighteen, more or less at random: perhaps none of these were more prodigiously gifted than Lorca, murdered at thirty-eight, and Crane, self-drowned at thirty-two. Lorca and Crane actually met once, at a bar in New York City, but each was too preoccupied by the sailor sitting next to him to pay much attention to the other.

This is a book about genius, in which I juxtapose many figures, in the hope of isolating in each the specific originality that renders us reluctant to yield him or her up to the ongoing vanishing of our high culture. It would be difficult to select one of Lorca's volumes of poetry as his best or most characteristic, partly because his work is so varied. But—like Whitman, Pessoa, Hart Crane, Cernuda—Lorca has a tendency to convert every genre into lyrical elegy. Rather than select a particular poem for discussion, I choose the famous lecture of 1930 in Havana: "The Duende: Theory and Divertissement." This reads like a prose poem, and can be interpreted as an examination of the unique element in Lorca's own genius, for the *duende*, as he describes it, appears to be his own daemon.

Arturo Barea, as quoted by the poet and translator Ben Belitt, emphasized again that Lorca was an Andalusian, and that the *duende* is used in his native idiom:

Characteristically, Lorca took his Spanish term for daemonic inspiration from the Andalusian idiom. While to the rest of Spain the *duende* is nothing but a hobgoblin, to Andalusia it is an obscure power which can speak through every form of human art, including the art of personality.

The *duende,* Lorca forcefully tells us, is a power and a struggle: it is not an idea. You either have it or you don't, and you may not have it when you wish to, even if once it seemed on call. He quotes an old guitarist:

The *duende* is not in the throat; the *duende* comes up from inside, up from the very soles of the feet.

(translated by Ben Belitt)

After a long lifetime of reading poetry, I know what this means in a poet. Hart Crane and Lorca share the *duende,* as do Blake, Goethe, Shelley, Tennyson, Whitman, Eliot, and some others: their poetry has "black sounds." Lorca adds a little historical note on varying demons:

So much for the *duende,* but I would not have you confuse the *duende* with the theological demon of doubt at whom Luther, on a Bacchic impulse, hurled an inkwell in [Wartburg], or with the Catholic devil, destructive, but short on intelligence, who disguised himself as a bitch in order to enter the convents, or with the talking monkey that Cervantes' mountebank carried in the comedy about jealousy and the forests of Andalusia.

No, the *duende* I speak of, shadowy, palpitating, is a descendent of that benignest *daimon* of Socrates, he of marble and salt, who scratched the master angrily the day he drank the hemlock.

There is some playful obfuscation here. Dictionaries generally define *duende* as charisma, the power of attracting others through magnetism of personality. Spanish dictionaries tend to define *duende* as charm, from Spanish for a ghost, going back to Old Castilian for the lord of a house, *duen* (lord) deriving from the Latin *dominus.* But Lorca cleverly narrows the definition to music, dance, and the spoken poem, and he hints at the famous affinities of one group of his poems to flamenco singing and dancing. Many readers would love to hear a resurrected Lorca speaking his famous "Sleepwalking Ballad," with its hypnotic opening, rendered here by Will Kirkland:

Green oh how I love you green.
Green mind. Green boughs.
Ship on the sea,
Horse on the mountain.
With waist of shadow,
She dreams at her rail,

Green flesh, hair green,
And her eyes, cold silver.
Green oh how I love you green.
Beneath the gypsy moon
Things are looking at her,
And she can't look at them.

Lorca fights a contest with the *duende*, for this is an agonistic daemon, a genius reluctant to yield control. The *duende* is neither angel nor muse, but alter ego, the second and more crucial ancient Roman definition of genius. And Lorca's admonition is timelier than ever:

The great artists of southern Spain, both Gypsies and flamenco, whether singing or dancing or playing on instruments, know that no emotion is possible without the mediation of the *Duende*. They may hoodwink the people, they may give the illusion of *duende* without really having it.

Black sounds—this mark of the *duende* is Lorca's pragmatic aesthetic. His precursor was Lope de Vega, "the monster of literature," whose fecundity was astonishing, beyond the capacity of any single reader to absorb. Like Lope, Lorca transcended regionalism while remaining more Spanish than universalist. The contrast has to be Cervantes, who is as universal as Shakespeare, and still could be regarded by Unamuno as the origin of the true Spanish religion. It makes a kind of sense to say that Lope, like Lorca, had *duende*, yet would seem silly if we ascribed *duende* to Shakespeare as to Cervantes. Northrop Frye thought that the lyric was a genre dependent upon "the assumed concealment of the audience from the poet," which seems true of Lorca's mode, even in his stage dramas. Some of Lorca's voices seem anonymous, which was a Whitmanian ambition never accomplished by Whitman, but which is an essential achievement if one is to have mastered *duende*.

Lorca approached Whitman in *Poet in New York*, with his "Ode to Walt Whitman," which does not compare favorably with the outrageous "Salutation to Walt Whitman" of Pessoa's Álvaro de Campos. Lorca, obsessed by their shared homoeroticism, addresses Whitman as if that is all there was to the poet of the self:

Not for a moment, Walt Whitman, lovely old man,
Have I failed to see your beard full of butterflies,

Nor your corduroy shoulders frayed by the moon,
Nor your thighs as pure as Apollo's,
Nor your voice like a column of ash;
Old man, beautiful as the mist,
you moaned like a bird
with its sex pierced by a needle.
Enemy of the vine,
and lover of bodies beneath rough cloth . . .
            (translated by Greg Simon and Steven White)

That is Whitman as a not unsentimentalized sexual ideal. Campos, in a direct confrontation, achieves *duende:*

I can never read through all your poems . . . There's too much
    feeling in them . . .
I go through your lines as through a teeming crowd that brushes past
    me,
Smelling of sweat, of grease, of human and mechanical activity.
At a given moment, reading your poems, I can't tell if I'm reading or
    living them,
I don't know if my actual place is in the world or in your poems.
I don't know if I'm standing here with both feet on the ground
Or hanging upside down in some sort of workshop,
From the natural ceiling of your stampeding inspiration,
From the center of the ceiling of your unapproachable intensity.
                        (translated by Richard Zenith)

That is the finest and most accurate tribute Whitman has received, and it celebrates Whitman's *duende,* his "intensity." Campos's *duende* comes in the contest with Whitman that he intensifies by the apparently total surrender to his precursor. But Lorca, who is the "natural" and original poet that Alberto Caeiro was supposed to be, seems to have no precursor with whom to wage a struggle, Lope being safely distant, and Jiménez and Machado being like kindly uncles. Increasingly, Lorca became his own forerunner, struggling to free himself of the vivid image of Andalusian poet engendered by his earlier works.

The purely daemonic Lorca may seem less a poet of the Atlantic Sublime than are Whitman, Pessoa, Crane, and the somber Luis Cernuda. Except for Whitman, poetry in English was alien to Lorca. Pessoa is deeply embedded in the English High Romantics; so were Crane and Cernuda, but Lorca's

tradition was almost entirely Spanish, except for contemporary literary culture, a largely French surrealism. Yet *Poet in New York*, though not the aesthetic peer of *The Bridge*, nevertheless is a full-scale excursion into the
Atlantic Sublime. Walt Whitman's New York City finds three powerful repetitions in the visions of Pessoa/Campos, Crane, and Lorca. One wonders if
Lorca would have welcomed such a role. "I want to live without seeing myself," he cries out in "Song of the Barren Orange Tree," beautifully rendered
by William Merwin:

> Why was I born among mirrors?
> The day walks in circles around me,
> and the night copies me
> in all its stars.

LUIS CERNUDA

A divine hand
Raised your lands in my body
And there set a voice
That would speak your silence.

I was alone with you,
Believing in you alone;
Now to think your name
Poisons my dreams.

(translated by Reginald Gibbons)

These stanzas are from Cernuda's "A Spaniard Speaks of His Land," and make me recall that Octavio Paz described Cernuda as the least Christian, indeed least Spanish of Spanish poets. A member of the "Generation of 1927" (Lorca, Alberti, and so many others), Cernuda can seem more an English Romantic poet than an Andalusian singer, the tradition to which he was born.

Stubborn, irreconciled to any belief or ideology, Cernuda is an extraordinarily intense instance of poetic integrity. Though his inspiration was as daemonic and Orphic as theirs, Cernuda has failed to find the audience that Lorca had from his beginnings, and that Hart Crane has won posthumously.

Robert Browning, whose dramatic monologues had a strong effect upon Cernuda, echoes in Cernuda's "Lazarus" and in the great ode "The Clouds." Perhaps Cernuda can be understood best as one of Browning's obsessed monologists, another Childe Roland come to the dark tower to confront, not the expected ogre, but the ring of fire of the heroic precursors: Hölderlin, Nerval, Novalis, Blake, Goethe, Browning, Machado.

The High Sublime is a difficult mode for post-Romantic poetry. Secular transcendence came to Cernuda as a very hard-won achievement. No other twentieth-century poet of his genius was as solitary as the exiled Cernuda. He had no life but his poetry: if the art of poetry has its saints, like Dickinson and Paul Celan, then Luis Cernuda is among them.

LUIS CERNUDA
(1902–1963)

LUIS CERNUDA WAS A CENTRAL POET OF the twentieth century, but he suffered from exile as no other major Spanish poet has done. Several Spanish poets and critics ceased to think of him as Spanish at all. His elegy for Lorca is the best I have read, but Cernuda's tradition was Romanticism: Goethe and Hölderlin, Blake and Novalis, Browning and Leopardi, Baudelaire and Nerval, and in his final phase, T. S. Eliot, accurately viewed as one of the Late Romantics. Of all the great Spanish poets, Cernuda was the most alienated: from Spain, from Catholicism, from much of the national literary tradition.

If I think of the Sublime mode, in Romanticism and after, Shelley, Victor Hugo, and Cernuda come first to my mind. But Shelley and Hugo were revolutionary partisans: Cernuda, cut off in and from Mexico, lived as solitary a Sublime as those of Hölderlin and Nerval, and attempts no large social subjects. His concern is his own consciousness. Whatever equivocations Whitman and Pessoa had in regard to their homoeroticism vanish in the aggressive homosexuality of Lorca and Hart Crane, but neither Lorca nor Crane employ their sexual orientation as a critique of societal morals and manners. Quietly embittered, Cernuda does, in ways that further enhance the sense of sublime isolation in his strongest poems.

In his brief talk "Words before a Reading" (1935), Cernuda faced a public for the first time. His remarks, hermetic and self-directed, must have baffled his audience:

> The poetic instinct was awakened in me thanks to a more acute perception of reality—experiencing with a deeper echo the beauty and the attraction of the surrounding world. Its effect, as in some way occurs with that desire which provokes love, was the necessity— painful because of its intensity—of getting outside myself, negating myself in the vast body of creation. And what made that desire even more agonizing was the tacit recognition that it was impossible to satisfy it.

(translated by Reginald Gibbons)

From this impasse, Cernuda leaps to the daemonic, the subject of my study. Like the poetic, he insists, it cannot be defined, but it resembles the remark of a Sufi sage, who hears the sound of a flute and announces, "That is the voice of Satan, who weeps over the world," who laments, like the poet, the destruction of beauty. In the same spirit, Cernuda ends his talk by asking, What answer a poet can expect in this world? and replies that there is none.

This negativity is Cernuda's starting-point, and led him on to a pure poetry, which could have only a few readers. He reminds me of Alvin Feinman, a sparse poet of authentic genius in my own generation, except that Cernuda went on to a great handful of sublime odes: "The Poet's Glory," "To the Statues of the Gods," "To a Dead Poet" (an elegy for Lorca), "The Visitation of God," "Lazarus," "Ruins," and his masterpiece, "Apologia Pro Vita Sua." These are difficult poems, but Cernuda—like Hart Crane—is one of the most difficult of modern poets. Crane's difficulties emanate from his invocatory surge and his "logic of metaphor," and so do Cernuda's, who may never have heard of Crane, though for a poet who died in Mexico a third of a century beyond Crane's stormy sojourn there, that seems to me unlikely. Whatever Crane's affinities with Pessoa, his family resemblance with the Cernuda of the *Invocations* (1934–35) runs deeper, except that Cernuda's bitterness stands apart, a negativity so profound that only Nietzsche or Leopardi can rival it. Whitman, who activated Pessoa, and stirred Crane and Lorca, had no effect upon Cernuda, who preferred the formalistic T. S. Eliot, despite Eliot's Christian orthodoxy. I think Whitman would have benefited Cernuda, as he did Paz and Borges, Neruda and Vallejo, but the temperamental bitterness of Cernuda was too intense to absorb what moves me most in Whitman, the vitalistic, Falstaffian force that affirms life's perpetual renewal:

Dazzling and tremendous how quick the sun-rise would kill me,
If I could not now and always send sun-rise out of me.
We also ascend dazzling and tremendous as the sun,
We found our own O my soul in the calm and cool of the day-break.

At his most impressive, Cernuda is the polar opposite of this magnificent vitalism. He invokes instead a post-Baudelairean contempt for the unimaginative life:

Listen to their marmoreal precepts
On the useful, the normal, the beautiful;
Listen to them dictate law to the world, fix the norms of love, give
    rules for ineffable beauty,

While they delight their sense with delirious loudspeakers;
Contemplate their strange minds,
Attempting to raise, son by son, a complex edifice of sand
Whose grim, livid façade would negate the refulgent peace of the
    stars.

These, my brother,
Surround my solitary dying—
Specters that someday will spawn
The solemn scholar, the oracle
Who will display my words for alien students,
And therewith gaining renown,
Get a little country place in the tortuous mountains
Near the capital.
While behind your rainbow fog
You stroke your curly hair
And from the heights distractedly contemplate
This filthy earth where the poet slowly suffocates.

                                    (translated by Reginald Gibbons)

The Demon brother addressed may be Baudelaire himself, but more
likely it is Cernuda's own genius, his daemon, his "poet's glory." Cernuda,
like Shelley and Stevens, is a Lucretian poet, and his invocation of the gods
properly sees them as remote from humankind. Cernuda's Sublime, Atlantic only in its high negations, culminates in his elegy for Lorca, which attributes the Fascist motive for murder to have been a hatred for poetry. And
yet Lorca was shot side by side with a poor schoolteacher, as the Falange followed its program of "Death to the intellect!" Cernuda's passionate mis-
perception does not weaken the sublime pathos of his lament for a unique
value destroyed in its prime:

        You were the green in our barren land,
        And the blue in our dark air.

The poetic hyperbole takes its force partly from Cernuda's generous
pathos of implicitly recognizing his own limitations in contrast to the natural vitality of Lorca. No one, elegizing Cernuda, would have found in him
the earth's green, the sky's blue. His power, against the grain and remorseless, centered itself elsewhere.

LUSTRE 16

|

George Eliot, Willa Cather, Edith Wharton, F. Scott Fitzgerald, Iris Murdoch

|

I have gathered this second Lustre of *Hod* because these five novelists are all deeply concerned with what might be termed "moral majesty," a stance superbly exemplified by George Eliot, perhaps the most eminent moral imagination in the novel's history.

Willa Cather's heroines inspire our love, as they inspired Cather's, but Edith Wharton's interests were more complexly societal, as were Scott Fitzgerald's. Mrs. Wharton both influenced and encouraged Fitzgerald, in whom she accurately found a successor to her tragicomedies of societal morality.

Iris Murdoch was a philosopher of morals, profoundly conversant with Plato, and her ambitious attempts to be both a Platonist and a Shakespearean novelist were not altogether successful. But Murdoch, though she wished otherwise, was a genius at the pre-novelistic fiction we rightly should term "romance." As a depicter of visionary states of mind and of enchanted spaces, Murdoch also exemplified *Hod*, even though she has no single character as memorable as the personalities created by George Eliot or by Cather, Wharton, and Fitzgerald at their best.

GEORGE ELIOT

If I were called on to act in the matter, I would certainly not oppose any plan which held out a reasonable promise of tending to establish as far as possible an equivalence of advantages for the two sexes, as to education and the possibilities of free development. I fear you may have misunderstood something I said the other evening about nature. I never meant to urge the "intention of Nature" argument, which is to me a pitiable fallacy. I mean that as a fact of more zoological evolution, woman seems to me to have the worst share in existence. But for that very reason I would the more contend that in the moral evolution we have "an art which does mend nature"—an art which "itself is nature." It is the function of love in the largest sense, to mitigate the harshness of all fatalities. And in the thorough recog-

nition of that worse share, I think there is a basis for a sublimer resignation in woman and a more regenerating tenderness in men.

—letter to John Morely, May, 14, 1867

It is perhaps too easy for some contemporary feminists to misunderstand
George Eliot, even to the extent of judging a great novelist and a moralist
of genius to have been a "defeatist." Eliot blames *mere* "zoological emulation" as the culprit, judging nature itself to be unfair. Whether this sense of
the harshness of being a woman is now acceptable or not, Eliot's allusion to
The Winter's Tale, act 4, scene 4, lines 88–96, clearly refuses Shakespeare's
meanings. The art which is to mend nature, by itself being or becoming nature, is equated to a new kind of relationship between women and men.

Eliot does not intend "sublimer resignation" to be her final counsel for
women. Dorothea Brooke in *Middlemarch* and Gwendolyn Harleth in *Daniel
Deronda* ultimately are sublime in much more than resignation.

GEORGE ELIOT
(MARY ANN EVANS)
(1819–1880)

IT IS TRADITIONAL, AND PERFECTLY sound, to ascribe a sort of natural majesty to the genius of George Eliot, who followed the poet Wordsworth in revealing something of the moral beauty of the common life. Eliot's masterwork is *Middlemarch*, which I have discussed in my book *The Western Canon*. Readers generally favor *The Mill on the Floss* after *Middlemarch*, and I agree. Yet, as always here, my longing is to define the peculiar individuality of George Eliot's genius, and I return to *Silas Marner*, which I read and loved in my childhood, and reread frequently, moved by the novel's poignance, and grateful always for its happy ending. In old age, I accept unhappy endings in Shakespearean tragedy, Flaubert, and Tolstoy, but back away from them in lesser works. Desdemona, Cordelia, Emma Bovary, and Anna Karenina are slain by their creators, and we are compelled to absorb the greatness of the loss. Perhaps it trains us to withstand better the terrible deaths of friends, family, and lovers, and to contemplate more stoically our own dissolution. But I increasingly avoid most movies with unhappy endings, since few among them aesthetically earn the suffering they attempt to inflict upon us.

Silas Marner: The Weaver of Raveloe (1861) was Eliot's third novel, following *Adam Bede* and *The Mill on the Floss*. In a letter to the book's publisher, she connects the origin of *Silas Marner* to a memory singularly Wordsworthian:

I don't wonder at your finding my story, as far as you have read it, rather sombre: indeed, I should not have believed that anyone would have been interested in it but myself (since William Wordsworth is dead) if Mr. Lewes had not been strongly arrested by it. But I hope you will not find it at all a sad story, as a whole, since it sets—or is intended to set—in a strong light the remedial influences of pure, natural human relations. The Nemesis is a very mild one. I have felt all through as if the story would have lent itself best to metrical rather than prose fiction, especially in all that relates to the psychology of Silas; except that, under the treatment, there could not be an equal play of humour. It came to me first of all, quite suddenly, as a sort of legendary tale, suggested by my recollection of having once, in early childhood, seen a linen-weaver with a bag on his back; but, as my mind dwelt on the subject, I became inclined to a more realistic treatment.

Wordsworth had died in 1850, and undoubtedly would have been interested in Eliot's brief pastoral novel. It is part of the singularity of George Eliot's genius that it found the prime precursor in Wordsworth. Formal elements in the novel she learned from a diverse group of Sir Walter Scott, Jane Austen, and Charlotte Brontë, but none of these haunted her consciousness; Wordsworth did. The epigraph to *Silas Marner* is from Wordsworth's powerful pastoral "Michael":

> A child, more than all other gifts
> That earth can offer to declining man,
> Brings hope with it, and forward-looking thoughts.

Wordsworth, unexportable to the Continent, nevertheless is the most original poet of the European nineteenth century. We are alone in a bare place, and walled inside our own consciousness, though we want to see our natural context as benign, and we long to break through to others, and beyond them to a common life in a just society. And yet the solitude of the self is what in Wordsworth is most memorable. The shepherd Michael

> had been alone
> Amid the heart of many thousand mists
> That came to him, and left him, on the heights.

No poet since John Milton is so perpetually on the heights as Wordsworth. George Eliot's authentic moral grandeur places her, among novelists, almost uniquely on the heights. One thinks of Tolstoy as something more sublime, but Tolstoy is almost more than human. *Silas Marner,* a pastoral fable, can seem slight alongside Wordsworth's "The Old Cumberland Beggar" or Tolstoy's *Hadji Murad,* and yet it shares the heroic ecstasy that exalts the common life. Nor is *Silas Marner* sentimental, its fate on the television screen.

Silas is a weaver, a craft that in folklore has a long tradition of preternatural affinities, beautifully revived in Ursula K. Le Guin's fantasy *The Left Hand of Darkness.* Shakespeare makes Bottom a weaver, because he is the one human in *A Midsummer Night's Dream* able to see, hear, touch the world of the faery folk. Nothing occult happens to Silas: he is slandered and betrayed by a close friend, and loses both his beloved and his place in an obscure Protestant sect that is also his only community. In solitude, he endures his sense of outrage, while accumulating gold by his skill as a weaver. The gold is stolen, and in its place a child is given, while the weaver is caught up in one of his characteristic trances:

This morning he had been told by some of his neighbors that it was New Year's Eve, and that he must sit up and hear the old year rung out and the new rung in, because that was good-luck, and might bring his money back again. This was only a friendly Raveloe-way of jesting with the half-crazy oddities of a miser, but it had perhaps helped to throw Silas into a more than usually excited state. Since the on-coming of twilight he had opened his door again and again, though only to shut it immediately at seeing all distance veiled by the falling snow. But the last time he opened it the snow had ceased, and the clouds were parting here and there. He stood and listened, and gazed for a long while—there was really something on the road coming to-wards him then, but he caught no sign of it; and the stillness and the wide trackless snow seemed to narrow his solitude, and touched his yearning with the chill of despair. He went in again, and put his right hand on the latch of the door to close it—but he did not close it: he was arrested, as he had been already since his loss, by the invisible wand of catalepsy, and stood like a graven image, with wide but sight-less eyes, holding open his door, powerless to resist either good or evil that might enter there.

When Marner's sensibility returned, he continued the action which had been arrested, and closed his door, unaware of the chasm in his consciousness, unaware of any intermediate change, except that the light had grown dim, and that he was chilled and faint. He thought he had been too long standing at the door and looking out. Turning towards the hearth, where the two logs had fallen apart, and sent forth only a red uncertain glimmer, he seated himself on his fire-side chair, and was stooping to push his logs together, when, to his blurred vision, it seemed as if there were gold on the floor in front of the hearth. Gold!—his own gold—brought back to him as mysteri-ously as it has been taken away! He felt his heart begin to beat vio-lently, and for a few moments he was unable to stretch out his hand and grasp the restored treasure. The heap of gold seemed to glow and get larger beneath his agitated gaze. He leaned forward at last, and stretched forth his hand; but instead of the hard coin with the familiar resisting outline, his fingers encountered soft warm curls. In utter amazement, Silas fell on his knees and bent his head low to examine the marvel: it was a sleeping child—a round, fair thing, with soft yellow rings all over its head. Could this be his little sister come back to him in a dream—his little sister whom he had carried about in his arms for a year before she died, when he was a small boy without shoes or stockings? That was the first thought that darted across Silas's bleak wonderment. *Was* it a dream? He rose to his feet again, pushed his logs together, and, throwing on some dried leaves and sticks, raised a little flame; but the flame did not disperse the vision—it only lit up more distinctly the little round form of the child, and its shabby clothing. It was very much like his little sister. Silas sank into his chair powerless, under the double presence of an inexplicable surprise and a hurrying influx of memories. How and when had the child come in without his knowledge? He had never been beyond the door. But along with that question, and almost thrusting it away, there was a vision of the old home and the old streets leading to Lantern Yard—and within that vision another, of the thoughts which had been present with him in those far-off scenes. The thoughts were strange to him now, like old friendships impossible to revive; and yet he had a dreamy feeling that this child was somehow a message come to him from that far-off life: it stirred fibres that had never been moved in Raveloe—old quiverings of tenderness—old impressions of awe at the presentiment of some Power presiding over his life; for his imagination had not yet extricated itself from the sense of mystery in the child's sudden presence, and had formed no conjectures of ordinary natural means by which the event could have been brought about.

From lost gold through a lost little sister on to a found child, whom he will raise as his foster daughter: the power of this progression resides somewhere between myth and morality, and wins us by the quietude of its force. Contrast this with the uncanniness and dread of a vital moment in William Blake's manuscript ballad "The Mental Traveller":

> An aged Shadow soon he fades
> Wandring round an Earthly Cot
> Full filled all with gems & gold
> Which he by industry had got

And these are the gems of the Human Soul
The rubies & pearls of a lovesick eye
The countless gold of the akeing heart
The martyrs groan and lovers sigh

They are his meat they are his drink
He feeds the Beggar & the Poor
And the wayfaring Traveller
For ever open is his door

His grief is their eternal joy
They make the roofs & walls to ring
Till from the fire on the hearth
A little Female Babe does spring

And she is all of solid fire
And gems & gold that none his hand
Dares stretch to touch her Baby form
Or wrap her in his swaddling-band

But She comes to the Man she loves
If young or old or rich or poor
They soon drive out the aged Host
A Beggar at another's door

He wanders weeping far away
Untill some other take him in
Oft blind & age-bent sore distrest
Untill he can a Maiden win

Little Eppie (who receives the name of Marner's dead sister) is anything but this Blakean infant Rahab, and it is almost infinitely moving to watch George Eliot's tracing of the mutual love that never abandons the two-year-old foundling and her weaver foster-father. Blake's apocalyptic vision of destructive sexuality is prophetic of our mode, while *Silas Marner* hardly could be more out of fashion in our wretched universities. One Professor of Resentment to whom I commended the novel snapped that if I read a little Karl Marx I might be cured of George Eliot. Marxist academic cheerleaders, waving their pom-poms, reduce George Eliot as uselessly as they reduce

Shakespeare, with whom she shares many qualities, including a mastery of dramatic dialogue.

She had learned from Shakespeare also how to distance an overwhelming pathos, which emerges at the conclusion of *Silas Marner*, and renders me tearful, despite Eliot's artful fabling. Eppie's natural father, Godfrey Cass, and his wife, Nancy, who is rather more principled, call upon Silas and Eppie to reveal Godfrey's sixteen-year guilt of abandonment, after his secret wife, Eppie's opium-crazed mother, had died in the snow near Silas's cottage. Belatedly, the Casses request that the eighteen-year-old Eppie leave Silas, and come to them:

"Eppie, my dear," said Godfrey, looking at his daughter, not without some embarrassment, under the sense that she was old enough to judge him, "it'll always be our wish that you should show your love and gratitude to one who has been a father to you so many years, and we shall want to help you to make him comfortable in every way. But we hope you'll come to love us as well; and though I haven't been what a father should have been to you all these years, I wish to do the utmost in my power for you for the rest of my life, and provide for you as my only child. And you'll have the best of mothers in my wife— that'll be a blessing you haven't known since you were old enough to know it."

"My dear, you'll be a treasure to me," said Nancy, in her gentle voice. "We shall want for nothing when we have our daughter."

Eppie did not come forward and curtsey, as she had done before. She held Silas's hand in hers, and grasped it firmly—it was a weaver's hand, with a palm and finger-tips that were sensitive to such pressure—while she spoke with colder decision than before.

"Thank you, ma'am—thank you, sir, for your offers—they're very great, and far above my wish. For I should have no delight i' life any more if I was forced to go away from my father, and knew he was sitting at home a-thinking of me and feeling lone. We've been used to be happy together every day, and I can't think o' no happiness without him. And he says he'd nobody i' the world till I was sent to him, and he'd have nothing when I was gone. And he's took care of me and loved me from the first, and I'll cleave to him as long as he lives, and nobody shall ever come between him and me."

"But you must make sure, Eppie," said Silas, in a low tone—"you must make sure as you won't ever be sorry, because you've made your choice to stay among poor folks, and with poor clothes and things, when you might ha' had every thing o' the best."

His sensitiveness on this point had increased as he listened to Eppie's words of faithful affection.

"I can never be sorry, father," said Eppie. "I shouldn't know what to think on or to wish for with fine things about me, as I haven't been used to. And it 'ud be poor work for me to put on things and ride in a gig, and sit in a place at church, as 'ud make them as I'm fond of think me unfitting company for 'em. What could *I* care for them?"

Nancy looked at Godfrey with a pained questioning glance. But his eyes were fixed on the floor, where he was moving the end of his stick, as if he were pondering on something absently. She thought there was a word which might perhaps come better from her lips than from his.

"What you say is natural, my dear child—it's natural you should cling to those who've brought you up," she said mildly; "but there's a duty you owe to your lawful father. There's perhaps something to be given up on more sides than one. When your father opens his home to you, I think it's right you shouldn't turn your back on it."

"I can't feel as I've got any father but one," said Eppie, impetuously, while the tears gathered. "I've always thought of a little home where he'd sit i' the corner, and I should fend and do everything for him: I can't think o' no other home. I wasn't brought up to be a lady, and I can't turn my mind to it. I like the working-folks, and their victuals, and their ways. And," she ended passionately, while the tears fell, "I'm promised to marry a working-man, as 'll live with father, and help me to take care of him."

I quote this at length to seek George Eliot's genius in its rightness at dialogue and moral economy at representing the heart's affections. One rhetorical false step, and this scene would plunge into the abyss of bathos: Eliot, superbly aware of the danger, writes with the massive simplicity and directness of Wordsworth. The apparent commonplaceness of the style allows Eliot to evade, without any overt allusiveness, the Wordsworth of *The Ruined Cottage* and "Michael," and the reconciling conclusion of *The Winter's Tale*. The aesthetic effect mingles Wordsworth's blessing of the dead Margaret "in the impotence of grief" yet also in the "secret spirit of humanity," with the restoration of the lost Perdita, who here needs no restoration, having long ago found the best of foster fathers.

Moral authority, whatever we may take it to be, rarely fuses with aesthetic strength. George Eliot seems to me unique in this regard, since

Isaiah, Plato, Wordsworth, and Tolstoy all relied upon transcendent beliefs, while she had dismissed God and immortality as illusions. Keats, who asserted that he believed only in the holiness of the heart's affection and the truth of the imagination, had no interest in teaching us to make moral decisions. George Eliot's beliefs were essentially akin to Keats's naturalistic humanism, but she was also a sage, composing wisdom-narratives. When the erudite and courageous Mary Ann Evans first became George Eliot, she took on a persona that already was her daemon, the otherness of her subtle genius.

WILLA CATHER

She was a battered woman now, not a lovely girl; but she still had that something which fires the imagination, could still stop one's breath for a moment by a look or gesture that somehow revealed the meaning in common things.

—*My Ántonia*, book 5, chapter 1

It is because Willa Cather was so intensely in love with Ántonia that the sensitive reader so easily comes to share the passion, but Cather's art is exquisitely subtle in rendering her love. Shadowed by Henry James, towards whose social scene she manifested acute ambivalence, Cather can be said to have moved her master outdoors, onto the Western prairie. Pragmatically, that obliged the Virginia-born Cather to be retrospective: she studies the nostalgias of lost or unfulfillable love, appropriate for her veiled lesbian stance in early twentieth-century America.

Jim Burden, Cather's surrogate, is obsessed with Vergil's *Aeneid*, and *My Ántonia* is a profoundly Vergilian novel. Cather's genius, like Vergil's, centers upon regret, upon honorable because hopeless erotic defeats.

Cather's aesthetic Americanizes Walter Pater, rather as Wallace Stevens does. Stevens preferred Cather to almost all their contemporaries, and their affinities help explain his judgment. She is the novelist of a retrospective glory, of the beauty of loss, even as Stevens is its poet. The Connecticut of Wallace Stevens necessarily is remote from the Nebraska of Willa Cather, but both are in the Evening Land aspect of America. East or West, we represent Europe's last stand. Cather brings the fading culture of Europe to the prairie as a counterpoise to Henry James's passionate American pilgrims, who search in European society for those values of moral choice and aesthetic sensibility that Europe no longer possesses, or holds on to only in decline.

Geniuses of nostalgia are rare: the only great critic who worked in that mode was William Hazlitt, the English High Romantic friend of John Keats. Walter Pater provided Willa Cather with materials for her mastery of regret, but the evasive Pater would not commit himself to anything. Willa Cather, searching for antique values, was able to incarnate them beautifully in her lost ladies.

WILLA CATHER
(1873–1947)

WILLA CATHER WAS ONE OF THE MAJOR American novelists of the first half of the twentieth century, fully the peer of Theodore Dreiser, Ernest Hemingway, and F. Scott Fitzgerald. Only William Faulkner, among her direct contemporaries, has an eminence beyond Cather's. Her genius, for me, emerges most clearly in two lyrical short novels, *My Ántonia* (1918) and *A Lost Lady* (1923). Since what I quest for is insight into the perpetual freshness of these two beautiful narratives, I engage directly with Cather's literary origins, and her swerve into her own originality.

Alexander's Bridge (1912), her first novel, is a remarkably successful work, and appeared when she was thirty-eight, a late start. Cather had published a volume of poetry in 1903 and a book of stories in 1905, but she found herself in the novel. Aside from *My Ántonia* and *A Lost Lady*, her principal fictions are *O Pioneers!* (1913), *One of Ours* (1922), *The Professor's House* (1925), and *Death Comes for the Archbishop* (1927).

In 1916, after a long relationship, Cather lost her first love, Isabelle McClung, to the Jewish violinist Jan Hambourg. This loss is the undersong of *My Ántonia* and still reverberates in *My Lost Lady*. Faithful to Romantic tradition, Cather's imagination transformed experiential loss into aesthetic gain. Unfortunately, her human bitterness manifested itself in a curious assimilation of her resentments of male aggressivity and of Jewishness, as though they were a single entity. *The Professor's House* is gratuitously marred by this mythic blending, and her later essay on the storywriter Sarah Orne Jewett expresses her disdain for "Jewish critics." Lionel Trilling delivered a temperate response:

> Miss Cather's later books are pervaded by the air of a broadening ancient wisdom, but if we examine her mystical concern with pots and pans, it does not seem much more than an oblique defense of gentility.

A lament for pots and pans would be well enough in Edward Lear or Lewis Carroll, but not in American fiction of the earlier twentieth century. A Vergilian dirge for a universal erotic bereavement, artfully handled, would be splendid anywhere, and is Cather's lasting glory in *My Ántonia* and *A Lost Lady.*

I have loved *My Ántonia* since I was fifteen, which means that, like the narrator, Jim Burden, I have been in love with Ántonia Shimerda for a lifetime. That seems to me Cather's richest gift; here is Jim Burden's memory of what Walter Pater would have called the "privileged moment" of Jim's falling in love with Ántonia, when they are both children:

> We sat down and made a nest in the long red grass. Yulka curled up like a baby rabbit and played with a grasshopper. Ántonia pointed up to the sky and questioned me with her glance. I gave her the word, but she was not satisfied and pointed to my eyes. I told her, and she repeated the word, making it sound like "ice." She pointed up to the sky, then to my eyes, then back to the sky, with movements so quick and impulsive that she distracted me, and I had no idea what she wanted. She got up on her knees and wrung her hands. She pointed to her own eyes and shook her head, then to mine and to the sky, nodding violently.
>
> "Oh," I exclaimed, "blue; blue sky."
>
> She clapped her hands and murmured, "Blue sky, blue eyes," as if it amused her. While we snuggled down there out of the wind, she learned a score of words. She was quick, and very eager. We were so deep in the grass that we could see nothing but the blue sky over us and the gold tree in front of us. It was wonderfully pleasant. After Ántonia had said the new words over and over, she wanted to give me a little chased silver ring she wore on her middle finger. When she coaxed and insisted, I repulsed her quite sternly. I didn't want her ring, and I felt there was something reckless and extravagant about her wishing to give it away to a boy she had never seen before. No wonder Krajiek got the better of these people, if this was how they behaved.

The passage is not sentimental, but myth or magic. Jim's recalcitrance is ambiguous, because as Cather's surrogate, his "repulse" of Ántonia stands for the eternal sorrow of the loss of Isabelle McLung's love. But Jim's only apparent rejection of Ántonia's love is not what will hold on in the reader's memory. "She was quick, and very eager": the sexual promise, never to be fulfilled, will never leave the narrator. Blue sky, gold tree, silver ring: these are the emblems that will haunt Jim, that justify his name of "Burden."

Cather wanted to find a woman precursor in Jewett, but she remained always the heir of two great aesthetes, Walter Pater and Henry James.

Like Pater and James, Cather is erotically evasive in her art, homoeroticism in their eros being limited by societal taboos. All three were skilled at intimating their authentic desires, yet Cather seems to me the most original in her intimations, as in Jim's celebrated dream of Ántonia's friend Lena Lingard:

> One dream I dreamed a great many times, and it was always the same.
> I was in a harvest-field full of shocks, and I was lying against one of
> them. Lena Lingard came across the stubble barefoot, in a short skirt,
> with a curved reaping-hook in her hand, and she was flushed like the
> dawn, with a kind of luminous rosiness all about her. She sat down
> beside me, turned to me with a soft sigh and said, "Now they are all
> gone, and I can kiss you as much as I like."

The erotic intensity of this remains undiminished, in force and suggestiveness. Lena becomes the harvest-girl of Keats's magnificent ode "To Autumn," where the stubble-fields testify to a sexual repletion and fulfillment. That curved reaping-hook in the hand of the rosy, short-skirted Lena testifies to her prowess as a harvester, indeed as a phallic woman. And yet Jim's dream does not find in Lena a figure of menace, a Belle Dame sans Merci. Rather she offers completion to female and male alike, as Keats yields to Cather's mode of lesbian receptivity.

The reader learns to see *My Ántonia* as an antiphony of two goddesses, Ántonia as Proserpina/Persephone, and Lena as Venus. It hardly matters that Jim Burden/Willa Cather remains ambiguously unresolved. You can, if you wish, regard *My Ántonia* as the most persuasive of lesbian novels in English. To me, that somewhat undervalues the book. Cather, for all her resentments, had the advanced aesthetic vision of her mentors Walter Pater and Henry James. The sexual nostalgia of *My Ántonia* touches the universal: whatever one's sexual orientation, one meets one's own nostalgias for a lost eros in the book. Wallace Stevens, a great student of those nostalgias, rather startled me by asserting, the one time I met him, that Cather was the best we had. The judgment was generous but not extravagant.

A Lost Lady is as central to that nostalgia as *My Ántonia*, but something in me could not clarify my confusions about Cather's most exquisite book until I first discussed it, decades ago, with the poet John Hollander. He caught the sense in which it parallels Eliot's *Waste Land*, as another fragment shored against the author's ruin. Though *A Lost Lady* takes us back to the American 1880s, it is another vision of 1922, when the world had broken apart. A cultural continuity ends in *A Lost Lady*, where the nostalgia becomes as cultural as it is erotic.

Niel Herbert, the narrator of *A Lost Lady*, is another surrogate for the lesbian Cather, but Cather's art has augmented, and Niel coheres as Jim Burden could not. This protagonist is a Flaubertian young aesthete, but he is also sturdy enough to be older brother to Hemingway's surrogate, Nick Adams, and to the Nick Carraway of *The Great Gatsby* of Scott Fitzgerald. I would cite Pater again as the authentic mentor of Niel Herbert's sensibility, for it is Pater who hovers in Niel Herbert's luminous epiphany of his "lost lady," Mrs. Forrester:

> Her eyes, when they laughed for a moment into one's own, seemed to provide a wild delight that he had not found in life. "I know where it is," they seemed to say, "I could show you!" He would like to call up the shade of the young Mrs. Forrester, as the witch of Endor called up Samuel's, and challenge it, demand the secret of that ardour; ask her whether she had really found some ever-blooming, ever-burning, ever-piercing joy, or whether it was all fine play-acting. Probably she had found no more than another; but she had always the power of suggesting things much lovelier than herself, as the perfume of a single flower may call up the whole sweetness of spring.

If this is illusion, nevertheless we want to dwell in it. There is a particular genius, in literature, that evokes lost happiness, not so much the happiness we never found anyway, but the illusion of happiness that we saw once (we think), even if only by glimpses. To suggest things much lovelier than herself is a rare gift in a handful of young women, whom one remembers among the pitifully few enlargement of life. Experience darkens Mrs. Forrester throughout *A Lost Lady*, but never to the point of obscuring her. *A Lost Lady* is a permanent book because it holds together, in a coherent vision, the icon of Mrs. Forrester as an image of the love and beauty that may haunt us in the hour of our deaths.

EDITH WHARTON

If the recurrence of this date is more than a coincidence—and for my part I think it is—then I take it that the strange woman who twice came up the drive at Whitegates on All Souls' eve was either a "fetch," or else, more probably, and more alarmingly, a living woman inhabited by a witch. The history of witchcraft, as is well known, abounds in such cases, and such a messenger might well have been delegated by the powers who rule in these matters to summon Agnes and her fellow servants to a midnight "Coven" in some neighboring solitude. To learn what happens at Covens, and the reason of the irresistible fascination they exercise over the timorous and superstitious, one need only address oneself to the immense body of literature dealing with these mysterious rites. Anyone who has once felt the faintest curiosity to assist at a Coven apparently soon finds the curiosity increase to desire, the desire to an uncontrollable longing, which, when the opportunity presents itself, breaks down all inhibitions; for those who have once taken part in a Coven will move heaven and earth to take part again.

This comes close to the end of Mrs. Wharton's "All Souls'," one of the finest ghost stories in the language, and the last story she sent off to a publisher before she died. Edith Wharton's ghosts are rather like her living characters in that they are as much absences as presences, except for Undine Spragg, the present-all-too-present protagonist of *The Custom of the Country*.

Edith Wharton fiercely resented any designation of her as the female Henry James, and her regard for Proust's achievement was larger than her estimate of James's. Though Mrs. Wharton and Henry James were good (if uneasy) friends, she found the novels of his major phase unreadable, while he increasingly came to resent and even fear her "deranging and desolating, ravaging, burning and destroying energy . . . The angel of Devastation."

Mrs. Wharton's life-force was extraordinary and augmented with each year, even when she aged. Her "All Souls'" contrasts wonderfully with a Jamesian ghost story like "The Jolly Corner," which is a parable of the unlived life, whereas Mrs. Wharton's story implies an orgiastic underlying reality always ready to break in upon the social surfaces of existence.

Edith Wharton's genius (it cannot be judged less) is vitalistic: she is a profoundly sexual writer, and her stories and novels subtly intimate an erotic realism that is stronger for being implicit. She had the great gift of writing her fictions as if she indeed had lived them, with more passion even than they overtly expressed.

EDITH WHARTON
(1862–1937)

GENIUS IS NOT ALWAYS LOVABLE. WHARTON, like T. S. Eliot and the shattering Dostoevsky, belongs to that small band of writers I am compelled to admire, but do not like. Celine, whom I find unreadable, is a different phenomenon: he is in my garbage bin, with Wyndham Lewis and all but a few fragments of Ezra Pound. Eliot's hallucinatory poetry and Dostoevsky's great nihilists, Svidrigalov and Stavrogin, impose themselves upon any authentic reader. Wharton, who had an original genius for representing changing social realities, and for seeing deeply into the war between men and women, is for me a very mixed reading experience. But unpleasant genius is an essential part of what forms the genius of language. I don't like what Wharton sees or how she sees it, but she teaches me to see what I can't quite behold without her. In these harsh years of George Bush II, Wharton is a grand guide to the advent of a new Gilded Age.

After rereading virtually all of Wharton, I have to settle for *The Custom of the Country* as her best book, and the disturbing Undine Spragg as her strongest character. Becky Sharp in *Vanity Fair* always makes me fall in love with her again, but you have to be coldly depraved to lose your soul to Undine. Wharton, a grand artist schooled despite herself by the master, Henry James, coolly appropriates Becky Sharp from Thackeray, and then transforms her into the virulent Undine Spragg. This is as it should be; Thackeray was no menace. Though Henry James and Wharton became close, lifelong friends, she fought hard against all insinuations that he overinfluenced her books. R. W. B. Lewis, Wharton's distinguished biographer, also deprecates the influence, and yet it seems to me palpable. Wharton's drive towards satire, particularly of the artistic life, reads to me as a reaction-formation against James. It was only after the death of Henry James (1916) that Wharton's complex (and loving) defenses against his influence began to give way, so that her later work is her most Jamesian: *The Age of Innocence, Old New York, Hudson River Bracketed, A Backward Glance.* It seems to me a classic instance of the anxiety of influence, in which the strong will of the latecomer diverts her from her natural mode, and makes her labor against the grain. Wharton's best fiction—*The House of Mirth, Ethan Frome, The Custom of the Country,* and the finest of her short stories—all benefit from the antithetical strain in them. Her vision is darker than that of James; after he was a memory, she was free to study the nostalgias.

The story of Undine Spragg, as created by Edith Wharton, has epic dimensions and thuggish protagonists, a contrast that keeps it lively. Undine is an unstoppable sexual force, almost occult in her destructive drive. She is a kind of troll or *huldre,* as her given name intimates, a descendant of Adam's first wife, Lilith. Fouqué's *Undine* (1811) tells the tale of a water-nymph turned loose among humans. Undine Spragg, however, boils up out of Kansas into New York City, where she marries the wealthy socialite and would-be artist Ralph Marvell. Later, she gives herself to Peter van Degen for a two-month affair. After rejecting poor Marvell, inducing his suicide, Undine devours a French aristocrat, Raymond de Chelles, and then returns to her first, secret Kansan marriage with Elmer Moffatt, now a New York billionaire. That is the gist of Wharton's fable; Elaine Showalter sees Undine as the answer to Freud: "While Freud asks, 'What do women want?,' Wharton replies 'What have you got?' "

As readers we follow Wharton in disliking Undine, but we become aware that Undine has an exasperating relationship to Edith Wharton. R. W. B. Lewis alarmingly suggests that Undine is what Wharton would have been without her more gracious and redeeming aspects:

So imagined, we see in Undine Spragg how Edith somehow appeared to the view of the harried and aging Henry James: demanding, imperious, devastating, resolutely indifferent to the needs of others, something like an irresistible force of nature.

Undine then is Wharton's anti-genius, the enemy of the novelist's daemonic sympathy for otherness. Wharton of course was a snob, an anti-Semite, a racist: it went with her era and social class, and while unpleasant, it is not particularly virulent, as it is in the Anglo-Catholic moralist T. S. Eliot. Undine is certainly the most memorable character in Wharton, but is she a fully achieved representation of a personality? Thackeray's Becky Sharp is a person; Showalter accurately observes that Undine "lacks Becky's spirit, irreverence, and humor." Wharton, enthralled by a daemonic antiself to her own genius, is content to mythify Undine as a grand villain, a truly fatal woman.

R. W. B. Lewis, immensely sympathetic to Wharton, is content to describe her as "a writer of near genius." Like Iris Murdoch, Edith Wharton can be undervalued if you make demands upon her that belong more to the novel than to the romance. Can there be, on a high aesthetic level, romances of society? In romance, states of being and places that are visionary, however realistic they seem, substitute for the representation of character. Edith Wharton's Kansas, that is to say Undine Spragg's Kansas, is a purely visionary locale, like Oz. But are the New York City and the Paris in which Undine exercises her sexual powers not equally visionary?

Perhaps Wharton was only a near-genius, except in the best of her short stories, like the ghostly tale "All Souls'." If her literary achievement needs to be bolstered, in our current fashion, by gender concerns and sociological contexts, then it would fall short of the qualities of innovation and continual freshness that genius ought to encompass. I am not sure that her life story, as recounted by Lewis, is more than the history of a will, rather than of an imagination.

In her later years, Wharton confessed her strong admiration for the novels of Colette, who had conveyed a more accurate sense of female sexuality than Joyce and Lawrence had achieved. Except for a posthumous fragment like "Beatrice Palmato," Wharton's good manners had prevented her from anticipating Colette. Whether one reads *The Custom of the Country* as realistic novel or as a romance myth, we are left with too cold a splendor in the depiction of Undine. Her sexual power is asserted, but never truly demonstrated, by which I do not mean that we wish to behold her in full action. But consider Hawthorne's *The Scarlet Letter,* where Hester Prynne's sexual splendor is subtly and powerfully conveyed, by all the nuances of which a genius of romance is capable. Inhibition is not the issue; the grace of genius is.

F. SCOTT FITZGERALD

The day before Doctor Diver left the Riviera, he spent all his time with his children. He was not young any more with a lot of nice thoughts and dreams to have about himself, so he wanted to remember them well.

—*Tender Is the Night*, chapter 12

He would come back some day; they couldn't make him pay forever. But he wanted his child, and nothing was much good now, beside that fact. He wasn't young anymore, with a lot of nice thoughts and dreams to have by himself.

—"Babylon Revisited"

Fitzgerald's repetition of that plangent sentence may have been indeliberate, though since it comes after the emotional defeat of Dick Diver, and at the close of one of the best stories, I suspect he was conscious of his own self-appropriation. It could go equally well in *The Crack-Up*, the posthumous collection put together by Fitzgerald's friend the literary critic Edmund Wilson. Whether those nice thoughts and dreams are about the self, or indulged in the solitude of the self, they fade with the passage of youth. As his own youth, with its superb promise, waned into an alcoholic and aesthetically stalled middle age, Fitzgerald had earned the repetition of that nostalgic sentence.

John Keats haunted Fitzgerald, whose own narrative style sometimes has a Keatsian lyricism. The "Ode to a Nightingale" seems to have been Fitzgerald's favorite poem, a preference that his life and his work also earned. One thinks of Scott Fitzgerald as one of Keats's tragic questers:

Ay, in the very temple of Delight
    Veiled Melancholy has her sovereign shrine,
        Though seen of none save him whose strenuous tongue
Can burst Joy's grape against his palate fine;
    His soul shall taste the sadness of her might,
        And be among her cloudy trophies hung.

F. SCOTT FITZGERALD
(1896–1940)

LIKE HIS EQUIVOCAL FRIEND, HEMINGWAY, Francis Scott Key Fitzgerald has joined American literary mythology. *The Great Gatsby* (1925) is a short novel of genius; it and a few stories center Fitzgerald's legacy. After *Gatsby*, there were fifteen years of falling off, and then the Keatsian novelist died. Like nearly everyone else, I have written about *The Great Gatsby* several times before, but never from the perspective of testing the book's genius.

In the nineteenth century, our national myth was Ralph Waldo Emerson's American Adam. The American Dream tended to be our characteristic myth in the twentieth century, and Scott Fitzgerald was both the prime celebrant and the great satirist of that dream-turned-nightmare. Now, at the start of the twenty-first century, it is unclear, just what—if anything—we entertain as a sustaining myth. Shall we say, in this new Gilded Age of George W. and his Robber Barons, Boom or Bust?

Scott Fitzgerald is reputed to have possessed by memory all of T. S. Eliot's *Waste Land* (1922), allusions to which populate *The Great Gatsby*. The subtlest allusion, though, is to Keats's "Eve of Saint Agnes," as I will show, and perhaps the poetic dialect of *The Great Gatsby* is its enforced attempt to fuse the incompatible strains of Keats and of Eliot.

After three-quarters of a century, *The Great Gatsby* retains its freshness. I cannot recall how often I have read it, and I am surprised, rereading it yet once more, that the stairway of surprise is still there. Even *The Sun Also Rises* has become a period piece, but not *Gatsby*. Here at least, and in a few short stories ("The Rich Boy" and "Babylon Revisited" among them), the daemon knew how it was done. When his gift for lyrical narrative and for an answerable style of characterization worked together, Fitzgerald touched an eminence that *Tender Is the Night* could not reach. John O'Hara, disciple of Fitzgerald and of Hemingway, is inspired by them in his memorable first novel, *Appointment in Samarra*, but then dwindled into their caricaturist. Fitzgerald does not have so pronounced a manneristic style as Hemingway, but in his way he is baroque enough to be highly recognizable.

The influence of Joseph Conrad upon Fitzgerald, Hemingway, and Faulkner is one of the odder phenomena of modern American fiction. It worked better for Fitzgerald than for the others because Nick Carraway is

an aesthetic improvement upon Marlow, whom Henry James had deprecated as "the mystic mariner." Some critics have protested that Carraway is
intrusive while Marlow is transparent, but I think they have this the wrong
way round. Marlow is an obscurantist, particularly in *Heart of Darkness*, but
Carraway, Horatio to Gatsby's Hamlet, is likable, helpful, and mediates for
us not Gatsby, who is not quite there, but the Platonic idea of Gatsby, who
as a gangster-poet sets a pattern for some contemporary rappers. Carraway,
moved by Gatsby (perhaps with repressed homoeroticism), senses what
Gatsby himself is too rapt to express:

> Through all he said, even through his appalling sentimentality, I was
> reminded of something—an elusive rhythm, a fragment of lost words
> that I had heard somewhere a long time ago. For a moment a phrase
> tried to take shape in my mouth and my lips parted like a dumb man's
> as though there was more struggling upon them than a wisp of star-
> tled air. But they made no sound, and what I had almost remembered
> was incommunicable forever.

Carraway and Fitzgerald almost remember a passage in Keats's *Fall of Hyperion* where the quester, unable to speak or move, is almost destroyed:

> One minute before death, my iced foot touched
> The lowest stair; and as it touched, life seemed
> To pour in at the toes.

We know that Horatio/Carraway is the foil, recalcitrant and puzzled, to
Hamlet/Gatsby's woe and wonder, the vitalism of a ceaseless quester who
cannot understand that he is subject and object of his own quest. But that
is the Keatsian condition, as the goddess is always unattainable, and would
lose divinity if achieved.

Why does Fitzgerald allow his quester to be killed? Critics who bring *The
Great Gatsby* too close to *The Waste Land* see Gatsby as a ritual sacrifice, who
will revive the dead land, which needs to absorb drowned poets. Everything
in America is cyclic; four years after Gatsby came the Wall Street panic and
crash. In 2001, we are back in 1925, or in the earlier Gilded Age.

Jay Gatsby is one of the Platonic poems of our climate, one of the flawed
words, stubborn sounds that go drifting on.

All of *The Great Gatsby* takes place in one summer, and lives on only in the
memory of Nick Carraway. Because Gatsby cannot tell his story, Carraway
will. Precisely why the story needs to be told, Carraway is more uncertain

than he realizes. He survives to tell Gatsby's story as Horatio draws his breath in pain to tell Hamlet's, lest Hamlet bear a wounded name. Carraway wants us to get Gatsby right, but there is no way to do that. There is no realistic warrant for Gatsby; as a Platonic conception of the self, Gatsby is neither real nor knowable. We are moved by Carraway's recalcitrant love for Gatsby as we are by Horatio's freer love for Hamlet, but Gatsby is all aspiration and no mind, drive without meaning.

And yet his story, as told by Carraway, has poignance. Is it all Carraway's interpretation? One critic speaks of Carraway's "pompous moralizing," but I myself cannot hear that. *The Great Gatsby* is more romance than novel, and Carraway is squire to Gatsby's knight. Reservations need to be made; Carraway is not going to adopt a Gatsby-like career as a front man for mobsters. His qualified apprenticeship to Gatsby is of a different nature, and begins when the two first meet:

> It was one of those rare smiles with a quality of eternal reassurance in it, that you may come across four or five times in life. It faced—or seemed to face—the whole eternal world for an instant, and then concentrated on you with an irresistible prejudice in your favour. It understood you just as far as you wanted to be understood, believed in you as you would like to believe in yourself, and assured you that it had precisely the impression of you that, at your best, you hoped to convey. Precisely at that point it vanished—and I was looking at an elegant young roughneck, a year or two over thirty, whose elaborate formality of speech just missed being absurd.

This is the Nick Carraway who can describe Gatsby's personality as an "unbroken series of successful gestures." That there is something else in Gatsby, not so much a dream of value, but the value of a dream, is what fascinates Nick, and the reader. Gatsby is a Son of God, self-engendered. He seeks what all the great American monomaniacs—fictive and historical—have sought: wealth, love, a home, a place in society. Fitzgerald is not Faulkner, whose Sutpen in *Absalom, Absalom!* seeks all this in the context we have learned to call Southern gothic. Gatsby is a parody of Emersonian self-reliance, and yet he remains as American as Emerson. Or should one say: as American as F. Scott Fitzgerald of St. Paul, Minnesota, whose dream of love led him to Princeton, to Zelda Sayre, and on to New York City, Paris, Hollywood, and Sheilah Graham.

My favorite passage in *The Great Gatsby* comes near the end of chapter 5, when Gatsby is showing Daisy and Nick his house. In Gatsby's bedroom,

Daisy picks up his hairbrush of "pure dull gold" and smoothes her hair. In a moment of shared ecstasy, Gatsby is transmogrified:

> "It's the funniest thing, old sport," he said hilariously. "I can't— When I try to—."
>
> He had passed visibly through two states and was entering upon a third. After his embarrassment and his unreasoning joy he was consumed with wonder at her presence. He had been full of the idea so long, dreamed it right through to the end, waited with his teeth set, so to speak, at an inconceivable pitch of intensity. Now, in the reaction, he was running down like an overwound clock.
>
> Recovering himself in a minute he opened for us two hulking patent cabinets which held his massed suits and dressing-gowns and ties, and his shirts, piled like bricks in stacks a dozen high.
>
> "I've got a man in England who buys me clothes. He sends over a selection of things at the beginning of each season, spring and fall."
>
> He took out a pile of shirts and began throwing them, one by one, before us, shirts of sheer linen and thick silk and fine flannel, which lost their folds as they fell and covered the table in many-colored disarray. While we admired he brought more and the soft rich heap mounted higher—shirts with stripes and scrolls and plaids in coral and apple-green and lavender and faint orange, and monograms of Indian blue. Suddenly, with a strained sound, Daisy bent her head into the shirts and began to cry stormily.
>
> "They're such beautiful shirts," she sobbed, her voice muffled in the thick folds. "It makes me sad because I've never seen such—such beautiful shirts before."

With great skill, Fitzgerald gives us a displaced allusion to John Keats's Gatsby, Porphyro in "The Eve of Saint Agnes" who piles up, for the sleeping Madeline, "a heap / Of candied apples, quince, and plum" and other spiced "dainties" and "delicates." On the same impulse, Gatsby heaps up his soft, rich, multicolored shirts, into which Daisy erotically weeps. It does not matter that poor, empty-headed Daisy is no Madeline or Belle Dame sans Merci; she is perfectly adequate to an elegant roughneck possessed by the American Dream in 1925.

Fitzgerald's genius, small but pure and precise, was for Keatsian prose poetry, adapted to the literary universe of Joseph Conrad and T. S. Eliot. To come alive in one short novel and three or four stories is a lesson in the adequacy and authenticity of genius.

IRIS MURDOCH

In morals and politics we have stripped ourselves of concepts. Literature, in curing its own ills, can give us a new vocabulary of experience, and a truer picture of freedom. With this, renewing our sense of distance, we may remind ourselves that art too lives in a region where all human endeavor is failure. Perhaps only Shakespeare manages to create at the highest level both images and people.

—"Against Dryness" (1961)

Shakespeare can influence only the strongest writers without destroying them: Milton, Goethe, Dickens, Dostoevsky, Ibsen, Joyce. Iris Murdoch, a supremely intelligent and talented writer, bravely sought Shakespeare's influence, with very mixed results. A. S. Byatt shrewdly noted that Murdoch's aesthetic drove her to confront Shakespeare: "Shakespeare is the Good, and contemplation of the best is always to be desired."

I myself delight in Murdoch's novels, but I regard them as romances, sometimes fantasies, a judgment she probably would have repudiated. Perhaps Murdoch is best viewed as a near-genius, who in approaching Shakespeare had to sustain a fairly honorable defeat. *The Black Prince* remains an admirable entertainment, almost an enchantment, but its reliance upon *Hamlet* nearly sinks it, while *A Word Child* barely survives its allusions to *King Lear*.

A Platonist novelist is an oxymoron, while a Shakespearean novelist can be refreshingly audacious, as Stendhal is in *The Charterhouse of Parma*, with its clear links to *Romeo and Juliet*. Murdoch, uneasily transcendental, exploits the preternatural while purporting to reject it. But I feel ungrateful in such an observation. Is there a living English novelist who manifests Murdoch's fusion of intellectual exuberance and storytelling drive?

IRIS MURDOCH
(1919–1999)

AN INCESSANT READER AND INSOMNIAC, I still have failed to reread all twenty-six of the late Iris Murdoch's novels before writing these pages. Yet I have reread my favorites: *Bruno's Dream, The Black Prince, A Word Child, The Sea, the Sea,* and *The Good Apprentice.* Lovers of Murdoch's fictions do not agree as to which is best, and I am uncertain I agree with myself. Of Murdoch's genius I entertain no doubts, even though I do not know which of her novels will prove to be permanent. This confuses me: can one be a great novelist, true heir of Dickens, and not have written a great novel? I prefer to believe that we, and time, have not yet sorted out so astonishingly fecund a narrative gift. Genius, as I keep perceiving, sometimes concentrates itself, and produces a canonical work, but often diffuses and fails to crystallize the singular masterpiece.

Murdoch set for herself only the highest models: Shakespeare, Dante, Tolstoy, Jane Austen, Dickens, Henry James. By that standard, how many could survive? Her characters, as she knew, never attain that level of memorability. Moral imagination was one of Murdoch's strengths, but the representation of character finally evaded her. Was she a victim of her own very original, quasi-religious Platonism?

Murdoch quested for the Good. Such a quest has been accommodated by the novel in George Eliot and Dickens, in James and Austen, in Dostoevsky and in Tolstoy, though not, I think, in Flaubert and Joyce. James and Austen were not less self-conscious novelists than Flaubert and Joyce, so that Murdoch's Platonism (to call it that: "Murdochism" might be better) cannot be faulted for its high sense of what she called "unselfing," since she agreed with T. S. Eliot that the greatest literary art was "impersonal." It isn't, though Murdoch is more interesting in her contention than is Eliot, who was fleeing the Late Romanticism of which he was so distinguished an embodiment. Murdoch, a professional philosopher, argued that certain writers, Shakespeare and Tolstoy and Homer and Dante, show us the real world, our own, which otherwise we generally don't see. I prefer A. D. Nuttall's variant, which is that Shakespeare allows us to see aspects of reality that otherwise we *could not see,* unless he showed them to us. Does Hamlet not refuse to cut down Claudius because he fears that Claudius may be his real father? Marc Shell, sensitive to the anxieties of cuckoldry and incest that pervade Shakespeare's plays, suggests this, and he may be right. But that intimates an even more personal reality for all of us, rather than an impersonal one.

I don't think that the impersonal ideal sabotaged Murdoch's creation of character, though it didn't help. The culprit seems to have been her notion of "unselfing," a Protestant variant of Simone Weil's "decreation" or flight from the ego. D. H. Lawrence also distrusted the "old ego," but his apocalyptic vitalism allowed him the Brangwen sisters, Ursula and Gudrun, who vivify *The Rainbow* and *Women in Love*. Murdochian "unselfing" is a severely moral mode, and too many of Murdoch's men and women are wild without being persuasive. Even her fiercest eccentrics blend into one another. She unselfs them, and is too strong for them. Murdoch is rather like a mother who upstages all her children, so that in comparison to her they appear lacking in personality. Reading *The Black Prince* or *The Good Apprentice* side by side with *The Rainbow* or *Women in Love* will tend to fade the Murdoch novels into very readable period pieces, but only because Bradley Pearson and Edward Baltram come just short of that invisible line which they must cross if they are to be more than names upon a page.

I am unhappy at observing this because I have read Murdoch with enthusiastic pleasure since her first novel, *Under the Net*, in 1954. Meeting her at Yale in 1959, I remember asking her if she felt any affinities with the novelists of her own British generation. She replied with a single "No," and frowned so that I subsided. There are few affinities, except perhaps with the admirable Antonia Byatt, in the generation after: novelists I also now admire, like Will Self, Peter Ackroyd, and John Banville, are very different from Murdoch. Philosopher-novelists are rare in English, as opposed to French or German. One wants Murdoch to be a novelist who matters as much as Hardy, Lawrence, Virginia Woolf, and E. M. Forster, and so I will keep worrying this, because again she certainly possessed uncanny and daemonic powers.

Was Murdoch too preoccupied with what her moral admirers call "the search for human goodness"? She was certainly a religious fabulist of a very original and unorthodox kind. By "religious" I mean something of that Romantic rationalism that she found in Sartre but far more enduringly in Plato. I don't mean the Hermetist or Gnostic strain that appears so often throughout Western literature, and is so beautifully expressed in the romances of John Crowley. Murdoch is her own revisionist of Plato, and intends to be friendlier to imaginative literature than Plato was, but I surmise that her Platonic severity tended to flatten out her characters. She certainly was aware of this danger, argued against Plato on behalf of art, and desired above all to create characters as unlike herself as Shakespeare had done. I am a little wary of calling Simone Weil Murdoch's evil genius, because I don't like reading Weil, whose Jewish self-hatred is—to understate it—deplorable. Weil permeates Murdoch's thinking to the extent that only *King Lear* is harsh enough (in all Shakespeare) to be admitted to the sufferer's canon, which for Weil centers upon the odd pairing of the *Iliad* and the Gospels.

Yet it may be that we, and the late Iris Murdoch, mistook her form for the novel, when she generally writes prose romance, the cast-off precursor of the novel of Cervantes and all his followers down to Proust, Joyce, and Mann. Religious fable, even of a Platonic kind, calls for romance, where sacred places, houses, landscapes, states of being count for more than personality, and romance thrives on incomplete and imperfect knowledge, since full knowledge destroys enchantment. *The Sea, the Sea, The Good Apprentice,* and the other strong Murdoch narratives rely upon magic, absurd passions, and gothic intrusions, and this is all in the mode of romance. Unselfing is inevitable in romance, where all identities are fluid.

In a 1988 interview, Murdoch observed:

> My problem is not being great. I'm in the second league, not among the gods like Jane Austen, and Henry James and Tolstoy. My characters are not as memorable as theirs.

Austen, James, and Tolstoy were novelists: memorable characterization was crucial to their art. But great romance writers, like Robert Louis Stevenson, Kipling, G. K. Chesterton, Richard Hughes, and John Crowley do not invest themselves in characters, but in story, imagination, visionary space. Murdoch is curiously mixed: she has the novelist's concern with moral imagination and the romancer's pragmatic disinterest in character. Her moral intensity and her London surfaces give us expectations appropriate to the realistic novel, but her personages belong to the typology of romance. There are her passionate, violent young women, sly and obsessive, who pursue narcissistic older men, who have great charm but little hold on reality, and are wavering skeptics. Then there are her older women, frequently unfulfilled and angry, and who fall in love with terrible suddenness. And there are Murdoch's mages, male Jewish charismatics, her "alien gods," as she once termed them. None of these types allows much individuation in personality, but they fit well into the cosmos of romance.

Perhaps then we will bring more accurate expectations to Murdoch if we think of her characters as deriving more from J. M. Barrie's *Peter Pan* than from George Eliot's *Middlemarch.* A very paradoxical Platonist, Murdoch may well have found her genius's appropriate form in her overplotted romance-novels, a very mixed genre yet perfectly expressive of her highly individual genius.

IX

YESOD

LUSTRE 17

|

Gustave Flaubert, José Maria Eça de Queiroz, Joaquim Maria Machado de Assis, Jorge Luis Borges, Italo Calvino

|

Yesod, roughly to be translated as "foundation," tends to have two related meanings—the male sexual drive, and the mystery of balance between female and male in natural processes. As *Yesod*'s first Lustre, I have grouped five masters of fiction who again can be regarded as tragic ironists, starting with Flaubert, artist-of-artists, in the novel, particularly in *Madame Bovary*.

Eça de Queiroz, Portugal's major novelist of the nineteenth century, and Machado de Assis, the black Brazilian novelist contemporary with Eça, extended Flaubert's ironies into satiric fantasies that reflected their national dilemmas.

In what was our own time, the Argentine Borges and the Italian Calvino were the authentic geniuses of fantastic fiction, providing an alternative to Chekhov's dominance of the short story. A playfulness with fictiveness itself, already manifest in Eça and Machado, attains an extraordinary expansion in Borges and Calvino, who seem between them to have set a limit beyond which the fantastic story has not been able to go.

GUSTAVE FLAUBERT

The first months of her marriage, her rides in the forest, the viscount who had waltzed with her, and Lagardy singing, all repassed before her eyes . . . And Léon suddenly appeared to her as far off as the others.

"I do love him!" she said to herself.

No matter! She was not happy, she never had been. Why was her life so unsatisfactory, why did everything she leaned on instantly rot and give way? . . . But suppose there existed somewhere some one strong and beautiful, a man of valor, passionate yet refined, the heart of a poet in the form of an angel, a bronze stringed lyre, playing elegiac epithalamia to the heavens, why might she not someday happen on him? What a vain thought! Besides, nothing was worth the trouble of seeking it; everything was a lie. Every smile concealed a yawn of boredom, every joy a curse, every pleasure its own disgust, and the sweetest kisses left upon your lips only the unattainable desire for a greater delight.

(translated by Eleanor Marx Aveling, with revisions by Paul de Man)

Emma Bovary is Gustave Flaubert, and almost all the rest of us as well. *Madame Bovary* is a kind of universal biography, not so much of the female Quixote, but of a sensual Quixote, female or male, whose quest is in no way metaphysical, whose desire is low romantic rather than High Romantic. Emma is a true alternative to Hamlet and Don Quixote: she is a genius of sensuality. The objects of her desire—Léon and Rodolphe—are interchangeable, and she is not destroyed by losing them. Emma dies because she cannot comprehend anything that she has not fully experienced. Her suicide has nothing to do with eros: she is victimized by her own inability to straighten her financial affairs into a minimal order. Flaubert's detachment from Emma remains extraordinary: an heroic effort at distancing makes the book possible—heroic because for Flaubert it was a self-estrangement. Like Emma, he was most himself when in a state of erotic reverie. Emma dies partly because of financial anxiety, but also because she foresees a life ahead that will alternate emptiness with arbitrary passion.

Her authentic poverty was imaginative need: if Flaubert is cruel towards her, it is in denying her any richness of consciousness whatsoever.

And yet Baudelaire was accurate in saying that Emma has real greatness, and provokes our pity. I wonder indeed if she does not provoke our fear as well, since she involuntarily exposes the contingency of most of our passions. Even our most violent attachments frequently are functions of mere juxtapositions of time and space. Her greatness is Quixotic: like the Knight, she rushes wholeheartedly into her amour, and dies only when she has surrendered her quest. Flaubert, the genius of style, paradoxically goes through all this for a heroine who has no style, thus establishing his own Quixotic authenticity.

GUSTAVE FLAUBERT
(1821–1880)

At six o'clock this evening, as I was writing the word "hysterics," I was so swept away, was bellowing so loudly and feeling so deeply what my little Bovary was going through, that I was afraid of having hysterics myself. I got up from my table and opened the window to calm myself. My head was spinning. Now I have great pains in my knees, in my back, and in my head. I feel like a man who has ——ed too much (forgive me for the expression)—a kind of rapturous lassitude.
>   —Flaubert to Louise Colet, December 23, 1853

I will not echo the Lycanthrope [Petrus Borel], remembered for a subversiveness which no longer prevails, when he said: "Confronted with all that is vulgar and inept in the present time, can we not take refuge in cigarettes and adultery?" But I assert that our world, even when it is weighed on precision scales, turns out to be exceedingly harsh considering it was engendered by Christ; it could hardly be entitled to throw the first stone at adultery. A few cuckolds more or less are not likely to increase the rotating speed of the spheres and to hasten by a second the final destruction of the universe.
>   —Baudelaire on *Madame Bovary*

The societal scandal of *Madame Bovary* is as remote now as the asceticism of the spirit practiced by Flaubert and Baudelaire, who seem almost self-indulgent in the era of Samuel Beckett. Rereading *Madame Bovary* side by side with, say, *Malone Dies* is a sadly instructive experience. Emma seems as boisterous as Hogarth or Rabelais in the company of Malone and Macmann. And yet she is their grandmother, even as the personages of Proust, Joyce, and Kafka are among her children. With her the novel enters the realm of inactivity, where the protagonists are bored, but the reader is not. Poor Emma, destroyed by usury rather than love, is so vital that her stupidities do not matter. A much-more-than-average sensual woman, her capacity for life and love is what moves us to admire her, and even to love her, since like Flaubert himself we find ourselves in her.

Why is Emma so unlucky? If it can go wrong, it will go wrong for her.

Freud, like some of the ancients, believed there were no accidents. Ethos is the daemon, your character is your fate, and everything that happens to you starts by being you. Rereading, we suffer the anguish of beholding the phases that lead to Emma's self-destruction. That anguish multiplies despite Flaubert's celebrated detachment, partly because of his uncanny skill at suggesting how many different consciousnesses invade and impinge upon any single consciousness, even one as commonplace as Emma's. Emma's *I* is an other, and so much the worse for the sensual apprehensiveness that finds it has become Emma.

"Hysterics suffer mainly from reminiscences" is a famous and eloquent formula that Freud outgrew. Like Flaubert before him, he came to see that the Emmas—meaning nearly all among us—were suffering from repressed drives. Still later, in his final phase, Freud arrived at a vision that achieves an ultimate clarity in the last section of *Inhibitions, Symptoms, and Anxiety,* which reads to me as a crucial commentary on Emma Bovary. It is not repressed desire that ensues in anxiety, but a primal anxiety that issues in repression. As for the variety of neurosis involved, Freud speculated that hysteria results from fear of the loss of love. Emma kills herself in a hysteria brought on by a fairly trivial financial mess, but underlying the hysteria is the terrible fear that there will be no more lovers for her.

The most troubling critique of *Madame Bovary* that I know is by Henry James, who worried whether we could sustain our interest in a consciousness as narrow as Emma's:

> The book is a picture of the middlings as much as they like, but does Emma attain even to *that?* Hers is a narrow middling even for a little imaginative person whose "social" significance is small. It is greater on the whole than her capacity of consciousness, taking this all around; and so in a word, we feel her less illustrational than she might have been not only if the world had offered her more points of contact, but if she had had more of these to give it.

That *sounds* right enough, yet rereading the novel does not make us desire a larger or brighter Emma. Until she yields to total hysteria, she incarnates the universal wish for sensual life, for a more sensual life. Keats would have liked her, and so do we, though she is not exactly an Isabel Archer or Millie Theale. A remarkable Emma might have developed the hardness and resourcefulness that would have made her a French Becky Sharp, and fitted her for survival even in mid-nineteenth-century Paris. But James sublimely chose to miss the point, which Albert Thibaudet got permanently right:

She is more ardent than passionate. She loves life, pleasure, love itself much more than she loves a man; she is made to have lovers rather than a lover. It is true that she loves Rodolphe with all the fervor of her body, and with him she experiences the moment of her complete, perfect and brief fulfillment; her illness, however, after Rodolphe's desertion, is sufficient to cure her of this love. She does not die from love, but from weakness and a total inability to look ahead, a naivete which makes her an easy prey to deceit as well as in business. She lives in the present and is unable to resist the slightest impulse.

I like best Thibaudet's comparison between Flaubert's attitude towards Emma and Milton's towards his Eve: "Whenever Emma is seen in purely sensuous terms, he speaks of her with a delicate, almost religious feeling, the way Milton speaks of Eve." One feels that Milton desires Eve; Flaubert indeed is so at one with Emma that his love for her is necessarily narcissistic. Cervantes, not Milton, was in some sense Flaubert's truest precursor, and Emma (as many critics have remarked) has elements of a female Quixote in her. Like the Don, she is murdered by reality. Milton's Eve, tough despite her yielding beauty, transcends both the order of reality and the order of play. Emma, lacking a Sancho, finds her enchanted Dulcinea in the paltry Rodolphe. Flaubert punished himself harshly, in and through Emma, by grimly mixing in a poisonous order of provisional social reality, and an equally poisonous order of hallucinated play, Emma's fantasies of an ideal passion. The mixing in is cruel, formidable, and of unmatched aesthetic dignity. Emma has no Sublime, but the inverted Romantic vision of Flaubert persuades us that the strongest writing can represent ennui with a life-enhancing power.

Sartre, very early in his endless meditations upon Flaubert, sensibly observed that "Flaubert despised realism and said so over and over throughout his life; he loved only the absolute purity of art." *Madame Bovary* has little to do with realism, and something to do with a prophecy of impressionism, but in a most refracted fashion. All of poor Emma's moments are at once drab and privileged; one remembers Browning's Andrea del Sarto intoning, "A common greyness silvers everything." The critical impressionism of Walter Pater is implicit in *Madame Bovary;* imagery of hallucinatory intensity is always a step away from suddenly bursting forth as secularized epiphanies. The Impressionist painters and Proust lurk in the ironies of Flaubert's style, but the uncanny moral energy remains unique:

The priest rose to take the crucifix; then she stretched forward her neck like one suffering from thirst, and glueing her lips to the body of the Man-God, she pressed upon it with all her expiring strength the fullest kiss of love that she had ever given. Then he recited the *Misereatur* and the *Indulgentiam*, dipped his right thumb in the oil, and began to give extreme unction. First, upon the eyes, that had so coveted all worldly goods; then upon the nostrils, that had been so greedy of the warm breeze and the scents of love; then upon the mouth, that had spoken lies, moaned in pride and cried out in lust; then upon the hands that had taken delight in the texture of sensibility; and finally upon the soles of the feet, so swift when she had hastened to satisfy her desires, and that would now walk no more.

This is Flaubert's elegy for Emma, and ultimately transcends its apparent ironies, if only because we hear in it the novelist's deeper elegy for himself. He refuses to mourn for himself, as befits the high priest of a purer art than the novel knew before him, yet his lament for Emma's sensual splendor is an authentic song of loss, a loss in which he participates.

One need hardly be a feminist to observe that Flaubert murders Emma Bovary. What is his motive? Self-punishment of course is involved, but Flaubert was too tough to be destroyed, prematurely, by the reality principle. Emma is at once far less tough and far more vital than her creator. I am afraid that the motive for murder is envy of her vitality, so that authorial sadism becomes as crucial in Emma's tragedy as is authorial masochism. The Flaubert who was to compose the dreadfully magnificent *Salammbô* (1858–63) is already present in the making of *Madame Bovary* (1852–56). Sensations are more extreme in *Salammbô*, the colors are far gaudier, the temperature extravagantly rises, and yet desire, ours and Flaubert's, seems less prevalent. As a hopelessly old-fashioned literary critic, who remembers falling in love with Marty South in Thomas Hardy's *The Woodlanders* when he was a boy, I continue to lust after Emma Bovary each time I reread Flaubert's masterwork. This seems to me as valid an aesthetic experience as being moved to desire by staring at a Renoir nude. Emma may be the most persuasively sensual of all fictive beings. Shakespeare's Cleopatra, like his Falstaff, is too witty not to be ironic about her own capacities, but poor Emma is a literalist of her own sexual imagination. Clearly this is a very different mode of fantasy than that of the narrator of *Madame Bovary* or of Flaubert himself. The narrator is considerably less fond of Emma than Flaubert is (or we are), and yet Flaubert, and not the narrator, is the murderer. One might transpose the novel into Shakespearean terms by seeing the narrator as Iago, Flaubert as Othello, and Emma as Desdemona. Of these three identifications (all knowingly outrageous), that of the narrator as Iago is the least fantastic. I have the same uneasy respect for Flaubert's narrator that I have for Iago; both of them propose emotions to themselves, and only then experience the emotions.

Emma, despite her hysterias, is not the heroine of a tragicomedy. The narrator intends otherwise, but Emma has the greatness of her vitality, the heroic intensity of her sexuality, and that eminence makes her an oddity, a tragic heroine in a literary work stoical, ironic, and sometimes grotesquely comic. Flaubert's savage and superb artistry conveys an embodied image of desire that is close to universal; Emma's aura is comprehensive enough to subsume both female and male sexuality. The objects of her desire do not much matter, whether to Flaubert or to the reader. They may mean more to the narrator than they do to Emma, whose concern is only that there always be one, or at least another one beyond, in a series not to be ended. Emma is thus representative of both the average sensual male and the average sensual female, though the sensual is the one domain in which she is above average. She is to the ideal of erotic passion what Don Quixote is to the ideal of playfulness, and like the Don she is at last murdered by reality, whose name is Flaubert, or Cervantes. Human playfulness is a much wider realm than erotic fantasy, and the Don certainly dwarfs Emma in aesthetic dignity. But her own aesthetic strength remains considerable; whom can we prefer to her in Flaubert's major fictions? She was the best available to Flaubert's imagination, and her progeny necessarily are with us still. Emma has fed herself on the erotic debasement of popular romances even as Don Quixote has sustained himself upon romance of knight-errantry. The Don is sublimely crazed, in terms of the order of reality, but he is sublime in the order of play. No order of play is available for Emma, and in the world of reality-testing she is almost absurdly suicidal. Her self-immolation contrasts weirdly with that of Tolstoy's Anna Karenina. Tolstoy's apocalyptic moralism destroys Anna, and yet there is a tragic relief we experience at Anna's death; her sufferings are too large to be allowed to continue. Emma's sufferings seem petty in comparison, and yet Emma is too pleasure-loving to sustain them. Her death lacks grandeur, and yet we are grandly moved because such a loss of sexual vitality is a defeat for the biblical sense of the Blessing, which is: more life. The death of Emma means less life, less possibility of natural pleasure for almost all of us, less of ourselves that we can spend in the days remaining to us.

One feels that, on a much-muted level, Emma belongs in a poem by Keats or by Wallace Stevens. Her narcissism is a value, but Flaubert's novel declines to provide her with contexts in which her self-absorption can acquire any aura of radiance. Hopelessly drab in mind and spirit, incapable of singling out a proper object of desire, she cannot bore us because she herself, despite everything, remains an image of desire. We are endlessly moved by that element in her that cannot accept erotic loss. We suffer our losses, and either we sublimate them, or we harden with them. Emma is as far as she can be from Nietzsche's admirable apothegm, "That which does not destroy me strengthens me." Her losses weaken her, and then destroy her. She represents therefore something stubborn in all of us, perhaps something childlike, that refuses to believe any object is lost forever. What Freud beautifully called "the work of mourning" is not available to her. But it is available to Flaubert, and through Flaubert to his readers. Though he murders her, Flaubert performs the work of mourning for her, a work that takes the shape of his masterpiece, the purest of all novels in form, economy, and the just representation of general nature.

JOSÉ MARIA EÇA DE QUEIROZ

On the walls I hung the images of the noblest saints, as a gallery of spiritual ancestors from whom I received a constant example in the difficult path of virtue. Indeed, there was no saint in heaven, however obscure, to whom I did not dedicate a scented offering of paternosters aflower. It was I who introduced to Auntie St. Telesforo, St. Secundia, the blessed Antony Estronconio, St. Restituta, St. Umbelina, sister of St. Bernard, and our beloved and charming countrywoman St. Basilissa, who is celebrated with St. Hypatius on the festal day of August when the penitents embark for Atalaya.

(translated by Aubrey F. G. Bell)

That is the delightful scamp, Raposo, the playboy-hero of *The Relic,* a comic masterpiece that deserves rediscovery. Eça is one of the great nineteenth-century European novelists, comparable to Balzac in quality, though much less prolific. *The Maias* and *Cousin Bazilio* are admirable realistic novels, but *The Relic* is something rarer: a novel of absolute comic genius, an invention provocative of outrageous laughter.

Raposo's narration of his sublimely absurd and hypocritical quest in the Holy Land is at once superb satire and a disturbing spiritual voyage, one that transcends both his expectations and his own. Who could expect the poignant portrait of Christ that forces its way into Raposo's vision?

Eça's other major works are haunted by the theme of incest, which was his most disturbing metaphor for the national decadence of Portugal in the nineteenth century. The genius of laughter exorcises the haunting in *The Relic*, which paradoxically goes beyond its satiric exuberance to proclaim a redemptive cleansing of Portugal's malaise.

JOSÉ MARIA EÇA DE QUEIROZ
(1845–1900)

PORTUGAL'S PRINCIPAL NOVELIST BEFORE our contemporary, José Saramago, is largely unknown and unread in the English-speaking world. We are puzzled even by his name: he spelled it Queiroz, but since an agreement with Brazil in 1945, the spelling of Portuguese has been standardized, and the name is now Queiros. As my emphasis here is on his marvelous seriocomic novel *The Relic*, translated by Aubrey Bell (1954), where the title page gives him as Queiroz, I will sometimes keep to his own spelling. Satirical imp as he could be, he would have avenged himself for the violence done to his authorial signature.

Though Alexander Coleman entitled his useful study *Eça de Queiros and European Realism* (1980), nineteenth-century "realism" was a wild category, and could mean everything and anything, as Coleman knew. Queiros loved Balzac and Flaubert, and their France, with an equivocal and evasive passion. Ironist as he was, he realized that his France was a metaphor, despite his long residence in Paris. The metaphor stood for everything lacking in the Portugal of the second half of the nineteenth century, which makes it a large metaphor indeed. The national myth of Sebastianism, explicit in the poet Fernando Pessoa, tends to be implicit in Eça. If one considers the major Portuguese writers, starting with the epic poet we call Camoens in English, one has to go beyond the eras of Eça de Queiros and of Pessoa, and into the present age of Saramago, before Sebastianism can be put to rest. The catastrophe of the boy-king Sebastian effectually killed Camoens also; the epic poet of Portugal could not survive the ruin of Portuguese imperial messianism on the sands of North Africa.

The skeptical Eça did not regret the evanescence of Sebastianism, but the dilemmas of Portugal's decline have a peculiar, almost ineluctable effect upon the author of *The Relic* and *The Maias*. *The Relic* has no genre whatsoever, and even *The Maias* declines the formal conventions it only seems to embrace. And yet Eça seems to me, at least in these two narratives, a writer of genius. That genius was wayward and unreliable, and probably was totally incompatible with the French influences that Eça sought to absorb. Flaubert and Zola were not good for Eça, Balzac was, and yet must have caused him despair. Everyone in Balzac, Baudelaire observed, is a genius.

Like Tom Wolfe in our America, Eça aspired to write the Balzacian novel, rather more successfully anyway than Wolfe so far has managed.

Alexander Coleman sensibly remarks that in the 1880s, with *The Mandarin* and *The Relic*, Eça for a while gave up the novel and adopted the romance form, with Flaubert being displaced by Robert Louis Stevenson. *The Mandarin* is a rather slight fantasy, but *The Relic* is a masterpiece, a work as fresh in 2001 as it was in 1887. Its protagonist, the outrageous Teodorico, desperately needs to be favored by his wealthy Aunt Titi's will, and she is an unthinking Catholic ritualist. Teodorico is a scamp: wildly hypocritical, an obsessed hunter of women, the archetypal pious fraud, and an orphan perpetually stalking every opportunity for personal aggrandizement. He is a delightful comic invention, not in mode, but in his single-mindedness, which makes us admire him for his endless gusto. I cannot resist him: each time he pretends piety to gratify his aunt's fetishes, he compensates himself with another whore. All the older conflicts in Eça: between France and Portugal, reform and tradition, realism and romance, fall away as the novelist yields to his happy hypocrite. Teodorico is almost free of the superego, and refreshes us all, since we are not free, Eça in particular.

Aunt Titi is a sublime monster, whose only complaint against God is his error in creating two sexes. Teodorico lives under her reign of terror, since a single mistake would disinherit him:

> My precautions were now therefore such that in order to prevent the delicious scent of Adelia from remaining on my clothes or skin I carried in my pocket loose pieces of incense. Before going up the gloomy steps of the house I would go furtively into the deserted stables at the further end of the courtyard and on the lid of a barrel burn a piece of the holy resin, and remained there bathing in its purifying odour the lapels of my coat and my manly beard. Then I went up and had the satisfaction of hearing Auntie sniff delightedly and say: "Heavens, what a good smell of church"; and with a modest sigh I would murmur: "It is I, Auntie."

Alas, Adelia deceives him and takes another lover. Fearful that, despite his enormous devotions, his mad aunt may leave everything to the church, Teodorico accepts her command: to go, as her surrogate, on a pilgrimage to the Holy Land, and bring back "a miracle-working relic." Until now a fiercely comic book, *The Relic* undergoes transformation into something radically different, an original blend of farce and troubled humanism, uneasy with its own skepticism.

Queiroz, an unbeliever, followed Renan in denying the divinity of Jesus, while proclaiming him a genius, a visionary suspiciously like Unamuno's Don Quixote, a madman who expiates for our dread of mortality. But before our Teodorico, questing for Auntie's relic, reaches Jerusalem, he arrives in the sensualist's true home: Alexandria. Here he links up with the illustrious and learned Dr. Topsius, an amiable fellow also bound for Jerusalem, to do research for his *History of the Herods*. There is a touch of Dr. Pangloss in Topsius, and we begin to feel that *The Relic* acquires a flavor of Voltaire, though Teodorico is not exactly a Candide! His more crucial link is with Mary, an English whore, with whom mutual ecstasy is established.

So happy indeed is this relationship that the reader, already captivated by Teodorico's exuberance, rebels against Eça and begins to identify with the picaroon. That rebellion truly is not against the deepest aspect of the novelist, who loves his creation, but against all the incessant ambivalences that haunt the author of *The Relic*. And yet precisely those ambivalences provide Eça with his story's best invention:

In his [Teodorico's servant] search among the blankets he had come upon a long lace night-dress, with ribbons of light-coloured silk. He shook it out, and from it came a sweet and lovely scent of violets. Alas, it was Mary's night-dress, still warm from my arms. "That belongs to Dona Mary. It is your night-dress, my love," I groaned as I went on dressing. My little gloveseller rose white and trembling, and in a poetical passionate impulse rolled it up and threw it into my arms as ardently as if its folds contained her heart.

"I will give it to you, Theodorico. Take it, Theodorico. It is a memorial of our tenderness. Take it to keep it by your side. But wait, wait, my love. I will write some words of dedication."

She ran to the table, where were remains of the prim paper on which I had been writing to Auntie the edifying history of my fasts in Alexandria, and of my nights spent in living the Gospel story. And I, with the scented night-dress in my arms and two tears rolling down my beard, sought anxiously where to put this precious relic. The trunks were locked, the canvas bag was full. Topsius had impatiently pulled out his silver watch from the depths of his breast-pocket; and our Lacedaemonian at the door was muttering: *"Don Teodorico, es tarde, es muy tarde."*

But now my love was holding up the paper on which she had written in large letters, frank and impetuous as her love: "To my Theodorico, my fine little Portuguese, in remembrance of all our joy."

"O my precious one, and where I am to put it? I can't carry a night-dress thus openly and unpacked."

Already Alpedrinha on his knees was desperately unstrapping the bag, when Mary in a moment of delicate inspiration seized a piece of brown paper and picked up some red string from the floor. The gloveseller's deft fingers swiftly made up a round handy and elegant parcel which I placed under my arm, pressing it jealously, passionately, against my side. Then there was a hurried murmur of sobs and kisses and soft words. "Mary, dear angel."—"Theodorico, my love."—"Write to me at Jerusalem."—"Remember your pretty little one."

Thus the catastrophe of the two precious relics slyly intrudes itself into Teodorico's life. Tearfully seasick aboard the *Shark*, bound from Alexandria to Jaffa, the increasingly surprising fortune-hunter dreams his first dream of the Christ. Accompanied by his two carnal lovers, Adelia and Mary, and by the disconsolate Devil, Teodorico has arrived in time to view the Ascension. After some amiable conversation, in which he attempts to cheer the Devil, his dream ends with a dreadful manifestation of his aunt:

Thinking that Lucifer was in low spirits, I sought to comfort him: "Never mind, there will always be plenty of pride and dissolution and blood and fury in the world. Do not regret the holocausts of Moloch. You shall have holocausts of Jews."

He answered in amazement: "I? What do I care about any of them, Raposo? They pass and I remain."

Thus carelessly conversing with Satan, I found myself in the Campo de Sant'Anna; and while he was disentangling his horns from the branches of one of the trees, I heard a yell: "See Theodorico with the Swine-Devil." I turned round. It was Auntie. And Auntie, livid, terrible, raised her prayer-book to beat me with.

Aside from the accurate shudder of the prophecy—"You shall have holocausts of Jews"—this alerts us to the true horror of Auntie; she herself is a devil, employing her prayer-book as a cudgel.

In his Jerusalem hotel Teodorico safely bestows his relic, Mary of York's scented night-dress, in a mahogany wardrobe, "which I opened as one opens a reliquary to place in it my sacred parcel." He then descends to the boredom of the hotel dining room, to be enchanted by a large-limbed gold beauty, Miss Ruby of Switzerland. But first he proceeds to the Church of

the Holy Sepulchre to find it guarded by Muslim soldiers, for reasons explained by Potte, his boisterous Montenegrin guide:

> But the festive Potte explained to me that those serious men
> smoking their pipes were Mussulman soldiers guarding the Christian
> altars to prevent the rival priests who celebrate their rival rites there
> from coming to blows round the mausoleum of Jesus: Catholics like
> Padre Pinheiro, orthodox Greeks for whom the cross has four arms.
> Abyssinians and Armenians, Copts descended from those who of yore
> worshipped Apis the bull at Memphis, Nestorians who come from
> Chaldea, Georgians who come from the Caspian Sea, Maronites who
> come from Lebanon, all Christians, all ferociously intolerant. Then I
> saluted in gratitude those soldiers of Mahomet who, in order to pre-
> serve peace and quiet round the dead Christ, keep armed watch,
> serenely smoking at the door.

Soon enough, our tireless quester is spying upon Ruby in her bath, only
to be caught and kicked by her father. An unsuccessful visit to a deceptive
bordello heightens the pilgrim's unhappiness, which is not dispelled by a
somber ride to the Jordan. Here he confronts the Tree of Thorns, from
which the mocking crown of Jesus was reft. From it, at the advice of Topsius, he cuts a bough, to be his dread Auntie's sacred relic. But though he
goes to sleep happily, he dreams a great and disturbing dream. With Topsius, he departs for Roman-occupied Jerusalem, where he sensibly wishes to
sojourn with a Babylonian prostitute, but is dragged off by Topsius to the
ordeal of Jesus of Nazareth:

> It did not occur to me that that spare dark man was the Redeemer
> of mankind. I became strangely anterior in time. I was no longer
> Theodorico Raposo, a Christian Bachelor of Law; my identity had
> fallen from me like a cloak as we hurried from the house of Gamaliel.
> The antiquity of the things around me had infused into me a new
> being, and I too had become one of the ancients. I was Theodoricus,
> a Lusitanian, who had come from the sounding shores of the Great
> Promontory and was travelling in the reign of Tiberius through lands
> tributary to Rome. And the man before me was not Jesus Christ nor
> the Messiah, but a young man of Galilee who, filled with a great
> dream, had come down from his green village to transform the world
> and renew the kingdom of heaven; and an elder of the Temple had
> bound him and sent him to the Praetor on an audience day, between

a thief who had robbed on the Sichem road and another who had used his knife in a quarrel at Emath.

In a space paved with mosaics, in front of the Praetor's curule chair under the Roman Wolf, stood Jesus with His hands crossed and lightly bound by a cord which fell to the ground. An ample cloak of coarse wool, striped in brown and edged with a fringe of blue, fell to His feet and He wore sandals worn by the ways of the desert and tied with thongs of leather. His brow was not pierced by that inhuman crown of thorns of which I had read in the Gospels; it was covered with a white turban formed of a long roll of linen, the ends of which fell over either shoulder; he was bound by a cord under his pointed curly beard. His unanointed hair, brushed back behind his ears, fell in curls on his back; and in his thick sunburnt face, under the long continuous line of the thick eyebrows, his black eyes gleamed with infinite depth and splendour. He did not move, but stood strong and calm before the Praetor. Only a tremor of His bound hands betrayed the tumult of His heart, and at times He drew a deep breath as though His breast, accustomed to the clear free air of the hills and lakes of Galilee, was stifled among those marbles, under that heavy Roman awning and by the narrow formalism of the law.

This is a humane and humanistic Jesus, but neither God nor God's Son. The wanton Teodorico merges into the skeptic Eça, as we watch and hear the familiar Gospel scene of Pilate, under pressure from the Israelite hierarchy, considering the fate of Jesus. After further phantasmagorias, Teodorico beholds Jesus dying on the cross. Further adventures follow, and the Portuguese playboy joins those who have rescued Jesus *alive* from the cross, and placed him in safety, and so the extraordinary dream ends.

After that, Palestine weighs upon our fortune-hunter, who carefully prepares his crown of thorns and lesser relics for the fetish-loving Auntie. But fate (or Providence) pursues Teodorico; absentmindedly he leaves behind the packet of Mary's night-dress, but the inconvenient object follows him through the streets of Jerusalem, and will accompany him back to Portugal. The dangerous parcel, he thinks, is thrown to a weeping woman, but we suspect already that he has flung away his crown of thorns.

And so we come at last to Eça's tragicomic epiphany, as nephew and aunt reunite to view the sacred relic. Here is the sublime moment of the unwrapping:

"Oh, what a scent; oh, I shall die," sighed Auntie, overcome with devout joy, the whites of her eyes showing above her dark spectacles.

"It is for my dear Aunt and for her only, owing to her great virtue, to unwrap the parcel."

Awaking from her languor, pale and trembling, but with the gravity of a high priest, Auntie took the parcel, made obeisance to the saints, and placed it on the altar. Then devoutly she untied the knot of red string, and carefully, as one anxious not to injure a body which was divine, she undid one by one the folds of the brown paper. A whiteness of linen appeared. Auntie held it in her finger-tips and suddenly shook it, and on to the altar, among the saints, over the camellias, at the foot of the cross fell in its ribands and laces Mary's night-dress. Mary's night-dress! In all its shameless luxury. Fold on fold. And pinned upon it, clear in the light of the candles, was the paper offering it to me in a round hand: "To my Theodorico, my valiant little Portuguese, in memory of our past joy." Two initials signed it: M. M. I scarcely know what happened in the flowered oratory. I found myself all in a swoon in the green curtain, with my legs hanging down. Crackling like logs thrown into a furnace I could hear the accusations hurled against me by Padre Negrao into Auntie's ear: "Dissolute ways. A mockery. The night-dress of a prostitute. An insult to Dona Patrocinio." A profanation of the oratory. I saw his boot furiously propelling the white rag into the passage. I saw my friends pass out one by one like long shadows in a raging wind. The wicks of the candles flickered in affliction. And, bathed in sweat amid the folds of the curtain, I saw Auntie coming towards me, slow and stiff, livid, frightful. She paused. Her cold ferocious spectacles went through me; and through clenched teeth she uttered but one word: "Swine," and went out.

After this delicious catastrophe, Teodorico is expelled from Auntie's house, never to return. A lesser scamp would have been obliterated, but our man could say, with Shakespeare's Parolles, in *All's Well That Ends Well,* "Simply the thing I am / Shall make me live." He cheerfully sells off his minor Holy Land relics. For a time he prospers, but then Catholic Portugal is flooded with his offerings, and business falls off. In another epiphany, too dark for comedy, Teodorico is confronted by the god Conscience, and at last acknowledges his own hypocrisy. He makes an honest marriage, to the squint-eyed but amiable and well-dowried Doña Jesnina, and leads a worthy and prosperous life. Let us praise him for his vision of the final epiphany, which even his audacity had not been sufficient to carry off:

Yes, when in place of the martyr's crown appeared the wicked night-dress, I should have shouted without blenching: "This is the relic. I wished it to be a surprise. It is not the Crown of Thorns. It is better still. It is the night-dress of St. Mary Magdalene. She gave it to me in the desert." And I would prove my assertion by means of the paper written in so clear a hand: "To my valiant little Portuguese, in memory of our past joy." It was the letter which the saint had written when she gave me the night-dress. There were her initials M. M., and there was the convincing confession: Our past joy, the great joy that I had experienced when the saint wafted my prayers to heaven and the great joy of the saint in receiving my prayers.

And who would dare to doubt it? Do not the holy missionaries of Braga in their sermons display notes from the Virgin, sent down from heaven without a stamp? And does not the *Nacao* guarantee the divine authenticity of these notes, which preserve in their folds a scent of Paradise? The two priests, Pinheiro and Negrao, aware of their duty and their natural eagerness to prop up a tottering faith, would at once acclaim in the night-dress, the letter and the initials a miraculous triumph of the Church. Aunt Patrocinio would have fallen upon my breast, calling me her son and heir. And I would have been rich. And holy. My portrait would have hung in the sacristy of the Cathedral; the Pope would have sent me his apostolic blessing telegraph. Thus my social ambitions would have been satisfied.

The fantasia continues magnificently as Eça's own imagination takes flight, in a final paragraph that is his apotheosis as a writer:

Thus cherished by the Church, admired by the universities, with my corner assured to me in eternal blessedness and likewise a page in history, I could peacefully grow fat on the fortune of G. Godinho. And all that I had lost. Why? Because for an instant I had lacked that shameless heroism of affirmation which stamps its foot vigorously on the earth or gently raises its eyes to heaven, and amid the universal illusion founds new sciences and religions.

This is a prophecy of James Thurber's "The Secret Life of Walter Mitty," and has its own splendor. I love in particular, "Renan, the sentimental heresiarch, would refer to his dear colleague Raposo." In an ecstasy of creative delirium, Eça is transported by the delight of having transcended his own limitations in having brought his outrageous comic romance to its true conclusion. Teodorico, marvelous wastrel, has realized his own failing: he had lacked only that "shameless heroism of affirmation" that allowed Joseph Smith to found Mormonism or Alfred Jarry to found Pataphysics: "*the* science, which we have only just invented and for which there is a crying need."

One hails Eça de Queiroz, to give him his true name, as a master who in *The Relic* has done the improbable. He has united Voltaire and Robert Louis Stevenson in a single body, and given us a genial romance that is also a superb satire, a unique literary triumph.

JOAQUIM MARIA MACHADO DE ASSIS

CVII
A Note

"Nothing happened, but he suspects something. He's very serious and not talking. He just went out. He smiled only once, at Nhonhô, after staring at him for a long time, frowning. He didn't treat me either badly or well. I don't know what's going to happen. God willing, this will pass. Be very cautious for now, very cautious."

CVIII
Perhaps Not Understood

There's the drama, there's the tip of Shakespeare's tragic ear. That little scrap of paper, scribbled on in art, crumpled by hands, was a document for analysis, which I'm not going to do in this chapter, or in the next, or perhaps in all the rest of the book. Could I rob the reader of the pleasure of noting for himself the coldness, the perspicacity, and the spirit of those few lines jotted down in haste and, behind them, the storm of a different brain, the concealed rage, the despair that brings on constraint and meditation, because it must be resolved in the mud, in blood, or in tears?

As for me, if I tell you that I read the note three or four times that day, believe it, because it's the truth. If I tell you, further, that I reread it the next day, before and after breakfast, you can believe it; it's the naked truth. But if I tell you the upset I had, you might doubt that assertion a bit and not accept it without proof. Neither then nor even now have I been able to make out what I felt. It was fear and it wasn't fear. It was pity and it wasn't pity. It was vanity and it wasn't vanity. In the end, it was love without love, that is, without delirium, and all that made for a rather complex and vague combination, something that you probably don't understand, as I didn't understand it. Let's just suppose that I didn't say anything.

(translated by Harriet De Onís)

Brás Cubas, in his *Posthumous Memoirs,* receives a note from his married mistress that her husband *may* know the truth, and proceeds to ponder his own lack of coherent reaction. Machado de Assis, Laurence Sterne's foremost disciple in the New World, writes his masterpiece in 1880, in a slave-holding Brazil, he himself the grandson of freed slaves. But Machado, an ironist of genius, never attacks his society directly, and works against it with sly comedy and a withering nihilism. His Brás Cubas is superbly alienated and marvelously likable: he never suffers, and so we never suffer with him. And yet an uncanny coolness rises up from his *Posthumous Memoirs,* an atmosphere so original that I can compare it to no other fiction whatsoever, despite its initial debt to Sterne.

Machado's true subject is our common mortality, hardly the subject for a shrug and a jest, and provocative in *The Posthumous Memoirs of Brás Cubas* of a perspective at once detached and hilarious.

The genius of irony has given us few equals of the African-Brazilian Machado de Assis, who seems to me the supreme black literary artist to date. Machado would have shrugged that away as another Shandean joke.

JOAQUIM MARIA MACHADO DE ASSIS
(1839–1908)

THIS MOST REFRESHING OF BRAZILIAN novelists once was represented only by inadequate translations, an unhappy situation now fully remedied by Gregory Rabassa in his eloquent versions of *The Posthumous Memoirs of Brás Cubas* (1997) and *Quincas Borba* (1998), and by John Gledson's equally fine *Don Casmurro* (1997). Machado de Assis is a great ironist, in the mode of his favorite novel, Laurence Sterne's *The Life and Opinions of Tristram Shandy* (1759–67). *Tristram Shandy* has influenced a cavalcade of novelists, from Goethe and Diderot through Balzac and Dickens on to Thomas Mann, James Joyce, and Samuel Beckett. In the twentieth century, Sterne has been probably the major English precursor of the Hispanic-American novelists. Machado de Assis, who wrote his principal novels in the 1880s and '90s, is closer to Sterne in spirit than anyone else has been, even the Dickens of *The Pickwick Papers*. Sterne died in 1768; a century later his ghost or daemon, let us say his genius, drifted across the water (like Maupassant's Horla) and possessed Machado. This is not to deny originality and creative zest to the Brazilian master, but only to remark that Sterne's spirit freed Machado from any merely nationalistic demands that his Brazil might have hoped to impose upon him.

Machado de Assis is a kind of miracle, another demonstration of the autonomy of literary genius in regard to time and place, politics and religion, and all those other contextualizations that falsely are believed to overdetermine human gifts. I had read and fallen in love with his work, *The Posthumous Memoirs of Brás Cubas* in particular, before I learned that Machado was a mulatto, and the grandson of slaves, and this in a Brazil where slavery was not abolished until 1888, when he was almost fifty. Reading Alejo Carpentier, I first wrongly assumed that he was what we call "black." Reading Machado de Assis, I first wrongly assumed that he was what we call "white" (but which E. M. Forster charmingly called "pinko-grey"). Carpentier, in *The Kingdom of This World*, writes from what we now regard as a black perspective. Machado, in *Posthumous Memoirs*, ironically adopts a rather decadent Portuguese-Brazilian white perspective.

Laurence Sterne's mode of satire owes much to Jonathan Swift and Alexander Pope, but with a gentle difference that renders Sterne unique.

As narrative, the Shandean mode is original: madly digressive (perhaps with a bow to Swift's *Tale of a Tub*) but also endlessly inventive. Yorick, Sterne's alter ego, dies but returns a few times after his death, resurrections that inspired Machado de Assis to allow Brás Cubas his posthumously composed memoirs. Sterne begins with the moment of Tristram Shandy's conception; Machado starts out with sly flair:

> For some time I debated over whether I should start these memoirs at the beginning or the end, that is, whether I should put my birth or my death in first place. Since common usage would call for beginning with birth, two considerations led me to adopt a different method: the first is that I am not exactly a writer who is dead but a dead man who is a writer, for whom the grave was a second cradle; the second is that the writing would be more distinctive and novel in that way. Moses, who also wrote about his death, didn't place it at the opening but at the close: a radical difference between this book and the Pentateuch.
>
> With that said, I expired at two o'clock on a Friday afternoon in the month of August, 1869, at my beautiful suburban place in Catumbi. I was sixty-four intense and prosperous years old, I was a bachelor, I had wealth of around three hundred *contos*, and I was accompanied to the cemetery by eleven friends. Eleven friends! The fact is, there hadn't been any cards or announcements. On top of that it was raining—drizzling—a thin, sad, constant rain, so constant and so sad that it led one of those last-minute faithful friends to insert this ingenious idea into the speech he was making at the edge of my grave: "You who knew him, gentlemen, can say with me that nature appears to be weeping over the irreparable loss of one of the finest characters humanity has been honored with. This somber air, these drops from heaven, those dark clouds that cover the blue like funeral crepe, all of it is the cruel and terrible grief that gnaws at my deepest insides; all that is sublime praise for our illustrious deceased."
>
> (translated by Gregory Rabassa)

Brás Cubas, noting that Moses as putative author of the Torah described his own death at the end, reverses the scriptural procedure. The whole of his narrative is written from the perspective of eternity, about which Machado tells us absolutely nothing, thus implying that there is nothing to tell. A skeptical ironist who plays with the possibility of madness—but only as Cervantes, Swift, and Sterne do—Machado is beyond belief, though hardly beyond a belief in the European literary tradition.

Don Casmurro is as subtle and beautiful a fiction as *Brás Cubas,* but captivates me less, perhaps because it is not as joyful a Shandean work. Brás Cubas, unlike Bento Santiago (nicknamed "Don Casmurro," the quiet, aristocratic person who withdraws from others), would not believe that life is an opera composed by Satan. Still, a choice between *Brás Cubas* and *Don Casmurro* is between greatnesses, whereas the very interesting *Quincas Borba* I find uneven, partly because it is narrated in the third person, which is not Machado's mode. He needs the protagonist as his speaker, in order to keep the reader perpetually off balance, where we are happiest.

The dedication of *The Posthumous Memoirs of Brás Cubas* I find too grisly to quote, and is a poor indication of the book's tone. Though Machado says of Brás Cubas that he had put a few fretful touches of pessimism into his *Memoirs,* the book's ironies are quite gentle, Sternean and not Swiftian, except that Machado has no residuum of Christian faith. The skepticism of Brás Cubas is pragmatically a nihilism, in which all of reality, eros included, falls away to nothingness. Here is Brás Cubas, attempting to hold on to the love of his life, Virgília, with whom he has an adulterous relationship:

Whatever it was, everything had been explained, but not forgiven, much less forgotten. Virgília had some harsh things to say to me, threatened me with separation, and ended up praising her husband. There, yes, you had a worthy man quite superior to me, charming, a model of courtesy and affection. That's what she said while I, sitting with my hands on my knees, looked at the floor, where a fly was dragging an ant that was biting its leg. Poor fly! Poor ant!

"But, haven't you got anything to say?" Virgília asked, standing over me.

"What is there for me to say? I've explained everything. You persist in getting angry. What is there for me to say? Do you know what I think? I think you're tired, that you're bored, that you want to stop . . ."

"Exactly!"

She put on her hat, her hand trembling, enraged . . . "Goodbye, Dona Plácida," she shouted to the back. Then she went to the door. She was going to leave. I grabbed her by the waist. "It's all right, it's all right," I said to her. Virgília still struggled to leave. I held her back, asked her to stay, to forget about it. She came away from the door and sat down on the settee. I sat down beside her, told her a lot of loving things, some humble, some funny. I'm not sure whether our lips got as close as a cambric thread or even closer. That's a matter of dispute. I do remember that in the agitation one of Virgília's earrings had fallen off and I leaned over to pick it up and that the fly of a little while back had climbed onto the earring still carrying the ant on its leg. Then I, with the inborn delicacy of a man of our century, took that pair of mortified creatures into the palm of my hand. I calculated the distance between my hand and the planet Saturn and asked myself what interest there could be in such a wretched episode. If you conclude from it that I was a Barbarian, you're wrong, because I asked Virgília for a hairpin in order to separate the two insects. But the fly guessed my intention, opened its wings, and flew off. Poor fly! Poor ant. And God saw that it was good, as Scripture says.

This is from chapter 103, accurately entitled "Distraction" (though the book is just two hundred pages, it has one hundred and sixty chapters). As a major crisis in illicit eros, it resolves itself through Brás Cubas's charming (and daft) concern for the fly and the ant. Machado's art triumphs in the juxtaposition of "the inborn delicacy of a man of our century" and "God saw that it was good." The reader cannot linger over this, because in the very next chapter there is a surprise visitation by Virgília's husband, compelling Brás Cubas to hide himself in the bedroom. Safely out of this moment, Brás Cubas receives a note from Virgília, reporting her husband's suspicion, and reacts with a superb sentence: "There's the drama, there's the tip of Shakespeare's ear." But the full ear we never see, Machado not being a tragedian. We receive instead, for the novel's remainder, the philosophy of Quincas Borba, watch-stealing friend of Brás Cubas. This is Humanitism, "a philosophical system destined to be the ruination of all others."

Quincas Borba is insane, or getting there, and it is never lucidly explained to me exactly what Humanitism precisely teaches. In the meantime, the passionate affair with Virgília ends, Brás Cubas turns fifty, and delivers a major address to the Brazilian parliament, advocating a reduction in size of the National Guard's shakos. We near the void: Quincas Borba turns unmistakably mad, various girlfriends of Brás Cubas's youth come to bad ends, and suddenly he is on his deathbed, with Virgília paying a farewell visit. He dies without complaint or remorse, and with a sense of being ahead of the game, as he explains in the novel's final sentence:

Because on arriving at this other side of the mystery I found myself with a small balance which is the final negative in this chapter of negatives—I had no children, I haven't transmitted the legacy of our misery to any creature.

There has not been much misery in the *Posthumous Memoirs,* and the reader again may be a little surprised. The book is comic, adroit, evasive, and a joy to read, from sentence to sentence. Machado's genius negates all pathos, while gently subverting all supposed values, morals, principles. It is as though Laurence Sterne had slipped away from Christianity, exchanged the absurdities of eighteenth-century British monarchy for the comic-opera inanities of nineteenth-century Brazilian empire (complete with black slavery, to temper the irreality).

It is remarkable that, throughout the novel, Machado modulates his astonishingly lucid and untroubled tonality without ever violating its consistency. The exquisite nihilism of the book is not Shandean, and manifests a superbly original stance and perspective. I read it and simultaneously I am profoundly diverted, yet also chilled. Here is Brás Cubas, at fifty, saying farewell to eros, in chapter 135, properly titled "Oblivion":

And now I have the feeling that if some lady has followed along these pages she closes the book and doesn't read the rest. For her, the interest in my love, which was love, has died out. Fifty years old! It isn't invalidism yet, but it's no longer sprightliness. With ten more years I'll understand what an Englishman once said, I'll understand that "it's a matter of not finding anyone who remembers my parents and the way in which I must face my own OBLIVION."

Put that in small caps. OBLIVION! It's only proper that all honor be paid to a personage so despised and so worthy, a last-minute guest at the party, but a sure one. The lady who dazzled at the dawn of the present reign knows it and, even more painfully, the one who displayed her charms in bloom during the Paraná ministry, because the latter is closer to triumph and she is already beginning to feel that others have taken her carriage. So if she's true to herself she won't persist in a dead or expiring memory. She won't seek in the looks of today the same greeting as in yesterday's looks, when it was others who took part in the march of life with a merry heart and a swift foot. *Tempora mutantur.* She understands that this whirlwind is like that, it carries off the leaves of the forest and the rags of the road without exception or mercy. And if she has a touch of philosophy she won't envy but will feel sorry for the ones who have taken her carriage because they, too, will be helped down by the footman OBLIVION. A spectacle whose purpose is to amuse the planet Saturn, which is quite bored with it.

Unlike Saturn, I am amused but not bored, knowing I too soon must face my own OBLIVION. The genius of Machado de Assis is to keep hold of his reader, address him frequently and directly, while avoiding mere "realism" (which is never realistic). *The Posthumous Memoirs of Brás Cubas*, written from the grave, almost uniquely renders oblivion entertaining.

JORGE LUIS BORGES

There are two observations that I wish to add: one, with regard to the nature of the Aleph; the other, with respect to its name. Let me begin with the latter: "aleph," as we all know, is the name of the first letter of the alphabet of the sacred language. Its application to the disk of my tale would not appear to be accidental. In the Kabbala, that letter signifies the En Soph, the pure and unlimited godhead; it has also been said that its shape is that of a man pointing to the sky and the earth, to indicate that the lower world is the map and mirror of the higher. For the *Mengenlehre*, the aleph is the symbol of the transfinite numbers, in which the whole is not greater than any of its parts. I would like to know: Did Carlos Argentino choose that name, or did he read it, *applied to another point at which all points converge,* in one of the innumerable texts revealed to him by the Aleph in his house? Incredible as it may seem, I believe that there is (or was) another Aleph; I believe that the Aleph of Calle Garay was a *false* Aleph.

Carlos Argentino Daneri is a palpable satire upon the Stalinist Chilean poet Pablo Neruda, but the Aleph—true or false—is high Kabbalistic fantasy, and vital to Borges's genius. Borges, a highly self-conscious Gnostic in his storytelling art, affirmed his enthusiasm for the doctrine of the Gnostic heresiarch Basilides (second century C.E.): "What greater glory for a God, than to be absolved of the world?" The Gnostic alien or stranger God, exiled from this cosmos, created neither it nor ourselves. In Borges's story "Tlön, Uqbar, Orbis Tertius," a Gnostic sage of Uqbar is quoted as having said that "mirrors and fatherhood are abominable because they multiply and disseminate [the] universe."

Borges observed of his first story, "Pierre Menard, Author of the *Quixote*," that it is exhausted and skeptical, because it comes "at the end of a very long literary period." The fictive Menard, a parody of a French Modernist man of letters, reproduces *Don Quixote* word for word, but asserts his triumph over Cervantes, since Menard's *Quixote* is centuries belated, and so reverberates more powerfully.

The ironies of Borges, for me, achieve their apotheosis in "Death and the Compass," an overtly Kabbalistic story where Red Scharlach the Dandy, an Argentine Jewish gangster-lord who resembles Isaac Babel's Benya Krik, traps the detective Erik Lönnrot in an Aleph-like labyrinth of false clues. Before executing Lönnrot, who dryly critiques the labyrinth's redundant lines, Scharlach proclaims, "The next time I kill you, I promise you that labyrinth, consisting of a single line which is invisible and unceasing."

Like Shelley, but in a lighter spirit, Borges came to see all great literature as a single cyclic, storytelling poem, written and rewritten throughout the centuries. I have never recovered from the initial wound I received when first reading Borges's fictions some forty years ago, but it seems always to be the same wound. Borges would not regard that as his limitation, but Shakespeare wounds us a thousand different ways.

JORGE LUIS BORGES
(1899–1986)

THE FAME OF BORGES IS FOUNDED ON HIS fictions, the finest of which generally do not exceed a dozen to fifteen pages in length. A considerable poet as well, Borges nevertheless has to be regarded primarily as an essayist of genius, in the modes of his most authentic precursors, the English Romantic critic Thomas De Quincey (1785–1859) and the twentieth-century English intellectual roustabout and person of letters Gilbert Keith Chesterton (1874–1936). Here I will center mostly upon Borges's nonfictions, having commented elsewhere upon his stories that greatly move me: "Tlön, Uqbar, Orbis Tertius," "Death and the Compass," "The Immortal," "The Theologians," and "The Aleph."

Like the Portuguese poet Fernando Pessoa, Borges grew up speaking and reading English, and is reported to have read Cervantes in English before absorbing the original. There was for Borges, from the start, little distinction between reading as a kind of rewriting, and writing itself. Though his biographer, Emir Rodriguez Monegal, accurately associated Borges with the writers (Rabelais, Cervantes, Laurence Sterne) who overtly make their readers into co-authors, I think De Quincey—in whom reading, plagiarism, and rewriting rarely can be distinguished—gave the young Borges the initial impetus towards mixing parody, translation, dreams and nightmares, and literary criticism into the "nonfictions" we now call Borgesian.

De Quincey, who led an improvident and sorrowful life, habituated to opium, earned his living as a journalist and miscellaneous writer, and covered a vast mass of subjects: metaphysics, history, politics, literature, linguistics. It was in De Quincey that Borges first found one of his cardinal principles, that language organizes and rewrites the cosmos:

> Even the articulate or brutal sounds of the globe must be all so many languages and ciphers that somewhere have their corresponding keys—have their own grammar and syntax; and thus the least things in the universe must be secret mirrors of the greatest.

Mirrors, like labyrinths and compasses, famously abound in Borges: they are answering metaphors to the riddle of the Theban Sphinx: what is Man?

From De Quincey, Borges had learned that Oedipus himself, and not man in general, was the profound solution to the riddle. Blind Oedipus, Homer, Joyce, Milton, Borges: they form a five-in-one. Borges's mother died at ninety-nine, after many devoted years as her son's secretary. Urbane, ironic, beautifully mannered, Borges loses his composure only when Freud is mentioned to him. Let us honor Borges by attaching to him Oedipus the man rather than the complex. The genius of Borges, particularly his nonfictions, is to exemplify what is man: the subject and object of his own quest. Borges remarked of his debt to De Quincey that it was "so vast that to point out only one part of it may appear to repudiate or silence the others."

One lesson Borges learned from De Quincey was to abhor all historicisms, including those that would explain away the individuality of genius. History, Borges quotes De Quincey as writing, is a highly indefinite discipline, subject to infinite interpretations. That includes necessarily the history of culture, and the late Michel Foucault's pernicious historicism, which has destroyed humanistic study in the English-speaking world. I offer Borges, and through him imaginative literature itself, as an antidote to Foucault and his resentful followers. Borges—who stood courageously against Argentine Fascism and anti-Semitism—always urges us away from ideology and towards Shakespeare.

In a sense, Borges wrote no major essays; nearly everything, like the stories, is quite short. Two rare exceptions are "A History of Eternity" (1936), which condenses eternity into sixteen pages, and "A New Refutation of Time" (1944–47), which needs only fifteen. These are both grand performances, but have meant less to me than many brief fragments and squibs, generally of three or four pages. In particular, there is the two-and-a-half-page "Kafka and His Precursors" (1951), with its crucial sentence: "The fact is that each writer *creates* his precursors." A fierce literary idealist, Borges thought that polemic and rivalry had no part in the drama of influence, which I believe is not so. And yet Borges may be almost a unique instance, since his crucial ancestors wrote in English and German, and he in Spanish. De Quincey, Chesterton, Sir Thomas Browne, the inescapable Edgar Poe, Robert Louis Stevenson, Walt Whitman, and Kafka affected Borges's work more strongly than did Cervantes and Quevedo. Borges's precursors (as he warns us) are innumerable: his poems echo Robert Browning's only less intensely than they do Whitman's, and Unamuno sometimes seems to me closest among Spanish writers. A Borgesian labyrinth beckons, which I dart out of, since it is from Borges one learns that Shakespeare was everyone and no one, so that Shakespeare himself is the living labyrinth of literature.

Borges has an extraordinary two-page story about Shakespeare, "Everything and Nothing," with that English phrase serving as the title in the original Spanish printing. Borges's Shakespeare—whose Iago invented European nihilism—is himself pragmatically the first nihilist, convinced that "There was no one inside him." This feeling of hollowness takes him to his career as an actor, and then as dramatist:

> Haunted, hounded, he began imagining other heroes, other tragic fables. Thus while his body, in whorehouses and taverns around London, lived its life as body, the soul that lived inside it would be Caesar, who ignores the admonition of the sibyl, and Juliet, who hates the lark, and Macbeth . . . No one was as many men as that man—that man whose repertoire, like that of the Egyptian Proteus, was all the appearances of being.

After twenty years of inhabiting "that guided and directed hallucination," Shakespeare is overwhelmed by the horror of otherness, and departs for Stratford permanently a "retired businessman." Borges dares a final paragraph, which works, though it touches a limit of representation:

> History adds that before or after he died, he discovered himself standing before God, and said to Him: *I who have been so many men in vain, wish to be* one, *to be myself.* God's voice answered him out of a whirlwind: *I, too, am not I; I dreamed the world as you, Shakespeare, dreamed your own work, and among the forms of my dream are you,* who *like me are many, yet no one.*

The undersong is plangent, reflecting the tragic sense of life that Borges shares with Unamuno, yet the tribute to the miracle of Shakespeare's universalism provides an affirmative force to the pathos. At the close of his career, a quarter-century later, Borges wrote his final fiction, "Shakespeare's Memory." Going on eighty-five, the great fabulist fails his own high standard, and the fiction remains inert. A German professor of Shakespeare improbably is given the equivocal gift of the poet's memory, but nothing not already known is revealed to us before, in distress, he hands Shakespeare's memory on to another. But then the aged Borges gives us a final, sublime moment. After yielding the memory up, the professor repeats "like a wish, these resigned words":

Simply the thing I am shall make me live.

It is the great line defiantly spoken by Parolles, the wordy, braggart soldier, after he has been humiliated and exposed in *All's Well That Ends Well:*

> Yet am I thankful: if my heart were great,
> 'Twould burst at this. Captain I'll be no more;
> But I will eat and drink, and sleep as soft
> As captain shall: simply the thing I am
> Shall make me live. Who knows himself a braggart,
> Let him fear this, for it will come to pass
> That every braggart shall be found an ass.
> Rust, sword! cool, blushes! and, Parolles, live
> Safest in shame! being fool'd, by foolery thrive!
> There's place and means for every man alive.
> I'll after them.

This, in context, makes us shudder, and Borges brilliantly wishes us to
contextualize. We, and Borges, cannot *be* Shakespeare, but simply the thing
we are shall make us live.

ITALO CALVINO

Already the Great Khan was leafing through his atlas, over the maps of the cities that menace in nightmares and maledictions: Enoch, Babylon, Yahooland, Butua, Brave New World.

He said: "It is all useless, if the last landing place can only be the infernal city, and it is there that, in ever-narrowing circles, the current is drawing us."

And Polo said: "The inferno of the living is already here, the inferno where we live every day, that we form by being together. There are two ways to escape suffering it. The first is easy for many: accept the inferno and become such a part of it that you can no longer see it. The second is risky and demands constant vigilance and apprehension: seek and learn to recognize who and what, in the midst of the inferno, are not inferno, then make them endure, give them space."

(translated by William Weaver)

That beautiful injunction is the conclusion of Italo Calvino's *Invisible Cities*, and is the humane legacy of his genius for fantasy. Marco Polo has spent the entire book describing his imaginary journeys to invisible cities, while Kublai Khan listens, until at last the aged emperor realizes that all the cities are one city, and it is at last the city of the damned, the inferno. Marco Polo, speaking for Calvino, offers two alternatives to damnation. The first is to become ourselves so infernal that we can no longer see where we are. The second, though risky and demanding, is an injunction to read better and live better:

> seek and learn to recognize who and what, in the midst of the inferno, are not inferno, then make them endure, give them space.

A superbly comic fabulist, Calvino frequently instructs us by laughter, as he does in *The Non-Existent Knight*. It is a laughter free of scorn, a healing laughter. His invisible cities are potential women, improbable but, more often than not, madly attractive. Perhaps the most disturbing, to me, is Valdrada:

> Valdrada's inhabitants know that each of their actions is, at once, that action and its mirror-image, which possesses the special dignity of images, and this awareness prevents them from succumbing for a single moment to chance and forgetfulness. Even when lovers twist their naked bodies, skin against skin, seeking the position that will give one the most pleasure in the other, even when murderers plunge the knife into the black veins of the neck and more clotted blood pours out the more they press the blade that slips between the tendons, it is not so much their copulating or murdering that matters as the copulating or murdering of the images, limpid and cold in the mirror.

ITALO CALVINO
(1923–1985)

ITALO CALVINO COMPILED AN ANTHOLOGY of *Fantastic Tales* with the subtitle *Visionary and Everyday,* a superb characterization of his own work. His masterpiece is rightly held to be *Invisible Cities* (1972), but as I have discussed that elsewhere, my concern will be the earlier fantasy *The Non-Existent Knight* (1959). I begin, however, with a marvelous obituary in today's *New York Times* (March 25, 2001, page 44, by Douglas Martin) devoted to the life of the president of the International Flat Earth Research Society. The Flat Earthers go back to 1832 but of course assert a longer lineage. They seem to me endearing compared to, say, the Oxfordians, who send me quite vicious letters when I assert that Lucy Negro, the celebrated East Indian whore, has a much better claim to have written Shakespeare's plays than the Earl of Oxford, since she at least slept with Shakespeare.

Flat Earthers, like Oxfordians, literalize their fantasies. As a literary critic, one prescribes Kafka or Borges or Calvino to heal this malady. "An empty suit of armor that persuades itself it is a man and carries on through its own will-power": that is Calvino's brief summary of *The Non-Existent Knight,* a tale of true genius, whose one hundred pages cheer me even on the gloomiest of my days.

Charlemagne reviews his paladins, until he encounters one entirely in white armor, who identifies himself as "Agilulf Emo Bertrandin of the Guildivern and of the Others of Corbentraz and Sura, Knight of Selimpia Citeriore and Fez." I should have written, "which identifies itself," because the armor itself speaks. Charlemagne, old and a little tired, observes that Agilulf, for someone who doesn't exist, seems in fine form, which understates Agilulf's skill and devotion. He is a model soldier, and therefore disliked by all, except the reader, for whom he is a delight, if also a mystery. Calvino disdains any explanation as to how, when, why this armor willed its identity into being, but then I meet suits almost every day, who must have done the same. Unlike those, Agilulf has a personality. He is a kind of better-natured Malvolio, punctilious and overbearing: "attentive, nervy, proud; the bodies of people with bodies gave him a sense of unease not unlike envy, but also a stab of pride, of contemptuous superiority." And yet he has no ill will; he needs all his will to keep going.

A heroic squire, Raimbaud of Roussillon, arrives, determined to avenge his father's death at the hands of the Muslim champion, the Argalif Isohar. The youth's anguish impels Agilulf to comfort him:

> States of confusion or despair or fury in other human beings im-
> mediately gave perfect calm and security to Agilulf. His immunity
> from the shocks and agonies to which people who exist are subject
> made him take on a superior and protective attitude.
>
> (translated by Archibald Colquhoun)

I think that the narrator is being unfair, but we do not learn until a few pages later that not Calvino, but Sister Theodora, nun of the order of Saint Columba, is telling the tale:

> we country girls, however noble, have always led retired lives in re-
> mote castles and convents; apart from religious ceremonies, triduums,
> novenas, gardening, harvesting, vintaging, whippings, slavery, incest,
> fires, hangings, invasions, sacking, rape and pestilence, we have had
> no experience.

Sister Theodora overprotests, and the reader suspects, even before the book's closing revelation, that this storytelling nun actually is the warrior Bradamante, a gorgeous Amazon with whom Raimbaud falls unhappily in love, since she is enamored of the immaculate Agilulf, who is necessarily un-moved by her passion.

But, before all that high romance, we go into battle between Moors and Christians, all shouting insults in a mad variety of languages:

> So interpreters took part in this phase of the battle, light-armed men
> swiftly mounted on fast horses which swiveled around, catching in-
> sults on the wing and translating them there and then into the lan-
> guage of destination.

Calvino, with a bow to Borges, asserts that Robert Louis Stevenson and Voltaire are his precursors, yet I hear Swift in this exuberant inventiveness, worthy of *A Tale of a Tub* or *The Battle of the Books*. Young Raimbaud charges the Argalif Isohar, only to discover that he faces the Argalif's spectacle-bearer, the Moorish hero being nearsighted. Enflamed, Raimbaud shatters the spectacles:

At the same instant, as if the sound of lenses in smithereens had been a sign of his end, Isohar was pierced by a Christian lance.

"Now," said the optician, "he needs no lenses to gaze at the houris in Paradise," and off he spurred.

This equivocal triumph precedes Raimbaud's infatuate first meeting with Bradamante, who (as I have recounted) is hopelessly in love with Agilulf, who has acquired a squire more or less named Gurduloo, who does not know inside from outside, and whose motto is: "all is soup!" Then there is young Torrismund of Cornwall, who confronts poor Agilulf and propels the non-existent knight into a crisis. Agilulf was granted his (or its) knighthood for having saved, fifteen years before, the king of Scotland's virgin daughter Sophronia from rape by brigands. Torrismund, who is twenty, insists that Sophronia is his mother, and that his father is the sacred Order of the Knights of the Holy Grail, taken as a whole. A double quest ensues, with Agilulf in search of Sophronia, and Torrismund of his composite father. But I will go mad if I attempt any more of this plot summary, since Calvino plainly intends the plot to drive us (me) mad:

> for now begin the real ramifications of the plot, Agilulf's and his squire's intrepid journeys for proof of Sophronia's virginity, interwoven with Bradamante's pursuit and flight, Raimbaud's love, and Torrismund's search for the Knights of the Grail. But this thread, instead of running through my fingers, is apt to sag or stick.

And yet it does not sag or stick; the novella's final twenty pages are its triumph. Agilulf is vindicated by finding and again rescuing Sophronia. Torrismund arrives where Agilulf has left her for safekeeping, and he and Sophronia instantly fall in love. They subsequently are exonerated of incest when it is revealed that she is *not* his mother, and we then proceed to Agilulf's apotheosis and self-immolation. He has spent an enchanted night with a beautiful temptress, Priscilla, and charmed her, before departing at dawn, to complete his final mission. We are not told why he abandons his armor and sword in a clearing, with a note: "I leave this armor to Sir Raimbaud of Roussillon." Presumably, erotic frustration has sapped the non-existent knight's extraordinary willpower. The story is soon completed; after some initial resistance, Bradamante is happy with Raimbaud, who goes forth to battle in Agilulf's armor.

Calvino spoke of this novella's themes as being "empty forms and the concrete nature of living, awareness of being in the world and building one's own destiny." That seems to me too wide a vista for the story of Agilulf. By a miracle of Calvino's comic genius, Agilulf metamorphoses from a martinet to a romantic doom-seeker, who dies (if that is the right word) by erotic despair. I hardly would have thought that an achieved pathos could culminate this zany tale. *Invisible Cities* is Calvino's masterpiece, but *The Non-Existent Knight* seems to me his funniest and most endearing work.

LUSTRE 18

|

William Blake, D. H. Lawrence, Tennessee Williams, Rainer Maria Rilke, Eugenio Montale

|

Yesod is the foundation of the passional life, and in its second Lustre I have brought together five visionaries, at once very diverse yet allied by their intensity and their transformative power.

William Blake and D. H. Lawrence were prophetic geniuses, mythmakers concerned to free us from nature's tyranny over us. Though Lawrence is out of favor as we begin a new century, feminist critics are likely to rethink their rejection of his work, if only because his more extreme stances matter little compared to the aesthetic and spiritual power of his best stories, novels, and poems. In a longer perspective, Lawrence will be seen as comparable to Blake.

Tennessee Williams, in his most accomplished plays, remains the only major American dramatist of unquestioned literary quality. Rilke, whatever reservations he can provoke, is one of the handful of twentieth-century European poets who was a persuasive seer, as well as a great artist.

Eugenio Montale fulfilled in himself all the major strains of Italian poetic tradition, from Dante to Leopardi, and was the peer of Valéry and of Rilke.

WILLIAM BLAKE

I have been very near the Gates of Death and have returned very weak and an Old Man feeble and tottering, but not in Spirit and Life not in The Real Man The Imagination which Liveth for Ever. In that I am stronger and stronger as this Foolish Body decays.

That is from a letter Blake wrote on April 12, 1827, four months before his death. After a lifetime of reading and studying Blake, I find he still refreshes me with a continual sense of wonder. The delusion that he was essentially a mystic cannot be dismissed, as I keep discovering. A poet-painter who considered the Bible to be the Great Code of Art, Blake more properly should be regarded as a visionary, akin to Dante, Milton, and Shelley.

"The Real Man The Imagination" is neither mystical nor Promethean: it is a consciousness into which you mature, whether as an artist or as an appreciator of art. Blake ascribes immortality to the Real Man the Imagination, by which he did not mean literal immortality but something very close to the story of Enoch in the Yahwist: "And Enoch walked with God, and he was not, because God took him." Kabbalah (with which Blake was conversant) interpreted this to mean that Enoch, taken up, became the angel Metatron, the Lesser Yahweh. The American Mormons, like the Kabbalists and Hermetists, believe in this transfiguration, and identify their prophet, seer, and revelator—Joseph Smith—with Enoch.

I myself find, as I age in my reverence for Blake, that it seems persuasive for Blake himself to have been another Enoch, and thus resurrected before he died, which is what the ancient Gnostics (like those Paul argued against at Corinth) believed of Jesus: *first* he was resurrected, and *then* he died.

Poetry and painting were, for Blake, prophecy. His poetry is shadowed by Milton, as his painting is haunted by Michelangelo, but his composite art has unique value as a prophecy of the Real Man the Imagination.

WILLIAM BLAKE
(1757–1827)

WHEN I WAS A SMALL BOY, NINE OR TEN, I copied out Blake's longer poems in my notebooks, so that I would have them with me whenever I had to return the perpetually renewed Nonesuch Blake (edited by Geoffrey Keynes) that I kept out of the Melrose branch of the Bronx Public Library. I never emulated Tennessee Williams, who liberated for himself the Washington University (St. Louis) Library copy of my other favorite poet, Hart Crane. Crane's and Blake's poetry were the first books I ever owned, birthday presents from my older sisters. I say this because I cannot begin to discuss the genius of William Blake without recalling that my reverence for Blake goes back sixty years. Doubtless so long a personal attachment precludes (at least for me) historical perspective, but this book is a continuous protest against historicizing and contextualizing the imagination of genius. At the start, I quoted Blake's assertion that genius is always above the age, and I am happy to return to it here.

Blake's genius was multiform: his painting was formidable, though never, I think, of the aesthetic eminence of his poetry. His most important poetry—his "brief epics" or "prophecies"—remains very difficult for the common reader, despite a tradition of distinguished exegesis. That which could be made explicit to the idiot, he snapped, was not worth his care. His conceptual powers were extraordinary; his mind was as powerful and original as Dante's, Shakespeare's, and Milton's, and he frequently concedes less to the careless reader than these precursors are willing to do. Shakespeare, richest of all poets, plays at conceding almost everything, though ultimately his innermost art makes demands at least equal to Dante's or Milton's. Blake, rather like the Joyce of *Finnegans Wake,* wants his reader to yield totally to a highly organized vision, which many regard as eccentric. Joyce, like Shakespeare, is not attempting to provide spiritual salvation for the reader. Blake, like Dante and Milton, attempts no less. The era of T. S. Eliot, who regarded Blake as homemade furniture, is long past, but *The Four Zoas, Milton,* and *Jerusalem*—Blake's principal poems—remain forbidding works to many readers of curiosity and goodwill.

I will use as proof-texts here for Blake's genius crucial passages from *The Four Zoas, Milton,* and *Jerusalem,* rather than the apparently more accessible lyrics of *Songs of Innocence and Experience* and from Blake's Notebook, though I will comment on the luminous quatrains that form the epilogue of *The Gates of Paradise,* a little emblem book that Blake reissued in 1818.

Blake was a heretical Protestant, who carried English Dissent further than John Milton had, though I incline to agree with A. D. Nuttall's estimate that Milton is the bridging figure between the speculations of Christopher Marlowe and Blake's large-scale "system" of extravagant vision. Milton's own work, particularly *Paradise Lost,* is the Mountain of Vision that most of the High Romantics climbed. His influence blended with Shakespeare's and Edmund Spenser's to provide Blake, Wordsworth, Shelley, Coleridge, Keats, and others with a sense that they constituted a renaissance of the English Renaissance.

I myself deprecate the academic fashion of referring to the European Renaissance as Early Modern Europe. Instead, I propose that we go back to the idea of the post-Enlightenment, a large-scale movement that separates Milton (to some degree) from Shakespeare, and then sees literature from Milton to the present as a vast continuity, embracing Pope, Dr. Johnson, Goethe, Blake, Wordsworth, Byron, Pushkin, Stendhal, Victor Hugo, Tolstoy, Emerson, Whitman, Dostoevsky, Balzac, Dickens, Flaubert, Joyce, and Proust, among so many others. Romanticism, so-called Modernism, the even more arbitrary Postmodernism, seem to me only phases of the post-Enlightenment sensibility. Shakespeare, Cervantes, Montaigne are so large that they contain movements yet to come: you never can reach the end of them. They were inwardly rich enough to absorb Western culture with relatively little anxiety. Milton and Goethe, Blake and Tolstoy, were giants of consciousness, but their stances, sometimes aggressive, other times evasive, towards the cultural past, are different in kind from those of Shakespeare, Cervantes, Montaigne.

As this book shows on every page, I am an Emersonian: there is no history, only biography. I have never encountered a social energy, though I have confronted a fair number of social hysterias. I do not know how one can be more enlightened than Shakespeare, or Montaigne. Many scholars assure me that Shakespeare, Cervantes, and Montaigne were believing Christians. I do not believe them. These greatest of post-Dantean writers were secularists, though who would expect them to have said so? In the United States of 2001–2, you cannot be elected dogcatcher if you do not declare your allegiance to a Supreme Being. Socially, in much of the nation, you are more acceptable as a Muslim or a Buddhist or a New Age crystal-rubber than as a declared atheist. That is in fairly direct continuity with much worse things that would have happened had Shakespeare, Montaigne, and Cervantes not conformed. I don't know whether Shakespeare was a secret Catholic or not, but I doubt it. Eros appears pragmatically to have been Shakespeare's God. Montaigne was a politic Catholic, following Henry of Navarre in mediating between Calvinists and Catholics, while Cervantes, had he expressed a few ironies too many, would have encountered the Inquisition. Montaigne's mother, whom he scarcely mentions, came from a family of converted Spanish Jews, and no one is certain whether Cervantes was of Old Christian stock or not. If Milton was a Protestant Christian, it was finally as a sect of one, as was Blake. Goethe was not a Christian, and Tolstoy was a Tolstoyan. Post-Enlightenment literature essentially is post-Christian. The United States, most Christian of nations, is in fact post-Christian, though no one will acknowledge this, including scholars of American religion. I hasten to observe that the United States is the most religious of nations, but how much has the American Religion in common with ancient medieval or modern European Christianity? Institutionally, theologically, culturally, how much of historical Protestantism have we retained? There is an American God, and an American Christ, but who or what are they? Perhaps they are what Blake meant by his "To the Accuser Who Is the God of This World":

> Truly My Satan thou art but a Dunce
> And dost not know the Garment from the Man
> Every Harlot was a Virgin once
> Nor canst Thou change Kate into Nan

> Though thou art Worshipped by the Names Divine
> Of Jesus and Jehovah: Thou art still
> The son of Morn in weary Nights decline
> The lost travelers' Dream under the Hill

Do we worship the Accuser? I don't doubt that Blake, resurrected among us, would think so. Partly Blake means the Accuser of Sin, or superego (if you want that translation) who got Job into trouble. But Blake would be confused by our America, *where God loves us,* according to eighty-nine percent of the population. Blake was a prophet; so was D. H. Lawrence. Who else, in England? How many authentic American prophets have there been? There was Joseph Smith, seer of the Mormons, who was martyred by the Illinois state militia. There was Emerson, whose hatred of the South augmented his rather-too-early senility. We have had prophetic poets, like Whitman and Hart Crane, but though aesthetic splendors they were hardly specific seers. The current Mormon hierarchy pragmatically reduces Joseph Smith to a pious reaffirmer of Christ, but that is absurdly inadequate. Smith, like the ancient Hermetists and certain Kabbalists and Gnostics, sought to end the distinction between the human and the divine, which was also the burden of Blake's strenuous prophecy. Blake advocated free love, but was not in a personal or social situation to realize it. Joseph Smith, in his final phase at Nauvoo, established Plural or Celestial Marriage for an Elite. It prevailed in the theocracy of Brigham Young, and then ended (officially) after John Taylor, who went to prison for it. After Utah became a state, it had a vexed, underground existence, and now divides off the Brighamite heretics from the Mormon Established Church. I need to leave Smith to get back to Blake, but hope to go on juxtaposing them elsewhere in a book on Immortality.

Blake, like Shelley, began as something of a revolutionary activist. Pitt's measures against protestors silenced Blake. Not wishing to be shipped off to Australia, or to an English prison, he confined himself to raging in his Notebooks and in his prophecies. But hiding yourself has its costs, particularly if your genius essentially is prophetic. Prophets do not secretly rage; their mission always has required total honesty. Blake subtly began to distrust political revolution; the Promethean Orc ceased to be the heroic rebel of Blake's poetry, and was replaced by Los, the prophet with a hammer, the poet-engraver locked in very dubious battle with his own Spectre of Urthona, his tendency to self-righteousness.

That in itself is an extraordinary story in Blake. The Spectre of Urthona is a crucial figure in Blake's definitive "brief epic," *Jerusalem, The Emanation of the Giant Albion,* upon which he worked from 1804 on, revising until perhaps 1815, when he began engraving the poem, a process complete by 1820, at the latest. Allegorizing Blake is frequently a dismal project, and need not be attempted here, since my only purpose is to isolate and define Blake's genius. A major aspect of that genius is an originality in detecting and depicting splits in the self. Freud perhaps rivals Blake in such an originality; Whitman, who cannot define anything, is as suggestive but necessarily less precise.

Jerusalem turns upon a severe internal struggle between Blake's prophetic gift, dramatized by Los, and Blake's imaginative despair, voiced by the Spectre of Urthona with frightening pathos:

> But my griefs advance also, for ever & ever without end
> O that I could cease to be! Despair! I am Despair
> Created to be the great example of horror & agony: also my

Prayer is vain I called for compassion: compassion mockd[,]
Mercy & pity threw the grave stone over me & with lead
And iron, bound it over me for ever: Life lives on my
Consuming: & the Almighty hath made me his Contrary
To be all evil, all reversed & for ever dead: knowing
And seeing life, yet living not; how can I then behold
And not tremble; how can I be beheld & not abhorrd

Milton's Satan and Edmund Spenser's Despair are echoed by the Spectre, who on his own terms is absolutely accurate: he expresses Blake's personal situation as outcast prophet, poet, and painter. I shudder, as a reader, when Los hammers the poor Spectre upon the anvil, a sublimely painful image for the strenuous overcoming of depression, the sickness unto death, by the poet-engraver's labor. Anyone who works on, in whatever way, while despairing and desiring only to cease, will find herself or himself in Blake's transcendence of his own agony.

In Blake's *Milton*, the prelude to his *Jerusalem*, a redeemed John Milton casts off an earlier version of the Spectre, "the idiot Questioner," and makes an extraordinary declaration of the freed imagination:

To bathe in the Waters of Life; to wash off the Not Human
I come in Self-annihilation & the grandeur of Inspiration
To cast off Rational Demonstration by Faith in the Savior
To cast off the rotten rags of Memory by Inspiration
To cast off Bacon, Locke & Newton from Albions covering
To take off his filthy garments, & clothe him with Imagination
To cast aside from Poetry, all that is not Inspiration
That it no longer shall dare to mock with the aspersion of Madness
Cast on the Inspired, by the tame high finisher of paltry Blots,
Indefinite, or paltry Rhymes; or paltry Harmonies.
Who creeps into State Government like a catterpiller to destroy
To cast off the idiot Questioner who is always questioning,
But never capable of answering; who sits with a sly grin
Silent plotting when to question, like a thief in a cave;
Who publishes doubt & calls it knowledge; whose Science is Despair,
Whose pretence to knowledge is Envy, whose whole Science is
To destroy the wisdom of ages to gratify ravenous Envy;
That rages round him like a Wolf day & night without rest
He smiles with condescension; he talks of Benevolence & Virtue
And those who act with Benevolence & Virtue, they murder time on time

These are the destroyers of Jerusalem, these are the murderers
Of Jesus, who deny the Faith & mock at Eternal Life!
Who pretend to Poetry that they may destroy Imagination;
By imitation of Natures Images drawn from Remembrance
These are the Sexual Garments, the Abomination of Desolation
Hiding the Human Lineaments as with an Ark & Curtains
Which Jesus rent; & now shall wholly purge away with Fire
Till Generation is swallowd up in Regeneration.

The imagery of removing false garments goes on through all of *Milton*, and goes back to a pattern of such images in Shakespeare's *Macbeth*. The idiot Questioner inhabits each of us, as the Spectre does, and pragmatically can be regarded, as the polar opposite to Emerson's Self-Reliance, or to Blake's Fourfold Vision. These bad days, Blake is badly misunderstood when he speaks of "Sexual Garments" or "Female Love," as he is both an apostle of human sexuality and nothing of a misogynist. "Sexual," "Female," "Male" for him all fall short of the liberated human eros, and Blake's Jesus comes to destroy all Mystery, all concealment. Blake, an independent Gnostic, who had created his own mythic "system," might go over to the Spectre of Urthona again if, in Eternity, he came to know how weakly he is misread by the current covens of the culturally correct.

What drives Blake's epics onward is their furious rhetorical energy, which should carry the reader through initial difficulties to an authentic moment of self-recognition. Like Victor Hugo and Nietzsche, Blake crosses into the dithyrambic, as here in the extraordinary opening of "Night the Ninth, Being the Last Judgment" in his epic *The Four Zoas:*

And Los & Enitharmom builded Jerusalem weeping
Over the Sepulcher & over the Crucified body
Which to their Phantom Eyes appear'd still in the Sepulcher
But Jesus stood beside them in the Spirit Separating
Their Spirit from their body. Terrified at Non Existence
For such they deemd the death of the body. Los his vegetable hands
Outstretchd his right hand branching out in fibrous Strength
Seized the Sun. His left hand like dark roots coverd the Moon
And tore them down cracking the heavens across from immense to immense
Then fell the fires of Eternity with loud & shrill
Sound of Loud Trumpet thundering along from heaven to heaven
A mighty sound articulate Awake ye dead & come
To Judgment from the four winds Awake & Come away

Folding like scrolls of the Enormous volume of Heaven & Earth
With thunderous noise & dreadful shakings rocking to & fro
The heavens are shaken & the Earth removed from its place
The foundations of the Eternal hills discoverd
The thrones of Kings are shaken they have lost their robes & crowns
The poor smite their oppressors they awake up to the harvest
The naked warriors rush together down to the sea shore
Trembling before the multitudes of slaves now set at liberty
They are become like wintry flocks like forests stripd of leaves
The opressed pursue like the wind there is no room for escape
The Spectre of Enitharmon let loose on the troubled deep
Waild shrill in the confusion & the Spectre of Urthona
Recievd her in the darkning South their bodies lost they stood
Trembling & weak a faint embrace a fierce desire as when
Two shadows mingle on a wall they wail & shadowy tears
Fell down & shadowy forms of joy mixed with despair & grief
Their bodies buried in the ruins of the Universe
Mingled with the confusion. Who shall call them from the Grave

It is difficult to find the equivalent of this strenuous eloquence in more than a double handful of other literary works. "And tore them down cracking the heavens across from immense to immense" is, in and out of context, an astonishing line. Even more remarkable is the despairing reunion of the Spectres: "their bodies lost they stood / Trembling & weak a faint embrace a fierce desire as when / Two shadows mingle on a wall." Most of us recall our own equivalents of erotic waning, but Blake phrases his apocalyptic version with inevitability.

Blake's Vision (for him, the central term) and his power of conceptual metaphor are crucial elements in his gift, yet after a lifetime's reading of his work, I would locate his genius elsewhere. William Butler Yeats once spoke of Blake's "beautiful, laughing speech," and there is an exuberance in Blake's writing so individual as to constitute its own kind of beauty:

The Last Judgment is an Overwhelming of Bad Art & Science. Mental Things are alone Real; what is call'd Corporeal, Nobody Knows of its Dwelling Place: it is in Fallacy, & its Existence an Imposture. Where is the Existence Out of Mind or Thought? Where is it but in the Mind of a Fool? Some People flatter themselves that there will be No Last Judgment & that Bad Art will be adopted & mixed with

Good Art, That Error or Experiment will make a Part of Truth, & they
Boast that it is its Foundation; these People flatter themselves: I will
not Flatter them. Error is Created. Truth is Eternal. Error, or Creation, will be Burned up, & then, & not till Then, Truth or Eternity
will appear. It is Burnt up the Moment Men cease to behold it. I assert for My Self that I do not behold the outward Creation & that to
me it is hindrance & not Action; it is as the Dirt upon my feet, No
part of Me. "What," it will be Question'd, "When the Sun rises, do
you not see a round disk of fire somewhat like a Guinea?" O no, no, I
see an Inumerable company of the Heavenly host crying "Holy, Holy,
Holy is the Lord God Almighty." I question not my Corporeal or Veg-
etative Eye any more than I would Question a Window concerning a
Sight. I look thro' it & not with it.

That is from Blake's commentary upon his last painting, *A Vision of the
Last Judgment.* To say of nature that "it is hindrance & not Action" is to declare one's freedom: as a visionary, a poet, a painter, a reader of the Bible as
"the Great Code of Art." The essence of Blake's genius is its exuberance
and its autonomy, its courage to rethink and resee everything for itself.

D. H. LAWRENCE

Nature responds so beautifully.
Roses are only once-wild roses, that were given an extra chance,
So they bloomed out and filled themselves with colored fullness
Out of sheer desire to be splendid, and more splendid.

"Roses" is only a four-line uncollected poem by D. H. Lawrence, but it charms and fortifies through its vitalism. Lawrence's was a remarkably varied literary genius, encompassing novels, stories, poems, essays, travel writings, apocalyptic commentaries, and nearly every other conceivable genre. Like Blake, Lawrence was a prophet whose religious vision was comprehensive, including society and nature. Between Blake and Lawrence came Marx and Freud, both of whom Blake anticipated and Lawrence disputed.

Lawrence perhaps is best called a prophetic novelist: for him, the novel was "the one bright book of life." The quickness given to the roses as "an extra chance" is the genius of Lawrence's work. What Lawrence said of Nathaniel Hawthorne—"Never trust the artist, trust the tale"—is our best guide to all of Lawrence.

Lawrence, as artist and as thinker, relied upon his prophetic drive to heal the malady he denounced as "sex in the head." As a novelist, he remained in the mode of Thomas Hardy; his poems pass from Hardy's influence to Walt Whitman's. His originality, his own creative genius, emerges most strongly in the novel *Women in Love,* and in the shorter novels and the stories. What Lawrence conveys, with a kind of eloquent desperation, is the necessity for both a spiritual rebirth in our mercantile society and a sexual resurrection in the body of the individual.

It is very easy to misread Lawrence: he is out of fashion because of feminist disfavor, which almost no male writer can survive at this time. But genius buries its undertakers, and Lawrence will rise in flames, like his mythological emblem, the Phoenix.

D. H. LAWRENCE
(1885–1930)

FASHIONS CHANGE; THE CURRENT neglect of Lawrence will not prevail. We are governed, in academic and journalistic circles these days, by feminist Puritanism. Lawrence, incorrect culturally and politically, is not acceptable to these archons. He concealed his homoeroticism, deprecated the female orgasm, and favored heterosexual anal intercourse. Yes, and also he wrote *The Rainbow* and *Women in Love*, two permanent novels, and scores of magnificent poems and stories. And though he was a confused and confusing prophet, he comes closer to prophetic status than any English writer since William Blake. A daemonic seer, he is as authentic a genius as twentieth-century literature offers. Seven decades after his death, his strongest pages continue to transmit fierce energies of spirit, will, and mind.

He is not Henry James or Wallace Stevens; Lawrence, except in certain moments of his travel writings, is not serene or composed. Part of his intensity was temperamental; part his anticipation of an early death from tuberculosis. For someone who died at forty-four, he was prodigiously productive: about seventy-five volumes, many of them published posthumously. A Lawrence enthusiast in youth, I had read most of them before I was twenty. These days I go on rereading *The Rainbow* and *Women in Love*, the best poems and stories, and much of the polemical and critical writing.

Lawrence wrote thousands of letters, though he cannot be said to have had a genius for friendship. E-mail has destroyed literary correspondence, and the personal letter threatens to become a dead form. Perhaps Lawrence, fifteen when Queen Victoria died, should be regarded as the last of the Victorian prophets: Carlyle, Ruskin, Newman, Arnold, Mill, Huxley, Morris, Butler. One might add Freud as an Austrian-Jewish adjunct. These seers could work all day and write letters until the dawn: I have attempted to read all of Ruskin, Freud, and Lawrence, but there is always more, in one place or another.

From 1912, when they ran off to Germany and Italy together, Lawrence's relationship to his wife, Frieda (they married in 1914), dominated his life. Shakespeare (I once wrote) teaches us a black box theory of marriage. We never know why we married, why marriage did or didn't work, and, after it crashes, we can't recover the black box. Lawrence and Frieda von Richthofen's marriage was an astonishing one, and after absorbing D. H. Lawrence—*The Story of a Marriage* by Brenda Maddox (1996)—I know everything and nothing about it, despite five hundred admirable pages by a skilled and sympathetic biographer. Frieda Lawrence herself found the clue in her late husband's life-long fear of women, a blind force that drove him on. Doubtless true, this is too reductive and too universal to be useful. You need not be a genius to fear women or not to fear them, so I suggest we look elsewhere, not to understand Lawrence as a prophet of sexuality, or as a husband, but as a novelist, poet, storyteller, essayist. Genius, and not marriage, is my subject, and the age-old advice not to marry a genius probably is sound enough.

My own best clue to Lawrence is his credo, "The novel is the book of life." Religiously, Lawrence overtly abandoned his Nonconformist Protestantism, under Darwin's impact, but in the depths his always remained a fiercely Protestant temperament, akin to Blake's. Writing became Lawrence's religion, and "more life" was the aim of everything he composed. Thomas Hardy and Walt Whitman were his authentic precursors, together with Shelley and (more personally) Robert Louis Stevenson. These were four very different authors, yet a displaced, romanticized Protestantism allies them with Lawrence's prophetic consciousness. The best way, here at the start of the twenty-first century, to get at this center of Lawrence is to read T. S. Eliot's ferocious Anglo-Catholic denunciation in *After Strange Gods:*

> I have already touched upon the deplorable religious upbringing which gave Lawrence his lust for intellectual independence: like most people who do not know what orthodoxy is, he hated it. And I have already mentioned the insensibility to ordinary social morality, which is so alien to my mind that I am completely baffled by it as a monstrosity. The point is that Lawrence started life wholly free from any restriction of tradition or institution, that he had no guidance except the Inner Light, the most untrustworthy and deceitful guide that ever offered itself to wandering humanity. It was peculiarly so of Lawrence, who does not seem to have been gifted with the faculty of self-criticism, except in flashes, even to the extent of ordinary worldly shrewdness. Of divine illumination, it may be said that any man is likely to think that he has it when he has it not; and even when he has it, the daily man that he is may draw the wrong conclusions from the enlightenment which the momentary man has received: no one, in short, can be the sole judge of whence his inspiration comes. A man like Lawrence, therefore, with his acute sensibility, violent prejudices

and passions, and lack of intellect and social training, is admirably fitted to be an instrument for the forces of evil.

This is so bad that it is good: turn it upside down, and you have the strength of Lawrence's tradition, the Inner Light invoked by John Milton and by William Blake, the Protestant radicalism that offended Eliot's Anglo-Catholic royalism. Lawrence's struggles with sexual identity and the wars between men and women have their spiritual basis as well as their psychoanalytic overtones. His awareness of spiritual difference emerges in Lawrence's confused struggle with Freud, whom he could not understand, or perhaps just did not want to understand. The First World War had been a crisis for Lawrence and for Freud, as for everyone else. Freud's rationalistic reaction to the mindless slaughter was not acceptable to Lawrence, who read Freud as a new dogma, which was untrue. Both men were post-Christian and post-Judaic, but Lawrence desired a Protestantism without Christ, the vision of his wonderful story "The Man Who Died," which is an exaltation of desire over everything else.

Lawrence's spirituality was apocalyptic, and that is a mode of which many of us are a little weary as we begin another millennium. Yet it remains authentic spirituality, in itself and in Lawrence. I do not know whether Lawrence was aware that Gnostic sects, like the Bogomils and at least some of the Cathars, had advocated heterosexual anal intercourse, which is celebrated in his poems and novels as the true liberation into the Holy Ghost. Norman Mailer, in *Ancient Evenings*, extended this Lawrentian myth into a brilliant but literal doctrine of immortality, but Lawrence fortunately remained more symbolic, even as he relied upon his own sexual apotheosis with Frieda.

Perhaps Lawrence should have been as explicit about his doctrine of heterosexual buggery in *Women in Love* and the poems of *Look! We Have Come Through!* as he was in *Lady Chatterley's Lover*, which is as unreadable now as it ever was. Chapter 23, "Excurse," is crucial to *Women in Love*, but its language is so carefully indefinite that many readers get impatient with it, which is a loss. I myself was bothered by the chapter, in my youth, until George Wilson Knight told me to read it more carefully. He himself believed that Ursula and Birkin were only experimenting with digital caresses, but a close reading shows that Lawrence celebrates the anal reentry into Eden. "Why make such a fuss about it!" was the recent reaction of a learned friend, irritated by this mix of sex and the spirit. One can make jokes about the missionary posture, if one wishes, and Lawrence's principal aesthetic defect is that, like John Milton, he is deficient in comedy. Sexuality and religion, however, cannot be kept apart, something to remember these days as President George W. Bush continues to trumpet his "faith-based initia-

tives." Apocalyptic sexuality follows its own conventions. T. S. Eliot, an ironist, considered Lawrence to be a bad poet. I follow the sacred Oscar Wilde
in his maxim that all bad poetry is sincere, but there is some (not much)
sincere poetry that is magnificent, and Lawrence wrote a considerable number of permanent poems, more in fact than Eliot did.

Lawrence excelled in the novella and the short story, as he did in the
double-novel, *The Rainbow* and *Women in Love.* Here I will turn only to his
poetry, which rivals the major English poets of the twentieth century (setting
Yeats, who admired Lawrence, aside as Anglo-Irish): Hardy, Edward Thomas,
Housman, Wilfred Owen, Geoffrey Hill. Like Hardy, who worshipped Shelley,
Lawrence's earlier poetry follows Romantic procedures, and the young
Lawrence can sound as much like Hardy in his first poems as *The White Peacock,*
an early novel, can seem a new novel by Thomas Hardy. In the middle phase
of *Look! We Have Come Through!* and *Birds, Beasts, and Flowers,* Lawrence indi-
viduates his poetry, partly through the catalyst of Walt Whitman, whose accent
is heard clearly in the great self-elegies of *Last Poems.*

Lawrence celebrated the early phase of his marriage in the poems of
Look! We Have Come Through! They tell the same story as "Excurse" but far
more directly, as in "Paradise Re-Entered":

> But we storm the angel-guarded
> Gates of the long-discarded
> Garden, which God has hoarded
> Against our pain.

That is not Lawrence in full voice; this is, in the wonderful "Song of a
Man Who Has Come Through:"

Not I, not I, but the wind that blows through me!
A fine wind is blowing the new direction of Time.
If only I let it bear me, carry me, if only it carry me!
If only I am sensitive, subtle, oh, delicate, a winged gift!
If only, most lovely of all, I yield myself and am borrowed
By the fine, fine wind that takes its course through the chaos of the
    world
Like a fine, an exquisite chisel, a wedge blade inserted;
If only I am keen and hard like the sheer tip of a wedge
Driven by invisible blows,
The rock will split, and we shall come at the wonder, we shall find
    the Hesperides.

Oh, for the wonder that bubbles into my soul,
I would be a good fountain, a good well-head,
Would blur no whisper, spoil no expression.

What is the knocking?
What is the knocking at the door in the night?
It is somebody wants to do us harm.

No, no, it is the three strange angels.
Admit them, admit them.

I hear Shelley, in his "Ode to the West Wind," asking to be lifted up as a leaf, to be carried by the wind to a resurrection. Lawrence, explicitly sexual, revises this to the resurrection of his body, the phallic hardness that propels him to his new heaven, new earth:

The rock will split, we shall come at the wonder, we shall find the
    Hesperides.

The fortunate islands of the Western star of Venus are an earthly paradise, and having reached them in *Look! We Have Come Through!*, Lawrence, like a New Adam, explores them throughout *Birds, Beasts, and Flowers*. In the most prophetic of these poems, "The Evening Land," Lawrence faces towards Whitman's America, protesting the boundlessness of Whitman's love. In the greatest of these poems, "Snake," Lawrence watches, in Sicily, a poisonous golden snake drink at the poet's water-trough, and is ambivalent, feeling both fear and the honor of a god's visit. As the snake departs, Lawrence throws a log after it, and then associates this act with the Ancient Mariner's murder of the albatross.

And I thought of the albatross,
And I wished he would come back, my snake.
For he seemed to me again like a king,
Like a king, uncrowned in the underworld
Now due to be crowned again.

And so, I missed my chance with one of the lords
Of life,
And I have something to expiate;
A pettiness.

*   *   *

"The Lords of life" is taken from Emerson, and the poem is another prelude to Lawrence's marvelous perspective in his *Studies in Classic American Literature* (1923). The final chapter, and the purpose of the book, is Walt Whitman. Complaint follows complaint: Whitman is condemned for an excess of democratic merging. But suddenly, the voice that is great within Lawrence speaks:

> Whitman, the great poet, has meant so much to me. Whitman, the one man breaking a way ahead. Whitman, the one pioneer. And only Whitman. No English pioneers, no French. No European pioneer-poets. In Europe the would-be pioneers are mere innovators. The same in America. Ahead of Whitman, nothing. Ahead of all poets, pioneering into the wilderness of unopened life, Whitman. Beyond him, none. His wide, strange camp at the end of the great high-road. And lots of new little poets camping on Whitman's camping ground now. But none going really beyond. Because Whitman's camp is at the end of the road, and on the edge of a great precipice. Over the precipice, blue distances, and the blue hollow of the future. But there is no way down. It is a dead end.
>
> Pisgah. Pisgah sights. And Death. Whitman like a strange, modern, American Moses. Fearfully mistaken. And yet the great leader. The essential function of art is moral. Not aesthetic, not decorative, not pastime and recreation. But moral. The essential function of art is moral.
>
> But a passionate, implicit morality, not didactic. A morality which changes the blood, rather than the mind. Changes the blood first. The mind follows later, in the wake.
>
> Now Whitman was a great moralist. He was a great leader. He was a great changer of the blood in the veins of men.

A great prose chant develops in Lawrence, as he joins Whitman in celebrating the Open Road:

> The true democracy, where soul meets soul, in the open road. Democracy. American democracy where all journey down the open road. And where a soul is known at once in its going. Not by its clothes or appearance. Whitman did away with that. Not by its family name. Not even by its reputation. Whitman and Melville both discounted that. Not by a progression of piety, or by works of Charity. Not by

works at all. Not by anything, but just itself. The soul passing unen-
hanced, passing on foot and being no more than itself. And recognized, and passed by or greeted according to the soul's dictate. If it
be a great soul, it will be worshipped in the road.

The love of man and woman: a recognition of souls, and a communion of worship. The love of comrades: a recognition of souls, and a
communion of worship. Democracy: a recognition of souls, all down
the open road, and a great soul seen in its greatness, as it travels on
foot among the rest, down the common way of the living. A glad
recognition of souls, and a gladder worship of great and greater souls,
because they are the only riches.

Love, and Merging, brought Whitman to the Edge of Death!
Death! Death!

But the exultance of his message still remains. Purified of MERG-
ING, purified of MYSELF, the exultant message of American Democracy, of souls in the Open Road, full of glad recognition, full of fierce
readiness, full of the joy of worship, when one soul sees a greater soul.

The only riches, the great souls.

This is Lawrence in Lobo, New Mexico, making his peace at last with
his and our father Walt Whitman. It opens the way to Lawrence's own *Last
Poems*, where he transmutes Whitman to his own dying needs. These are
Lawrence's best poems: "Bavarian Gentians," "The Ship of Death," and the
extraordinary "Shadows," with its Jobean descent into total despair:

> And if, in the changing phases of man's life
> I fall in sickness and in misery
> My wrists seem broken and my heart seems dead
> And strength is gone, and my life
> Is only the leavings of a life.

The aesthetic dignity of this transcends its poignance and prepares for
the battered sense of renewal, as "odd, wintry flowers" appear upon Lawrence's "withered stem" and the old Nonconformist ecstasy returns:

> Then I must know that still
> I am in the hands of the unknown God,
> He is breaking me down to his own oblivion
> To send me forth on a new morning, a new man.

TENNESSEE WILLIAMS

[*Blanche turns weakly, hesitantly about. She lets them push her into a chair.*]
BLANCHE. I can smell the sea air. The rest of my time I'm going to spend on the sea. And when I die, I'm going to die on the sea. You know what I shall die of? [*She plucks a grape*] I shall die of eating an unwashed grape one day out on the ocean. I will die—with my hand in the hand of some nice-looking ship's doctor, a very young one with a small blond mustache and a big silver watch. "Poor lady," they'll say, "the quinine did her no good. That unwashed grape has transported her soul to heaven." [*The cathedral chimes are heard*] And I'll be buried at sea sewn up in a clean white sack and dropped overboard—at noon—in the blaze of summer—and into an ocean as blue as [*Chimes again*] my first lover's eyes!

This is the poignant moment in *A Streetcar Named Desire*, just before a doctor and a matron arrive to take Blanche DuBois to a state mental institution. Blanche's death-fantasy foreshadows Tennessee Williams's own desire to be buried in the Caribbean Sea at the spot where Hart Crane leapt to his death in 1932. This strange fusion of Blanche, Hart Crane, and Williams can be seen as the center of the lyrical dramatist's vision of American eros and its tragic trajectory.

Williams found in Crane a paradigm for his identification of homoerotic desire and artistic vocation. The persuasive aesthetic dignity of Blanche, so memorable in its pathos, is enhanced by her defeat, truly self-inflicted. Her desire for death is Williams's interpretation of American discomfort with its culture, and has an origin in Hart Crane's vision of a Gnostic Helen, the whore selected by Simon Magus as his image of a fallen though still divine eros. Blanche is akin to Hart Crane's Helen in his "For the Marriage of Faustus and Helen":

> But if I lift my arms it is to bend
> To you who turned away once, Helen, knowing
> The press of troubled hands, too alternate
> With steel and soil to hold you endlessly.

Like Crane's Helen, Blanche is burdened by guilt and by cultural exhaustion. She never can scrub herself clean, and her authentic obliteration results not from Stanley's brutality towards her, but from her troubled and accurate perception of the achieved heterosexual intensity of her sister's marriage to Stanley.

There is a disproportion between Blanche's wistful doom-eagerness and the intensely literary energies of the language endowed upon her by Williams. Perhaps that is only an indication that she—more than Tom Wingfield in *The Glass Menagerie* or Sebastian Venable in *Suddenly Last Summer*—is the incarnation of Tennessee Williams's own genius, which he himself identified with the poetry of Hart Crane.

TENNESSEE WILLIAMS
(1911–1983)

IT IS A CURIOSITY OF AMERICAN LITERATURE that the United States, an excessively dramatic nation, has had many superb poets and novelists, but few playwrights of eminence. In the nineteenth century, the novelists include Hawthorne, Melville, and Mark Twain; there are Walt Whitman and Emily Dickinson as poets, and Emerson and Thoreau as essayists. The drama comprises Clyde Fitch. In the twentieth century, the novelists are Henry James, Edith Wharton, Theodore Dreiser, Willa Cather, Scott Fitzgerald, Hemingway, Nathanael West, Flannery O'Connor, William Faulkner, Ralph Ellison, and more recent figures like Thomas Pynchon, Cormac McCarthy, Philip Roth, Don DeLillo. Poets of the last century, keeping the scope quite narrow, include Edwin Arlington Robinson, Frost, Stevens, Eliot, Pound, William Carlos Williams, Marianne Moore, Hart Crane, Robert Penn Warren, Elizabeth Bishop, May Swenson, James Merrill, A. R. Ammons, John Ashbery. Where are the dramatists? Eugene O'Neill, Thorton Wilder, Arthur Miller, Tennessee Williams, and Edward Albee are the figures most would cite, but even Williams, the best of these, is out of place in the company of Henry James and William Faulkner, Wallace Stevens and Hart Crane. I cannot solve the mystery of this, but I feel the poignance of it, particularly in juxtaposing Williams with Hart Crane, whom he worshipped, and whose influence upon him was abiding.

Though Williams learned much of his craft from Chekhov, his prime precursors were Hart Crane and D. H. Lawrence. Crane killed himself in 1932; Lawrence had died of tuberculosis in 1930. Williams, a young man when they died, fell in love with Crane's poetry in 1936, and with Lawrence's writing soon after; in 1939 he visited Frieda Lawrence in New Mexico. The influence of Crane and of Lawrence upon Williams was more than textual, indeed more than literary. It was personal, and in Crane's instance approached total identification. As a poet, Williams was cancelled by Crane; as a writer of prose fiction, drowned out by Lawrence. Fortunately, Williams was a lyrical dramatist, and free to find his own voice in his best plays: *The Glass Menagerie* (1945), *A Streetcar Named Desire* (1947), *Summer and Smoke* (1948), and *Suddenly Last Summer* (1958). The plays of his remaining quarter-century represent a falling away, and while he did not outlive his genius, he seemed more and more alienated from it. Yet even in his later phase, Williams writes more memorably and eloquently than any other American dramatist. Crane's rhetorical art had a benign and invigorating effect upon Williams's language. The taking of Crane's identity into his own was so comprehensive on Williams's part that I can think of no real parallel to it in all of literary history. Hart Crane himself, when intoxicated, would identify himself with Christopher Marlowe and with Rimbaud. Perhaps in that dangerous mode also he was Tennessee Williams's paradigm.

Can we speak of a writer, and a person, as having a genius for identification? I fell in love with Hart Crane's poetry when I was a child, but in much the same way that I became rapt with William Blake's work. The identification was with the poetry, not the poets. One writes books on Shelley, or on Wallace Stevens, or on Yeats, identifying with what most takes possession of one's own soul as a reader. With Shakespeare, it must be different: no single person can identify with that cosmos of poetry, so we identify with a particular character or characters. On some days I go about murmuring Sir John Falstaff's most outrageous speeches, and even have been outrageous enough to take on the role in stage readings. But these are all a critic's identifications, and not those of a poet, dramatist, or storyteller. Williams became a great dramatist, in at least four of his plays, by identifying as much (or more) with a poet as with the poetry. This process of merging with Hart Crane was so comprehensive that the two mothers, Grace Hart Crane and Edwina Estelle Dakin Williams, also fused, thus providing the models for Amanda Wingfield in *The Glass Menagerie* and Violet Venable in *Suddenly Last Summer*.

In his final, experimental plays, Williams moved towards the theater of Pirandello, but as an immensely rhetorical playwright he always had affinities with the Sicilian master, whom Eric Bentley places first among all dramatists since Ibsen, preferring Pirandello even over Beckett and Brecht. Pirandello was conscious of the Sicilian tradition of rhetoric, as inaugurated by Empedocles and developed by Gorgias the Sophist, opponent of Socrates and Plato. This rhetoric of *kairos,* the opportune word, a word that already is action, at the opportune moment, is based upon a will-to-identification, hence its utility in politics and law cases, as opposed to the Socratic will-to-distinguish the knower from the known. Williams's art depends upon the audience's will-to-identification, which is why he gives equal sympathy to the "realist" Kowalski and to Blanche DuBois, apostle of yearning. In Pirandello, Blanche would triumph, however equivocally, but Williams, against his own heart, identifies also with the world that destroys grace and wistfulness. Here his genius for identification served Williams well.

* * *

Tennessee Williams did not identify with D. H. Lawrence, a prophet he followed but did not love. It is interesting to compare two short plays by Williams: *I Rise in Flame, Cried the Phoenix*, with *Steps Must Be Gentle*. In the first, Lawrence and his wife, Frieda, and his disciple Brett share his final moments before he dies of tuberculosis. Defiant of the female principle until the end, the dying Lawrence affirms his apocalyptic vitalism, with singular male pride and force, despite his desperate physical weakness. The play might as well be titled *The Death of the Prophet*, and clearly there is no will-to-identification in it.

Steps Must Be Gentle (a title taken from Crane) is an occult dialogue between Hart Crane and Grace Hart Crane. Both are dead; the poet speaks from the bottom of the Caribbean, and his just-deceased mother (who outlived him by fifteen years) chides him for ignoring her during his four final years. Though he is coldly reserved, she recaptures him by emphasizing her devotion to his poetry during the fifteen years since his death, and her own struggle with poverty. His homosexuality remains a division between them, but the mother wins out, and Crane is again dependent upon her, losing the chilled peace of the drowned man.

Crane, allowed to speak some of his magnificent lines, remains the great poet as maternal victim, rather than a prophet resisting the quasi-incestuous embrace of the mother-wife. Of the two brief plays, *Steps Must Be Gentle* is the stronger; it has the pathos of personal confession, as Williams anticipates an after-death confrontation with his own mother. Williams had wished to have his own remains thrown into the Caribbean at the spot where Crane had made his final leap, but he thought better about this, and was buried by his mother's side in St. Louis. He might have feared that he also would be caught up in a mystic dialogue with his formidable mother, who died at age ninety-five in 1980, less than three years before him.

Hart Crane, in the second Roman meaning of "genius," the daemon or alter ego, indeed can be regarded as Tennessee Williams's genius. I take this precise suggestion from Gilbert Debusscher, a Belgian scholar who documented Williams's obsession with Crane in 1983, the year of the dramatist's death. That obsession or fusion of identities manifested itself in many ways. The Orphic theme in Williams's work, his vision of himself as the Orpheus of the American theater, is founded upon Hart Crane's Orphic self-acceptance:

> My eyes pressed black against the prow,
> —Thy derelict and blinded guest.

> Waiting, afire, what name, unspoke,
> I cannot claim: let thy waves rear
> More savage than the death of kings,
> Some splintered garland for the seer.

Williams also identified his despair with Crane's despair, though Crane had never enjoyed what Williams called "the catastrophe of success." Crane, a very difficult poet, had a tiny audience in his own lifetime, and not a much larger one since. Williams's plays and films reached millions, but this was little comfort to the tormented dramatist. Though Crane increasingly was alcoholic, and ended his life deliberately, convinced that his poetic gift had abandoned him, he was tragically mistaken, as "The Broken Tower," his superb valediction, demonstrates. Williams, whose gift and whose temperament were of a different order, could tolerate neither his own success nor the multiple sorrows of his familial context. His sister Rose, two years older, and truly the great, quasi-incestuous love of his entire life, was schizophrenic by sixteen, and at twenty-eight was committed to institutions. At thirty-four, she suffered the horror of a lobotomy. *The Glass Menagerie*, written the year after, essentially is an elegy for Rose, and the play's public success in 1945 did not solace Williams for long. In 1948, his parents separated, and soon afterwards he was able to move Rose to a private institution in Connecticut. Despite his prolonged relationship with Frank Merlo, from 1948 to Merlo's death in 1963, Williams suffered endless breakdowns, depressions, and drug and alcohol dependencies. Though Williams never said so, he must have wondered whether the long decline of his life and career was a better path than Crane's early suicide. Except for being an only child and thus having no Rose in his life, Hart Crane's circumstances and nature always seemed to Williams uncannily similar to his own.

Though Tom Wingfield, Blanche DuBois, and Sebastian Venable are all in a sense self-portraits of Williams, they also carry in them aspects of Hart Crane, and could be termed Williams's interpretations of Crane. Could we reverse time, and ask Crane for an elegiac interpretation of his disciple, he might have offered us (and Williams) this:

> Distinctly praise the years, whose volatile
> Blamed bleeding hands extend and thresh the height
> The imagination spans beyond despair,
> Outpacing bargain, vocable and prayer.

RAINER MARIA RILKE

> Otherwise this stone . . .
>
> would not, from all the borders of itself,
> burst like a star: for here there is no place
> that does not see you. You must change your life.
> —"Archaic Torso of Apollo"
> (translated by Stephen Mitchell)

Rilke was moved to these lines, not by an actual statue of Apollo, but by a fifth century B.C.E. torso of a youth, in the Louvre. The torso *found* Rilke, and issued the famous injunction: "You must change your life."

Once Rilke's consciousness fully was formed, his life never could change. With Georg Trakl and Paul Celan, Rilke unquestionably is one of the essential poets who wrote in German during the twentieth century. Though he is all but universally admired (exceptions include Samuel Beckett and the critic Paul de Man), Rilke's genius for portraying transcendental experience was accompanied by a humorless sense of his own election as the seer of the invisible. His extraordinary eloquence sometimes veils a certain emptiness in poetic argument: he would have benefited by absorbing more of Goethe's irony and self-understanding.

When I was young, a half-century ago, Rilke seemed to me beyond criticism. At his strongest, as here in the ninth *Duino Elegy*, he still speaks to me with such force that my increasing reservations seem ungrateful:

> *Here* is the time for the sayable, *here* is its homeland.
> Speak and bear witness. More than ever
> the things that we might experience are vanishing, for
> what crowds them out and replaces them is an imageless act.
> (translated by Stephen Mitchell)

"Think of the earth," the admonition that Keats accepted and that Nietzsche also urged, was Rilke's heroic doctrine. Like Keats and Nietzsche, Rilke was post-Christian, and his testimony to the earth as the primordial God is heartening: "The idea that we are sinful and need to be redeemed . . . is more and more repugnant to a heart that has comprehended the earth." As an oppositional spirit, Rilke's genius is always persuasive. When he passes to affirming his conceptualizations, sometimes I again long for the shrewdness and serene good humor of Goethe, but again I wonder at my own ingratitude.

RAINER MARIA RILKE
(1875–1926)

IT IS A CURIOSITY THAT LITERATURE composed in German has so powerful a tradition of lyric poetry, consistently stronger than prose narrative and drama. This lyric tradition long preceded Goethe, but was confirmed by his extraordinary eminence, still unrivaled by any Continental poet. As all would consent, Hölderlin is the other height of German lyric. Hofmannsthal, alas, abandoned that solitary art, but Rilke is one of several poets writing in German during the twentieth century who have enhanced the tradition. Whether he altogether sustains comparison with Yeats and Valéry, with Montale and Wallace Stevens, with Lorca and Hart Crane, I am uncertain, but any investigation of the phenomenon of literary genius ought to include Rilke, whose major elegies and sonnets resulted from experiences and visitations that he himself regarded as transcendental breakthroughs.

Rilke is also almost a paradigm of how writing shapes a life, rather than life forming the work. The major biography, Ralph Freedman's *Life of a Poet: Rainer Maria Rilke* (1996), argues that Rilke's poetry radically transformed not only his inward self but his relationships with friends, with lovers, and with other literary figures.

Rilke's attitude towards Goethe was necessarily ambivalent, as Goethe increasingly was an influence Rilke both feared and welcomed. We rightly think of Rilke as an elegiac poet, and Goethe provided him with the idea of the elegy. Goethe's "Euphrosyne" mourned Christine Neumann, an actress who died young, and this poem greatly modified Rilke's view of his inevitable precursor. A fusion of Goethe's elegies and Hölderlin's exalted hymns and odes has much to do with the form and procedures of the *Duino Elegies*. But Goethe's larger influence was as epistolary lover, one whose ideal mode precluded any encounters with the distant beloved. It is a little hard, in 2001, to accept this aspect of Goethe and of Rilke without some irony, particularly towards Rilke, who was about as problematical a lover as Franz Kafka. Goethe may not have invented the poetics of renunciation— that honor (if it is one) belongs to Petrarch—but Goethe may be regarded as the theoretician as well as the pragmatist of this mode. Rilke was always in love with the Dark Woman, but her incarnation kept shifting about. More even than Goethe, Rilke became the great celebrant of female erotic suffering. Much-battered patriarchal critic as I am, I find it difficult to suppress a modest hilarity at the self-deceptions of what might be called the Goethe-Rilke tradition of both exalting and separating from the muse, or, to be merely reductive, treating the woman more as a mother than as an erotic partner.

Goethe's way of renunciation (to follow him in calling it that) ultimately led to the Second Part of *Faust,* a work beyond critical dispute, a magnificently sustained outrage. The late Paul de Man was relatively unique in his severe questioning of Rilke's achievement, which he thought inflated by a spurious transcendentalism. The tenth and final *Duino Elegy* ends with a famous verbal gesture:

> And we, who have always thought
> Of happiness as *rising,* would feel
> The emotion that almost overwhelms us
> Whenever a happy thing *falls.*
> (translated by Stephen Mitchell)

I reflect, as I read this, that we speak of *falling* in love, and not of *rising* in it. Freedman, Rilke's biographer, quotes this passage and rather impressively responds with a litany of Rilkean muses:

Here the process of separation becomes Rilke's own: Lou first, then Clara, Paula Becker, later Loulou Lasard, Merline: each "served" to raise the poet to a higher stage away from encumbrance.

As to the evocative power of Rilke's rhetoric, no cavils could be credited: I have carried hundreds of his lines in my head for more than a half-century, though many of them are from the two volumes of *New Poems.* And yet the spiritual assertions of the *Duino Elegies* have a self-conscious grandeur that can be puzzling. The grandeur I join most readers in finding persuasive; the implicit sense of election to the Sublime can be a trouble. Essentially the *Duino Elegies* center upon love and death: they cannot be faulted for being less interesting upon death than is Prince Hamlet, and they certainly must be respected for their genius at extolling the sufferings and renunciations of love. The sufferings are those of Rilke's lovers, though the Renaissance poet Gaspara Stampa figures significantly, doubtless because of Rilke's conviction that, but for a time warp, she would ecstatically have joined the company of those he loved and then renounced. Again, like Goethe, like

Kafka, Rilke had another genius in him, which was to become an immortal fixation for remarkably impressive women, graciously superior to those great writers in compassion, understanding, and the capacity to remain in love.

I hope to be plain on this: there is no reason to deplore Rilke's high-minded mining of his affections, because his poetic economy demanded it, and the superb company of Lou Andreas-Salome, Clara Westhoff (Rilke's wife and mother of his daughter), Paula Becker, Loulou Albert-Lasard, and Merline (Baladine Klossowska) all encouraged it and yielded to its purpose: to render their poet's imagination autonomous. These of course are merely the major muses; Rilke, to keep running (as it were), had to recruit them on a constant basis. Since all this ended seventy-five years ago, what matters is what Rilke was able to make of it, which returns me to the *Duino Elegies*.

It is one of Rilke's glories, everywhere in his work, but in the *Elegies* particularly, that he is the poet of loneliness, making Shelley and Wallace Stevens seem positively gregarious in contrast. Since even Shelley had nothing like Rilke's montage of muses (though Mary Shelley, Emilia Viviani, and Jane Williams probably could have joined Rilke's entourage), and Stevens had only Elsie Stevens, one sees more clearly the mode of Rilke's imaginative project: the more magnificent ecstasies, the more intense solitude and emptiness. You could not achieve the sumptuous destitution of the *Elegies* unless you could renounce taking the next train to any of a bevy of wise women, while knowing that they always still would be there. Thus, there is the splendid conclusion of the remarkable fifth elegy:

Angel! If there were a place that we didn't know of, and there,
on some unsayable carpet, lovers displayed
what they never could bring to mastery here—the bold
exploits of their high-flying hearts,
their towers of pleasure, their ladders
that have long since been standing where there was no ground, leaning
just on each other, trembling,—and could master all this,
before the surrounding spectators, the innumerable soundless dead:
　　　　　Would these, then, throw down their final, forever saved-up,
forever hidden, unknown to us, eternally valid
coins of happiness before the at last
genuinely smiling pair on the gratified
carpet?

Though Stephen Mitchell has done his best, this is untranslatable, and is outrageously impressive in the original. That the carpet should be gratified is an amiable metaphor, though it is liable to remind us that the daemonic Rilke, unlike the even more daemonic Goethe, lacks a sense of humor. He proposes—out of space and time—sacred orgies upon magic carpets—which like his Angel suggests a Koranic influence. As a scholar, indeed a historian-collector, of exalted women in love, Rilke has no peer. In one crucial letter, he lists his champions, all historically inaccessible:

> in the situation of Gaspara Stampa, Louize Labe, certain Venetian courtesans, and, above all, Marianna Alcoforado, that incomparable creature, in whose eight heavy letters woman's love is for the first time charted from point to point, without display, without exaggeration or mitigation, drawn as if by the hand of a sibyl. And there—my God—there it becomes evident that, as a result of the irresistible logic of woman's heart, this line was finished, perfected, not to be continued any further in the earthly realm, and could be prolonged only toward the divine, into infinity.
>
> —to Annette Kolb, January 23, 1912

As the poet of transfigurations, Rilke is hardly to be mocked. If the poetry were not so absolute as, at its best, it is, he might begin to be a figure of fun. He is eternal, and would flourish just as well now (I am convinced) in our own postfeminist age as he would have in the Renaissance or in his twentieth-century Middle Europe. Perhaps he was the creation of his muses, none of whom seems to have been surprised or deceived. No one has taken the religion of art farther, whether into the impasses of serial High Romantic love or into the abyss of speculations about the influence of love upon poetry. His genius fused poetic art and the erotic life more inextricably than ever was accomplished before.

EUGENIO MONTALE

True poetry is similar to certain pictures whose owners are unknown and with which only a few initiates are familiar. Yet poetry does not live only in books or school anthologies. The poet does not know— often he will never know—whom he really writes for.

> —Nobel Prize address (1975)
> (translated by Jonathan Galassi)

To be the most considerable poet in Italian after Leopardi is to have inherited an extraordinarily strong tradition, one that only an authentic genius could have hoped to fulfill, extend, modify. Montale refreshes because he found the power to enhance his tradition without resorting to ideologies: political, religious, philosophical. A skeptical humanist, Montale preferred to confront poetry directly, asking only whether it *was* poetry.

An Italian poet of genius finally must struggle with Dante, who is as dangerous to imitate as is Shakespeare. T. S Eliot, whom Montale admired rather excessively, helped created the unfortunate Anglo-American tradition in which Dante's achievement is regarded as inseparable from his theology.

Montale, far closer to Dante's poetry, believed that Dante wished to be "a poet and only a poet." Though he would not say so, Montale's relationship to Dante (and to Leopardi) was essentially agonistic. Dante could not be surpassed but he was not the representative of a poetry of belief. Rather, he taught Montale the lesson that "true poetry is always in the nature of a gift, and that it therefore presupposes the dignity of its recipient." That aesthetic dignity, in Montale as in Leopardi, implies a loving separation from Dante, a complex re-visioning of Dante's art, both as necessary burden and as spur to Montale's own highly original achievement.

EUGENIO MONTALE
(1896–1981)

THOUGH ITALIAN POETRY OF THE TWENTIETH century was so rich—D'Annunzio, Campana, Ungaretti, Quasimodo, Saba, and others—Montale is rightly regarded as the strongest poet in the language since Leopardi, and perhaps even the culmination of the tradition of Dante and Petrarch. In English, Montale has enjoyed two superb (and very different) translators: the late William Arrowsmith, and Jonathan Galassi, both of whom I shall draw upon here. Montale is a difficult poet for any reader, because, at least on the surface or rhetorical level, he can seem rugged, almost the antithesis of Leopardi's sparse and chastened diction. Genius in Montale is allusive, assimilative, dense, extraordinarily self-aware, and definitively addressed in the poem of that title, "Il genio," in the volume *Satura: 1962–1970*. Since, regrettably, genius speaks through another's mouth (being the alter ego), it leaves only footprints in the snow, and these are effaced, and so the world cannot read them. That is the tenor of *Satura* (Latin for a stew or mixed dish), where the sequence "Xenia II" ends with a flood, literal and metaphorical, that destroys Modernist literary culture in Florence, obliterating that aspect of the European mind.

Satura, and the poetry of Montale's old age, constitute a palinode, an ironic commentary upon the poet's major achievements as published from 1920 to 1954. The effect is very curious in this second Montale: he seems at times more an Anglo-American than an Italian poet, closer perhaps to the later T. S. Eliot than to the earlier Eugenio Montale. To define Montale's genius, you go back to the earlier work, where he is more wholeheartedly in the celebratory tradition of Petrarch, addressing or commemorating an erotic ideal. To have both extended and revised the most characteristic genre of Italian poetry, as the younger Montale accomplished, was astonishing, and established a freshness and unexpected originality that the later Montale could not undo.

For the common reader, of whatever nation, the canonical Montale of 1920–54 is going to seem rather more the revisionist of Dante and Petrarch than their extender into a very different era. The High Modernism of Valéry, Eliot, and Pound, again on the surface, is initially far more evident in *Cuttlefish Bones*, *The Occasions*, and *The Storm*, than is the continuity of major

Italian poetry: Dante, Petrarch, Foscolo, Leopardi. But Montale's three canticles, as he called them, though they lead to no salvation, are more Dantesque than not, once the reader descends into them by repeated expeditions. Montale is difficult more in the mode of Hart Crane—whom I believe he never mentions—than in Eliot's way, which he mentions too often, though with augmenting wariness. Like Crane, Montale relies upon a "logic of metaphor," and upon a poetic texture shockingly impacted. There the similarity concludes: Hart Crane is an incantatory rhapsode, a Pindar of the Machine Age, as he said. Montale is as memorable as Crane, but by and large you can't hear in him the Whitman–Hart Crane high chant as "the voice that is great within us rises up" (Wallace Stevens).

The hermetic element in Montale, particularly in *The Occasions,* doubtless has some relation to the burdens of writing an authentic poetry in pre-Fascist, Fascist, and post-Fascist Italy, where everything was politicized. If your obsessions are love, renunciation, and the great poetry of the past, then you internalize in a political time, as Montale did. *The Storm* (1956), generally taken to be Montale's summit, is much more open to the reader, and seems to me particularly heartening in 2001, when poetry and its absorption alike have been all but destroyed by the creeping plague so appropriately called "political correctness." Much of *The Storm* is Montale's war poetry of the early 1940s, and reflects the agony of an Italy only very slowly retaken by the Allies, against tenacious German resistance, and with violence perpetual in occupied Italy between the partisans and the Nazi-Fascist forces.

I want to examine only one poem here, "The Hitler Spring," which takes its origin from a meeting between Hitler and Mussolini in Florence in 1938. The poem cannot be understood without invoking Montale's Beatrice or Laura, whom he called Clizia, and who is identified with the American Dante scholar Irma Brandeis. Theirs was evidently a relationship of renunciation, in the mode exalted by Dante and by Petrarch. The name Clizia is Ovidian and refers to a girl who falls in love with Apollo and is transformed into a sunflower. Frequently Montale also calls her Iris or rainbow. She has no consistent symbolic meaning in Montale's work, and later is essentially angelic or visionary, ultimately perhaps associated by the poet with his dead sister and his dead mother. But here in the oxymoronic Hitler Spring, she too is oxymoronic, doubtless with a hidden pun upon her name, both firebrand and ice. As Jonathan Galassi notes, the poem organizes itself around this antithetical image-structure.

"Hitler Spring" opens with a white cloud of crazed moths whirling about the parapets and streetlights of Florence, which follows a notation of Montale's that speaks of white butterflies, like snow, coming down upon the Arno River. They are an emblem of the unseasonable, apt for Hitler, Hell's messenger, coming down the acclaiming street, in a city where no one still can be considered blameless.

The poet and his muse, Clizia, are exchanging vows and long farewells in this infernal context, against the background of celebratory fireworks for Hitler. What follows is powerful and difficult, and so I give three translations, successively William Arrowsmith's, Jonathan Galassi's, and George Kay's plain prose version:

All for nothing then?—and then Roman
candles in San Giovanni slowly blanching
the horizon, and the vows, and the long farewells
strong as any christening in the sad, sullen waiting
for the horde (but a jewel furrowed the air, dropping
Tobias's angels, all seven, on the icefloes and rivers
of your shores, sowing them
with the future), and the sun-seeking flowers sprouting
from your hands—all scorched, sucked dry
by pollen hissing like fire, stinging
like wind-whipped snow

All for nothing then?—and the Roman
candles at San Giovanni, slowly whitening
the horizon, and the vows and long farewells
definitive as baptism in the dismal
vigil of the horde (but a jewel scored the air,
sowing the icy edges of your beaches
with the angels of Tobias, the seven,
seed of the future) and the sunflowers born
of your hands—all burned, sucked dry
by pollen that hisses like fire
and stings like hail . . .
                                    Oh the wounded spring
     is still a festival if it will chill

All for nothing, then?—and the roman candles, at Saint John's day,
that slowly paled the skyline, and the tokens and the long farewells
strong as a baptism in the mournful waiting of the horde (but a gem
streaked the air, scattering on the ice, and the shores of your coastline,

Tobias's angels, the seven, the seed of the future) and the heliotropes born from your hands—all burnt and sucked dry by a pollen that hisses like fire, and has the sharpness of driving snow.

San Giovanni—Saint John—is Florence's patron saint, presiding over an obscene parody of his feast day. We see now that what we thought were moths or white butterflies were shattered angels' wings, alluding to the breakup of the Chariot of the Soul in Plato's *Phaedrus*. To this are opposed the seven angels of Tobias in the Apocryphal Book of Tobit. The poet and Clizia make their farewell vows under the angelic protection of those who will guide her on her return journey to the New World. Unquestionably brilliant (and overtly owing something to the second elegy in Rilke's *Duino Elegies*), this packed stanza is followed by the poem's conclusion, which I give only in Kay's literal translation:

Oh the wounded springtime is still holiday if it freezes this death in death! Look up again, Clizia, it is your fate, you who though changed, keep your love unchanged, until the blind sun you bear in you is dazzled in the Other and is destroyed in Him for everyone. Perhaps the sirens, the tolling bells that greet the monsters on the evening of their witches' Sabbath are already mingling with the sound that, unloosed from heaven, descends, conquers,—with the breathing of a dawn that tomorrow, for everyone, breaks again, white, but without wings of horror, over the scorched wadis of the south.

All but apocalyptic, this seems to me Montale at his most powerful. "The scorched wadis of the south" refers to the origins of Clizia's Jewish tradition and the poet's Christian heritage in ancient Israel. Clizia, a Dante scholar, author of *The Ladder of Vision*, is suddenly associated with Beatrice at the very start of *Paradiso*, where Dante's beloved, with the gaze of an eagle, stares directly into the Sun that is emblematic of God. Dante/Montale, no eagle, looks upon Beatrice/Clizia, and begins his own ascent to hope. Here and now, in a Florence given over to the Nazi-Fascist witches' Sabbath celebrating Hitler, the "blind sun" carried in Clizia "is dazzled in the Other and is destroyed in Him for everyone." Montale, not a believing Catholic, adopts Dante's gnosis, brilliantly employing *his* Beatrice as an involuntary Christ-bearer (Irma Brandeis being Jewish). To invoke Dante against Hitler and Italian Fascism is a superb stroke, carried through with an audacity founded upon Montale's own poetic authority, which is its own evidence in this magnificently conceived poem.

X

MALKHUT

LUSTRE 19

|

Honoré de Balzac, Lewis Carroll, Henry James, Robert Browning, William Butler Yeats

|

The tenth and final *Sefirah* is the richest and most diverse in its implications. *Malkhut*, the "kingdom," is the presence of God in the world, displayed in the radiant glory of the *Shekhinah*, the "descent" of the Divine as a woman.

Balzac wrote esoteric novels (*Louis Lambert, Seraphita*), but he figures in the first Lustre of *Malkhut* as the creator of the vast kingdom of this world throughout his *Human Comedy*. The visionary writings of Lewis Carroll (which we miscall "Nonsense") are another version of *Malkhut*, as is the enormous fictive cosmos of Henry James, who praised "the lesson of Balzac," and who created his own mythology in the major phase of his work.

The dramatic monologues of Robert Browning and the dramatic lyrics of William Butler Yeats (founded on his personal occult system of *A Vision*) fit also in this more transcendental Lustre of *Malkhut*.

HONORÉ DE BALZAC

"But where do you suppose you'll find an honest man? Here in Paris, an honest man's the one who keeps his mouth shut and doesn't let anyone else in on the deal. I'm not talking about those poor peons, and they're all over the place, who never really get paid for all they do: they're what I call the lay brothers of God's Order of the Rundown Shoes. There's a kind of virtue in being that stupid, but it's the virtue of poverty. If God decides to play a bad joke on us, and stay away when the Last Judgment comes, oh, I can just see their faces!

"So if it's a fast fortune you want, you either have to be rich already or else look as if you are. Getting rich around here means you have to be a high-stake gambler, otherwise you're wasting your time, bye-bye baby! Just look at a hundred professions you might go into: if you find ten men who've made their fortunes quickly, everyone will tell you they're thieves. Draw your own conclusions. This is the way things are. Life's no prettier than a kitchen, it stinks just as bad, and if you want to get anything done you have to get your hands dirty: just make sure you know to wash them off: that's the beginning and the end of morality, these days."

(translated by Burton Raffel)

That is Vautrin, genius of crime, in *Père Goriot*, instructing Rastignac on Parisian morality. For me, to think of Balzac is to remember Vautrin, before all the other persons who throng *The Human Comedy*. Vautrin is the incarnation of Balzac's superhuman energies, of the fierce vitalism that animates each of the novels in which "Death-Dodger" (Vautrin's nickname) appears.

Marcel Proust wonderfully said of Balzac, "He hides nothing; he says everything." Vautrin has everything to hide, and paradoxically says all but everything, precisely because he knows everything about everyone, just as Balzac did.

Why did Balzac, in 1834, so boldly present his great hero-villain as a homosexual? Doubtless Vautrin represents many of Balzac's own concealed drives, but I would place the emphasis elsewhere. Vautrin is the classical outcast—outside the law, beyond the social contract. Balzac, with superb irony, will conclude Vautrin's career by making him head of the Parisian police establishment. Who could be better qualified?

Henry James, who could not abide the novels of Tolstoy ("loose, baggy monsters"), loved Balzac's fictions, which are far looser and baggier. Balzac's incredible energy—indeed his energetics—seduced Henry James. Like Baudelaire, James saw that Balzac was a visionary, not a mere realist. When I meditate upon Vautrin, I think also of Milton's Satan, and of William Blake's *Marriage of Heaven and Hell*.

HONORÉ DE BALZAC
(1799–1850)

BAUDELAIRE OBSERVED, FAMOUSLY, that "every one of Balzac's characters, even the janitors, has some sort of genius." Balzac, rather like Victor Hugo, outrageously was possessed by a genius, a daemonic will that drove him through the ninety novels and novellas that constitute *The Human Comedy*, deliberate rival to Dante's *Divine Comedy*. Reading the admirable Graham Robb's *Balzac: A Biography*, one comes away with the startled impression that Balzac cannot always be distinguished from his daemon. Since genius is my sole subject in this book, I will feel free to mix observations on Balzac himself with my account of his extraordinary character-of-characters, the master criminal Vautrin, also known as Jacques Collin and as the Abbé Carlos Herrera. Vautrin is crucial in *Père Goriot* (1834–35), *Lost Illusions* (1837–43), dominant in *A Harlot High and Low* (1838–47), and was the hero-villain of the play *Vautrin* (1840), banned after one performance by the Ministry of the Interior, to no great aesthetic loss.

Henry James, a superb literary critic except when he felt himself menaced (as by Hawthorne, Dickens, George Eliot), was at his best on Balzac, who for James possessed "a kind of inscrutable perfection." This appeared to James the prime lesson that Balzac taught other novelists:

> The lesson of Balzac, under this comparison, is extremely various, and I should prepare myself much too large a task were I to attempt a list of the separate truths he brings home. I have to choose among them, and I choose the most important; the three or four that more or less include the others. In reading him over, in opening him almost anywhere to-day, what immediately strikes us is the part assigned by him, in any picture, to the *conditions* of the creatures with whom he is concerned. Contrasted with him other prose painters of life scarce seem to see the conditions at all. He clearly held pretended portrayal as nothing, as less than nothing, as a most vain thing, unless it should be, in spirit and intention, the art of complete representation. "Complete" is of course a great word, and there is no art at all, we are often reminded, that is not on too many sides an abject compromise. The element of compromise is always there; it is of the essence; we live

with it, and it may serve to keep us humble. The formula of the whole matter is sufficiently expressed perhaps in a reply I found myself once making to an inspired but discouraged friend, a fellow-craftsman who had declared in his despair that there was no use trying, that it was a form, the novel, absolutely too difficult. "Too difficult indeed; yet there is one way to master it—which is to pretend consistently that it isn't." We are all of us, all the while, pretending—as consistently as we can—that it isn't, and Balzac's great glory is that he pretended hardest. He never had to pretend so hard as when he addressed himself to that evocation of the medium, that distillation of the natural and social air, of which I speak, the things that most require on the part of the painter preliminary possession—so definitely require it that, terrified at the requisition when conscious of it, many a painter prefers to beg the whole question. He has thus, this ingenious person, to invent some *other* way of making his characters interesting—some other way, that is, than the arduous way, demanding so much consideration, of presenting them to us. They are interesting, in fact, as subjects of fate, the figures round whom a situation closes, in proportion as, sharing their existence, we feel where fate comes in and just how it gets at them. In the void they are not interesting—and Balzac, like Nature herself, abhorred a vacuum. Their situation takes hold of us because it is theirs, not because it is somebody's, any one's, that of creatures unidentified. Therefore it is not superfluous that their identity shall first be established for us, and their adventures, in that measure, have a relation to it, and therewith an appreciability. There is no such thing in the world as an adventure pure and simple; there is only mine and yours, and his and hers—it being the greatest adventure of all, I verily think, just to *be* you or I, just to be he or she. To Balzac's imagination that was indeed in itself an immense adventure—and nothing appealed to him more than to show *how* we all are, and how we are placed and built-in for being so. What befalls us is but another name for the way our circumstances press upon us—so that an account of what befalls us is an account of our circumstances.

An exquisite account of Balzac's other characters, does this work for the master criminal Vautrin, Balzac's alter ego, perhaps his daemon? Rastignac, Lucien de Rubempré, Cousin Pons, Old Goriot, Eugénie Grandet, Baron Hulot, and all the other grand protagonists are indebted to Balzac for his showing *how* they are, and how they are placed. Vautrin is larger, as Balzac himself is. Graham Robb writes, "Balzac is both the embodiment of his age and its most revealing exception." I transpose that to: Vautrin is both the embodiment of *The Human Comedy* and its most revealing exception. The outcast Vautrin, Satan of the criminal life of Paris, ends as head of the Sûreté. Balzac, the hack writer from Tours, received the final tribute at his funeral from the inevitable Victor Hugo, his only literary rival in sublime madness and unbelievable fecundity. Robb tells us that Balzac's friends called him "Vautrin"; one surmises that the novelist's genius, had it not exhausted itself in his vast *Human Comedy*, could have been converted into either career: master criminal or master detective.

W. B. Yeats revered *Louis Lambert*, one of Balzac's occult performances, because it exalts a visionary energy, but so does the rest of *La Comédie Humaine*. Like his Louis Lambert, Balzac desired to write a *Theory of the Will*, or Human Force, and he did compose it in his *Comedy*, with Vautrin as its star manifestation. Ernst Robert Curtius, studying Balzac's energetics, emphasizes the novelist's obsession with economizing his vitality. Like Dickens, Balzac worked himself to death, though not as a public performer of his own works. Always apocalyptically in debt, he wrote in a frenzy, sometimes sleeping just two hours a night while drowning himself in coffee. Subject to hallucinations both auditory and visual, Balzac revived in himself the ancient association of genius with madness. Though as grand a monomaniac as Victor Hugo, and as much a force of nature and an occult energy, Balzac was wholly a novelist, and therefore *seems* saner than Hugo, who wrote enormous novels, yet who was the poet proper, the poet of his language, however unfashionable in our tasteless era.

When we first encounter Vautrin in *Père Goriot*, we are not precisely aware of what titanism he conceals, but we are told this tough forty-year-old has "appalling depths within." Vautrin's literary lineage is more High Romantic than gothic: he is a Byronic hero-villain, but a survivor. No one in Byron ever reaches forty, and one of Vautrin's nicknames in the criminal cosmos is "Death-Dodger." Vautrin is not a quester, and he is at war with a society he despises, but then he would be subversive of any nation, anywhere, anytime. He is pragmatically an anarchist, but this is pure paradox, since he has totally organized and imperiously rules over the entire criminal world. Since he is Parisian, not Sicilian, his Satanic pride is individual rather than familial. His drive is homoerotic, but it remains ambiguous whether his desire for handsome young disciples is primarily sexual or a displaced paternalism, as Balzac's perhaps was. Vautrin is free of sexual jealousy, so long as his young men fall in love and form liaisons only with women.

Sainte-Beuve, the major literary critic of the era of Victor Hugo, who had very mixed feelings about Balzac's work, envied Balzac the enthusiastic response he evoked among women readers. They sensed possibly a female element in the ferociously sexual Balzac, which I myself cannot locate. Balzac's orientation, like Shakespeare's, is too multiform to be reduced into our categories. I find this analogous to the question of Balzac's literary ancestry, which is also a puzzle. He has a vague debt to Sir Walter Scott's Waverley novels, but not to classical French fiction. Though the disapproving New Critic Martin Turnell found in Balzac the influence of Corneille, I agree with Graham Robb that the authentic precursor is Molière, who might have written a *Vautrin* if only his audience (and King Louis XIV) would have tolerated it.

Vautrin's criminal genius is dramaturgical: he wants to mold Balzac's characters, Rastignac and the poet Lucien, into something grander, and he is a superb scene-setter. Trapped in a police ambush, in part 3 of *Père Goriot*, he dodges death by an extraordinary art of command over his own fury:

> "In the name of the law, and the name of the King," announced one of the officers, though there was such a loud murmur of astonishment that no one could hear him.
>
> But silence quickly descended once again, as the lodgers moved aside, making room for three of the men, who came forward, their hands in their pockets, and loaded pistols in their hands. Two uniformed policemen stepped into the doorway they'd left, and two others appeared in the other doorway, near the stairs. Soldiers' footsteps, and the readying of their rifles, echoed from the pavement outside, in front of the house. Death-Dodger had no hope of escape; everyone stared at him irresistibly drawn. Vidocq went directly to where he stood, and swiftly punched Collin in the head with such force that his wig flew off, revealing the stark horror of his skull. Brick-red, short-clipped hair gave him a look at once sly and powerful, and both head and face, blending perfectly, now, with his brutish chest, glowed with the fierce, burning light of a hellish mind. It was suddenly obvious to them all just who Vautrin was, what he'd done, what he'd been doing, what he would go on to do; they suddenly understood at a glance his implacable ideas, his religion of self-indulgence, exactly the sort of royal sensibility which tinted all his thoughts with cynicism, as well as all his actions, and supported both by the strength of an organization prepared for anything. The blood rose into his face, his eyes gleamed like some savage cat's. He seemed to explode into a gesture of such wild energy, and he roared with such ferocity that, one and all, the lodgers cried out in terror. His fierce, feral movement, and the general

clamor he'd created, made the policemen draw their weapons. But seeing the gleam of cocked pistols, Collin immediately understood his peril, and instantly proved himself possessor of the highest of all human powers. It was a horrible, majestic spectacle! His face could only be compared to some steaming apparatus, full of billowing smoke capable of moving mountains, but dissolved in the twinkling of an eye by a single drop of cold water. The drop that doused his rage flickered as rapidly as a flash of light. Then he slowly smiled, and turned to look down at his wig.

"This isn't one of your polite days, it is, old boy?" he said to Vidocq. And then he held out his hands to the policemen, beckoning them with a movement of his head. "Gentlemen, officers, I'm ready for your handcuffs or your chains, as you please. I ask those present to take due note of the fact that I offer no resistance."

(translated by Burton Raffel)

"The highest of all human powers" here is the art of the great dramatist, Shakespeare or Molière, in representing sudden change in a great character, an Iago or a Tartuffe, or a Vautrin. Balzac's apotheosis in this art comes with "The Last Incarnation of Vautrin," the final section of *A Harlot High and Low*. Vautrin, bereft of Lucien through the poet's suicide, is transformed, phase after phase, from the Satan of the underworld to the God of the Parisian police establishment. Balzac dazzles the reader throughout the shock of this transformation, but he leaves me very uncertain what has happened to Vautrin's Rousseau-inspired lifelong battle against society. Vautrin goes over to Balzac's side, thus becoming a legitimist, a royalist, and a prime preserver of the oligarchy. Though Vautrin has been all but traumatized by Lucien's suicide, his conversion to the established order does not seem a reaction to this loss. Perhaps the explanation is the Balzacian energetics of power. Vautrin is now older, and even his diabolic energy may be on the verge of waning, while presumably the power of enforcement requires less strain than the power of subversion. Or again, perhaps the act of usurpation is the supreme accolade for Vautrin, Balzac's prime surrogate.

One of Balzac's great inventions is the intricate dance of recruitment that is performed by Granville, the dignified and honorable attorney-general, and the endlessly metamorphic Vautrin, who in a sense is seduced by Granville's authentic moral grandeur. The greatness of Vautrin recognizes, and is raised to a state of exaltation by, the rival greatness of Granville. As a reader, I sorrow at losing Vautrin to the state; it is rather as though Satan repented fully in *Paradise Lost*, and rejoined the angelic orders.

But Balzac was guiding his genius to safe harbor; he lived only three years beyond Vautrin's metamorphosis from Death-Dodger to society's ultimate weapon against disorder. He needed Vautrin to be an allegory of his own posthumous destiny: to become a guardian of the human comedy he had so exuberantly imagined.

LEWIS CARROLL

> He thought he saw an Argument
>> That proved he was the Pope:
> He looked again, and found it was
>> A Bar of Mottled Soap.
> "A fact so dread," he faintly said,
>> "Extinguishes all hope!"
>>> —"The Mad Gardener's Song"

Lewis Carroll is the greatest master of literary fantasy, a mode of romance still alive in our era, where I find much of Carroll's spirit in John Crowley's *Little, Big* and his *Ægypt* series.

The masterpieces of Carroll are the *Alice* books—*Wonderland* and *Through the Looking-Glass*—as well as the long poem *The Hunting of the Snark*, which opens superbly:

> "Just the place for a Snark!" the Bellman cried,
>> As he landed his crew with care;
> Supporting each man on the top of the tide
>> By a finger entwined in his hair.

> "Just the place for a Snark! I have said it twice:
>> That alone should encourage the crew,
> Just the place for a Snark! I have said it thrice:
>> What I tell you three times is true."

The Snark turns out to be a dread Boojum, a Carrollian version of Melville's Moby-Dick, and the poem closes on a note of implicit dread that remains insouciantly joyous. Carroll's genius is not truly for nonsense writing, like Edward Lear's, but for warding off mortality, the quest that story-telling shares with wisdom literature. Such a quest must fail for some, and those who come through may be disreputable personages like the Walrus and the Carpenter, who in their marvelous poem devour those poor innocents, all the little oysters:

"It seems a shame," the Walrus said,
    "To play them such a trick.
After we've brought them out so far,
    And made them trot so quick!"
The Carpenter said nothing but
"The butter's spread too thick!"

"I weep for you," the Walrus said:
    "I deeply sympathize."
With sobs and tears he sorted out
    Those of the largest size,
Holding his pocket-handkerchief
Before his streaming eyes.

"O Oysters," said the Carpenter,
    "You've had a pleasant run!
Shall we be trotting home again?"
    But answer came there none—
And this was scarcely odd, because
    They'd eaten every one.

LEWIS CARROLL
(CHARLES LUTWIDGE DODGSON)
(1832–1898)

THE REVEREND CHARLES LUTWIDGE Dodgson, lecturer in mathematics at Christ Church College, Oxford University, is remembered primarily for his three totally original literary achievements: *Alice's Adventures in Wonderland* (1865), *Through the Looking-Glass and What Alice Found There* (1871), and *The Hunting of the Snark: An Agony in Eight Fits* (1876). The category of "children's literature" seems to me no longer useful as we commence the third millennium. Bad writing is bad for children, and the Harry Potter books (even if I am a minority of one on this) are cliché-heavy period pieces, and will end in dustbins. When there *was* children's literature, its masterworks were Carroll's. His three creations of genius abide securely with the varied perfections of nineteenth-century literature, the works of Manzoni and Leopardi, of Eça de Quieroz and Victor Hugo, of Balzac and Stendhal and Flaubert, Baudelaire and Rimbaud, Ibsen and William Blake, Wordsworth and Coleridge, Shelley and Keats, Tennyson and Dickens and Robert Browning, George Eliot and Oscar Wilde, Novalis and Heine, Pushkin and Gogol, Turgenev and Dostoevsky, Tolstoy and Chekhov. I list these as reminder and as true context, though only Blake and Coleridge, Wordsworth and Tennyson, can be regarded as authentic influences upon Lewis Carroll. Of these, Wordsworth matters most, and therefore is most destructively parodied by Carroll.

There is no precise literary term for Carroll's genre, except "romance," but that has been destroyed by modern popular usage, which has also demolished "fantasy." There remains "parody," but Carroll generally transcends that mode; his ironies frequently achieve Shakespearean resonance. Carroll is ultimately so strong a writer that he slyly can survive taking Shakespeare and Cervantes as his models. I say this of his three great works; the two *Sylvie and Bruno* novels fail, though their use of fairies appears to be the model for one of the finest unread fantasies of our time, John Crowley's wonderful *Little, Big*.

Carroll, in the *Alice* books and the *Snark*, is so original that he transmutes every possible source into an alchemical gold instantly recognizable as unique to him. In the outrageous chapter 6, "Pig and Pepper," of *Alice's*

Adventures in Wonderland, we enter, with Alice, a smoky kitchen to find ourselves breathing pepper, together with a sneezing Duchess, who holds what appears to be her screaming and sneezing baby. We behold also a huge, grinning Cheshire Cat, and a cook stirring soup in a cauldron. The cook proceeds to throw saucepans and dishes at the noisy Duchess, who roars forth, "Chop off her head!" while crooning a lullaby to the baby, shaking it violently and frequently:

"Speak roughly to your little boy,
And beat him when he sneezes:
He only does it to annoy,
Because he knows it teases."

Chorus

(in which the cook and the baby joined):—
"Wow! Wow! Wow!"

"Here! You may nurse it a bit, if you like!" the Duchess said to Alice, flinging the baby at her as she spoke. "I must go and get ready to play croquet with the Queen," and she hurried out of the room. The cook threw a frying-pan after her as she went, but it just missed her.

The baby turns out to be a pig, which the calm Alice sensibly releases. Wonderland, as the Cheshire Cat tells Alice, is a world where everyone is quite mad. The critic William Empson observed that Lewis Carroll seemed to equate sexual maturation with dying, a formula madder than anything explicit in the *Alice* books. Carroll, like John Ruskin, could only be attracted to pre-adolescent girls, a malady inherited by Humbert Humbert in Nabokov's *Lolita.* Certainly, Alice's extraordinary charm in both books has a palpably sexual aura. Aesthetically, this is enhancing, and any psychosexual reductions of Carroll's books are tiresomely superfluous. The *Alice* books are not secret manuals of sexual harassment, and the Madame Defarges who staff the Sexual Harassment Committee in each and every one of our English-speaking universities would never be able to knit Lewis Carroll into their indictments. The historical Alice Liddell was more Carroll's Dulcinea than his Beatrice, though Morton N. Cohen, in his *Lewis Carroll: A Biography* (1995), conjectures that Charles Dodgson, at thirty-one, proposed marriage to Alice Liddell, at eleven, presumably by venturing to speak to her parents. Certainly there was a lasting rift between Dodgson and the

Liddells by 1864. Carroll sent his illustrator, John Tenniel, a photograph of another child-friend, Mary Badcock, to use as a model for *Alice's Adventures in Wonderland*, and yet another child-friend, Alice Raikes, became the muse for *Through the Looking-Glass*. When *The Hunting of the Snark* was published, its dedication was to yet one more child-friend, Gertrude Chataway. Though he was never to marry, and died presumably without sexual experience, the resilient Dodgson manifested a healthy degree of what Freud was to term "narcissistic mobility." At fifty-nine, he continued to correspond with eleven-year-old beauties, quite blamelessly.

There is some complex relationship between Lewis Carroll's astonishing exuberance in both verse and prose, and Charles Dodgson's lifelong stammering. But, like all of those poignant friendships with eleven-year-old young ladies of good family, no facile connections between life and work are at all illuminating. Much more interesting, and more revelatory of the strangeness of Carroll's genius, would be to ask: how did the *Alice* books change Carroll's inward life, if at all? There is clearly a sense in which Alice, in both books, is more Carroll himself than she is a vision of his beloved child-friends. Did he realize this? A sparse and fastidious person in his diet, Dodgson was always baffled that his child-friends had hearty appetites. His Alice is an eccentric delight, surrounded by aristocrats and royalty who seem to represent Dodgson's revenge against the snobbish Liddells, who may have felt that the son of a Yorkshire rector was not their social equal.

Our best clue to the effect of *Alice in Wonderland* upon Carroll is the very different *Through the Looking-Glass*, and the two *Alice* books together can be seen as modifying Carroll's stance towards reality in *The Hunting of the Snark*. The second *Alice* book has a visionary otherness that I cannot locate in the first; there seems to me both aesthetic gain in sophistication, and aesthetic loss in exuberance, as you read on from one book to the other. My favorite moment of *Alice in Wonderland* is not possible for the sequel:

> "Hold your tongue!" said the Queen, turning purple.
> "I won't!" said Alice.
> "Off with her head!" the Queen shouted at the top of her voice. Nobody moved.
> "Who cares for *you*?" said Alice (she had grown to her full size by this time). "You're nothing but a pack of cards!"

Alice splendidly casts away phantasmagoria, and returns to our normative reality. So cleanly abrupt a movement is not possible in *Through the Looking-Glass*, where Alice may be not much different, but Carroll is. It would be hard to vary Alice anyway, since uniquely in both books only she lacks personality. All the (what shall we call them?) inhabitants of Wonderland and the world on the other side of the looking-glass are madly eccentric, when not completely mad. One useful way of contrasting the two *Alice* books is to compare their invariably superb poems. *Alice in Wonderland* gives us the parodies "How doth the little crocodile," and "You are old, Father William," "The Lobster-Quadrille," "The Mock Turtle's Song," and "The White Rabbit's Verses." Though all pleasant, these are dwarfed by the poems of *Through the Looking-Glass*, which are among the best in the language: "Jabberwocky," "The Walrus and the Carpenter," "Humpty Dumpty's Song" ("In winter, when the fields are white"), and Carroll's finest poem, except for *The Hunting of the Snark*, "The White Knight's Ballad." The delicious sadism of "The Walrus and the Carpenter" would be out of place in Wonderland, where threats are made but no one can be devoured or beheaded. In *The Hunting of the Snark*, a poem comparable in power to Rimbaud's "Bateau ivre" or Coleridge's *Rime of the Ancient Mariner*, we arrive at the outer limit of Lewis Carroll's vision. The final four of the quest-poem's eight fits lead off with a stanza twice spoken earlier, so that we cannot get it out of our mind:

> They sought it with thimbles, they sought it with care;
> They pursued it with forks and hope;
> They threatened its life with a railway-share;
> They charmed it with smiles and soap.

One feels that is the heart of the matter, but what is the matter? "It" presumably is the Snark, but what is that? The distinguished poet-exegete John Hollander usefully replies "female sexuality," but that seems only partly appropriate. Despite Alice's disturbing ride on the railway in *Through the Looking-Glass*, one doesn't know why a railway-share would be more life-threatening to a female than a male. I suspect that "it" is death, our death, though for Dodgson/Carroll there isn't much difference between death and mature sexual experience, so I don't disagree much with Hollander. I am in considerable disagreement with Carroll's biographer, Morton Cohen, who insists that his author was not expressing any fear of death or annihilation, being too good a Christian for that. Yet Cohen also relates the Baker's annihilation, at the poem's end, to "the hallowed relationship of person to person, of Charles [Dodgson] to his child-friends, a sacredness that must never be violated." An actual embrace by Dodgson of any of his charming panoply of eleven-year-old princesses would have been not only illegal and immoral but annihilating. That appears to have been the audacious crime of the Baker, who plunges off the top of a crag into a love-death:

> Erect and sublime, for one moment of time.
> In the next, that wild figure they saw
> (As if stung by a spasm) plunge into a chasm . . .

Commentary seems unnecessary: "erect," "spasm," "chasm" tell one story and one story only. For once, a reductive interpretation is both sufficient and necessary, and certainly does not lessen this poem.

HENRY JAMES

"I can't escape unhappiness," said Isabel. "In marrying you I shall be trying to."

"I don't know whether you'd try to, but you certainly would: that I must in candour admit!" he exclaimed with an anxious laugh.

"I mustn't—I can't," cried the girl.

"Well, if you're bent on being miserable I don't see why you should make *me* so. Whatever charms a life of misery may have for you, it has none for me."

"I'm not bent on a life of misery," said Isabel. "I've always been intensely determined to be happy, and I've often believed I should be. I've told people that; you can ask them. But it comes over me every now and then that I can never be happy in any extraordinary way; not by turning away, by separating myself."

"By separating yourself from what?"

"From life. From the usual chances and dangers, from what most people know and suffer."

—*The Portrait of a Lady*, volume 1, chapter 14

Isabel Archer, declining Lord Warburton's marriage proposal, states Henry James's aesthetic credo: not to be separated from the common life. James, as much a high priest of the art of the novel as were Flaubert and Proust, does not immediately impress most readers as an apostle of the common life. James is hardly Tolstoy or even George Eliot, and his late masterpieces like *The Wings of the Dove* and *The Golden Bowl*, though eloquent and poignant, do not have the largeness and the universalism of *The Portrait of a Lady*.

Yet if you immerse yourself in Henry James's fictions, then you encounter the genius of the United States at its strongest and most characteristic. Isabel Archer is the portrait of the American woman: only Hawthorne's Hester Prynne in *The Scarlet Letter* is her rival. And there is a subtle sense in which Isabel is the representative of the genius of Henry James at its most generous and affirmative. Even the greatest of modern American novelists, William Faulkner, is not as central to the American imagination as Henry James continues to be. To understand the American psyche, three writers are essential above all others: Emerson, Walt Whitman, Henry James.

HENRY JAMES
(1843–1916)

HENRY JAMES IS THE MOST EMINENT writer of prose fiction that the United States has brought forth. He has only a few peers in his nation's literature: Whitman and Dickinson among the poets, and Ralph Waldo Emerson among the prophets. Hawthorne and Faulkner are the only artists of romance who approach his eminence, but his subtle achievement is more nuanced and more universal than theirs. If I had to answer the desert island question with only one American author, I would have to take Whitman because he is richer. Henry James has an almost Dantesque complexity in his vast temple of language, but he lacks Whitman's pathos and dramatic urgency. And while he seems more challenging than Whitman, he is not; Whitman is the more difficult and finally more demanding writer.

James is more than demanding enough. Since my subject is the genius of Henry James, I set aside the social lion and look for the lesson of the artist. The great novels—*The Portrait of a Lady, The Ambassadors, The Wings of the Dove, The Golden Bowl*—require more than a single tessera of my mosaic can provide, so I will seek James's genius in one of his stories, the ghostlier the better, because I like tales of ghosts and of hauntings.

Leon Edel, Henry James's biographer, judges some eighteen of the master's stories to be "supernatural." So artful is James that it is hard to know; some are romance fantasies, while others belong to no genre. James wrote just over a hundred stories, so eighteen is a high percentage. But if Joseph Sheridan Le Fanu is a ghost story writer, then Henry James is something else. He was not as receptive to psychic phenomena as his brother William James was, and yet they both were their father's sons. Henry James Sr. felt, with William Blake, that everything possible to be believed was an image of truth. Though the senior Henry loved (and was exasperated by) Emerson, he turned to the sublimely mad Emanuel Swedenborg after his celebrated *vastation,* a more-than-clinical depression that afflicted him in England, in 1844. William and Henry were babies, and could have had no immediate sense of what occurred, but the *vastation* became family mythology, not easily set aside by any among them.

Though the relationship between William and Henry James defies almost any characterization, on some level they were allied, thanks to their many different modes. Had they both been writers of fiction, like Thomas and Heinrich Mann, it would have been unfortunate for the love between them. Had they a common genius? The question, I am aware, is a peculiar one; it might be more coherent to speak of the common genius of the Brontë sisters, though Emily Brontë was an almost unique visionary, as individual as William Blake or D. H. Lawrence. We know, more or less, what we mean by "Brontëan," but what would "Jamesian" mean?

I suppose that, among active Swedenborgians, in Boston or elsewhere, one could still locate a person or two who was saved from depression by reading *Divine Providence* or *Divine Love and Wisdom.* Having read both, and much more Swedenborg, in my youth, when I was a scholar of William Blake, I well remember how depressed I became battling through the Swedish mystic's boomfog. Fortunately, the senior Henry James merely picked his way through Swedenborg, whom he regarded as a clever reporter who had visited the various heavens and hells, and returned to tell us they were much like Sweden. The principle that the father of William and Henry took from Swedenborg—that individual selfhood led to vastation—he would have found better expressed in Meister Eckhart: "Only the Self burns in Hell." James Sr. was a Swedenborgian only as so many people I knew in my youth were Freudian; you had dinner with them, or went to a movie together, and they carried along a volume or two by the founder of psychoanalysis.

The secret of Swedenborg, according to the first Henry James, was that redemption came through turning away from the self to others. This was not even a weak misreading of Swedenborg; it was not a reading at all, but that did not matter, at all. The senior James revived, and functioned, and changed his ideas only a little. It is an irony that both William and the younger Henry both found Emerson to have too benign a view of the world, while their fiercely optimistic father on many occasions lamented Emerson's lack of societal optimism, and continued to complain of the ironic seer, "O, you man without a handle!" The father's ambivalence towards the inventor of intellectual America was carried forward by the sons. Isabel Archer, in *The Portrait of a Lady,* is as much an Emersonian coming to some grief as is Hester Prynne in *The Scarlet Letter,* while William in his *Pragmatism* "corrected" Emerson in a vocabulary imparted from his father's frustrating friend, particularly from Emerson's greatest essay, "Experience."

If there is a common element to the Jamesian genius, it did not emanate from the opacity of their father's prose. Nor were their notions of the self consonant with their father's supposed rejection of it, since he never could shed that inescapable animal, one's self. Yet he remained for them what William called him after his death, "a religious prophet and genius," who firmly rejected all organized and historical religion. Henry rather regretted his father's prose style, but otherwise concurred in William's estimate. In truth, the senior Henry James was neither prophet nor genius, neither Joseph Smith nor Waldo Emerson. And yet his diffuse theism, his strong belief that there *was* a spiritual world, undoubtedly influenced both William's psychology of religious experience and Henry's subtle secularization of the spirit in a novel like *The Wings of the Dove.* Even more elusively, the fatherly preoccupation with the unseen gets into the ghostly tales of Henry James.

The more famous of those stories include "The Ghostly Rental," "Owen Wingrave," "The Turn of the Screw," and "The Jolly Corner," but I choose to write here about a particular favorite, "The Way It Came" (1896), originally titled "The Friends of the Friends." So subtle is "The Way It Came" that I can think of four or five meanings for that revised title, none of them indisputable. Few other stories defy summary interpretation so formidably. We are given two narrators—the outer one, who has only an opening paragraph, and then a remarkable woman, now deceased, writing in her diary. The frame-narrator usefully remarks that no names, not even initials, are given by the diarist, who handles her tale so skillfully that, at first reading, one may not realize that no one in the story *has* been named.

R. W. B. Lewis, in his *Jameses: A Family Narrative,* quotes William James's assertion that "the cases where the apparition of a person is seen on the day of his death are four hundred and forty times too numerous to be ascribed to chance." That emphatic but arbitrary "four hundred and forty" gives James's contention a certain gusto, and makes me recall how many times I have been told of such apparitions, though I haven't myself seen one. But the tradition involved is very ancient; Shelley in *Prometheus Unbound* tells us that Zoroaster (Zarathustra) met his own image while walking in a garden and died shortly afterward. Shelley in his last days similarly encountered his own image, and fainted when it asked him, "How long do you mean to be content?" Such images are also apparent to others. Another tradition, which Henry James exploits, maintains that one may behold the parent's phantom of the sex opposite to one's own, if she or he has died that day in a distant place.

"The Way It Came" is an occult love story twisted very fine. Our name-less diarist tells us that she had long expected to introduce to one another two of her friends, a woman and a man, who each had seen the phantom of

their father and mother respectively, not knowing that, at the same moment and far distant, the parent was dying. In a comedy of mischances, the
introduction never takes place, though both are receptive to it. After the
narrator is betrothed to the man, she insists on making a final attempt to
bring them together. When, the next day, her "dearest friend" informs the
narrator, by a note, that her estranged husband has just died, the diarist
reconsiders:

When she left me I began to wonder what she was afraid of, for she
had spoken as if she fully meant it. The next day, late in the afternoon, I had three lines from her: she found on getting home the an-
nouncement of her husband's death. She hadn't seen him for seven
years, but she wished me to know it in this way before I should hear
of it in another. It made however in her life, strange and sad to say, so
little difference that she would scrupulously keep her appointment. I
rejoiced for her—I supposed it would make at least the difference of
her having more money; but even in this diversion, far from forgetting
she had said that she was afraid, I seemed to catch sight of a reason
for her being so. Her fear, as the evening went on, became contagious,
and the contagion took in my breast the form of a sudden panic. It
wasn't jealousy—it was just the dread of jealousy. I called myself a fool
for not having been quiet till we were man and wife. After that I
should somehow feel secure. It was only a question of waiting another
month—a trifle surely for people who had waited so long. It had been
plain enough that she was nervous, and now she was free her ner-
vousness wouldn't be less. What was it therefore but a sharp forebod-
ing? She had been hitherto the victim of interference, but it was quite
possible she would henceforth be the source of it. The victim in that
case would be my simple self. What had the interference been but the
finger of Providence pointing out a danger? The danger was of course
for poor me. It had been kept at bay by a series of accidents unexam-
pled in their frequency; but the reign of accidents was now visibly at
an end. I had an intimate conviction that both parties would keep the
tryst. It was more and more impressed on me that they were approaching, converging. They were like the seekers for the hidden object in the game of blindfold; they had one and the other begun to
"burn." We had talked about breaking the spell; well, it would be effectually broken—unless indeed it should merely take another form
and overdo their encounters as it had overdone their escapes. This
was something I couldn't sit still for thinking of; it kept me awake—

at midnight I was full of unrest. At last I felt there was only one way of laying the ghost. If the reign of accident was over I must just take up the succession. I sat down and wrote a hurried note which would meet him on his return and which as the servants had gone to bed I sallied forth bareheaded into the empty gusty street to drop into the nearest pillar-box. It was to tell him that I shouldn't be able to be at home in the afternoon as I had hoped and that he must postpone his visit until dinner-time. This was an implication that he would find me alone.

I quote this long paragraph because it is a sinuous epitome of the entire story, including its failed prophecy: "At last I felt there was only one way of laying the ghost." Her woman friend arrives, is disappointed, and departs, having given up. The man, immensely disappointed, also yields the hope of ever meeting. In remorse, the diarist calls upon her woman friend the following day, only to be told that she died last night of a sudden heart attack. In some grief (and remorse) the diarist visits her betrothed, to impart the bad news, and to be told that the deceased friend had called upon him the night before.

There is an exquisitely rendered disagreement: he insists that the still-living woman visited him briefly, and *she that* he beheld an apparition. What passed between them is left ambiguous. But what now augments is a rift between the two living components of the triangle, in a foreshadowing of the memory of Milly Theale coming between Kate Croy and Merton Densher at the very close of *The Wings of the Dove*. Yet the story is occult, the novel not. The diarist dissolves her engagement, because she rightly surmises that there is an ongoing erotic relationship (no details are proffered) between her betrothed and the shade who visits him nightly: "we separated and I left him to his inconceivable communion."

That superbly ironic sentence precedes the story's superb final paragraph:

He never married, any more than I've done. When six years later, in solitude and silence, I heard of his death I hailed it as a direct contribution to my theory. It was sudden, it was never properly accounted for, it was surrounded by circumstances in which—for oh, I took them to pieces!—I distinctly read an intention, the mark of his own hidden hand. It was the result of a long necessity, of an unquenchable desire. To say exactly what I mean, it was a response to an irresistible call.

So much is left indefinite. Did an apparition or a living woman embrace her lover the night of her death? "The Way It Came," as a title, suggests that "it" was the apparition. With extraordinary and convincing quietude, a voice of enduring jealousy and regret has told us a story in which love is stronger than death, and it remains for the reader to decide how incredulous she or he ought to be.

Did either Henry or William James believe in the spirit's survival? The question may not be answerable in anything except their terms, and those are neither identical nor definite. In 1910, Henry James wrote an essay called "Is There Life after Death?" Frances Wilson, astutely commenting upon this, observes that "the James children became graveyards for their parents and for each other, and the family ideal of self-detachment became indistinguishable from the stranger idea that the self was the harborage of others."

As a title "Is There Life after Death?" is misleading, since the essay is not devoted to any traditional notions of survival or of immortality. What is a touch preternatural about the James family—William, Henry, and Alice in particular—is that they shared a kind of "over-consciousness," which is reflected in writings by all three. I don't believe that any idea of "over-consciousness" retains much interest if it does not imply a survival of one's own consciousness in someone else. I don't want to portray the House of James as the House of Usher, the Jameses being more Emersonian than Poesque, but we all know siblings, particularly twins, who seem to communicate across space and time without much speaking being involved. William and Henry were not twins, but there was only a year between them.

Henry James was a great artist of prose fiction, comparable in craft and vision to Marcel Proust. William James was a superb psychologist and religious thinker; I lack the competence to judge him or any other philosopher as such. The Jamesian genius, present also in Alice's disturbing diaries but hard to find in Henry Sr.'s opacities, is a genius of consciousness, carried on from William by Gertrude Stein, but inimitable in Henry. I have not space here to analyze *The Varieties of Religious Experience,* a work I find as permanently valuable and readable as *The Portrait of a Lady* or *The Wings of the Dove.* Yet I give the last word here to William James, from his postscript to *The Varieties:*

> The difference in natural "fact" which most of us would assign as the
> first difference which the existence of a God ought to make would, I
> imagine, be personal immortality. Religion, in fact, for the great ma-
> jority of our race means immortality; and whoever has doubts of

immortality is written down as an atheist without farther trial. I have said nothing in my lectures about immortality or the belief therein, for to me it seems a secondary point. If our ideals are only cared for in eternity, I do not see why we might not be willing to resign their care to other hands than ours.

ROBERT BROWNING

> What in the midst lay but the Tower itself?
>   The round squat turret, blind as the fool's heart,
>   Built of brown stone, without a counterpart
> In the whole world. The tempest's mocking elf
> Points to the shipman thus the unseen shelf
>   He strikes on, only when the timbers start.

Robert Browning has become too difficult for many readers in the Age of the Screen, but his genius remains unique and nurturing. His "dramatic monologues" are misleadingly named: they are subjective, lyrical antiphons in which many voices, usually dwelling in a single person, play against one another.

In a wonderful poetic monologue by the contemporary poet Richard

Howard ("November 1889") Browning is made to observe, "I am not interested in art, but in the obstacles to art." That brilliantly captures Browning's enterprise, a divided flame akin to the one in Dante's *Inferno* out of which Ulysses speaks, creating in Dante an absolute silence of response, in which the Christian poet tacitly acknowledges his affinity with the damned quester. Listening to Browning's speakers, we also pass into the profound silence of recognizing our complicity with an array of great failures: self-ruined poets and painters, disgraced questers, betrayed lovers, fanatics of near-genius, inspired charlatans, unimaginative monomaniacs, and talented confidence men capable now of deceiving only themselves.

Browning's bad dreams become one's own: his genius, like that of Dickens and of Kafka, was for the grotesque:

> . . . each oak
> Held on his horns some spoil he broke
> By surreptitiously beneath
> Upthrusting: pavements, as with teeth,
> Gripped huge weed widening crack and split
> In squares and circles stone-work erst.

ROBERT BROWNING
(1812–1889)

THERE ARE OTHER GREAT WRITERS OUT of fashion at our bad moment, but of all the major poets in English, Robert Browning now seems to me the most absurdly neglected. Because his genius is so original, his daemonic force still so astonishing, I hope to treat him rather fully here, though I have set my heart upon economy in this book, especially because there are more geniuses of language that should be considered than I have the time and space to accommodate. For reasons explained at the outset, I have excluded the living, but in my universe of the mighty dead, Robert Browning is so preeminent that I will allow him scope so that his gifts may seem finally beyond argument. His magnificent semi-invention was the dramatic monologue, and I will examine five of his best: "My Last Duchess," "Fra Lippo Lippi," "Childe Roland to the Dark Tower Came," "Andrea del Sarto," and "A Toccata of Galuppi's." Of these, "Childe Roland" haunts me most—I have spent many days of my life going about reciting it to myself—but I think the masterpiece is "Andrea del Sarto," and so I will examine it most closely.

"My Last Duchess" may be Browning's best-known poem, and has been widely parodied and imitated. The monologist, the murderous Duke, holds our attention because he is on the border of madness, poised at the abyss where familial pride and personal self-esteem cross over into an obsessional mania.

> She thanked men,—good! But thanked
> Somehow—I know not how—as if she ranked
> My gift of a nine-hundred-years-old name
> With anybody's gift. Who'd stoop to blame
> This sort of trifling? Even had you skill
> In speech—(which I have not)—to make your will
> Quite clear to such a one, and say, "Just this
> Or that in you disgusts me: here you miss,
> Or there exceed the mark"—and if she let
> Herself be lessoned so, nor plainly set
> Her wits to yours, forsooth, and made excuse.

E'en then would be some stooping; and I choose
Never to stoop. Oh sir, she smiled, no doubt
Whene'er I passed her; but who passed without
Much the same smile? This grew; I gave commands;
Then all smiles stopped together.

Rather than instruct your seventeen-year-old first wife in the deference due to a man of your degree, you have her poisoned! Since the Duke of Ferrara is showing off his art collection (including the portrait of "my last Duchess") to the emissary of the father of his next Duchess, this argues either for an immoderate sophistication or a certain madness, or perhaps even for both. But this is Browning at twenty-nine or thirty, in 1842, still in the process of teaching himself the monologue form, in a transition away from the Shelleyan lyric mode, and there is melodrama hovering too close with so glaringly wicked a Duke, fun though he is.

With "Fra Lippo Lippi," written eleven years later, we have the authentic Browning monologue, not a self-protrait of the artist but of the art. The historical Fra Lippo Lippi (1406–1469) was a superb naturalistic Florentine painter, and a wonderfully libertine friar of the Carmelite order. Of all Browning's speakers, he may be the most likable: he has a Chaucerian and Shakespearean vitalism, and is in rebellion against the highly spiritual art of Giotto, urged upon him by his Prior, who directs Lippi to "Paint the soul, never mind the legs and arms!", to which this roaring boy of an artist replies:

"Oh, that white smallish female with the breasts,
She's just my niece . . . Herodias, I would say—
Who went and danced, and got men's heads cut off!
Have it all out!" Now, is this sense, I ask?
A fine way to paint soul, by painting body
So ill, the eye can't stop there, must go further
And can't fare worse! Thus, yellow's simply black,
And any sort of meaning looks intense
When all beside itself means and looks nought.
Why can't a painter lift each foot in turn,
Left foot and right foot, go a double step,
Make his flesh liker and his soul more like,
Both in their order? Take the prettiest face
The Prior's niece . . . patron-saint—is it so pretty
You can't discover if it means hope, fear,

Sorrow or joy? Won't beauty go with these?
Suppose I've made her eyes all right and blue,
Can't I take breath and try to add life's flash,
And then add soul and heighten them threefold?
Or say there's beauty with no soul at all—
(I never saw it—put the case the same—)
If you get simple beauty and nought else,
You get about the best thing God invents:
That's somewhat: and you'll find the soul you have missed,
Within yourself, when you return him thanks.

What Lippi knows best is "the value and significance of flesh," and he integrates this avowed sensualism with his art. And yet Browning curiously renders Lippi as beset by aesthetic anxieties, including the premonition of an art to come that he himself cannot foreshadow:

> Oh, oh,
> It makes me mad to see what men shall do
> And we in our graves!

The actual Lippi was the student and disciple of Masaccio, the "Hulking Tom" of this monologue, who, however, appears here as Lippi's student, not a mistake that Browning would make unintentionally. Fiercely invested both in his own originality and in Lippi as his chosen surrogate, Browning inflates Lippi's originality. In the yet more fascinating "Andrea del Sarto," Browning does the reverse, deprecating the marvelous achievement of "The Faultless Painter." You can say that Browning simply follows Vasari's *Lives of the Painters*, where Andrea is seen as the perfect craftsman who lacks richness and force, but Vasari, who was Andrea's pupil, shows a personal animus against a personality clearly not as likable as Lippo Lippi's.

Browning, who hated compromise, had renounced his mother's Evangelical faith, at fourteen, under Shelley's influence. After a crisis with his mother, Browning yielded, and never got over his subsequent sense of inner betrayal. It is very difficult these days to say much about Browning's marriage to Elizabeth Barrett, an idealized but difficult relationship, because fierce feminist critics rise up instantly to bash one. There are a very few readable poems by Barrett Browning, but she is mostly an earnestly bad poet, endlessly sincere. She was also a fierce supporter of the tyrant Napoleon III, which did not make her husband, a man of the Shelleyan left, very happy. "Andrea del Sarto" is an intense twilight piece, in which "a common greyness silvers everything." The poem is in no way a Browningesque self-portrait: Andrea's wife is an adulterous gold-digger, the antithesis of the generous and virtuous Elizabeth Barrett. But there is a deep anxiety implicit in "Andrea del Sarto," quite apart from Andrea's ambivalence towards his own self-curtailments, in life and in art. Browning is in no danger of turning into Andrea, who nevertheless troubles him, and us, as an eloquent instance of hard-won defeat.

Andrea's subtly perverse stance parodies Browning's own aesthetic of imperfection, if only because Andrea rates his own potential as a painter very high, reaching to the realm of the greatest: Leonardo, Raphael, Michelangelo. Does he know that he deceives himself? Can he believe anything that he says? His language, beautifully wrought yet emotionally confused, is the most nuanced of any of Browning's monologists:

> You smile? Why, there's my picture ready made,
> There's what we painters call our harmony!
> A common greyness silvers everything,—
> All in a twilight, you and I alike
> —You, at the point of your first pride in me
> (That's gone you know),—but I, at every point;
> My youth, my hope, my art, being all toned down
> To yonder sober pleasant Fiesole.
> There's the bell clinking from the chapel-top;
> That length of convent-wall across the way
> Holds the trees safer, huddled more inside;
> The last monk leaves the garden; days decrease,
> And autumn grows, autumn in everything.
> Eh? The whole seems to fall into a shape
> As if I saw alike my work and self
> And all that I was born to be and do,
> A twilight-piece. Love, we are in God's hand.
> How strange now, looks the life he makes us lead;
> So free we seem, so fettered fast we are!
> I feel he laid the fetter: let it lie!

Is it God's autumn, or Andrea's? G. K. Chesterton concludes that Browning's two great theories were the imperfection of man and God's jealousy of this imperfection, a divine envy that provoked the Crucifixion. I suspect that to be a paradox more Chestertonian than Browningesque. Andrea is not so self-divided as he aspires to be, and he revels rather too deliciously in the silver-grey self-portrait he paints:

> I, painting from myself and to myself,
> Know what I do, am unmoved by men's blame
> Or their praise either. Somebody remarks
> Morello's outline there is wrongly traced,
> His hue mistaken; what of that? or else,
> Rightly traced and well ordered; what of that?
> Speak as they please, what does the mountain care?
> Ah, but a man's reach should exceed his grasp,
> Or what's a heaven for? All is silver-grey
> Placid and perfect with my art: the worse!
> I know both what I want and what might gain,
> And yet how profitless to know, to sigh
> "Had I been two, another and myself,
> Our head would have o'erlooked the world!"; No doubt.

It is Andrea, and not Browning, who utters the now notorious, "Ah, but a man's reach should exceed his grasp, / Or what's a heaven for?" Why has posterity given this sentiment to Browning, and not to his parody? Browning regularly storms the Sublime, and generally he grasps it pretty firmly, though he cheerfully converts the Sublime into the grotesque. Andrea sees himself as the perfect painter, aesthetically flawless, and deliberately uninspired. Browning, who is shrewder than his creation, refuses Andrea's self-consolation:

> I am grown peaceful as old age tonight.
> I regret little. I would change still less.
> Since there my past life lies, why alter it?

That is a more-than-hollow man, from whom Browning and the reader need not disengage, because he speaks only for and to himself. One reason that "Andrea del Sarto" seems Shakespearean is that it develops so fully the psychology of cuckoldry that floats through many of the plays, culminating in *Cymbeline* and *The Winter's Tale*. Andrea wanted, and secured, a wife who would cuckold him, and on the grand scale. This system could be called what you will, except for betrayal. Andrea writes a dismal tragicomedy, and sees it as the Faustian price of his art, which is not so much limited in perfection as it is perfect in limitation. Anything but a quester, Andrea is the point-by-point reversal of Browning's own stance as an artist.

* * *

With "Childe Roland to the Dark Tower Came," Browning externalizes his daemon or genius as the most remorseless quester among all his monologists. They are a very varied company: monomaniacs, charlatans, scoundrels, sophists, compromised artists, failed lovers, bad poets, religious fanatics, confidence men, self-deceivers and deceivers of others. The nameless, ruined quester of "Childe Roland to the Dark Tower Came" is the most extreme of all these figures.

It is traditional to call him Roland (or Childe Roland, a "childe" being a candidate for knighthood) even though the poem never identifies him.

The thirty-four six-line stanzas of this poetic romance were composed by Browning in one burst of writing, in less than a day. Something long stored up suddenly precipitated itself out, as though Browning, unaware, had been working on it for some time. The stimulus was a sudden recall of the fragmentary song of Edgar, disguised as a Tom O' Bedlam beggar, in *King Lear*, act 3, scene 4, 173:

> Child Rowland to the dark tower came,
> His word was still, "Fie, foh, and fum,
> I smell the blood of a British man."

"His word" refers not to Rowland, but to a presumed ogre who dwells in the Dark Tower. Browning's Roland (to call him that) is far gone in despair:

> Thus, I had so long suffered in this quest,
> > Heard failure prophesied so oft, been writ
> > So many times among "The Band"—to wit,
> The knights who to the Dark Tower's search addressed
> Their steps—that just to fail as they, seemed best,
> > And all the doubt was now—should I be fit?

How does one become fit to fail? In this nightmare poem, failure means total nihilism or purposelessness. Browning's irony of the grotesque takes over the poem, as we ride with Roland across a landscape in which everything is deformed and broken, *as the Childe sees it*. Whether the reader, if riding alongside, would see as Roland sees is eminently disputable.

> A sudden little river crossed my path
> > As unexpected as a serpent comes.
> > No sluggish tide congenial to the glooms;

This, as it frothed by, might have been a bath
For the fiend's glowing hoof—to see the wrath
        Of its black eddy bespate with flakes and spumes.

So petty yet so spiteful! All along,
        Low scrubby alders kneeled down over it;
        Drenched willows flung them headlong in a fit
Of mute despair, a suicidal throng:
The river which had done them all the wrong,
        Whate'er that was, rolled by, deterred no whit.

Which, while I forded,—good saints, how I feared
        To set my foot upon a dead man's cheek,
        Each step, or feel the spear I thrust to seek
For hollows, tangled in his hair or beard!
—It may have been a water-rat I speared,
        But, ugh! It sounded like a baby's shriek.

Roland's vision darkens his own path, producing a landscape of horror,
until suddenly Browning changes perspectives:

For, looking up, aware I somehow grew,
        'Spite of the dusk, the plain had given place
        All round to mountains—with such name to grace
Mere ugly heights and heaps now stolen in view,
How thus they had surprised me,—solve it, you!
        How to get from them was no clearer case.

Yet half I seemed to recognize some trick
        Of mischief happened to me, God knows when—
        In a bad dream perhaps. Here ended, then,
Progress this way. When, in the very nick
Of giving up, one time more, came a click
        As when a trap shuts—you're inside the den!

Burningly it came on me all at once,
        This was the place! Those two hills on the right,
        Crouched like two bulls locked horn in horn in fight;
While to the left, a tall scalped mountain . . . Dunce,
Dotard, a-dozing at the very nonce,
        After a life spent training for the sight!

What in the midst lay but the Tower itself?
> The round squat turret, blind as the fool's heart,
> Built of brown stone, without a counterpart
In the whole world. The tempest's mocking elf
Points to the shipman thus the unseen shelf
> He strikes on, only when the timbers start.

"Childe Roland to the Dark Tower" is a poem for chanting aloud, and at just this point demands a heightening and widening of voice, because the Childe suddenly understands that he has overprepared the event. Spend a lifetime training for a particular context, a site where your ultimate battle must be fought, and you are all too likely to be caught unaware when it actually comes upon you. Browning, his genius activated by his monologist's mingled dismay and exultation, gives us the insoluble paradox of the Dark Tower, windowless ("blind as the fool's heart"), commonplace ("Built of brown stone"), yet absolutely unique: "without a counterpart / In the whole world."

We are given ultimate irony, but no allegory. Is there an ogre living in the Dark Tower? Certainly, no one exits from the Tower to confront Roland. Instead, the Band of brothers, all disgraced, return from the dead to surround Roland, in a ring of fire. As before, we distrust what Roland thinks he sees, until a final vision is granted, summoned up by the great noise of what may be a tolling bell, rung by the ringers in the Tower:

> Not see? Because of night perhaps?—why, day
> > Came back again for that! before it left,
> > The dying sunset kindled through a cleft:
> The hills, like giants at a hunting, lay,
> Chin upon hand, to see the game at bay,—
> > "Now stab and end the creature—to the heft!"

> Not hear? When noise was everywhere! It tolled
> > Increasing like a bell. Names in my ears
> > Of all the lost adventurers my peers,—
> How such a one was strong, and such was bold,
> And such was fortunate, yet each of old
> > Lost, lost! one moment knelled the woe of years.

> There they stood, ranged along the hill-sides, met
> > To view the last of me, a living frame
> > For one more picture! in a sheet of flame

I saw them and I knew them all. And yet
Dauntless the slug-horn to my lips I set,
    And blew. *"Childe Roland to the Dark Tower came."*

The names are at once sound and vision, ringers and flame. "All the lost adventurers my peers" for Browning proudly would be headed by Shelley, whose "trumpet of a prophecy" ("Ode to the West Wind") is sounded by Roland in the dauntless blast of his slug-horn. This quester, no longer ruined, may be about to die (we don't know) but he certainly is no longer purposeless, and is the epitome of Browning's own dauntless genius.

As an epilogue to what I hope will send new readers to Robert Browning, I will glance, quite briefly, at his brilliant "touch piece" (toccata) or apparent improvisation, "A Toccata of Galuppi's." Baldassare Galuppi (1706–1785) was organist at St. Mark's in Venice. In just fifteen triads of verse, Browning demonstrates his astonishing mastery of technique, including juxtaposing very different tonalities in separate voices. The primary voice is that of the unnamed monologist, an Englishman never out of his own country, and so someone who knows Venice only through Shakespeare (who himself had never been out of England) and through Galuppi's music. Uncannily, two scenes of performance and listening are enacted simultaneously. One is Galuppi at his clavichord playing to Venice's masked revelers, with their voices alternately responding to and ignoring his music. The other is the monologist, who is hearing Galuppi played in the present, and hears also the Venetian voices evoked by the music. In the final four sections of the dramatic monologue, Galuppi's own voice directly addresses his modern auditor, through the music, and a final response is made.
    Browning begins with the monologist pretending a jocular reaction to Galuppi's fusion of sensual celebration and a foreboding of death's emptiness:

Was a lady such a lady, cheeks so round and lips so red,—
On her neck the small face buoyant, like a bell-flower on its bed,
O'er the breast's superb abundance where a man might base his head?

Well, and it was graceful of them—they'd break talk off and afford
—She, to bite her mask's black velvet—he, to finger on his sword,
While you sat and played Toccatas, stately at the clavichord?

What? Those lesser thirds so plaintive, sixths diminished, sigh on sigh,
Told them something? Those suspensions, those solutions—"Must we die?"
Those commiserating sevenths—"Life might last! We can but try!"

"Were you happy?"—"Yes."—"And are you still as happy?"—"Yes. And you?"
—"Then, more kisses!"—"Did *I* stop them, when a million seemed so few?"
Hark, the dominant's persistence till it must be answered to!

So, an octave struck the answer. Oh, they praised you, I dare say!
"Brave Galuppi! That was music! Good alike at grave and gay!
I can always leave off talking when I hear a master play!"

Browning's own heartening susceptibility to women is difficult to disengage
here from the monologist's, but that is all to the good of the reader's delight.
"The breast's superb abundance" will return in the darker, final lines of the
poem, as will be seen. Here, "the dominant's persistence" leads us on to the
monologist's dread of dissolution, expressed at the crest of Browning's power:

Then they left you for their pleasure: till in due time, one by one,
Some with lives that came to nothing, some with deeds as well undone,
Death stepped tacitly and took them where they never see the sun.

But when I sit down to reason, think to take my stand nor swerve,
While I triumph o'er a secret wrung from nature's close reserve,
In you come with your cold music till I creep through every nerve.

Yes, you, like a ghostly cricket, creaking where a house was burned:
"Dust and ashes, dead and done with, Venice spent what Venice earned.
The soul, doubtless is immortal—where a soul can be discerned."

Who or what is this monologist—a natural scientist, or philosopher of science, or simply an educated Darwinian? Browning will not tell us, but continues Galuppi's uncanny voice:

"Yours for instance: you know physics, something of geology,
Mathematics are your pastime; souls shall rise in their degree;
Butterflies may dread extinction,—you'll not die, it cannot be!

"As for Venice and her people, merely born to bloom and drop,
Here on earth they bore their fruitage, mirth and folly were the crop:
What of soul was left, I wonder, when the kissing had to stop?

"Dust and ashes!" So you creak it, and I want the heart to scold.
Dear dead women, with such hair, too—what's become of all the gold
Used to hang and brush their bosoms? I feel chilly and grown old.

Galuppi clearly insinuates that nothing was left of soul, when the kissing had to stop, and his final notes proclaim, " 'Dust and ashes!' " The monologist remains, breaking my own heart with: "Dear dead women, with such hair, too—what's become of all the gold / Used to hang and brush their bosoms?" I hear Browning (and many more of us) in that rhetorical question, and then the nameless monologist returns with: "I feel chilly and grown old." Galuppi, a sophisticated artist who gave his audience precisely what it required of him, has a very different auditor in Browning's monologist, but why does this English auditor stay with Galuppi? The truths of the toccata ravage him, but he cannot break from his fascination with Galuppi's world. He suffers from erotic nostalgias, and he studies them by hearing and rehearing Galuppi. Something enigmatic in Browning's own genius is stirred by Galuppi, by the fascination that achieves the erotic by crossing sexuality with death.

WILLIAM BUTLER YEATS

A girl arose that had red mournful lips
And seemed the greatness of the world in tears,
Doomed like Odysseus and the laboring ships
And proud as Priam murdered with his peers;

That is early Yeats lamenting the "Sorrow of Love" in *The Rose* (1893). The Odysseus of Homer sees his doom lift, and that weeping red-lipped Helen of Troy was also a great survivor, as was the poet Yeats, whose pride surpassed Priam's.

Back in the days of High Modernism (the 1950s, when I set out as a critic-teacher) the dogma was that late Yeats manifested genius, while the early work was dismissed as Aestheticism, Pre-Raphaelitism, belated Romanticism. Yeats, though he unfolded, never wandered far from his poetic origins, and in my old age I am enchanted by his genius as a very young lyrical writer in the modes of Blake, Shelley, William Morris, and Dante Gabriel Rossetti.

Yeats's whole enterprise is implicitly present in "The Madness of King Goll," where the legendary Celtic monarch runs off from governing and from battle to wander in the woods until he becomes a minstrel, singing of a sorrow that surpasses human suffering:

> I came upon a little town
> That slumbered in the harvest moon,
> And passed a-tiptoe up and down,
> Murmuring, to a fitful tune,
> How I have followed, night and day,
> A tramping of tremendous feet,
> And saw where this old tympan lay
> Deserted on a doorway seat,
> And bore it to the woods with me;
> Of some inhuman misery
> Our married voices wildly trolled.
> *They will not hush, the leaves a-flutter,*
> *round me, the beech-leaves old.*

The genius of refrain never abandoned Yeats. His is the poetry of refrain, of repetition in a finer tone, raised to the Sublime, at the limits of art.

WILLIAM BUTLER YEATS
(1865–1939)

No one can doubt the genius of Yeats, Anglo-Irish poet and visionary, even if the once-prevalent judgment of the critic R. P. Blackmur—that Yeats was the most considerable poet in English since the seventeenth century—seems now a touch inflated. Doubtless Blackmur was thinking of John Donne, another poet of genius, but not exactly William Shakespeare, even as Yeats was not necessarily of the eminence of William Blake and William Wordsworth, of Emily Dickinson and Walt Whitman. And yet Yeats was the first poet in the world for some things, and Blackmur's judgment, though hyperbolical, was as memorable an estimate as Ben Jonson's praise of John Donne.

With Yeats, I return to one of this book's sharpest concerns, the influence of the work of genius upon the life of the genius. Like Victor Hugo before him, and James Merrill later, Yeats was an occultist, sometimes even the table-rapping variety. I remember a meeting I attended, by invitation of some Cambridge University faculty occultists in the autumn of 1954, in which, with some disquiet, I observed and felt a table levitating, despite the common effort (in which I joined) to hold it down. This is mentioned in order to manifest my skepticism as to spooks, and to admit a certain battering such skepticism takes, from time to time. Unruly tables always can be dismissed, charlatanry being everywhere. More unsettling were conversations with the poet James Merrill, a person of unfailing charm, courtesy, and intelligence, who was more open to unknown modes of being than I was, or perhaps something in his complex nature allowed the dead poets to literalize their speaking to him. I avoid séances, because they upset me, and I would rather the dead speak to me through printed pages.

Yet Yeats, through his wife's mediations, entertained spirits on four hundred and fifty separate occasions. They arrived, according to Yeats, to bring him metaphors for poetry. Brenda Maddox, an excellent recent biographer, thinks they aided Mrs. Yeats in regulating her wayward husband. If they did double labor, then the time they consumed presumably was justified. Yeats, aesthetically a pragmatist, knew that poetry could only be made out of poetry, and his two versions of his "system," *A Vision* (1925, 1937), are less occult speculations than they are accounts of poetic tradition. But though I will discuss *A Vision*, I want to center upon a more beautiful work, the exquisite marmoreal reverie *Per Amica Silentia Lunae* (1917), the prelude to *A Vision*. This reverie is Yeats's book of the daemon, and so it is his meditation upon his own genius. Though descended from a line of clergymen of the Anglican Church of Ireland, the Anglican Yeats followed in the spiritual tradition of his father, the painter John Butler Yeats, who believed in "personality" rather than God. Like Goethe or Shelley, W. B. Yeats decidedly was not a Christian, whether as man or as poet. He believed in his daemon, but developed a powerful dramatic theory of the daemon, worked out particularly in *Per Amica*. The daemon is not just our other self, but an *opposing* self, allied with the beloved against one. This doctrine, based partly upon Yeats's obsessive and (mostly) frustrated passion for Maud Gonne, Irish beauty and revolutionary, goes on to insist that the daemon imposes upon the poet the hardest tasks, always just short of the impossible.

Like Emerson, Yeats encountered the doctrine of the daemon in Plutarch, and in Ralph Cudworth, seventeenth-century English Neoplatonist. But we have seen the daemon in Plato in the Eros of the *Symposium*, while Socrates in the *Apology* memorably speaks of listening to the voice of his daemon. The pre-Socratics had argued that ethos or character was the daemon or destiny, a grim doctrine, since everything that can happen to you is already built into your own nature. Knowing one's own character is necessarily to know one's fate. Fate, in this sense, is one's guiding genius, Goethe's notion, but akin also to Blake's myth of the emanation as the female will or opposing self of the poet. Yeats, disciple both of Blake and of Shelley, combined the Blakean emanation with the Shelleyan epipsyche, the soul out of one's own soul. Walter Pater, whose daemonic Mona Lisa we have glanced at, is probably the prime origin of the Yeatsian vision of the daemon, which may be why *Per Amica* is written in so Paterian a prose.

Yeats's relation to the daemon is both erotic and agonistic, and may recall Dante Gabriel Rossetti's fierce, destructive love affair with Jane Burden Morris, the muse viewed (no doubt unfairly) as the Queen of Hell. But Yeats has the advantage of seeing his daemon without ambivalence, since he theorizes that the enabling function of the daemon is to oppose him in all things, thus spurring his dramatic imagination to supreme efforts. At almost the final shore of Romantic tradition, Yeats rekindled the Romantic idea of genius by granting it tragic dignity:

> I am in the place where the Daimon is, but I do not think he is with
> me until I begin to make a new personality, selecting among those

images, seeking always to satisfy a hunger grown out of conceit with daily diet; and yet, as I write the words I select, I am full of uncertainty, not knowing when I am the finger, when the clay.

The poet cannot know whether he is the daemon's victim or accomplice; either way, the poet must change as a Shakespearean protagonist changes, startled by a new self-awareness. Antiself must replace self, if art is to become an "opposing virtue," since poetry has to be made "out of the quarrel with ourselves." Yeats mounts towards an astonishing eloquence, as memorable as any of his poems, in the final sentences of this declaration:

> He only can create the greatest imaginable beauty who has endured all imaginable pangs, for only when we have seen and foreseen what we dread shall we be rewarded by that dazzling, unforeseen, wing-footed wanderer. We could not find him if he were not in some sense of our being, and yet of our own being but as water with fire, a noise with silence. He is of all things not impossible the most difficult, for that which comes easily can never be a portion of our being; soon got, soon gone, as the proverb says. I shall find the dark grown luminous, the void fruitful when I understand I have nothing, that the ringers in the tower have appointed for the hymen of the soul a passing bell.

Yeats, in a prologue addressed to Maud Gonne's daughter, Iseult (under the cover name of "Maurice"), dates *Per Amica* May 11, 1917, a month short of his fifty-second birthday. On October 20 of that year, Yeats married Bertha Georgie Hyde-Lees, who had just turned twenty-five, and whom he had known, not at all intimately, since 1910 or 1911. Yeats was every sort of an occultist, including an astrologer, and always kept in mind that, at the moment of his birth, (10:40 P.M., June 13, 1865), Aquarius was ascending and entering the first "house," with moonrise coming in less than an hour and a half. He therefore was persuaded that his poetic characters resided *per amica silentia lunae,* "in the moon's friendly silence." Astrologically, his birth horoscope was erotically negative: the planet Venus was ninety degrees square to his Mars. Brenda Maddox tells us that astrological advisors convinced Yeats that the best time for him to marry was October 1917. The poet therefore made his fifth rejected marriage proposal to Maud Gonne, and several of the same to her daughter Iseult, before he successfully proposed marriage to Georgie Hyde-Lees, his third candidate in about a year. With considerable wisdom, the new Mrs. Yeats saved their marriage, after a first bad week, by a burst of magical automatic writing, the onset of what was to produce some thirty-six hundred pages of occult material.

But none of this was known to Yeats half a year earlier, when he wrote that magnificent sentence:

> I shall find the dark grow luminous, the void fruitful when I understand I have nothing, that the ringers in the tower have appointed for the hymen of the soul a passing bell.

The soul always will remain virginal because the daemon or genius is antithetical to it. Revelations made to the poet through the occult powers provoked *A Vision* and the poetry partly founded upon it, but Yeats had the good fortune to have married a medium, rather than his muse or her daughter. His genius flowered when he did understand that he *had* nothing, that inner solitude was its ultimate poetic blessing. This is part of the burden of the superb esoteric poem "The Double Vision of Michael Robartes," which closes Yeats's next volume of poems, the wonderful *Wild Swans at Coole* (1917). Robartes speaks for Yeats, undone by Maud Gonne, his Helen, "Who never gave the burning town a thought." Yet to be so undone is to rewarded by

> The commonness of thought and images
> That have the frenzy of our western seas
> Thereon I made my moan,
> And after kissed a stone,
>
> And after that arranged it in a song . . .

LUSTRE 20

|

Charles Dickens, Fyodor Dostoevsky, Isaac Babel, Paul Celan, Ralph Ellison

|

There is a second aspect of *Malkhut*, the swarming cities of descent: Dickens's London, Dostoevsky's St. Petersburg, Isaac Babel's Jewish Odessa. A realism that crosses into phantasmagoria is shared by these three geniuses of the grotesque. Dickens's eccentrics, Dostoevsky's nihilists, and Babel's gangsters enlarge the kingdom of imaginative literature on a scale virtually Shakespearean.

It is only a step from Babel (and from the poet Osip Mandelstam, another great Russian-Jewish writer destroyed by Stalin) to Paul Celan, whose poetry in German is the strongest achievement of post-Holocaust Jewish literature.

The Underground Man of Dostoevsky reappears in Ralph Waldo Ellison's *Invisible Man*, still the major work of African-American literature. This second Lustre of *Malkhut* comprehends the images of descent, Jonah-like, in Dickens, Dostoevsky, and Ellison. The dark personal ends of Babel and Celan add a poignance, here at the close of this book's mosaic of genius.

CHARLES DICKENS

Any iron ring let into stone is the entrance to a cave which only waits for the magician, and the little fire, and the necromancy, that will make the earth shake. All the dates imported come from the same tree as that unlucky date, with whose shell the merchant knocked out the eye of the genie's invisible son. All olives are of the stock of that fresh fruit, concerning which the Commander of the Faithful overheard the boy conduct the fictitious trial of the fraudulent olive merchant; all apples are akin to the apple purchased (with two others) from the Sultan's gardener for three sequins, and which the tall black slave stole from the child. All dogs are associated with the dog, really a transformed man, who jumped upon the baker's counter, and put his paw on the piece of bad money. All rice recalls the rice which the awful lady, who was a ghoul, could only peck by grains, because of her nightly feasts in the burial-place. My very rocking-horse,—there he is, with his nostrils turned completely inside-out, indicative of Blood!— should have a peg in his neck, by virtue thereof to fly away with me, as the wooden horse did with the Prince of Persia, in the sight of all his father's Court.

That is Dickens, in his *Christmas Stories*, delighting in the *Arabian Nights*, probably his truest precursor, except for Shakespeare. The universal appeal of the *Arabian Nights* remains a clue to Dickens's astonishing universality, in which he nearly rivals Shakespeare and the Bible.

Everything will happen in Dickens, where coincidence is the law of life. Or rather, there are *no* coincidences in Dickens, as there are no accidents in Freud. Samuel Taylor Coleridge, expounding his *Rime of the Ancient Mariner*, explained its albatross-curse as an analogue to the *Arabian Nights* tale in which a merchant idly throws the remnants of a date into a well. A genie emerges, who informs the unfortunate culprit that he is obliged to kill him, because the traveler has destroyed the only eye of the genie's invisible son.

Kafka loved Dickens, because a cosmos so Kabbalistically overdetermined was also his own. *The Castle* seems freedom itself compared to *Bleak*

House, where every event and relationship is prefigured, and where every omen is fulfilled.

John Ruskin praised Dickens for "stage fire," and Dickens was most himself in his prolonged suicide by giving his exhausting stage readings, the authentic Victorian achievement in drama. The genius of Dickens was "stage fire": *Hamlet* pervades the novels. After Shakespeare and Chaucer, Dickens vies with Jane Austen as the peopler of a world. It is all the better that so many of the Dickens people are grotesques: look around you.

CHARLES DICKENS
(1812–1870)

IF YOU THINK OF GENIUS IN REGARD TO a novelist writing in English, you begin and end with Dickens. In our Information Age, he joins Shakespeare and Jane Austen as the only writers evidently able to survive the dominance of the new media. Throughout the world, he is second only to Shakespeare as a universal author. Shakespeare is everywhere in Dickens, sometimes concealed, though Dickens's people began closer to Ben Jonson's incarnated humors than to Shakespeare's inwardness.

John Ruskin thought that Dickens's genius was essentially dramatic, and Dickens's public readings from his novels were one of the glories of the Victorian age. These were expensive glories, as they exhausted him, and may have contributed to his death in late middle age. What Ruskin called "stage fire" is central to Dickens, and redeems even his most melodramatic works, such as the unfinished *Mystery of Edwin Drood*.

Alexander Welsh, one of Dickens's most useful critics, emphasizes the importance of *King Lear, Macbeth*, and *Hamlet* to the novelist. I myself have wondered why Falstaff did not mean more to Dickens, whose Shakespeare was the tragedian, and not the comic genius that to me is the heart of Shakespeare's achievement.

As a child, I loved *The Pickwick Papers* best, and in old age I have not altered, though plainly *David Copperfield, Great Expectations, Dombey and Son, Little Dorrit*, and *Bleak House*, above all, are rightly considered to be the true foundation for Dickens's eminence. Welsh remarks that only *Don Quixote*, among novels, stands higher in general estimation than *Bleak House*, which is as it should be. No one expects Dickens to have the cosmological sweep of Cervantes, Shakespeare, Dante, and Chaucer. He is only just below them, fully as rammed with life, but not as preternatural as they can be in their control of perspectives, and except for Shakespeare, he is their equal in "stage fire."

I have written elsewhere about *Bleak House, Great Expectations*, and *David Copperfield*, and though *The Pickwick Papers* is early Dickens, I follow my lifelong passion and will contemplate his genius there, while acknowledging how much more depth and power were to come. It is rather like seeking Shakespeare's genius only in *Love's Labour's Lost*, and not in the *Henry IV* plays, *Hamlet, King Lear, Macbeth, Twelfth Night, Antony and Cleopatra*, and *The Winter's Tale*. And yet *Pickwick* remains one of the books for extremely intelligent children of all ages, and Dickens's stage fire burns on in it.

The Pickwick Papers are joyous until Mr. Pickwick enters debtor's prison, after he refuses to pay what a court unjustly imposes as costs and compensation for a supposed breach of a marriage proposal to the unfortunate Mrs. Bardell. My two sharpest memories of the book, across some sixty years, are of the learned barrister, Mr. Serjeant Buzfuz, denouncing Mr. Pickwick at the trial, and of Mr. Leo Hunter reciting to Mr. Pickwick two stanzas of Mrs. Leo Hunter's "Ode to an Expiring Frog," before the literary Public Breakfast given by the poetess:

> "Can I view thee panting, lying
> On thy stomach, without sighing;
> Can I unmoved see thee dying
> On a log,
> Expiring frog!

> "Say, have fiends in shapes of boys,
> With wild halloo, and brutal noise,
> Hunted thee from marshy joys,
> With a dog,
> Expiring frog!"

Against this I hear the countermelody of Serjeant Buzfuz:

"And now, gentlemen, but one word more. Two letters have passed between these parties, letters which are admitted to be in the handwriting of the defendant, and which speak volumes indeed. These letters, too, bespeak the character of the man. They are not open, fervent, eloquent epistles, breathing nothing but the language of affectionate attachment. They are covert, sly, underhanded communications, but, fortunately, far more conclusive than if couched in the most glowing language and the most poetic imagery—letters that must be viewed with a cautious and suspicious eye—letters that were evidently intended at the time, by Pickwick, to mislead and delude any third parties into whose hands they might fall. Let me read the first:—'Garraway's, twelve o'clock. Dear Mrs. B.—Chops and Tomata sauce. Yours, PICKWICK.' Gentlemen, what does this mean? Chops and Tomata sauce! Yours, Pickwick! Chops! Gracious heavens! and Tomata

sauce! Gentlemen, is the happiness of a sensitive and confiding female to be trifled away, by such shallow artifices as these? The next
has no date whatever, which is in itself suspicious.—'Dear Mrs. B., I
shall not be at home till to-morrow. Slow coach.' And then follows this
very, very remarkable expression—'Don't trouble yourself about the
warming-pan.' The warming-pan! Why, gentlemen, who *does* trouble
himself about a warming-pan? When was the peace of mind of man or
woman broken or disturbed by a warming-pan, which is in itself a
harmless, a useful, and I will add, gentlemen, a comforting article of
domestic furniture? Why is Mrs. Bardell so earnestly entreated not to
agitate herself about this warming-pan, unless (as is no doubt the
case) it is a mere cover for hidden fire—a mere substitute for some
endearing word or promise, agreeable to a preconcerted system of correspondence, artfully contrived by Pickwick with a view to his contemplated desertion, and which I am not in a condition to explain?
And what does this allusion to the slow coach mean? For aught I know,
it may be a reference to Pickwick himself, who has most unquestionably been a criminally slow coach during the whole of this transaction,
but whose speed will now be very unexpectedly accelerated, and
whose wheels, gentlemen, as he will find to his cost, will very soon be
greased by you!"

G. K. Chesterton preferred *The Pickwick Papers* to all the rest of Dickens,
though it was written at the age of twenty-four, his second book:

> Even as a boy I believed that there were some more pages that were
> torn out of my copy, and I am looking for them still . . . If we had a se-
> quel of Pickwick ten years afterwards, Pickwick would be exactly the
> same age . . . It is first and foremost, a supernatural story. Mr. Pick-
> wick was a fairy. So was old Mr. Weller . . . Dickens has caught, in a
> manner at once mild and convincing, the queer innocence of the af-
> ternoon of life. The round moon-like spectacles of Samuel Pickwick
> move through the tale as emblems of a certain spherical simplicity . . .
> Dickens went into the Pickwick club to scoff, and Dickens remained
> to pray.

As an enthusiast, but in a very different critical mode, Steven Marcus revisited *Pickwick* two-thirds of a century after Chesterton, and praised Dickens's great genius in this exuberant work of his young manhood, while
finding in this first and freest of his novels a negativity at its dramatic cen-

ter, but a negativity of the Hegelian sort, which is necessary if freedom is to be persuasively represented. A third critic, the late Northrop Frye, deftly described the formulaic elements in *The Pickwick Papers.*

Most of the standard types of humor are conspicuous in Dickens, and could be illustrated from *Bleak House* alone: the miser in Smallweed; the hypocrite in Chadband; the parasite in Skimpole and Turveydrop; the pedant in Mrs. Jellyby. The braggart soldier is not much favored: Major Bagstock in *Dombey and Son* is more of a parasite. Agreeably to the conditions of Victorian life, the braggart soldier is replaced by a braggart merchant or politician. An example, treated in a thoroughly traditional manner, is Bounderby in *Hard Times.* Another Victorian commonplace of the braggart-soldier family, the duffer sportsman, whose pretensions are far beyond his performance, is represented by Winkle in *The Pickwick Papers.* There are, however, two Winkles in *The Pickwick Papers,* the duffer sportsman and the pleasant young man who breaks down family opposition on both sides to acquire a pleasant young woman. The duality reflects the curious and instructive way that *The Pickwick Papers* came into being. The original scheme proposed to Dickens was a comedy of humors in its most primitive and superficial form: a situation comedy in which various stock types, including an incautious amorist (Tupman), a melancholy poet (Snodgrass), and a pedant (Pickwick), as well as Winkle, get into one farcical predicament after another.

Can the adventures of Samuel Pickwick, in which Dickens first found himself, serve to define the particular quality of Dickens's genius? Though we ordinarily speak of Dickens as a novelist, he writes romances, though after *The Pickwick Papers* they will *look* more like novels. Jane Austen, George Eliot, and Henry James write novels; Dickens writes a mixed genre, mingling Sir Walter Scott and Tobias Smollett and obliterating them in the originality of his perpetual newness. There is something waiflike in Dickens's genius: it makes a universal appeal, because it calls out to the waif in each of us, unlikely as most of us must seem if we assumed the roles. The young Henry James, who had extraordinary critical gifts, nevertheless nodded twice in 1865, with ghastly reviews of Walt Whitman's *Drum-Taps* and Dickens's *Our Mutual Friend.* James more than changed his mind about Whitman, but his defensive resentment of Dickens proved permanent. Yet James is supremely useful in defining Dickens's genius if we merely turn the critic inside out:

What a world were this world if the world of *Our Mutual Friend* were an honest reflection of it! But a community of eccentrics is impossible. Rules alone are consistent with each other; exceptions are inconsistent. Society is maintained by natural sense and natural feeling. We cannot conceive a society in which these principles are not in some manner represented. Where in these pages are the depositories of that intelligence without which the movement of life would cease? Who represents nature?

The Pickwick Club is of course a community of eccentrics: in Dickens's waiflike vision the cosmos is peopled by eccentrics, and nature itself is eccentric, as is society. Henry James was not exactly a waif, and his strictures reflect a normative viewpoint that became more generous as he matured. James desperately wanted theatrical success and never could achieve it. Dickens had only to mount a stage and read Dickens aloud, and audiences surged in. His genre is dramatic romance, which is almost unique to him, and which he reinvents in *The Posthumous Papers of the Pickwick Club*, to give its full title.

I have just completed a rereading of *Pickwick* across several joyous days, deliberately slowing myself down, with many pauses, to enjoy the book as long as possible. Somewhere Dostoevsky surprisingly admits that his Prince Myshkin in *The Idiot* compounds Mr. Pickwick and Don Quixote. The mind of Dostoevsky is, to me, a very dark place, and perhaps, through Karamazov's eyes, Don Quixote and Myshkin have their affinities, but what would the prince and Samuel Pickwick have had to say to one another? I can find more of Shakespeare than of Cervantes in Dickens, and Mr. Pickwick and Sam Weller would fit better in Smollett's *Humphry Clinker* than in *Don Quixote*. If there is a metaphysical aspect to Dickens's first full-scale narrative, as Marcus suggests, then it is too deeply implicit to be explicated. Don Quixote attacks reality; Samuel Pickwick accepts it, except when imprisoned in the Fleet, where he endures the irreality. If Mr. Pickwick is too cheerful to resemble the sad Knight, Sam Weller is too insouciant to challenge the massively grounded Sancho Panza, genius of the common life.

Dickens's characters, as Northrop Frye suggested, resemble Ben Jonson's, whose *Every Man in His Humour* Dickens produced and took on tour. Thus, Pickwick represents "genial, generous, and lovable" humors, while Sam Weller incarnates loyalty and resourcefulness. The sublime Pickwick begins the book as an amiable enough pedant, but then catches fire as Dickens's genius flares up. It is as though Pickwick cannot remain for more than a few chapters in Ben Jonson's cosmos; instead, he inaugurates what critics call "the Dickens world." That world darkens considerably after *The Pickwick Papers,* and yet its parameters remain comic, though it sounds odd to call *Bleak House* a comic romance.

The language of the Pickwickians has been studied adroitly by Marcus. Here I want to invoke only one aspect of *The Pickwick Papers:* the central relationship, master and man, between Mr. Pickwick and Sam Weller. The Knight and his squire, Quixote and Sancho, are equals: after only a few pages, no hierarchy exists between them, they become friends and brothers, quarrelsome but loving. Samuel Pickwick and Sam Weller truly become father and son, equally loving, but Dickens places old Mr. Weller in the book so as to preserve the formal relationship of master and man. The loyalty towards one another of Pickwick and Sam Weller is absolute—it is not accidental that they are both Samuels—but of the two, Sam Weller is finally the stronger and more obstinate will, rugged as Pickwick's is, and Sam's will prevails. Though Pickwick, in an ultimate act of fatherly love, attempts to release Sam into marriage, Sam will not leave Pickwick, and marries only when the housekeeper's role is available for his new wife.

It feels odd to say it, but the bachelor, childless Samuel Pickwick is the center of a community of love, which would be impossibly idealized outside the pages of *The Pickwick Papers.* Everyone in the book is redeemable, except lawyers (Mr. Perker being the exception), who for Dickens as for Shakespeare constituted the Devil's profession. There is no overt religion in *The Pickwick Papers;* Angus Wilson called the book's faith New Testament Christianity, without explaining what he thought that meant. Pickwick does not need anyone to redeem him; he is Original Goodness itself, Adam early in the morning, beyond temptation and in no need of an Eve. His freedom from sexual desire has a subtle relation to his freedom from financial anxieties.

Chesterton, a natural Pickwickian and a Roman Catholic, found "popular religion, with its endless joys" to be the essence of *The Pickwick Papers.* Chesterton meant a sort of "folk Catholicism," which he fancied had been the norm in Chaucer's time. Pickwick may indeed be from Fairyland, but I know of no religion, popular or formal, which features "endless joys," and *The Pickwick Papers,* in my experience of it, is beautifully secular. Mr. Pickwick is neither a churchgoer nor a Bible-reader. He is an adventurer, always out upon the roads, heading his loyal and absurd followers into innocent but difficult pleasures. When, at the end, he is too old and infirm to wander, he sits at home, listening to Sam Weller read aloud, with commentaries by the

irrepressible Sam. The work's final sentence, after more than eight hundred
pages of benign exuberances, concludes with the heart of the matter:

> on this, as on all their occasions, he is invariably attended by the faith-
> ful Sam, between whom and his master there exists a steady and rec-
> iprocal attachment, which nothing but death will terminate.

FYODOR DOSTOEVSKY

Now I would like to tell you, gentlemen, whether or not you want to hear it, why it is that I couldn't even become an insect. I'll tell you solemnly that I wished to become an insect many times. But not even that wish was granted. I swear to you, gentlemen, that being overly conscious is a disease, a genuine, full-fledged disease. Ordinary human consciousness would be more than sufficient for everyday human needs—that is, even half or a quarter of the amount of consciousness that's available to a cultured man in our unfortunate nineteenth century, especially to one who has the particular misfortune of living in St. Petersburg, the most abstract and premeditated city in the whole world. (Cities can be either premeditated or unpremeditated.) It would have been entirely sufficient, for example, to have the consciousness with which all so-called spontaneous people and men of action are endowed. I'll bet that you think I'm writing all this to show off, to make fun of these men of action, that I'm clanging my saber just like that officer did to show off in bad taste. But, gentlemen, who could possibly be proud of his illnesses and want to show them off?

(translated by Michael R. Katz)

Dostoevsky's *Notes from Underground* features a narrator-monologist, the Underground Man, whom no reader can like or forget. The power of this protagonist is that he contaminates us: he speaks for and to our universal masochism, and we worry whether truly we share his lovelessness.

One can name Dostoevsky as the genius of contamination. I read him, and shudder. His obscurantism, which he calls Russian Christianity, embraces a worship of tyranny, a hatred of the United States and of all democracy, and a profound and vicious anti-Semitism. He loathes nihilistic terrorism, but endorses the state terrorism of the Russian empire and church.

And yet Dostoevsky is indispensable: he is the satirist who joins Jonathan Swift in exposing our egoism, our cruelty, our hypocrisies, above all our crippling self-consciousness. We are not the same after recognizing the Underground Man in ourselves. His treatment of Liza exposes the male resentment and fear of women so vividly that we are brought back to Shakespeare, where Othello yields so readily to an Iago who speaks for what already is Othello's.

Dostoevsky, who eagerly learned from Shakespeare, may be the Shakespeare of novelists, in that his greatest figures are vibrant with the energy of consciousness that we recognize as Shakespearean. The Underground Man is his own Iago, except that Iago is incapable of shame. That final lesson even Shakespeare could not teach Dostoevsky.

FYODOR DOSTOEVSKY
(1821–1881)

SIGMUND FREUD, RATHER POLEMICALLY, placed *The Brothers Karamazov* first among all novels ever written, approaching Shakespeare in aesthetic eminence. The judgment was excessive, but the book certainly is the strongest that Dostoevsky composed, and is where his genius should be sought. It is his final work and his intended revelation, published a year before his death at fifty-nine. His only son, Alyosha, had died at the age of three in 1878, which is prelude to *The Brothers Karamazov*, whose hero is Alyosha, the youngest brother. Had Dostoevsky lived, there would have been a second volume to the novel, centering almost wholly upon the fully mature Alyosha.

But we have only *The Brothers Karamazov* in one substantial novel of seven hundred and seventy-six pages, in the strong translation of Richard Pevear and Larissa Volokhonsky (1990), which I will employ here. Most readers regard the novel's protagonist as being either Dmitri, poetic sufferer, or Ivan, prideful intellectual, or both together, rather than the realistic and loving Alyosha. The book's glory is that we are fascinated by all three brothers (despite Dostoevsky's palpable dislike for Ivan) as we also are enchanted by their dreadful father, the vitalistic monster Fyodor Pavlovich, and interestingly are repelled by their bastard brother, the cook Smerdyakov. These five Karamazovs are the genius of the novel; the principal women, Grushenka and Katerina Ivanovna, seem to me to divide male fantasy between them, and they fail to persuade as personalities. Tolstoy could create women; Dostoevsky could not, though he studied Shakespeare, hoping to learn the secret.

To invoke the genre of the novel does not help much in reading *The Brothers Karamazov*. We might call it Scripture, though that would be too broad a designation, since Dostoevsky seems to combine the Book of Job with the Revelation of Saint John the Divine, with much of the rest of the Bible implied. Critics, following Mikhail Bakhtin, speak of the book as a polyphony, but why that applies more to it than to Dickens or Proust is unclear to me. There is a peculiar narrator, who seems to represent the public in general, though Dostoevsky sometimes breaks in. *The Brothers Karamazov* could be called gloriously unsteady, which is appropriate for the wild Old

Karamazov and his volatile sons, who in different but parallel ways share in his outrageous nature.

Freud overpraised the novel because it confirmed his theory in *Totem and Taboo*, where the Primal Father appropriates all the women for himself, and finally is slain by his sons. Hatred of the father, according to Freud, is the source of our unconscious sense of guilt. But, except for Alyosha, all the Karamazov sons explicitly hate their ferocious father, and Alyosha is saved from that hatred only by having found a replacement in the monk, Father Zosima.

It is Mitya's novel, but Dostoevsky gave his own first name to Old Karamazov (who is actually fifty-five), and the sensual exuberance of this worst of fathers makes us feel his absence after he is murdered by Smerdyakov. Dostoevsky, in his *Notebooks*, declared that "we are all, to the last man, Fyodor Pavloviches," since we all are sensualists and nihilists, however we attempt to be otherwise. Dostoevsky, who compelled himself to religious belief, was anything but a mystic, and was the ancestor of Kafka's passionate motto: "No more psychology!" There are almost no normative personalities among Dostoevsky's characters: they are what they will to be, and their wills are inconstant. And so is Dostoevsky's. His unfairness to Ivan is exasperating, but Dostoevsky intends to exasperate us. He certainly would have declined to care about the reactions of Jewish critics, since he himself was a vicious anti-Semite, comparable to Ezra Pound. It is important to remember that Dostoevsky was an obscurantist, and a supporter of Czarist tyranny and Russian Orthodox theocracy. He was a vehement parodist of Westernization, and firmly believed that Russians were the Chosen People and that Christ was the Russian Christ. Admirers of Dostoevsky should read his *Diary of a Writer*, a fascinating and obnoxious book. It is one thing to be passionate and provocative, and quite another to preach hatred of non-Russians in anticipation of the End of the World.

Dostoevsky's genius was for dramatizing character and personality, and he seems to me to have a deeper relationship with Shakespeare than criticism so far has revealed. His nihilists are Shakespearean: Svidrigailov, Stavrogin, Ivan Karamazov. And there is something of a Falstaffian parody in Fyodor Karamazov, though I find it distressing. Western literary tradition was not for Dostoevsky the nightmare it constituted for Tolstoy, but I am uncertain that Dostoevsky could see the differences between Shakespeare and the novels of Victor Hugo, whose vision of the wretched of the earth was not far from Dostoevsky's own.

The genius of Dostoevsky faltered when it came to representing religion, which is the flaw of *The Brothers Karamazov*, since Dostoevsky's Russian Christianity was purely a disease of the intellect, a nationalistic virus, devoid of spiritual insight. Are we to be moved by Zosima's assertion, "Whoever does not believe in God is not going to believe in God's people"? That sounds uncomfortably like Southern Baptist conviction that Christ favors the Republican Party. It ought to be a scandal that an agnostic or atheist cannot be elected dogcatcher in the United States, but it is a weary fact we must accept. Dostoevsky's obscurantist religiosity is plain tiresome, though critics mostly will not say so. At the close of *The Brothers Karamazov*, Alyosha joyously kisses the Russian earth, and Dostoevsky is immensely moved by this heroic act. The novel ends with the young prophet preaching to a group of boys, in memory of one of their group who has died:

"I am speaking about the worst case, if we become bad," Alyosha went on, "but why should we become bad, gentlemen, isn't that true? Let us first of all and before all be kind, then honest, and then—let us never forget one another. I say it again. I give you my word, gentlemen, that for my part I will never forget any one of you; each face that is looking at me now, at this moment, I will remember, be it even after thirty years. Kolya said to Kartashov just now that we supposedly 'do not care to know of his existence.' But how can I forget that Kartashov exists and that he is no longer blushing now, as when he discovered Troy, but is looking at me with his nice, kind, happy eyes? Gentlemen, my dear gentlemen, let us all be as generous and brave as Ilyushechka, as intelligent, brave, and generous as Kolya (who will be much more intelligent when he grows up a little), and let us be as bashful, but smart and nice, as Kartashov. But why am I talking about these two? You are all dear to me, gentlemen, from now on I shall keep you all in my heart, and I ask you to keep me in your hearts, too! Well, and who has united us in these good, kind lives, who, if not Ilyushechka, that good boy, that kind boy, that boy dear to us unto ages of ages! Let us never forget him, and may his memory be eternal and good in our hearts now and unto ages of ages!"

"Yes, yes, eternal, eternal," all the boys cried in their ringing voices, with deep feeling in their faces.

"Let us remember his face, and his clothes, and his poor boots, and his little coffin, and his unfortunate, sinful father, and how he bravely rose up against the whole class for him!"

"We will, we will remember!" the boys cried again, "he was brave, he was kind!"

"Ah, how I loved him!" exclaimed Kolya.

"Ah, children, ah, dear friends, do not be afraid of life! How good life is when you do something good and rightful!"

"Yes, yes," the boys repeated ecstatically.

"Karamazov, we love you!" a voice, which seemed to be Kartashov's, exclaimed irrepressibly.

"We love you, we love you," everyone joined in. Many had tears shining in their eyes.

"Hurrah for Karamazov!" Kolya proclaimed ecstatically.

"And memory eternal for the dead boy!" Alyosha added again, with feeling.

"Memory eternal!" the boys again joined in.

"Karamazov!" cried Kolya, "can it really be true as religion says, that we shall all rise from the dead, and come to life, and see one another again, and everyone, and Ilyushechka?"

"Certainly we shall rise, certainly we shall see and gladly, joyfully tell one another all that has been," Alyosha replied, half laughing, half in ecstasy.

"Ah, how good that will be!" burst from Kolya.

"Well, and now let's end our speeches and go to his memorial dinner. Don't be disturbed that we'll be eating pancakes. It's an ancient, eternal thing, and there's good in that, too," laughed Alyosha. "Well, let's go! And we go like this now, hand in hand."

"And eternally so, all our lives hand in hand! Hurrah for Karamazov!" Kolya cried once more ecstatically, and once more all the boys joined in his exclamation.

(translated by Richard Pevear and Larissa Volokhonsky)

Someone not fond of this passage unkindly suggested that it had the aura of a Boy Scout rally, an event of which I know nothing. Whatever it resembles, it divides readers. To me, it is of a badness not to be believed, and reminds me that Tolstoy grudgingly approved of Dostoevsky only to the extent that this rival prophet could be termed the Russian Harriet Beecher Stowe.

Yet all that I try to indicate is that Dostoevsky was neither a religious genius nor a genius of religion. In spiritual matters, he merely was a bigoted know-nothing, whose authentic anti-Semitism was the only evidence of his election as a Russian prophet. *The Brothers Karamazov* is not *The Diary of a Writer*, and the genius of Dostoevsky is strongest where it brings Old Karamazov and Mitya into confrontation:

"Dmitri Fyodorovich!" Fyodor Pavlovich suddenly screamed in a voice not his own, "if only you weren't my son, I would challenge you to a duel this very moment . . . with pistols, at three paces . . . across a handkerchief! across a handkerchief!" he ended, stamping with both feet.

Old liars who have been play-acting all their lives have moments when they get so carried away by their posturing that they indeed tremble and weep from excitement, even though at that same moment (or just a second later) they might whisper to themselves: "You're lying, you shameless old man, you're acting even now, despite all your 'holy' wrath and 'holy' moment of wrath."

Dmitri Fyodorovich frowned horribly and looked at his father with inexpressible contempt.

"I thought . . . I thought," he said somehow softly and restrainedly, "that I would come to my birthplace with the angel of my soul, my fiancée, to cherish him in his old age, and all I find is a depraved sensualist and despicable comedian!"

"To a duel!" the old fool screamed again, breathless and spraying saliva with each word. "And you, Pyotor Alexandrovich Miusov, let it be known to you, sir, that in all the generations of your family there is not and maybe never has been a woman loftier or more honorable—more honorable, do you hear?—than this creature, as you have just dared to call her! And you, Dmitri Fyodorovich, traded your fiancée for this very 'creature,' so you yourself have judged that your fiancée isn't worthy to lick her boots—that's the kind of creature she is!"

"Shame!" suddenly escaped from Father Iosif.

"A shame and a disgrace!" Kalganov, who had been silent all the while, suddenly cried in his adolescent voice, trembling with excitement and blushing all over.

"Why is such a man alive!" Dmitri Fyodorovich growled in a muffled voice, now nearly beside himself with fury, somehow raising his shoulders peculiarly so that he looked almost hunchbacked. "No, tell me, can he be allowed to go on dishonoring the earth with himself?" He looked around at everyone, pointing his finger at the old man. His speech was slow and deliberate.

"Do you hear, you monks, do you hear the parricide!" Fyodor Pavlovich flung at Father Iosif. "There is the answer to your 'shame'! What shame? This 'creature,' this 'woman of bad behavior' is perhaps holier than all of you, gentlemen soul-saving hieromonks! Maybe she fell in her youth, being influenced by her environment, but she has 'loved much,' and even Christ forgave her who loved much . . ."

"Christ did not forgive that kind of love . . . ," escaped impatiently from the meek Father Iosif.

"No, that kind, monks, exactly that kind, that kind! You are saving your souls here on cabbage and you think you're righteous! You eat gudgeons, one gudgeon a day, and you think you can buy God with gudgeons!"

"Impossible! Impossible!" came from all sides of the cell.

But the whole scene, which had turned so ugly, was stopped in a most unexpected manner. The elder suddenly rose from his place. Alyosha, who had almost completely lost his head from fear for him and for all of them, had just time enough to support his arm. The elder stepped towards Dmitri Fyodorovich and, having come close to him, knelt before him. Alyosha thought for a moment that he had fallen from weakness, but it was something else. Kneeling in front of Dmitri Fyodorovich, the elder bowed down at his feet with a full, distinct, conscious bow, and even touched the floor with his forehead. Alyosha was so amazed that he failed to support him as he got to his feet. A weak smile barely glimmered on his lips.

"Forgive me! Forgive me, all of you!" he said, bowing on all sides to his guests.

Dmitri Fyodorovich stood dumbstruck for a few moments. Bowing at his feet—what was that? Then suddenly he cried out: "Oh, God!" and, covering his face with his hands, rushed from the room. All the other guests flocked after him, forgetting in their confusion even to say good-bye or bow to their host. Only the hieromonks again came to receive his blessing.

"What's that—bowing at his feet? Is it some sort of emblem?" Fyodor Pavlovich, who for some reason had suddenly grown quiet, tried to start a conversation, not daring, by the way, to address anyone in particular. At that moment they were just passing beyond the walls of the hermitage.

This wonderful passage is an epitome of *The Brothers Karamazov,* and more than redeems it from all of Dostoevsky's spurious spirituality. We are free to interpret as we will the elder's terrifying obeisance to Mitya, but dramatically it prophesies the martyrdom he must undergo when he is unjustly convicted of his father's murder. Everything in the passage has a marvelous aesthetic appropriateness, including Old Karamazov's denunciation of the monks for their diet of cabbage and gudgeons—small, tasteless fish good only for bait—which he regards as another mark of their hypocrisy. A gourmet as to food, Old Karamazov will devour any woman whatsoever: "There are no ugly women!" The peculiar intensity of the father's buffoonery, with its outrageous challenge to a duel, inevitably provokes the passionate Mitya to the sinful threat of patricide. Father and son, fascinating monster and poignant poet, share in the one nature, villain and hero alike. This is the genius of Dostoevsky at full play, almost Shakespearean in its splendor.

ISAAC BABEL

At the wedding feast they served turkey, roast chicken, goose, stuffed fish, fish-soup in which lakes of lemons gleamed nacreously. Over the heads of defunct geese, flowers swayed like luxuriant plumages. But does the foamy surge of the Odessa sea cast roast chicken on the shore?

All that is noblest in our smuggled goods, everything for which the land is famed from end to end, did, on that starry, that deep-blue night, its entrancing and disruptive work. Wines not from these parts warmed stomachs, made legs faint sweetly, bemused brains, evoked belches that rang out sonorous as trumpets summoning to battle. The Negro cook from the *Plutarch*, that had put in three days before from Port Said, bore unseen through the customs fat-bellied jars of Jamaica rum, oily Madeira, cigars from the plantations of Pierpont Morgan, and oranges from the environs of Jerusalem. That is what the foaming surge of the Odessa sea bears to the shore, that is what sometimes comes the way of Odessa beggars at Jewish weddings.

This is Benja Krik's wedding feast in Babel's "The King," from *The Odessa Tales.* James Falen, much in Babel's own spirit, emphasizes the high exoticism of the passage, with its very mixed overtones, ranging from Hebrew tradition to modern and contemporary gangsterism. Go to "Little Odessa," Brighton Beach, New York, on a Saturday night, and you will see that Benja Krik's world is alive and well, bubbling with an exuberance that convinces me that the Little Odessa mob has read Isaac Babel, and in the Russian original. Nowhere else, except in the pages of Babel, have I seen men in orange suits and raspberry waistcoats, and women in scarlet frocks and men's boots. Babel's epic farce or heroic travesty has obeyed the law of Oscar Wilde, which is that life must imitate art. In Tel Aviv and Brighton Beach, if no longer in Odessa, Babel's reprobates thrive.

Babel, though so highly stylized, is a storyteller of primordial power, almost Tolstoyan in his directness and natural intensity. Of Jewish writers of Russian fiction, Babel remains the magnificent and turbulent source. Gogol and Maupassant were Babel's formal precursors, but again and again I recall Sholom Aleichim as I reread Babel. Sholom Aleichim is wry where Babel is wildly bitter, but the ironic stance is very close: sometimes one detects—at a distance—the overtones of Yiddish wit in Babel, who joins Kafka and Freud as one of the seminal Jewish writers of the twentieth century.

ISAAC BABEL
(1894–1940)

BABEL, MURDERED BY THE STALINIST secret police, comes first to my mind, after Kafka, when I brood on genius in modern Jewish fiction. Open him at random, as I have just done, and your eyes hover on almost any sentence, which reverberates and will go on:

> My grandfather was once a rabbi in Belaya Tserkov, but he was banished from there for blasphemy and with much fuss and in great poverty, lived another forty years, studied modern languages and began to go mad in the eightieth year of his life.
>
> (translated by David McDuff)

A story in itself, like so many of Babel's sentences, this reminds one of his audacious stylistic economy as a writer. McDuff, Babel's best translator, speaks of the contrast between the shadowy life of Babel and the writer's personality: humor, intelligence, lyrical depth. In the Russia first of civil war, and then of Stalin, a superbly vivacious, comic, wise Jewish writer had to become as shadowy as possible. Babel finally attempted to save himself by withdrawing into silence, but even that did not work. Between this silence, and Stalinist elimination at forty-five, Babel's achievement was gravely truncated, which was an immense aesthetic loss.

So far, there are at least two sources for hearing Babel plain, his *1920 Diary* of the Polish-Soviet war of 1919–20, and *At His Side*, a memoir by his second wife, A. N. Pirozhkova. Here is her account of his arrest by the secret police on May 15, 1939; he was taken to prison, tortured into a "confession" (which he recanted), and executed on January 27, 1940:

> When the search of Babel's room was completed, they put all his manuscripts into folders and ordered us to put on our coats and go to the car. Babel said to me: "they didn't let me finish."

As a writer of short stories, Babel rivals Turgenev, Chekhov, Maupassant, Gogol, Joyce, Hemingway, Lawrence, Borges: he is in many ways, like them, the genius of the form. But, like Kafka's, his genius is peculiarly one of dichotomy. Kafka writes in a purified German very much his own; Babel is a master of Russian literature, but both uncannily are Jewish writers: ambivalently, estranged from tradition, and yet they have become the Jewish literary tradition. Nothing else allows one to hold Kafka and Babel within the confines of the same sentence. As writers, they have almost no common features. Even as Jewish writers, they diverge; Kafka had traces of something like Jewish self-hatred, which he worked through and transcended. There is nothing of that in Babel; despite his ironies, and his awareness of the difficulties of being a Russian-Jewish writer (and the impossibility of being a Soviet-Jewish author), he always remained aware of what was most his own.

Babel's most famous works (though not, in my judgment, his best) are the Cossack stories of *Red Cavalry*, first published as a book in 1926, but widely available for three years before that. Though the eminent critic Lionel Trilling interpreted *Red Cavalry* as "trying to come to terms with the Cossack ethos," he appears to have been misled by Babel's irony, sometimes too large to be seen (as Chesterton said of Chaucer's):

And then I trampled on Nikitinksy, my master. I trampled on him for an hour or more than an hour, and during that time I got to know him and his life. Shooting—in my opinion—is just a way of getting rid of a fellow, to shoot him is to pardon him, and a vile compromise with yourself; with shooting you don't get to a man's soul, where it is in him and how it shows itself. But usually I don't spare myself, usually I trample my enemy for an hour or more than an hour, I want to find out about the life, what it's like with us.

The speaker is the Red general, the Cossack Matuey Pavlickenko, formerly a pigkeeper in the employ of Nikitinsky the landowner, whom "the headstrong Pavlickenko" gets to know rather thoroughly. More pungent demonstrations of "the Cossack ethos" abound elsewhere in *Red Cavalry*:

I ended up billeted in the house of a red-haired widow who smelled of widows' grief. I washed off the grime of the journey, and went out into the street. On the noticeboards were bills saying that the divisional military commissar Vinogradov would that evening deliver a lecture on the Second Congress of the Comintern. Directly under my window several Cossacks were shooting an old Jew with a silvery beard for espionage. The old man was screaming and trying to tear himself free. Then Kudrya from the machine-gun detachment took the old man's head and put it under his arm. The Jew calmed down and stood with his legs apart. With his right hand Kudrya pulled out his dagger and carefully cut the old man's throat, without splashing any blood on himself. Then he knocked on the closed window frame.

"If anyone's interested," he said, "they can come and get him. He's all yours."

Marshal Semyon Bodyonny, who commanded the Red Cavalry against the Poles, denounced Babel for slandering his valiant Cossacks, which at least got Babel's ironies accurately. For Babel, the Cossack is hardly a "noble savage," and in time the ironist of genius was slain for his ironies. In his *1920 Diary*, Babel tells himself that, accompanying the Cossacks, he is present at "an endless funeral." If we—and Babel—are to have a funeral, let it be in the exuberant Jewish mode of his magnificent "How It Was Done in Odessa," the crown of his *Odessa Stories*, which together with his "autobiographical" tales far surpass *Red Cavalry*:

And the funeral took place the following morning. About that funeral ask the beggars of the cemetery. Ask the beadles from the Synagogue of Kosher Poultry Vendors or the old woman from the Second Almshouse about it. Such a funeral as Odessa had never seen before, and the world will never see again. That day the policemen put on cotton gloves. In the synagogues, twined with greenery and with doors open wide, electricity burned. Black plumes swayed on the white horses that were harnessed to the hearse. Sixty choristers walked at the head of the procession. The choristers were boys, but they sang with the voices of women. The elders of the Synagogue of Kosher Poultry Vendors helped Auntie Pesya along by the arm. Behind the elders walked the members of the Society of Jewish Shop Assistants, and behind the Jewish Shop Assistants, barristers, doctors of medicine and doctors' assistant-midwives. On one side of Auntie Pesya were the female poultry sellers from Stary Bazaar, and on her other side were the honourable dairymaids from Bugayevka, tucked up in orange shawls. They were stamping their feet like gendarmes on parade on their holiday. From their broad hips came a smell of sea and milk. And behind them trudged the employees of Ruvim Tartakovsky. There were a hundred of them, or two hundred, or two thousand. They were dressed in black frock-coats with silk lapels and new boots that squeaked like piglets in a sack.

This gorgeous affair is organized by Benya Krik, gangster king of Jewish Odessa, for the late Josif Muginshteyn, unfortunately shot by one of Benya's gunmen (who was intoxicated) during a raid upon the office of Tartakovsky, who had declined to pay protection money. Confronting the hysterical Auntie Pesya, bereaved mother of Muginshteyn, Benya, attired in a chocolate jacket, cream trousers, and raspberry-colored lacing boots, utters a magnificent apologia:

"Auntie Pesya," Benya said then to the disheveled old woman who lay on the floor, "if you need my life you can have it, but everyone makes mistakes, even God. There has been a huge mistake, Auntie Pesya. But was it not a mistake on God's part to settle the Jews in Russia, where they have been tormented as if in hell? And what would be the harm if the Jews were to live in Switzerland, where they would be surrounded by first-class lakes, mountain air and nothing but Frenchmen? Everyone makes mistakes, even God. Listen to me with your ears Auntie Pesya. You have five thousand in hand and fifty roubles a month until you die—live a hundred and twenty years. Iosif's funeral will be first class: six horses like six lions, two hearses with wreaths, the choir from the Brody Synagogue. Minkovsky himself will come to sing the burial service for your departed son."

How often, reading about the Jews of Russia, have I repeated Benya's eloquence. God, who could have put the Jews in Switzerland, placed them in Russia, where they have been tormented as if in hell, as Babel was tormented by the secret police before they shot him. Victor Erlich, celebrating Babel's command of color and line, asked what other storyteller had fused Gogol and Maupassant. In another great story, "Guy de Maupassant," Babel relates his experience at twenty in St. Petersburg, where he assists the full-breasted Madam Raisa Bendersky in her translating Maupassant. Impressed by his skill in revising her, she asks, "How did you do it?":

Then I began to speak of style, of the army of words, an army in which all kinds of weapons are on the move. No iron can enter the human heart as chillingly as a full stop placed at the right time. She listened, her head inclined, her painted lips slightly open. A black gleam shone in her lacquered hair, smoothly drawn back and divided by a parting. Her legs, with strong, soft, calves, in shiny stockings, were placed apart over the carpet.

There is Babel's credo: "No iron can enter the human heart as chillingly as a full stop placed at the right time." After a passionate encounter with his hostess and a bottle of Muscadet 1883, Babel staggers home to read a critical biography of Maupassant, dead in a madhouse at forty-two:

> I read the book to its end and got out of bed. The fog had come up to the window, obscuring the universe. My heart was constricted. I was brushed by a foreboding of truth.

There "Guy de Maupassant" ends, with four full stops placed at the right time. Uncannily prescient, perhaps Babel (on some level) anticipates his own close at forty-five. Truncated by Stalin's murderous anti-Semitism, Babel's literary career, with its fewer than sixty stories, nevertheless radiates his extraordinary gift, his genius at portraying the dichotomy imposed upon him by history, geography, and his own imaginative eminence. He is not to be thought of as a victim, because his greatest stories transcend victimization: they give nothing away to the anti-Semites. One does not remember him ultimately as an ironist but as the comic celebrator of the personality of "the King," Benya Krik, and of the Jews of Odessa: "the stout and jovial Jews of the South, bubbling like cheap wine."

PAUL CELAN

Reachable, near and not least, there remained amid the losses this one thing: language.

It, the language, remained, not lost, yes in spite of everything. But it had to pass through its own answerlessness, pass through frightful muting, pass through the thousand darknesses of deathbringing speech. It passed through and gave back no words for that which happened; yet it passed through this happening. Passed through and could come to light again, "enriched" by all this.

—Bremen Prize speech (1958)
(translated by John Felstiner)

Felstiner, Celan's prime critic and biographer, notes the intricate ironies of allusion here: "the thousand darknesses" invoke Hiter's "Thousand-Year Reich," and "the word *angereichert* ('enriched') buries Hiter's *Reich* within itself." Celan's prose is as subtle as his poetry, another analogue between the Jewish poet whose native language (in Bukovina province, Romania) was German, and Emily Dickinson, whose poetry he translated superbly. Both are masters of the abyss, employing a wit beyond wit to express what cannot be said, only intimated.

Celan's poetry, which is as difficult as Dickinson's, is also nearly as rewarding (to be compared to Dickinson is, after all, as dangerous as being contrasted with Shakespeare). What lasts is founded by poets, Hölderlin, the great German Romantic, had proclaimed, and Celan lasts. Though Celan, in his exquisite and unique poignance, seems to me a universal poet, his dilemma, as *the* post-Holocaust poet in German, has a particular relevance in our new Age of Terror, which is not likely to pass by quickly. Again like Dickinson's, Celan's poetry powerfully performs what Freud called "the work of mourning." In his isolation and fear of fresh madness, Celan ended himself at forty-nine. One badly wants what would have been the poetry of his later years.

PAUL CELAN (PAUL ANTSCHEL)
(1920–1970)

LIKE FRANZ KAFKA IN PRAGUE, PAUL Antschel (changed first to Ancel and then to the poetic anagram Celan) grew up in a community of German-speaking Jews, Czernowitz in Bukovina, a province of Romania. In 1942, the Nazis murdered Celan's mother in a camp, after his father had died there of typhus. Celan himself survived a Romanian labor camp—the Romanians also being Nazis and murderous anti-Semites—and eventually settled in Paris, where he taught German literature until he drowned himself at forty-nine. A difficult, laconic poet of extraordinary power and originality, he sustains aesthetic comparison with Kafka, that being a juxtaposition that destroys most writers.

Celan (like Kafka) subverts any attempt I can make to isolate his innate poetic genius from a daemonic otherness, particularly because "otherness" is overtly recast by Celan as a central component in his work. In a famous speech, "The Meridian," given in Darmstadt in 1960, Celan said that

> The poem intends another, needs this other, needs an opposite. It goes toward it, bespeaks it.
>
> For the poem, everything and everybody is a figure of this other toward which it is heading.
>
> (translated by Rosmarie Waldrop)

Beneath the urgency of this, one hears the horror of one's parents' deaths, and of the destruction of most of European Jewry by the Germans and their willing helpers. The poem makes a figuration of otherness, and yet there is no other, no God and no redemptive reader. Since no other exists, the poem is only a brief fiction of duration, a metaphor of time replacing otherness:

> Only the space of this conversation can establish what is addressed, can gather it into a "you" around the naming and speaking I. But this "you," come about by dint of being named and addressed, brings its otherness into the present. Even in the here and now of the poem—and the poem has only this one, unique, momentary present—

even in this immediacy and nearness, the otherness gives voice to
what is most its own: its time.

(translated by Rosmarie Waldrop)

Celan insisted that his poetry was not hermetic, but of course it is, like
the poetry of Walt Whitman, Emily Dickinson, and Hart Crane. Emily
Dickinson and Celan had authentic affinities, as his remarkable translations
from her show. In his own language (how odd to call German that), Hölderlin and Rilke are Celan's precursors, and they are hermetic also. But Celan's
difficulty is very individual, and centrally Jewish. Though he survived the
Nazi era by almost a quarter-century, the Holocaust never left his consciousness. Inevitably there were terrible depressions, paranoia, breakdown, and at last suicide. When Celan identifies (momentarily) with King
Lear's madness, he holds on to the peculiar authority of his own genius,
which returns me to the difficulty of distinguishing, in this extraordinary
poet, between the slain fathering and mothering force, and the opening to
an otherness that is scarcely even a postulate.

If you can imagine Kafka as a Holocaust survivor, then you would approach nearer to Celan, whose poetry, like Kafka's prose, purifies the German language of many elements that make Jews uneasy. Celan's choice was
not the state of Israel, which greatly moved him, but "to live out to the end
the destiny of the Jewish spirit in Europe." His poetic German, though as
much his own as Kafka's language, nevertheless remained German, and
Celan, who knew Hebrew well, was not prepared to become a Hebrew poet.

I do not know what the destiny of the Jewish spirit in the United States
will be. The best American-Jewish poet remains Moshe Leib Halpern, who
wrote in Yiddish; American English has yet to bring forth a Kafka or a Celan.
But Kafka is of the eminence of Proust and Joyce, and Celan shares the
greatness of Valéry and Mandelstam, both of whom he translated superbly.
Though he is so difficult for the common reader, Celan is an essential poet,
and hardly for Jews alone. His severe formalism teaches what poetry is: at
once a rejection of barbarism and an assertion (however qualified) of the
power of mind over every universe of death, whether natural or Nazi.
Celan's poems urge us, with something close to the terrible inwardness of
King Lear, to use only the highest of our abilities to remember what must
never be forgotten.

Like Kafka, Celan approached a negative or Gnostic Kabbalah, more personal than traditional, a new Kabbalah, protesting God's alienation or exile.
The history of Jewish Gnosticism, as outlined by Gershom Scholem and
(very differently) by Moshe Idel, is a more-than-Borgesian labyrinth, and

Celan, again like Kafka, is both suggestively and disputably placed in that immense tradition. How can there be Kabbalah without God, since all Kabbalah is an elaborate phantasmagoria on the names of God? Ian Fairley, a recent translator of Celan, argues (as have others) that Celan is estranged from Kabbalah, but to me it hardly seems that any poet whatsoever could be more in the spirit of the Gnostic as opposed to the Neoplatonic strain in Kabbalah. Shira Wolosky, in her *Language Mysticism* (1995), makes a convincing demonstration of Celan's knowing relationship to the Kabbalah of Isaac Luria, with its catastrophic vision of the Breaking of the Vessels. A protest against, or argument with, a God whose highest name is *Ayin* or nothingness is not an argument against God, but is a deep component in the most negative of all theologies.

So far, I have not cited or discussed a single poem by Paul Celan, but one needs to wind one's way into his work. There is a superb biographical-critical study (1995), by John Felstiner, which is a miracle of sympathetic understanding and of a poignant love for Celan, and I will owe much to it, and to Wolosky's book, in what follows. As always, my concern is limited to the question of genius, so palpable in Celan's astonishing control of language that you have to be tone-deaf or an ideologue not to recognize it.

Paul Celan is a difficult poet, but so were Wallace Stevens and Hart Crane, or Friedrich Hölderlin and Georg Trakl. So indeed was Dante, or Shakespeare upon his heights. Genius is the only justification for stunning difficulty, because only genius can reward enormous demands made upon the reader. Emily Dickinson, though we remain slow to recognize this, actually is more difficult than Celan, or almost anyone else, because her cognitive originality is as immense as Dante's or Shakespeare's or William Blake's. Celan breaks up the surface of his poems, as Dickinson does not, but she finally is the more elliptical of the two.

If those who speak the mother tongue murdered your mother, then you must write as though there is no audience. I think that Dickinson attracted Celan because she is so free of the burden of an audience. And yet Celan was drawn even more intensely to Shakespeare, the greatest master at gratifying an audience (though Shakespeare increasingly grew ambivalent at his own mastery of such gratification). Celan, himself virtually untranslatable, became much the strongest twentieth-century translator of great poetry into German.

If your desire is to define and to characterize Celan's genius, then you must resort to endless paradox, which returns me to Kabbalah, the science of divine paradox, that takes a step away both from Talmudic Judaism and from Neoplatonism by becoming obsessed with the question of evil. The *Zohar*, central work of Kabbalah, assigned ten *Sefirot* or emanations to *the other side*, to worlds that God had made and then destroyed. This is not yet the Gnostic Kabbalah of Luria and Moses Cordovero, but the "nothing" that is God is on the way to becoming equivocal. That is part of the burden of one of Celan's best-known poems, "Psalm," which I render here for myself, but with close attention to the versions of Felstiner, Wolosky, and Michael Hamburger:

> Noone molds us again out of earth and clay,
> Noone speaks about our dust
> Noone.
>
> Praised are you, noone.
> For your sake
> We would flower.
> Against
> You.
>
> A Nothing
> Were we, are we, will
> We remain, flowering:
> The Nothing—, the
> Noone's rose.
>
> With
> Our pistil soul—bright,
> With our stamen heaven-wasted,
> Our corolla red
> From the Purpleword that we sang
> Over, O over
> The thorn.

This seems to me the only legitimate twentieth-century candidate for inclusion in the Hebrew Bible's Book of Psalms, though no one is likely to put it there. As the hymn of the Holocaust, what could match this? Paraphrase of this "Psalm" is possible, but not without demeaning or distorting it: "Us," the Jews throughout history, praise/protest Noone, both *Ayin* and the Yahweh who molded Adam out of the *Adamah*, moistened red clay, but who utters no word about his slaughtered people, who are Noone's rose. To sing over o over the thorn is to prefer the Original Testament to the Belated One, even if no credence still can be given to the covenant cut with Noone.

"Psalm" is simplicity itself compared with Celan upon his heights: "The Sluice," "A Boomerang," "Snow-Bed," and seventy to eighty other elliptical lyrics. But again, my concern is not to mediate Celan's poems, but to define, as best I can, a genius beyond all limits of anguish. The Yiddish poet H. Leivick, speaking of his art and that of his peers—Moshe Leib Halpern, Mani Leib, Glatstein—best prophesied Celan's genius:

> A song means filling a jug, and even more so breaking the jug. Breaking it apart. In the language of the Kabbalah we perhaps might call it: Broken Vessels.

RALPH ELLISON

Meanwhile I enjoy my life with the compliments of Monopolated Light & Power. Since you never recognize me even when in the closest contact with me, and since, no doubt, you'll hardly believe that I exist, it won't matter if you know that I tapped a power line leading into the building and ran it into my hole in the ground. Before that I lived in the darkness into which I was chased, but now I see, I've illuminated the blackness of my invisibility—and vice versa. And so I play the invisible music of my isolation. The last statement doesn't seem just right, does it? But it is; you hear this music simply because music is heard and seldom seen, except by musicians. Could this compulsion to put invisibility down in black and white be thus an urge to make music of invisibility? But I am an orator, a rabble rouser—Am? I *was,* and perhaps shall be again. Who knows? All sickness is not unto death, neither is invisibility.

Invisible Man speaks to us towards the close of his prologue, hinting that, after he has told his life story, he may come up again. Despair, Kierkegaard said, was the sickness unto death, and invisibility—the African-American situation a half-century ago—is thus carefully distinguished from despair.

Ellison's superb first (and only completed) novel won its fame as a profound vision of African-American consciousness. So much has changed, in the American half-century, that *Invisible Man* might be reduced to a period piece if it were primarily a vision of African-American dilemmas. The novel's permanence stems from its universality: it is one of the major American visions of what Emerson and Whitman regarded as the infinite possibilities of life in the United States. If I wince a little now on rereading—a month after September 11, 2001—it is because Ellison sounds an unintentional prophecy as to what can destroy possibility for all of us:

But my world has become one if infinite possibilities. What a phrase—still it's a good phrase and a good view of life, and a man shouldn't accept any other; that much I've learned underground. Until some gang succeeds in putting the world in a strait-jacket, its definition is possibility.

RALPH WALDO ELLISON
(1914–1994)

THOUGH HE LIVED TO BE EIGHTY, ELLISON never again approached the aesthetic splendor of his *Invisible Man* (1952). The posthumously published quasi-novel *Juneteenth,* is not representative of his genius, and should have stayed in manuscript, following his own judgment. The final quarter-century of his life (I base this on a number of conversations with him) seemed less shadowed by his inability to finish a second novel that would meet his own high standards than it was by social pressures that could have been relieved only if he had abandoned his own very individual stance. He was an African-American literary artist, the peer of the greatest masters of jazz: Louis Armstrong and Charlie Parker. To debase his art in the supposed service of black nationalist or separatist movements had no appeal for a legitimate heir of Melville and Dostoevsky, T. S. Eliot and Hemingway, Faulkner and Malraux.

Kenneth Burke remarked to me that *Invisible Man* was as intricate as *The Brothers Karamazov* or *The Magic Mountain.* In some respects, it may be more intricate, since it is, as Ellison said, "jazz-shaped," that is, agonistic, involved in a creative cutting contest, as John Coltrane was with Parker, or Charles Mingus with the totality of jazz tradition. *Invisible Man,* an experimental novel that never wears out, engages in a contest with the long novelistic tradition of the self-portrait of the young artist, unnamed by Ellison.

I have reread *Invisible Man* every other year or so in the almost half-century since its publication, but its rich complexities make it difficult to keep wholly in mind. A five-hundred-page novel that consists of a prologue, twenty-five chapters, and an epilogue, it is as organized as Joyce's *Ulysses,* and similarly fuses symbolism and naturalism. The nameless young African-American narrator maintains an ironic reserve throughout. In the prologue we find him living underground on the outskirts of Harlem, in a large room illuminated by 1,369 light bulbs. He taps into Monopolated Light & Power, which cannot locate him, while he listens to a recording of Louis Armstrong performing "What Did I Do to Be So Black and Blue." Descending, "like Dante," into the song's depth, he hears the antiphony of a black preacher and his congregation, with the preacher crying out, ". . . It'll put you, glory, glory, Oh my Lord, in the WHALE'S BELLY." The Book of Jonah, read in the synagogue on the afternoon of the Day of Atonement (as Ellison knew), provides *Invisible Man* with a fundamental structural paradigm. Jonah, an unwilling prophet, is always in flight until he is put in the whale's belly.

The new Jonah's autobiography takes him from a horrible racist "celebration" following a high school graduation through misadventures at a black college on to Harlem and the Brotherhood, or Communist Party. He befriends Tod Clifton, a black organizer for the Brotherhood, and confronts the marvelous Ras the Exhorter, a black nationalist leader. After Clifton is murdered by the police, Invisible Man is expelled by the white powers of the Brotherhood. Disguising himself with dark sunglasses and a broad-brimmed hat, he is mistaken for Rinehart, reverend and runner: preacher, pimp, mobster. Ras, now the Destroyer and not the Exhorter, leads a Harlem race riot, and the narrator escapes to the underground sanctuary where we first meet him.

I intend this not as a plot summary (virtually impossible with *Invisible Man*) but as a Jonah's progress into the whale's belly, remarkably illuminated by 1,369 bulbs. The biblical Jonah is shocked when his prophecy is heeded, and Nineveh repents. This new, black Jonah concludes by preparing to ascend:

In going underground, I whipped it all except the mind, the *mind*. And the mind that has conceived a plan of living must never lose sight of the chaos against which that pattern was conceived. That goes for societies as well as for individuals. Thus, having tried to give pattern to the chaos which lives within the pattern of your certainties, I must come out, I must emerge. And there's still a conflict within me: With Louis Armstrong one half of me says, "Open the window and let the foul air out," while the other says, "It was good green corn before the harvest." Of course Louis was kidding, *he* wouldn't have thrown old Bad Air out, because it would have broken up the music and the dance, when it was the good music that came from the bell of old Bad Air's horn that counted. Old Bad Air is still around with his music and his dancing and his diversity, and I'll be up and around with mine. And, as I said before, a decision has been made. I'm shaking off the old skin and I'll leave it here in the hole. I'm coming out, no less invisible without it, but coming out nevertheless. And I suppose it's damn well time. Even hibernations, since there's a possibility that even an invisible man has a socially responsible role to play.

"Ah," I can hear you say, "so it was all a build-up to bore us with his buggy jiving. He only wanted us to listen to him rave!" But only partially true: Being invisible, and without substance, a disembodied voice, as it were, what else could I do? What else but try to tell you what was really happening when your eyes were looking through? And it is this which frightens me:

Who knows but that, on the lower frequencies, I speak for you?

This conclusion, ironic though almost hopeful, has not found favor with certain African-American critics, and yet it is remarkably balanced in its realism. The *mind*, the most terrible force in the world, will compel Invisible Man to come up from the whale's belly. And the mind ought to compel any reader to become that *you*, to and for whom the narrator speaks. Of Ellison's many symbolic figures in this strong fable, the most memorable is Rinehart, more even than Ras or Tod, unless you want to cite the Ulysses-like survivor, Invisible Man himself. The Reverend Rinehart is chaos, according to Ellison, but his middle name is Proteus, the Confidence Man, so that he is also the United States, perpetually in change. He is the novel's other invisible man, and is everywhere and nowhere. Shall we not call the Reverend Rinehart also Ralph Ellison's own genius, his daemon?

The narrator chooses Louis Armstrong as forerunner, since Armstrong, in the 1920s, changed jazz into an individualistic art form, by an extraordinary originality. But Ellison wisely knew that our precursors choose us, and Invisible Man is found by Rinehart the Runner. The origins of jazz are in the cosmos of Rinehart, which takes over Ellison's novel in chapter 23. Here is Rinehart's persuasive handbill:

Behold the Invisible
Thy will be done O Lord!
I See all, Know all, Tell all, Cure all.
You shall see the unknown wonders.
        —REV. B. P. RINEHART,
        Spiritual Technologist

The old is ever new
Way Stations in New Orleans, the home of mystery,
Birmingham, New York, Chicago, Detroit and L. A.

No Problem too Hard for God.

Come to the Way Station.

BEHOLD THE INVISIBLE!
Attend our services, prayer meetings Thrice weekly
Join us in the NEW REVELATION of the OLD
   TIME RELIGION!

BEHOLD THE SEEN UNSEEN
BEHOLD THE INVISIBLE
       YE WHO ARE WEARY COME HOME!

I DO WHAT YOU WANT DONE! DON'T WAIT!

The truth is always a lie, and Rinehart is the truth, being the key to Invisibility, and to the freedom of chaos. Ellison's narrator says that there is an alternative freedom, imagination, and the permanence of the novel, *Invisible Man*, is evidence of that difficult freedom. The art of *Invisible Man* is a difficult pleasure, and persuades us to forsake easier pleasures. Ellison's genius did not abandon him after the publication of *Invisible Man*, but it became displaced into the irony of commentary, and his legitimate pride would not permit him to publish a less-achieved second novel. *Juneteenth*, even if it had been finished, was an ironic repetition of *Invisible Man*, and a lessening of it. Perhaps Ellison should have followed his daemon and composed a different novel, *Rinehart: Reverend and Runner*. Genius follows its own laws, and my suggestion is only wistful, and is intended as homage to a great individualist, as self-reliant as the Concord sage for whom he was named.

CODA:

The Future of Genius

A book that has excluded all living literary geniuses, and almost all who died recently, needs to be tentative in prophesying the future of genius. Information technology may transform the relations between writer and reader, but can have little effect upon the question of genius. If you contemplate the wide span from Homer to Samuel Beckett, what leaps out at you is how minimal the changes have been in the qualities that sustain the identity of genius.

Teaching imaginative literature for a half-century can be a considerable self-education, and has not diminished my passion for greatness, for what the ancient Hellenistic critic Longinus called the Sublime. Shakespeare, of all writers I have ever read, still dwells apart, uniquely able to give the illusion that he differs from all others in kind, not just in degree. To think about him and discuss him only in regard to the attributes he shared with his contemporaries has been the curse of twentieth-century Shakespeare criticism. I have urged a fierce Bardolatry as an antidote, and assert that almost all of the hundred figures appreciated in this book share, to one extent or another, the Shakespearean timelessness.

Every era exalts works that, in a few generations, prove to be period pieces. A pragmatic definition of a genius of language is that she or he is not a producer of period pieces. With only a double or triple handful of exceptions, everything we now freshly acclaim is a potential antique, and antiques made out of language wind up in dustbins, and not in auction houses or museums.

Without genius, literary language stales quickly, and resists revival, even upon the sacred grounds of gender, ethnicity, skin pigmentation, sexual orientation, and all the other criteria that dominate our media, including their sub-branch, our campuses. Even parody cannot prevail in a bad time that deprecates genius. A few years back, ironically responding to the zealots who insist that Shakespeare was written by the Earl of Oxford, I countered with the suggestion that Lucy Negro, Elizabethan London's leading East Indian sex worker, had been both the Dark Lady of the Sonnets and the author of all of Shakespeare's better plays. An epidemic of letters showered upon me, expressing either outrage or the joy of discovery. I wished only that I could summon up Antony Burgess at a séance, so as to have his moral support: "At least she slept with Shakespeare!"

Time, which destroys us, reduces what is not genius to rubbish. I finished writing this book a few days after my seventy-first birthday, saddened by the number of friends dead or dying. If there is a secular immortality, it belongs to genius. A few figures—Goethe, Tolstoy, Ibsen—played with the fantasy that nature would make a literal exception for those with preternatural gifts of creativity. There is a heroic pathos in such play, but the future of genius is always metaphorical.